10,000 Famous Freemasons

William R. Denslow

Volume II
E to J

10,000 Famous Freemasons

A Cornerstone Book
Published by Cornerstone Book Publishers
Copyright © 2007 by Cornerstone Book Publishers

Cornerstone Book Publishers
New Orleans, LA

www.cornerstonepublishers.com

ISBN: 1-887560-79-3
ISBN 13: 978-1-887560-79-5

MADE IN THE USA

10,000 Famous Freemasons

E

Henry P. Eames (1872-1950) Pianist and lecturer. b. Sept. 12, 1872 in Chicago, Ill. Studied in U.S. and abroad under private teachers including Madam Clara Schumann and Ignace Paderewski. Graduate of Northwestern U. in 1894. He established the Omaha School of Music and was connected with the musical departments of several schools including U. of Nebr., Illinois Wesleyan U.; U. of Calif.; U. of Hawaii; U. of N. Mex. Published over 30 songs and choruses. Made 14 annual concert-lecture tours of America and several abroad. Member of Lancaster Lodge No. 54, Lincoln, Nebr., receiving degrees on March 13, April 17 and May 29, 1903; suspended April 7, 1916. d. Nov. 25, 1950.

Harry B. Earhart (1870-1954) Ship owner, manufacturer and oil executive. b. Dec. 21, 1870 at Worthington, Pa. From 1888-1904 he was owner of vessels on the Great Lakes; from 1904-10 was engaged in the manufacture of machinery and from 1910-32 was president and chairman of the board of the White Star Refining Co., and during the same period was director of Vacuum Oil Co. He was director of the National Safety Council at one time. Raised Nov. 13, 1893 in Ionic Lodge No. 186, Duluth, Mimi. and affiliated with Palestine Lodge No. 357, Detroit on April 13, 1913, becoming a life member of same Jan. 7, 1937. Member of Scottish Rite. d. Oct. 21, 1954.

R. E. W. Earl American artist. Painted numerous portraits of Andrew Jackson, q.v., member of Cumberland Lodge No. 8, Nashville, Tenn.

Clarence E. Earle (1893-1953) Chemical engineer. b. Aug. 27, 1893 at Bengies, Md. He graduated from George Washington U. in 1923. Employed by U.S. government and many private firms as a chemical engineer and was president of Breco Mfg. Co. and director of Medical Chemicals, Inc., as well as Insl-X Co. He discovered and developed lithium soap lubricating greases used in aircraft manufacture. Also originated and developed all-purpose hydraulic oil and chemical polar compounds for thin film preservation of metallic surfaces against corrosion. He developed an aircraft carbon monoxide detector and pioneered the discovery of a series of chemical compounds known as phenylammonio salts used as a mycotic drug in South Pacific. Raised in Delnorta Lodge No. 105, Delnorta, Colo. and affiliated with Jephthah Lodge No. 222 (Md.) on June 17, 1952. d. Nov. 15, 1953.

George H. Earle Governor of Pennsylvania, 1935-39. b. Dec. 5, 1890 in Devon, Pa. Holds honorary degrees from several universities. Associated with father in sugar industry at Philadelphia and later in Chicago. He founded Flamingo Sugar Mills in Philadelphia and was active in various business activities until appointed envoy and minister (E.E. and M.P.) to Austria in 1933-34. In 1940-41 he was minister to Bulgaria and in 1943 assistant naval attaché at Istanbul, Turkey. Served in army on Mexican Border and in WWI entered navy and was commander of U.S.S. Victor, submarine chaser. Received Navy Cross. Member of Lodge No. 9 in Philadelphia, Pa. and Shriner.

Roy B. Earling Vice president of U. S. Smelting, Refining & Mining Co. and in charge of Alaska operations since 1935. b. May 29, 1887 at Milwaukee, Wis. With U. S. Smelting since 1925. Mason.

Claudius M. Easley (1891-1945) Brigadier General, U.S. Army. b. July 11, 1891 at Thorp Spring, Tex. Graduated from Texas A. & M. Coll. in 1916 and graduate of several Army service schools. Commissioned in 1917 and advanced through grades to brigadier general. Mason. d. June 19, 1945 and buried in 96th Infantry Div. Cemetery in Okinawa.

Edmund P. Easterbrook (1865-1933) Chief of chaplains, U.S. Army, 1928-30. b. Dec. 22, 1865 in Torquay, England. He was ordained as a Methodist minister in 1889. He served as a chaplain in the Spanish-American War and in Cuba with the Army of Occupation. He was commissioned a chaplain in the Army by President McKinley in 1900 and served as such in the Philippine Insurrection from 1900-05. He was in WWI with U.S. forces in Germany from 1919-23. On return to U.S. was stationed at Fort Sam Houston, Tex. and Fort Monroe, Va. Mason. d. Jan. 18, 1933.

Rufus Easton (1774-1834) First postmaster West of the Mississippi River (St. Louis) and first attorney general of Missouri. b. May 4, 1774 at Litchfield, Conn. He studied law in the office of Ephraim Kirby, q.v., and was admitted to the bar in 1795. In 1803 he went to Washington, D.C. where he met a number of prominent statesmen. Following his death, letters were found in his effects from Col. Aaron Burr, Postmaster General Gideon Granger, Governor DeWitt Clinton and others. It was his intention to locate in New Orleans, but upon reaching Vincennes, Ind. in 1804 he decided to remain there and practice in the courts of the territory. He accompanied General Harrison to St. Louis and took up residence there. In 1815 President Jefferson gave him a commission as judge of the Territory of Louisiana. Following Missouri's admission as a state, President Monroe appointed him U.S. attorney general for the state, an office which he held until his retirement in 1826. He also served Missouri in the U.S. Congress. As postmaster of St. Louis he had difficulties with General James Wilkinson, q.v., who was one of the conspirators with Aaron Burr. Easton supported the policies of Jefferson and complained of "spies and informers" of the Wilkinson camp. He entered Freemasonry through Roman Lodge No. 82 of New York and assisted in the organization of Western Star Lodge No. 107, Kaskaskia, Ill. When St. Louis Lodge No. 111 was organized, he became a charter member and officer. Easton was one of the incorporators of the first territorial bank of St. Louis in 1813, being elected a director in 1814. He also was land agent from 1808-18. In 1822 he moved to St. Charles, Mo., where he died July 5, 1834. He left a large family, one daughter marrying Henry S. Geyer, later U.S. senator; another married Governor Hamilton Gamble. His daughter, Mary, married George C. Sibley and together they founded Lindenwood College at St. Charles in 1831.

Stanley A. Easton President of Bunker Hill & Sullivan Mining and Concentrating Co.—one of the largest lead and silver mines in the world. b. April 7, 1873 at Santa Cruz, Calif. Graduate of U. of Calif. Coll. of Mines in 1894. He is also president of Sullivan Mining Co. and Caledonia Mining Co. Mason.

Barney E. Eaton (1878-1944) President of Mississippi Power Co. from 1924. b. Dec. 5, 1878 at Taylorsville, Miss. Graduate of Millsaps Coll., Jackson. Admitted to the bar in 1903 and practiced at Hattiesburg. He affiliated with Gulfport Lodge No. 422 on May 1, 1919, Gulfport, Miss. and dimitted Aug. 3, 1933. d. July 18, 1944.

Hubert Eaton Originator of the "memorial-park" plan for cemeteries, substituting tablets set level with the lawn for tombstones, providing art collections, historical buildings, etc., thereby revolutionizing cemeteries throughout the U.S. He is known as "the builder" of Forest Lawn Memorial Park, Glendale, Calif., which is noted for its collection of stained glass works of American sculptors and recreations of Last Supper and Calvary. b. June 3, 1881 at Liberty, Mo., he graduated from William Jewell Coll. in Liberty in 1902. A chemist, he has been associated with many of the main mining companies of America including Anaconda, Teziutlan Copper (Mexico), Adaven Mining (Nev.). Raised in Euclid Lodge No. 58, Great Falls, Mont. in 1905 and presently member of Southern California Lodge No. 278, Los Angeles. Member of Liberty Chapter No. 3, R.A.M., Liberty, Mo., Los Angeles Commandery No. 9, K.T., Al Malaikah Shrine of Los Angeles and of Shrine Patrol. Served as junior deacon of his lodge.

James M. Eaton Vice President of American Overseas Airlines. b. Feb. 15, 1888 at Palatka, Fla. Graduated from U. of Maine in 1910. Eaton became interested in airplanes when he made his first flight with Ed Wiggins in 1913. In 1914 he assisted in establishing service between Tampa and St. Petersburg, Fla. (21 miles), which is now credited as the world's first scheduled airline. In 1920 he went to Europe to investigate the possibility of using wartime aircraft for commercial operation, but concluded they were not adequate. He was later with Pan American Airways and president of Ludington Airlines (New York to Washington every hour). Mason.

John H. Eaton (1790-1856) U.S. Secretary of War under Jackson, 1829-31; U.S. Senator from Tennessee; Governor of Territory of Forida, 1834-36; U.S. Minister to Spain, 1836-40. b. in Tenn. He studied law and after admission to the bar, practiced in Nashville. He is the author of Life of Andrew Jackson (1824), and was a personal friend of the president. Eaton was a member of Cumberland Lodge No. 8, Nashville; was elected an honorary member of Federal Lodge No. 1 at Washington, D.C. on Jan. 4, 1830; was an honorary member of the Grand Lodge of Florida. He was present at the communication of the Grand Lodge of Tenn. in 1825 and participated in the meeting at the U.S. Capitol in 1822 for the purpose of forming a general grand lodge. He is also recorded as a visitor at Nashville Lodge No. 37 (Tenn.) on June 2, 1825. d. Nov. 17, 1856.

William Eaton (1764-1811) Soldier and early political figure. b. Feb. 23, 1764 at Woodstock, Conn. He entered the Revolutionary army at age of 16 and served 19 years. He graduated at Dartmouth in 1790 and in 1797 was appointed consul to Tunis and for several years was engaged in altercations with the bey in regard to the annual "blackmail" payments this country made to Tunis to prevent them from molesting

American ships. He returned to the U.S. in 1803 and was appointed U.S. naval agent to the Barbary states. In this capacity he embarked on a romantic attempt to restore the exiled pasha, Hamet, to the throne, carrying out a small war with 500 men on his own initiative and utilizing two ships of the U.S. fleet. His attempt failed, but Mass. granted him 10,000 acres of land for his "heroic enterprise." In 1806 Aaron Burr, q.v., attempted to enlist Eaton in his conspiracy and at Burr's trial in Richmond, Eaton was one of his accusors. He was made a Mason in North Star Lodge, Manchester, Vt. in 1792. At one time he wrote a eulogy for George Washington, "composed for the celebration of St. George at Monson, 22nd inst." The last verses conclude: "Approving Heaven, with fostering hand, Gave Masons triumph through this land; And firmly to secure our craft, From bigot rage and envy's shaft, Sent a Grand Master, Freedom's son, The God-like patriot, Washington!" d. June 1, 1811.

William R. Eaton (1877-1943) U.S. Congressman, 71st and 72nd Congresses (1929-33) from 1st Colorado dist. b. Dec. 17, 1877 at Pugwash, N.S., Canada and brought to U.S. by parents the following year. Graduate of U. of Denver in 1909, he was admitted to the bar that year. He served two terms in the state senate. Raised March 22, 1902 in Union Lodge No. 7, Denver, Colo.; exalted Feb. 14, 1912 in Colorado Chapter No. 29, R.A.M. and knighted March 14, 1922 in Denver Commandery No. 25, K.T., all of Denver. Received 32° AASR (SJ) on Oct. 22, 1921 in Colorado Consistory No. 1, Denver and was KCCH. d. Dec. 16, 1942.

Charles H. Ebbets (1859-1925) Owner of the Brooklyn Dodgers (National League) and non-playing manager for the team in 1898. b. Oct. 29, 1859 in New York City. He was president of the National League from 1898-1925 and is a member of Baseball's National Hall of Fame as an owner. Ebbets Field is named for him. Member of Greenwood Lodge No. 569, New York City. d. April 18, 1925.

George A. Eberly Associate Justice, Supreme Court of Nebraska, 1925-43. b. Feb. 9, 1871 at Ft. Wayne, Ind. Received LL.B. and LL.M. from U. of Mich. Resident of Nebraska from 1873 and admitted to the bar in 1893. He served in the Spanish-American War in 1898 and Mexican border service in 1916. He was a colonel in WWI. In 1949 he was commander-in-chief of the Spanish-American War Veterans. Member and past master of Northern Light Lodge No. 41, Stanton, Nebr. He holds membership in the York Rite bodies of Omaha and is 32° AASR (SJ) in the Valley of Omaha; National Sojourner, and member of Tangier Shrine Temple, Omaha.

Frederick H. Ecker President of Metropolitan Life Insurance Co. 1929-36. b. Aug. 30, 1867 in Phoenicia, N.Y. With Metropolitan since 1883; comptroller in 1905; treasurer in 1906; director in 1909, vice president in 1919, and chairman of board of directors after retirement as president in 1936. Also vice-president and trustee of Union Dime Saving Bank; trustee of Consolidated Edison Co. and director of Chase National Bank and Western Union Telegraph Co. Member of Kane Lodge No. 454, New York City, receiving degrees on May 20, June 3 and June 17, 1902; received 50-year membership award in 1953; served a number of years on the Kane-Peary Room committee of his lodge.

Henry Eckford (1775-1832) Early American naval architect. b. March 12, 1775 in Irvine, Scotland. At 16 he was placed with a naval constructor at Quebec and in 1796 moved to New York, where he introduced important changes in the art of shipbuilding. His vessels were superior in strength and speed to all others and in the War of 1812 he was employed by the U.S. government to build ships. Following the war he built the steamer Robert Fulton. In 1820 he was appointed naval constructor at Brooklyn and he built six ships of the line including the famous Ohio which was claimed to be the finest in the world. Disagreeing with the naval commissioners, he left government service and built a sloop-of-war for Sultan Mahmoud of the Ottoman empire and was solicited to enter his service. This led him to a visit to Turkey where he established a navy yard and died at Constantinople on Nov. 12, 1832. He was a member of Fortitude Lodge No. 48 (now No. 19) of Brooklyn, N.Y. and was first junior warden of the lodge.

Karl F. Eckleff (1723-1789) German physician who was active in the propagation of the high grades of Freemasonry in Sweden between 1752 and 1759. It was in the latter year that the "secret constitutions" were adopted. In 1766 he sold to Berlin Masons such rights and rituals as he held and tried to do the same insofar as Sweden was concerned. However, he finally relinquished all rights to the Duke of Sudermania, q.v. in 1774 and the duke (later King Charles XIII, q.v.), who gained control of the symbolic degrees through the resignation of Count Scheffer, became the head of all forms of Freemasonry in Sweden.

Zales N. Ecton U.S. Senator from Montana, 1948. b. April 1, 1898 at Weldon, Ia. He was state representative from 1933-37 and state senator, 1937-46. He is secretary and director of the Flying D, Inc., a ranch and cattle company at Gallatin Gateway, Mont. Mason, 32° AASR (SJ) and Shriner. At one time he was in the line of the Grand Lodge of Montana and at the annual communication in 1952 addressed the grand lodge.

Prince Edwin The English Ancient manuscripts claim that he called a great communication of operative Masons at York in the year 926. This legend is not accepted by modern historians.

Paul D. Eddy President of Adelphi College, Garden City, N.Y. since 1937. b. Feb. 18, 1895 in Montgomery, Ala. Graduate of U. of Pennsylvania and ordained to ministry of Methodist Church, serving several Pennsylvania churches. He was director of the Wesley Foundation in the Philippines in 1929-30 and executive director of the Religious Educational Foundation, 1931-37. Served in U.S. Navy in WWI. Member of Garden City Lodge No. 1083, Garden City, L.I., N.Y. and chaplain of same several years.

Samuel Eddy (1769-1839) Chief Justice, Supreme Court of Rhode Island, 1827-35 and U.S. Congressman, 1819-25. b. March 31, 1769 in Johnston, R.I., he graduated at Brown U. in 1787 and studied law. He was clerk of the R.I. supreme court in 1790-93 and secretary of state from 1798-1819. Member of St. John's Lodge No. 1 at Providence, being initiated Feb. 1, 1792. d. Feb. 2, 1839.

William H. Eddy (1817-1859) Hero of the Donner Party trapped in the Sierra Nevada mountains in winter of 1846-47. b. in Providence, R.I. in 1817. In 1845 he was working as a wheelwright in Belleville, Ill. He joined the Donner Party for the trip to California and with James Frazier Reed, q.v., and William McCutchen, q.v., is referred to as one of the "big three" of that ill-fated group. Eddy's privations and experiences were particularly harrowing, for his wife and two children perished of cold and starvation. He led the "Forlorn Hope" group—ten men and five women, who made a desperate attempt to escape from their snowy prison and obtain relief for the rest of the party. It took them 32 days to get out and all the men except Eddy and a William Foster died on the way. They left bloody footprints on the snow as their shoes wore out and their shredded clothing was frozen to their bodies. His exertions led to his early death on Dec. 24, 1859 of angina pectoris. On July 11, 1850 he was one of the 15 brethren at San Jose who petitioned the grand lodge for a dispensation to open a lodge in that city. His name later appears on the records of San Jose Lodge No. 10 as a charter member. This shows he was a Mason before coming to San Jose, but there is no available record of his original membership. Unfortunately he was suspended NPD in 1857.

William Eden (1744-1814) (Lord Auckland) English barrister who served at different times as Secretary of State for Ireland, privy councilor and ambassador to France, Spain and Holland. Was made an Irish peer in 1789 with the title Baron Auckland, receiving the same title in the English peerage in 1793. He was one of the three commissioners sent by Lord North in 1788 to treat with the Americans. In 1770 he was grand steward of the Grand Lodge of England. d. May 28, 1814.

Arthur H. Edens President of Duke University since 1949. b. Feb. 14, 1901 at Willow Grove, Tenn. Degrees from Emory and Harvard U. Was dean at Emory Jr. Coll. and Emory U. until 1948. Mason.

Walter E. Edge (1873-1956) U.S. Senator from New Jersey, 1919-29; Governor of New Jersey during WWI and also WWII (1917-19 and 1943-46) and ambassador to France 1929-33. b. Nov. 20, 1873 in Philadelphia. He began as a printer's "devil" on the Atlantic Review, Atlantic City, N.J., and during his lifetime made a fortune in the advertising and publishing business. He is credited with helping to promote Atlantic City into prominence as a vacation spot. He was one of the first prominent men to back Eisenhower for the presidency in 1951. As ambassador to France, he won the admiration and respect of the French people and was instrumental in negotiating important trade treaties. He was raised Feb. 4, 1896 in Trinity Lodge No. 79, Atlantic City and affiliated with Belcher Lodge No. 180, Atlantic City on April 9, 1904. He was a visitor to the grand lodge sessions in 1917. Member of Evergreen Forest No. 49, Tall Cedars of Lebanon at Milford, Del. on June 9, 1923 and member of Crescent Shrine Temple, Trenton, N.J. d. Oct. 29, 1956.

Alonzo Jay Edgerton (1827-1896) U.S. Senator from Minnesota, March-Oct., 1881. b. June 7, 1827 in Rome, N.Y. Graduate of Wesleyan U. at Middletown, Conn. and settled in Mantorville, Minn. in 1855 where he practiced law. Was brigadier general in Civil War. Served terms in state senate. Moved to Kasson, Minn. in 1878. He was appointed chief justice of the territorial supreme court of Dakota and when South Dakota was admitted as a state, he was made U.S. judge of that district. He served as president of the constitutional convention of South Dakota. Made a Mason in 1851 in Grenada Lodge No. 31 of Miss. and later a member of Mantorville Lodge No. 11, Mantorville, Minn. He was grand scribe of the Grand Chapter, R.A.M. of Minn. in 1875 and also served as senior grand warden of the Grand Lodge of Minnesota. d. Aug. 9, 1896.

Harold E. Edgerton Electrical engineer and inventor of stroboscopic high-speed motion and still photography apparatus. b. April 6, 1903 in Fremont, Nebr. Graduate of U. of Nebr. and Mass. Institute of Tech. Employed as electrical engineer by Nebr. Light & Power Co., and General Electric Co. and professor at M.I.T. Member of Acacia fraternity. Raised in Aurora Lodge No. 68, Aurora, Nebr. and presently a member of Richard C. Maclaurin Lodge, Cambridge, Mass.

H.R.H. Prince Philip, Duke of Edinburgh Consort of Queen Elizabeth, q.v. b. June 10, 1921. Although a prince of the royal house of Greece, Philip is a descendant of the English royal house and of Queen Victoria. Victoria's third child, H.R.H. Princess Alice, who married Prince Louis, grand duke of Hesse, was the mother of Victoria Alberta, who married the Marquess of Milford Haven. Their eldest child, Alice, married Prince Andrew of Greece. They, in turn had five children, Philip being the youngest. He married H.R.H. Princess Elizabeth in November, 1947. Philip was initiated in Navy Lodge No. 2612 of London on Dec. 5, 1952.

Present at the initiation were the Earl of Scarbrough, grand master, q.v., and Geoffrey Fisher, archbishop of Canterbury. The lodge has many ties with the royal family as King Edward VII served as its first master in 1896 when he was Prince of Wales, q.v., King George VI, q.v., served as master when he was Duke of York. In 1928 H.R.H. Duke of Kent, q.v., was master and later became grand master of the Grand Lodge of England.

William Henry, Duke of Edinburgh (see Duke of Gloucester) Douglas L. Edmonds Justice, Supreme Court of California, 1936-56. b. in Chicago, Ill. Admitted to California bar in 1910 and practiced in Los Angeles until 1926 when he became municipal court judge and later superior court judge. Mason.

George W. Edmonds (1864-1939) U.S. Congressman, 63rd to 68th and 73rd Congresses (1913-25 and 1933-35) from 4th Pa. dist. b. Feb. 22, 1864 (and thus named George Washington). Was in retail drug business until 1887, when he became an organizer of the Black Diamond Coal Co. He continued throughout his life in the wholesale coal business. Received his degrees in Washington Lodge No. 59, Philadelphia on Jan. 10, March 14 and Oct. 9, 1906; affiliated with Olivet Lodge No. 607, Philadelphia on Sept. 24, 1907. d. Sept. 28, 1939.

Ed Edmondson U.S. Congressman to 83rd through 85th Congresses from 2nd Okla. dist. b. April 7, 1919 in Muskogee, Okla. Brother of J. Howard Edmonson, q.v., governor of Okla. Graduate of U. of Oklahoma and Georgetown U. Was a newspaperman with the Muskogee Daily and United Press, 1936-40 and a special F.B.I. agent, 1941-43. In

1946-47 while studying law at Georgetown U., he was Washington correspondent for four Okla. newspapers. Admitted to the bar in 1947 and practiced in Muskogee with his brother. Served as a Naval lieutenant in WWII. Member of Muskogee Lodge No. 28; 32° AASR (SJ) in Indian Consistory at McAlester and member of Bedouin Shrine Temple of Muskogee.

J. Howard Edmondson Elected Governor of Oklahoma in 1958. b. Sept. 27, 1925 in Muskogee, a brother of Congressman Ed Edmondson, q.v. Graduated in law from U. of Oklahoma and served four years as county attorney of Tulsa Co., Okla. Served in Air Force in WWII and was flight commander. Member of Oriental Lodge No. 430, Muskogee, Okla. and 32° AASR (SJ) in Indian Consistory of McAlester, Okla.

George F. Edmunds (1828-1919) U.S. Senator from Vermont, 1866-91, resigning in the latter year. b. Feb. 1, 1828 at Richmond, Vt. Graduate of U. of Vt. in 1855. Member of Vermont lower house, 1854-59 and upper house, 1861-62. He authored the act in 1882 for suppression of polygamy in Utah and disfranchisement of those practicing it. It was known as the "Edmunds Act." He was president pro-tem of the U.S. Senate during Arthur's presidency. Received 34 votes for Republican presidential nomination in 1880 and 93 in 1884. Member of Washington Lodge No. 3, Burlington, Vt. d. Feb. 27, 1919.

William R. Edrington (1872-1932) Capitalist. b. Feb. 22, 1872 in Madison Parish, La. He began in the investment business at Fort Worth, Texas in 1897, and became president of the Edrington-Minot Corp., Edring-ton Investment Co., and vice president of Minot Holding Corp. Member of Fort Worth Lodge No. 148, Fort Worth, Texas, receiving degrees on Dec. 27, 1897, May 13, 1898 and Feb. 13, 1899. d. Nov. 6, 1932.

Samuel C. Edsall (1860-1917) Episcopal Bishop. b. March 4, 1860 in Dixon, Ill. Was ordained deacon in 1888; priest in 1889. He founded St. Peter's Mission of Chicago in 1887. From 1889-99 he was rector of St. Peter's Church, Chicago and became missionary bishop of N.D. in 1899. In 1901 he was elected coadjutor bishop of Minn. d. Feb. 17, 1917. He was a member of Minneapolis Lodge No. 19, Minneapolis, Minn.

Merritt A. Edson (1897-1955) Major General, U.S. Marine Corps. b. April 25, 1897 in Rutland, Vt. Advanced to brigadier general in 1943, retiring as major general in 1947. Awarded Congressional Medal of Honor. Was with Marines in France in WWI and later served as a Marine aviator in the Pacific and Central America. A small arms expert, he taught and served in ordnance depots. From 1937-39 he was with 4th Marines in China and as commander of 1st Raider bn. participated in the Tarawa operations. He was assistant division commander of 2nd Marines in Saipan-Tinian operations and later commanding general of the service command of the Fleet Marine Force, Pacific. From 1946-47 he was member of staff of Chief of Naval Operations. After his retirement he became Vermont's first public safety commissioner. Raised in Olive Branch Lodge No. 64, Chester, Vt. on Feb. 24, 1926. d. Aug. 14, 1955.

Edward VII (1841-1910) King of England, 1901-10. Of the house of

Saxe-Coburg, he was called The Peacemaker. Eldest son of Queen Victoria, he was created Prince of Wales in 1841. Studied at Edinburgh, Oxford, and Cambridge and served as a colonel in the army in 1858. He was the first British royal prince to visit a colony, visiting Canada in 1860, where on Sept. 1, he laid the cornerstone of the Canadian Parliament building at Ottawa. It is interesting to note that the government would not allow the Freemasons to take part in the ceremonies, but told them that they were welcome to appear in their regalia. It was on this trip that he visited the St. Louis, Mo. agricultural and mechanical fair on Sept. 26, arriving from Canada by way of Detroit and Chicago, and by steamer from Alton. He bought a fast trotting horse at the fair and dined on buffalo tongue, quail, prairie chicken and Missouri wine, departing the next day for Cincinnati. In 1863 he took a seat in the house of lords as Duke of Cornwall. His mother, Queen Victoria, would not allow him to take part in foreign negotiations until Gladstone's last ministry in 1892-94. He was chancellor of the U. of Wales, arranged the queen's jubilees, assisted in promoting the Royal College of Music, and won the Derby three times with his horses. As king, he promoted international amity by visits to European capitals. He brought the crown into active participation in public life and with all sections of the empire. He was initiated into Freemasonry in 1868 at Stockholm, Sweden by King Adolphus Frederick, q.v., who was also grand master of Sweden. He was master of Apollo University Lodge at Oxford in 1873; master of Prince of Wales Lodge No. 250, London and also of Royal Alpha Lodge, London. He was patron of the Grand Lodge of Scotland and Ireland and was honorary member of Edinburgh

Lodge No. 1. He was patron of the Supreme Council of the 33° of England. Edward was elected grand master of the Grand Lodge of England on April 28, 1875 and installed that date in a ceremony at Albert Hall conducted by the Earl of Carnarvon, q.v., in the presence of 10,000 brethren. It was probably the most brilliant Masonic function ever held. He served as grand master until 1901 when he ascended the throne and took the title of "protector of the craft." Queen Alexandria Lodge No. 2932 of London was named for his queen with her permission and good wishes.

Edward VIII King of England, Jan. 20-Dec.11, 1936, abdicating to marry Mrs. Wallis Simpson, an American. Eldest son of George V. and Queen Mary, his full name is Edward Albert Christian George Andrew Patrick David. Before ascending to the throne, he was Prince of Wales, and after abdication, Duke of Windsor. He was prepared for the Navy at Osborne and Dartmouth and created Prince of Wales and Earl of Chester in 1911. At his investiture in Carnarvon Castle, he was the first English prince to address the Welsh in their own tongue. He served as a midshipman on the H.M.S. Hindostan and in WWI was with the B.E.F. in Flanders, France and on the Italian front. He was on the staff of the commander of the Mediterranean Force in Egypt and also with the Canadian Corps. Taking up his public duties in 1919, he toured Canada, U.S., Africa, and South America as England's favorite "Ambassador of the Empire." When he succeeded his father in 1936, he was the first bachelor king in 176 years. When he proposed to marry Mrs. Simpson nee Warfield and elevate her as queen, it raised a storm of protest resulting in his abdication. He later visited Germany to study social and housing conditions, and in 1939 was a major general attached to the B.E.F. staff in liaison work in France. From 1940-45 he was governor of the Bahama Islands. Edward was initiated by H.R.H. Arthur, Duke of Connaught and Strathearn, q.v., on May 2, 1919 in the Household Brigade Lodge No. 2614—one of the lodges of which the grand master is permanent master. He was appointed senior warden of the lodge in 1920 and elected deputy master in 1921. On Oct. 25, 1922 he was installed as senior grand warden of the Grand Lodge of England in Royal Albert Hall in the presence of nearly 9,000 brethren. He was named provincial grand master for Surrey on July 22, 1924 and grand master of the Grand Lodge of England in 1936. He also served as grand superintendent of Royal Arch Masonry for Surrey. He was an honorary 33° of the Supreme Council, Scottish Rite of England.

Edward Augustus (Duke of Kent) (1767-1820) Fourth son of George III of England and father of Queen Victoria. A soldier, he became major general in 1793; lieutenant general in 1796, and full general in 1799. He was commander-in-chief of the forces in British North America in 1799-1800. From 1802-03 he was governor of Gibraltar and in 1805 was created field marshal. He was initiated in 1790 in Union Lodge of Geneva. In 1813 he was elected grand master of the Athol Grand Lodge, accepting the office in order to unite the two rival grand lodges. When his purpose had been accomplished, he resigned the grand-mastership and suggested his younger brother, Augustus Frederick, q.v., Duke of Sussex as grand master. This was accomplished, and Augustus Frederick became the first grand master of the

United Grand Lodge of England, serving from 1813-43. While serving in the British military establishment in North America, Edward Augustus was on the rolls of the Craft in Nova Scotia.

Clarence R. Edwards (1860-1931) Major General U.S. Army. b. Jan. 1, 1860 at Cleveland, Ohio and graduated U.S. Military Academy in 1883. Commissioned in the latter year, he advanced through grades to major general in 1917. He organized the 26th Infantry Division and commanded it for 10 months on the front lines in France. Held numerous commands on his return to the U.S. He retired in 1922. Member of Euclid Lodge in Boston, Mass. d. Feb. 14, 1931.

Edward I. Edwards (1863-1931) U.S. Senator from New Jersey, 1923-29 and Governor of New Jersey, 1920-23. b. Dec. 1, 1863 at Jersey City, N.J. He was connected with the First National Bank of Jersey City from 1882. He was a state senator from Hudson Co. in 1919, resigning to become governor. Member of Bergen Lodge No. 47, Jersey Ctiy, being initiated on Feb. 6, 1891. 32° AASR and Shriner. d. Jan. 26, 1931.

Gus Edwards (1879-1945) Theatrical producer, composer and vaudeville star. Raised Jan. 16, 1904 in Independent Lodge No. 185, New York City. Dimitted May 4, same year and reaffiliated May 19, 1906.

Henry W. Edwards (1779-1847) U.S. Senator from Connecticut, 1823-27 and Governor of Connecticut, 1833-38. b. in New Haven, Conn., the son of Pierpont Edwards, q.v., first grand master of Connecticut. He studied at the Litchfield law school and settled in New Haven where he was twice elected to congress as a Democrat, serving from 1819-1823. He also served in the two state legislative bodies. He was initiated in Hiram Lodge No. 1 of New Haven on Feb. 2, 1809 and elected secretary of the lodge the same year. He was exalted in Franklin Chapter No. 2, R.A.M. of New Haven on June 14, 1810 and greeted in Harmony Council, R. & S.M. on Oct. 16, 1818. d. July 22, 1847.

John Edwards (1748-1837) One of the first two U.S. Senators from Kentucky, 1791-1795. Born in Virginia, he moved to that portion of the state now comprising Kentucky in 1780, where he owned some 23,000 acres of land. He was a member of the state legislature from 1781-85 and again from 1795-1800. He was elected to the convention that ratified the Federal constitution as well as his own state conventions of 1785-88. Member of Abraham Lodge No. 8, Louisville, Ky.

Morton Edwards English sculptor. Made a Mark Master in Thistle Lodge No. 8, London, England on Oct. 1, 1869.

Ninian Edwards (1775-1833) U.S. Senator from Illinois, 1818-24; Governor of Illinois Territory, 1809-18 and Governor of Illinois, 1826-30. Born in Maryland, he was educated at Dickinson College in Pennsylvania and moved to Kentucky at age of 20. At one time his education was directed by William Wirt, q.v., the presidential candidate on the anti-Masonic ticket. A lawyer, he became chief justice of the supreme court of Kentucky at the age of 32. He moved to Illinois when President Madison appointed him governor of the territory and remained there until his death. He was one of the first two U.S.

Senators from Illinois just as his uncle, John Edwards, q.v., had been in Kentucky. He was a member of Lexington Lodge No. 1, Lexington, Ky. d. July 20, 1833.

Pierpont Edwards (1750-1826) Member of the Continental Congress of 1787-88. b. April 8, 1750 in Northampton, Mass., his father was a missionary to the Stockbridge (Mass.) Indians and young Pierpont became so proficient in the Indian language that he said he "often thought in Indian." He graduated from Princeton in 1768 and began practice of law in New Haven, Conn. in 1771. He was appointed administrator of the estate of Benedict Arnold, q.v., at the time of his treason. He took an early stand in favor of independence and served in the Revolutionary Army, taking part in two battles. At the time of his death he was a judge of the U.S. district court. He was initiated in Hiram Lodge No. 1, New Haven, Dec. 28, 1775, serving as master of the lodge in 1777-78, and was the first grand master of the Grand Lodge of Connecticut, 1789-90. His son, Henry W., q.v., became U.S. senator and governor of Connecticut. d. April 5, 1826.

Willard E. Edwards Originator of The Perpetual Calendar. b. Dec. 11, 1903 at Chatham, Mass. He was educated at Mass. Inst. of Tech.; B.S., U. of Oklahoma and graduate work at U. of Southern Calif. He originated The Perpetual Calendar in 1919, which was officially endorsed by Hawaiian legislature in 1943 and by Mass. in 1952. The calendar has been proposed by congressional resolution in 1943, 45, 47, 49, 51, and 53. A writer and lecturer since 1922, he has been a research engineer with Radio Corp. of America, Alexander Aircraft Co., American Telephone &

Telegraph Co. and others. In WWII he served as a lieutenant commander in the U.S. Navy. Raised in Wollaston Lodge, Quincy, Mass. on March 17, 1925. He later affiliated with Norman Lodge No. 38, Norman, Okla. (1929-33); Silveyville Lodge No. 201, Dixon, Calif. (1933-35); Fullerton Lodge No. 339, Fullerton, Calif. (1936-46) and Honolulu Lodge No. 409, Honolulu, Hawaii since 1947. Received AASR (SJ) degrees in 1958. Life member of Square and Compass Club of Midway Island.

Edwin Early Masonic tradition claims him as the son of Athelstan (895-940), King of England, who was the son of King Edward the Elder and grandson of King Alfred. Practically all of the Old Charges, after the first two, refer to Athelstan as having a son called Edwin, "and hee loued masons much more than his father ... and a Comifsion to hould euer yeare and Afsembly." By tradition, the first was held at York in 926. Whether Athelstan had a son named Edwin is doubtful. Historians have agreed that he had a brother of that name, but the brother was drowned in his youth (933). A theory has been advanced that the "Edwin" referred to in the Old Charges may have been Edwin, King of Northumberland (585?-633).

David Edwin (1776-1841) American engraver. b. Dec., 1776 in Bath, England. His father, John, was a comedian. David was apprenticed to Jossi, a Dutch engraver residing in England, who soon returned to Holland, taking David with him. Disagreeing with his master, he left before his apprenticeship was over and shipped as a sailor on an American vessel bound for Philadelphia, hoping eventually to reach London. He arrived in Philadelphia in December of 1797, and obtained employment from an

English publisher, and later worked for Edward Savage, the painter. His specialty was engraving portraits and his work was credited with being the best produced in America up to that time. His copies of Gilbert Stuart's paintings were especially good. He made copies of portraits by the artists Peale, Waldo, Wood, Jarvis, Sully and Neagle. After 20 years of application, his eyesight failed and he was compelled to resort to other work to earn a living. He was initiated in Columbia Lodge No. 91, Philadelphia on March 1, 1806 and later served as master of the lodge. d. Feb. 22, 1841.

Stillman W. Eells (1873-1937) American foreign service officer and businessman. b. April 24, 1873 at Cleveland, Ohio. Graduated from Yale in 1895. Became president of the Wheeler Mfg. Co. and the Alignum Co., retiring from active business in 1904. From 1918-35 he served as U.S. consul in British East Africa, Bermuda, Kenya, Madeira, Leeds, England, Ceylon, Cardiff, Wales, and Valencia, Spain. Member of Albion Lodge No. 26, New York City, receiving degrees on Jan. 9, Jan. 23 and Feb. 13, 1899. He was junior warden of his lodge in 1901-02. d. May 12, 1937.

Charles Howard, 2nd Baron of Effingham (1536-1624) Of the English house of Howard, he was also the 1st Earl of Nottingham. Ambassador of Effingham to France in 1559; lord chamberlain from 1574-85, and as lord high admiral from 1585-1618, he held the chief command against the Spanish Armada in 1588, which he defeated. He was the commissioner for the trial of Mary, Queen of Scots in 1586. According to William Preston, q.v., he was grand master of England from 1579-88.

Thomas, 3rd Earl of Effingham Served the Grand Lodge of England as pro grand master from 1782-90 in place of the Duke of Cumberland, who was of royal blood.

Philippe Egalite (see Due de Chartres)

W. Grant Egbert (1869-1928) Musician. b. Dec. 28, 1869 at Danby, N.Y. Received M.A. in music from Syracuse U. in 1904 and studied in Europe under several masters. He made his debut at age of eight as a violinist, touring the U.S. and the capitals of Europe. He was concertmeister and assistant conductor of the Sevcik Orchestra at Prague for three years, and in 1892 founded and directed the Ithaca Conservatory of Music, bringing Cesar Thomson and 0. Sevcik to the U.S. as instructors. Member of Fidelity Lodge No. 51, Ithaca, N.Y., receiving degrees on April 15, May 6 and May 20, 1902. d. Dec. 18, 1928.

Edward Eggleston (1837-1902) American author. b. Dec. 10, 1837 in Vevay, Ind. He was a Methodist pastor and Bible agent in Minnesota from 1858-66, but his poor health forced him to turn to other occupations for a living, which as he stated were "always honest, but sometimes undignified." In 1866 he moved to Evanston, Ill., where he was associate editor of the Little Corporal, a children's paper, to which he had previously contributed. Within a year he became the editor of Sunday School Teacher and gained a reputation as a speaker. During this time he was a contributor to the New York Independent, and in 1870 moved to New York and became its literary editor, and later the editor. In 1871 he became editor of Hearth and Home, but resigned in a year due to ill health, and spent the remainder of his life writing. Among his novels depicting early life in Indiana are The Hoosier Schoolmaster; The End of the World; The Circuit Rider; Roxy; The Hoosier Schoolboy; The Graysons, and The Faith Doctor. He received his degrees in Ancient Landmark Lodge No. 5, St. Paul, Minn., in 1863.

William H. Egle (1830-1901) Historian and physician. b. Sept. 17, 1830 in Harrisburg, Pa. He spent three years as a printer on the Pennsylvania Telegraph and later became editor of Literary Companion and also Daily Times. He graduated in medicine from U. of Pennsylvania in 1859 and served during the Civil War as a surgeon, being chief medical officer of General Birney's division. From 1871, he turned his attention to historical research, and, in 1887 was appointed state librarian of Pennsylvania. Most of his writings are on Pennsylvania history including Notes and Queries Relating to Interior Pennsylvania; History of the Commonwealth of Pennsylvania; Pennsylvania in the Revolution, and many others. He was a member of Perseverance Lodge No. 21 of Harrisburg, Pa., receiving degrees on Oct. 9, Nov. 9, 1854, serving as master in 1866 and resigning in 1870. d. in 1901.

Alexander, 10th Earl of Eglinton Grand Master Mason (15th) of Scotland in 1750. House of Montgomerie.

Archibald, 16th Earl of Eglinton Grand Master Mason (82nd) of Scotland in 1920. Also Earl of Winton.

Archibald William, 17th Earl of Eglinton House of Montgomerie, Scottish peer of the realm. Initiated in Apollo University Lodge No. 357 in

1936. Affiliated with Lodge No. 0 in 1947 and master of same in 1953. Substitute grand master in 1955.

Leopold Garcia Ehlers Mexican architect and Grand Master of the Grand Lodge, Valle of Mexico. b. July 8, 1913 in Concordia, Puebla, Mexico. His father, also a Freemason, fought in the revolution in the Zapatistas and Carrancistas forces. The son became a graduate engineer in 1936 and then specialized as a civil sanitary engineer. He has been a professor of mathematics and architectural composition at the National Polytechnic Institute since 1937. Since 1937 he also has been engineer in charge of the water and drainage dept. of the Federal District (Mexico City). He has designed and built residences, apartments, factories, churches, schools, etc. The present new grand lodge building of the Grand Lodge, Valle de Mexico at Sadi Carnot No. 75 is of his design. He donated his services to the grand lodge on this work. In 1959 he became grand master of the Grand Lodge, Valle de Mexico.

Fausto Ehluller, with the Arago brothers, is said to have established the first Masonic lodge in Mexico City; he enlisted the support of the most distinguished men of Mexico, including the Mexican national hero, Miguel Hidalgo, curate of the village of Hidalgo, state of Guanajuato; he later was known as the father of Mexican Independence. He was initiated in 1808. He was defeated at the River Santiago, 1811, and betrayed into the hands of the Spaniards, q.v.

John C. B. Ehringhaus (1882-1949) Governor of North Carolina, 1933-37. b. Feb. 5, 1882 at Elizabeth City, N.C. Graduate of U. of N.C., and admitted to bar in 1903,

practicing at Elizabeth City. After a term as governor, he practiced at Raleigh. Member of Eureka Lodge No. 317 of Elizabeth City (EA Nov. 13, 1917; FC Feb. 18, 1918; MM Feb. 26, 1918). Exalted in Cherokee Chapter No. 14, R.A.M. on Oct. 14, 1920 and knighted in Griggs Commandery No. 14, K.T. on Feb. 1, 1921—all of Elizabeth City, N.C. d. July 29, 1949.

Robert L. Eichelberger Lieutenant General, U.S. Army. b. March 9, 1886 at Urbana, Ohio. Graduate of U.S. Military Academy in 1909 and advanced through grades to major general in 1941 and lieutenant general in 1942. He served on Mexican border in 1911, Canal Zone, 1911-15, and major of infantry in 1918-19. He was with the Siberian Expeditionary Forces in 1918; Philippines, 1920; China and Japan, 1920-21; General Staff, 1921-24; adjutant general of U.S. Military Academy, 1931-35; sec. General Staff at Washington, 1935-38; commander of the Presidio, San Francisco and 30th Infantry, 1938-40; superintendent of U.S. Military Academy, 1940-42. In WWII he commanded the 77th Infantry div., 1st Corps, and participated in Philippines reoccupation, New Guinea and New Britain campaigns. He commanded the 8th Army from 1944-48 and the allied and U.S. occupation forces of Japan from 1946-48 when he retired. Author of *Our Bloody Jungle Road to Tokyo*. Member of Pike Lodge No. 36, Washington, D.C., 32° AASR in Army Consistory, Fort Leavenworth, Kans. on Nov. 28, 1925. d. Sept. 26, 1961.

Rudolph Eickemeyer (1831-1895) American inventor. b. in Altenbamberg, Bavaria, coming to the U.S. in 1850. He patented about 150 inventions including a hat-manufacturing machine that helped revolutionize that industry; a differential gear for mowing and reaping machine in 1870; many electrical machines and devices, including the first symmetrical drum armature iron-clad dynamo, direct-connected railway motor and others. He was the discoverer and first employer of Charles P. Steinmetz. Member of Rising Star Lodge No. 450, Yonkers, N.Y.

Carl Ben Eielson (1897-1929) Aviator and Arctic explorer. b. July 20, 1897 at Hatton, N.D. Early Arctic aviator who taught others about Arctic flying and flew Sir Hubert Wilkins over the North Pole. The plane in which they made the trip is in the North Dakota state historical building at Bismarck, where it is deposited as a memorial to Eielson. A member of Garfield Lodge No. 105 at Hatton, N.D., his degrees were conferred March 31, June 3, Sept. 16, 1921. He was lost while on a rescue mission in the Siberian Arctic on Nov. 9, 1929.

Arthur B. Eisenhower (1886-1958) Executive Vice President of Commerce Trust Co., Kansas City, Mo., and brother of President Eisenhower. b. Nov. 11, 1886 at Hope, Kans. With the Commerce Trust since 1905. Was a director of several banks and corporations including TWA airlines. Member of Rural Lodge No. 316 of Kansas City. Member of Orient Chapter No. 102, R.A.M. and Oriental Commandery No. 35, K.T., but withdrew from each in 1937. Also withdrew from Ararat Shrine Temple in 1938. d. Feb., 1958.

Dwight D. Eisenhower President of the United States. He is not a Freemason, but holds the fraternity in high regard. On February 24, 1955 he addressed 1,100 Freemasons at a breakfast given by Frank S. Land in the Statler Hotel in Washington, D.C.

At this time he stated: "I feel a distinct sense of pride in appearing before this group which takes on its own shoulders the care and welfare of the unfortunate. This group, by action, recognizes the responsibilities of brotherhood by helping one another . . . you are setting an example to all of us that we must do our duty if we are to prove the Communists to be in error—to be liars."

Milton S. Eisenhower President of Pennsylvania State University since 1950. b. Sept. 15, 1899 at Abilene, Kans. Graduate of Kansas State Coll. in 1924. Honorary degrees from 17 colleges and universities. City editor of the Abilene Daily Reflector in 1918 and 1920-21. From 1924-26 he was U.S. vice consul at Edinburgh, Scotland. From 1926-40 he was with the U.S. department of agriculture as assistant to the secretary and director of information. He was director of the War Relocation Authority in 1942 and associate director of the Office of War Information 1942-43. From 1943-50 he was president of Kansas State Coll. He has served on many national and international committees on education, relief, etc., including membership on the executive board of UNESCO special ambassador and personal representative of the Presidenton Latin American affairs, and director of Freedoms Foundation. Made a Mason "at sight" by the Grand Lodge of Pennsylvania on Nov. 5, 1951 by William E. Yeager, grand master; petitioned State College Lodge No. 700 at State College, Pa., on May 13, 1952 and was admitted June 10, 1952.

Walter E. Ekblaw (1882-1949) Geographer. Geologist and botanist on Crocker Land Arctic Expedition of 1913-17. b. March 10, 1882 at Rantoul, Ill. Graduate of U. of

Illinois including Ph.D. He was re-search associate of American Museum of Natural History, 1917-22, consultant geologist until 1924 and editor of Economic Geography from 1924. Member of Rantoul Lodge No. 470, Rantoul, Ill., receiving degrees on June 5, June 21 and Aug. 30, 1906. d. June 5, 1949.

Samuel Elbert (1743-1788) Revolutionary Brigadier General; Governor of Georgia, and last grand master of Georgia to be appointed by the United Grand Lodge of England. b. in Prince William parish, S.C., he was orphaned at an early age and went to Savannah. In 1774, he was elected captain of a grenadier company and entered the Continental army with rank of lieutenant colonel in 1776. He participated in an expedition against the British in East Florida and later captured Fort Oglethorpe. At the action of Brier Creek, where he commanded 60 continentals and 160 militia, he was surrounded on three sides and made a valiant stand. He was captured and wounded in this action and according to accounts was saved by a British officer who drew him out of the line of fire when he had given a Masonic sign. He was a member of Solomon Lodge No. 1, Savannah. He resigned as grand master of the Provincial Grand Lodge of Georgia (under English constitution) on Dec. 16, 1786 in order that the new Grand Lodge of Georgia might be organized. He was made brigadier general in 1783 and subsequently held the rank of major general of Georgia militia. Elbert county, Ga., was named in his honor. d. Nov. 2, 1788.

Samuel H. Elbert (1833-1899) Governor of Colorado Territory in 1873. b. in Logan Co., Ohio. Following his term as governor, he was justice of the supreme court of Colo-

rado. He was initiated in Plattsmouth Lodge No. 6 of Nebraska and was a charter member and first master of Union Lodge No. 7, Denver, Colo. in 1863, serving again in 1869. He was also a charter member of Denver Chapter No. 2, R.A.M. and member of Colorado Commandery No. 1, K.T., Denver. d. Nov. 27, 1899.

Duc d'Elchingen (see under Michel Ney).

Francis, Lord Elcho Grand Master Mason (57th) of Scotland in 1827-29. He was later the 8th Earl of Wemyss.

Francis Charteris, Lord Elcho Grand Master Mason (36th) of Scotland in 1786-87.

Bowman Elder (1888-1954) President of Southern Indiana Railway and veterans' organization executive. b. March 4, 1888 at Indianapolis, Ind. Entered real estate business with father in 1912. Vice president of Circle Agencies, Inc., and consular agent for France at Indianapolis, 1934-40. Served in France during WWI. In 1927 he was chairman of the France Convention Committee of the American Legion when 20,000 legionaires, known as the "2nd A.E.F." went to France. It was the largest peace time movement in history. He was national treasurer of the American Legion, 1928-33. Received his degrees in Oriental Lodge No. 500, Indianapolis, Ind., on Oct. 21, Oct. 28, Nov. 4, 1919. d. June 10, 1954.

Harry S. Eldred Executive Vice President of Armour & Co., since 1950. b. Jan. 21, 1889 at Colfax, Ind. He was an auditor from 1909 until 1919 when he became plant manager of Morris & Co., Kansas City. In

1923 he went with Armour as plant accountant, becoming general auditor in 1925, assistant to vice president in charge of operations in 1930, general manager of plants in 1934, vice president in charge of operations in 1936 and executive vice president and member of executive committee since 1950. Mason.

Charles, 5th Earl of Elgin Grand Master Mason (23rd) of Scotland, 1761-62. Also the 7th Earl of Kincardine.

Edward James Bruce, 10th Earl of Elgin Grand Master Mason (83rd) of Scotland, 1921-22. Also 14th Earl of Kincardine. Initiated in Lord Elgin and Bruce Lodge No. 1077 in 1912 and served as master in 1913 and 1922. He affiliated with Lodge No. 77 and was master in 1914. Also member of Old Etonian Lodge No. 4500 (English) and master of it in 1928. Founding member of Librarius Lodge No. 6966 (English); member of Royal Altha Lodge No. 16 (English) and master of same in 1948. Honorary past master of Elgin Lodge No. 7 (Quebec) in 1923. He is past senior grand warden of the Grand Lodge of England and an active Royal Arch Mason. He is the head of the Royal Order of Scotland, an organization traditionally founded by his ancestor, Robert le Bruce. The earl lives at Broomhall, Dunfermline, and in the entrance hall is displayed the famous sword of Robert le Bruce, q.v., that has been handed down through the family.

John Eliot (1604-1690) "Apostle of the Indians," minister and author. b. in Widford, Hertfordshire, England on Aug. 5, 1604. He graduated from Cambridge in 1622, and after teaching school, he entered the holy orders of the Church of England.

On Nov. 4, 1631 he landed in Boston, Mass. He first preached in a Boston church and then moved to Roxbury where he taught the Indians for 60 years. He saw much of his work with the Indians destroyed by King Philip's War. He was the author of *A Primer or Catechism, in the Massachusetts Indian Language* (1654); *Up-Bookum Psalmes* (1663) and many others. His Indian translation of the Bible in 1663 was the first Bible printed in North America. Although he is thought to have been a Freemason, no record has been found. *Mackey's Encyclopedia* shows a facsimile of a shipping mark with Masonic emblems sent to Eliot from England.

Elizabeth I (1533-1603) Queen of England and Ireland from 1558-1603. Anderson referred to her in his first Book of Constitutions of the Grand Lodge of England. After stating that no woman should be admitted as a member of a Masonic lodge, he said: "The learned and magnanimous Queen Elizabeth, who encourag'd other Arts, discourag'd this; because, being a Woman, she could not be made a Mason, tho', as other great Women, she might have much employ'd Masons like Semiramis and Artemisia." He continued, "Elizabeth being jealous of any Assemblies of her Subjects, whose Business she was not duly appris'd of, attempted to break up the Annual Communication of Masons, as dangerous to her Government. But as old Masons have transmitted it by Tradition, when the noble Persons her Majesty had commissioned, and brought a sufficient Posse with them at York, on St. John's Day, were once admitted into the Lodge, they made no use of Arms, and returned the Queen a most honorable Account of the ancient Fraternity, whereby her political fears and doubts were dispell'd, and she let them alone as a People much respected by the Noble and Wise of all the polite Nations, but neglected the Art all her Reign." In his edition of 1738, Anderson added the following:"Now Learning of all Sorts revived, and the good old Augustan Style began to peep from under its rubbish. And it would have soon made great progress if the Queen had affected Architecture. But hearing the Masons had certain secrets that could not be reveal'd to her (for that she could not be Grand Master) and being jealous of all Secret Assemblies, she sent an armed force to break up their annual Grand Lodge at York on St. John's Day, 27th December, 1561. But Sir Thomas Sackville, Grand Master, took care to make some of the chief men sent Free-Masons, who then joining in that Communication, made a very honourable report to the Queen, and she never more attempted to dislodge or distrust them, but esteem'd them as a peculiar sort of men that cultivated peace and friendship, arts and science, without meddling in the affairs of Church and State." This is undoubtedly pure fiction.

Elizabeth II Queen of England. She is grand patroness of each of the three Royal Masonic Benevolent Institutions conducted by the Grand Lodge of England—one for old people and one each for boys and girls. When she married Lord Mountbatten, now Philip, Duke of Edinburgh, q.v., the United Grand Lodge of England presented her with a gift costing $2,500 in appreciation of the services her father, King George VI, q.v.; rendered to the Craft.

Stephen B. Elkins (1841-1911) U.S. Secretary of War, 1891-93, and U.S. Senator from West Virginia, 1895-1911. b. Sept. 26, 1841 in Perry Co., Ohio, moving to Missouri in his youth and attending the U. of Missouri in 1860. He served as a captain of the 77th Missouri regiment in the Civil War and later went to New Mexico, where he was admitted to the bar in 1864. He accumulated a fortune in stock raising and mining and was a member of the territorial legislature in 1865-66 and U.S. district attorney in 1870-72. He was then elected a delegate to congress and served two terms, 1873-77. In 1875 he became interested in West Virginia railroads, founding the town of Elkins, W.Va. and moving there about 1890. He was a member of Montezuma Lodge No. 109, New Mexico. At one time he was captured by Quantrill's band, tied up and ready to be shot, when, it is claimed, he gave a Masonic sign and was enabled to make his escape. While in Washington as a representative for Territory of New Mexico, he met and married the daughter of Henry Gassaway Davis, q.v., U.S. senator from W. Va. Davis, a man of great wealth, brought Elkins to W. Va., and although one was a Democrat and the other a Republican, they worked together in both business and politics. They founded Davis-Elkins Coll.

William L. Elkins Founder of the Pennsylvania Masonic Home for Girls. He became a member of Harmony Lodge No. 52 of Philadelphia on June 4, 1864.

Henry Ellenbogen U.S. Congressman, 73rd to 75th Congresses (1933-38) from 33rd Pa. dist. b. April 3, 1900. Graduate of Duquesne U. He has been judge of the court of common pleas of Allegheny Co. since 1938. Active in labor arbitration, he is a member of the national panel of arbitrators of American Arbitration Assn. Member of Oakland Lodge No.

535, Pittsburgh, Pa.; Mizpeh Chapter No. 288, R.A.M. and Allegheny Council No. 18, R. & S.M. of Pittsburgh and Islam Grotto.

William Ellery (1727-1820) Signer of the Declaration of Independence. b. Dec. 22, 1727 at Newport, RI., where his father was a successful merchant and politician. Like his father, he attended Harvard, graduating in 1747. He later engaged in business in Newport and began the practice of law there in 1770. He took his seat in the Continental Congress in May, 1776 and was an influential member. In 1785 he was an active supporter of Rufus King, q.v., in his effort to abolish slavery throughout the country. He served in congress until 1786 with the exception of the years 1780 and 1782. d. Feb. 15, 1820. It cannot be said for certain that Ellery was a Freemason. There is record of a "William Ellery" being made a Mason in St. John's Lodge of Boston on Oct. 12 and also Oct. 25 of 1748. Ellery had graduated from Harvard in Boston the year before. The same Ellery was present at the celebration of St. John the Evangelist Day by the Grand Lodge of Massachusetts on Dec. 27, 1753 and also attended a sermon with the grand lodge at Boston's Trinity church on Oct. 1, 1755. His name on the list of members of St. John's gives the date of reception, but under the column for withdrawal or death, no entry was made, indicating they had no knowledge of what became of him. There was also such a name on the rolls of St. John's Lodge No. 4, Hartford, Conn., showing he was admitted Feb. 8, 1763 and was treasurer of the lodge later in the year.

Aaron Elliott (?-1811) First American physician west of the Mississippi and first master of the first lodge west of that river. He came to Missouri from Connecticut, settling near Ste. Genevieve. Land records of 1798 show that he purchased a tract from Maxwell, the Cure, that year. He probably received his degrees in the East, for he is found as a visitor at Kaskaskia No. 107 (across the river in Illinois) on Dec. 27, 1806 at the feast of St. John the Evangelist. He next appears as one of the signers of the application for a dispensation for Louisiana Lodge No. 109, being recommended in the petition (to the Grand Lodge of Pennsylvania) as master of the lodge. The first returns of the lodge (1808) gives his name as master and charter member. When St. Louis Lodge No. 111 applied for a dispensation on Aug. 2, 1808, it had to have the approval of the nearest lodge —which was No. 109 at Ste. Genevieve. Their action was prompt, for six days later, on Aug. 8, Elliott as master signed the request directed to the Grand Lodge of Pennsylvania, stating . . . "we do further recommend Brother Meriwether Lewis, q.v., a Past Master Mason, Thomas Fiveash Riddick, q.v., a Master Mason, and Brother Rufus Easton, q.v., a Master Mason, as proper persons to fill the respective offices to which they have been nominated in a new Lodge to be constituted in the town of St. Louis. . . ." His family was closely allied with the old established families of Ste. Genevieve, one daughter marrying William C. Carr and another Leon Delassus. d. July, 1811.

Byron K. Elliott President of John Hancock Mutual Life Insurance Co. b. May 5, 1899 at Indianapolis, Ind. Degrees from Indiana and Harvard universities. Admitted to Indiana bar in 1921, practicing at Indianapolis. Was judge of the superior court of Indiana from 1926-29, resigning in the latter year. President of the

Curtis-Wright Flying Service of Ind. 1927-29. Went with John Hancock in 1934 as a solicitor, becoming general counsel, director, executive vice president and president. Served as lieutenant in WWI. Mason, receiving 33° AASR (NJ) in Sept., 1957.

Erroll T. Elliott College president, editor and executive of Friends of America. b. Nov. 10, 1894 at Carthage, Mo. Degrees from Friends U. (Wichita, Kans.) and U. of Colorado. A pastor of the Friends church from 1926-30 and secretary of Five Years Meeting of Friends in America, 1930-36. President of William Penn Coll. at Oskaloosa, Ia., 1942-44. Since 1944 he has been executive secretary of Five Years Meeting of Friends and editor of The American Friend at Richmond, Ind. Mason.

Francis P. Elliott (1861-1924) Editor. b. July 29, 1861 at Nashville, Tenn. Taught and supervised schools in early years. With Harper & Bros., New York, 1898-1900; managing editor of Home Magazine, New York, 1900-03; The New Age, Washington, 1903-04; The Great Southwest, Denver, 1906-08. Author of Pals First; Lend Me Your Name; and The Shadow Girl. Mason. d. Aug. 13, 1924.

I. H. Elliott Union Brigadier General, Civil War. Breveted March 13, 1865 in Volunteers. Member of Bureau Lodge No. 112, Princeton, Ill.

James D. Elliott (1859-1933) U.S. District Judge, District of South Dakota, 1911-33. b. Oct. 7, 1859 at Mt. Sterling, Ill. Admitted to S.D. bar in 1884 and practiced at Tyndall, and later, Aberdeen. Raised in Mount Zion Lodge No. 6, Springfield, S.D. on March 27, 1887, affiliating with Bon Homme Lodge No. 101 at Tyn-

dall as a charter member on June 18, 1888; was senior deacon of the latter in 1889-90. d. Jan. 30, 1933.

Kenneth B. Elliott Vice President of the Studebaker Corp. from 1941. b. Jan. 22, 1896 at Lebanon, Mo. Graduate of Drury Coll., Springfield, Mo. in 1916. Began as an accountant and auditor. Went with the Studebaker Corp. in 1928 as assistant treasurer and was later assistant comptroller and assistant to president. Member of Laclede Lodge No. 83 and Lebanon Chapter No. 64, both of Lebanon, Mo.

Clyde T. Ellis U.S. Congressman, 76th and 77th Congresses (1939-43) from 3rd Ark. dist. b. Dec. 21, 1908 near Garfield, Ark. Admitted to bar in 1933 and practiced at Garfield and Bentonville. Served terms in both bodies of the state legislature. Member of Bentonville Lodge No. 48, Bentonville, Ark.

Crawford H. Ellis President of Pan American Life Insurance Co. from 1912 and Vice President of United Fruit Co. from 1909. b. Aug. 26, 1875 at Selma, Ala. He began as an accountant in 1893 and in 1899 was manager of the United Fruit Co., serving in that capacity until 1909 when he became vice president. Mason and Knight Templar.

Griffith O. Ellis (1869-1948) Editor, publisher and Boy Scout founder. b. Nov. 19, 1869 at Urbana, Ohio. Graduate of U. of Michigan. Became connected with the Sprague Publishing Co., Detroit in 1891 and was president of it from 1908-39. He was editor of the American Boy published by the above house from 1908-40. Also president of the Wm. A. Scripps Co. He participated in the organization of the Boy Scouts of

America in 1910 and has served on the national council since that time. Received the award of Silver Buffalo in 1931 from Boy Scouts. Was an officer of two banks and president of the Detroit Street Railway Commission from 1920-30 which municipalized Detroit's system. Raised April 11, 1911 in Oriental Lodge No. 240; 32° AASR (NJ). d. Feb. 4, 1948.

John Valentine Ellis (1835-1913) Canadian Senator, journalist and publisher. b. Feb. 14, 1835 in Halifax, N.S. Was a member of the House of Assembly, N.B., 1882-1900 and appointed Canadian senator in 1900, serving until death in 1913. Raised June 6, 1856 in The Lodge of Social & Military Virtues, Montreal (now The Lodge of Antiquity No. 1). Was active in the formation of the Grand Lodge of New Brunswick in 1867 and was grand master of same in 1872-74, 1884-86. An active leader in all branches of Masonry, he was grand high priest of the Grand Chapter of New Brunswick, 1894-98. He revived the Grand Council of Maritime Provinces in 1892 and was grand master of same that year. In 1899-1900 he was supreme grand master of the Sovereign Great Priory of Canada, and instituted the Scottish Rite in N.B. under Supreme Council of Scotland in 1871. He was member of first supreme council for Canada in 1874 and sovereign grand commander in 18861902. Was provincial grand master of Royal Order of Scotland, 1895-1913. d. July 10, 1913.

John W. Ellis (1820-1861) Governor of North Carolina, 1858-61, dying in office. b. Nov. 25, 1820 in Rowan Co., N.C. Graduate of U. of North Carolina in 1841 and admitted to bar following year. A member of the state house of commons from 1844-48 when he was elected judge of the superior court of N.C. As governor he took possession of the U.S. arsenal at Fayetteville and the U.S. mint at Charlotte in 1861. He was a member of Fulton Lodge No. 99, Salisbury, N.C. and master of same in 1853. In 1850 he represented Wm. R. Davie Lodge No. 119 at the grand lodge sessions. Also member of Salisbury Chapter No. 20, R.A.M.

Thomas Q. Ellis General Grand High Priest of the General Grand Chapter, Royal Arch Masons, 1954-57. b. Dec. 11, 1890 near Bolling Green, Miss. Educated in public schools and business college. For 20 years he was a train dispatcher for the Illinois Central Railroad, but turning to politics in 1931, he was elected clerk of the supreme court of Mississippi over five opponents in the largest vote ever given a statewide candidate, and took office in Jan., 1932. Since that time he has been reelected five times without opposition. He is a life member of Valley City Lodge No. 402, Water Valley, Miss., and past grand master of the Grand Lodge of Mississippi; life member of McConico Chapter No. 96, R.A:M., Water Valley, and grand high priest of the state in 1941; life member and past master of J. J. Melton Council No. 50, R. & S.M.; life member and past commander of St. Cyr Commandery No. 6 and past grand commander of the Grand Commandery, K.T. of Mississippi. He is past sovereign of St. Leonard Conclave, Red Cross of Constantine; member of Delta Consistory, AASR (SJ) and KCCH. Ellis is much in demand as a public speaker.

William H. Ellis (1867-1948) Justice, Supreme Court of Florida, 1911-38. b. Sept. 17, 1867 in Pensacola, Fla. Admitted to bar in 1889. Served Florida as state auditor and attorney general. Mason. d. April 14, 1948.

George R. Ellison (1881-1957) Judge, Supreme Court of Missouri, 1931-1955. b. July 22, 1881 at Canton, Mo. Graduate of Harvard U. in 1903, he studied law at U. of Missouri and was admitted to bar in 1904, practicing at Maryville. He was a commissioner of the state supreme court from 1927-30. Member of Nodaway Lodge No. 470, Maryville, Mo., receiving degrees on Jan. 13, June 13, Aug. 1, 1912. d. July 17, 1957.

Lee Ellmaker (1896-1951) Publisher. b. Aug. 7, 1896 at Lancaster, Pa. Began as a newspaper reporter in 1913; vice president of the National City Bureau in Washington, D.C. 1918-25; correspondent for International News Service, 1919-23. In 1926 he organized the Philadelphia Daily News, and has since been its publisher. While with the Macfadden Publications from 1927-31, he published Liberty and other publications for them. From 1931-33 he published Pictorial Review and from 1932-40, Woman's World. Served with U.S. Navy in WWI. Member of Keystone Lodge No. 271, Philadelphia, receiving degrees on Dec. 8, 1919, Nov. 29, 1920 and April 18, 1921. d. March 27, 1951.

Oliver Ellsworth (1745-1807) Third Chief Justice of U.S. Supreme Court; first U.S. Senator from Connecticut. b. April 29, 1745 in Windsor, Conn. He entered Yale U. in 1762, but afterward went to Princeton U. where he was graduated in 1766 with high honors. It was while a student at Princeton that he became a charter member of St. John's Lodge at Princeton, N.J. on Dec. 27, 1765. He studied theology for a year and abandoned it for law, being admitted to the bar in 1771. In 1778 he took his seat

as a delegate to the Continental congress, serving until 1783. In 1784 he accepted the assignment of judge of the Connecticut superior court and held it until he became a member of the Constitutional convention of 1787. It was through his insistence that the words "national government" were removed from the draft and "government of the United States" substituted. He was an advocate of state's rights at the convention, but did not have an opportunity to sign the Constitution as he was called home at that time. He was U.S. senator from Connecticut from 1789 to 1796 and was on the committee for organizing the U.S. judiciary, the bill being in his own handwriting. He was the Federalist leader in the senate. The mission of John Jay to England in 1794 was at his suggestion; and in 1799 he was named with Patrick Henry and William R. Davie for a special mission to France to negotiate with that country at a time of strained relations. He later served as chief justice of the supreme court of Connecticut, but ill health forced his resignation after serving a short term. d. Nov. 26, 1807.

Dave Elman Actor, radio writer and director. b. May 6, 1900, in Park River, N.D. From 1914-22 he was an actor and from 1922-24 a song writer. In the latter year he became a radio writer, director and producer. He originated and produced the radio feature Hobby Lobby in 1938. He is a lecturer on the value of hobbies and in 1939 wrote Hobbies on Parade. Mason.

Charles H. Elston U.S. Congressman to 78th through 81st Congresses (1939-51) from 1st Ohio dist. b. Aug. 1, 1891 at Marietta, Ohio. Admitted to Ohio bar in 1914 and practiced at Cincinnati. In aviation service during WWI. Member of Walnut Hills Lodge No. 483, Cincinnati, receiving degrees on March 16, April 27 and May 25, 1915; 32° AASR (NJ), Shriner, member of Royal Order of Jesters and Grotto.

Julian Eltinge (1883-1941) Actor. b. May 14, 1883 at Boston, Mass. He began his professional career at Keith's Theatre, Boston. He was famous for his female impersonations. Eltinge was a member of Pacific Lodge No. 233 of New York City and a charter member of the "233 Masonic Club" of Hollywood, Calif. d. March 7, 1941.

Ford Q. Elvidge Governor of Guam, 1953-56. b. Nov. 30, 1892 at Oakland, Calif. Admitted to Washington bar in 1918 and practiced at Seattle. Active in many civic enterprises and organizations. Served as a lieutenant in WWI with 13th Infantry. Governor of Washington State Bar Assn., 1943-46; past president of English Speaking Union. A past master of Arcane Lodge No. 87, Seattle, he was grand master of the Grand Lodge of Washington for 16 months (1944-45). He served on the grand lodge jurisprudence committee from 1945-53. A member of both York and Scottish Rites, he received his 33° AASR (SJ) on Dec. 11, 1943. In 1956 he was vice president of the American Baptist convention. Grand Sovereign of the national Red Cross of Constantine (1957).

John W. Elwood Business executive. b. July 17, 1895 at Illion, N.Y. He was assistant to vice president of General Electric Co. in 1947-48 and assistant secretary of same in 1918-22. Later he was secretary of Radio Corp. of America and vice president of Federal Telegraph Co. of Delaware. In 1927-29 he was assistant to the president of National Broadcasting Co., program manager of the same from 1928-29 and vice president, 1929-34. For a time he was a public relations consultant. He was manager of the international division of NBC and since 1942 has been general manager of NBC-KNBC at San Francisco. Mason.

Philip H. Elwood, Jr. Landscape architect and regional planner. b. Dec. 7, 1884 at Fort Plain, N.Y. Graduate of Cornell U. Organized department of landscape architecture at Ohio State U. in 1915 and head of same department at Iowa State Coll. since 1923. Landscape engineer for Argonne cemetery (France) in 1919. At various times he has been consultant or advisor to Columbus, Ohio; Iowa Conservation plan, Iowa Planning Board, National Resources Commission, Missouri Valley Regional Planning Commission, Ames, Iowa; Iowa Roadside Improvement Council, American Association of Highway Officials, U.S. Army Engineers, Boys Town, Nebr.; Pi Beta Phi settlement school (Tenn.), and National Park Service. Mason, 32° AASR.

Frank C. Emerson (1882-1931) Governor of Wyoming, 1927-30. b. May 26, 1882 at Saginaw, Mich. Graduate of U. of Michigan in 1904. Entered general engineering practice in Wyoming in 1904 and was chief engineer of the Wyoming Land & Irrigation Co. and Wyoming Irrigation Co., 1907-15. From 1915-19 he was superintendent of the Big Horn Canal Association and Lower Hanover Canal Association and also state engineer of Wyoming from 1919-27. He was made a Mason Feb. 5, 1807 in Cheyenne Lodge No. 1 at Cheyenne and affiliated with Greybull Lodge No. 34, Greybull on June 5,

1914. On Jan. 25, 1919 he affiliated with Cloud Peak Lodge No. 27 at Worland. He was made a Knight Templar in Wyoming Commandery No. 1 and received 32° AASR (SJ) on Dec. 13, 1907. d. Feb. 18, 1931.

Nehemiah Emerson A captain in the Revolutionary War who was one of the guards at the execution of Major Andre, q.v. Received his degrees in Washington Lodge No. 10 (military) and was later a member of Merrimack Lodge at Haverhill, Mass.

DeWitt McKinley Emery (18961955) Founder of National Small Business Men's Association in 1937 and president of same. b. Dec. 12, 1896 at Grove City, Pa. President and treasurer of Monroe Letterhead Co. since 1929. Mason. d. July 23, 1955.

Louis L. Emmerson (1863-1941) Governor of Illinois, 1929-33. b. Dec. 27, 1863 at Albion, Ill. He entered the mercantile business in Mt. Vernon, Ill. in 1883 and in 1901 organized and was president of the Third National Bank, Mt. Vernon. Active in Republican politics, he was chairman of the state central committee, served on state board of equalization and was elected secretary of state in 1916, 1920 and 1924. He was initiated on Dec. 8, 1890 in Mt. Vernon Lodge No. 31 and was grand master of the Grand Lodge of Illinois in 1929. 33° AASR (NJ). He was also grand commander of the Grand Commandery, K.T. of Illinois and in 1929 was appointed grand treasurer of the Grand Encampment, K.T. In 1913 he was grand high priest of the Grand Chapter, R.A.M. of Illinois. d. Feb. 4, 1941.

Raoul Engel Belgian Masonic martyr. A past grand master of the Grand Lodge of Belgium. He was one of 112 Freemasons murdered during the Nazi occupation of this country. Others included Georges Petre, grand commander of the Scottish Rite in Belgium, the lieutenant grand commander, General Emile Lartigue and eleven of the twelve members of the supreme council. Broadcasts over the Nazi radio stations in 1941 accused Freemasonry thusly: "To sabotage everything, to befoul everything, to lead the people to ruin, to sow hatred and despair everywhere, sums up the whole activity of the Freemasons."

Fred Englehardt (1885-1944) President of the University of New Hampshire from 1937. b. April 15, 1885 at Naugatuck, Conn. Graduate of Yale, Columbia and Harvard universities. Taught and administered schools until 1919. Was director of administration in Pennsylvania state department of education and professor and dean at U. of Pittsburgh and U. of Minnesota. Member of No. Constellation Lodge No. 291, Malone, N.Y. d. Feb. 3, 1944.

Elbert H. English (1816-1884) Chief Justice of Supreme Court of Arkansas, 1854-1884. b. March 6, 1816 in Madison Co., Ala. He studied law and practiced at Athens, Ala. until 1844 when he moved to Little Rock, Ark. He was general grand high priest of the General Grand Chapter from 1874-77. Raised in Athens Lodge No. 16, Athens, Ala. In 1843 he affiliated with Western Star Lodge No. 2 in Little Rock and was master in 1845 and served as grand master of Arkansas in 1849. In 1859 he was again elected grand master and served continuously for ten years. He was exalted in Union Chapter No. 2, Little Rock, in 1846 and was a member of the convention that formed the Grand Chapter of Arkansas in 1851, being elected first grand high priest in 1851, 1857, 1858, 1869 and 1870. The cryptic degrees were communicated to him by Albert Pike, q.v., in 1853 for the purpose of organizing Occidental Council No. 1. When the Grand Council of Arkansas was organized in 1860, he was elected grand recorder. In 1865, 1866, 1871 and 1872 he was grand master of the same. English was knighted in Hugh de Payens Commandery No. 1, Little Rock, on its organization in 1853 and assisted in organizing the Grand Commandery of Arkansas in 1872. He was grand commander in 1876-77. Received 33° AASR (SJ) in 1859 and made grand inspector general and honorary member of the Supreme Council. d. Sept. 1, 1884.

James E. English (1812-1890) U.S. Senator and Governor of Connecticut. b. March 13, 1812 in New Haven, Conn. He was apprenticed in a carpenter's shop and by the time he reached his majority was a master builder. He engaged in the lumber business, real estate, banking and manufacturing and became one of the richest men in the state. He served in both legislative bodies of the state in the 1850's and was U.S. congressman from 1861-65. Served as governor of Connecticut from 1867-70 and elected U.S. senator in 1875. Member of Trumbull Lodge No. 22, New Haven. d. March 2, 1890.

William E. English (1854-1926) U.S. Congressman to 48th Congress (1883-85), from Indiana. He declined reelection. b. Nov. 3, 1854 at English-ton Park, Ind. He practiced law at Indianapolis until 1882. Served in both state legislative houses and was in the Spanish-American War under General Joseph Wheeler, being seriously wounded in the battle of Santiago. Raised in Cen-

tre Lodge No. 23, Indianapolis on March 17, 1890 and was master of same in 1893, 1894 and 1898, serving as grand master of the Grand Lodge of Indiana in 1904. A member of Indianapolis Chapter No. 5, R.A.M. he was high priest in 1900; greeted in Indianapolis Council No. 3, R. & A.M., he was master in 1900; knighted in Raper Commandery No. 1, K.T. and member of AASR (NJ) at Indianapolis. He is the author of History of Masonry in Indianapolis (190.). d. April 29, 1926.

William H. English (1822-1896) U.S. Congressman from Indiana, 1853-61. b. Aug. 27, 1822 in Lexington, Ind. A lawyer, he was secretary of the state convention that framed the constitution for Indiana, and was a member and first speaker of the house of representatives. From 1853-61 he was one of the regents of the Smithsonian Institution. He was nominated for vice president in 1880 on the Democratic ticket with General Hancock. Author of Conquest of the Northwest and other works. He became a member of Center Lodge No. 23, Indianapolis, when past 71 years of age (1893). d. Feb. 7, 1896.

John Entick (1703-1773) Church of England clergyman and schoolmaster. He is chiefly remembered in Freemasonry for his edition of the Book of Constitutions, published in 1756. It omitted some additions to the ancient charges which had marred Anderson's second edition of 1738. He was grand steward in 1755 and junior grand warden in 1758. His name appears on the title page of the next Book of Constitutions (1767), but it is improbable that he had much to do with its preparation as at that time he was in ill repute Masonically, as a complaint had been lodged against him regarding his administration of accounts of his lodge. His Latin dictionary was in use for many years by schools.

Eugene C. Eppley President of Eppley Hotels Co. since 1915, operating 20 hotels. b. April 8, 1884 at Akron, Ohio. Began with McKinley Hotel at Canton, Ohio in 1903. He is a director of the Sheraton Corp. of America, Mid-Continent Airlines, and served as national food administrator for hotels in WWI. In WWII he was food consultant to the secretary of war. He is a director of the Mt. Rushmore National Memorial Society of the Black Hills (S.D.) and was King Ak-Sar-Ben of the legendary Nebraskan Empire of Quivera at Omaha in 1933. Mason, 32° AASR and Shriner.

Jean Jacques Duval Epremesnil (1746-1794) Sometimes spelled Epremenu/ and Espremesnil. French jurist and politician. b. Dec. 5, 1745 at Pondicherry, India. He was educated in Paris and became a member of the French parliament, where, in 1788, he vigorously defended its rights against the royalty. For this he was imprisoned for four months. On his return to Paris, he was hailed as a hero and was chosen first deputy by the nobility. When he defended the royal cause as a member of the national assembly in 1791, and protested against the new constitution, he was attacked by a mob, wounded and rescued by the state troops. He escaped to his property near Havre, but was arrested there and condemned to death by a revolutionary tribunal at Paris and was guillotined on April 22, 1794. His wife, Francoise Augustine, who was called Mere des Pauvres, because of her many charities, was guillotined at the same time. Epremesnil was a member of the famous Lodge of the Nine Sisters at Paris, his name being on

the calendar for 1788 as a "deputy" of the lodge.

George B. Erath (1813-1891) Indian fighter, soldier, surveyor. b. Jan.1, 1813. He was a major in the battle of San Jacinto, Texas and later surveyed the site on which the city of Waco is located. Erath County, Texas is named for him. His original lodge is not known, but he was a charter member and first treasurer of Bosque Lodge No. 92, Waco (now Waco No. 92) in 1852. He served as secretary through 1855, was suspended NPD on Aug. 1, 1889, but reinstated in Dec. of that year. d. May 13, 1891.

Otto Linne Erdmann (1804-1869) German chemist who was known for his research on nickel, indigo, illuminating gas, and for determinations of atomic weights. Bulletin of International Masonic Congress (1917) states he was a Freemason.

John E. Erickson (1863-1946) U.S. Senator and Governor of Montana. b. March 14, 1863 at Stoughton, Wis. Admitted to Kansas bar in 1891 and moved to Montana in 1894 where he practiced at Kalispell; was county attorney and district judge. He was governor of Montana two terms, 1925-33, and on March 14, 1933 was appointed U.S. senator to fill a vacancy, serving until Nov. 6, 1934. He was a member of Choteau Lodge No. 44, later dimitting to Kalispell Lodge No. 42, which he served as master. Member of Cyrene Commandery No. 10, K.T. at Kalispell; 32° AASR (SJ) at Helena and Algeria Shrine Temple at Helena. d. May 25, 1946.

Leif Erickson Justice, Supreme Court of Montana. b. July 29, 1906 at Cashton, Wis. Graduate of U. of Chicago, he was admitted to Montana bar in 1934, serving as justice on supreme court from 1939-45. He received Democratic nomination for governor in 1944 and U.S. senator in 1946. Mason.

Milton S. Erlanger President of B.V.D. Co., 1929-48 and chairman of board of directors since 1948. b. Feb. 28, 1888 in Baltimore, Md. Graduate of Johns Hopkins U. in 1907. Joined B.V.D. Co. in 1907 and was elected vice president in 1909. Also director of N.C. Finishing Co., Salisbury-Erlanger Mills, Inc., Alexander Mfg. Co., and Lynchburg Garment Co. Member of Mount Neboh Lodge No. 257, New York City and Mecca Shrine Temple, New York City.

Mitchell L. Erlanger (1857-1940) Justice, Supreme Court of New York. He received a public school education and was self-educated in the classics. As sheriff of New York Co. in 1904-05 he effected many reforms and secured the release of many prisoners. Served on supreme court bench from 1907-1927 when he retired and was appointed official court referee for life. Received his degrees in True Craftsmen's Lodge No. 651, New York City on Jan. 23, Feb. 13 and Feb. 27, 1889; affiliated with Munn Lodge No. 190, New York City on April 13, 1893; affiliated with Pacific Lodge No. 233, New York City on Oct. 1, 1903. Member of the grand lodge committee on Hall and Asylum, 1905-06. d. Aug. 30, 1940.

Ernest Augustus (see Duke of Cumberland)

Ernest II, Duke of Saxony-Coburg (1818-1893) Full name was August Karl Leopold Alexander Eduard. The older son of Ernest I, he became duke on his death in 1844.

Born in Coburg, he was educated at Bonn and traveled extensively. He fought successfully in the war against Denmark in 1849. His liberal policies prevented disturbances in his duchy during the revolutionary crisis of 1848-49. A nationalist, he favored Austrian leadership and long opposed Bismarck, later siding with Prussia in the Seven Weeks' War, and took part in Franco-Prussian War of 1870. He was known as an excellent musician and wrote several operas. He was a cousin of Queen Victoria of England and a brother of the Prince consort, Albert, and nephew of Leopold I of Belgium. He founded the *Lodge Ernst zum Compass* at Gotha in 1857 and was master of the same.

Ernest Ludwig II. Duke of SaxeGotha-Altenburg (1745-1804) Initiated in Lodge Kosmopolit at Altenburg in July, 1774. In 1775 he accepted grandmastership of the National Grand Lodge of Berlin, but was obliged to resign the office a year later.

Ernst Gottlob Albert, Prince of Mecklemburg-Strelitz (1742-1785) Brother of Duke Karl Ludwig Friedrich. He became a major general in the English Army. Member of Lodge Irene zu den drei Sternen at Rostock from 1773 until his death.

Richard P. Ernst (1858-1934) U.S. Senator from Kentucky, 1921-27. b. Feb. 28, 1858 in Covington, Ky. B.A. at Centre Coll. in 1878 and LL.D. from same college. LL.B. from U. of Cincinnati in 1880. Admitted to bar in 1880, entering practice at Covington. Long active in educational and church (Presbyterian) work. Raised in Temple Noyes Lodge No. 32, Washington, D.C., and became member of Col. Clay Lodge No. 159 at Covington. d. April 13, 1934.

Leon Errol (1881-1951) Movie comedian. Member of Pacific Lodge No. 233, New York City.

Lord Henry Erskine (1746-1817) Scottish orator and wit. He was lord advocate of Scotland in 1783, and again in 1806, and dean of the faculty of advocates from 1785-95. He failed at reelection because of his condemnation of the government's sedition and treason bills as unconstitutional. He was an eloquent and witty orator at the Scottish bar and was the author of *The Emigrant, an Eclogue*, and several poems. He was master of Canongate Kilwinning Lodge at Edinburgh in 1780.

Robert Erskine (1735-1795) Surveyor General and Geographer to the Army of the United States during the Revolutionary War. b. Sept. 7, 1735 in Scotland, the son of a Presbyterian minister, he graduated at the U. of Edinburgh and became a renowned mathematician and hydraulic engineer. He was honored with membership in the Royal Society at the same time as Benjamin Franklin. He invented a hydraulic pump used in draining coal, mines and wrote on bridge design, water flow in navigation, canal improvement and tidal influences. In 1770 he came to America as a representative of a London syndicate to salvage some of their investment in the New Jersey iron mines at Ringwood. At the outbreak of the Revolution, he espoused the colonial cause and turned the iron production over to the American army. It was Erskine's iron that formed the chain boom across the Hudson at West Point. His many field survey parties ran their lines all the way from Philadelphia to Boston, and up the Hudson and into the Mohawk Valley. More than 200 maps, the results of his cartographic skill, may be seen among the collections of the New York Historical Society. He is on record as one of the visitors to American Union Lodge at Morristown on Dec. 27, 1779, when the famous military traveling lodge entertained a distinguished assemblage, headed by General Washington. Erskine is supposed to have been made a Mason in Edinburgh or London. d. March 9, 1795.

Lord Thomas Erskine The 14th Grand Master Mason of Scotland in 1749.

Samuel J. Ervin, Jr. Justice of Supreme Court of North Carolina since 1948. Congressman from N.C. in 1946-47. b. Sept. 27, 1896 at Morganton, N.C. Degrees from U. of North Carolina and Harvard. Admitted to bar in 1919, he served as judge of criminal and superior courts. Served with First Infantry division (28th regiment) in WWI and was twice wounded in action. Member of Catawba Valley Lodge No. 217, Morganton, N.C.; Catawba Chapter No. 60, R.A.M., Hickory, N.C.; Lenoir Commandery No. 33, K.T., Lenoir, N.C. and 32° AASR (SJ) at Charlotte, N.C.

James B. Erwin (1856-1924) Brigadier General, U.S. Army. b. July 11, 1856 at Savannah, Ga., he graduated from U.S. Military Academy in 1880. He advanced through the grades to brigadier general in 1917. He participated in the Indian campaigns of 1885-86 and in 1897-98 he was superintendent of Yellowstone National Park. In WWI he commanded the 6th and 92nd divisions in France and took part in two major offensives as commander of the 12th brigade. Mason. d. July 10, 1924.

Marion C. Erwin Rear Admiral, U.S. Navy. b. March 15, 1893 at

Hartsville, Tenn. He enlisted in the Navy as an apprentice seaman in 1910; was commissioned ensign in 1917 and advanced through grades to rear admiral in 1946, retiring from active duty that year. In WWI he was with the armed guard and British grand fleet. In WWII he was with the amphibious forces in Africa, Solomons, Guam, Iwo Jima, Philippines and Japan landings (1941-45). Mason.

Von Steinbach Erwin (1244?-1318) A distinguished German architect, who, as his name implies, was born at Steinbach, near Buhl. He was master of the works at the Cathedral of Strasburg. He was the head of the German fraternity of stonemasons, who were the precursors of the modern Freemasons. He began the cathedral tower in 1275 and finished it and the doorway before his death in 1318. His son, namesake, and successor worked with him on the Strasburg cathedral.

Mariano Escobedo (1827-1902) Mexican General, who as commander-in-chief of the Mexican army defeated, captured and executed Maximilian, q.v., at Queretaro in 1867. Born in Galeana, state of Nuevo Leon, of humble parentage, he first tasted the military life when he fought against General Zachary Taylor in the war with the United States. From that time on he was almost constantly fighting for political causes. He aligned himself with Juarez, q.v., and the liberal party and fought against the Roman Catholic church parties. When Juarez established his government in Mexico City, in January, 1861, he made Escobedo a brigadier general. He was twice taken prisoner and escaped. At the intervention of Napoleon III in Mexican affairs, he began his long fight against the for-

eign rule. When the empire was established in June, 1864, with Maximilian as emperor of Mexico, he was obliged to give up the struggle and escaped into Texas where he set up a resistance headquarters at San Antonio. By November, 1865, he was ready to return to Mexico with a recruited force of American Negroes, ex-confederate soldiers and Mexican refugees. With the capture of the garrison at Monterrey, his good fortune continued until he had control of all the northern states and an army of 15,000 men. In 1867 Juarez made him commander-in-chief of all the Mexican republican armies, and he rapidly pushed into the interior and broke the French rule with the capture of Emperor Maximilian himself. He then retired, but was called back to put down a revolution of the church party in 1874. He led forces against General Diaz's, q.v., revolution in 1876 and was named secretary of war. When it became apparent that the revolution was a success, he organized a body of troops and made possible the escape of President Lerdo de Tejada and his cabinet to the Pacific coast where the entire party sailed to New York. He again found his way to San Antonio and issued a manifesto against Diaz. Later Diaz allowed him to retire to his estate in San Luis Potosi and eventually he even held a government position under Diaz' government. Escobedo was a member of the Supreme Council of the Scottish Rite of Mexico.

Joseph B. Esenwein (1867-1946) Editor and author. b. May 15, 1867 in Philadelphia, Pa. Editor and manager of Lippincott's Magazine, Philadelphia, 1905-14 and editor of *The Writer's Monthly* from 1915. He was an instructor in public speaking and a lecturer on educational, ethical and popular topics. Among his many writings are *Writing the Short Story; Lessons in the Short Story; Writing the Photoplay; The Art of Story Writing; Writing for Magazines; The Art of Public Speaking* (with Dale Carnegie). He also published many songs and hymns. Member of Franklin Lodge No. 134, Philadelphia, receiving degrees on Jan. 31, Feb. 28 and March 30, 1907. He was master of his lodge in 1912. d. Nov. 7, 1946.

Ascension Esquivel President of the Republic of Costa Rica, 1902-06. He was also secretary of state; a diplomat and jurist. Member of Esperanza Lodge No. 2 and Union Fraternal No. 19.

Jesse F. Essary (1881-1942) Journalist. b. Aug. 22, 1881 at Washburn, Tenn. Began on a Virginia paper as a reporter in 1903. In 1908 he became financial editor of the Baltimore Star, and, in the period 1910-12, he was Washington correspondent for the Baltimore News, New Orleans Item and Boston Journal. He served the Baltimore Sun in that capacity from 1912. In 1926 he was London correspondent for the Sun. Mason. d. March 11, 1942.

Count Estaing (see D'Estaing) Joe E. Estes U.S. District Judge at Dallas, Texas since 1955. b. Oct. 24, 1903 at Commerce, Tex. Graduate of U. of Texas and admitted to bar in 1923. Member of John Peavy Lodge No. 1162, Fort Worth, Texas; 32' AASR (SJ) at Dallas and member of Hella Shrine Temple, Dallas.

Emerson Etheridge (1819-1902) U.S. Congressman from Tennessee, 1853-57 and 1859-61. b. Sept. 28, 1819 in Currituck, N. Car. Admitted to the bar in 1840 and prac-

ticed at Dresden, Tenn. Served in both state legislative branches. From 1861-63 he was clerk of the national house of representatives. Member of Dresden Lodge No. 90, Dresden, Tenn. d. Oct. 21, 1902.

Alvin C. Eurich University president and vice president and director of the Ford Fund for Advancement of Education since 1951. b. June 14, 1902 at Bay City, Mich. Degrees from North Central Coll., U. of Maine and U. of Minnesota, with honorary degrees from a number of other institutions. He was acting president of Stanford U. in 1948 and first president of State U. of New York, 1949-51. He was raised in Justice Lodge No. 753, New York City.

William Eustis (1753-1825) Governor of Massachusetts 1823-25; Secretary of War, 1807-13; U.S. Congressman from Mass., 1801-05 and 1820-23. b. June 10, 1753 at Cambridge, Mass., he graduated from Harvard in 1772, studied medicine under Dr. Joseph Warren, q.v., and entered the Revolutionary army as a regimental surgeon, serving throughout the war. For some years he was stationed opposite West Point, at the house of Col. Beverly Robinson, where Arnold had his headquarters. He was U.S. minister to Holland from 1814-18. Eustis was raised in St. Andrew's Lodge of Boston on Feb. 6, 1795. d. Feb. 6, 1825.

Edward A. Evans Brigadier General in Officers Reserve Corps and executive director of the Reserve Officers Association of the U.S. b. Sept. 17, 1895 in Muskogee, Okla. He was commissioned in the reserve in 1919 and advanced through grades to brigadier general. He saw active duty in both World Wars. Member of Monrovia Lodge No. 308;

Foothill Chapter No. 129, R.A.M.; Foothill Commandery No. 63, K.T., all of Monrovia, Calif. He served as senior warden of his lodge and is past commander of his commandery. Member of Mahi Shrine Temple and Miami Court No. 88, Royal Order of Jesters, both of Miami, Fla.

Henry C. Evans (1843-1921) U.S. Congressman from Tennessee, 1889-91; Assistant Postmaster General, 1889-93; U.S. Consul General at London,1902-05. b. June 18, 1843 in Juniata Co. Pa. Served as an enlisted man in Civil War with 41st Regiment, Wisconsin Vol. Inf. He settled in Chattanooga, Tenn. in 1870, where he manufactured freight cars. He was mayor of the city in 1881, organized the public school system and served as first school commissioner. In 1894 he was elected governor of Tenn. on the face of the returns, but a legislative recount declared his opponent elected. Member of Temple Lodge No. 430 and Hamilton Chapter No. 49, R.A.M., Chattanooga. d. Dec. 12, 1921.

Henry R. Evans (1861-1949) Author, student of psychical research and Masonic antiquities. b. Nov. 7, 1861 at Baltimore, Md. Graduate of U. of Maryland in 1884. Among his Masonic writings are *History of the York and Scottish Rites*, and *Cagliostro and His Egyptian Rite of Freemasonry*. Other writings include: *The Napoleon Myth; The Spirit World Unmasked; The Old and the New Magic; The House of the Sphinx; Adventures in Magic; Life and Adventures of Robert Houdin*, etc. He was raised May 16, 1894 in Benjamin B. French Lodge No. 15, Washington, D.C., receiving 32° AASR (SJ) in Washington, D.C. in 1902 and 33° on Oct., 1907. He was editor of the *New Age* and wrote many articles in that publication in his name and under his pen name, *Mysticus*. d. March 29, 1949.

Sir Horace Evans English doctor who was physician in ordinary to Queen Mary and was in attendance at her death in March, 1953. He enjoyed the personal confidence of the queen. A Freemason, he was consultant physician at the Royal Masonic Hospital.

Hugh I. Evans (1887-1958) National head of the Presbyterian Church, U.S.A. in 1950-51. b. March 6, 1887 in Delaware, Ohio. Graduate of Wooster (Ohio) Academy and Coll. of Wooster and Princeton Theological Seminary. Was a Presbyterian pastor at Gallipolis, Marysville, Portsmouth, and Dayton, Ohio. Retired from active ministry in 1955 and became director of the Foundation of the Presbyterian Church at N.Y.C. He was moderator of the 162nd General Assembly of the Presbyterian Church, U.S.A. in 1950-51. He was past president of the Board of National Missions, and represented the U.S. at the meeting of World Council of Churches in Holland in 1948. Raised in Palestine Lodge No. 158, Marysville, Ohio and affiliated with Horace A. Irvin Lodge No. 647, Dayton, on Sept. 19, 1928. Was grand chaplain of Grand Lodge of Ohio in 1926. Member of Unity Chapter No. 16, R.A.M.; Reese Council No. 9, R. & S.M. and Reed Commandery No. 6, K.T., all of Dayton. 32° AASR (NJ) in Columbus, affiliating later with Valley of Dayton and received 33° on Sept. 25, 1946. d. April 23, 1958.

John Evans (1814-1897) Second Territorial Governor of Colorado in 1862-65. He helped establish the Chicago public school system and was a planner of Northwestern University. Evanston, Ill., where the University is located, is named for him, as is Evans Lodge No. 524, which was established there in 1866, while he was yet alive. b. March 9, 1814 in Waynesville, Ohio, he studied medicine. In 1842 he campaigned for a state mental institution for Indiana and was later made superintendent of it. He came to Chicago as a lecturer at Rush Medical Coll. President Lincoln named him territorial governor of Colorado in order to save that territory for the Union cause. When he arrived there, he found that many of the Freemasons in Denver Lodge No. 5 were outspoken against the Union, so he and others organized Union Lodge No. 7 in 1863. He was raised July 6, 1844 in Attica Lodge No. 18, Attica, Ind., and was first master of Marion Lodge No. 35 at Indianapolis. He became a Royal Arch Mason in Indianapolis Chapter No. 5 in 1846. He was a charter member of Colorado Commandery No. 1, K.T. in Denver. As president of the Denver Pacific Railway, he drove the last spike to complete its entry into Denver in 1870. He was also an incorporator of the Denver Street Car System. He was buried by Union Lodge No. 7 and Colorado Commandery No. 1, K.T. on July 6, 1897. d. July 3, 1897.

John Gary Evans (1863-1942) Governor of South Carolina, 1894-97. b. Oct. 15, 1863 at Cokesbury, S.C. Admitted to bar in 1886 and served terms in both state legislative bodies. In 1895 he was president of the S.C. constitutional convention. Served in Spanish-American War as a major and assisted in organizing the civil government of Havana after the war. Member of Spartan Lodge No. 70, Spartanburg, S.C. d. June 27, 1942.

John W. Evans (1855-1943) Artist, engraver, philosopher and idealist. b. March 27, 1855 at Brooklyn, N.Y. He exhibited at the Chicago Exposition of 1893, Paris Exposition of 1900, and also in London, Berlin, Vienna, Munich and New York. He won the bronze medal at the Buffalo Exposition in 1901, St. Louis Exposition in 1915, and silver medal at Panama Exposition of 1915. He was a member of Commonwealth Lodge No. 409, New York City and master of same in 1886. d. March 10, 1943.

Lewis A. Evans President and General Manager of The Belt Railway Co. of Chicago since 1953. b. June 22, 1907 at Brownsville, Pa., he graduated from Carnegie Inst. of Tech. in 1928 and began his railroad career as engineer assistant with the Pennsylvania Railroad in 1928. He became superintendent of the Indianapolis division in 1948 and resigned in 1951 to become vice president and general manager of the C. & W.I. as well as the Belt in Chicago. Mason.

Ray O. Evans (1887-1954) Cartoonist. b. Dec. 1, 1887 at Columbus, Ohio. Graduate of Ohio State U. in 1910, began as an advertising artist for the Columbus Dispatch in 1910. He later was a cartoonist for the Dayton News, Baltimore American, and member of Puck art staff. He returned to the Columbus Dispatch in 1922 and has remained there since. He has created several special features including Maryland Movies; Snapshots at Annapolis; Pertinent Portraits; Kindly Karicatures and Uncle Funny Bunny for children. Member of Humboldt Lodge No. 476, Columbus, Ohio, receiving degrees on Jan. 10, Feb. 9, and Mar. 1, 1948; 32° AASR (NJ) in Columbus and member of Aladdin Shrine Temple, Columbus. d. Jan. 18, 1954.

Hal G. Evarts (1887-1934) Author. b. Aug. 24, 1887 at Topeka, Kans. In his early life he was a surveyor in the Indian Territory, rancher, trapper and guide. Among his writings are Passing of the Old West; The Yellow Horde; The Settling of the Sage; Fur Sign; Tumbleweed; Spanish Acres; The Painted Stallion; The Moccasin Telegraph; Fur Brigade; Tomahawk Rights; The Shaggy Legion and Short-grass. Mason. d. Oct. 18, 1934.

Sir Richard Everard (?-1733) Last proprietary governor of North Caro-lina (1725-1729) and first governor under the Crown (1728-1731). He took the place of George Burrington, q.v. in July, 1725 and was succeeded by him on Feb. 25, 1731. His administration was disturbed by frequent disagreements with the council. He is recorded as a member of the Ross Tavern Without Temple Bar, London, England in the returns of 1730. This lodge was founded in 1730, and erased in 1736. d. Feb. 17, 1733 in London.

David C. Everest (1883-1955) President and General Manager of the Marathon Corp. b. Oct. 13, 1883 in Pine Grove, Mich. He began as office boy for Bryant Paper Co. in Kalamazoo, Mich. and has been with the Marathon Corp. paper and food package manufacturers at Rothschild, Wis. since 1909, and president of same since 1939. He is also president of the Wausau Paper Mills Co. and vice president of Masonite Corp. and Longview Fibre Co. Received his degrees in Forest Lodge No. 130, Wausau, Wis. March, 1906, Nov., 1912 and Jan., 1913. Member of Wausau Chapter No. 51, R.A.M. (1914); Wausau Council No. 22, R. & S.M. (1918) and St. Omer Commandery No. 19, K.T. (1914) all of Wausau; 32° AASR (NJ), Tripoli Shrine Temple, Royal Order of Jesters. d. Oct. 28, 1955.

Frank F. Everest Major General, U.S. Air Force. b. Nov. 13, 1904 at Council Bluffs, Ia. Graduate of U.S. Military Academy in 1928 and Air Corps Technical School in 1933. He transferred to the Air Corps in 1928, having previously held a commission in the Field Artillery. In WWII he was commanding officer of the 11th Heavy Bomb Group and Army air commander of the South Pacific from 1942-43. In 1944-45 he was a member of the joint war plans commission of Joint Chiefs of Staff and later commanded the Yukon Sector of Alaska Air Command. In 1948 he was assigned to headquarters of the Air Force as assistant deputy chief of staff. Member of Bluff City Lodge No. 71, Council Bluffs, Iowa, receiving degrees on Nov. 16, Dec. 26 and Dec. 29, 1928.

Edward Everett (1794-1865) Anti-Mason; Governor of Massachusetts, 1836-40; U.S. Congressman, 1825-35; U.S. Minister to Great Britain, 1841-45; President of Harvard, 1846-49; U.S. Secretary of State, 1852. b. April 11, 1794 in Dorchester, Mass. He was a Unitarian clergyman and orator of great ability. He took sides in the politics maintained by the friends of John Quincy Adams, q.v., another anti-Mason. In 1860 he ran on the Constitutional-Union ticket for vice-president with John Bell, q.v., a Tennessee Mason, as the presidential candidate. They received 39 electoral votes. In his famous orations on Washington, q.v., and General Warren, q.v., he failed to mention either of their Masonic connections. He wrote a letter to the secretary of the Anti-Masonic Committee of Middlesex Co., Mass. on June 29, 1833, stating among other things "The supremacy of the laws is the fundamental principle of civil society. The allegiance due to the country is the highest human obligation of all men who enter into civil society; and I conceive the institution of Freemasonry to be at war with both these principles." d. Jan. 15, 1865.

Sir Raymond Evershed English Baron and Lord Justice of Appeal. Knighted in 1944 and baroneted in 1955. He was appointed lord justice in 1947, and two years later made master of the rolls. b. Aug. 1889 at Burton-on-Trent, he was educated in Clifton Coll., Bristol, afterwards attending Oxford. Served as an officer of the Royal Engineers in WWI. He was initiated in Chancery Bar Lodge No. 2456 in April, 1947 by Edward, Prince of Wales, afterwards King Edward VII, q.v. He is a past grand warden of the Grand Lodge of England.

William G. Everson (1879-1954) Baptist clergyman and Major General of National Guard. b. July 1, 1879 in Wooster, Ohio, he was ordained in the Baptist ministry in 1901 and served churches in Ind., Mass., Ky., Ohio, Colo., and Oregon. He was president of Linfield Coll., McMinnville, Oreg. from 1939-43. From 1919 he was a chautauqua and lyceum lecturer. He served in the Spanish-American War and in WWI in France, Italy, Austria, Dalmatia, Serbia and Montenegro, commanding the only American sector in Italy and all the U.S. troops east of Adriatic Sea. He represented the U.S. at Fiume and supervised investigations of food distribution in Austria and Serbia after armistice. He was discharged in 1919 with rank of colonel. In 1922 he was promoted to brigadier general in the reserves and commanded the 76th Inf. Brigade. In 1929 he was made major general, U.S. Army and chief of the National Guard Bureau until 1931; retired in 1945 with rank of major general. A member of Willamette Lodge No. 2, Portland, Oreg., he affiliated with it on Jan. 3, 1944 from Delaware Lodge No. 46 of Muncie, Ind. Was 32° AASR, Knight Templar, Shriner and member of Red Cross of Constantine. He was chairman of the advisory committee of the Shriners Hospital for Crippled Children at Portland, Oreg. from 1944-47. d. Sept. 3, 1954.

Frank L. Eversull Educator. b. April 19, 1892 at Cincinnati, Ohio. A.M. and Ph.B. from U. of Chicago; Ph.D. from Yale; D.D. from Marietta Coll. He was ordained to the Presbyterian ministry in 1917, serving several pastorates in Illinois. He was school principal in St. Louis and East St. Louis, and then an instructor in education at Yale. From 1934-38 he was president of Huron Coll. (S. Dak.), and president of the North Dakota Agricultural Coll., 1938-46. In 1946-47 he was associated with higher education in Korea as advisor to Ewah College, Seoul, and member of the board of regents of Seoul National U. Since 1950 he has been a professor at Washington U., St. Louis, and pastor of the Belleville (Ill.) Presbyterian church. He is founder of the Korean Association for Advancement of Science and Korean Academy of Science. In 1946 he was selected as the distinguished graduate of the U. of Chicago and has been an elector of New York U. Hall of Fame since 1938. He has been decorated by King Christian of Denmark with the Medal of Liberation (1946). Made a Mason in Belleville Lodge No. 24 in 1918. Also member of Belleville Chapter No. 106, R.A.M. and Tancred Commandery No. 50, K.T. all of

Belleville, Ill.; AASR (NJ) membership at East St. Louis and is 33°. He is past sovereign of the Red Cross of Constantine at St. Louis. In 1937 he was grand orator of the Grand Lodge of South Dakota. Member of Ainad Shrine Temple, East St. Louis, Ill.

Harry K. Eversull (1893-1953) Clergyman and educator. b. Sept. 20, 1893 at Cincinnati, Ohio, a brother of Frank L. Eversull, q.v. He was a graduate of Wabash Coll. and Yale and was ordained to the Congregational ministry in 1922, serving pastorates in East Haven, Conn., and Cincinnati, Ohio until 1937 when he became president of Marietta Coll., serving until 1942. In 1946 he became a Presbyterian and was pastor at Walnut Hills Presbyterian Church (Cincinnati) from 1946. He received his degrees in Gothic Lodge No. 582, East St. Louis, Ill. on Jan. 15, Feb. 9 and Feb. 20, 1915 and affiliated with Hyde Park Lodge No. 589, Cincinnati, Ohio on June 3, 1930. He was master of Hyde Park Lodge in 1951. Harry K. Eversull Lodge No. 573, Cincinnati, has been named for him. He served asgrand chaplain for both the Grand Lodge of Ohio and Grand Council, R. & S.M. of Ohio; was 33° AASR (NJ) and wrote the 17th degree of that Rite (NJ) as now used. He was also a member of chapter, council, commandery, shrine and jesters. d. Sept. 13, 1953.

Joseph L. Evins U.S. Congressman, 80th to 84th Congresses (1947-55) from 4th and 5th Tenn. districts. b. Oct. 24, 1910 in DeKalb Co. Tenn. Graduate of Vanderbilt U. and Cumberland U. and admitted to bar in 1934, engaging in general law practice at Smithville, Tenn. Assistant secretary of Federal Trade Commission 1938-40. Served in WWII, European Theatre from 1943-45 and dis-

charged as a major in 1946. Member of Liberty Lodge No. 77, Smithville, Tenn. and 32° AASR (NJ) in Chicago.

Ezra P. Ewers (1837-1912) Brigadier General, U.S. Army. b. April 13, 1837 in Wayneport, N.Y. Entered the army as a private of Co. E, 1st Battalion, 19th Infantry in 1862 and commissioned the following year. Later served with 37th Infantry and 5th and 9th Infantry divisions, becoming brigadier general of volunteers in 1898. He retired from the volunteers in 1899 and became a colonel with the 10th Infantry (regulars). Was retired by operation of law in 1904 as a brigadier general. Member of Sackets Harbor Lodge No. 135, Sackets Harbor, N.Y. d. Jan. 16, 1912.

Arnold H. Exo Christian Science Church official. b. in Muscatine, Iowa. He was a district advertising manager for Household Finance Corp. from 1931-41, and in 1942 became a Christian Science practitioner and later a reader. He has been 1st reader of the First Church of Christ Scientist in Boston since 1956. Mason.

F

Eberhard Faber (1859-1946) Head of the Eberhard Faber Pencil Co. at Brooklyn, N.Y. and Eberhard Faber Rubber Co. at Newark, N.J. b. March 14, 1859 in New York City, he was educated in the Columbia School of Mines. In 1879 he entered the office of his father, the well-known lead-pencil manufacturer, and took charge of the business. He was a life member of Chancellor

Walworth Lodge No. 271, New York City. d. May 16, 1946.

Bernard R. Fabre-Palaprat (?- 1838) The restorer, or organizer, of the Order of the Temple at Paris, of which he was elected grand master in 1804. He died at Pau, in the lower Pyrenees, Feb. 18, 1838.

James G. Fair (1831-?) Wealthy gold and silver miner of Comstock bonanza fame and U.S. Senator from Nevada from 1881-87. b. Dec. 3, 1831 near Belfast, Ireland, coming to the U.S. with his parents in 1843. The family settled in Illinois where he attended public schools and completed his education in Chicago, where he gave much attention to scientific studies. He went to Calif. in 1849, and engaged in mining until he moved to Nevada and amassed a fortune of 50 million dollars. He was successful in the construction of quartz mills, water works, and chlorinizing furnaces. In 1865 he became superintendent of the Ophir mine, and in 1867 of the Hale and Norcross mine. In the latter year he formed a partnership with John W. Mackay, James C. Flood and Wm. T. O'Brien and purchased control of several well-known mines. He was raised in Bear Mountain Lodge No. 76 at Angels Camp, Calif. in 1858, serving as secretary in 1861 and treasurer in 1862-64.

Alfred Fairbank (1887-1945) President of Central States Life Insurance Co., St. Louis, from 1938. b. Aug. 3, 1887 at DeSoto, Mo. Taught school in Cleveland and St. Louis from 1905-11. Admitted to Missouri bar in 1909. He entered investment banking in 1920 and was vice president and trust officer of Boatmen's National Bank in St. Louis from 1930-38. Member of Tuscan Lodge No.

360, St. Louis, Mo., receiving degrees on March 3, March 17 and May 15, 1914. d. March 6, 1945.

Charles W. Fairbanks (1852-1918) Twenty-sixth Vice President of the United States. b. May 11, 1852 on a farm near Unionville Center, Ohio. Received A.B. and A.M. from Ohio Wesleyan U. He was agent for the Associated Press at Pittsburgh and Cleveland from 1872-74. He was admitted to the Ohio bar in 1874, and established practice at Indianapolis, Ind. Prominent in Republican politics, he was chairman of the Indiana Republican conventions of 1892, 1898, 1914 and delegate to national conventions of 1896, 1900, 1904, 1912. He was U.S. senator from Indiana for term 1897-1903, but resigned in 1905 to become vice president under Theodore Roosevelt for term, 1905-09. He was again selected as vice presidential nominee with Charles E. Hughes by the national convention of 1916 and defeated by a narrow margin. Was made a Mason "at sight" in Oriental Lodge No. 500, Indianapolis, Ind. on Dec. 27, 1904. He became a Royal Arch Mason in Keystone Chapter No. 6 at Indianapolis on March 20, 1905 and was knighted in Raper Commandery No. 1, K.T. at Indianapolis on June 26, 1905. He received his 32° AASR (NJ) in Indiana Consistory at Indianapolis on Nov. 8, 1905 and became a member of Murat Shrine Temple, Indianapolis on April 12, 1907, being a life member of the same. On June 7, 1905 he was the orator of the day at the laying of the cornerstone of the Federal building at Flint, Mich. On Oct. 29, 1906 he was elected an honorary member of American Union Lodge No. 1 at Marietta, Ohio. During his life, he is recorded as a visitor of lodges from coast to coast. At one time he said: "I am a firm believer in the virtue of Masonry. The foundation principles of the organization are everlastingly sound." d. June 4, 1918.

Douglas Fairbanks, Sr. (1883-1939) Movie star of the silent film era. b. May 23, 1883 in Denver, Colo. He attended Jarvis Military Academy at Denver, East Denver High School and the Colorado School of Mines. He had three marriages. He made his first stage appearance in New York City in 1901. On the stage he appeared in Hawthorne of the U.S.A.; Frenzied Finance; All for a Girl; A Gentleman from Mississippi; The Cub; Gentleman of Leisure; Comes Up Smiling; Henrietta; Show Shop. He entered motion pictures and was head of his own producing company in 1916. His later productions were His Majesty the American; When the Clouds Roll By; The Mollycoddle; The Mark of Zorro; The Nut; The Three Musketeers; Robin Hood; The Thief of Bagdad; Don Q, Son of Zorro; The Black Pirate; The Gaucho; The Iron Mask; and The Taming of the Shrew. He was raised in Beverly Hills Lodge No. 528 on Aug. 11, 1925 and was a member of the "233 Club"—whose members were Freemasons of the movie colony. d. Dec. 11, 1939.

Lucius Fairchild (1831-1896) Governor of Wisconsin for six terms. b. Dec. 27, 1831, in Kent, Ohio. His family moved to Wisconsin in 1846 when it was still a territory. When gold was discovered in Calif., he left for that state, although only 18 years old. After several years of fruitless labor, he returned to Wis. in 1885. He entered the Union service early in the Civil War, and distinguished himself at Bull Run, Antietam, Gettysburg, losing his left arm in the latter battle at Seminary Hill. While recovering from his wounds he was commis-

sioned brigadier general. In 1863 he was elected secretary of state in Wisconsin, serving until 1865 when he was elected for the first of his six consecutive terms as governor. He was consul general in Paris in 1878-80 and U.S. minister to Spain, 1880-82. In 1886 he was elected national commander-in-chief of the G.A.R. A member of Hiram Lodge No. 50, Madison, Wis., he received his degrees on March 19, April 16 and May 21, 1860. He was exalted in Madison Chapter No. 4, R.A.M., Madison, Wis. in Dec. 1863 and was knighted in Robert Macoy Commandery No. 3, K.T. at Madison on July 19, 1864. He also received 95 degrees in the "Egyptian Masonic Rite of Memphis." d. May 21, 1896.

Louis W. Fairfield (1858-1930) U.S. Congressman, 65th to 68th Congresses (1917-25) from 12th Ind. dist. b. Oct. 15, 1858 near Wapakoneta, Ohio. A teacher, he was professor of physics and philosophy at Tri-State College from 1885-1917. Member of Angola Lodge No. 236, Angola, Ind. receiving degrees on June 23, June 30 and July 21, 1913. d. Feb. 20, 1930.

Guy L. Fake (1879-1957) Judge of U.S. District Court of New Jersey since 1929 and chief Federal judge since 1948. Retired in 1951, but assigned to continue in service. b. Nov. 15, 1879 at Cobleskill, N.Y. Admitted to N.J. bar in 1903 and practiced at Rutherford. He had served as a member of the state general assembly and district judge. Served in the Spanish-American War. Raised in Boiling Spring Lodge No. 152, Rutherford, N.J. on Nov. 26, 1907. d. Sept. 23, 1957.

Juan C. Falcon (1820-1870) President of Venezuela from June 15,

1863 to 1868. His regime was over-thrown by revolution in the latter year. b. in Paraguana. He was a political leader and Venezuelan general. Falcon was the 7th sovereign grand commander of the Supreme Council, 33°, AASR in 1864-65. During his administration as president of Venezuela, he frequently delegated his charge, and among those Masons who served as president by his delegation were General Antonio Guzman Blanco, 33° (who was later to be elected to three terms himself); General Jose Desiderio Trias, 18°; Rafael Arvelo, 18°; General Miguel Gil, 30°; and General Manuel E. Bruzual, 33°.

James W. Fannin (1800-1836) Texas patriot and pioneer. b. in North Carolina about 1800, he was executed by the Mexican general, Santa Anna, q.v., with 357 others on March 27, 1836. Fannin was a captain in the Texas service in 1835. On Oct. 28th of that year, with Capt. Bowie and 90 men, he defeated a superior Mexican force near Bexar. General Houston, q.v., soon afterward made him a colonel and inspector-general. In January of 1836 he set out to reinforce Dr. James Grant who was in command of an unauthorized expedition to Matamoras. When he learned that Grant's force had been destroyed, he fell back to Goliad, but by Houston's order, he marched toward Victoria, and on March 19 was attacked on the Coleta River by a Mexican force under General Urrea. When the Mexicans were reinforced by 500 men on the 20th, the American force capitulated and it was agreed that the Texans should be treated as prisoners of war and sent back to the U.S. as soon as possible. After surrendering their arms, they were taken to Toliad, where, on the 26th, a dispatch was received from Santa Anna ordering their execution.

At daybreak the next morning all of the 357 prisoners but four physicians and their helpers were marched out under various pretexts "and shot in groups. Fannin was last to be killed. When Holland Lodge No. 36 of La. (later No. 1 of Texas) was organized at Brazoria, Texas, Fannin was present and acted as senior deacon, but it does not appear he became a member of that lodge. He is believed to have been a Mason before he left Georgia.

John C. Fant (1870-1929) President of Mississippi State College, 1920-29. b. Jan. 15, 1870 near Macon, Miss. Was superintendent of schools at Water Valley and Meridian, Miss., from 1895-1910 and then professor of secondary education for the state until 1920. Received his degrees in Meridian Lodge No. 308, Meridian, Miss. on Aug. 7, 1903, June 3 and June 10, 1904. Dimitted, March 1, 1927. d. Nov. 8, 1929.

Charles B. Faris (1864-1938) Judge Supreme Court of Missouri and Federal Judge, Eastern District of Missouri. b. Oct. 3, 1864 near Charleston, Mo. Graduate of U. of Missouri and admitted to bar in 1891. Practiced in Caruthersville, serving as city and prosecuting attorney. Served in lower house, judge of 28th judicial circuit and judge of the supreme court for term 1912-22, resigning in 1919 to become judge of the Eastern district. He was a member of the board of curators of the U. of Missouri and member of control board of Cottey Coll. for women at Nevada, Mo. Member of Caruthersville Lodge No. 461, Caruthersville, Mo., receiving degrees on Sept. 4, Dec. 18, 1900 and Jan. 21, 1901. Suspended, NPD, June 7, 1927. d. Dec. 18, 1938.

James I. Farley (1871-1948) U.S. Congressman to 73rd to 75th Congresses (1933-39) from 4th Ind. dist. b. Feb. 24, 1871 at Hamilton, Ind. Began as a teacher in public schools in 1889, and then as a salesman for Studebaker Corp. in 1906. In 1908 he joined the Auburn Automobile Co. as a salesman, rising to presidency and retiring in 1926. He affiliated with De-Kalb Lodge No. 214, Auburn, Ind. on Dec. 3, 1907 from Spartan Lodge No. 226 at Millersburg, Ohio. d. June 16, 1948.

James T. Farley (1829-?) U.S. Senator from California 1879-1885. b. Aug. 6, 1829 in Virginia. He moved first to Missouri and then to California where he studied law and was admitted to the bar in 1854. He served two terms in the state assembly and eight years in the state senate. He was recognized as the leader of the Democratic party in California for many years. He was a member of Volcano Lodge No. 56, Volcano and Amador Lodge No. 65 at Jackson as well as Sutter Chapter No. 11, R.A.M. at Sutter Creek, Calif.

Theodore Farley Vice president of Caterpillar Tractor Co. since 1940. b. Nov. 22, 1894 at Ipswich, Mass. He was with the Holt Mfg. Co. of Peoria, Ill. from 1919-25 as export manager. When the company merged with the C. L. Best Tractor Co. in 1925 to form the Caterpillar Co., he became assistant export manager, rising to assistant to president in 1935. Served in WWI as a captain. Mason, Shriner and Jester.

Lord Farnham (?-1957) Irish Peer. In 1908 he was elected to a seat in the house of lords as an Irish representative peer. He served in the South African War in 1901-02 with the 10th Hussars and was mentioned in dispatches. He joined the newly raised North Irish Horse and went to France in WWI in command of a battalion of the Royal Inniskilling Fusiliers in the Ulster division. He was awarded the Distinguished Service Order. In the spring of 1918 he was taken prisoner, but escaped and made his way through Germany to Holland. He was a member of the General Synod of the Church of Ireland and a member of the representative church body. He was president of the Hibernian Church missionary society and the Adelaide hospital. He was initiated in Lodge No. 90 at Cavan in 1901, and served as master in 1910. He was also a member of Meridian Lodge No. 12 of Dublin from 1903, and served as master in 1911. From 1928 until his death on Feb. 5, 1957, he was provincial grand master of the province of Meath and was senior grand warden of the grand lodge of Ireland at the time of his death.

David G. Farragut (1801-1870) First Admiral of the U.S. Navy. b. July 5, 1801 at Campbell's Station, near Knoxville, Tenn., son of George Farragut, naval and army officer of the American Revolution. He was adopted in 1808 by Commander Porter who educated him at Washington, D.C. and Chester, Pa. He was a midshipman at 91/2 years of age and was placed in command of a prize ship when only 12. He was on routine naval duty from 1810-47 and commanded the ship Saratoga during the Mexican War. He was on duty on the ship that carried Ambassador Joel Poinsett, q.v., to Mexico, and also in the convoy that escorted Lafayette, q.v., back to France in 1825. He was detailed to establish the Mare Island Naval Base in San Francisco Bay. He was the outstanding naval officer of the Civil War. He was in command of the West Gulf blockading squadron with orders to take New Orleans, which he did in 1862 without bloodshed, bombarding Fort Jackson and running his ships past Fort Jackson and Fort St. Philip. In 1863 he ran his flagship, Hartford, and one other vessel past Port Hudson and thereby controlled the Mississippi between Port Hudson and Vicksburg. Back into the Gulf, he silenced Fort Morgan, ran a blockade of mines, dispersed the Confederate fleet and captured Forts Morgan and Gaines. In Dec., 1864, Congress created the rank of vice admiral for him and in 1866 created the rank of admiral. He is a member of the American Hall of Fame. His lodge is not known, but he is thought to have been made a Mason on the island of Malta in 1818, when he was 17 years of age, serving in the Mediterranean under Bainbridge. He died Aug. 14, 1870, and was buried with Masonic honors by the grand master of New Hampshire and St. Johns Lodge No. 1 of Portsmouth. Admiral George W. Baird, q.v., wrote the following of him: "While Farragut's Masonic connection is beyond doubt, the writer has been unable to identify his lodge. Naval Lodge No. 87 was instituted at Vallejo, opposite the Navy Yard at Mare Island, and there are members of that lodge still living (1920) who greeted the admiral when he visited there. Surgeon General John Mills Brown, q.v., of the Navy, who was grand master of California as well as master of Naval Lodge and also an active 33rd, was intimate with the admiral in California and remembered him as a Mason and a promotor of Masonry. He did not, however, remember the name of his lodge." Admiral Baird wrote another interesting incident in connection with Farragut: "After the unveiling of the statue (of Farragut in Washington, D.C., Bar-

tholomew Dig-gins, a member of Brightwood Lodge No. 24 in the District of Columbia, who had been in Farragut's gig crew all during the war, asked for his old flag and offered a new one for it. The secretary of the Navy granted his request. Many years afterwards, when Dewey returned from the Philippines, Diggins asked the writer, who was about to go to New York to make arrangements for Dewey's reception, to present the flag to Dewey. The flag was duly presented and it was the only admiral's pennant ever flown by Farragut or Dewey."

Bernard G. Farrar (1785-1849) Pioneer Missouri physician. b. July 4, 1785, he was the first physician of the St. Louis area. He arrived in St. Louis in 1807. Originally a Virginian, he came from the same county as did Edward and Frederick Bates, q.v., settling first in Kentucky, near Frankfort, where he practiced medicine for a time. A brother-in-law, Judge Coburn, having received the appointment as judge of the Louisiana Territory, he was encouraged to move farther west. In St. Louis, he formed a partnership with Dr. David V. Walker. In 1815 he was one of a group who started the newspaper Western Journal in St. Louis. Farrar fought the first duel recorded west of the Mississippi in 1810. It was with James A. Graham. Farrar was hardly to be blamed for his participation, for at first, he was merely the bearer of the challenge to Graham. Graham declined to accept the challenge, giving as his plea that the challenger "was not a gentleman." Under the code that prevailed, Farrar became the principal. It was fought on Bloody Island, scene of many later encounters and Graham received severe wounds from which he never recovered, dying on his way East about a year later. Farrar was also the surgeon in the Benton-Lucas duel.

Frank G. Farrington (1872-1933) Justice, Supreme Court of Maine, 1929-33. b. Sept. 11, 1872 at Augusta, Me. Admitted to bar in 1902 and practiced at Augusta. Served in both branches of Maine legislature. Raised March 31, 1903 in Augusta Lodge No. 141, and exalted Feb. 24, 1921 in Cushnoc Chapter No. 43, both of Augusta, Maine. d. Sept. 3, 1933.

Wallace R. Farrington (1871-1933) Governor of Hawaii, 1921-29. b. May 3, 1871 at Orono, Me. Graduate of U. of Maine in 1891, he began newspaper work that year with the Bangor Daily News. Worked on newspapers in Kennebec, Augusta, and was managing editor and one of the founders of the Rockland Daily Star—all of Maine. Moving to Hawaii in 1894, he became editor of the Pacific Commercial Advertiser and president of the Hawaiian Gazette Co. in Honolulu. He later became president of the Honolulu Star Bulletin. Active in many activities of the territory, particularly in the educational field, and a regent of the College of Hawaii. Mason and past master of Lodge Progress d L'Oceania No. 37. Member of AASR in Hawaii. d. Oct. 6, 1933.

Charles B. Farwell (1823-1903) U.S. Senator from Illinois 1887-91. b. July 1, 1823 at Painted Post, N.Y. In 1838 he removed to Ogle Co., Ill. and worked at farming and on government surveys until 1844 when he went to Chicago on a load of wheat with ten dollars in his pocket. Worked first as a bank teller and later county clerk of Cook Co. Formed the firm of John V. Farwell with his brother in 1891 and became presi-

dent of the same. He and his brother built the Texas state capitol in 1887 and received in turn three million acres of land for it on which they stocked 150,000 head of cattle. Was a member of U.S. congress from 1871-76. Listed in *Who Was Who as a Mason*, but grand lodge records of Illinois do not show membership. d. 1903.

Orval E. Faubus Governor of Arkansas from 1955. b. Jan. 7, 1910 at Combs, Ark., he was educated in the public schools of that state. His first ten years (1928-38) were spent as a rural school teacher; iri 1939 he became circuit clerk and county recorder at Huntsville. In 1946-47 he was acting postmaster of Huntsville, and from 1953-54, postmaster. He is the editor, owner and publisher of Madison County Record at Huntsville since 1947. From 1949-53 he held the positions of highway commissioner, administrative assistant to the governor and directory of highways for Arkansas. He served as rural scout commissioner for Northwest Ark. for 14 years and was an Infantry major in WWII. In September, 1957 he became the most controversial figure in the United States when he refused to allow integration of white and Negro students in the Little Rock high schools. Integration was later enforced by Federal troops and the episode rocked the Southern states and focused the international spotlight on Faubus. He is a member of Huntsville Lodge No. 367, Huntsville, Ark., receiving his degrees on April 8, May 27 and June 24, 1947. Received the 32° AASR (SJ) on Oct. 28, 1953 at Fort Smith, Ark.; belongs to Sahara Shrine Temple at Pine Bluff and the Grotto at Fort Smith, and is a member of the Northwest Arkansas Scottish Rite Club.

Charles J. Faulkner, Jr. (1847-1929) U.S. Senator from West Virginia, 1887-99. b. Sept. 21, 1847 in Martinsburg, W. Va. He received an early education in France and Switzerland and entered Virginia Military Inst. in 1862. He served with the cadets of the school at the battle of New Market and afterwards as aide to generals Breckenridge and Wise in the C.S.A. Graduated from U. of Virginia in 1868 and admitted to bar same year. He served seven years as a circuit judge and was a member of the British-American Joint High Commission in 1898. He was the 8th grand master of the Grand Lodge of West Virginia, serving in 1880. He was a member of Equality Lodge No. 136 (Va. charter), now No. 44 of West Virginia charter, receiving the degrees on Dec. 12, Dec. 26, 1868 and Jan. 9, 1869. He served as master of the same from 1876 to 1878. At the time of his death on Jan. 13, 1929 he was the oldest past grand master of West Virginia.

Charles J. Faulkner, Sr. (1806-1884) U.S. Minister to France in period preceding the Civil War. b. in 1806, Martinsburg, Va., he graduated at Georgetown U. and was admitted to the bar in 1829. As a member of the Virginia lower house, he introduced a bill for the gradual abolition of slavery in Virginia. He was elected to the U.S. congress four successive terms from 1851-59, accepting the ministry to France in the latter year. While in France, he encouraged Louis Napoleon to sympathize with the southern cause, and as a result was recalled by Lincoln, arrested and confined in Fort Warren as a disloyal citizen, but released on a prisoner exchange. He was disbarred from citizenship until 1872. He served another term in the U.S. congress from 1875-77. A Mason, he delivered a Masonic address on Nov. 13, 1852 at Martinsburg. His son, Charles J. Jr., q.v. became U.S. senator and grand master of the Grand Lodge of West Virginia. He received his degrees in old Equality Lodge No. 136 (Va. charter) in 1867 and affiliated with the same lodge under West Va. charter in 1879. The lodge was then Equality No. 44. His son was a member of the same lodge. d. Nov. 1, 1884.

Edwin J. Faulkner President and director of Woodmen Accident & Life Co. and Woodmen Central Life Ins. Co. since 1954. b. July 5, 1911 at Lincoln, Nebr. Graduate of U. of Nebraska and Pennsylvania. He became treasurer of the Woodmen Central Assurance Co. in 1932, and vice president of the Woodmen Central Life Ins. Co. in 1938. Member of Lancaster Lodge No. 54, Lincoln, Nebr., receiving all three degrees in 1940.

Roy H. Faulkner Automobile executive. b. Feb. 11, 1886 at Allegheny, Pa. Automobile salesman from1916 until he became sales manager of Oakland-Pittsburgh Co., and later general manager of Nash-Cincinnati Motor Co. He joined Auburn Automobile Co. as sales manager in 1922, advancing to vice president in 1931, resigning that year to become vice president of Studebaker Sales Corp. and Pierce-Arrow Motor Co. He returned to Auburn Co. as president in 1934. He is now owner of Roy H. Faulkner & Associates in Auburn, Ind. Mason.

Francois Felix Faure (1841-1899) Sixth President of the Republic of France. He was a cabinet officer in the department of commerce and colonies in the 1880's, and later minister of marine under President Casimir Perier whom he succeeded as president in 1895, serving until his death in 1899. The bulletin of the International Masonic Congress of 1917 states that he was a Freemason.

George D. Fawcett (1861-1939) Actor. b. Aug. 25, 1861 in Virginia. He attended the U. of Virginia for four years and made his debut in the Manhattan Theatre in New York City in 1886. He supported Tomasso Salvini in 1890, and Alexander Salvini in 1894. In 1895-96 he was in repertoire with Nat Goodwin and with Maude Adams from 1897-99. He appeared in many productions of his own company, the Fawcett Stock Co., and in 1917 played the title role in Great John Ganton at Aldwych Theater in London. Later he was in vaudeville and motion pictures. He was a member of Pacific Lodge No. 233, New York City and of the "233 Club" in Hollywood. d. June 6, 1939.

Novice G. Fawcett President of Ohio State University. b. March 29, 1909 at Gambier, Ohio. Graduate of Ohio State in 1937. Taught and was superintendent of schools in Gambier, Defiance, Bexley, Akron and Columbus. He was named president of Ohio RR Robert Fechner State in 1956, assuming his duties on Aug. 1. He is a member of Ohio Lodge No. 199 at Bladensburg, Ohio, and received the Scottish Rite degrees in November, 1955 in the Valley of Columbus.

Bernard Fay Author, professor and anti-Mason. b. in 1893, this French historian specialized in books on American history. His writings included: *Revolutionary Spirit in France and America* (1927); *Franklin, the Apostle of Modern Times* (1929); *George Washington, Republican Aristocrat* (1931) and *Revolution and*

Freemasonry, 1680-1800 (1935). The latter book, published by Little Brown was definitely unfriendly to Freemasonry though purporting to be "factual" and "objective." The Masonic world, therefore, could not be expected to grieve when the following was published in the New York Times on Dec. 5, 1946: "Bernard Fay, former professor of American civilization at the College de France and writer on *Franco-American Relations*, was sentenced to life imprisonment at hard labor today after his conviction on a charge of intelligence with the enemy. M. Fay has been charged with publishing documents and lists of the Freemasons for the Vichy (Nazi dominated) government. This had resulted, according to the prosecution, in deportation or death for thousands of them."

Jonas Fay (1737-1818) American patriot, who with two other members of Vermont Lodge No. 18 (Ira Allen, q.v., and Thomas Chittenden, q.v.) led the fight that established Vermont as the 14th state. b. Jan. 17, 1737 in Hardwick, Mass. He received a good education and became a physician. He moved to Bennington, Vt. in 1766 and became prominent among the settlers on the New Hampshire grants, going as their agent to New York with Seth Warner in 1772 to lay their grievances before English Governor Tryon. It was on this trip that Fay and Warner spent some time in Albany where they were made Masons in Masters' Lodge No. 5. He was clerk of the convention of March, 1774, that resolved to defend by force Ethan Allan and the others who were outlawed by the legislature of N.Y. Dr. Fay was surgeon under Allen at Ticonderoga, and, afterward in Col. Warner's regiment. He was a member of the convention of Jan., 1777, which declared Vermont an independent state. For all practical purposes it was an independent republic from this date until 1791 when it was admitted to the Union and Dr. Fay—"learned, sagacious and well versed in political economy"—was mainspring and balance wheel of the movements. He was accredited to the Continental Congress year after year, but was not officially recognized as a delegate. He was secretary to the council of safety, helped draft the first constitution for Vermont and served as a member of the governor's council from 1778-85. He was probate judge at Bennington for five years and judge of the supreme court in 1782. Dr. Fay was admitted to Vermont Lodge at Springfield in 1782 and in 1793 was a charter member of Temple Lodge at Bennington. d. March 6, 1818.

Louis H. Fead (1877-1943) Justice, Supreme Court of Michigan, 1928-37. b. May 2, 1877 at Lexington, Mich. and graduated U. of Michigan in 1900. He practiced law at Newberry and served as prosecuting attorney and circuit judge. Raised in Lexington Lodge No. 61, Lexington, Mich. on July 12, 1902 and affiliated with McMillen Lodge No. 400, Newberry, Mich. on Sept. 2, 1905; was grand master of the Grand Lodge of Michigan in 1917; 33° AASR (NJ). d. Feb. 4, 1943.

Robert Fechner (1876-1939) First director of the Civilian Conservation Corps in 1933. President F. D. Roosevelt, by executive order, set aside 72,000 acres of public land on Massanutten Mountain in Virginia as the "Robert Fechner Memorial Forest" in his honor. b. March 22, 1876 in Chattanooga, Tenn., he was a machinist, foreman and master mechanic from 1896-1912. He then became executive officer of the Interna-

tional Association of Machinists until 1933 when he became director of the C.C.C. He was a member of Clinton Lodge No. 56, Savannah, Ga. and Mt. Pleasant Chapter No. 13, R.A.M. of Washington, D.C. d. Dec. 31, 1939.

Ladislav   Feierabend Czechoslovakian cabinet officer under President Benes, q.v. He was one of the organizers of the Grand Lodge "Comenius" in exile in England. Others who helped form the grand lodge were Dr. Vladimir Klecanda, grand master, q.v.; Dr. P. R. Korbel, grand secretary, q.v.; and Jan Masaryk, q.v., son of the first president of Czechoslovakia.

Lorenza Feliciana Also known as Madam Cagliostro, wife of the Count Alessandro di Cagliostro, q.v. When Cagliostro set up his "Egyptian Rite," his wife became grand mistress of the Lodge of Isis, which, in 1784, counted among its adepts some of the most prominent of the French titled women. It is said that she and her husband assumed the leading roles in the initiation. She delivered an oration advocating the emancipation of woman which was followed by the appearance of her husband as the "Grand Copt" in the nude. He then commanded the initiates to disrobe, for if they were to receive the truth, they must be "naked as truth." It is recorded that when Cagliostro was tried by the Inquisition, she was the chief witness against him.

Grant Fellows (1865-1929) Justice, Supreme Court of Michigan, 1917-29.b. April 13, 1865 in Hudson, Mich. Admitted to bar in 1886 and practiced in Hudson, Mich. He was attorney general of Michigan from

1913-17. Raised in Lebanon Lodge No. 26. d. July 16, 1929.

John Quincy Adams Fellows (1825-1897) Louisiana Freemason who headed all York Rite bodies of that state. b. April 3, 1825 at Topham, Vt., moving to New Orleans shortly after 1850. He was raised in Rising Sun Lodge No. 7 in Vermont in 1850 and affiliated with Marion Lodge No. 283 in New Orleans. He was elected grand master of the Grand Lodge of Louisiana in 1860 and served during the stormy six years of the Civil War. By his skill and ability, he was able to keep the passions of war outside the doors of the lodges, and the Blue and the Grey met in Louisiana lodges and forgot for the moment that they were sworn enemies. It is said that he facilitated the passage of many Union Masons out of Confederate camps when they revealed to him they were brethren. Exalted in Orleans Chapter No. 1 in 1852 he was grand high priest in 1859. Greeted in Louisiana Council No. 2 R. & S.M. he was grand master in 1868. Knighted in Indivisible Friends Commandery No. 1, he was grand commander in 1865 and grand master of the Grand Encampment, U.S.A. in 1871. He also rose to grand scribe in the General Grand Chapter. He was a 33° AASR (SJ). d. Nov. 28, 1897.

Christian Fenger (1840-1902) Surgeon and pathologist. b. in Copenhagen, Denmark and graduated as a doctor from the U. of Copenhagen in 1867. For the next ten years he served in a Copenhagen hospital; was a surgeon in the International Ambulance Assn. during Franco-German War; lectured at U. of Copenhagen; and went to Egypt where he was appointed medical officer in the Khalifa quarter of Cairo.

He came to Chicago in 1877 and was chief pathologist of the Cook County Hospital from 187993; professor of surgery at College of Physicians & Surgeons in New York City, 1884, returning to Northwestern U. in 1893 in the same capacity; and with Rush Medical College in 1899. He was raised in a Copenhagen lodge and affiliated with Ashlar Lodge No. 308 of Chicago. d. March 2, 1902.

Hart E. Fenn (1856-1939) U.S. Congressman to 67th to 71st Congresses (1921-31) from first Conn. dist. b. Sept. 12, 1856 in Hartford, Conn. He was city editor of the Hartford Post for many years and served in both legislative bodies of Conn. From 1909-14 he headed the fisheries and game department of Conn. Mason. d. Feb. 23, 1939.

Ivor D. Fenton U.S. Congressman since the 76th Congress (1939) from 12th Pa. dist. b. Aug. 3, 1889 at Mahanoy City, Pa. A physician by profession, he received his M.D. degree from Jefferson Medical Coll. in 1912 and began practice in Mahanoy City in 1914. He served in WWI as a captain in the Medical Corps with the 79th Division, A.E.F. A member of Mahanoy City Lodge No. 357, he received his degrees on March 23, April 27 and May 25, 1914. He was exalted in Mizpah Chapter No. 252, R.A.M. on June 10, 1915 and knighted in Ivanhoe Commandery No. 31, K.T. on March 23, 1916; both being in Mahanoy City. He is a member of the Scottish Rite at Bloomsburg, Rajah Shrine Temple at Reading, and Tall Cedars of Lebanon Forest No. 50 at Pottsville.

Ferdinand (see Duke of Brunswick) Ferdinand IV (1751-1825) Anti-Mason. King of the Two Sicilies. Also known as Ferdinand I, and Ferdinand III. He was the son of Don Carlos of Bourbon (later Charles HI of Spain). He was King of Naples from 1759-1806 and again from 1815-25 as Ferdinand IV. He expelled the Jesuits in 1767, and married Maria Carolina of Austria in 1768. Under her influence, he joined the coalition against France in 1793. At Napoleon's victory he fled to Palermo and then to Sicily, where in 1806 he ruled as Ferdinand III while Naples was ruled by Joseph Bonaparte, q.v., and Murat, q.v. He was restored to Naples in 1815, and made king of the two Sicilies as Ferdinand I. He ruthlessly repressed liberal opinion and his tyranny brought on the revolution of 1820. His last years were an era of cruel vengeance and persecution. On Sept. 12, 1775, he issued an edict forbidding the meeting of Freemasons in lodges in his dominions under the penalty of death. He revoked the edict in 1777 at the solicitation of his queen, Caroline, but in 1781 the decree was renewed.

Ferdinand VI (1713-1759) Anti-Mason. King of Spain, 1746-59. He was the second son of Philip V and Maria Louisa of Savoy. He kept Spain neutral during the first part of the Seven Years' War. He suffered from extreme melancholy which developed into insanity. His government was generally administered by ministers Jose de Carvajal and Ensenada. At the solicitation of Joseph Torrubia, visitor of the Holy Inquisition, he enforced the Bull of Excommunication of Pope Benedict XIV, q.v., and forbade the congregation of Freemasons under the highest penalties of law (1751).

Ferdinand VII (1784-1833) Anti-Mason. King of Spain, 1814-20 and 1823-33. Son of Charles IV, he was proclaimed king after the forced

abdication of his father in 1808, but Napoleon captured him on a ruse and held him prisoner until 1814, when he reinstated him. He had no sooner ascended the throne than he reestablished the Inquisition, which had been abolished by his predecessor. He ordered the closing of all lodges under the heaviest penalties. In Sept following, 25 persons, among whom were several distinguished noblemen, were arrested as "suspected of Freemasonry." On March 30, 1818, a still more rigorous edict was issued, by which those convicted of being Freemasons were subjected to severe punishment, exile or death. His rule was cruel and tyrannical and was overthrown in 1820, but the Holy Alliance, using French troops, restored him in 1823. His further reign lost Spain all its colonies in North and South America and relegated the country to a second rate power.

Roger H. Ferger Publisher of *Cincinnati Enquirer* (Ohio) since 1944. b. Jan. 5, 1894 in Cincinnati. He graduated from U. of Pennsylvania in 1916. Until 1920 he was an advertising agency executive, and in that year became advertising manager for the Enquirer. He returned to the advertising field on the Pacific coast until 1933 when he became business manager of the *Milwaukee Sentinel* (Wis.), and in 1936, of the *Pittsburgh Post Gazette* (Pa.). He returned to the Enquirer in 1940 as assistant publisher. Director of several companies and active in city and state service organizations. Member of Hyde Park Lodge No. 584, Cincinnati, since 1922; 32° AASR, (NJ) at Cincinnati, and Syrian Shrine Temple.

Homer Ferguson U.S. Senator from Michigan, 1943-54 and U.S. Ambassador to Philippines since 1955. b. Feb. 25 in Harrison City, Pa.

Graduate of U. of Michigan in 1913. He was admitted to the bar in 1913 and practiced until 1929, when he became a circuit judge. He was elected to the U.S. Senate in 1943, following his investigation of rackets in Detroit in 1939. City and county officials including the mayor, chief of detectives, prosecuting attorney, and sheriff were indicted as a result of his fact-finding. He also served as a professor at the Detroit College of Law. His appointment as ambassador to the Philippines was approved March 11, 1955. He is a member of Golden Rule Lodge No. 159, in Ann Arbor; Palestine Chapter No. 159, R.A.M. and Detroit Cornmandery No. 1, K.T., both of Detroit. He received his 32° AASR (NJ) in Detroit Consistory and 33° in 1952.

Homer L. Ferguson (1873-1953) Shipbuilder and President of Newport News Shipbuilding & Dry Dock Co. (Va.) from 1915-46 and chairman of board, 1940-53. b. March 6, 1873 at Waynesville, N.C. He was with the Newport News company from 1905. Previously he had been in naval construction for private firms and the U.S. Navy from one coast to the other. Mason. d. March 14, 1953.

James E. Ferguson (1871-1944) Governor of Texas 1915-16. b. Aug. 31, 1871 in Bell Co., Texas. He spent two years on Pacific coast and in the Rocky Mountains as a laborer, teamster, miner and became a foreman on bridge-building crews on various Texas railways. He next engaged in farming in Bell Co. and became an extensive landowner. He was admitted to the Texas bar in 1897, and practiced at Belton, and later in Temple. He was a member of Knob Creek Lodge No. 401 at Temple and 32° AASR (SJ). d. Sept. 21, 1944.

Malcolm P. Ferguson President and Director of Bendix Products of Bendix Aviation Corp. since 1946. b. June 20, 1896, at Elmira Heights, N.Y. Graduate of Syracuse U. in 1918. He was with the Eclipse Machine Co. of Elmira, N.Y., before coming to Bendix as assistant general manager in 1936. Mason and Knight Templar.

Sterling P. Fergusson Meteorologist who conducted the first experiment of elevating a recording instrument by kites in 1894. b. Nov. 8, 1868 at Dixon's Springs, Tenn. He has been with the Blue Hills Observatory (Harvard), U.S. Weather Bureau, and with the Hobbs Greenland expedition in 1926-27, as meteorologist. He has devised many instruments and methods for use in his field. Mason.

Bert M. Fernald (1858-1926) Governor and U.S. Senator from Maine 1916-19. b. April 3, 1858 at West Poland, Maine. He was a packer of canned goods from 1888 and president of the National Canners' Assn. in 1910. He was state senator two terms and governor of Maine from 1909-11. Raised in Tyrian Lodge No. 73 on June 25, 1896 and exalted May 27, 1910 in St. Andrews Chapter No. 51, R.A.M., both of Mechanic Falls, Maine. d. Aug. 23, 1926.

Karl Ludwig Fernow (1763-1808) German writer on art. A painter himself, he was a member of Goethe's circle. b. Nov. 19, 1763 at Pomerania, Germany. He was in Rome from 1795-1802 lecturing on archaeology. When he returned to Germany he became a professor of Italian literature at Jena. In 1804 he was librarian for the Duchess Amalia at Weimar. He was a member of the lodge Amalia, which honored his memory by a special assembly in 1809. d. Dec. 4, 1808.

Francisco Guardia Ferrer (1859-1909) Spanish free-thinker, revolutionary, educator and martyr. He was bequeathed a legacy by a Catholic woman for the purpose of founding a school. Upon learning of this, the French ecclesiastical authorities unsuccessfully sought to utilize the legacy for a church school, but Ferrer founded the Escuela Moderna at Barcelona in 1901, where he refused to teach a religious curriculum and spoke against the existing Spanish regime. In 1907 he was acquitted on charges of complicity in an attempt to assassinate the king and queen of Spain the preceding year. He went to England in 1909, but returned when he learned of an uprising in Barcelona. He was arrested on charges of aiding the uprising, convicted, and executed on Oct. 13, 1909. His trial caused the downfall of the Maura ministry and created violent antagonism abroad against Spain and Catholicism. Although his lodge is not known, he is referred to by the Bulletin of the International Masonic Congress in 1917 as a Freemason.

Robert, 5th Earl of Ferrers Real name was Robert Shirley. Grand Master of Grand Lodge of England (Moderns), 1762-63. He sheltered the famous Chevalier D'Eon de Beaumont, q.v., at his home, Staunton Harold near Ashby-de-la-Zouch at one time when it appeared that the latter might be kidnapped.

David L. Ferris (1864-1947) Protestant Episcopal Bishop. b. Dec. 31, 1864 at Peekskill, N.Y. A deacon in 1893 and priest in 1894, he served churches in New York, Conn. and Pa. from 1893 until 1920 when he was named bishop suffragan, diocese of Western New York. He was bishop coadjutor in 1924-29 and bishop, 1929-32. From 1932-38 he was bishop of diocese of Rochester, N.Y., and resigned in 1938. Raised May 19, 1908 in Hail-man Lodge No. 321, Pittsburgh, Pa.; grand chaplain of Grand Lodge of Pennsylvania from 1908-12; affiliated with Frank R. Lawrence Lodge No. 979, Rochester, N.Y. on Feb. 10, 1913; was grand chaplain of Grand Lodge of New York from 1916-17, 1920-23; exalted in Pittsburgh Chapter No. 268, R.A.M. on Dec. 20, 1909; greeted in Doric Council No. 19, R. & S.M. in May, 1916; knighted in Monroe Commandery No. 12, K.T. in March, 1914; joined Damascus Shrine Temple in 1912; received 32° AASR (NJ) in Pittsburgh in 1909; affiliated with Rochester (N.Y.) Consistory Feb. 6, 1915; crowned 33° AASR Sept. 18, 1919. d. June 9, 1947.

Woodbridge N. Ferris (1853-1928) Governor and U.S. Senator from Michigan. b. Jan. 6, 1853 at Spencer, N.Y. In the educational field, he served as a teacher in a business college at Freeport, Ill.; a professor at Rock River U. at Dixon, Ill.; principal of the Dixon and Pittsfield, Ill., schools; and in 1885 founded, and was president, of the Ferris Institute. He was elected governor of Michigan two terms, 1913-16 and was U.S. Senator from 1923-29. He was raised in Big Rapids Lodge No. 171, Big Rapids, Mich., on Feb. 12, 1891. d. March 23, 1928.

Elisha P. Ferry Governor of Washington, 1872-80. Member of Harmony Lodge No. 13 at Olympia, Wash., and past master of same. Grand master of the Grand Lodge of Washington and 32° AASR (SJ) at Olympia. Deceased.

Jules F. C. Ferry (1832-1893) French lawyer, statesman and Premier of France, 1880-81, 1883-85. Born at Saint Die, in the Vosges in 1832, he was admitted to the bar in 1851. Active in the establishment of the Republic of France, he turned to politics and opposed the party of Louis Napoleon. He gained fame for himself while serving as minister of public instruction. Through his efforts, the rule of the Jesuits was broken in 1879, and in 1882, he was instrumental in the passage of a law which made primary education free, compulsory and non-clerical. While prime minister, he directed the acquisition of colonies in Africa and Asia. At the siege of Paris during the Franco-Prussian War (1870-71), he was prefect of the besieged city and conceived the novel idea of getting the mail out by balloons, thus founding the world's first "air mail." He was a member of the Lodge Alsace-Lorraine which was constituted at Paris in Sept. 1872 under the jurisdiction of the Grand Orient of France.

Simeon D. Fess (1861-1936) U.S. Senator from Ohio, 1923-35. b. Dec. 11, 1861 in Allen Co., Ohio. Three degrees from Ohio Northern U. at Ada, Ohio. A professor of law from 1896-1900, he then served two years as vice president of his alma mater, and later was a lecturer at the U. of Chicago. From 1907-17 he was president of Antioch Col., Yellow Springs, Ohio. He was a member of the 63rd to 67th U.S. congresses (1915-23) before becoming a member of the U.S. Senate for two terms. A member of Yellow Springs Lodge No. 421, he was a 33° AASR (NJ) and member of Antioch Shrine Temple at Dayton. d. Dec. 23, 1936.

Samuel Fessenden (1784-1869) Lawyer and Major General of Massachusetts militia. b. July 16, 1784 in Fryeburg, Maine. Graduate of Dartmouth in 1806. In 1828 he declined the presidency of that institution. He was admitted to the bar in 1809, and began practice at New Gloucester. He was on the general court of Mass. (of which Maine was then a part) for two years and represented his district in the state senate and legislature. He served 14 years as a major general of the 12th Mass. militia. Raised Sept. 25, 1805 in Pythagorean Lodge No. 11, Fryeburg, he affiliated with Cumberland Lodge No. 12, New Gloucester on Oct. 16, 1809 and with Portland Lodge No. 1 (Portland) on March 24, 1823. He served in the grand lodge line from 1822 until 1828, when he was elected grand master. He was exalted in Mt. Vernon Chapter No. 1, R.A.M. of Portland on July 11, 1823, elected an honorary member in 1849, and served as deputy grand high priest of the Grand Chapter of Maine in 1826-27; knighted in Maine Encampment No. 1, Portland on Nov. 24, 1823, he was commander in 1825, 1845 and 1846. In 1845 he was grand captain general of the Grand Encampment of Mass. and R.I. d. March 13, 1869.

Aurelius Fessler (1756-1839) Hungarian ecclesiastic, historian and Masonic reformer. b. May 18, 1756 at Czarendorf, Hungary. He was educated in the Jesuit school of Raab, and took the orders in 1772. He was sent to the Capuchin monastery in Vienna. When he exposed the monastic abuses to Emperor Joseph II, he was dismissed from the order in 1781, and was converted to Lutheranism in 1791. He then taught oriental languages at the U. of Lemberg and served as private tutor to the son of Prince of Crolath. From 1791 to 1806, he was a superintendent of schools in Berlin. It was during this period that he made the attempted revision of the Royal York Lodge in Germany and documented the Rite of Fessler. He was initiated at Lemberg in 1783. He studied Freemasonry and thought it incapable of producing the moral reforms he wished. He therefore established a secret order called the Evergreen in 1788 while in Breslau. It bore a resemblance to Freemasonry, but it later failed. In June, 1796, while in Berlin, he affiliated with the Lodge Royal York, zur Freundschaft, became one of its officers, and eventually saw it grow into a grand lodge, of which he became deputy grand master. He was charged with revising the ritual, which was based on the French system of advanced degrees. Fessler, himself, did not believe in any degrees beyond that of "Master." He worked on its revision for many years and incorporated parts of the Swedish system. When the brethren would not accept his revisions, he wearied of his opposition and renounced all the offices he had filled, resigning in 1802. His revised rite, which was soon abandoned by the grand lodge in favor of the English system, contained nine degrees—Entered Apprentice, Fellowcraft, Master Mason, The Holy of Holies, Justification, Celebration, True Light, The Country, and Perfection. He later received relief from the German lodges. In 1808 he became a professor in the U. of St. Petersburg, Russia; ecclesiastical president of the Consistory at Saratow, and in 1827 on the invitation of Emperor Alexander, he was made ecclesiastical counselor. In Russia he became master of The Polar Star Lodge which was organized about 1809 and met in the private apartments of Baron Rosenkampf. They were called "Illuminati" or "hateful revolutionaries" by the Russian Rosicrucians. Fessler's early renunciation of the priesthood

followed him all his life and forced him from one position to another as he was constantly attacked for his liberal views.

John E. Fetzer Radio executive. Co-owner Detroit Tigers Baseball Club, Am. League, since 1956. b. March 25, 1901 in Decatur, Ind. Graduate of Purdue U. in 1921. After doing experimental work on spark and vacuum tube transmitters, he built and operated the pioneer Southwest Michigan radio station KFGZ in 1923. He then did research in England, Holland, France, Germany and Switzerland. Returning to the U.S. he became president and owner of WKZO at Kalamazoo, Mich. (1939). He then established station WJEF at Grand Rapids and became vice president of KXEL at Waterloo, Ia. From 1944-46 he was assistant director of U.S. censorship in charge of radio and as such supervised 900 domestic radio stations and all shortwave overseas broadcasts, all wire services and network news rooms. Visited Europe in 1945 at invitation of General Eisenhower to study problems of use of radio in postwar Europe. Member of Anchor Lodge No. 87; Kalamazoo Chapter No. 13, R.A.M.; Peninsular Commandery No. 8, K.T., all of Kalamazoo, Mich. 32° AASR (NJ) at Grand Rapids, Mich., and Saladin Shrine Temple of same city.

Wade Fetzer President of The Fidelity & Casualty Co. of New York. b. Nov. 22, 1879 at Ottumwa, Ia. Has been in the insurance business at Chicago, Ill., since 1897. He has been president of the W. A. Alexander & Co. since 1927 and now chairman; president of Fidelity of New York since 1930, now director. He is also director of the Continental Insurance Co. of N.Y.; La Salle National

Bank of Chicago and First National Bank of Hinsdale, Ill. He was the first president of the Insurance Federation of America in 1913, and again in 1920. Mason.

Anthony Fiala (1869-1950) Explorer. b. Sept. 19, 1869 in Jersey City Heights, N.J. Began as a designer of lithography, and later a newspaper artist and cartoonist with Grit publications. He studied photoengraving, and installed the plant for the Brooklyn Daily Eagle in 1894, and was in charge of the same. While serving in the Spanish-American War, he acted as war correspondent for that paper. He later established and was president of Fiala Outfits, Inc. He was photographer for the Baldwin-Ziegler Polar Expedition of 1901-02, and commanding officer of the Ziegler Polar Expedition of 1903-05, the latter reaching 82° 4' north and discovering and mapping new islands. They also discovered and mapped accurately the greater part of Franz Joseph Archipelago. He accompanied Col. Theodore Roosevelt, q.v., on his trip through the Brazilian wilderness in 1913-14 and explored the Papagio River and descended the Jurnena and Tapajos Rivers of Brazil. Served in the Mexican border affair and as a major in WWI. Member of Kane Lodge No. 454, New York City. d. April 8, 1950.

Johann Gottleib Fichte (1762-1814) German philosopher. Educated at Jena and Leipzig, Germany. After tutoring in Zurich, Switzerland, he was appointed professor of philosophy at the U. of Jena in 1793 and here wrote some of the books for which he became internationally famous. In 1798, a theological furor arose over an article which appeared in a journal he edited, and he resigned. Taking up residence in Berlin, he drew up a plan for the U. of Berlin and was its first rector (1810-14). He was the exponent of a system of transcendental idealism, emphasizing self-activity of reason, and setting forth a perfected Kantian system, or science of knowledge, in which he connected practical reason with pure reason. He was the author of Versucheiner Kritik alter Offenbarung, which was first attributed to Kant. Fichte was made a Mason in Zurich. There was no lodge in Jena, so he went to Rudolstadt in Thuringia, a duchy where the reigning prince was a patron of Masonry. When he went to Berlin in 1799, he became acquainted with Fessler, q.v., deputy grand master of the Royal York grand lodge and co-operated with him on the philosophical phase of additional degrees. Among his writings was a book entitled The Philosophy of Masonry.

Crosby Field Inventor. b. March 12, 1889 at Jamestown, N.Y. Graduate of New York and Cornell Universities. He has over 100 U.S. patents in his name for electrical, mechanical and chemical processes. His inventions include the Oxide Film Lightning Arrester (1912) and continuous ice ribbon freezing process (1923). He was first with General Electric and then in private practice as a consulting engineer. From 1919-23 he was with National Aniline & Chemical Co. in charge of all engineering; from 1923-45 he was vice president of Brillo Mfg. Co.; has been president of Flak Ice Corp. since 1923. As an officer of Army Ordnance Dept. since 1917, he served in both World Wars. He received his third degree in Wappingers Lodge No. 671, Wappingers Falls, N.Y., on May 15, 1916 and has been in good standing since that time.

Robert Field (1769-1819) Portrait painter. b. in England in 1769. He resided at Philadelphia from 1795-1800; Washington, D.C., 1800-02; Annapolis, Md., 1802-03; Baltimore, Md., 1803-05; Fort Boston, Mass., 1805-08 and Halifax, N.S., 1808-16. He moved to Kingston, Jamaica in 1816 and died there in 1819 of yellow fever. He was a leading portrait painter of his time and his biographer claimed he was "second only to Gilbert Stuart in his work." Some of the leading citizens painted by Field were Sir John Wentworth, Sir George Prevost, Sir John C. Sherbrooke. George and Martha Washington commissioned him to paint miniatures of them. He was raised in Annapolis Lodge No. 36 (now 69), Annapolis, Md., on Dec. 29, 1802 and in 1812 was master of St. Johns Lodge No. 211 (Eng.). d. in 1819 at Kingston, Jamaica.

Stephen J. Field (1816-1899) Justice, U.S. Supreme Court, 1863-97. b. Nov. 4, 1816 at Haddam, Conn., he was admitted to the bar in 1841. He was the last justice appointed by Lincoln. His decisions were important in the development of constitutional law. He resigned in 1897. He was a member of Corinthian Lodge No. 9 (formerly Lavely Lodge) at Marysville, Calif., and in 1866 was made a life member for his liberal donations to the lodge. d. April 9, 1899.

William C. Fields (1880-1946) Comedian of stage, motion picture and radio. b. Jan. 29, 1880 at Philadelphia, Pa. He was in vaudeville for several years and appeared in musical productions on Broadway including the Ziegfield Follies and Earl Carroll's Vanities. Among his motion pictures were: *So's Your Old Man, It's the Old Army Game, The Potters, Six of a Kind, One in a Million, It's a Gift, David Copperfield, Mississippi, The Man on a Flying Trapeze, Poppy, The Big Broadcast of 1938, The Bank Dick, Never Give a Sucker an Even Break* and *My Little Chickadee*. In 1937 he starred on the Chase and Sanborn Radio Hour. He was famous for his bulbous nose and his Fieldisms such as "my little chickadee" and "imagine that—a check for a short beer." He was a member of E. Coppee Mitchell Lodge No. 605, Philadelphia, Pa. d. Dec. 25, 1946.

Willam J. Fields (1874-?) Governor of Kentucky, 1924-27 b. Dec. 29, 1874 in Willard, Ky. Farmer, lawyer and real estate dealer at Olive Hill, Ky., and then a commercial traveler for wholesale groceries and dry goods from 1899-1910. Member of 62nd to 68th Congresses (1911-25). Resigned to become governor. Original lodge not known, but was admitted to Little Sandy Lodge No. 712 on Aug. 21, 1915 from "Ashland" (grand secretary's records do not locate him in any lodges around Ashland). He was suspended Aug. 20, 1921; reinstated July 21, 1923; suspended June 20, 1925. Deceased.

James, 4th Earl of Fife Fiftieth Grand Master Mason of Scotland, 1814-15.

Howard W. Files (1893-1957) Vice President of Pillsbury Mills, Inc. since 1933. b. Feb. 18, 1893 at Sioux Falls, S.D. He has been employed by Pillsbury since 1912, advancing to vice president in 1933, and vice president in charge of sales and advertising since 1940. Served in WWI both as an enlisted man and officer. Member of Khurum Lodge No. 112, Minneapolis, receiving degrees July 23, Aug. 16 and Aug. 20, 1915; 32°

AASR (NJ) on Nov. 12, 1921. d. Dec. 7, 1957.

Jose Quirce Filguera Costa Rican architect who reconstructed the Cathedral of San Jose. On a voyage to Guatemala he organized Freemasonry in that country. He was master of Caridad Lodge No. 26.

Vincente Filisola Mexican general, second in command to Santa Anna during the Texas revolution. He was senior warden of La Independencia Lodge.

Everett R. Filley (1894-1958) Vice President of The Texas Company from 1953; President of Texas-Zinc Minerals Corp. and Texaco Exploration Co. b. Sept. 5, 1894 in Filley, Nebr. Graduate of Baker U. in 1915. Went with the Texas Company in 1915 in production department and rose to executive secretary, assistant division manager, division manager, assistant manager, and vice president. Affiliated with Holland Lodge No. 1, Houston, Texas, Dec. 25, 1946 from Delta Lodge No. 425, Tulsa, Okla. d. March 21, 1958.

Millard Fillmore (1800-1874) Thirteenth President of the United States. Was an Anti-Mason. At the beginning of the Anti-Masonic period he was one of the most bitter critics of the fraternity which he characterized as "organized treason." Later in life his views seemed to mellow, for on July 4, 1851, as President, he was present at the Masonic cornerstone laying of the extension of the Capitol in Washington and took part in the exercises, examined the stone, pronounced it laid, and said, "The Most Worshipful Grand Master of the District of Columbia will now please examine the stone and see that it is well laid." In Sept., 1872, he attended

another Masonic cornerstone laying at the Buffalo State Asylum for the Insane. His uncle, Jesse Millard of Michigan, was a Mason.

William P. Filmer (1866-1942) President of the Golden Gate Bridge and Highway District from 1929-38. b. March 2, 1866 in New York City and educated in California public schools. Began as a farmer and then went into the printing business, becoming president of the Filmer Bros. Electrotype Co. from 1900. Initiated in King Solomon's Lodge No. 260 in July, 1898, he was master in 1903, and held the office of treasurer from 1903 until his death. Member of chapter, council and commandery, he received the Scottish Rite in 1900, and was grand treasurer general, 33° of the AASR (SJ). He was grand master of the Grand Lodge of California in 1911 and grand treasurer of the same from 1913 until his death on Nov. 22, 1942.

John Filson (1747-1788) Explorer and historian. b. in Chester Co., Pa. An early explorer of the western country, he had traveled throughout the central part of North America before he was 37. After spending several years in Kentucky collecting information for a history of the country, he purchased one-third interest in the present site of Cincinnati, Ohio, from Mathias Denman. While exploring the country between his new land and the Great Miami, he disappeared on Oct. 1, 1788 and was presumed to have been killed by hostile Indians. He became a member of Lodge No. 14 at Christina Ferry, Del. on Dec. 16, 1784, on a trip to Wilmington to have his first book printed, i.e., The Discovery, Settlement and Present State of Kentucky. He also published A Map of Kentucky; A Topographical Description of the Western Territory of North America and other works.

Alexander Edward, Viscount of Fincastle Sixty-first Grand Master Mason of Scotland in 1835. He was later the 6th Earl of Dunmore.

William Finch (1772-1818) Controversial character of early English Freemasonry. Claimed by some to be a Masonic charlatan and imposter, he is supported by others as being a genuine student of Freemasonry. He was initiated in what is now the United Industrious Lodge No. 31 of Canterbury. He gave up his trade as a tailor and went to London to write Masonic books, which he published in great number. The first, published in 1801, was *A Masonic Treatise, With an Elucidation on the Religious and Moral Beauties of Freemasonry, etc*. It was approved by the provincial grand master for Kent. Five years later he was censured by the grand lodge. In 1807 he was again censured by the grand lodge. He set up his own "Independent" lodge in his home in Westminster where he conducted initiations and imparted Masonic instruction and even offered correspondence courses in Freemasonry. His rituals were printed in a cypher or *The Master Key* which he varied from time to time. The first was one using Z for A, Y for B, etc. He made considerable profit from his lodge and books, but in 1815 an engraver named Smith sued him for money due for printing and Finch instituted a countersuit for money due him for initiating and instructing Smith in Freemasonry. When the grand lodge officers were called into court as witnesses, they denied that Finch had the right to make Freemasons and he lost the suit, later dying in poverty.

William G. H. Finch Inventor and radio executive. The inventor of automatic high speed radio printing system; radio relay, and recorder; high fidelity transmission system (both black and white and color); and radio broadcast facsimile system. b. June 28, 1895 in Birmingham, England, coming to the U.S. in 1906. In early years, he was an electrical engineer and radio specialist with several companies. Since 1921 he has been radio engineer and editor of Internation News Service, and radio editor of *New York American* and patent advisor for *Popular Radio* and *Wireless Age* since 1925. He established the first radio-typewriter press circuit between New York City and Chicago in 1932, and the first international circuit between New York City and Havana in 1933. He is the chief consulting engineer of the Hearst Newspapers, and chief engineer and secretary of Hurst's *American Radio News Corp*. In 1931 he was communications aide to the Wilkins-Ellsworth Transarctic Submarine Expedition. He is vice president of WCAE, Pittsburgh, and owner of WGHF. Member of DeMolay Lodge No. 498, Buffalo, N.Y., since 1919; Ancient Chapter No. 1, R.A.M. and Columbia Commandery No. 1, K.T., both of New York City; 32° AASR (SJ) at Alexandria, Va., and Washington, D. C. Chapter of National Sojourners; Mecca Shrine Temple, New York City.

Gottfried Joseph G. Findel (1828-1905) German Masonic writer, noted mainly for his General History of Freemasonry, published in 1861 and translated into English versions in 1865 and 1869. This was the forerunner of Gould's later work. He was initiated in Lodge Eleusis zur Vershwiegenheit at Bayreuth on Oct. 19, 1856. He founded the Union of

German Freemasons in 1860 and was the editor of an interesting Masonic journal at Leipzig in 1858, entitled *Craft Lodge*. In 1874 he published *Genius and Form of Freemasonry*. Of interest to Americans is the fact that in 1860 the Prince Hall (Negro) Grand Lodge of Mass. made him honorary past grand master and named him representative of the Prince Hallgroups in Germany. They presented him with a jewel, collar, and gauntlets which were on display in the museum of the grand lodge at Bayreuth before WWII. When the Nazis overran Germany, all items were confiscated except the jewel and it is again on display in the museum. d. in 1905.

William Findlay (1768-1846) Governor of Pennsylvania 1817-20 and U.S. Senator from Pennsylvania, 1821-24. b. June 20, 1768 in Mercersburg, Pa., he became a farmer and active in Democratic politics. He was elected to the state legislature in 1797 and 1803. From 1807-17 he was state treasurer. He was treasurer of the U.S. mint at Philadelphia from 1827-40. Member of a Pennsylvania lodge. d. Nov. 12, 1846.

Benjamin Fine Journalist and Education Editor for *The New York Times*. In 1943 he won the Pulitzer Award for the New York Times for "the most disinterested and meritorious public service rendered by an American newspaper during the year." b. Sept. 1, 1905 in New York City, he is a graduate of Rhode Island State Coll., and Columbia U. He was taught and lectured in education in a number of institutions of higher learning. Among his books are *A Giant of the Press; Educational Publicity*; and *Admission to American Colleges*. Raised in Justice Lodge No. 753, New York City in 1937, he was mas-

ter in 1946 and named representative of New Mexico near the Grand Lodge of New York in 1955; 32° AASR (NJ) and member of Mecca Shrine Temple of New York; chairman of education committee of New York Times Square Club.

John S. Fine Governor of Pennsylvania, 1950-54. b. April 10, 1893 near Nanticoke, Pa. Graduate of Trinity Coll. and U. of Dublin. Admitted to bar in 1915, he practiced in Wilkes-Barre until 1927 when he became judge of court of common pleas of Luzerne Co. In 1947 he was named to the bench of the superior court of Pa., serving until elected governor in 1950. Mason.

George K. Finlay (1877-1938) Protestant Episcopal Bishop. b. Oct. 1, 1877 at Greenville, S. Car. Ordained deacon in 1902 and priest in 1903. He was missionary in charge of Trinity Chapel at Clemson Coll. (S. Car.) from 1902-07, and rector of Trinity Church at Columbia from 1907-21, when he was consecrated bishop coadjutor of diocese of South Carolina. From 1922 he was bishop for diocese of upper South Carolina. Mason. d. Aug. 27, 1938.

David E. Finley Director, National Gallery of Art at Washington, D.C. since 1938. b. Sept. 13, 1890 at York, S. Car. Graduate of U. of South Carolina and George Washington Law School. He practiced law at Philadelphia from 1915-17, and after service as a lieutenant in WWI, went with the War Finance Corp. and later with the U.S. treasury. From 1933-37 he practiced law in Washington, D.C. He was president of American Association of Museums from 1945-49 and has served on national and international museum commissions. Mason.

Member Philanthropic Lodge No. 32, York, S.C.

George Washington Finley (1858-1932) Piankesha Indian Chief whose tribal name was Te-Wah-Guah-Kelllon-Ga b. b. Oct. 7, 1858 near Paola, Kans. He was raised in Miami Lodge No. 140, Miami, Okla. on Sept. 24, 1913 and served that lodge as tyler for 15 years. He received his 32° AASR (SJ) at McAlester, Okla. on Jan. 25, 1917 and was a member of Akdar Shrine Temple at Tulsa, Okla. d. Nov. 16, 1932.

Woolsey Finnell (1866-1955) Alabama engineer who sponsored the erection of a monument to the memory of Ephriam Kirby, q.v., the first general grand high priest of the General Grand Chapter, U.S.A. at Mt. Vernon, Ala. in 1953. b. Oct. 24, 1866 near Tuscaloosa, Ala. He was an engineering graduate of the U. of Alabama. Served in Engineer Corps as a colonel in WWI and was cited for meritorious service by General Pershing, q.v. Was judge of probate in Tuscaloosa Co. following the war and later state director of highways for Ala. Finnell was one of the cofounders of the American Legion. Raised Sept. 26, 1896 and served as head of the grand chapter, grand council and grand commandery of Alabama. Member of Red Cross of Constantine; K.Y.C.H.; 33° AASR (SJ). He was awarded the General Grand Chapter's gold distinguished service award in 1954 for his part in the erection of the Kirby monument. d. Jan. 26, 1955.

Charles G. Finney (1792-1875) Anti-Mason, clergyman, abolitionist and president of Oberlin College (Ohio) from 1851-65. He received his degrees in Meridian Sun Lodge No. 32, Warren, Conn. in

1816, and in June, 1818, made his first visit to Rising Sun Lodge No. 125 at Adams, N.Y. Although not a member of the latter lodge at the time, he was voted to serve as secretary, pro tern at a meeting on Feb. 24, 1820. On Dec. 14, 1820 he was admitted a member of the lodge and named secretary at the same meeting. On May 6, 1824, he was discharged by his own request. It was in this year that he was licensed as a minister by the St. Lawrence Presbytery, and two years later he began conducting religious revivals throughout the Middle and Eastern states. He wrote and preached anti-Masonry wherever he was, and with Jonathan Blanchard, a Presbyterian minister and president of Wheaton College, published an anti-Masonic newspaper called The Christian Cynosure. He was active with Blanchard and Bishop David Edwards in the formation of the National Christian Association in 1868, whose purpose was to oppose all secret societies. This grew into the American Party in 1872, and this short-lived organization ran candidates in the 1876 and 1880 elections. Eventually dissension and petty jealousies in the anti-Masonic ranks caused the movement to die. As one biographer stated: "Were he alive today, how surprised he would be to learn that there are more Masons among the undergraduates and graduates of Oberlin College than existed during the Morgan affair in the entire state of New York."

Joseph Firrao Anti-Mason. Roman Catholic Cardinal and secretary of state to Pope Clement XII, q.v., who after his famous Bull of Excommunication on April 24, 1738 entitled *In Eminenti Apostolatus Specula*, caused Firrao to issue a still more stringent edict for the Papal states on Jan. 14, 1739 of which subjected Freemasons to death and confiscation of property, without hope of mercy—"sotto Pena della morte, e confiscazione de deni da incorressi, irremisstbilmente senz a speranza di grazia."

Leo H. Fischer Sports editor. b. Sept. 20, 1897 at Chicago, Ill. Has been a reporter and sports writer for *Chicago Examiner, Chicago Herald-Examiner, Chicago Journal, Chicago American*. Has been sports editor for *Chicago Herald-American* since 1941. He was founder and president of the Amateur Softball Assn. in 1930-38; president of the National Professional Basketball League in 1940-44. Served in the Navy in WWI. Member of Monroe C. Crawford Lodge No. 1042, Chicago, Ill., receiving degrees on May 27, July 1, and Sept. 9, 1921. Served as senior warden at one time. Member of National Sojourners and Heroes of '76.

Bert Fish (1875-1943) U.S. Envoy and Minister. b. Oct. 8, 1875 at Bedford, Ind. Graduate of John B. Stetson U. Admitted to Florida bar in1902, practiced in De Land, retiring in 1926. He served as envoy extraordinary and minister plenipotentiary to Egypt (1933), Saudi Arabia (1939), and Portugal from 1941. In 1937 he was chairman of the delegation to the Capitulations Conferences at Montreaux, Switzerland. He also was engaged in the citrus industry in Florida. Member of St. Johns Lodge No. 37, De Land, Fla., receiving degrees on Feb. 14, March 14 and March 28, 1899; 32° AASR (SJ). d. July 21, 1943.

Edward L. Fishburne Justice, Supreme Court of North Carolina since 1935. b. Nov. 4, 1883 at Walterboro, S. Car. Graduate of The Citadel (S.C.). Admitted to bar in 1907 and practiced in Walterboro. Served four years in the lower house of his state. Mason.

John W. Fishburne (1868-1937) U.S. Congressman to 72nd Congress (1931-33) from 7th Va. dist. b. March 8, 1868 in Albemarle Co., Va. Law degree from U. of Virginia in 1896, he practiced at Charlottesville. Served in lower state house and was circuit judge from 1913-30. Mason. d. June 26, 1937.

Geoffrey F. Fisher Archbishop of Canterbury. b. May 5, 1887 at Higham Rectory, Numeaton, England. He was a student at Marlborough Coll. from 1901-06 and received a B.A. from Exeter Coll., Oxford, in 1910 and an M.A. in 1913. He was ordained as a deacon in the Church of England in 1912, priested in 1913, and consecrated bishop in 1932, as bishop of Chester; bishop of London in 1939, and archbishop of Canterbury since 1945. He is known for his tolerance and unconventionality. When enthroned in 1945 as archbishop, he became one of the youngest primates of England in modern times. He has been privy councilor since 1939. Initiated in Old Reptonian Lodge No. 3725 in 1916, he later became a member of Tyrian Lodge No. 253 in Derby, and as bishop of Chester, he joined St. Anselms Lodge No. 5166 at Chester in 1935, and served as master in 1936. He has twice been grand chaplain of the Grand Lodge of England-1937 and 1939 and served as provincial grand master for Norfolk.

Henry C. Fisher (1867-1936) Brigadier General, U.S. Army Medical Corps. b. May 20, 1867 in Montgomery Co., Md. Received his M.D. degree at Georgetown U. in 1891, and appointed 1st lieutenant and assistant surgeon in the Army in the same year, advancing through grades to brigadier general and assistant surgeon general in 1929, retiring in 1931. He served in the Spanish-American War, Philippine Insurrection and WWI. He commanded hospitals at Hot Springs, Ark., Walter Reed General Hospital, and Army Medical School at Washington, D.C. Mason. d. Dec. 18, 1936.

John S. Fisher (1867-1940) Governor of Pennsylvania, 1927-31. b. May 25, 1867 in South Mahoning Twp., Pa. Graduate of Indiana State Normal School of Pa. in 1886 and honorary degrees from several institutions. Admitted to the bar in 1893, he practiced at Indiana, Pa. He was chairman of the board of National Union Fire Insurance Co. and was chairman of the investigating committee which exposed the frauds in connection with furnishing the state capitol at Harrisburg. In 1919 he was appointed state commissioner of banking. He was made a Mason "at sight" by the grand master of Pennsylvania at a special communication of the Grand Lodge of Pennsylvania on March 7, 1928, and was elected to membership in Indiana Lodge No. 313 of Indiana, Pa. d. June 25, 1940.

Joshua Fisher (1748-1833) Surgeon on a privateer during the Revolutionary War. b. May 17, 1748, in Dedham, Mass. He graduated from Harvard in 1776, studied medicine and began his practice until the hostilities with Great Britain began in 1775, when he volunteered as a surgeon on a privateer out of Marblehead. He was captured, but escaped to France, again entering the service. After the war, he settled in Beverly, Mass. and attained a high reputation in his profession. He bequeathed $20,000 to found a Harvard profes-

sorship in natural history. He was president of the Massachusetts Medical Society and published A Discourse on Narcotics in 1806. He was a member of Unity Lodge at Ipswich, Mass. and served as secretary of the lodge. d. March 15, 1833.

0. Clark Fisher U.S. Congressman to 78th to 80th Congresses from 21st Texas dist. (1943-51). b. Nov. 22, 1903 near Junction, Texas. Admitted to bar in 1929, he served as county attorney, state representative and district attorney. Member of Concho Lodge No. 1260, San Angelo, Texas since 1922 and past master of same. Member of Acacia Fraternity, Eastern Star and Shrine.

George A. Fitch Secretary of the International Committee on Y.M.C.A. since 1909. b. Jan. 23, 1883 in Soo-chow, China. An ordained Presbyterian pastor, he entered the Y.M.C.A. work in 1909, and has served in Shanghai, Nanking, Chungking, Lan-chow, China, and in Korea since 1947. He was director of the Nanking Safety Zone during the siege and occupation of 1937-38. He has been executive adviser to Chinese Industrial Cooperatives; deputy director of UNRRA; vice president of Chinese-Foreign Famine Relief; trustee of Institution for Chinese Blind, and honorary adviser to Chinese Mission to Lepers. Mason and member of O.E.S.

John Fitch (1743-1798) Inventor of steamboats. b. Jan. 21, 1743 in East Windsor, Conn. His early years were marked by ill-treatment from his father and elder brother, and an unfortunate marriage. After serving an apprenticeship as a watchmaker, he became a wanderer in 1769. First a gunsmith to the American forces of the Revolution, he later joined the New Jersey troops and wintered at Valley Forge, later resuming his watch-making trade in Bucks Co., Pa. As a deputy surveyor for the state of Virginia he also combined the job of selling merchandise in the back country and on one trip was captured and held prisoner by the Indians throughout one winter (1782-83) until he escaped. He first conceived the idea of steam as a motive-power in April, 1785 while in Warminster, Pa. He had been initiated into Bristol Lodge No. 25 of Bristol, Pa., just three months earlier (Jan. 4, 1785). His first thought was to use it for carriages, but then he returned to vessels. He completed his first model of a steamboat that year. Although he besieged the Continental Congress as well as the Pennsylvania legislature for aid in his project, he failed to receive it, and with $800 of his own capital, he formed a company and began a boat of 60 tons. His second boat made its trial trip on the Delaware at Philadelphia on Aug. 22, 1787, in the presence of the members of congress met in convention to frame the Federal constitution. A still larger boat was completed in October, 1788, and another in April, 1790, the latter running the entire summer as a regular passenger boat between Philadelphia and Burlington with a speed of eight miles per hour. In 1791 he received a patent for his inventions from the government. In 1793 he went to France to build a boat, but found the country in revolution and left his plans and specifications with the American consul at L'Orient and went to London. In his absence, his drawings and papers, it is claimed, were lent to Robert Fulton who was then in Paris. He returned to America in 1794 disappointed and penniless. He then constructed one more steamboat and another model, but sometime between June 25 and

July 18, 1798, he committed suicide by poison and died in a tavern in Bardstown, Ky. He wrote: "The day will come when some more powerful man will get fame and riches from my invention; but nobody will believe that poor John Fitch can do anything worthy of attention." In 1817, at the instigation of Governor Ogden of N.J. the original patents, drafts, specifications and models of both Fitch's and Fulton's boats were presented before a committee of the New York legislature which reported: "the steamboats built by Livingston and Fulton were in substance the invention patented to John Fitch in 1791, and Fitch during the term of his patent had the exclusive right to use the same in the United States."

Lord Frederick Fitzclarence. Sixty-Fifth Grand Master Mason of Scotland, 1841-42.

A. L. Fitzgerald (1840-1921) President of Pacific Methodist College, 1871-75 and Chief Justice, Supreme Court of Nevada, 1907. b. Oct. 27, 1840 in Ruffin, N. Car. Graduate of U. of N. Car. Serving in the Civil War, he saw action in the battles of the Wilderness, Petersburg, and the siege of Richmond. Went to Calif. after the war and taught Greek and Latin in the Pacific Methodist College. He later became deputy superintendent of Public Instruction of the state and returned to the college in 1871 as president. He read law and was admitted to the bar in 1878, moving in that year to Eureka, Nev. He was elected district judge in 1887, and elevated to the supreme court bench in 1900. Raised in Rockwell Lodge No. 600, Ruffin, N. Car., he received the chapter and commandery degrees in Petersburg, Va. in 1863. In Nevada he affiliated with Eureka Lodge No. 16 and St. Johns Chapter

No. 5, heading both bodies and becoming grand high priest of the Grand Chapter of Nevada in 1884 and grand master of the Grand Lodge of Nevada in 1887. He received his AASR (SJ) degrees in Santa Rosa, Calif., in 1870, 33° and sovereign grand inspector general for Nevada. d. Aug. 21, 1921.

Edward Fitzgerald (1809-1883) English poet and translator. Educated at Cambridge, he is best known for his translation in rhymed verse of the Rubaiyat of Omar Khayyam (1859). He was the author of two plays of Sophocles and six dramas of Calderon. Member of Doric Lodge No. 96 at Woodbridge, England.

Frank D. Fitzgerald (1885-1939) Governor of Michigan, 1935-36. b. Jan. 27, 1885 at Grand Ledge, Mich. In the service of his state from 1913, he was variously a proofreader of the lower house, bill clerk, clerk in office of secretary of state, executive secretary of Michigan Federal Food Administration, deputy secretary of state, business manager of state highway department, secretary of state, 1931-34. He was raised in Grand Ledge Lodge No. 179 on Nov. 7, 1920, and was a member of the Scottish Rite (NJ) at Grand Rapids, Mich. d. March 16, 1939.

John Fitzgerald Aide-de-Camp to General Washington in Revolutionary War. A major of the 9th Virginia Regiment, he served as Washington's aide from Nov. 1776 to July 1778. Member of Williamsburg Lodge No. 6 in Virginia.

Roy G. Fitzgerald U.S. Congressman, 67th to 71st Congresses (1921-31) from 3rd Ohio dist. b. Aug. 25, 1875 at Watertown, N.Y. Admitted to bar in 1896. He served in WWI as an infantry captain overseas. He is the author of the cumulative codification system for statutory law of U.S. and District of Columbia, and has been a delegate to the conference of the Inter-parliamentary Union in 1927, 1928 and 1929. Member of Mystic Lodge No. 405, Dayton, Ohio, receiving degrees on Dec. 23, 1902, Feb. 4 and Feb. 16, 1903; 32° AASR (NJ).

Charles Fitzsimmons (1835-1905) Brigadier General, U.S. Volunteers. b. Dec. 26, 1835 in New York. He entered Union Army in 1861 as a captain of 3rd N.Y. Cavalry. Wounded in 1863, returned to service in Oct. that year as lieutenant colonel. Was wounded again at Ashley's Gap in 1864. Served on Western plains until mustered out in 1866 with brevet rank of brigadier general. Entered contracting business in Chicago; was active in Ill. National Guard, becoming brigadier general U.S.V. in June 1898 during Spanish-American War, but resigned shortly afterward. Member of Yonnondio Lodge No. 163 of Rochester, N.Y. d. in 1905.

Burton S. Flagg President of Federated Mutual Fire Insurance Co. and Cambridge Mutual Fire Insurance Co. b. Nov. 10, 1873 in Littleton, Mass. Graduate of Brown U. in 1896. Started in insurance business at Fitchburg, Mass. in 1897. Officer and director of many companies. Raised in St. Matthews Lodge, Andover, Mass. on Nov. 2, 1903; knighted in Bethany Cornmandery No. 17, Lawrence, Mass. on May 28, 1907; received 32° AASR (NJ) in Massachusetts Consistory, Boston, April 28, 1911; entered Aleppo Shrine Temple, Boston, on Dec. 30, 1910.

Edmund Flagg (1815-?) Author. b. Nov. 24, 1815 in Wiscasset, Maine. He graduated at Bowdoin in

1835 and taught school in Louisville, Ky. and wrote for the Louisville Journal for 30 years. He read law in St. Louis and was admitted to the Mo. bar in 1837, also editing the St. Louis Commercial Bulletin. In 1840-41 he practiced law in Vicksburg, Miss., and was editor of the Whig at the same time. At this time he was seriously wounded in a duel with the editor of the Vicksburg Sentinel. In 1842 he owned the Gazette at Marietta, Ohio, and in 1844-45 the St. Louis Evening Gazette. He subsequently acted as official reporter of the courts of St. Louis and reported on the debates of the constitutional convention of Mo. In 1849 he was secretary of the U.S. legation at Berlin, and in 1850-51 was U.S. consul at Venice and also correspondent for several New York papers. On his return in 1852 he took charge of a Democratic paper in St. Louis. He was afterward placed in charge of the bureau of statistics in the department of state at Washington, D.C. From 1858-60 he acted as Washington correspondent for the western press. From 186170 he was in charge of the U.S. copyright office and then practiced law at Falls Church, Va. Among his writings are The Far West; The Howard Queen; Blanche of Artois; Edmond Dantes (a sequel to Monte Cristo); Venice, the City of the Sea; De Molai, the Last of the Military Grand Masters. Although his lodge is not known, he was a member of Louisville Chapter No. 5, Louisville, Ky. and created a Knight Templar on April 26, 1851 in Louisville Commandery No. 1, K.T. He was a life member of the latter body, but dimitted to affiliate with Washington Commandery No. 1 of Washington, D.C. on March 8, 1854.

Harris Flanagin Former Governor of Arkansas. Member of Arkadelphia Lodge No. 19, Arkadelphia, Ark. In 1859 he was chairman of the committee on education of the Grand Lodge of Arkansas and junior grand deacon in 1862. A member of Whitfield Chapter No. 4, R.A.M., Camden, Ark., he became high priest of Merrick Chapter, U.D. at Arkadelphia and was deputy grand high priest of the Grand Chapter, R.A.M. of Arkansas in 1860. He served as grand master of the Grand Council, R. & S.M. of Arkansas. Deceased.

John W. Flannagan, Jr. (1885-1955) U.S. Congressman to 72nd to 80th Congresses (1931-49) from 9th Va. dist. b. Feb. 20, 1885 at Trevilians, Va. Began law practice at Appalachia, Va. in 1907 and later settled in Bristol. Mason and Shriner. d. April 27, 1955.

Reuben H. Fleet President of Consolidated Aircraft Corp. b. March 6, 1887 at Montesano, Wash. He began in 1907 as a real estate operator, specializing in timber and in May, 1923, organized the Consolidated Aircraft Corp., of which he was president and general manager until 1941 and senior consultant since 1942. Served as a major in Army Air Force in WWI. Mason.

Hans Kirkgaard Fleischer (1803-1884) Norwegian Lieutenant General and Lord Steward of the King. Master of the Norwegian Steward Lodge, and later provincial grand master, at which time Norway worked under the Grand Lodge of Sweden. K.C. of the Order of King Charles XIII.

Samuel S. Fleisher (1872-1944) Wool manufacturer and philanthropist. Particularly active in juvenile fields. b. in Philadelphia, Pa., he was vice president of S. B. & B. W. Fleisher, Inc., manufacturers of worsted yarn, but retired to devote himself to community projects in Philadelphia as well as those on a national scale. Member of Keystone Lodge No. 271, Philadelphia, receiving degrees on April 6, May 9 and June 12, 1914. d. Jan. 20, 1944.

Sir Alexander Fleming (1881-1955) British discoverer of penicillin. Graduate of St. Mary's Hospital Medical School. A professor of bacteriology at the U. of London and lecturer of Royal Coll. of Surgeons. He discovered penicillin in 1928 for which he was awarded the Nobel prize in 1945. Discovered lysozyme in 1929. He was knighted by King George VI, q.v., in 1944. He was awarded the distinguished service citation of the Grand Lodge of New York in 1953. A member of several English lodges, he was master of Misericordia Lodge No. 3286 in 1935, and later served as treasurer. He was master of Santa Maria Lodge No. 2682 in 1925, and later secretary. In 1942 he was elected senior grand deacon of the United Grand Lodge of England and promoted to past grand warden in 1948. He served as high priest of Aesculapius Chapter and in 1942 was past grand sojourner of the Supreme Grand Chapter, R.A.M. of England, and later was named past grand scribe. In the Scottish Rite, he was 30° and was sovereign of Victory Chapter of Rose Croix. He was also a member of the London Scottish Rifles Lodge No. 2310 and took special pride in the fact that he has served as a private in the Scottish Rifles Regiment of London for 14 years. d. March 11, 1955.

Dewey L. Fleming Newspaperman and Pulitzer prize winner. b. July 19, 1898 at Whitmer, W. Va. Was a reporter with Elkins Inter-Mountain (W. Va.) and Baltimore American until 1923, when he went with the Baltimore Sun. Since that time he has been with the Washington Bureau, New York correspondent, Chicago correspondent, London correspondent and chief of the Washington Bureau since 1941. He was awarded the Pulitzer prize for reporting on national affairs in the year 1943. Mason.

Raymond H. Fleming Brigadier General, U.S. Army. b. July 5, 1889 at Waxahachie, Texas. Graduate of Trinity U. (Texas) and postgraduate work in economics and labor relations at Tulane. He enlisted as a private in the La. national guard in 1916 and was commissioned in 1917, advancing to brigadier general in the guard in 1928 and in the U.S. Army in 1940. He served in the Mexican border conflict and with the field artillery overseas in WWI. In WWII he was state director of selective service (La.) and in 1948 was assistant director of selective service at Washington, D.C. Member of Louisiana Lodge No. 102, New Orleans, La. since 1917 and a National Sojourner.

Wallace B. Fleming President of West Virginia Wesleyan College, 1915-22 and president of Baker University, 1922-36, and now president emeritus. b. Nov. 22, 1872 in Cambridge, Ohio, he holds degrees from Muskingum (Ohio), Drew, Columbia, West Virginia, Wesleyan and Baker. Ordained a Methodist Episcopal minister in 1897, he served pastorates in Paterson and Bayonne, N.J. and was later professor of Hebrew and Greek at Drew Theological Seminary (N.J.). Raised in Maple Lodge No. 196, N.J. on June 16, 1911. Later affiliated with Madison Lodge No. 93, N.J. and with Franklin Lodge No. 7, Buckhannon, W.Va. in 1918 dimitting in 1923.

Walter M. Fleming (1838-1913) Cofounder of the Ancient, Arabic Order of the Nobles of the Mystic Shrine with William J. Florence, q.v., on June 6, 1876 and was its first imperial potentate, serving for 12 years. b. June 13, 1838 in Portland, Maine. A physician, he was raised in Rochester Lodge No. 660 on Feb. 13, 1869 and affiliated with New York Lodge No. 330 on Dec. 3, 1872. He became a member of Columbian Commandery No. 1, K.T. at New York City on Dec. 2, 1871 and was its commander from 1873-77. d. Sept. 9, 1913.

William Fleming (1734-1824) American patriot and jurist. A graduate of William and Mary CO11. in 1763, he was a member of the house of burgesses and of the Virginia conventions in 1775-76 and a member of the committee on independence in May, 1776. He became judge of the general court and presiding judge of the court of appeals. He served as a delegate from Virginia to the Continental Congress in 1779-81. His lodge is not known, but he attended the sessions of the Grand Lodge of Virginia in Oct. 1791. d. Feb. 2, 1824.

Hugh J. Flemming Prime Minister of New Brunswick from 1952. b. at Peel, Carleton Co., N.B., Canada. Engaged in potato farming and lumbering early in life. He became a county councilor and was later elected to the New Brunswick legislature and became the leader of the opposition, in which capacity he served until the election of 1952, when the Conservatives came into power and he was called upon to form a new government. His father, John K. Flemming was premier of New Brunswick from 1911-14. He was raised in Carleton Lodge No. 35 in 1925 and took his chapter work in Woodstock Chapter No. 8, R.A.M. and was made a Knight Templar in 1929. As premier of the province, he encouraged legislation to widen the social services and develop the potential hydro resources.

Duncan U. Fletcher (1859-1936) U.S. Senator from Florida 1909-36. b. Jan. 6, 1859 at Sumter Co., Ga. Degrees from Vanderbilt U. and John R. Stetson U. He was admitted to the bar in 1881 and practiced at Jacksonville, Fla. He served as mayor of Jacksonville two terms, was a member of the lower house in Florida, and chairman of the Democratic state committee from 1905-08. He was raised in Solomon Lodge No. 20 of Jacksonville in 1882. d. June 17, 1936.

Esten A. Fletcher (1869-?) Imperial Potentate of the Shrine in 1931-32. b. July 23, 1869 near Toronto, Canada.

Robert C. Fletcher One of the founders of Rotary International. Member of LaGrange Lodge No. 770 at LaGrange, Ill. and recorder of Trinity Commandery No. 80, K.T. of LaGrange.

Thomas C. Fletcher (1827-1899) Governor of Missouri, 1865-69. b. Jan. 22, 1827 at Herculaneum, Mo., his family came from Maryland in 1818. When 22, he was elected circuit clerk of Jefferson Co. He was admitted to the bar in 1855 and became land agent for S.W. branch of the Pacific Railroad. In 1857 he and his brother-in-law, Louis J. Rankin, laid out the town of DeSoto, Mo. In the Civil War he volunteered in April, 1861, and in 1862, recruited the 31st Missouri Infantry and was commissioned as colonel. He was wounded and captured at Chickasaw Bayou. In

1864 he organized state troops to resist the invasion of General Price, and for his successful defense of Pilot Knob under General Ewing, he was brevetted brigadier general by President Lincoln. Elected governor in Nov. 1864, he was the first native-born Missourian and the first Republican to serve as governor of the state. One of his first acts was to issue an emancipation proclamation on Jan. 11, 1865. He created a new and larger public school fund; reorganized and improved the public school system; made the first appropriation from the general revenue for the U. of Missouri; established an an-migration board and sold railroads owned by the state through failure of the companies to pay interest on state-guaranteed bonds. At the conclusion of his term in 1869, he practiced law in St. Louis and then in Washington, D.C. He was a member of Joachim Lodge No. 164, Hillsboro, Mo. (of which his father was also a member) and of Jefferson City Chapter No. 34, RA.M., receiving the Mark and Past Master degrees on Dec. 29, 1868 and Royal Arch on Jan. 23, 1871. He dimitted to St. Louis Chapter No. 8 on Feb. 4, 1876. He was knighted in Ivanhoe Commandery No. 8, K.T., St. Louis on May 25, 1871 and served as commander in 1874. When he moved to Washington, he dimitted from both chapter and commandery and it is presumed that he affiliated with those bodies in the east. d. March 25, 1899.

Charles W. Flint Methodist Bishop. b. Nov. 14, 1878 at Stouffville, Ont., Canada. Received degrees from Victoria Coll. (Ont.), Drew Theological Sem.; Columbia U. and Wesleyan U. He entered the Methodist ministry in 1900, and served pastorates in Iowa, New York and Conn. From 1915-22 he was president of Cornell Coll. (Ia.) and chancellor of

Syracuse U. from 1922-36. Named as bishop in 1936, he first served the Atlanta area until 1939 and then the Syracuse area until 1944. In 1944 he was moved to the Washington, D.C. area. He is a member of Mt. Vernon Lodge No. 112, Mt. Vernon, Iowa. Received the 32° AASR (SJ) in Iowa on Feb. 1, 1918, withdrawing in 1919, and later affiliating with the northern jurisdiction and receiving 33°.

Frank P. Flint (1862-1929) U.S. Senator from California, 1905-11. b. July 15, 1862 in North Reading, Mass., moving to San Francisco with parents in 1869. Studied law, became clerk in U.S. marshal's office and admitted to the bar. He served as U.S. attorney for Los Angeles and later to Southern District of Calif. Member of Eastgate Chapter No. 103, R.A.M. of Los Angeles. d. Feb. 11, 1929.

Thomas Barnard Flint (1847-?) Member of Canadian House of Commons, 1891-96, 1900-02. b. April 28, 1847 in Yarmouth, N.S. He was a graduate of Mt. Allison U., Sackville, N.B. and Harvard Law School. He was clerk of the house of commons, 1902-17 and a recognized authority on parliamentary procedure. An eloquent and forceful speaker, he was raised in St. Andrews' Lodge No. 1, Halifax, N.S., on Jan. 5, 1871; master of Scotia Lodge No. 31, Yarmouth in 1877 and grand master of Grand Lodge of Nova Scotia in 1897-99. Deceased.

Charles T. Floquet (1828-1896) President of the French Chamber of Deputies, 1885-88. A French politician and lawyer, he opposed the second empire, and was active in government of national defense in 1870. He attempted a reconciliation between the revolutionary leaders and Versailles government during the Commune, but was briefly imprisoned at Paris for his radical sentiments (1871). In 1875 he entered the chamber of deputies. From 1888-89 he was president of the council and minister of interior. He was again president of the chamber in 1889-93. Said by the bulletin of the International Masonic Congress (1917) to be a Freemason.

William Jermyn Florence (1831-1891) The stage name for Bernard Conlin, an American actor who is recognized as the founder of the Ancient and Arabic Order, Nobles of the Mystic Shrine. b. July 26, 1831 in Albany, N.Y. He excelled in dialect impersonation. During one of his trips abroad, he conceived the idea of the Shrine while in North Africa, and on his return conveyed the idea to his friend, Dr. Walter M. Fleming, q.v., and the two founded the organization in New York City on June 6, 1876 with Fleming as first potentate of Mecca Temple. He received all three degrees by special dispensation in Mt. Moriah Lodge No. 155, Philadelphia, Pa. on Oct. 12, 1853 and "joined" the lodge on Nov. 22 of that year. He became a member of Zerubbabel Chapter No. 162, R.A.M. on June 12, 1854and of Pittsburgh Commandery No. 1, K.T. on June 13, 1854. He was a 33° AASR (NJ). d. Nov. 19, 1891. He was buried in a Protestant cemetery with Catholic rites, the latter being arranged by his wife.

Jean P. C. Florian (1755-1794) French author who wrote fables, romances and plays. Member of the Lodge of Nine Sisters, Paris.

Robert L. Flowers (1870-1951) President of Duke University, 1941-48. b. Nov. 6, 1870 in N. Car.

He was a graduate of the U.S. Naval Academy in 1891. He was professor of mathematics at Duke U. from 1891-1934; vice president from 1925-41; trustee from 1910; treasurer 1928-48 and chancellor from 1948. Member of Durham Lodge No. 352, Durham, N. Car., receiving degrees on July 6, 20, 27, 1925. d. Aug. 24, 1951.

John B. Floyd (1807-1863) Governor of Virginia, 1850-53; Secretary of War, 1857-60; Brigadier General in Confederate Army. b. June 1, 1807 in Blacksburg, Va. He graduated from Coll. of South Carolina in 1826 and moved to Arkansas for three years, returning to Virginia in 1839 to practice law. He served one term in the lower house of Virginia before becoming governor in 1850. In 1861 he was indicted in Washington as having given aid to secession leaders while he was secretary of war by dispersing the army to remote parts, transferring muskets from northern to southern arsenals and other charges. He demanded an immediate trial and in Jan. 1861, a committee from the house of representatives completely exonerated him. In that same year he was made brigadier general in the Confederate Army. He was a member of St. Johns Lodge No. 36, Richmond, Va. and was present at a special communication of the Grand Lodge of Virginia on Feb. 21, 1850. He delivered the oration at the cornerstone laying of the Washington monument. d. Aug. 26, 1863.

Robert Fludd (1574-1637) An Oxonian philosopher who introduced Rosicrucianism into England. He wrote many works on the "Rosy Cross," all of which were in Latin. He claimed that the Rose Croix symbolically signified the cross dyed with the blood of the Saviour—a Christian idea which was in advance of the original Rosicrucians. Although he probably was not a member of the craft, his ideas may have had an influence on speculative Freemasonry in England. He was often called "Robertus de Fluctibus."

John J. Flynt, Jr. U.S. Congressman, 83rd and 84th Congresses from 4th Georgia dist. b. Nov. 8, 1914 at Griffin, Ga. Graduate of U. of Georgia and George Washington U. Admitted to bar in 1938. Served in U.S. Army from 1936-37 and 1941-45. Member of Meridian Sun Lodge No. 26, Griffin, Ga., receiving degrees on Sept. 3, Oct. 1, and Oct. 15, 1946.

Nandor Fodor Psychoanalyst. b. May 13, 1895 in Beregszasz, Hungary. Graduate of Royal Hungarian U. of Science, Budapest, in 1917. From 193438 he was director of research for the International Institute of Psychical Research at London, and London editor of the Journal of American Society for Psychical Research from 1935-39. Since 1939 he has been a practicing psychoanalyst in New York City. He is the author of *Encyclopedia of Psychic Science; Those Mysterious People; The Search for the Beloved; Freud—Dictionary of Psychoanalysis*. Mason.

James W. Foley, Jr. (1874-1939) Author and newspaperman. b. Feb. 4, 1874 in St. Louis, Mo. Student at U. of South Dakota. He began newspaper work on the Tribune at Bismarck in 1892 and was associate editor of the Evening Post at Pasadena, Calif., from 1919-29. He was the author of many poems and stories for children, and in 1924 the state department of public instruction in N.

Dak. ordered his birthday to be celebrated by all public schools of that state and to be observed annually. Among his writings are *Boys and Girls, Plains and Prairie, Life and Laughter—Completed Verses* (1911); *Old Friends in Joyous Verses* (1912); *The Way of Smiles* (1913); *Tales of the Trail* (1914); *The Friendship Series* (which included 10 subjects in 1915); *The Voices of Song* (1916). He also produced several outdoor plays including *In Old Virginia; With Happiness to You* and *White Gods and Red*. Affiliated with Starr King Lodge No. 344, Calif. on Dec. 4, 1919 from Bismarck Lodge No. 5, S. Dak. d. May 17, 1939.

John H. Folger U.S. Congressman to 72nd and 78th to 80th Congresses (1943-49) from 5th N.Car. dist. b. Dec. 18, 1880 at Rockford, N.Car. Practiced law in N.Car. since 1901. Served in both branches of state legislature and was mayor of Mt. Airy for two terms. Mason and Shriner.

Joseph W. Folk (1869-1923) Governor of Missouri, 1905-09. b. Oct. 28, 1869 at Brownsville, Tenn. Graduated from Vanderbilt U. in 1890 and admitted to bar that year. He practiced in Brownsville, Tenn. for four years, and then moved to St. Louis, Mo. in 1894. While serving as circuit attorney of St. Louis (1900-04), he exposed a vast amount of political and official corruption and prosecuted numerous bribery cases, some involving influential St. Louis citizens. He lost two races for U.S. Senate and at one time was mentioned as a presidential candidate. He made a lecture tour of the U.S. in 1909-10 and was chief counsel for the Interstate Commerce Commission from 1914-18. He was raised in Occidental Lodge No. 163 at St. Louis on June

30, 1903 by the grand master of the state, Dr. William F. Kuhn, q.v. d. May 28, 1923.

Martin Folkes (1690-1754) English scholar and antiquarian. b. Oct. 29, 1690 in Westminster, England. He entered Cambridge U. in 1707 and in 1713 was elected a fellow of the Royal Society and in 1723 was named its vice president. At the death of Sir Isaac Newton in 1727, he became a candidate for its presidency, but was defeated by Sir Hans Sloane. At the resignation of Sloane in 1741 Folkes became president and held the office until 1753, when he resigned due to ill health. He was elected a member of the Royal Academy of Sciences in Paris in 1746, and in the same year received Doctor of Laws degrees from both Oxford and Cambridge. In 1750 he was elected president of the Society of Antiquaries, holding that position until his death. It seems that he was induced to take a part in Freemasonry through his association with Sir Christopher Wren, q.v., and Dr. Desaguliers, q.v. Few records remain of his Masonic life. In 1725 he was appointed deputy grand master of the Grand Lodge of England, serving under the Duke of Richmond. He is recorded as having given considerable attention to his duties, and presided over the grand lodge in May of that year. He is supposed to have given an address at that meeting which was preserved as the "Folkes M.S." but since lost. He visited Italy and is said to have established a lodge named Fabius Maximus in Rome. In 1742 the Freemasons of that country struck a medal in his honor with Masonic symbols on one side and his likeness on the obverse. d. June 28, 1754.

A. J. Folley Former Justice, Supreme Court of Texas. b. Nov. 28, 1896 at Oletha, Texas. Graduate of Baylor U. in 1921 and 1925. He first taught in Frederick, Okla., and in 1923, was a teacher in Baylor U. Admitted to bar in 1925, he practiced in Floydada, serving as district attorney, district judge, and associate justice of court of civil appeals. Now in private practice in Amarillo. Received his degrees in Mart Lodge No. 636, Mart, Texas in 1918 and holds dual membership in Floydada Lodge No. 712 and Amarillo Lodge No. 731, being past master of the latter and past district deputy grand master of the 96th dist. He is also a member of the chapter and council at Floydada.

Frederick V. Follmer U.S. District Judge for Eastern, Middle and Western Districts of Pennsylvania since 1946. b. Dec. 13, 1885 at Milton, Pa. Graduate of Bucknell U. and Harvard. Admitted to bar in 1910, he practiced at Milton and later served as district attorney and U.S. attorney. Member and past master of Milton Lodge No. 256, Milton, Pa.; 32° AASR (NJ) at Williamsport, Pa.

James E. Folsom Governor of Alabama since 1947. b. Oct. 9, 1908 in Coffee Co., Ala. He was a district agent of Emergency & Aid Insurance Co. at Elba, Ala., from 1937-40 and became state manager for same in 1940. He is a member of Marshall Lodge No. 209 at Guntersville and belongs to the chapter and commandery at Birmingham. In 1956 he extended his greetings to the Grand Lodge of Alabama at their annual communication. Shriner.

Jellis A. Fonda Revolutionary War officer. Sometimes referred to as "Jules" or "Jelles." He was a major in Col. Willett's New York Regiment. Originally initiated in St. Patrick's Lodge No. 8 at Johnstown. This lodge became famous when the Revolution split its membership between the colonies and the crown. Such famous members as Sir William Johnson, q.v., Sir John Johnson, q.v., Col. Guy Johnson, q.v., and Col. John Butler, q.v., were British leaders while others such as Gen. Nicholas Herkimer, q.v., and Rev. Samuel Kirkland, q.v., fought with the colonies. Fonda later became a member of St. George's Lodge No. 1 at Schenectady and served as master in 1797, 1799-1803 and in 1805.

Marquis Louis de Fontanes (1757-1821) French writer and statesman. b. March 6, 1757 at Niort, France. He was president of the Corps Legislatif in 1804, having been a member from 1802. In 1810 he was a senator under Napoleon I, q.v. He was also a member of the privy council and was created a marquis and a peer by Louis XVIII. He was a member of the famous Lodge of the Nine Sisters at Paris, his name appearing on the lists of members between 1783 and 1806. d. March 17, 1821.

Percy W. Foote Rear Admiral, U.S. Navy. b. Aug. 13, 1879 at Roaring River, N.Car. Graduated from U.S. Naval Academy in 1901 and served through the grades to that of rear admiral in 1936, when he was retired. He was recalled to active duty in May, 1942 as inspector of Naval material at Houston, Texas. He was again retired in 1945. He commanded the U.S.S. President Lincoln when it was sunk in an engagement with the German submarine U-90 in 1918, and was in command of forces from the U.S.S. Baltimore during the Chinese uprising of 1905. From 1937-39 he was commander of the Pennsylvania motor police. Former member of Harmony Lodge No. 17, Washington, D.C., now dimitted.

Joseph B. Foraker (1846-1917) U.S. Senator from Ohio, 1897-1909 and Governor of Ohio, 1885-89. b. July 5, 1846 near Rainsboro, Ohio. He graduated from Cornell in 1869 after he had served in the Civil War with the 89th Ohio Infantry from 1862 to the end of the war. He was admitted to the bar and began practice at Cincinnati in 1869. He served as judge of the superior court of Cincinnati. Running for governor four times, he was twice elected and twice defeated. A delegate to eight national Republican conventions, he presented the name of William McKinley for nomination in 1896 and 1900. He became a member of Walnut Hills Lodge No. 483 of Cincinnati on May 19, 1885 and was also a member of Walnut Hills Chapter No. 151, R.A.M., Cincinnati Cornmandery No. 3, K.T. and Al Koran Shrine Temple of Cincinnati. d. May 10, 1917.

James, 16th Baron of Forbes Nineteenth Grand Master Mason of Scotland in 1754.

Aaron L. Ford U.S. Congressman, 74th to 77th Congresses (1935-43) from 4th Miss. dist. b. Dec. 21, 1903 at Potts Camp, Miss. Graduate of Cumberland U. Admitted to bar in 1927. From 1943-45 he acted as special attorney for special committee of House of Representatives to investigate acts of bureaus exceeding their authority. Vice president of Burma-Cola Co. and Bantam Beverages, Inc. Former member of Ackerman Lodge No. 1191, Ackerman, Miss. Dates of degrees—Nov. 15, Dec. 6, 1928, Jan. 8, 1929; dimitted Jan. 5, 1954.

Benson Ford Vice president of Ford Motor Co. and general manager of Lincoln-Mercury division as well as vice president and group director of Mercury and special products division of Ford Motor Co. b. July 20, 1919 at Detroit, grandson of Henry Ford, q.v., founder and long-time president of the company. He was educated in the Detroit U. school, Hotchkiss school and Princeton U. From 1940-41 he was assistant purchasing agent for Ford Motor Co. and assistant superintendent, 1941-42. He is a director of the company. He is a member and trustee of The Ford Foundation and trustee and president of the Henry Ford Hospital at Detroit. Served in WWII as a captain in the Air Force. Both Benson and his brother William, q.v., were raised in Corinthian Lodge No. 241 of Detroit on May 1, 1950. On April 28, only a few days earlier, Benson had addressed 1600 Scottish Rite Masons in the Detroit temple on "A Practical Approach to Brotherhood." He is a 32° AASR (NJ).

Henry Ford (1863-1947) Automobile manufacturer and philanthropist. b. July 30, 1863 in Wayne Co., Mich. His inventive genius helped change the methods of transportation of the world. Early in life he learned the machinist's trade and was chief engineer for Edison Illuminating Co. In 1903 he organized the Ford Motor Co. and built it into the largest automobile company in the world. In 1914 he made the unprecedented announcement that the company would institute a profit-sharing plan involving the distribution of 10 to 30 million dollars annually to employees. In 1915 he chartered a ship at his own expense to conduct a party to Europe with the object of organizing a conference of peacemakers to influence the belligerent governments to end the war. He returned home after reaching Christiania, Norway, but other members of his party proceeded to Stockholm, Copenhagen

and through Germany to The Hague. In 1918 he was an unsuccessful candidate for the U.S. Senate. He was raised in Palestine Lodge No. 357, Detroit, Mich. on Nov. 28, 1894. The degree team was composed of men in overalls with whom he worked at the Edison company. He continued a staunch member of this lodge for almost 53 years. On March 7, 1935 he was made a life member of his lodge and presented with a testimonial plaque commemorating his 75th birthday. Ford made many visitations to lodges near his summer home at Traverse City and his winter residence in Georgia. He also made several visits to Zion Lodge which his brother-in-law, William R. Bryant, served as master in 1932. On Nov. 21, 1928 he was made an honorary member of Zion Lodge No. 1 (Michigan's oldest lodge). When he received the 33° AASR (NJ) in Sept., 1940, he stated: "Masonry is the best balance wheel the United States has, for Masons know what to teach their children." Henry's only son, Edsel, was not a Mason, but two of his grandsons, Benson and William q.v., are. The third grandson, Henry II, became a Roman Catholic. d. April 7, 1947.

Hiram C. Ford U.S. District Judge, Eastern District of Kentucky since March, 1935. b. July 28, 1884 in Scott Co., Ky. Graduate of Georgetown Coll. (Ky.) and Transylvania Coil. of Law. Admitted to bar in 1907 and practiced in Georgetown. He served as county attorney and district judge of 14th state district. Member of Mt. Vernon Lodge No. 14, Georgetown, Ky., since 1915 and past master of same.

Samuel C. Ford Governor of Montana, 1940-48 (two terms). b. Nov. 7, 1882 in Albany, Ky. Began law practice in Helena, Mont. in 1906 and served as the first assistant U.S. Attorney for Montana from 1908-14. He was attorney general of the state from 1917-21 and associate justice of the supreme court from 1929-33. Since that date he has been in private practice. He was raised in Tyrian Lodge No. 246, Garden City, Kans. in 1905 and later affiliated with Helena Lodge No. 3, Helena, Mont. Member of Helena Chapter No. 2, R.A.M.; Helena Council No. 1, R. & SM.; and Helena Commandery No. 2, K.T., and 32° AASR (SJ), all of Helena, Mont.

Stanley H. Ford Major General, U.S. Army. b. Jan. 30, 1877 at Columbus, Ohio. Graduate of Ohio State U. in 1898. Commissioned a lieutenant in 1898 (Infantry), he advanced through grades to brigadier general in 1930 and later to major general. Served in Cuba during Spanish-American War, and in China from 1914-17. Was chief of staff of the 27th Division throughout its operations in Belgium and France in 1918, and was assistant chief of staff in Washington from 1927-30. He received the 2nd and 3rd degrees in George W. Lininger Lodge No. 268 at Omaha, Nebr. by special dispensation of the grand master. Five past grand masters were present for the occasion.

William C. Ford Vice President of Lincoln and Continental divisions of the Ford Motor Co. b. March 14, 1925 at Detroit, he is the grandson of Henry Ford, q.v., the founder of the Ford automotive empire. Graduated from Yale in 1948. He began with the company in 1942 as a laboratory technician, later in labor relations and quality control. He has been a director since 1948 and is president of the Edison Institute and Edsel B. Ford Institute for Medical Research. He is a trustee of the Thomas A. Edison Foundation and Henry Ford Hospital. He was raised in Corinthian Lodge No. 241, Detroit, Mich. on May 1, 1950 at the same time as his brother Benson, q.v. A 32° AASR (NJ) and Knight Templar.

Edwin Forrest (1806-1872) American tragedian. b. March 9, 1806 in Philadelphia, Pa. His first New York success was at Park Theatre as Othello on June 23, 1826, although he had played in small stock companies in the rural areas previous to this. He appeared in London's Drury Lane Theatre as Spartacus in 1834. After years of success, he began a feud with the actor, Macready, over an imagined insult. As a result a mob attacked the Astor Place Opera House in London on May 10, 1849, where Macready was appearing and attempted to wreck the building. When the militia fired on them, 22 persons were killed and 36 wounded. From that time on he was given to brooding and melancholy, although during the period he appeared in some of his most successful performances. His chief roles were Lear, Coriolanus, Richard III, Virginius and Damon. He bequeathed a fortune to establish a home in Philadelphia for aged actors, but the claims of his divorced wife crippled the legacy. His lodge is not known, but in 1860 he donated $500 he received from a libel suit to the Grand Lodge of New York for the widows and orphans home of New York. d. Dec. 12, 1872.

Sir James Forrest (of Comiston) Sixty-third Grand Master Mason of Scotland in 1838. He was provost of Edinburgh.

Nathan B. Forrest (1821-1877) Lieutenant General of the Confederate Army. b. July 13, 1821 in

Bedford Co., Tenn. He first farmed in Hernando, Miss. but moved to Memphis, Tenn. in 1852, and became a real estate dealer and broker in slaves. Entering the war in 1861 as a lieutenant colonel of cavalry, he distinguished himself with daring cavalry raids and was promoted to brigadier general after the attack on Murfreesboro in 1862. Following the battle at Chickamauga, he was transferred to northern Miss. and made a major general. His harassment of the Union forces by cavalry raids and his capture of Fort Pillow in April, 1864 lead to his promotion to lieutenant general in Feb., 1865. His actions at Fort Pillow, when he moved his troops to a commanding position under a flag of truce and then gave no quarter to the Negro troops, is questioned. His own report stated: "We busted the port at ninerclock and scattered the niggers. The men is still a cillanem in the woods." He was an entered apprentice in Angerona Lodge No. 168 at Memphis, Tenn. d. Oct. 29, 1877.

James H. Forsee Brigadier General, U.S. Army Medical Corps. Deputy Commander of Walter Reed Medical Center and chief of its Professional Services in 1959. Member of Aurora Lodge No. 156, Colorado and 32° AASR (SJ) in Colorado Consistory.

Weidman W. Forster Editor of the Pittsburgh Press since 1950. b. Nov. 27, 1899 at Mercersburg, Pa. He did editorial work on the Ladies' Home Journal from 1916-17, and was with the Pittsburgh Leader from 1917-23. Going with the Press in 1923 he was successively reporter, financial editor, sports editor, news editor and managing editor. In WWI he served with the U.S. Navy. Mason.

James M. Forsyth (1842-1915) Rear Admiral, U.S. Navy. b. Jan. 1, 1842 in the Bahamas, B.W.I. and was brought to the U.S. in 1853. He went to sea as a sailor before the mast in 1858, when only 16 years old. Although he served throughout the Civil War and was in many engagements including the capture of Forts Clarke and Hatteras, with Farragut on the Mississippi, and Forts Sumter and Moultrie, he was not commissioned until 1868, when he won in a competitive examination. He was promoted through the grades to captain in 1899 and retired in 1901 at his own request, as a rear admiral. He was made a Mason in Peru and later affiliated with Union Lodge No. 121, Philadelphia. He was a member of Shamokin Chapter No. 264 and Shamokin Commandery No. 77, K.T. both of Shamokin, Pa. On Nov. 5, 1909 he addressed Shamokin Lodge No. 255 on "Freemasonry Abroad." d. Aug. 3, 1915.

George F. Fort (1848-1909) Masonic author. b. Nov. 20, 1848 at Absecon, N.J. He edited the Keystone, a Masonic publication at Philadelphia and wrote several Masonic books including: Early History and Antiquities of Freemasonry; A Historical Treatise on Early Builders' Marks; and Medieval Builders. He was initiated in Camden Lodge No. 15, Camden, N.J. and was a founding member and second master (1871) of Trumble Lodge No. 117 of Camden. He was a scholar with an encyclopedic mind. He studied at Heidelburg U. and was noted for his studies of history and archeology. d. March 30, 1909.

Greenbury L. Fort (1825-1883) U.S. Congressman to 43rd through 46th Congresses, 1873-81. b. Oct. 17, 1825 at French Grant,

Ohio. Moved with parents to Marshall Co., IR. in 1834. Studied law, and was admitted to the bar in 1847, practicing at Lacon, Ill. He served as sheriff, county clerk, county judge and in the state senate. He served in the Civil War with the 11th Regiment, Ill. Infantry from first lieutenant to lieutenant colonel (brevet). Knighted in Peoria Commandery No. 3, K.T., Peoria, Ill. on March 24, 1882. d. Jan. 13, 1883.

John F. Fort (1809-1872) Governor of New Jersey, 1850-54. b. in May, 1809 in Pemberton, N.J. Graduated in medicine at the U. of Pennsylvania in 1830 and became a successful practitioner. In 1844 he was a member of the state constitutional convention, and subsequently elected to the state senate. After his service as governor, he was judge of the court of errors and appeals. He was said to be made a Mason in Kane Lodge No. 55, Newark, N.J. on Sept. 18, 1885 and affiliated with Hope Lodge No. 124, East Orange, N.J. on July 20, 1898. Dates of his degrees do not coincide with his life span. It is therefore presumed that he was not a Mason. He is sometimes credited with writing *Early History and Antiquities of Freemasonry*, but this was the work of his nephew, George F. Fort, q.v., who in turn is often mistaken as the former governor of New Jersey. d. April 22, 1872. Death date questioned.

Michael J. Fortier Vice President, Director and General Manager of Sherwin-Williams Co. (paint). b. Dec. 6, 1903 at Jeanerette, La. He began with the company in 1931 as a sales representative, later became division manager and district manager in both St. Louis and Cleveland. He was vice president and director from 1944, and vice president, director and general manager since 1945. He is also vice president and director of the following companies owned by Sherwin-Williams: Acme White Lead and Color Works; John Lucas & Co.; Rogers Paint Products; Martin-Senour; Hemingway & Co.; Texarkana Paint. Mason.

Joseph J. Foss Governor of South Dakota; U.S. Marine flying ace in WWII and holder of Congressional Medal of Honor. b. April 17, 1915 in Sioux Falls, S.Dak. He received an A.B. from the U. of South Dakota in 1940. He has been president of the Foss Motor Co. of Sioux Falls since 1953, and governor of South Dakota since 1955. He served in the lower house of the state from 1949-53. During WWII he served as a major in the U.S. Marine Corps, and as a pilot downed 26 Japanese planes, to become a national hero. He has been a brigadier general in the U.S.A.F. reserve, as well as the S.Dak. Air National Guard, since 1953. Foss was raised in Minnehaha Lodge No. 5 of Sioux Falls, June 29, 1943. He received the 32° AASR (SJ) in Los Angeles and is a member of El Riad Shrine Temple at Sioux Falls. Interested in crippled children, he is president of the South Dakota Society of Crippled Children, and in 1956 was chairman of the Easter Seal campaign for the National Society for Crippled Children and Adults.

Addison G. Foster (1837-1917) U.S. Senator from Washington, 1899-1905. b. Jan. 28, 1837 at Belchertown, Mass. He taught school in Illinois and moved to Wabasha, Minn. in 1859 where he engaged in the grain and real estate business until 1875. He then moved to St. Paul, and eventually to Tacoma, Wash. where he was in the lumber business and active in the development of coal mines and railways, retiring in 1914. He became a member of Wapahasa Lodge No. 14 at Wabasha, Minn. in 1861. When he moved to St. Paul, he affiliated with Ancient Landmark Lodge No. 5, and later with Summit Lodge No. 163 of St. Paul. d. Jan. 16, 1917.

Arthur B. Foster Justice, Supreme Court of Alabama, 1928-53 and now supernumerary justice. b. Oct. 19, 1872 at Clayton, Ala. Graduate of U. of Alabama. He practiced law at Troy, served in the house of representatives, was circuit judge, and then resumed practice in Birmingham until named to the supreme court bench. Mason.

Charles Foster (1828-1904) U.S. Secretary of the Treasury, 1891-93.b. April 12, 1828 near Tiffin, Ohio. His father was the founder of Fostoria, Ohio, said city being named for him. He became a partner in his father's general store at 18, and was in full charge the following year. He served his district in the U.S. Congress from 1871-79. He was governor of Ohio from 1880-84. President Harrison named him as chairman of a commission to negotiate a treaty with the Sioux Indians. He was long identified with the business interests of Fostoria and was a member of Fostoria Lodge No. 288. d. Jan. 9, 1904.

Ellsworth D. Foster (1869-1936) Encyclopedia editor. b. Oct. 2, 1869 at Clayton, Mich. He first taught school; was superintendent at Columa, Mich., until 1898, when he became associated with a textbook publisher. He began his Reference Library in 1907 and in 1914 became editor of *The World Book*. In 1931 he went to *Volume Library* as editor, and from 1935 was editor-in-chief of *The American Educator*. Member of

Woodlawn Park Lodge No. 841, Chicago, Ill., receiving degrees on Sept. 25, Oct. 23 and Oct. 30, 1916. He was secretary of the lodge in 1920-21, 1923-25; dimitted Feb. 22, 1932. d. Nov. 7, 1936.

Ephraim H. Foster (1795-1854) U.S. Senator from Tennessee, 1837-39. Studied law and was admitted to the bar and practiced in Nashville. In 1829 he was speaker of the state house of representatives. He was again elected to the senate in 1843. In 1847 he was the unsuccessful Whig candidate for governor. He was a member of Cumberland Chapter No. 1, R.A.M. of Nashville. Inasmuch as the old records of the Grand Lodge of Tenn. were destroyed during the occupation of Nashville in the 1860's, it is difficult to determine exact membership dates. Foster was grand treasurer, pro tem, of the Grand Lodge of Tenn. on Oct. 2, 1820, and was elected grand treasurer at that meeting for the next year. In the proceedings of 1824, he is listed as a member and past grand treasurer. In the proceedings of 1820, he is listed as a past master of Cumberland Lodge No. 8, but in the records of 1825 he is not mentioned. The grand secretary of Tenn. doubts if he was actually a past master of that particular lodge, as he is not in the past master list of that lodge, published in 1951. In 1825 he was a member of Nashville Lodge No. 37 (existed from 1821-1828). The assumption of the grand secretary is that he was a member of Cumberland Lodge No. 8 in 1820 and became a charter member of Nashville Lodge No. 37 in 1821. d. Sept. 4, 1854.

John Gray Foster (1823-1874) Major General Union Army, Civil War. b. May 27, 1823 at Whitefield, N.H. Graduated from U.S. Military Academy in 1846. Served in Mexican War and was wounded severely. As a lieutenant, he was an assistant professor of engineering at West Point in 1855-57. Early participant in Civil War, he was made brigadier general in 1861, and, in quick succession, lieutenant general and major general. He was in charge of the departments of Virginia and North Carolina at one time, and of Florida at another. His submarine engineering operations in Boston and Portsmouth harbors were very successful and in 1869 he published Submarine Blasting in Boston Harbor. Said to be a Freemason by *Freemason's Monthly Magazine* (Boston), Oct. 1864. d. Sept. 2, 1874.

Richard C. Foster (1895-1941) President of the University of Alabama from 1937. b. July 12, 1895. A.B. and LL.D. from U. of Alabama and LL.B. from Harvard. Admitted to bar in 1919. Served as captain in Field Artillery in WWI. Mason. d. Nov. 19, 1941.

Robert Foster A captain of the Minute Men in the Revolutionary War who said "hoist the draw." He was master of Essex Lodge, Salem, Mass. Birth and death dates unknown.

Wilbur F. Foster (1834-1922) Engineer. One of the organizers of the Masonic Veterans' Association (for Civil War veterans). b. April 13, 1834 at Springfield, Mass. Past master of Cumberland Lodge No. 8, Nashville, Tenn., having been raised March 26, 1857. Member and past high priest of Cumberland Chapter No. 1, Nashville. He became grand master of the Grand Lodge of Tennessee and grand high priest of the Grand Chapter of Tennessee. d. March 26, 1922.

William B. Foster Father of Stephen Foster, the songwriter. He was a member of Hamilton Lodge No. 173 of Lawrenceville, Pa. The lodge was organized in 1819 and constituted Feb. 20, 1820 with William B. Foster, Sr. as treasurer. William B. Foster, Jr., a brother of Stephen, was initiated in 1828, but his certificate of membership was not issued until Sept. 19, 1831 at which time he was secretary of the lodge. The warrant of the lodge was vacated in 1837—for non-payment of dues. There is no record of Stephen Foster being a Freemason.

William W. Foster, Jr. (1849-1933) President of Clarke University, Atlanta, Ga., from 1912-18. b. July 27, 1849. Ordained a Methodist minister in 1873, serving churches in Vermont, New York and Mass. Retired in 1921. Trustee of Rust U., Beaver Coll. and Clark U. Mason. d. Feb. 22, 1933.

Roberto Brito Foucher Outstanding Mexican lawyer, known for his work among underprivileged children. A past grand master of the Grand Lodge, Valle de Mexico, he was featured in an article in Reader's Digest in May, 1952 entitled Doctor Ragpicker Finds the Forgotten Ones.

William Foulkes (1690-1754) English scholar who was elected to the Royal Society in 1714 when only 23. He was vice president of the society in 1722-23, and frequently presided in the absence of Sir Isaac Newton, the president. He was elected president in 1741 and served until 1753. In 1742 he was elected a member of the French Academy, and the same year was appointed as deputy grand master of the Grand Lodge of England, being the third person to hold this office. His contemporary, the painter William Hogarth, q.v., executed two paintings of him. He was born Oct. 29, 1690 on Queen St., Lincoln's Inn Fields, which almost a century later became the headquarters of Freemasonry. As a youth he attended the U. of Saumur near Tours, France, and was there recorded as "a choice youth of penetrating genius and master of the beauties of the best Roman and Greek writers." He later entered Clare College, Cambridge and was graduated in 1717 as a Master of Arts. He was made a Mason before 1723 at which date his name appears in the list of members of Bedford Lodge, Covent Garden. He is known to have been intimately connected with the Duke of Richmond. When the duke was made grand master in 1724, he appointed Foulkes as his deputy in succession to Dr. Desaguliers, q.v. On May 11 of that year, Foulkes attended the Maid's Head Lodge at Norwich Inn and thus constituted the earliest lodge in Norfolk, which seven years later raised Francis of Lorraine, later emperor of Germany, who was on a visit to England, and who had been initiated earlier at a special lodge held at The Hague by Dr. Desaguliers.

Fernand Foureau (1850-1914) French explorer in Africa who made a special study of the Sahara region. The bulletin of the International Masonic Congress (1917) states he was a Freemason.

John B. Fournet Chief Justice, Supreme Court of Louisiana since 1949. b. July 27, 1895 at St. Martinville, La. Graduate of Louisiana State U. and admitted to bar in 1920. Practiced in St. Martinville, Baton Rouge, and Jennings. He served in the lower house of the legislature and was speaker of the same from 1928-

32. In 1932-35 he was lieutenant governor of Louisiana. Named associate justice of the supreme court of Louisiana in 1934, he has been chief justice since Sept., 1949. Received his degrees in Albert Rousseau Lodge No. 301, St. Martinville, La. in 1916-17 and is past master of same; 32° AASR (SJ) at New Orleans and member of Jerusalem Shrine Temple of New Orleans.

Winfred E. Fouse Co-organizer of General Tire and Rubber Co., Akron, Ohio in 1914 and director of same since. b. Dec. 24, 1877 at Akron. Employed by B. F. Goodrich and Diamond Rubber Co. from 1902-05, he was credit manager for Firestone Tire & Rubber Co., 1905-09. Organized the Western Rubber & Supply Co. in Kansas City in 1909 with W. O'Neil and the General Tire Co. at Akron in 1914. Received his degrees in Gate City Lodge No. 522, Kansas City, Mo. on April 23, May 4 and May 21, 1910; admitted to Akron Lodge No. 83, Akron, Ohio, March 7, 1916. Exalted in Orient Chapter No. 102, Kansas City on April 13, 1912 and admitted to Washington Chapter No. 25, R.A.M. of Akron on March 10, 1916. Greeted in Akron Council No. 80, R. & S.M. on Nov. 22, 1946. Knighted in Oriental Commandery No. 35, K.T. Kansas City, Mo. on Dec. 21, 1912 and admitted to Akron Commandery No. 25 March 10, 1916; 32° AASR (NJ) at Canton, Ohio on April 13, 1934 and 33° Sept. 29, 1943. Joined Ararat Shrine Temple, Kansas City, March 21, 1913 and was a charter member of Tadmore Temple of Akron, being potentate of same in 1934. d. July 22, 1958.

Daniel G. Fowle (1831-1891) Governor of North Carolina, 1889-91. b. March 3, 1831 at Washington, N.Car. There is no record of his membership prior to 1864, when he was first listed as a member of Hiram Lodge No. 40, Raleigh, N.Car. On Jan. 13, 1891, while governor, he invited the members of the grand lodge to attend an informal reception at the executive mansion that evening. He was a member of Raleigh Chapter No. 10, R.A.M. receiving the degrees on Nov. 12, 1864; Jan. 27-28, 1865. d. April 7, 1891 and his funeral was conducted by Hiram Lodge No. 40, assisted by members of William G. Hill Lodge No. 218 on April 9.

Henry Fowle (1766-1837) Masonic ritualist and lecturer who was one of the organizers of the Grand Encampment, K.T. b. Sept. 1, 1766 at Medford, Mass. He was a pump and block maker. Initiated in Lodge of St. Andrew at Boston on April 10, 1793; he was first master of Mount Lebanon Lodge, Boston from 1801-03 and 1805. He returned to his mother lodge in 1805 and served it as master from 1810-17. In 1807-09 he was senior grand warden of the Grand Lodge of Massachusetts. He was the leading spirit in making several important changes in the ritual which were approved by his grand lodge and almost universally adopted by other states. He became a member of Saint Andrew's Royal Arch Chapter on Feb. 18, 1795 and served as high priest in 1804-08. He became deputy grand high priest of Mass. and was active in the General Grand Chapter. He received the Knight Templar degree in St. Andrew's Chapter on Jan. 28, 1795 and rose to deputy grand master of the Grand Encampment, U.S.A. in 1819. d. March 10, 1837.

Charles H. Fowler (1837-1908) Methodist Episcopal Bishop. b. Aug. 11, 1837 in Burford, Ont., Canada. He was educated in Genesee Coll. and Garrett Biblical Institute; studied law in Chicago, but never practiced. He was a pastor for 11 years in Chicago, and president of Northwestern U. from 1872-76. In 1876 he was appointed by the governor of Ill. to deliver an oration at the Philadelphia Centennial Exposition, and in that same year became editor of the New York Christian Advocate. He was elected bishop in 1884; visited South America in 1885; visited Japan, Korea and China in 1888. He organized Peking U. and Nanking U. in Central China and also, the first Methodist church in St. Petersburg, Russia. Returning to the U.S. after a trip around the world, visiting missions, he worked eight years on the Pacific coast and then established Maclay Coll. of Theology in Southern Calif. and assisted in founding Nebraska Wesleyan U. at Lincoln. He received his first degree in Vitruvius Lodge No. 81 at Wheeling, Ill., in 1862 and soon after moved to Minn. Jurisdiction was waived and he was raised in Minneapolis Lodge No. 19, Minneapolis, Minn. on Jan. 15, 1896. He was a member of Zion Commandery No. 2, K.T. of Minneapolis. When the Fowler Cathedral Church, bearing his name, was erected in Minneapolis, the commandery placed in the front of the church a rose window, 18 feet in diameter, with Knights Templar emblems in its design, as a tribute to him. In 1904 Bishop Fowler was grand chaplain of the Grand Lodge of New York and grand chaplain emeritus until his death on March 19, 1908 in New York City.

Edward B. Fowler (?-1896) Union Brigadier General of Civil War. Served with the 84th N.Y. Infantry, first as a lieutenant colonel, promoted to colonel on Dec. 9, 1862, and to brigadier general on March 13, 1865 for gallant and meritorious service. Mustered out June 6, 1864. Member of Lexington Lodge No. 310, Brooklyn, N.Y., receiving degrees on Oct. 23, Oct. 30 and Nov. 20, 1865 at the age of 30. d. Jan. 16, 1896.

H. Robert Fowler (?-1925) U.S. Congressman, 62nd and 63rd Congresses (1911-15) from 24th Ill. Dist. b. in Pope Co., Ill. Practiced law in Elizabethtown, Ill. Served in both legislative branches of the state and was state's attorney in Hardin Co. Received degrees in Eddyville Lodge No. 672, Eddyville, Ill., being raised July 20, 1878; dimitted Dec. 6, 1884 and on May 14, 1892; affiliated with Elizabeth Lodge No. 276, Elizabethtown, Ill.; suspended Aug. 4, 1898; reinstated Sept. 5, 1901; served as a lodge officer from 1903 until master in 1907. d. Jan. 5, 1925.

Marvin E. Fowler Provincial Grand Master of Royal Order of Scotland for United States since 1953. b. Oct. 12, 1904. Graduate of Central Coll., Fayette, Mo. in 1926 and of George Washington U. in 1931. Taught science in high school at Mexico, Mo., 1926-29. He is with the division of forest pathology of the U.S. Dept. of Agriculture and the author of many scientific publications. Raised in Hebron Lodge No. 354, Mexico, Mo. in 1927; knighted in Crusade Commandery No. 23, K.T., Mexico same year. In Washington, D.C. he became a member of Lafayette Lodge No. 19 and master in 1940; Columbia Chapter No. 1, R.A.M. and high priest in 1944; Adoniram Council No. 2 and master in 1944; Columbia Commandery No. 2, K.T. and commander in 1946. Received 32° AASR (SJ) in 1932 and 33° in 1943. Was grand master of the Grand Lodge, District of Columbia in 1950 and grand high priest of Grand Chapter,

District of Columbia in 1952. Past sovereign of St. Simon Stylites Conclave, R.C.C.; member of Almas Shrine Temple, Grotto, Tall Cedars, National Sojourners, Allied Masonic Degrees and York Cross of Honor.

George L. Fox (1900-1943) Methodist minister who was one of the "four immortal chaplains" who gave up their lifebelts to others when the U.S.S. Dorchester was torpedoed in the North Atlantic on Feb. 23, 1943. b. March 15, 1900, he served in WWI as a first aid man in Ambulance Co. No. 1, 2nd Division and won the Silver Star, Croix de Guerre with palms, Victory Medal with 6 battle bars and Purple Heart. He became a Methodist minister and was serving the Community Church of Gilman, Vt. in 1942 when he entered the Chaplain's Corps. He was a member of Moose River Lodge No. 82, Concord, Vt. He and the three other chaplains, who gave up their life belts to enlisted men and went down with the ship, were posthumously awarded the Distinguished Service Cross.

Herbert H. H. Fox (1871-1943) Protestant Episcopal Bishop. b. March 11, 1871 in Montclair, N.J. A deacon and priest in 1900, he first served a New York missionary district and then churches at Lockport, N.Y., Pontiac, Mich., and Detroit, Mich. and was consecrated suffragan bishop of Montana in November, 1920. He was elected co-adjutor bishop in May, 1925 and retired in 1939. Member of Ashlar Lodge No. 29; Billings Chapter No. 6, R.A.M.; Aldemar Commandery No. 5, K.T., all of Billings, Mont. He was grand prelate of the Grand Commandery of Montana from 1938-43. d. Nov. 24, 1943.

Philip Fox (1878-1944) Astronomer and director of Adler Planetarium and Museum of Science and Industry at Chicago. b. March 7, 1878 at Manhattan, Kans. Graduate of Kansas State Coll., Dartmouth, and student at U. of Berlin. Taught math and physics from 1899-1903 when he became a Carnegie research assistant at Yerkes Observatory, U. of Chicago and later a professor of astrophysics at that school. From 1909-29 he was professor of astronomy and director of the Dearborn Observatory at Northwestern U. He was director of the Adler Planetarium from 1929-37 and director of the Museum of Science and Industry from 1937-40. He served as a lieutenant in the Philippine Insurrection of 1898-99 with the 20th Kans. Infantry and in WWI was an Infantry major with the 7th Division. He entered WWII as a colonel and served until his death on July 21, 1944. Mason.

James Emory Foxx Named member of the Baseball Hall of Fame at Cooperstown, N.Y. in 1951. b. Oct. 22, 1907 at Sudlersville, Md. He played first and third bases and also was a catcher. He was noted for his batting —particularly as a home run hitter. He collected 534 home runs in 2,317 games and had a life-time batting average of .325. In three world series he compiled a mark of .344 and in seven all-star games batted .316. Playing from 1925-45, he was with the Philadelphia American League from 1925-35; Boston American League, 1936-42; Chicago National League, 1942-44 and Philadelphia National League in 1945. His nickname was "Beast." He received his degrees in George W. Bartram Lodge No. 298, Media, Pa. in 1930-31 while residing in Elkins Park, Philadelphia. He visited the lodge only once following his degrees and allowed himself to become suspended NPD on Dec. 9, 1946.

Joseph I. France (1873-1939) U.S. Senator from Maryland, 1917-23. b. Oct. 11, 1873. Graduate of Hamilton Coll. (N.Y.) and received M.D. degree from College of Physicians and Surgeons at Baltimore in 1903. He practiced medicine in Baltimore. He served in the Maryland senate from 1905-09. In 1931 he was a candidate against Herbert Hoover for the Republican presidential nomination. Member of Landmark Lodge No. 127, Baltimore, Md. He received his degrees on Dec. 27, 1922, Feb. 28 and March 14, 1923. d. Jan. 26, 1939.

Francis I (1708-1765) Holy Roman Emperor from 1745-1765. b. Dec. 8, 1708 at Nancy, France, the second son of Leopold Joseph Charles, "The Good," Duke of Lorraine. Francis Stephen succeeded his father to the duchy of Lorraine as Francis III in 1729. In 1737 he ceded it to Leszczynski, king of Poland. In 1736 he married Maria Theresa of Austria, q.v., with whom he was co-regent of Austria from 1740-45. At one time his wife issued an edict against Freemasonry. He was chosen emperor in 1745. He did not concern himself much with the wars of Frederick II, q.v., against his wife, nor the Seven Years' War. After his death, his wife associated her son, Joseph II, q.v., with her as ruler. Their daughter was the ill-fated Marie Antoinette. Francis received the first two degrees at a special lodge in The Hague in 1731, and in the same year was raised in an occasional lodge held a Houghton Hall, Norfolk, England, by the grand master, Lord Lovel. The event is mentioned in Anderson's Book of Constitutions. As grand duke, he refused to permit the promulgation of Pope Clement's Bull, q.v., against Freemasonry in Austria. He protected Freemasonry as far as he could during his reign, and was grand master when he died Aug. 18, 1765.

Francis II (1768-1835) Last Holy Roman Emperor, 1792-1806: When he was forced to abdicate in 1806 he became Francis .I, emperor of Austria, until his death in 1835. Son of Leopold II, q.v., he followed his father's course in suppressing Freemasonry. When he ascended the throne, he requested all the German princes under him to extirpate all secret societies, by whatever name they might be called. He insisted that any person officially employed should swear that he was not then, and would never become, a member of secret societies, Freemasons, Rosicrucians, Illuminati, or whatever name they might bear. He closed the lodges in 1789, and in 1794 proposed the suppression of Freemasonry to the Diet of Ratisbon. The diet, however, controlled by the influence of Prussia, Brunswick and Hanover, in which Freemasonry was strong, refused the proposition. In 1801 he renewed his opposition to secret societies, especially the Masonic group. Although he fought against Napoleon, q.v., in four wars, his daughter, Maria Louisa, married the French emperor (and Mason) in 1810.

Francis III, Duke of Lorraine (see Francis I).

David R. Francis (1850-1927) Governor of Missouri, Secretary of the Interior, Ambassador to Russia. b. Oct. 1, 1850 at Richmond, Ky. He moved to St. Louis with his parents in 1866 and graduated from Washington U. in 1870, and U. of Missouri in 1892. He went into the grain commission business and headed his own firm. He was president of the Merchant's Exchange and mayor of St. Louis from 1885-89.

From 1889-93 he was governor of Missouri, and in 1896-97 was secretary of the Interior in Cleveland's cabinet. In 1904 he was president of the Louisiana Purchase Centennial Exposition in St. Louis (World's Fair) and U.S. ambassador to Russia during WWI. He was a friend of public education and during his governorship, he increased the endowment of the state university. When the main building of the university at Columbia burned in 1892, he called a special session of legislature and personally visited Columbia to check a threatened exodus of students. He received his degrees in Nov.-Dec., 1891 in George Washington Lodge No. 9 of St. Louis and his capitular degrees in Oriental Chapter No. 78, R.A.M. on Feb. 5, 1892. He was knighted in Ascalon Commandery No. 16, K.T. on April 2, 1892 and was elected as its commander from the floor in 1893. He led his cornmandery in the official triennial parade in Denver, Colo., that year while governor of Mo. He withdrew from all bodies for political reasons. The dates of withdrawal are interesting for he first withdrew from his lodge. The dates of withdrawal are: lodge, June 14, 1898; chapter Nov. 17, 1898 and commandery Sept. 16, 1899. d. Jan. 15, 1927.

John B. Francisco (1863-1931) Artist and violinist. b. Dec. 14, 1863 at Cincinnati, 0. Studied painting and violin abroad. He settled in Los Angeles in 1887 and conducted an art school until 1901. He was a painter of figures and landscapes, especially of Calif. mountain scenes. Mason. d. Jan. 8, 1931.

Henry A. Francken (1720?-1795) The first deputy grand inspector general in the United States of the Scottish Rite and first propagator of these advanced degrees in America.

Probably born in Holland, but came to Jamaica in 1754, where he became a naturalized British subject in March, 1758, and rose to considerable prominence in the island. He occupied the posts of appraiser, marshal and sergeant-at-arms in the court of the vice-admiralty. Henry Moore, the lieutenant governor of Jamaica (and later governor of N.Y.), appointed Franck-en as interpreter of English and Dutch languages in the court. With the governor's permission, he came to New York in 1767 and founded the Sublime and Ineffable Lodge at Albany, creating several deputy inspectors general. The minutes of the Albany lodge state: "About the 7th October, 1767 Messrs. Pfister & Gamble were introduced at New York, to Mr. Henry Andrew Francken, who a day or two after, by Authority invested in him, initiated them in the 11 Degrees of Ancient Masonry, from the Secret Master being the 4th to the Perfection, which is the 14th and Known to be the utmost Limits of Symbolik Masonry. About a week after the above date Mr. Francken conferred on them the two first degrees of Modern Masonry or Masonry Revived, and proposed to them that if they chose he would erect a Lodge of Perfection at Albany and appoint William Bamble Master thereof (pro tempore) until Sir William Johnson, q.v., should have the refusal of it." Francken's next act was to establish a grand chapter of Sublime Princes of the Royal Secret at Kingston, Jamaica under warrant from Stephen Morin, q.v. This was done on April 30, 1770. After his return to Jamaica, he lived on government sinecure and became commissioner of the supreme court at Kingston. d. May 20, 1795.

Francisco Franco Spanish Generalissimo and dictator of Spain since 1939. Anti-Mason. Full name is Francisco Paulino Hermenegildo Teodulo Franco-Bahamonde. He served in the army in Morocco and was appointed chief of staff of Spanish army in 1935. At outbreak of the revolution, he organized the transport of foreign legionnaires and Moorish troops in Spain and became commander of the insurgents. He received aid from Nazi Germany and Fascist Italy, and indirectly from Great Britain and the U.S. through their "nonintervention" policy, thus enabling him to buy war supplies, whereas the constitutional government could not. In 1941 he signed a concordat with the Vatican which empowered him to designate Spanish bishops, subject to ratification by the Holy See. This unholy alliance was the beginning of a modern inquisition and since that date Freemasons have been persecuted, imprisoned, and executed in Spain. Franco holds that Freemasonry is as subversive as Communism—if not more so. After winning the civil war, one of his first acts was to set up a special tribunal for the "Repression of Masonry and Communism." It is a secret court and no reports of its activities appear in print.

Nicolas Louis Francois (1750-1828) French statesman and man of letters. Was called Francois de Neufchateau. He was minister of interior in 1797, member of the directory from 179798, president of the senate from 180406 and created a comte under the Empire. His works include the comedy *Pamela ou la Vertu Recompensee* and *Fables en Contes en Vers*. He was a member of the famous Lodge of the Nine Sisters in Paris and together with Comte Lacepede revived the lodge. He was on the membership list in 1783, 1784 and 1806. d. Jan. 10, 1828.

Christian J. Frank Movie actor who appeared in more than 200 pictures. He was raised in Reagan Lodge No. 1037, Houston, Texas, and was a member of the "233 Club" degree team and took the part of a deacon. This Masonic club was made up of Freemasons in the movies.

Eugene M. Frank Methodist Bishop. b. Dec. 11, 1907 in Cherryvale, Kans. Graduate of Kansas State Teachers Coll., 1930; Garrett Biblical Inst., 1932; Baker U. (Kans.) 1947. Ordained to ministry in 1932 and served the following Kansas pastorates Tonganoxie, Americus, Olathe, Kansas City, Topeka. Consecrated bishop in 1956 and bishop of Missouri at St. Louis same year. Member of Wyandotte Lodge No. 3, Kansas City, Kans. and grand orator of the Grand Lodge of Kansas in 1959-60.

Selby H. Frank Brigadier General, U.S. Army. b. Aug. 15, 1891 at Louisville, Ky. Graduate of U.S. Military Academy in 1913. Advanced through grades to brigadier general in 1945. Mason.

Walter H. Frank Major General, U.S. Air Force and business executive. b. April 23, 1886 at Humphrey, N.Y. Graduate of U.S. Military Academy in 1910. He advanced through grades to brigadier general in 1938, and major general in 1941, retiring in 1945. Assigned to the Aviation Section of the Signal Corps in WWI, he became chief of staff of the Air Force in 1938. Later a wing commander. In 1941-42 he was commanding general of the Third Air Force, and in 1942 commanded the Eighth Air Force Service Command in London, Eng. From 1942-44 he commanded the Army Air Forces Air Service Command and was a member of the Pearl Harbor Board in

1944. Since 1946 he has been president of Sears & Roebuck, S.A. Comercio e Indsl. and in charge of that companys' foreign expansion. Mason.

Benjamin Franklin (1706-1790) American statesman, scientist, philosopher and author. b. Jan. 17, 1706 in Boston, Mass. Apprenticed to his brother, James, a printer, when only 12, he left him five years later after disagreements, and settled in Philadelphia. First employed as a printer, he became proprietor of a printing business and published *The Pennsylvania Gazette*, 1730-48 and gained wide recognition with his *Poor Richard's Almanack*, 1732-57. In 1727 he organized the "Junto" club which became the American Philosophical Society, and in 1731 laid the foundations for a library which developed into the Philadelphia Public Library. He was instrumental in improving the lighting of city streets, invented a heating stove about 1744 (which is still being made), and, becoming interested in electricity, tried his famous kite experiments in 1752. In 1748 he sold his business to the foreman and retired to devote himself to public life. In 1754 he was Pennsylvania's delegate to the Albany Congress and from 1757-62 was in England representing Pa. in efforts to enforce taxes on proprietary estates. In 1766 he was called before the English House of Commons to explain colonial opposition to the Stamp Tax. He returned to Philadelphia when war became inevitable in 1775. He was a member of the second Continental Congress of 1775 and was on the committee to draft the Declaration of Independence, being one of its signers. In 1776 he was sent as one of a committee of three to negotiate a treaty with France. He became immensely popular during his stay which lasted until 1785, during which time he was U.S. minister. In 1781 he was named with Jay and Adams to negotiate peace with Great Britain and returned to Philadelphia in Sept. 1785. From 1785-87 he was president of the Pa. executive council. In 1727 he organized the "Leathern Apron Club" as a secret society in Philadelphia (non-Masonic); and on Dec. 8, 1730 printed an article in his paper pretending to reveal Masonic mysteries. Two months later (Feb., 1731) he received his degrees in St. John's Lodge of Philadelphia and became active in its work from the very beginning. He was secretary of the lodge from 1735-38; elected junior grand warden of the Grand Lodge of Pennsylvania on June 24, 1732 and the grand master on June 24, 1734. He was appointed provincial grand master (first native born) by Thomas Oxnard, q.v., of Boston on June 10, 1749. He was deposed as provincial grand master by William Allen on March 13, 1750, but immediately appointed deputy grand master. On March 12, 1752 he was named to a committee for building "the Free-Mason's Lodge" in Philadelphia and on June 24, 1755 took a prominent part in the dedication of the same as the first Masonic building in America. In 1760 he was named provincial grand master of Philadelphia. In 1734 he printed *Anderson's Constitutions* as Mason Book, which was the first Masonic book printed in America. In 1759 he was a visitor to Lodge Saint David at Edinburgh, Scotland and on Nov. 17, 1760 was present at the Grand Lodge of England, held at Crown & Anchor, London as "provincial grand master." An April 7, 1778 he assisted at the initiation of Voltaire, q.v., in the Lodge of the Nine Sisters in Paris, and affiliated with that lodge the same year. On Nov. 28, 1778 he officiated at the Masonic funeral services held by that lodge for Voltaire. On May 21, 1779 we find him elected master of the Lodge of Nine Sisters. He served as master for two years. On July 7, 1782 he was a member of the Respectable Lodge de Saint Jean de Jerusalem and on April 24, 1785 was elected honorary master of the same. He was also elected honorary member of the Loge des Bon Amis of Rouen, France in 1785. d. April 17, 1790.

Jesse Franklin (1760-1823) Governor and U.S. Senator from North Carolina. b. March 23, 1760 in Orange Co., Va. His father moved to N. Car. just before the Revolution in which young Jesse served as a major. He served in both the state house of delegates and senate and was a member of the U.S. congress from 1795-97 and U.S. senator from 1799-1805, and again from 1807-13. In 1816 he was appointed by the president to treat with the Chickasaw Indians, and in 1820 he was elected governor of N. Car. Franklin was made an entered apprentice at Fayetteville, N. Car. on Dec. 23, 1793. He later became a member of Liberty Lodge No. 45, Wilkesborough, N. Car. Although the records of the lodge were lost, he was recorded a member in 1811. d. in Sept., 1823.

William Franklin (1729-1813) Illegitimate son of Benjamin Franklin, q.v., and the last royal governor of New Jersey under the British. b. in Philadelphia. About a year after his birth, his father, who had married on Sept. 1, 1730, took the child into his home and brought him up as a son. He served in the Pa. forces during the French war of 1744-48 and became a captain before he was of age. He was at Ticonderoga. Returning to Philadelphia, where his father had gained both wealth and prestige, he became comptroller of the general post office and later clerk of the provincial assembly. At this time he also entered Freemasonry (about 1751) but it is uncertain whether he was a member of his father's lodge St. John's No. 1, or the Tun Tavern Lodge. He was grand secretary of the Grand Lodge of Pennsylvania in 1755. He accompanied his father to London in 1757, and was there admitted to the bar the following year. He was also with his father when he visited the Grand Lodge of England on Nov. 17th at the Crown & Anchor in London, and with his father recorded on the books as "provincial grand master," he was registered as "grand secretary." It was undoubtedly through his father's influence that William was appointed royal governor of New Jersey in 1762. He was the first native-born person to receive such an appointment. Originally he had been a Whig, but as the years advanced he became a Tory and an ardent supporter of the British. His father pled with him to join the American cause, both by letter from England and in personal visits. From this point on the two went separate ways. William was eventually placed under guard and sent to England after the war where the government granted him £1,800 remuneration for his losses and £800 yearly pension. Although father and son became partially reconciled in 1784, his father bequeathed him only some land in Nova Scotia and released him from all debts that the executors might find due him stating: "The part he acted against me in the late war, which is of public notoriety, will account for my leaving him no more of an estate he endeavored to deprive me of." d. Nov. 17, 1813.

Wirt Franklin Oklahoma oil producer and one of the discoverers of the Healdton oil field in 1913. b.

March 22, 1883 at Richmond, Mo. He was stenographer of the commission to the Five Civilized Tribes at Muskogee, Indian Territory from 1902-04. Admitted to the bar in 1906 and practiced at Ardmore. He is president of the Franklin Petroleum Corp. From 1929-35 he was president of the Independent Petroleum Association of America. Member of Ardmore Lodge No. 31 and past master of same. Also member of Ardmore Chapter No. 11, R.A.M.; Ardmore Council No. 11, and Ardmore Commandery No. 9, K.T. all of Ardmore, Okla. 32° AASR (S.J.) at South McAlester and member of Indian Shrine Temple of Oklahoma City, Okla.

Frank Frantz (1872-1941) Governor of Oklahoma, 1905-07. b. May 7, 1872 at Roanoke, Ill. He was with Roosevelt's Rough Riders in the Spanish-American War as a captain and participated in the Cuban campaign and the Battle of San Juan Hill. He became postmaster of Enid, Okla. in 1901 and Indian agent for the Osage Indians in 1903. After his term as governor he engaged in the real estate business and the production of oil, being president of the Roanoke Oil Co. and chairman of the board and general manager of Franko Co. Mason. d. March 9, 1941.

Alexander Fraser President of Shell Oil Corp. b. Oct. 11, 1889 at Glasgow, Scotland. Associated with the petroleum industry since 1910, and with the Shell Co. since 1929. President of Shell Petroleum Corp. since 1933; president of Shell Oil Co. 1939-47; president of Shell Union Oil Corp. since 1947. Mason.

Duncan Cameron Fraser (1845-1910) Justice, Supreme Court of Nova Scotia, 1906-10 and member of Canadian House of Commons,

1891-1904. b. Oct. 1, 1845 in New Glasgow, N.S. Was admitted to the bar in 1873. Member of legislative council of Nova Scotia and of the cabinet in 1875-78 and 1888-91. In 1906-10 he was lieutenant governor of Nova Scotia. He was raised in Truro Lodge No. 43, Truro, N.S. on Jan. 3, 1872; master of Albion Lodge No. 5, New Glasgow in 1882 and grand master of the Grand Lodge of Nova Scotia in 1892-93. d. Sept. 27, 1910.

Duncan W. Fraser President of American Locomotive Co. 1940-45 and chairman of board since 1945. b. June 2, 1875 at Churchville, N.S., Canada. Was vice president of the company from 1920-40. Director and officer of several other large corporations. Mason.

Harry W. Fraser (1884-1950) President of Order of Railway Conductors of America from 1941. b. June 7, 1884 at Topeka, Kans. Began as a railway clerk in 1900 and was later brakeman and conductor. In 1929 he became secretary to the president of the Order of Railway Conductors, followed by the offices of chief clerk; deputy president, vice president and president. Active in Boy Scout work, he was a member of the national council in 1943. Member of National Management-Labor Policy Committee, War Manpower Commission from 1943-45. Was delegate several times to International Labor Organization. Mason, Knight Templar, 32° AASR, Shriner and High Twelve. d. May 13, 1950.

William A. Fraser (1869-1932) President of Woodmen of the World Life Ins. Assn. from 1913 and Globe Insurance Co. from 1927. b. Jan. 29, 1869 in Woodside, Scotland. Began with the Woodmen company at Dallas, Texas in 1892. Mason. d. Nov. 6, 1932.

Samuel Fraunces (1722?-1795) Revolutionary tavern keeper and patriot. A West Indian Negro who was the keeper of "Fraunces Tavern," New York City, between 1762-65 and 1770-89. From 1789-94 he was household steward to George Washington. Member of Holland Lodge No. 8, New York City.

Everett W. Frazar (1867-1951) Inventor, business agent, and exporter. b. Aug. 17, 1867 in Shanghai, China, of American parents. He began with the Edison Phonograph Works at West Orange, N. J. in 1890, and later transferred to the laboratory of Thomas A. Edison. He went to Europe to demonstrate an electrically propelled and operated torpedo invented by Edison and Scott, and on returning to the U.S. assisted in the development of a pneumatic dynamite gun invented by Dana Dudley. In 1896 he joined the firm of his father, Frazar & Co. in Japan. He was in charge of the engineering department and also represented Henry Ford, Baldwin Locomotive Works, Victor Talking Machine Co. and many other American manufacturers. On declaration of war on Japan in 1941, all company assets were frozen. He was senior partner of Frazar & Co., New York and partner of Frazar and Hansen, San Francisco. Mason and 33° AASR. d. Oct. 14, 1951.

Harry H. Frazee (1880-1929) Theatrical producer and owner of Boston American League Baseball Club. b. June 29, 1880 in Peoria, Ill. At age of 16 he was on the road as an advance theatrical agent. His first road production was Uncle Josh Perkins in 1902-03. From 1904-07 he launched a number of musical comedy successes. He built and operated several theaters in Chicago and New York and produced shows in London. Among his productions were *Madame Sherry; Ready Money; Fine Feathers; A Pair of Sixes; Nothing but the Truth; My Lady Friends; No, No, Nanette; Yes, Yes, Yvette.* d. June 4, 1929. Member of Blair Lodge No. 382, Chicago, receiving degrees on Jan. 24, Jan. 31 and Feb. 14, 1906. d. June 4, 1929.

James B. Frazier (1856-1937) Governor and U.S. Senator from Tennessee. b. Oct. 18, 1856 at Pikeville, Tenn. Graduated from U. of Tenn. in 1878 and practiced law at Chattanooga. He was governor of Tennessee two terms, 1902-06, but resigned in 1905 to become U.S. senator from the term 1905-11. Member of McWhirtersville Lodge No. 375, Donelson, Tenn. d. March 28, 1937.

Joseph Frazier (1864-1925) Army officer. b. Dec. 8, 1864 at Rolling Home, Mo. Graduate of U. of Missouri and U.S. Military Academy. Served in the Boxer Rebellion in 1900 and is said to have been the first American to scale the Chinese Wall, July 13, 1900. He was cited for his action and received the D.S.C. He served 30 years in the Army and from 1905-09 was commandant of cadets at Missouri U. where he did more to build up the R.O.T.C. than any of his predecessors. In 1907 he took the entire corps of cadets to the Jamestown Exposition. Member of lodge, chapter and commandery at Columbia, Mo. d. March 13, 1925.

Russell G. Frazier Explorer and surgeon. b. July 5, 1893 at Fraziers Bottom, W. Va. Received medical degree from U. of Louisville in 1919 and in 1921 became mine surgeon of Utah Copper Co., Bingham

Canyon, Utah, a position he has held since that time. In 1933 he headed an expedition by boat on the Green River, Utah. In 1934 he headed another expedition from Grand Canyon, Colo., to Boulder Dam. In 1936 and 1937 he was a member of historical and archaeological expeditions in Utah, and in 1938 headed the expedition which discovered the most northern American cliff dwellings near Yampa River, Colo. He was physician and surgeon with Admiral Byrd's, q.v., third U.S. Antarctic Expedition, studying climatology and physiology from 1939-41. Now retired. Raised in Canyon Lodge No. 13, Bingham Canyon, Utah in Sept., 1914. Member of Eureka Chapter No. 101, R.A.M. of Louisville, Ky.; Utah Council No. 1, R. & S.M., Salt Lake City, Utah and Utah Commandery No. 1, K.T. as well as Shrine.

J. Allen Frear, Jr. U.S. Senator from Delaware since 1949. b. March 7, 1903 at Rising Sun, Del. Graduate of U. of Delaware in 1924. An agriculturist, he has been a director of the Federal Land Bank at Baltimore since 1938. He is a member of Union Lodge No. 7, Dover, and served as grand master of the Grand Lodge of Delaware in 1948-49. He is also a member of Kent Chapter No. 8, R.A.M. of Dover, and St. John's Commandery No. 1, K.T. of Wilmington. He has served as master of the Delaware Consistory of the AASR (NJ) and was coroneted 33° in Philadelphia in 1950.

Frederick I (1754-1816) King of Wurtemberg in 1805. Full name was Frederick William Karl. From 1797-1804 he was Frederick II, duke of Wurtemberg. Made an elector in 1803. He protected the lodges of the rite of Strict Observance and was first master of the lodge Frederica zum Schadel in Luben, Silesia in 1778.

Frederick II (1712-1786) Known as "The Great." King of Prussia from 1740-1786. Son of King Frederick William I. When 18, he tried to escape from his father's control, but was arrested, tried as a deserter and made to believe that he would receive severe punishment, but pardoned. As the royal prince, he engaged in literary and social pursuits from 1732 until he became king in May, 1740. Shortly thereafter he began warring against Maria Theresa, q.v., over the possession of Silesia. Her husband, Francis I, q.v., had little to do in helping his wife. His alliance with England in 1765 marked the beginning of the Seven Years' War in which he displayed great military genius and perseverance in face of great odds. Prussia emerged from the war a greatly strengthened state. He joined Russia in the first partition of Poland in 1772. A patron of literature, he invited Voltaire, q.v., to live at his court (1750-53). A skilled administrator of national economy, he encouraged agriculture and industrial improvements and instituted many social reforms. He took a special interest in the improvement of the Prussian army. He was greatly interested in the American Revolution and an admirer of Washington. He wrote much, and his complete works are published in 30 volumes. He was initiated on the night of Aug. 14-15, 1738 in a special lodge called at Brunswick. The degrees started at midnight and ended at 4 a.m. Baron von Bielfeld, q.v., an intimate companion of the prince, was present at the initiation and left a written record of the proceedings. Bielfeld also states that in 1739, Frederick invited the Baron von Oberg and himself to Reinsberg where they founded a

lodge into which Keyser-ling, Jordan, Moolendorf, Queis, and Fredersdorf, Frederick's valet, were admitted. Bielfeld also tells us that on June 20, 1740, shortly after he ascended the throne, Frederick held a lodge at Charlottenburg, and serving as master, initiated his brother, Henry Louis Frederick, prince of Prussia, q.v., Frederick William, q.v., duke of Holstein, and Charles, Margrave of Brandenburg. On July 16, 1774 Frederick granted his protection to the National Grand Lodge of Germany and officially approved of the treaty by that grand lodge with the Grand Lodge of England. He wrote the Lodge Royal York of Friendship in Berlin on Feb. 14, 1777 stating " . . . a society which employs itself only in sowing the seed and bringing forth the fruit of every kind of virtue in my dominions may always be assured of my protection. It is the glorious task of every sovereign, and I will never cease to fulfill it. And so I pray God to take you and your Lodge under his holy and deserved protection." It has been claimed by some that Frederick wrote and set up the Scottish Rite system of 33 degrees, but evidence indicates that it is the brain child of Stephen Morin, q.v., who in an effort to give his rite a royal background had faked Frederick's signature on the documents while in the West Indies.

Frederick William III (1770-1840) King of Prussia. Not to be confused with William Frederick III (1831-1888) who was emperor of Germany and his grandson, q.v. He was the son of King William Frederick II, q.v., and father of William I, q.v. Although he was not a Freemason, his father, son and grandson were. He was king of Prussia from 1797-1840. Shortly after ascending the throne, he wrote on Dec. 29, 1797 the following to the

Lodge Royal York of Friendship at Berlin: "I have never been initiated, as every one knows, but I am far from conceiving the slightest distrust of the intentions of the members of the Lodge. I believe that its design is noble, and founded on the cultivation of virtue; that its methods are legitimate, and that every political tendency is banished from its operations. Hence, I shall take pleasure in manifesting on all occasions my good-will and my affection to the Lodge Royal York of Friendship, as well as to every other Lodge in my dominions." He wrote three months later to Fessler, q.v., in a similar friendly tone, and when he issued an edict on Oct. 20, 1798 that forbade secret societies, he made a special exemption in favor of the Masonic lodges. He took part in the French campaigns of 1792-94. Napoleon completely subjugated him in 1801-05, and at the insistence of the queen, he opposed the French resulting in disastrous defeats at Jena and Auerstedt in 1806. The kingdom was then dismembered by treaty of Tilsit. The army was reorganized and finally the victory at Leipzig in 1813 liberated Germany. This was followed by Napoleon's defeat at Waterloo and Prussia was reestablished in 1814.

Frederick III (1831-1888) Emperor of Germany for three months (March 9 to June 15, 1888). Son of William I, q.v., and grandson of William Frederick III, q.v. As Frederick William, he was crown prince of Prussia from 1861-88. Educated in Bonn, he engaged in military duties and travel from 1851-58, marrying Victoria Adelaide Mary Louise, the eldest daughter of Queen Victoria, in the latter year. He was strongly opposed to Bismarck's policies for strengthening Prussia, and to the war with Austria in 1866, but took part in the war as a division commander and secured the victory at Koninggratz. He was in command of the armies of the southern states in the Franco-Prussian War in 1870, and took part in the battles of Worth, Sedan, and in the siege of Paris. He was a patron of literature and science. He developed cancer of the throat in the year before he became emperor, and his illness proved fatal in the third month of his reign. He was initiated Nov. 5, 1853 by his father in the royal palace at Berlin. The grand officers of the three Berlin grand lodges had been called together for the occasion and the degrees were given according to the ritual of the Grosse Landesloge. He became grand master of the National Grand Lodge of Germany in 1860.

Frederick VII (1808-1863) King of Denmark from 1848-63. He was the son of Christian VIII, q.v., and his predecessors since Christian VII (1766) were probably Freemasons. He was initiated in the lodge "Mary at the Three Hearts" in Odense. When he ascended the throne he became grand master of the Grand Lodge of Denmark. In 1855 he adapted the Swedish system to the Danish lodges. His father, Christian VIII, was protector of Freemasonry from 1836-1848. He promulgated a new constitution in 1849 which deprived him of absolute power. During much of his reign he was involved in disputes with Germany and Austria over the duchies of Schleswig and Holstein. He died childless as the last of the Oldenburg line.

Frederick VIII (1843-1912) King of Denmark, 1906-12. He was the son of Christian IX, q.v., whom he succeeded as king, and father of Haakon VII, q.v., King of Norway and of Christian X, who followed him on the Danish throne. He was made a past grand master of the Grand Lodge of England in 1897, while crown prince of Denmark, and was grand master of the Grand Lodge of Denmark from 1872 until May 14, 1912, when succeeded by his son Christian X. As many other of the rulers of Denmark, he carried the title Vicarius Salomonis, which means protector of the order. (Literally, "Vicar of Solomon.") Frederick Adolf (1750-1803) Duke of Ostogothland (Sweden). The third son of King Adolf Frederick, q.v., who reigned from 1751-71 as the first of the Holstein-Gottorp dynasty. In 1777 he was a member of the "high chapter" and was received in Turin in the German system of Strict Observance. In 1779 he was master of the military lodge in Stockholm.

Frederick Albert, Margrave of Brandenburg-Schwedt (1705-1762) Initiated in Charlottenburg in 1740, he was master of the Scottish lodge "Union" of Berlin in 1742. In 1761 he was elected master of the Scottish lodge "Harmony."

Augustus Frederick (1773-1843) (See Duke of Sussex.) Frederick Augustus (1740-1805) (See Prince of Brunswick.) Frederick Augustus, Duke of York (1763-1827) The title "duke of York" is frequently conferred by the British sovereign on his second son. Frederick was the second son of George III, and brother of George IV, q.v. He was initiated Nov. 21, 1787 in Britannic Lodge No. 29 (now 33) at a special lodge held at the Star and Garter Tavern, London. The lodge was called by the duke of Cumberland, q.v., who was his uncle and grand master of the grand lodge. He was sponsored by his brother, George III, who was Prince of Wales at that time. He succeeded his brother as master of the Prince of Wales Lodge in 1820.

Frederick Christian (?-1769) Margrave of Brandenburg-Bayreuth. An uncle of Frederick, Margrave of Brandenburg-Kulmbach, and succeeded him. He patronized the lodge in Bayreuth.

Frederick, Duke of Saxony-Hildburghausen (1763-?) Was duke of Saxony from 1780-1826. He was initiated in the lodge Karl zum Rautenkranz at Hildburghausen in 1789. The lodge had been constituted in 1787 by the Grand Lodge of England and became one of the five independent lodges of Germany.

Frederick Eugen (1732-?) Duke of Wurtemberg from 1795-97. He was the author of several Masonic lectures printed in 1784-85.

Frederick Heinrich Eugen (1758-1822) Prince of Wurtemberg. A lieutenant general in the Prussian Army, he was initiated in a military lodge and became an honorary member of two lodges in Stargard.

Henry Frederick (See H.R.H. the Duke of Cumberland.) Henry Frederick (1709-1788) Mar-grave of Brandenburg-Schwedt. Admitted in the Grand Lodge of The Three Globes in Berlin.

Henry Louis Frederick Prince of Prussia and brother of Frederick the Great, q.v. He was initiated by his brother, who served as master of a special lodge held in Charlottenburg on June 20, 1740.

Frederick, King of Sweden (See under Adolf Frederick.) Louis Frederick, Prince of Wales (1707-1751) Eldest son of King George II and Queen Caroline. Father of George III. b. in Hanover, Germany, he was the first royal member of the house of Hanover to become a Mason. He was initiated in a special lodge at Kew Palace by Dr. John T. Desaguliers, q.v., on Nov. 5, 1737. Three of his sons became Freemasons—the dukes of York, Gloucester and Cumberland, q.v. He was bitter against his father for vetoing his marriage to Wilhelmina, princess royal of Prussia, and also for refusing him an adequate allowance. For this reason, he either wrote or inspired the Histoire du Prince Titi in 1735, which was a caricature of his parents. His father refused him permission to command a British army against the Jacobites in 1745. He died as a result of a blow from a cricket ball. His son, William Henry, Duke of Gloucester and Edinburg, q.v., and grandson, William Frederick, Prince of Gloucester, q.v. were Freemasons.

Frederick Ludwig (?-1819) Grand Duke of Mecklemburg-Schwerin. Initiated in 1818 in Concordia Lodge in Berlin and became a member of the Grand Lodge "The Three Globes." d. 1819.

Frederick Ludwig (1751-1820) Landgrave of Hesse-Homburg. He was initiated in 1782 at Wilhelmsbad by Prince Charles of Hesse-Cassel.

Frederick Ludwig Alexander (1756-1823) Duke of Wurtemberg. A brother of Frederick I, king and prince of Wurtemberg, q.v. He served in the Prussian army and became a field marshal. He was initiated in the lodge of The Three Globes at Berlin in 1776.

Frederick, Margrave of Brandenburg-Kulmbach (1711-?) He was initiated by Frederick the Great, q.v., in 1740 and founded a lodge in his palace at Bayreuth which later

became the Grand Lodge Zur Sonne. He was succeeded by his nephew, Frederick Christian, q.v.

Frederick, Prince of Hesse-Cassel (1747-1837) A Dutch major general. He entered the rite of Strict Observance at Cassel in 1777. Also a land-grave of Hesse-Cassel.

Frederick Wilhelm Paul (1797-1861) Duke of Wurtemburg. He was initiated in the lodge Zum Verein der Menschenfreunde at Triers in 1817 and later became master of the lodge Zu den drei Cedern in Stuttgart and honorary member of the lodge in Heilbronn.

William Frederick II (1744-1797) (Also Wilhelm) King of Prussia, 1786-97. Grandson of Frederick William I; son of Prince Augustus William and nephew of Frederick the Great, q.v. His lack of administrative ability caused Prussia to decline. He joined Austria in support of French royalty in the French Revolution which involved him in war (1792-95). He was compelled by the Treaty of Basel, in the latter year, to give up Prussian territories west of the Rhine. He was made a Mason in the Lodge Drei Degen at Halle about 1769, and affiliated with the Lodge Drei Goldene &Mussel at Berlin, Oct. 1, 1777.

Frederick William, Duke of Holstein-Beck (also Friedrich Wilhelm) He was initiated on June 20, 1740 in the royal palace of Frederick the Great, q.v., who acted as master of the lodge. In 1741 he affiliated with the Grand Lodge of "The Three Globes" in Berlin, and was appointed fifth grand master of the same in 1747. He was governor of Berlin.

William Frederick, Prince of Gloucester (see under Gloucester)

Frederick William (1831-?) Prince of Hesse-Philippsthal-Barchfeld.   He served in the Prussian navy. Was a member of the lodge Urania in 1856, and an honorary member of the grand lodge, Royal York a l'Amitie, in Berlin.

Frederick William Charles (1797-1881) Prince of the Nether-lands. Son of King William I, and brother of King William II, q.v. He served in the Dutch army, and took part in the Belgian Revolution of 1830. In 1825, he married Princess Louise, the daughter of Frederick William III, q.v., king of Prussia. He was initiated in Berlin by a deputation of the grand lodge of "The Three Globes" in 1817, and the same year was appointed grand master of the National Grand Lodge of the Nether-lands. He was a Masonic reformer who denounced the advanced de-grees as being contrary to the true intent of Freemasonry, and in 1819, tried to introduce a new rite consisting of five degrees. This included the degrees of "Elect Master" and "Su-preme Elect Master," in addition to the three symbolic degrees. Only a few lodges accepted his new system.

John E Fredrick (1865-1943) Chairman of the board of Continental Steel Corp. b. Oct. 27, 1865 in Randolph Co., Ind. Received M.D. from Ohio Medical Coll. in 1892, and practiced medicine at Ridgeville, Ind. from 1892-96. Between 1896 and 1901, he organized the Kokomo Nail & Wire Co.; Kokomo Steel & Wire Co. and merged with others as Continen-tal Steel Corp. He was co-author of the Indiana workmen's compensation law, and president of the Indiana state chamber of commerce for 18 years. He affiliated with Howard Lodge No. 93 at Kokomo, Ind., June

1, 1898. His original lodge is not known. d. March 3, 1943.

Emerich B. Freed Federal Judge, Northern District of Ohio since 1941.

Alfred B. Freeman President of Louisiana Coca-Cola Bottling Co., 1943-47, and chairman of board since 1947. b. Jan. 13, 1881 in Dal-ton, Ga. He went with the Louisiana beverage company in 1906, as secre-tary and treasurer. He is also a direc-tor of Wesson Oil, and Snowdrift Co. of New Orleans, and a director of the Federal Reserve Bank of Atlanta, Ga. Mason.

James E. Freeman (1866-1943) Episcopal Bishop of Washing-ton, D.C., whose inspiration resulted in the building of the great national cathedral on Mt. St. Albans in Wash-ington. Like Hiram Abif, he never lived to see his dream completed. b. July 24, 1866, in New York City. After spending 15 years in the legal and accounting departments of the New York City and Hudson River Rail-ways, he completed a theological course under Bishop Henry C. Potter, and later received many honorary degrees from universities and col-leges throughout the U.S. He was ordained a deacon in 1894, and priest in 1895, in the Protestant Episcopal church. He then served churches in Yonkers, N.Y., Minneapolis, Minn., and Washington, D.C. He was con-secrated bishop of Washington in 1923, and although elected bishop coadjutor of Western Texas in 1911, he declined. He was the author of *If Not the Saloon, What?; Man and the Master; Themes in Verse*, and *The Ambassador*. He was raised in Nep-perhan Lodge No. 736, Yonkers, N.Y., Nov. 22, 1906, passed, Feb. 18, 1907, and raised, April 1, 1907. On

Oct. 12, 1922 he affiliated with Temple Noyes Lodge No. 32, Washington, D.C., and served as chaplain of the lodge. A 33° AASR, he first affiliated with the Southern Jurisdiction in Washington, and later with the Northern Jurisdiction in New York City. His bust is displayed in the national cathedral of which he is considered the "father." d. June 6, 1943.

Martin J. Freeman Author and English professor. b. May 17, 1899 at Ada, Ohio. Graduate of Ohio Northern U. and Ph.D. from U. of Chicago in 1934. Was a reporter on Ohio and Illinois newspapers from 1917-19, and editor of the Beaumont News (Texas) in 1922. After more newspaper work in Ohio, he taught English in Iowa State Coll., and U. of Chicago, and since 1941, has been professor of English at Hunter Coll. In WWI he was an infantry lieutenant. He is the author of *The Murder of a Midget; Murder by Magic; Written Communication in Business; The Case of the Blind Mouse; The Scarf on the Scarecrow*; and *Bitter Honey*, as well as others. Initiated in Beaumont, Texas, and presently a member of Ada Lodge No. 346, Ada, Ohio.

Orville Freeman Governor of Minnesota from 1955. b. May 9, 1918 at Minneapolis, Minn. Received B.A. and LL.B. from U. of Minnesota, and admitted to bar in 1947. Active in city and state civic movements. He served in WWII in the Marine Corps advancing from a 2nd lieutenant to major (1941-45). Named Secretary of Agriculture, 1961 by President Kennedy. Was initiated in 1950 and began in chairs in 1953. Was installed master of his lodge on Dec. 18, 1959 while governor. Member of Khuram Lodge No. 112, Minneapolis, and serving as junior warden at this time. Member of the Grotto. Initiated in

1950. Began in chairs, 1953; installed master Dec. 18, 1959.

Ralph M. Freeman Federal Judge, Eastern District of Michigan from 1954. b. May 5, 1902 at Flushing, Mich. Graduate of U. of Mich. in 1926. Was in private law practice in Flint, Mich. Member of Flint Lodge No. 23, Flint, Mich.

Richard P. Freeman b. Nov. 22, 1897 in Hungary, and came to U.S. in 1910. Graduate of Western Reserve U. Admitted to bar in 1919, and was in private practice from 191829, when he became assistant prosecuting attorney for Cuyahoga Co., Ohio, and later U.S. attorney for Northern Ohio. Mason.

Richard P. Freeman (1869-1944) U.S. Congressman to 64th to 72nd Al Walker B. Freeman Congresses (1915-33) from 2nd Conn. dist. b. April 24, 1869 at New London, Conn. Graduate of both Harvard and Yale (1891 and 1894). Practiced law in New London, Conn. Served in Spanish-American War as a sergeant. Became member of Brainard Lodge No. 102, New London, Conn., Oct. 27, 1897. d. July 18, 1944.

Walker B. Freeman (1843-1935) Commander in Chief of Confederate Veterans in 1925. b. Aug. 28, 1843 in Bedford Co., Va. He was in the mercantile business from 1869-87, and after that, an agent for New York Life Ins. Co. He enlisted in the Confederate Army in June, 1861, and surrendered at Appomattox in 1865. Mason. d. Feb. 9, 1935.

Ferdinand Freiligrath (1810-1876) German poet. His works include lyric and political poems such as Glaubensbekenninis and Ca Ira. He also did translations from Victor

Hugo, Shakespeare, q.v., and Burns, q.v. Initiated in 1842, according to the bulletin of the International Masonic Congress.

Freire de Andrade (1685?-1763) Portuguese general and administrator. Full name was Freire de Andrade de Gomez. b. in Coimbra. He was governor and captain general of Rio de Janeiro from 1733-63. He is celebrated in Gama's epic poem *Epicos Brasileiros*. A Freemason.

John C. Fremont (1813-1890) American explorer and army officer, known as "the pathfinder." Often referred to as a Freemason, but no proof of membership can be found. He was a son-in-law of Thomas H. Benton, q.v.

Augustus C. French (?-1864) Former governor of Illinois. Listed as both a member of Lebanon Lodge No. 110, Lebanon, Ill., and Springfield Lodge No. 4, Springfield, Ill. There is no record of his original lodge, and first record is affiliation with Lebanon Lodge No. 110 in 1862. d. Sept. 5, 1864.

Benjamin B. French (1800-1870) Grand Commander of the Grand Encampment, K.T. in 1859, and Grand Secretary of the General Grand Chapter, 1850-59. b. Sept. 4, 1800 at Chester, N.H. He moved to Washington, D.C. in 1813, and became president of the board of aldermen and the common council. He was chief clerk of the U.S. House of Representatives and commissioner of public buildings and grounds. As grand master of the Grand Lodge of the District of Columbia, he laid the cornerstones of the Smithsonian Institution, the Washington Monument, the Capitol extension, many other public buildings, and churches.

(1846-55 and 1868) He served as master of Corinthian Lodge No. 28, Newport, N.H., and as grand marshal of the grand lodge in that state. In Washington, he affiliated with National Lodge No. 12 in 1846, and was elected grand master the same year. He was knighted in DeWitt Clinton Encampment, Brooklyn, N.Y., April 5, 1847, and became commander of Washington Commandery No. 1 (D.C.) on its revival in 1847, serving for 11 years. In 1850 he became grand recorder of the Grand Encampment, K.T. and served until 1859 when he became grand master of the same. At the time of his death he was lieutenant grand commander of the AASR (SJ). d. Aug. 12, 1870.

Burton L. French (1875-1954) U.S. Congressman, 58th to 72nd Congresses (1903-33) from 1st Idaho dist. with the exception of two congresses. b. Aug. 1, 1875 at Delphi, Ind., moving to Nebraska, and then to Idaho. Graduate of Idaho and Chicago universities. He was professor emeritus of government at Miami U., Oxford, Ohio. Member of Federal Loyalty Review Board in 1947. Received the degrees in Kendrick Lodge No. 26, Kendrick, Idaho, May 11, Oct. 12, and Nov. 9, 1899, withdrawing from same, May 13, 1909, and affiliating with Paradise Lodge No. 17, Moscow, Idaho, July 17, 1909; he was a member at the time of his death, Sept. 20, 1954.

Domingo French (1783-1825) Argentine patriot and Colonel who took part in many engagements in the War of Independence, especially at the siege of Montevideo in 1814, and in Peru in 1815. He exiled himself to the U.S. from 1817-19. A Freemason.

Sir John D. P. French (1852-1925) British Field Marshal and 1st Earl of Ypres. He served in the British Navy from 1866-70, and in the army from 1874. He distinguished himself in the Nile expedition in 1884, and as a cavalry commander in the Boer War, 1899-1901. He was promoted to general in 1907, was chief of the imperial general staff in 1912-14, and field marshal in 1913. He was placed in supreme command of the British Army on the Western front in WWI and prevented the Germans from reaching Calais by the battle at Ypres. He resigned in 1915, under criticism for costly advances. He later became commander-in-chief of the United Kingdom, and lord lieutenant of Ireland (1918). He was raised June 15, 1906 in Jubilee Masters Lodge No. 2712 of London.

Hubert J. W. Frere-Orban (1812-1896) Prime minister of Belgium. A lawyer, he was leading liberal member of the lower house from 1847-94, minister of public works in 1847, minister of finance, 1848-52 and 1857-70. He was minister of state in 1861, and prime minister from 1867-70 and 1878-84. The bulletin of the International Masonic Congress states that he was a Freemason.

Wilhelm Frick (1877-1946) German politician who was minister of interior from 1933-43 under Hitler and was hanged as a war criminal in 1946. Anti-Mason. Hitler's newspaper Voelkischer Beobachter announced the final dissolution of all Masonic lodges in Germany on Aug. 8, 1935. The paper blamed the Order for the incidents leading to WWI, saying that Freemasonry believed the time had come for a "bloody war between nations and the erection of a world republic." The National Socialist press gave the lodges a final obituary in

which they were accused of all imaginable historic crimes, including the undermining of the German empire and the assassination at Sarajevo which precipitated WWI. Acting under a decree that had been issued by President von Hindenburg, which charged that the Masonic lodges had engaged in "subversive activities," Dr. Frick, then minister of interior, called for the immediate disbandment of all lodges throughout Germany and the Saar and ordered a confiscation of their property. This was a step that the German Freemasons had expected for some time.

Alfred H. Fried (1864-1921) Austrian pacifist. b. in Vienna, he settled in Berlin in 1883, where he was a bookseller and author. In 1891 he founded and edited the first pacifist paper in Germany, *Die Waffen Nieder!* and in 1892 founded the German peace society. He took a leading part in all international peace movements, and in 1911, was co-winner of the Nobel Peace Prize. At the time of his death he was one of the oldest and most faithful members of Lodge Sokrates.

Theodore Friedlander President of Phoenix Hosiery Co. b. March 6, 1886 in San Francisco, Calif. Began with the hosiery company in 1909 at Milwaukee, and was later Pacific coast representative. Worked up as vice president and general manager. Mason.

Oscar J. Friend Author of Western stories. b. Jan. 8, 1897 at St. Louis, Mo. He was in the drug business with his father at Fort Smith, Ark., from 1916-23, and a freelance writer from 1923-28, returning to pharmacy in that year on the death of his father. From 1937-44 he edited western and detective magazines in

Standard and Better Publications, moving to California in 1944, and again did freelance work. He returned to New York in 1948, where he purchased Otis Kline Associates, a literary agency. He has Written dozens of western and mystery novels such as *The Round-Up; Gun Harvest; Bloody Ground; The Mississippi Hawk; The Long Noose; Range Doctor; The Red Kite Clue; The Hand of Horror; Murder-As Usual*, etc. He is the author of numerous short stories for American magazines. Mason and Knight Ternplar.

Amos A. Fries Major General, U.S. Army, who commanded the Chemical Warfare Service in WWI. b. March 17, 1873 at Debello, Wis. Graduate of U.S. Military Academy in 1898, and promoted through grades to brigadier general in 1918, and major general in 1925. He was chief of the Chemical Warfare Service from 1918-29, retiring on the latter date. He served in the Philippines in 190103, and from 1906-09, was in charge of the Los Angeles River and Harbor district, laying out a complete and modern harbor. He is a past master of Columbia Lodge No. 3, Washington, D.C.; received 32° AASR (SJ) at Washington, March 25, 1919, and 33°, Oct. 22, 1929. He was knighted in Brightwood Commandery No. 6, K.T. in Washington, June 30, 1927, and served as potentate of Almas Shrine Temple, Washington. He is also honorary past president of the National Sojourners.

Charles E. Friley President of Iowa State College since 1936. b. Aug. 27, 1887 in Ruston, La. Graduate of Sam Houston Teachers Coll., Texas A. & M., Columbia U. and U. of Chicago. He taught school in Texas and La. from 1907-10, and became registrar of Texas A. & M. in 1912,

and dean of the school of arts and sciences in 1924. He went with Iowa State in 1932, as dean of the division of science, became vice president in 1935. Mason, 33° AASR (SJ), and Shriner.

Frank F. Frisch Member of the Baseball Hall of Fame at Cooperstown, N.Y. b. Sept. 9, 1898 in New York City. Known as the "Fordham Flash," he jumped from college into the major league. He was an active player from 1919-37, and, from 1938, was a non-playing manager. Always with the National League, he played for New York from 1919-26, St. Louis from 1927-38, and Pittsburgh from 1940-46. He was an outstanding infielder, base runner, and batter. Had a lifetime batting mark of .316 and holds many records. Played in 50 world series games, and managed St. Louis from 1933 through 1938, winning the world series in 1934. He managed Pittsburgh from 1940 through 1946. Member of Beacon Lodge No. 3, St. Louis, Mo.

Lawrence G. Fritz Brigadier General, U.S. Air Force and vice president of American Air Lines. b. Aug. 7, 1896 at Marine City, Mich. He was a transport pilot in 1925, and a test pilot for the Ford Airways from 1925-27. From 1927-29 he was chief pilot of the Maddux Airlines, Los Angeles. 1929-31 he was vice president of Southwest Airfast Express, Tulsa, Okla., and regional superintendent for TWA from 1931-38. From 1938-42 he was vice president of TWA in charge of operations. After military duty from 1942-46, he became vice president of American Air Lines in 1946, and retired in 1956. He served in WWI with the aviation section of the Signal Corps, and, after graduating from advanced flying school at Kelly Field in 1924, was commissioned a 2nd lieutenant in the Air Corps reserve. He was made brigadier general in 1944, and major general of Air Force reserve in 1955. He was assistant chief of staff of Air Transport Command from 1942-43; commanding general of the North Atlantic Wing, 1943-44 and commanding general of North Atlantic division 1944-45. He was raised in Alamo Lodge No. 44 of San Antonio, Texas in 1923, while serving in the Air Corps at Kelly Field.

John Frizzell (1829-1894) General Grand High Priest of the General Grand Chapter, 1887-80. b. Sept. 8, 1829 in Bedford Co., Tenn. Served as registrar of the land office at Nashville when 21 years old. Admitted to bar in 1854. Served with the Confederate Army in the Civil War. He was a member of Cumberland Lodge No. 8; Cumberland Chapter No. 1, R.A.M.; Nashville Council No. 1, R. & S.M. and Nashville Commandery No. 1, K.T. He served as head of all York rite bodies in Tenn. Received 32° at hands of Albert Pike, and honorary 33° in 1886. d. Nov. 30, 1894.

Charles W. Froessel Justice, Supreme Court of New York, 1937-49, and associate judge of New York Court of Appeals since 1950. b. Nov. 8, 1892 in Brooklyn, he graduated from the New York Law School and was admitted to the bar in 1915. In 1935-37 he had charge of the slum clearance projects in New York City as special assistant to the U.S. attorney general. He is a trustee of the New York Law School, served with naval reserve in WWI, and member of the executive board, National Council, Boy Scouts of America. A member of Tadmor Lodge No. 923, Ridgewood, N.Y., he was master in 1926; district deputy grand master in 1927-28; grand lodge law enforcement

officer, 1928-39; grand treasurer, 1939-41; deputy grand master, 1942-44; grand master, 1944-46; chairman of committee on awards for distinguished achievement in 1946. On the latter committee, he has been primarily responsible for the selection of the following award recipients: General Omar Bradley, General Jonathan Wainwright, Rear Admiral Richard E. Byrd, Charles E. Wilson, J. Edgar Hoover, Warren R. Austin, John W. Davis, Sir Alexander Fleming, Thomas J. Watson, David Sarnoff, Sir Ernest H. Cooper, Cecil B. de Mille, Dr. Charles W. Mayo, qq.v. He was honored by the Grand Lodge of Connecticut with their Pierpont Edwards, q.v., award.

John Frost (1738-1810) Brigadier General in American Revolution. b. May 5, 1738 in Kittery, Maine. He served as a captain in the Canadian campaign of 1759, and, in 1775, was a lieutenant colonel at the siege of Boston. He won distinction in several engagements that preceded the retreat of Washington to Philadelphia, and when Burgoyne invaded New York, his regiment was placed under General Gates, and later, with Washington's central division. He participated in the action of Monmouth. He left the army with the rank of brigadier general. He was a member of St. Andrews Lodge of Boston, Mass. After the war he returned to Kittery, Maine, where he was county judge, and a member of the governor's council in Massachusetts, of which Maine was then a part. d. July, 1810.

Leslie M. Frost Premier of Ontario, Canada, from 1949. b. Sept. 20, 1895 at Orilla, Ont. Graduate of U. of Toronto. He was admitted to the Ontario bar in 1922, and created King's Counsel in 1933. He served in the Ontario legislature in 1937, 43, 45 and 48, and became leader of the Progressive Conservative Party in 1949. In addition to being prime minister of Ontario, he is also treasurer of the province. In WWI he was severely wounded near Arras, France, in March, 1918. He is a member of Faithful Brethren Lodge No. 77 at Lindsay, and a 32° AASR in the Moore Consistory at Hamilton.

M. M. Frost Vice president of Eastern Air Lines since 1950. b. July 10, 1898 at Nashville, Tenn. He was a sales executive for Portland Cement Co. in Tampa, Fla. from 1929-41. In 1945 he became vice president, and assistant to the president of Eastern Air Lines, N.Y.C. and has been vice president in charge of traffic and sales since 1950. During WWII (1942-45) he served as a colonel with the Air Force. Mason and Shriner.

George A. Fry Management consultant and chairman of George Fry & Associates, Inc. since 1946. b. Oct. 20, 1901 in Swayzee, Ind. Graduate of Northwestern U. in 1924. He was director of personnel at that university in 1924-25, becoming associated with Edwin G. Booz Surveys in the latter year. In 1936 he became a partner of Booz, Fry, Allen & Hamilton, and, in 1942, senior partner of Fry, Lawson & Co. In 1952 he was chairman of the Citizens for Eisenhower and Nixon Committee. Mason.

Joseph Frye (1711-1794) General in the Revolutionary War. b. April, 1711, at Andover, Mass. He was an ensign in Hale's regiment at the capture of Louisburg in 1745, and a colonel when Montcalm captured Fort William Henry in 1757. He escaped by killing an Indian that had charge of him. He was appointed major general by the Mass. provincial congress in June, 1775, and commissioned brigadier general by the Continental Congress, Jan. 10, 1776, but due to infirmities, resigned on April 23. His great grandson was William P. Frye, q.v., U.S. Senator from Maine. d. 1794 in Fryeburg, Maine. He was a member of a Mass. lodge.

William P. Frye (1831-1911) U.S. Senator from Maine, serving six terms from 1881-1911. b. Sept. 2, 1831 at Lewiston, Maine. He was the grandson of General Joseph Frye, q.v. Graduate of Bowdoin Coll., he practiced law. He was a member of the Maine legislature in 1861, '62, and '67. He served as mayor of Lewiston and attorney general of Maine. From 1871-81 he was U.S. congressman to 42nd through 46th congresses. Member of Ashlar Lodge No. 105, Lewiston, Maine. d. 1911.

Dr. R. H. Fuhrmann (?-1937) St. Louis physician who, as an amateur photographer, compiled an historical collection of photographs of the growth of St. Louis. He left the collection to the St. Louis Scottish Rite bodies, stipulating that they could not be sold, and could be used only for educational, display, and entertainment purposes. They were printed in *the St. Louis Globe Democrat* about 1955. He learned photography from the professional, Emil Boehi, and together they took many pictures. When Boehi died in 1919, Dr. Fuhrmann bought the hundreds of negatives he had, that date back to the Civil war, and continued to record the history of St. Louis until his own death, Dec. 20, 1937. Member of West Gate Lodge No. 445, St. Louis, Mo., he received his degrees on Feb. 23, March 1, and March 29, 1904.

James F. Fulbright (1877-1948) Judge and U.S. Congressman to 68th, 70th and 72nd Congresses from 14th Mo. dist. b. Jan. 24, 1877 in Millerville, Mo. Admitted to the bar in 1903. Served as prosecuting attorney of Ripley Co. and mayor of Doniphan, Mo. He was a member of the lower house three terms. In 1938 he was named judge of the Springfield court of appeals, and became presiding judge. Member of Composite Lodge No. 369, Doniphan, Mo., receiving degrees, March 4, 20, and 31, 1905. Suspended NPD June 22, 1937; reinstated Jan. 22, 1946. d. April 5, 1948.

Alfred C. Fuller President of the Fuller Brush Co. b. Jan. 13, 1885 in Welsford, Nova Scotia, Canada; he became a U.S. citizen in 1918. He established the Fuller Brush Co. at Somerville, Mass., in 1906, and since, has been president and chairman of the board. He is a director of the national Better Business Bureau in New York City. Mason, 32° AASR, Knight Templar, and Shriner.

Alvan T. Fuller (1878-1958) Governor of Massachusetts, 1925-29. b. Feb. 27, 1878 in Boston. He was a wealthy auto dealer (Packard) in Boston. He was a member of the state legislature in 1915, and U.S. congressman to 65th and 66th congresses (1917-21) from Mass. He served as lieutenant governor from 1921-25. He never cashed a paycheck as governor or congressman. As governor, he was beset by pressure from near and far to intervene in behalf of the condemned Nicola Sacco and Bartolomeo Vanzetti. After a full investigation by a committee appointed by him, he decided to back up the state judiciary, and they were executed for murder. Agitators charged that Fuller was predisposed against the immigrant, anarchist Ital-

ians because of his wealth and position. He was raised in Converse Lodge, Malden, Mass. in 1906; exalted in Tabernacle Chapter, R.A.M. in 1923, greeted in Melrose Council, R. & S.M., and knighted in Beauseant Commandery, all of Malden in 1923. He received the 32° AASR (NJ), at Buffalo, N.Y., in 1926, and 33° in 1926; member of Aleppo Shrine Temple and Omar Grotto of Boston. d. May, 1958.

Ben H. Fuller (1870-1937) Major General and Commandant of the U.S. Marine Corps. b. Feb. 27, 1870 in Big Rapids, Mich. Attended U.S. Naval Academy. He was appointed a naval cadet in 1885, and transferred to the Marine Corps as a 2nd lieutenant in 1891, advancing through grades to brigadier general in 1918, and major general in 1930. He served on the U.S.S. Columbia in the Spanish-American War, and was in the Philippines during the 1899-1901 insurrection. He was with the Boxer Relief Expedition to Peking, China in 1900, and commanded the 2nd Brigade of Marifies in Santo Domingo in 1918. He served as commandant of the U.S. Marine Corps from 1930, until his retirement in 1934. Mason and member of Washington Chapter No. 3, National Sojourners. d. June 8, 1937.

Justin K. Fuller U.S. Public Health Service. b. Aug. 28, 1888 at Marysville, Calif. Graduate of Stanford U. and U. of Calif. In the public health service he rose from assistant surgeon in 1916, to medical director in 1942, and assistant surgeon general in 1944, resigning in 1948 to become medical consultant of the department of correction and health authority of Calif. Active in penal and correctional institution work, he served as clinical director of the U.S.

narcotic farm at Lexington, Ky., from 1935-37, and was medical director of the bureau of prisons of the U.S. justice dept. 1937-42. Member of Washington Centennial Lodge No. 14, Washington, D.C.

Levi K. Fuller (1841-1896) Governor of Vermont in 1892-94. b. Feb. 24, 1841 at Westmoreland, N.H., moving to Brattleboro in 1854, where he was educated in the public schools. From 1866 he was associated with the Estey Organ Co., and was vice president for many years. He was a member of the state senate in 1880, and held many town and municipal offices. He organized and commanded the Fuller Light Battery of the national guard. He was lieutenant governor from 1886-88. He was raised in Columbian Lodge No. 36, Brattleboro, Feb. 19, 1863; exalted in Fort Dummer Chapter No. 12, R.A.M. in Brattleboro, April 20, 1864; and knighted in Vermont Commandery No. 4, K.T. at Windsor, prior to 1867, dimitting in 1868. d. Oct. 10, 1896.

Walter D. Fuller President of Curtis Publishing Co. 1934-50. b. June 5, 1882 at Corning, Ia. He began as a bank clerk and salesman (1899-1904), and became associated with the publishing business in 1904. He was with the Crowell Publishing Co. in 1906; the S. S. McClure Company until 1908, associating himself with the Curtis Co. in that year and advanced through various positions to president. Has been a member of Rising Star Lodge No. 126, Philadelphia, Pa., for 48 years.

Hampton P. Fulmer (1875-1944) U.S. Congressman to 67th to 78th Congresses (1921-45) from 2nd S.Car. dist. b. June 23, 1875 near Springfield, S.Car. He was a farmer. In Congress, he was the author of the

U.S. standard cotton grading act and agricultural adjustment act. Mason. d. Oct. 19, 1944.

Robert Fulton (1765-1815) American engineer and inventor. Often called the inventor of the steamboat, but claim is a little broad as John Fitch, q.v., had a steamboat in operation before Fulton. Fulton is often referred to as a Mason, but no proof of his membership can be found.

Will H. Fulton Judge, Kentucky Court of Appeals, 1939-44 and chief justice from 1943-44. b. Aug. 8, 1888 in Bardstown, Ky. Graduate of U. of Va. Admitted to bar in 1909. Was circuit court judge for eight years. Resigned from court of appeals to engage in private practice. Served overseas in WWI with field artillery. Mason.

William J. Fulton Judge, Supreme Court of Illinois since 1942. b. Jan. 14, 1875 at Lynedoch, Ont., Canada. Came to U.S. in 1881, and naturalized in 1887. Graduate of U. of Illinois, and admitted to bar in 1901. He served as law clerk, court reporter, city attorney, and circuit judge. Member of Sycamore Lodge No. 134, Sycamore, Ill., receiving degrees, March 4, April 22, 1910, and Nov. 24, 1911.

Charles E. Funk (1881-1957) Dictionary editor. b. April 4; 1881 at Springfield, Ohio. Graduate of U. of Colorado. From 1904-11 he was an engineer in the western states and then associate editor of *The Engineering Magazine*, becoming managing editor from 1915-17. From 1916-22 he was editor and secretary of the Industrial Extension Institute. His lexicography work began in 1921, as associate editor of the *New Standard*

Dictionary, and in 1939, he became editor, serving as such until 1947. He was also associate editor of *New Standard Encyclopedia* in 1931, and editor of New International Year Books from 193238. He was consulting editor of Funk & Wagnalls Co. from 1947. He was also the author of *25,000 Words Spelled, Divided and Accented; A Hog on Ice and Other Sayings; New Comprehensive Dictionary, 1937; Standard Junior Dictionary, 1939; New Practical Standard Dictionary, 1946; and New College Standard Dictionary, 1947.* Mason. d. April 16, 1957.

Eugene D. Funk (1867-1944) Founder and President of Funk Brothers Seed Co. at Bloomington, Ill., in 1901. b. Sept. 3, 1867 at Shirley, Ill. He began plant breeding in 1892, after studying both in the U.S. and abroad. He was primarily interested in corn, and he became one of the largest producers of hybrid seed corn in the world. Member of Shirley Lodge No. 582, Shirley, Ill., receiving degrees Nov. 27, Dec. 15, and Dec. 23, 1893; 32° AASR (NJ). d. Nov. 28, 1944.

Frank H. Funk (1869-1940) U.S. Congressman to 67th and 69th Congresses (1921-27) from 17th Ill. dist. b. April 5, 1869 at Bloomington, Ill. Was farmer and stock raiser on family farm, "Funk's Grove," from 1891. Served in state senate and was nominee for governor and U.S. senator. Raised in Bloomington Lodge No. 43, Bloomington, Ill., July 6, 1893 and dimitted Jan. 1, 1932. d. Nov. 24, 1940.

Henry Fuqua (1865-1926) Governor of Louisiana, 1924, '26, dying in office. b. Nov. 8, 1865 at Baton Rouge, La. Began with corps of engineers on Construction of the Yazoo & Miss. Valley Railroad, and later engaged in bridge building. He then entered the hardware business in Baton Rouge, and in 1892, organized the Fuqua Hardware Co. In 1916 he became warden of the state prison, serving until 1924. This also included the management of three large plantations owned by the state. d. Oct. 11, 1926. Member and past master of St. James Lodge No. 47 at Baton Rouge. Received his degrees, June 1, July 16, Aug. 24, 1894.

Stephen 0. Fuqua (1874-1943) Major General, U.S. Army. b. Dec. 25, 1874 at Baton Rouge, La. He was the younger brother of Henry Fuqua, q.v., governor of Louisiana. Attended Tulane and U. of La. as well as U.S. Military Academy. He was commissioned a captain of volunteers in 1898, and advanced to rank of major general in 1929, when he became chief of Infantry. He served at one time as military attaché of the U.S. embassy in Madrid, Spain, and, after his retirement, was military affairs editor of *Newsweek* magazine in New York. Member of Sackett's Harbor Lodge No. 135, Sackett's Harbor, N.Y., receiving degrees, Feb. 26, March 12, and March 26, 1906. d. May 12, 1943.

Charles M. Furman (1797-1872) Seventh Grand Commander of the Southern Supreme Council, Scottish Rite, 1858. b. Oct. 17, 1797 in Charleston, S.Car. He was admitted to the bar in 1819, and later served as state treasurer, comptroller, and, in 1850, president of the state bank. He "resigned" from head of the AASR in the same year as he was named grand commander, and Albert Pike, speaking the year Furman died, stated "he has been as one dead to us for 13 years." He was initiated in Solomon's Lodge No. 1 of Charleston in 1824, and became master of Kilwinning Lodge No. 4, same city. In 1838-40 he was grand master of the Grand Lodge of South Carolina, and held the same position again in 1847-48. He was high priest of Union Chapter No. 3 in 1846, and deputy grand high priest of the Grand Chapter, R.A.M. of S.Car. in 1847. In 1850 he was commander of South Carolina Encampment No. 1, K.T.

Robert W. Furnas (1824-1905) Governor of Nebraska, 1873-75. b. May 5, 1824 in Miami Co., Ohio. He was a resident of Nebraska from 1855 until his death. During the Civil War, he was a colonel in the 2nd Nebr. cavalry. He was president of the Nebraska State Board of Agriculture. On retiring from public life, he engaged in farming and tree culture. He was a member of Capitol Lodge No. 3 at Omaha, and later served as master of Nemaha Lodge No. 4 at Brownville, Nebr. He was grand master of the Grand Lodge of Nebraska in 186566, and grand secretary from 1858-62. d. June 1, 1905.

Jonas Furrer (1805-1861) First President of the Swiss Confederation and founder of the Grand Lodge Alpina of Switzerland. A Swiss statesman and lawyer, he was a member of the grand council from 1934-46, and president of the same in 1837 and 1846. In 1848 he was a member of the diet council.

Joseph H. Fussell (1863-1942) Theosophist. b. in Nottingham, England, he came to the U.S. in 1890. He first taught in a private school in Savannah, Ga., and was later private tutor in N.J. and N.Y. In 1893 he became private secretary to William Q. Judge, and later secretary to Katherine Tingley (1896-1929). He was secretary general of The Theosophical Society, and a trustee of Theosophical Univ. He wrote Theosophy and Occultism; More Light—A Study of Theosophy and Freemasonry. Mason; received 32° AASR (SJ), July 31, 1912, at San Diego, Calif. and withdrew Aug. 16, 1932. He had affiliated with San Diego Lodge No. 35 in Feb. 1907, from Ancient Lodge No. 724, N.Y., and withdrew in May, 1934. d. May 7, 1942.

Junius M. Futrell Governor of Arkansas, 1933-35. b. Aug. 14, 1871 in Green Co., Ark. Member of Paragould Lodge No. 368, Paragould, Ark., and received AASR (SJ) degrees in May, 1926.

G

William IL Gabbert (1849-1923) Justice of Supreme Court of Colorado from 1898-1917 and Chief Justice, 1904-07, and 1915-16. b. Oct. 12, 1849 in Scott Co., Ia. Began law practice in Davenport, Ia. in 1870, and moved to Colo. in 1879, settling at Telluride. From 1893-97 he was district judge. In 1916 he resumed private practice. Member of Union Lodge No. 7, Denver. d. July 18, 1923.

Clark Gable Movie actor. b. in 1907 in Cadiz, Ohio. Attended Akron U. (Ohio). He began as a worker in rubber plants and oil fields. He first won recognition as an actor in *The Last Mile*, and made his film debut in *The Painted Desert*. He has appeared in many films *including Hell Divers; Strange Interlude; It Happened One Night; Mutiny on the Bounty; Strange Cargo; Gone With the Wind; The Hucksters; The Wide*

Missouri; Lone Star; Mogambo; Soldier of Fortune; and *Idiot's Delight.* He received the award (Oscar) of the Academy of Motion Picture Arts and Sciences for his role in *It Happened One Night,* in 1934. In WWII he was a 2nd lieutenant in the 8th Air Force, resigning with the rank of major. He was raised in Beverly Hills Lodge No. 528, Oct. 31, 1933, having received his other degrees on Sept. 19, Oct. 17 of same year. d. Nov. 17, 1960.

James Gadsden (1788-1858) U.S. Army officer and diplomat who, as U.S. minister to Mexico, concluded the treaty with that country for the re-adjustment of the boundary line between the two nations, and the acquisition of the tract of land after-wards known as the "Gadsden Purchase." b. May 15, 1788 in Charleston, S.Car. He graduated from Yale in 1806, and moved to Florida, where he was a planter, until he joined the army and was appointed lieutenant colonel of engineers. He served with distinction in the War of 1812, and as an aide-de-camp to General Jackson, q.v., in the campaign against the Seminole Indians in 1818, and aided in the capture of the leaders Arbuthnot and Ambrister. He went with Jackson to Pensacola when the latter took possession of Florida, and was active in settling a dispute between Jackson and the Spanish governor. After his retirement from the army, he returned to farming and was a member of the legislative council of the Florida Territory. He removed the Seminoles to the southern part of Florida under a commission from President Monroe. He later returned to his native state of S.Car. and became president of the South Carolina Railroad and engaged in rice culture. In 1853, President Pierce made him minister to Mexico, and on Dec. 30 of that year he negotiated the famous treaty, setting up

the new boundary. He was an early member of Jackson Lodge No. 23 at Tallahassee, Fla. which was then under the Grand Lodge of Alabama. It is now No. 1 of Florida jurisdiction. d. Dec. 25, 1858.

Johann C. Gaedicke (1763-?) Ger; man bookseller who published a number of Masonic books including the *Freimaurer-Lexicon* in 1818 which was later published in English. b. Dec. 14, 1763. He was initiated in 1804.

Henry T. Gage (1852-1924) Governor of California from 1899-1903. b. Nov. 25, 1852 near Geneva, N.Y. He was educated in the public schools of Michigan and under private tutors. He practiced law in Los Angeles. He was U.S. minister to Portugal in 1909-11. As a lawyer, he was counsel for the Southern Pacific Railroad and other corporations. He was raised in Ancient Landmarks Lodge No. 503 of Saginaw, Mich. Sept. 18, 1872. d. Aug. 28, 1924.

Jonathan Gage (1759-1841) One of the organizers of the General Grand Chapter, Royal Arch Masons. A shipbuilder and owner, his sloop Polly was stolen by the British, and his brig Ranger by the French prior to 1800. He built a turnpike road; was an incorporator of the Newburyport Academy (Mass.), and also helped found a marine insurance company and a savings association. From 1802-03 he was a selectman of Newburyport, Mass., and from 1805-16, a representative of his city to the Massachusetts general legislature. He was master of St. Peter's Lodge of Newburyport in 1791. In 1797 he met with Thomas Smith Webb, q.v., and others in Boston to plan the organization of the General Grand Chapter. Both Webb and Gage were on the committee with Benjamin Hurd, q.v., to bring together the Royal Arch Masons of the various states. They met in Hartford, Conn., to perfect the organization. In 1798 he was elected first grand treasurer of the Grand Chapter of Massachusetts, and was grand high priest of the same in 1820-22. He was a member of King Cyrus Chapter at Newburyport and served as high priest in 1801-02.

Edmund P. Gaines (1777-1849) Major General in War of 1812. b. March 20, 1777 in Culpepper Co., Va. Commissioned as a 2nd lieutenant in the 6th Infantry in 1799, and advanced to major general in 1814. He was active on the frontier for many years and was instrumental in arresting Aaron Burr, q.v. He resigned from the army in 1811, intending to become a lawyer, but returned when the War of 1812 threatened. As a brigadier general he conducted the defense of Fort Erie in Aug. 1814, and was severely wounded in repelling a superior force. In 1816 he was appointed one of the commissioners to treat with the Creek Indians, and was in the southern military district in 1817, when the Creeks and Seminoles began their depredations against Georgia and Alabama. He was a member of Phoenix Lodge No. 8, Fayetteville, N.Car. d. June 6, 1849.

John P. Gaines (1795-1858) Governor of Oregon Territory 1850-53. b. in Walton, Ky., he was admitted to the bar, and began practice in his city of birth. He served in the Mexican War as a major of Marshall's Kentucky cavalry volunteers, and was taken prisoner in Jan., 1847. He was subsequently aide-de-camp to General Scott, and distinguished himself at the battle of Molino del Rey. While still held a prisoner, he was elected to the 30th Congress as a Whig, and served from Dec. 1847 to March 1849. President Fillmore appointed him as territorial governor in 1850, and he never returned to the east. He was a member of Multnomah Lodge No. 1, Oregon City, Oreg.

Sir Charles Gairdner British Lieutenant General and Governor of Western Australia in 1952. He was initiated in Shamrock Lodge No. 101 (Irish constitution) and affiliated with Military Lodge No. 15 (Western Australia constitution), March 21, 1952. He was given the rank of past master of this lodge, and later named senior grand warden of the Grand Lodge of England.

John W. Galbreath Owner and President of the Pittsburgh Pirates Baseball Club. b. Aug. 10, 1897 in Derby, Ohio. Graduated from U. of Ohio in 1920, he entered the real estate business and organized the John W. Galbreath & Co., Columbus, in 1924. He was raised in University Lodge No. 631 of Columbus, Nov. 28, 1922, and received the 33° AASR (NJ) in Boston in 1954.

Eduardo Rincon Gallardo Mexican General. b. April 27, 1900 in Guadalajara, Jalisco, Mexico. Attended the Heroica Colegio Military, later becoming an instructor in this military school and a general of the Army. He was director of the Dept. of Transit, Mexico City; administrator of the Port of Tampico; chief of the Import Dept. and Federal treasurer. In the last ten years he has been head of the Automobile Club of Mexico. He was initiated in 1925 in the lodge Gnosis No. 6 under the jurisdiction of the Grand Lodge, Occidental Mexicana. On this same day another distinguished Mexican Freemason was initiated—Lazaro Cardenas—later a

general and president of Mexico. Gallardo served as treasurer, senior and
junior warden of the lodge Masones
Mexicanos No. 51. He became grand
master of the Grand Lodge, Valle of
Mexico and president of the Inter-
american Masonic Confederation.

Jacob H. Gallinger (1837-
1918) U.S. Senator from New Hampshire for five terms, 1891-1921, dying
in last term. b. March 28, 1837 in
Cornwall, Ont., Canada. Received
medical degree from Medical Institute
of Cincinnati in 1858, and practiced in
Concord, N.H. from 1862-85. He was
surgeon general of N.H., with the
rank of brigadier general, in 1789-90.
He served in both legislative bodies
of his state and was a member of its
constitutional convention in 1876. He
served in the 49th and 50th U.S. congresses (1885-89) but declined renomination. Raised in Eureka Lodge
No. 70, Concord, N.H. on Dec. 13,
1883. d. Aug. 17, 1918.

Floyd E. Galloway (1890-
1955) Brigadier general in Army Air
Service. b. Sept. 11, 1890 in Fal-
mouth, Ky. Graduate of several early
Air Corps schools, and commissioned
lieutenant in 1917, advancing through
grades to brigadier general in 1942.
In WWI he served with the A.E.F. in
Siberia and later commanded Bolling
Field, Washington, D.C.; Maxwell
Field, Montgomery, Ala.; Crissy Field,
San Francisco; and Albrook Field,
Canal Zone. He organized and com-
manded the Air Force Service Com-
mand in the Caribbean Area. Mason.
d. Sept. 19, 1955.

Joseph Galloway (1729-
1803) Pennsylvania lawyer of pre-
revolutionary period, who was an
intimate friend of Benjamin Franklin,
q.v. b. in Anne Arundel Co., Md., he
studied law and practiced in Philadel-

phia where he became intimate with
Franklin. When the latter went to England in 1764, he left his valuable papers with Galloway for safe keeping.
He was a member of the Pennsylvania assembly almost continuously
from 1757 until the Revolution, serving as speaker from 1766 to 1774. In
the early part of the colonial struggle,
he sympathized with the British and
grew to be an active Tory. As a
member of the provincial congress in
1774, he proposed a scheme of government to consist of a president-
general, to be appointed by the king,
and to hold office during his pleasure,
and a grand council, to be chosen
once in three years by the assemblies
of the various colonies. In 1775 he
retired to his country place, where
Franklin visited him, attempting in
vain to swing him to the cause of the
colonies. In 1776 he joined General
Howe, the British commander and on
the taking of Philadelphia, was
named superintendent of the police,
thus becoming virtual head of the civil
government. At the evacuation of the
city he retired with the British and left
for England, never to return. In 1788
the Pennsylvania assembly found him
guilty of high treason and ordered his
estate sold. He was a member of
Lodge No. 2, Philadelphia. d. Aug.
29, 1803.

**Randolph, 12th Earl of Gal-
loway** 94th Grand Master Mason of
Scotland, 1945-48 and First Grand
Principal of the Grand Chapter of
Scotland, R.A.M. since 1953.

Juan Manuel Galvez President of Honduras, 1949-55. Initiated
in Lodge Agustin Disdier of the Orient
of La Ceiba.

**George, 8th Viscount of Gal-
way** (1882-1943) (George Vere Arun-
dell Monckton-Arundell) British soldier

and colonial governor. He served in WWI and was quartermaster general from 1917-19. From 1935-41 he was governor general of New Zealand. He was a past grand master of the Grand Lodge of New Zealand.

Leon Gambetta (1838-1882) Premier of France, lawyer and statesman. b. April 2, 1838 at Cahors. He studied law at Paris and won fame as an orator. Opposing the rupture with Germany, and leader of the party in opposition to the reign of Napoleon III, he was a member of the Government of National Defense (1870). On Oct. 8, 1870 he made a spectacular escape from the Prussian-besieged city of Paris, by balloon. He raised an army and fought to the finish. He founded the influential journal *La Republique Francaise*; succeeded in the adoption of a new constitution and massed effective opposition to the restoration of the Pope's temporal power. He was president of the chamber of deputies from 1879-81. An accidental shot from a pistol cut his life short, Dec. 31, 1882. He was initiated in a lodge at Bordeaux, France, and July 8, 1875, he, with two others, affiliated with the lodge La Clemente Amitie at Paris.

Hamilton R. Gamble (1798-1864) Civil War Governor of Missouri. b. Nov. 29, 1798 in Winchester, Va. Educated in Hampden-Sidney Coll. and admitted to Va. bar when 18 years old. In 1818 he came to Missouri and settled in Old Franklin, Howard Co., where he petitioned Franklin Union Lodge No. 7, Jan. 4, 1822, receiving his degrees Jan. 12, 26, and Feb. 23 of that year. In March, 1822 he was secretary of the lodge, senior warden in October, and master in December. In 1824 he was named secretary of state, holding the office one year. He then moved to St.

Louis where he became a successful lawyer, and presiding judge of the supreme court of the state. In St. Louis he affiliated with Missouri Lodge No. 1, Nov. 2, 1824, and was master in 1826-27. He was elected grand master of the Grand Lodge of Missouri in 1832. When Governor Claiborne F. Jackson joined the secession party, the state constitutional convention of 1861 named Gamble governor. Serving in a difficult time, he is credited with saving the state for the Union, but his duties were demanding, and he died on Jan. 31, 1864. He married Louisa, daughter of Col. Rufus Easton, q.v.

Robert J. Gamble (1851-1924) U.S. Senator from South Dakota, 1901-13. b. Feb. 7, 1851 in Genesee Co., N.Y. Graduate of Lawrence U. (Wis.) in 1874, admitted to the bar the following year, and practiced at Yankton, S.D. He served as district and city attorney, state senator, and chairman of the state Republican convention. He represented his state in the 54th and 56th U.S. congresses. He became a member of St. John's Lodge No. 1, June 8, 1880 and belonged to DeMolay Commandery, K.T., and Oriental Consistory AASR (SJ), at Yankton. He was a member of El Riad Shrine Temple at Sioux Falls. d. Sept. 22, 1924.

Frank E. Gannett (1876-1957) Owner of Brooklyn Eagle and 21 other newspapers. b. Sept. 15, 1876 in Bristol, N.Y. Graduate of Cornell in 1898. He first entered the newspaper field as editor of the Ithaca Daily News (N.Y.) in 1900, and built a $3,000 stake into a newspaper empire, owning all, or controlling interest in 22 newspapers, four radio stations, and three television stations. Most of the newspapers are in New York state. Member of Hobasco

Lodge No. 716 of Ithaca, N.Y.; he was a Knight Templar and Shriner. d. Dec. 3, 1957.

James Ganson (1774-1858) Morgan trial defendant. b. in Salem, Mass. He settled in Avon, N.Y. with his father and brother about 1789. He achieved notoriety in 1826 as one of the defendants in the Masonic trials for the abduction of William Morgan, q.v. He was acquitted. He was probably initiated in Genesee Lodge No. 130 at Avon, N.Y. as he is listed in the returns of 1806-12 in both the "initiation" and "quarterages" columns. He is also listed as a member on the returns of the same lodge, 1812-14. In 1816 he is listed as the charter senior warden of LeRoy Lodge No. 260, LeRoy, Genesee Co., N.Y. His attic once served as a lodge room. Rob Morris states that he was secretary of Western Star Chapter No. 35, R.A.M. of LeRoy when William Morgan was exalted to the Royal Arch degree. He moved to Jackson, Mich. in 1827 or 1828 and died there on May 4, 1858.

Calixto Garcia-Iniguez (1836?-1898) Cuban patriot and lawyer. As a revolutionist, he became a leader in the Ten Years' War against Spain (1868-78), and led the Cuban force at El Caney in the Spanish-American War. In that year he was appointed to represent Cuba in negotiations with the U.S. for Cuban independence. Widely remembered in the U.S. through Elbert Hubbard's inspirational essay A Message to Garcia. Mason.

William Y. Gardiner Governor of Maine, 1929-33. b. June 12, 1892 at Newton, Mass. Graduate of Harvard in 1914. Admitted to Mass. bar in 1917, and Maine bar in 1919; practiced at Augusta. Served in Maine lower house 1921-25. Served in both World Wars. In WWI he was with the 56th Pioneer Infantry, and advanced from private to lieutenant. In WWII he was a major with the U.S. Air Force from 1942-45. Made a Mason March 16, 1920 in Hermon Lodge No. 32, Gardiner, Maine, and is a 33° AASR (NJ).

Frederick D. Gardner (1869-1933) Governor of Missouri 1917-21. b. Nov. 6, 1869 in Hickman, Ky. He moved to St. Louis when 17 years old and was employed by the St. Louis Coffin Co.; he became its owner. It was during his term, that the Missouri State Highway Commission was established as a nonpartisan governmental bureau. He received his degrees in Cornerstone Lodge No. 323 of St. Louis in Jan., Feb. and March, 1891, and March 21, 1893, affiliated with Tuscan Lodge No.360. He was exalted in St. Louis Chapter No. 8, R.A.M., and knighted in Ascalon Commandery No. 16, K.T. in 1892. Also a member of the St. Louis Scottish Rite Consistory and Moolah Shrine Temple. In his will he left substantial amounts to the Masonic Home of Missouri and the Shrine Hospital. d. Dec. 18, 1933.

Henry J. Gardner (1819-1892) Governor of Massachusetts, 1855-1858. Member of Revere Lodge, Boston, Mass. and a Knight Templar. Dimitted Jan. 5, 1869.

William S. Gardner (1827-1888) Masonic writer and historian. He was grand master of the Grand Lodge of Massachusetts three terms, and was 8th grand master of the Grand Encampment, Knights Templar. Received 32° AASR (NJ), in 1857, and 33° May 16, 1861. b. Oct. 1, 1827. d. April 4, 1888.

James A. Garfield (1831-1881) Twentieth President of the United States. b. Nov. 19, 1831 in Cuyahoga Co., Ohio. He was a teacher, and head of Hiram College, Hiram, Ohio from 1857-61. At the outbreak of the Civil War in 1861, he was a colonel in the Ohio volunteers, rising to brigadier general in 1862, and major general in 1863. From 1863-80 he was a member of the U.S. congress, and Republican leader of the same from 1876. He was elected president in 1880, and inaugurated, March 4, 1881. On July 2, 1881 he was shot, in the Washington railroad station, by Charles J. Guiteau, and died Sept. 19, 1881. He was initiated in Magnolia Lodge No. 20 of Columbus, Ohio, Nov. 22, 1861; passed, Dec. 23, 1861. Owing to war duties, he did not receive the third degree until three years later, when, by request of Magnolia lodge, it was conferred on him by Columbus Lodge No. 30, Nov. 22, 1864. On Oct. 10, 1866, he affiliated with Garrettsville Lodge No. 246, and served as chaplain in 1868-73. Even before he was a member of the latter lodge, he visited them April 26, 1865, and was appointed on a committee to draft resolutions on the death of President Lincoln. His membership remained in Garrettsville lodge until he became a charter member of Pentalpha Lodge No. 23 of Washington, D.C., May 4, 1869. He was one of the petitioners for the charter. He was exalted in Columbia Chapter No. 1, R.A.M. of Washington, D.C., April 18, 1866. On May 18 of the same year, he was knighted in Columbia Commandery No. 2, K.T. of Washington. He was made an honorary member of Hanselmann Commandery No. 16, K.T. of Cincinnati, Ohio, July 19, 1881. He received 4-14° AASR (SJ), Jan. 2, 1872 from Albert Pike, q.v., in Washington. On April 10, 1871 he attended the banquet given in honor of the Earl de Grey and Ripon, q.v., then grand master of the Grand Lodge of England. The banquet was given by the Grand Lodge of the District of Columbia. In 1876 he allowed himself to be suspended in the chapter for nonpayment of dues, but was reinstated in 1877. At his inauguration as president, an honor guard of five platoons was appointed by his commandery of Knights Templar (Columbia No. 2), as an escort. On May 20, 1881, he reviewed five commanderies from Mass. and R.I. at the White House, and the following day gave a reception to DeMolay Commandery of Boston, and St. John's No. 1 of Providence, R.I., at the White House. When his body lay in state at the U.S. capitol from Sept. 21-23, Columbia Commandery No. 2 formed part of the guard of honor and escorted his remains from Washington to Cleveland, Ohio. At the funeral, Sept. 26, nearly all the officers of the Grand Commandery of Ohio, 14 commanderies of that state, and eight commanderies from adjacent jurisdictions were present and participated in the funeral cortege. Benjamin Dean, grand master of the Grand Encampment, U.S.A. also was present.

Giuseppe Garibaldi (1807-1882) Italian liberator and the "George Washington" of Italy. b. July 4, 1807 at Nice, the son of a sailor. He became associated with another Freemason and liberator—Mazzini, q.v., in 1833, joining his secret revolutionary society, Young Italy. An ill-timed plot sent him into exile in France, with a death penalty imposed upon him, in 1834. He fled to South America in 1836, where he first engaged in trade, and then joined the revolt in southern Brazil. Captured, he was tortured and held prisoner for six months. Back in Montevideo, Uruguay, he headed a small army of his own, and was an important factor in the signing of Uruguay's freedom. Hearing that Europe was on the threshold of revolution, Garibaldi sailed for Italy with a picked company of his legion, and landed at Nice in June, 1848. He served in the army of the Roman Republic, and with his red-shirted volunteers amazed Europe with his stubborn defense of Rome in a nine-week siege. When Rome was finally captured, he fled to the U.S. where he became a naturalized citizen. For a year he was employed as a candle-maker on Staten Island, N.Y., and for three years captained trading vessels on the Atlantic and Pacific. By this time his presence in Italy was not feared, and he returned to Genoa in May, 1854, and purchased the island of Caprera, where he built a home. On May 5, 1860 he left Genoa with 1,000 hand picked men known as "red-shirts" and captured Sicily, then, crossing to the mainland of Italy, expelled the anti-Mason, Francis II, q.v., thus defeating the so-called Kingdom of the Two Sicilies. He retired after Victor Emmanuel of Sardinia was named as king of Italy. Thus for the first time, Italy became partially united. Only Rome, in the hands of the French, and held by the Austrians, stood in the way of Garibaldi's dream of complete independence. Twice he organized expeditions (1862 and 1867) and marched against Rome, and was defeated by regular Italian troops. Twice, he was placed in prison. Venetia was won in 1866, and in 1870, France was compelled to withdraw her garrison from Rome to fight the Prussians. Although Garibaldi had nothing to do with the latter two actions, they fulfilled his life's aim. In 1874 he was elected deputy for Rome in the Italian parliament. He became a member of the Lodge Les

Amis de Patrie of Montevideo, Uruguay, about 1844, and when he came to the U.S., affiliated with Tompkins Lodge No. 471, Stapleton, N.Y. In 1860 he became grand master of the grand lodge at Palermo, and in 1867, called a convention to unite all the Italian bodies, but this project was not successful. He was an honorary member of the Egyptian Rite of Memphis. In 1863 he was elected grand commander of the Supreme Council, 33° AASR, in Italy. Garibaldi Lodge No. 542, New York City, was named in his honor. Warranted on June 11, 1864, while Garibaldi was grand master of Italy, he wrote, March 14, 1864, sending the lodge his blessing and good wishes. d. June 21, 1882. The Garibaldi monument erected in Rome had large bronze wreaths superimposed on it, acknowledging him as the grand master of Italy. In the Mussolini period, they were removed, but, in 1956, replaced. Said Garibaldi: "Whenever there is a human cause, we are certain to find Freemasonry, for it is the fundamental basis of all true liberal associations. Thank all of my brethren and tell them that I am always with them with all my heart, and that forever I will pride myself upon my Masonic connection."

Clement L. Garner Hydrographic and geodetic engineer with the U.S. Coast and Geodetic Survey since 1907. b. Sept. 22, 1884 at Bogue, N.C. Was chief of survey party from 1913-23, and commander of the ship Discoverer from 1923-27. He was chief of the service from 1937-45. From 1938-40 he was chairman of the Federal Board of Surveys and Maps. Member of Dawson Lodge No. 16, Washington, D.C.; received 32° AASR (SJ) in Albert Pike Consistory, Washington, May

23, 1922. National Sojourner and member of Heroes of '76.

Alexander C. Garrett (1832-1924) First Protestant Episcopal Bishop of Dallas, Texas. b. Nov. 4, 1832 in Ballymot, Ireland. Graduated from Trinity Coll., Dublin U. in 1855. Ordained deacon in 1856, and priest in 1857. Was curate at East Worldham, Hampshire, England, from 1856-59; and from 1859-69, served as a missionary in British Columbia. He then served as a rector in San Francisco, and dean at Omaha, Nebr. from 1870-74, when, in the latter year, he was elected missionary bishop of Northern Texas, and later of Dallas. Mason and 33° AASR. He was a member of Dallas Lodge No. 760, Dallas, Texas, and served as an officer of the same. d. Feb. 18, 1924.

Finis J. Garrett (1875-1956) U.S. Congressman to 59th through 70th Congresses, 1905-29 from Tenn. b. Aug. 26, 1875 near Ore Springs, Tenn. Graduate of Bethel Coll., McKenzie, Tenn. in 1897. Before completing his college courses, he was editor of country newspapers at Dresden and McKenzie. After teaching school at Como and Milan, Tenn., he studied law and began practice in Dresden in 1899. President Coolidge appointed him judge of the U.S. Court of Customs and Patent Appeals and he became presiding judge of the court under Franklin D. Roosevelt. Raised in Dresden Lodge No. 90, Dresden, Tenn. on June 3, 1905. d. May 25, 1956.

David Garrick (1717-1779) Regarded as the greatest actor in the history of the English stage. b. Feb. 19, 1717 in Hereford, England, of Huguenot descent, he met Samuel Johnson, q.v., while a student at Lichfield grammar school and became his first pupil at Edial. In 1737 he accompanied Johnson to London, where he made his reputation by acting in Richard III, Oct. 19, 1741. His success continued in other Shakespearean plays and he became co-manager of Drury Lane Theatre in 1747. Amassing a fortune, he retired to Hampton in 1776. He enjoyed the friendship of Dr. Johnson and his circle of distinguished persons of that day. A Mason, he is thought to have belonged to St. Paul's Lodge No. 194. This lodge has a snuff box which, the old minutes state, "replaces one presented to the lodge by Bro. David Garrick." d. Jan. 20, 1779.

James P. Garrick (1875-?) President of Morris College (S.C.) from 1939. b. Aug. 7, 1875 at Weston, S.C. Teacher, and Baptist minister, serving several S.C. pastorates. Mason. Deceased.

Stuart Garson Former Minister of Justice of Canada and Premier of Manitoba. b. Dec. 1, 1898 at St. Catharines, Ont. Law graduate of U. of Manitoba in 1918. He was elected to the Manitoba legislature five times, serving from 1927-48. In 1936 he was appointed treasurer of Manitoba, and in 1941, minister in charge of Manitoba Power Commission. He was sworn in as premier of Manitoba in 1943, and resigned in 1948. He became minister of Justice in St. Laurent's cabinet in that year. Mason.

Schuyler E. Garth (1898-1947) Methodist Bishop. b. Sept. 1, 1898 at Saffordville, Kans. Graduate of Baker U., Garrett Biblical Inst., and Ohio Wesleyan U. Ordained Methodist minister in 1920, serving churches in Kansas, Illinois, Florida, Pa., and Ohio. He was consecrated a bishop in 1944, and assigned to the Wisconsin area. He was later assigned, with his wife, to make a survey of the Chinese mission field. He was killed in an airplane crash near Hankow, China, Jan. 28, 1947, and buried in the International Cemetery near that city. Mason.

Will M. Garton (1875-1946) Rear Admiral, U.S. Navy. b. Oct. 31, 1875 at Des Moines, Ia. A physician, he received his M.D. from the U. of Iowa in 1896, and was commissioned an ensign in the Navy in 1898, advancing through grades to rear admiral in 1930, retiring in 1939. He served in the Spanish-American War, Mexican Border, World War I, and Haitian and Dominican campaigns. Mason, 32° AASR, and Shriner. d. June 7, 1946.

Frank B. Gary (1860-1922) U.S. Senator from South Carolina, 1908-09. b. March 9, 1860 at Cokesbury, S.C. He was admitted to the bar in 1881, and practiced at Abbeville, S.C. He was a member of the lower house of his state from 1890-1900, and again in 1906, serving as speaker five years. He was a member of the constitutional convention of 1895. Mason, and potentate of Oasis Shrine Temple in Charlotte, N.C. d. Dec. 7, 1922. His father, Franklin F. Gary, q.v., was grand high priest of the Grand Chapter of S.C. in 1880.

Franklin F. Gary (1829-1897) Surgeon in the Confederate army and grand high priest of the Grand Chapter, R.A.M. of S.C. in 1880. His son, Frank B. Gary, q.v., was U.S. Senator from S.C. b. Nov. 4, 1829 at Cokes-bury, S.C., he was a member of state legislature several terms. He served as president of the S.C. Medical Society and was chairman of the state board of health for many years. He was elected a delegate to the Medical Congress of the

World at Geneva, Switzerland, but died on Dec. 31, 1897 before it convened.

Hunter L. Gary (1884-1946) Telephone company executive. b. May 27, 1884 in Macon, Mo. He was a partner of Theodore Gary & Partners, N.Y. He was also president and director of the Nemo Corp.; Adaven Corp; National Service, Inc.; Nevada Trust Co.; Natser Corp. (all of Reno, Nev.) and the Gary-Loomis Co. and Walnuts Residence Co. of Kansas City, Mo. He was chairman of the board of Associated Telephone & Telegraph Co. of Wilmington, Del., and vice president of the Anglo-Canadian Telephone Co. (Montreal); Compania Dominican de Telefonos (Dominican Republic). His chairmanships included Theodore Gary & Co. (Kansas City); York Investment Co.; Allied Syndicate, Inc.; General and Telephone Investment, Inc. (of Wilmington). He was a director in many other companies. Member of Censer Lodge No. 172, Macon, Mo. Exalted in Macon Chapter No. 22 April 17, 1907; knighted in Emanuel Commandery No. 7, K.T., May 21, 1909, both of Macon, Mo. withdrew from chapter Jan. 21, 1915, and corn-mandery, March 22, 1915. d. Nov. 30, 1946.

J. Vaughn Gary U.S. Congressman, 79th to 81st Congresses (1945-51) from 3rd Va. dist. b. Feb. 25, 1892 at Richmond, Va. Graduate of U. of Richmond in 1912 and 1915. A lawyer, he first taught school. He served as counsel on the Virginia Tax Board, and later was secretary of the National Agricultural Advisory Commission in Washington. He served in the lower house of Virginia (1926-33). Raised June 14, 1918 in St. Johns Lodge No. 36, Richmond, Va. and was master of same in 1926. 18° AASR (SJ) .

Allard H. Gasque (1873-1938) U.S. Congressman, 68th to 75th Congresses (1923-39) from 6th S.C. dist. b. March 8, 1873 in Florence Co., S.C. Graduate of U. of South Carolina. He taught in the public schools and served as county superintendent of Florence Co. Died in office, June 17, 1938. Mason.

Percy L. Gassaway (1885-1937) U.S. Congressman to 74th Congress (1935-36) from 4th Okla. dist. b. Aug. 30, 1885 at Waco, Texas, moving into Indian Territory (Oklahoma) early in life. Admitted to bar in 1919, he was a district judge from 1926-34. Mason. d. May 15, 1937.

Cadet de Gassicourt A Parisian apothecary, who, in 1796, wrote a work against the Masonic fraternity. However, he later acknowledged that he had written something he knew nothing about, and in 1805, was initiated in the Lodge l'Abeille at Paris and became its master.

John Gaston Grand Duke of Tuscany. An anti-Mason, he inaugurated a persecution against the Freemasons in his dominions in 1737.

William Gaston (1820-1894) Governor of Massachusetts, 1875-76. b. Oct 3, 1820 in South Killingly, Conn. Graduate of Brown U. in 1840 and began law practice in Roxbury, Mass. in 1846. He served as mayor of Roxbury, and also mayor of Boston. He was a member of the Mass. legislature and also a state senator. He was raised in Washington Lodge, Roxbury, June 7, 1855. d. Jan. 19, 1894.

Thomas L. Gatch Rear Admiral, U.S. Navy and hero of WWII when, as captain of the battleship South. Dakota, his ship downed 32 Japanese planes in one battle in the Solomon. He is a member of Pacific Lodge No, 50, Salem, Oreg. His grandfather was grand master of the Grand Lodge of Oregon in 1873.

Floyd B. Gates Midget, 49 inches high and weighed 60 pounds. He was past master of James E. Dillon Lodge No. 466 at Mesick, Mich. and was frequently hailed as the "smallest past master in the world."

Horatio Gates (1728-1806) Major General of Continental Army in American Revolution. b. in Maldon. England. He entered the British army and joined Braddock's army in Virginia in 1755, and was wounded at Monongahela. In 1760 he was a brigade-major under Moncton at Fort Pitt, and was his aide in 1762 at the capture of Martinique. In 1772 at the invitation of Washington, he took up land in Virginia and settled down to develop it. When the Revolution broke out, he sided with the colonies and was appointed an adjutant-genera with the rank of brigadier, by congress in July, 1775. The next year hi was made major general and place in command of the northern army that had been commanded by Arnold Wooster, Montgomery, and Sullivan. He was at Fort Ticonderoga for the next two years and received credit for the success in repulsing Burgoyne's army from the north, although Schuyler and Benedict Arnold, q.v., were responsible for the defense. In fact he was later charged with cowardice at this action. At this juncture his friends formed the noted Conway Cabal to place him as commander-in-chief instead of Washington. It failed, and in 1780, he lost the disastrous battle of Camden, S.C. for which he was relieved of his command; he returned to his plantation. He asked official inquiry into his conduct at the battle of Camden, but it was 1782 before congress got around to acquitting him. He served loyally under Washington for the remainder of the war. His wealthy wife spent most of her fortune on the cause of the colonies, and nursed the patriot Thaddeus Kosciusko for six months in her home, after he was wounded. Gates was probably a member of a regimental lodge at Annapolis Royal, Nova Scotia, Canada. There was an active regimental lodge there between 1738 and 1755, with the Philipp's or 40th Foot. Practically all the officers of the regiment were members. On Dec. 18, 1778 the Grand Lodge of Massachusetts invited "the Hon'bl General Gates and such of his family who are Masons, be waited upon and invited to dine at the Feast (St. John's Day). The minutes of St. John's Day (Dec. 28) that followed show Gates was present. d. April 10, 1806.

John H. Gates (1865-1927) Judge, Supreme Court of South Dakota. b. Oct. 26, 1865 at Waterloo, Ia. Graduate of State U. of Iowa in 1888. Admitted to bar in 1890, and practiced at Sioux Falls, S.D. He was an associate judge of the supreme court of South Dakota from 1913, serving as presiding judge in 1917, 1920, and 1926. Member of Minnehaha Lodge No. 5, of Sioux Falls, S.D., receiving degrees, Sept. 17, Nov. 16 and Dec. 17, 1904; served in lodge line from 1905 until he was master in 1909. d. Nov. 8, 1927.

Ralph F. Gates Former Governor of Indiana. b. Feb. 24, 1893 at Columbia City, Ind. He is a member of Columbia City Lodge No. 189, receiving his degrees June 3, June 17, and July 1, 1935. Now practices law at Columbia City.

Richard J. Gatling (1818-1903) Inventor of the "Gatling Gun," the World's first practical repeating guns which changed the tactics of warfare throughout the world. b. Sept. 12, 1818 in Hertford Co., N.C. As a boy he assisted his father in perfecting a machine for sowing cottonseed, and another for thinning cotton plants. He subsequently invented and patented a machine for sowing rice, and when he moved to St. Louis in 1844, adapted it to drilling wheat. Although he studied medicine, he never practiced as a physician. He conceived the idea of his revolving battery gun in 1861. The first was made at Indianapolis in 1862. Twelve were later manufactured and used by General Butler on the James River, Va. In 1865, he further improved his invention, and it was adopted by the U.S. army. It was also made in Austria and England and used by several European governments. The first gun fired about 250 rounds per minute, but later improvements with a motor drive raised it to 3,000 rounds per minute. He was a member of Center Lodge No. 23, Indianapolis, Ind. d. Feb. 26, 1903.

Ga-wa-so-wa-neh (See under Dr. Arthur C. Parker.) Edward K. Gaylord Newspaper editor. b. March 5, 1873 at Muscotah, Kans. Began as clerk of district court at Colorado Springs, Colo. in 1897 and went with the Colorado Springs Telegraph in 1901. In 1902 he was business manager of the ,St. Joseph (Mo.) Gazette. Since 1903 he has been general manager of the Daily Oklahoman, Oklahoma City Times, and Oklahoma Farmer-Stockman. He has been president of the Oklahoma Publishing Co. since 1918. He has been a director of the Associated Press, and president of several firms, including radio and real estate companies. In 1918 he was a member of the commission to construct the Oklahoma state capitol. Mason.

Frank R. Gaynor (1852-1920) Judge, Supreme Court of Iowa, 1912-20. b. Sept 2, 1852 in Hamilton, Ont., Canada, and brought to U.S. at age of three. Graduate of State U. of Iowa in 1877, and practiced in Marshalltown and LeMars, Iowa. Mason. Died, 1920.

John H. Gear (1825-1900) U.S. Senator and Governor of Iowa. b. April 7, 1825 at Ithaca, N.Y. He moved to Galena, Ill. in 1836, and then to Fort Snelling, Iowa Territory in 1838. In 1843 he moved to Burlington, and was mayor of that city in 1863. He was in the state legislature six years, and speaker four years. He was governor of Iowa from 1878-82, and a member of the U.S. congress from 1887-91, and again from 1893-95. From 1892-93 he was assistant secretary of the U.S. treasury. Elected as U.S. Senator in 1894, he served until his death in 1900. Member of Des Moines Lodge No. 1, Burlington, Iowa.

John W. Geary (1819-1873) Governor of two states and Major General in the Civil War. b. Dec. 30, 1819 near Mount Pleasant, Pa. Admitted to bar, but never practiced. Employed as a civil engineer in Ky., he was named assistant superintendent of the Alleghany Portage railroad. He commanded a regiment in the Mexican War of 1846 as a lieutenant colonel, and was wounded at Chapultepec. He was made the first commander of the city of Mexico. In 1849 he was appointed the first postmaster of San Francisco. In 1850

he became the first mayor of the city and took a leading part in the formation of the new constitution for Calif. In 1852 he retired to his farm in Westmoreland Co., Pa., and remained in private life until 1856, when he was appointed territorial governor of Kansas, serving one year. At the beginning of the Civil War he raised the 28th Pa. volunteers. In 1862 he was commissioned brigadier general, and promoted to major general in 1865. He fought in the battles of Bolivar Heights, Cedar Mountain, Chancellorsville, Gettysburg, and Lookout Mountain. His son, Edward, was killed in the last mentioned battle. After the war, he was elected governor of Pennsylvania (1866) and served until two weeks before his death. He received the three degrees of Masonry "at sight" on Jan. 4, 1847 in St. John's Lodge No. 219, Pittsburgh, Pa., while on the way to Mexico with his troops. He never became a member of this lodge, but on June 11, 1855 was admitted a member to Philanthropy Lodge No. 225, Greensburg, Pa. He was a charter member of California Lodge No. 13 (now No. 1) of San Francisco, and its first secretary. On returning to Pennsylvania in 1851 he severed his connection with the California lodge. It is thought he affiliated with Concordia Lodge No. 67 of Philadelphia, on his return, as he is listed as a member in May, 1860. He received the chapter degrees in Zerubbabel Chapter No. 162, R.A.M., of Pittsburgh on July 14, 1848, as a sojourner, and the commandery orders in Pittsburgh Commandery No. 1 on Oct. 2, 1848—but resigned two days later! d. Feb. 8, 1873.

John Geddes (1773-1828) Governor of South Carolina, 1818-20. b. in Charleston, S.C. He was the son of a merchant. He studied law and was admitted to the bar in 1797, serving several terms in the state legislature. He was made brigadier general of militia. A past master of St. John's Lodge No. 13, Charleston, he was grand master of the Grand Lodge of South Carolina in 1826. d. March 5, 1828.

Arthur H. Geissler (1877-1945) U.S. Minister to Guatemala, 1922-29, and Siam from 1929. b. Oct. 30, 1877. Admitted to bar in 1896. He was an instructor in modern languages, president of a bank, and also of an insurance company in Oklahoma City, Okla. In 1918 he was president of the national association of Republican state chairmen. Mason and Shriner. d. Feb. 18, 1945.

Walter Geist (1894-1951) President of Allis-Chalmers Manufacturing Co. from 1942. b. Dec. 1, 1894 at Milwaukee, Wis. Joined Allis-Chalmers in 1909 and advanced from errand boy to draftsman, designer, engineer, manager, general sales manager, vice president, and president. He was a director of many large corporations. Mason and member of St. Wilfred Conclave, Red Cross of Constantine. He received his lodge degrees in Independence Lodge No. 80 of Milwaukee, March 6, May 20 and Sept. 23, 1921. 32° AASR (NJ) in Valley of Milwaukee. d. Jan. 29, 1951.

George I King of Greece (1845-1913) Full name was Christian William Ferdinand Adolphus George. He was king from 1863 to 1913. The second son of Christian IX, q.v., king of Denmark, and served in the Danish navy. After the deposition of Otto I, he was elected king of the Hellenes (Greece), in 1863, by the Greek national assembly. He married Grand Duchess Olga, niece of the czar of Russia. During his reign the greater part of Thessaly and part of Epirus were incorporated into Greece. He was involved in the First Balkan War of 1912-13, and was assassinated at Salonika. His son, Constantine I, as well as his grandson, George II, q.v., were Freemasons. George I was initiated in Denmark before becoming king of Greece.

George II King of Greece (1890-1947) He was the eldest son of Constantine I, a Freemason, and grandson of George I, q.v. b. July 20, 1890 at Tatoi, Greece. He was king from 1922-23, when his father abdicated in his favor, and again from 1935-47. He ruled with little actual authority, and was deposed by the military junta in 1923. He was recalled to the throne by a plebiscite in 1935, but he was overshadowed by Metaxas, who became dictator in 1936, and in 1941 George fled to England for the second time to escape the Nazis. He was again restored to the throne by a plebiscite in 1946. He was initiated, Sept. 16, 1930, during his first 12-year exile in England, in Wallwood Lodge No. 5143 of London. The ceremony took place in the Grecian Temple, Great Eastern Hotel, London. On Feb. 1, 1933, he was installed as master of this lodge and served with zeal. He was a past grand warden of the Grand Lodge of England at the time of his death. He was also a 33° AASR, being created in Sept. 1943.

George III (1738-1820) King of Great Britain and Ireland, 1760-1820. Although he was not a Freemason, the majority of the male members of the immediate royal family were. It is thought that his early accession to the throne (at age of 22) prevented him from joining the Craft. A grandson of King George II, his father, Frederick, Prince of Wales, was initiated in 1737. His younger brother, Prince William Frederick of Gloucester, was initiated in Britannic Lodge in 1795. Six of his seven sons as well as his nephew and son-in-law were Masons. His six Masonic sons were: George, Prince of Wales (later George IV and grand master) initiated in 1787, in a special lodge at the Star and Garter, Pall Mall; Prince William Henry, later King William IV, in Prince George Lodge No. 86 at Plymouth; the Duke of York, in Britannic Lodge No. 29, London, in 1787; Prince Edward, Duke of Kent (later grand master of the "Antients" and father of Queen Victoria) in Lodge Union des Coeurs, Geneva; Prince Ernest, later Duke of Cumberland and King of Hanover, at the house of the Earl of Moira in 1796; and Prince Augustus William, Duke of Sussex, and grand master of the United Grand Lodge, at the Royal York Lodge of Friendship in Berlin in 1798. The only non-Mason son was Adolphus, Duke of Cambridge.

George IV King of England (1762-1830) Full name was George Augustus Frederick, of the house of Hanover. He was the son of George III. His first marriage to Mrs. Fitzherbert in 1785 was declared illegal, and he deserted her in 1794. In 1795 he married his cousin, Caroline of Brunswick, but when crowned king in 1820, he refused to allow Queen Caroline to be present at his coronation. In 1800 he attempted to get Mrs. Fitzherbert to return, but she refused until she gained assurance of papal approval of marriage. He gained the ill will of his father for his extravagances and dissolute habits. He assumed the throne when his father became permanently deranged, first, as regent in 1811, and as king in 1820. During his reign the Catholic

Emancipation Act was passed. He was initiated in a special lodge, Feb. 6, 1787, meeting at the Star and Garter at London, by his uncle, the duke of Cumberland, then grand master. He succeeded his uncle in office in 1790. He joined Prince of Wales Lodge No. 259, London, April 16, 1787, and was master of the lodge from that date until 1820. He served as grand master of the Grand Lodge of England for 23 years, and in 1805 was grand master of the Grand Lodge of Scotland. When he became king, the Duke of Sussex was elected grand master, and the king took the title of grand patron. The Duke of Sussex, his younger brother, was able to bring about a union of the two English grand lodges in 1813.

George V King of England (1865-1936) Full name, George Frederick Ernest Albert of house of Saxe-Coburg-Gotha, which in 1917 changed its name to the house of Windsor. His father was Edward VII, q.v., whom he succeeded on the throne at the latter's death, May 6, 1910, and ruled until his own death in 1936. Although not a Freemason, he became grand patron of three Masonic charities of the Grand Lodge of England when he ascended the throne.

George V Last King of Hanover (1819-1878) Full name was George Frederick Alexander Karl Ernest August, son of Ernest Augustus, q.v., duke of Cumberland. He ruled Hanover from 1851-66. He refused to yield to Prussia's demands, and sided with Austria in the Seven Week's War of 1866, being forced to abdicate as a result of this conflict. In 1852 he was proclaimed protector of Freemasonry, and when he was initiated, Jan. 14, 1857 in Lodge Zum schwarzen Bar (Black Bear), the initiation ceremonies were not abbreviated at his own request. A lodge room, including ante-room and preparation chambers were set up in the royal palace and 300 brethren assembled to assist in his initiation. He was initiated at 7:15, retired, returned, and passed at 8:00; retired again, and introduced at 8:15 for the Master Mason degree. At the conclusion of the initiation he said: "I am now one of you—received and accepted as a member of your noble fraternity. I may, therefore, now say, without hesitation, that I have always longed and designed to become a worthy member of your noble institution. I was not satisfied to be merely the protector of Freemasonry; I felt that I ought to be in it and of it—that I ought to have the privilege to be called by you a brother. You have gratified my wish, to your utmost ability, by opening wide for me the doors of the lodges of my country, and by having honored me with membership in each. For those favors bestowed upon me, accept my sincere gratitude, and with it the assurance that I will endeavor to so discharge my duty that you shall find in me all you have a right to expect. In order that I may worthily fulfill this promise, I pray that the Grand Architect may grant me the power to carry out, in practice, what is now only a sincere desire, and that I thus may prove myself a true and faithful brother to you and all good Masons." This he did, for he became grand master of the Grand Lodge of Hanover, and although blind, regularly attended meetings of the lodges.

George VI King of England (1895-1952) Full name was Albert Frederick Arthur George of the house of Windsor (formerly Saxe-Coburg-Gotha). A son of George V, q.v., he reigned from the time his brother, Edward VIII, q.v., abdicated in 1936,

until his death in 1952. He studied in Trinity College at Cambridge and served in WWI. He was created duke of York in 1920. He was initiated in Naval Lodge No. 2612 in Dec., 1919, the ceremony being conducted by Lord Ampthill. In 1922 he was appointed senior grand warden of the Grand Lodge of England, and in 1924 was made provincial grand master for Middlesex. He was invested and installed by his great uncle, H.R.H. the Duke of Connaught, q.v. He held the latter position until he ascended the throne in 1938. As king, he accepted the rank of past grand master of the Grand Lodge of England, and was ceremonially installed at the Albert Hall in London before an audience of Masons from all parts of the world. In 1936 he accepted and was installed grand master mason of Scotland, and affiliated with the lodge of Glamis, Scotland, where his father-in-law, the Earl of Strathmore, was a past master. He created the precedent of the English sovereign's active participation in Masonic ceremonies, and personally conducted the installation of three grand masters—the Duke of Kent at Olympia in 1939; the Earl of Harewood in Freemason's Hall in 1943; and the Duke of Devonshire in Albert Hall in 1948. Only his last illness prevented his installing the Earl of Scarbrough in 1951. Toward the end of his reign, he stated that he had always regarded Masonry as one of the strongest influences of his life. He was a Royal Arch Mason and was a first principal. He was a past grand master of the Mark Lodge and former ruler of the Mark province of Middlesex (1931-37). He held the rank of past grand master, and of knight commander of the Temple, was a 33°, and grand inspector general in the Ancient and Accepted Rite of Rose Croix. Said he of Masonry: "The world today does require spiritual and moral regeneration. I have no doubt, after many years as a member of our Order, that Freemasonry can play a most important part in this vital need."

George August (1748-?) Prince of Mecklemburg-Strelitz. Brother of Duke Karl Ludwig Friedrich and Prince Ernst Gottlob Albert. Initiated in Naples Lodge Vittoria in 1768, and in 1773 affiliated with the Lodge Irene zw den drei Sternen in Rostock.

George Frederic Karl Duke of Saxony-Meiningen. Brother of Karl Frederick III. Initiated in 1777.

Harold L. George Lieutenant General, U.S. Air Force. b. July 19, 1893 at Somerville, Mass. Began as secretary to U.S. comptroller of currency in 1917. Commissioned lieutenant in U.S. Air Force in 1917, and advanced through grades to lieutenant general in 1944. Commanded the 2nd Bombardment Group in 1939; director of tactics and strategy, Air Corps Tactical School from 1932-35; assistant chief of staff for war plants, 1941; commanding general of Air Transport Command, AAF, 1942-46. President of Peruvian Airways, Lima, Peru, 1947-48. Since 1948 he has been vice president of Hughes Tool Co. and general manager of Hughes Aircraft Co. Raised in Aberdeen Lodge No. 187, Aberdeen, Md. about 1922. Received chapter, council, and commandery at Aberdeen about 1923.

George Karl Prince of HessiaDarmstadt. b. 1754. In 1778, he introduced the system of strict observance in Holland.

George Ludwig Prince of Holstein Gottorp (1710-1763) Became a field marshal in the Russian army. He was initiated in Dresden in

1741, and became a member of the Lodge Absalon zu den drei Nesseln in Hamburg in 1742. The second lodge Sankt Georg in Hamburg was named in his honor.

H.R.H. Prince George Duke of Kent (1902-1942) English Royal Prince. Full name was George Edward Alexander Edmund. He was the son of George V, q.v., and brother of George VI, q.v. He was initiated at an emergency meeting of Navy Lodge No. 2612, held in the Cafe Royal, London, on April 12, 1928. He was proposed for membership by his brother, H.R.H. the Prince of Wales, and seconded by his brother, H.R.H. the Duke of York, the latter being permanent master of the lodge at the time. He received his third degree in the same lodge, June 28, 1928. On Dec. 4, 1931, he was installed as master of the lodge, and, on April 26, 1933, he was invested as senior grand wardenof the Grand Lodge of England. On July 19, 1934, he was installed provincial grand master for Wiltshire by Lord Arnpthill, q.v. He was installed first grand principal of the Supreme Grand Chapter, Royal Arch of England, May 3, 1939, by the Earl' of Harewood, and installed grand master of the Mark Grand Lodge, June 6, 1939, by the Earl of Stradbroke. On July 19, 1939 he was formally installed grand master of the Grand Lodge of England by his brother, King George VI. He was killed, August 25, 1942, in an airplane accident. He was grand master only three years, which is the shortest tenure for this office on record—the longest being the Duke of Connaught, for 38 years, q.v.

Sir Robert A. George British Air Vice Marshal and Governor of South Australia. b. 1897 at Invergordon, Ross-Shire. Served in WWI with the Seaforth and Gordon Highlanders, and later with the Royal Flying Corps. From 1919-24 he was with the R.A.F. on the Northwest frontier of India, and from 1924-31 was with the R.A.F. College at Cranwell. He was senior air staff officer with the Far East Command; air attaché to Turkey and Greece; with the R.A.F. in the Middle East; air officer commanding Iraq and Persia in 1944-45; and from 1945-51 was head of the R.A.F. delegation in Paris, air attaché of the British embassy, and with NATO and SHAPE. Appointed governor of South Australia in 1952. Initiated in Hope Lodge No. 337 (S.C.), March 8, 1920, and raised in Hardinge Lodge No. 3754 (E.C.), a service lodge at Risalpur, India. Returning to England he affiliated with Lodge Daedalus, a R.A.F. Lodge which met in the Air Force College at Cranwell. He is still a member of that lodge, but affiliated with Lodge St. Alban No. 38 in South Australia, and served as warden and master. In 1956 he was elected grand master of the Grand Lodge of South Australia, being the fourth governor to be so honored.

Walter F. George (1878-1957) U.S. Senator from Georgia for 34 years, 1922-57. b. Jan. 29, 1878 at Preston, Ga. Began law practice in Vienna, Ga. in 1901. He served his state as superior judge, judge of the court of appeals, and justice of supreme court of Georgia. In 1957 he was serving as Eisenhower's personal representative to the North Atlantic Treaty organization. As a foreign policy and fiscal leader, he was admired by both Democrats and Republicans. Although a Democrat, he was strongly bi-partisan when it came to foreign relations policy and was the senior member of that committee in the Senate. He was a member of Vienna Lodge No. 324, Vienna, Ga.,

and belonged to both the York and Scottish Rites. d. Aug. 4, 1957.

Joseph C. Gephart Editor. b. Sept. 7, 1902 at Bedford, Pa. Attended Columbia U. and was sports correspondent for the *New York Times* from 1921-25, and from 1927-28 a copyreader on that paper. He served as editor of the *McKeesporter* (Pa.) and of the Calumet Index (Ill.). From 1928-35 he was again with the *New York Times* as sports editor, and from 1936-43 as news picture editor. He has been editor of the *New York Times Index* since 1943, and editor of the *New York Handbook and Guide* from 1932-42. Member of Aliquippa Lodge No. 375, McKeesport, Pa., receiving degrees in 1925.

Alexander A. Gerebzov Russian Major General and courtier. He was raised in a Paris lodge and opened the lodge Les Amis Reunis at Petersburg, Russia, June 10, 1802. His own lodge was impregnated with French ideas, and represented the "liberal" branch of Russian Freemasonry, believing in abolishing religion, national and social differences, arid forming a true brotherhood of man. Among its famous members were the Grand Duke Konstantin, q.v.; Alexander, Duke of Wurtemburg, q.v.; Count Stanislaus Kosta-Potocky, q.v.; and Count Alexander Ostermann-Tolstoy, q.v. From 1815-17 he was grand master of the provincial grand lodge of Russia, following the dissolution of the Directorial Lodge Vladimir zur Ordnung. He was also grand prefect of Chapter Phoenix, which was in reality a ruling body for the Swedish rite union of lodges in Russia at that time.

Charles L. Gerlach (1895-1947) U.S. Congressman, 76th to 78th Congresses (1939-45) from 9th

Pa. dist. b. Sept. 14, 1895 at Bethle-
hem, Pa. He was treasurer of the
Allentown Supply Co. Member of
Bethlehem Lodge No. 283, Bethle-
hem, Pa., receiving degrees, April 6,
May 9 and June 12, 1914; 32° AASR
(NJ); Shriner. d. May, 1947.

Elbridge Gerry (1744-1814)
Signer of Declaration of Independence, Vice President of the United
States, 1813-14, and Governor of
Massachusetts, 1810-11. b. July 17,
1744 in Marblehead, Mass. He was a
member of the Mass. provincial congress from 1774-75, and of the Continental Congress from 1776-81 and
1782-85. He signed the Declaration
of Independence, and also the Articles of Confederation, but as a delegate to the Constitutional Convention
of 1787, he opposed the constitution
as drafted. From 1789-93 he was a
U.S. congressman. Gerry was a
member of the famous XYZ mission
to France in 1797-98, but was at odds
with the other two negotiators, and
attempted to obtain a separate treaty
from Talleyrand. For this he was recalled. It was through his efforts of
redistricting Massachusetts to give
Republicans continued control that
the term "gerrymander" was coined.
Although no definite proof is available, it is generally understood by his
friends and surviving family that he
was a member of Philanthropic Lodge
of Marblehead, Mass. The records of
this lodge are missing from the period
1760-78 when he logically would
have been initiated. d. Nov. 23, 1814.

Clark H. Getts Lecture manager. b. Aug. 5, 1893 at Whitehall,
Wis. Graduate of U. of Wisconsin in
1914, Columbia U. in 1916. In college
days he managed Chautauqua tours
for Wm. Howard Taft, Frederick
Warde and others. Going to the Orient, he was a newspaper representative in China from 1920-26, returning
to the U.S. where he lectured on the
Orient until 1932. With National
Broadcasting Co.' from 1930-32,
booking tours for Paderewski, Rach-
maninoff, Kreisler, and others, until
he established himself as Clark H.
Getts, Inc., lecture bureau, in 1937.
Has done radio shows and managed
the Johnson expedition to Africa,
making the Stanley and Livingston
motion picture for 20th Century Fox.
He has arranged national tours for
hundreds of personalities including
Dale Carnegie, Eleanor Roosevelt,
Pearl Buck, Harold Stassen, Alexander Woollcott, Amelia Earhart, etc.
Mason.

Peter Getz Goldsmith and
engraver of Lancaster, Pa. who is
said to have engraved the George
Washington Masonic medal of 1797.
He was master of Lodge No. 43 at
Lancaster, Pa.

Henry S. Geyer (1790-1859)
U.S. Senator from Missouri, 1851-57;
pioneer jurist. b. Dec. 9, 1790 in Fred-
ericktown, Md. He began the practice
of law in that city in 1811. In 1813 he
was commissioned a first lieutenant
in the 38th Infantry, and later regimental paymaster, serving until June,
1815. He then moved to St. Louis,
Mo., which was a frontier village at
that time. Here he married the daughter of Rufus Easton, q.v., first postmaster of St. Louis. He was a member of the territorial legislature in
1818, and a captain of the first militia
company in the territory. He was a
delegate to the state constitutional
convention of 1820, and was chosen
for the legislature five times, serving
as speaker of the first three general
assemblies of the state. In 1825 he
was one of the revisers of the statutes, and contributed largely to the
adoption of a code, which was at that

time superior to that of any other western state. He declined the post of secretary of war offered him by Fillmore in 1850, and was then elected U.S. senator over Thomas H. Benton, q.v., on the 40th ballot, by a majority of five votes. While in Washington, he was a counsel in the Dred Scott case. He also compiled a digest of the laws of the Missouri Territory in 1817. Geyer was a member of Missouri Lodge No. 12 of St. Louis, which was established under the Grand Lodge of Tennessee in 1815. Geyer was a member at least by 1820, as his name is found in the annual report for that year. In 1816 he had a duel with George H. Kennerly, wounded his opponent in the knee, but later they became fast friends.

Lee E. Geyer (1888-1941) U.S. Congressman to 76th Congress (1939-41) from 17th Calif. dist. b. Sept. 9, 1888 at Wetmore, Kans. He was a high school teacher in Kans. and Calif. Mason. d. Oct. 11, 1941.

Felice di Giardini (1716-1796) Italian violinist and composer of violin pieces, chamber music, and several operas. An early member of the Lodge of the Nine Muses No. 325 in London, England.

Edward Gibbon (1737-1794) English historian who is famous for his *History of the Decline and Fall of the Roman Empire*. b. April 27, 1737 at Putney, England. He spent 16 years in compiling his monumental work, the first volume being published in 1776, and the last in 1788. He was a member of the British parliament from 1774-80, and 1781-83. In his early days he was a Roman Catholic. He became a member of Friendship Lodge No. 6, London, England in March 1775. His close friend and fellow member of parliament, Row-

land Holt, was treasurer of the lodge from 1767 to 1783, and it was Holt and Thomas Dunckerley, q.v., who proposed Gibbon's name for the Royal Arch degree. In the circle in which Gibbon and Holt moved were such as Pope, Swift, Arbuthnot, Samuel Johnson, Boswell, Garrick, Gay, Darner, Gascoine. The majority of them were Masons, and the last two were members of Friendship lodge. The Duke of Buccleuch, q.v., a member of this lodge, became the first patron of Sir Walter Scott, q.v. Friendship lodge was constituted in 1721, only four years after the erection of the first grand lodge. In 1767 it moved from the Haymarket-Picadilly Pall Mall area to the Thatched House Tavern on Pall Mall, which was frequented by members of parliament. d. Jan. 16, 1794.

Herbert A. Gibbons (1880-1934) American author. b. April 9, 1880 at Annapolis, Md. Graduate of Princeton and U. of Pa. Ordained Presbyterian minister in 1908; from 1908-18 was correspondent for the New York Herald in Turkey, Egypt, the Balkans, and France. He also represented Century and Harper's magazines in Europe. Served in A.E.F. in WWI. Served as a history professor in both European and American universities. He managed the trans-Atlantic flight of Byrd, q.v. in 1927. Among his many books are The Foundation of the Ottoman Empire; France and Ourselves; Introduction to World Politics; Life of John Wanamaker; Europe of Today; Contemporary World History. Raised in Princeton Lodge No. 38, Princeton, N.J., Dec. 19, 1921, and dimitted Dec. 11, 1933. d. Aug. 7, 1934.

George S. Gibbs (1875-1947) Major General, U.S. Army and industrialist. b. Dec. 14, 1875 at

Harlan, Iowa. Graduate of State U. of Iowa in 1897. Entered military service as a private with the 51st Iowa Infantry in 1898, advancing to brigadier general in WWI, and promoted to major general in 1928, retiring from active service in 1931. He served in the Philippines in the Spanish-American War; the Philippine Insurrection; built north central section of the Alaska telegraph system in 1901-03. He was chief signal officer in Army of Cuban Pacification. In WWI he was assistant chief signal officer of the A.E.F. in France from 1917-18, followed by two years on the general staff. In 1924 he was in charge of laying the new Alaska cable. From 1928 to retirement in 1931 he was chief signal officer of the U.S. Army. At his retirement he became vice president of International Telephone and Telegraph Corp. and president of Postal Telegraph-Cable Co. Mason and Knight Templar. d. Jan. 9, 1947.

Willis B. Gibbs (1889-1940) U.S. Congressman, 76th Congress (1939-41) from 8th Ga. dist. b. April 15, 1889 at Dupont, Ga. A lawyer practicing in Jessup, Ga. Member of Jessup Lodge No. 112, Jessup, Ga., raised March 6, 1916. He was master of same in 1921, 1922, 1923 and 1937. d. Aug. 7, 1940.

Colin Wm. G. Gibson Canadian cabinet member. b. Feb. 16, 1891 at Hamilton, Ont. He was educated in the Royal Military College at Kingston. Called to the Ontario bar in 1915, and practiced at Hamilton, Ont., since 1919. Created Kings Counsel, and elected to house of Commons in 1940, serving until 1945. He was named minister of national revenue in 1940, and minister of national defense for air in 1945. In 1946 he was secretary of state, and minister of mines and resources in 1949.

Since 1950 he has been an appellate judge of the supreme court of Ontario. Served in WWI rising from captain to colonel. Was international president of Alpha Delta Phi fraternity in 1948. Mason and 32° AASR.

Edward R. "Hoot" Gibson Movie cowboy of the silent film era. He was a member of Truth Lodge No. 628 of Los Angeles, Calif.

Ernest Willard Gibson (1871-1940) U.S. Senator from Vermont. b. Dec. 29, 1871, at Londonderry, Vt., he was a graduate of Norwich U. in 1894 and 1896. He practiced law at Brattleboro from 1899. He served terms in both legislative bodies of Vermont, and was U.S. congressman to 68th to 73rd Congresses (1923-35) from 2nd Vt. dist. He was appointed to the U.S. senate in 1933 to fill an unexpired term, and reelected twice to the office. When he died, June 20, 1940, his son, Ernest William, q.v., was appointed to take his senate seat. Raised in Olive Branch Lodge No. 64 of Chester, Vt., Nov. 14, 1895, and later affiliated (Aug. 20, 1900) with Brattleboro Lodge No. 102 at Brattleboro. He was exalted in Fort Dummer Chapter No. 12, R.A.M.; admitted to Connecticut Valley Council No. 16, R. & S.M. in 1921; and knighted in Beauseant Commandery No. 7, March 27, 1902. He remained a member of the above Brattleboro bodies until his death.

Ernest William Gibson U.S. Senator and Governor of Vermont. b. March 6, 1901 at Brattleboro, Vt. Graduate of Norwich U. in 1923. He served as a teacher in a private military academy, and later as a mathematician with Geodetic Survey; was admitted to Vermont bar in 1926, practicing law at Brattleboro since 1927. He served as secretary of the

Vermont state senate from 1933-40, resigning in the latter year to be appointed U.S. senator on the death of his father, who had filled the office since 1933. He was elected governor of Vermont in 1947, reelected in 1948, but resigned in 1950 to accept appointment as Federal district judge. Served overseas in WWII as an army captain. He became a member of Columbian Lodge No. 36 of Brattleboro, Vt., Jan. 22, 1929. His father, Ernest Willard, q.v., was a member of Brattleboro Lodge No. 102, of the same city. He is a 32° AASR (NJ) in the Valley of Montpelier, and joined the Mt. Sinai Shrine Temple at Montpelier on May 13, 1949.

Herbert D. Gibson Brigadier General, U.S. Army. b. Oct. 27, 1891 at Schenectady, N.Y. Commissioned a second lieutenant in 1917, and advanced through grades to brigadier general in 1942. He served with the A.E.F. in 1917-19 in WWI, and, between that time and WWII, was a military professor in several colleges and universities, including Cornell. He commanded the Canton Island Army Task Force in 1942, and was first army commander of the Marshall Islands in 1944. From 1944-46 he was organizer and commander of the replacement training command of the Air Force for the Pacific Ocean areas. Raised in DeWitt Clinton Lodge No. 15, Northfield, Vt. in 1916, and member of King Solomon Chapter No. 7, R.A.M., Montpelier, Vt. Retired on disability from combat wounds in 1946.

J. Bannister Gibson (1780-1853) Chief Justice, Supreme Court of Pennsylvania, 1827-53. b. Nov. 8, 1780 at Carlisle, Pa. He graduated at Dickinson Coll. in 1800, and was admitted to Pa. bar in 1803, practicing in Carlisle and Beaver counties. He

served in the state legislature in 1813, and was named to the supreme court bench in 1816, becoming chief justice in 1827. He was raised Dec. 30, 1811 in Lodge No. 43, Lancaster, Pa. and in March, 1814 affiliated with Lodge. No. 61 at Wilkes-Barre. He served as inn John Gibson master of the latter from 1815-16, and Dec. 1, 1823, was elected grand master of the Grand Lodge of Pennsylvania. d. May 3, 1853.

John Gibson (1740-1822) Secretary of Indiana Territory and acting Governor of Indiana Territory. b. May 23, 1740 in Lancaster, Pa. He joined an expedition against the Indians in 1757. He then settled as a trader at Fort Pitt, where he was taken prisoner, but rescued from the stake by a squaw who adopted him. He married the sister of Logan, an Indian chief, and became familiar with the Indian language and customs. He again settled at Fort Pitt, and in 1774 was conspicuous in Lord Dunmore's expedition against the Shawnee towns. In the treaty that followed the Battle of Point Pleasant, he negotiated between Logan and Lord Dunmore and helped free many Indian captives. At the beginning of the Revolution, he commanded a regiment, served in New York, and in the Jersey retreat; he commanded the western military department from 1781 until peace was established. In 1788 he was a member of the Pennsylvania convention, and subsequently associate judge of court of common pleas of Alleghany Co., and major general of militia. Jefferson appointed him secretary of the Indiana territory in 1801, and he was acting governor of the territory from 1811-13. He received his first and second degrees in Lancaster, Pa., and his third degree in Vincennes Lodge, Indiana, March 14, 1809. He is said to have been the first candidate to receive the Master's degree in Indiana territory. d. April 10, 1822.

Sir John Morison Gibson (1842-1929) Canadian Major General in WWI; first president of Canadian Red Cross; Governor of Province of Ontario for six years. b. in Peel Co., Ontario in 1842. He was graduated from U. of Toronto in 1863 and became a barrister in 1869. He was a member of the 13th Royal Regiment (Canada) and rose from private to major general. He was elected to the provincial legislature of Ontario, serving from 1879-95. Was initiated Nov. 19, 1867 in Strict Observance Lodge No. 27, Hamilton, Ontario, and was grand master of the Grand Lodge of Ontario. He was sovereign grand commander of the Scottish Rite in Canada, 1904-13 and 1922-23. d. June 3, 1929.

John S. Gibson U.S. Congressman, 77th to 79th Congresses (1941-47) from 8th Ga. dist. b. Jan. 3, 1893 at Folkston, Ga. Began as a railroad laborer in 1917, and was admitted to bar in 1923, practicing at Douglas, Ga. Received his degrees in Douglas Lodge No. 386, Douglas, Ga., Nov. 9, Nov. 19, and Dec. 3, 1920.

Robert M. Gibson (1869-1949) U.S. District Judge, Western District of Pennsylvania from 1922. b. Aug. 20, 1869 at Duncansville, Pa. Graduate of Washington and Jefferson Coll. in 1889. Received degrees in Allegheny Lodge No. 23, Pittsburgh, Pa., June 24, Sept. 8, and Nov. 11, 1918, resigning Dec. 8, 1924 to become charter member and master of John Marshall Lodge No. 734, Pittsburgh, Dec. 18, 1924. d. Dec. 19, 1949.

Thomas Gibson (1750-1814) Revolutionary soldier and first state auditor of Ohio. b. in Virginia. He served in the Revolution, and became the auditor of the Northwest Territory. When Ohio became a state, he was its first auditor. He was an early member of Nova Caesarea Lodge No. 10, Cincinnati, Ohio, and the first master of Scioto Lodge No. 2, Chillicothe, Ohio, from 1805-07. He was exalted in Cincinnati Chapter No. 2, R.A.M., Dec. 11, 1799. d. May 3, 1814.

Joshua R. Giddings (1795-1864) U.S. Congressman from Ohio from 1838 to 1858. U.S. Consul General in Canada from 1858 until death in 1864. b. Oct. 6, 1795 in Athens, Pa. His parents moved first to New York, and in 1806 to Ashtabula Co., Ohio. He served in the War of 1812. After the war he became a teacher, studied law, and was admitted to the bar in 1820. He was elected to the Ohio legislature in 1826, but refused re-election. In the U.S. congress, he was a champion of abolition, fighting the slavery movement for 20 years. He was raised in Jerusalem Lodge No. 19, Hartford, Ohio in 1819, and later affiliated with Tuscan Lodge No. 342 at Jefferson, Ohio. At one time he was grand junior warden of the Grand Lodge of Ohio. d. May 27, 1864 in Montreal, Canada.

Charles L. Gifford (1871-1947) U.S. Congressman to 67th to 72nd Congresses from 15th Mass. dist. (1923-47) . b. March 15, 1871 at Cotuit, Mass. He was in the real estate business from 1900, and served on the Mass. general court and in state senate. Raised in De Witt Clinton Lodge, Sandwich, Mass. on Oct. 2, 1900. d. Aug. 23, 1947.

Emilio Portes Gil President of Mexico, 1928-30. b. in 1891 in Victoria City, Tamaulipas, Mexico. A lawyer, he served several years in a legal capacity with the war and navy as well as military justice departments. He was a congressional deputy to the 27th, 29th and 30th legislatures. He was provisional governor of Tamaulipas in 1917 and constitutional governor, 1925-29. From 1930 he was secretary of the government and afterwards (until 1959) was president of the executive committee of the National Revolutionary Party. He has served his government as minister to the French government and first representative of Mexico at the League of Nations in Geneva. He also has been Mexican ambassador to the Dominican Republic and India. Since 1959 he has been president of the national commission on insurance. The recipient of several honorary doctorates and decorations from foreign governments, he is the author of 15 books on both legal subjects and in the field of the humanities. While he was president he put down a revolution of fanatics who had been encouraged by the Catholic hierarchy. He occupied a number of Masonic offices, and from 1933-34 was grand master of the Grand Lodge, Valley of Mexico.

Lucio Martinez Gil (?-1957) Spanish Freemason, who as grand master of the Grand Lodge of Spain, was forced to seek exile in Mexico in 1939, when Franco banned Freemasonry. The grand lodges of Mexico offered asylum to him. d. April 13, 1957 in Mexico City.

Albert C. Gilbert President of Gilbert Paper Co., Menasha, Wis. from 1926. b. Nov. 20, 1887 at Neenah, Wis. Became associated with the company in 1907, serving as treasurer, director, and vice president. Mason and 32° AASR.

Harvey W. Gilbert Industrialist. b. Feb. 18, 1884 in Beaumont, Texas. Began in the oil and lumber business in Texas in 1903. He is president of the Harvey W. Gilbert Petroleum Co.; Gilbert Lumber Co.; Gilbert Tidewater Industrial Sites; Gilbert Tidewater Industries; Nona Oil Co.; Nona Lumber Mills, and Cheltenham Import & Export Co. He was the pro-motor of the Beaumont-Port Arthur Ship Channel, and builder of the Kansas City Southern Industrial R.R. Belt Line. He is also the builder and pro-motor of several other railroads, canals, highways, and dams. Mason and 32° AASR (SJ).

Henry E. Gilbert President of the Brotherhood of Locomotive Firemen and Enginemen since 1953. b. Oct. 5, 1906 in Ethel, Mo. He has been with the labor group since 1927, first as local chairman, member of executive board, board of directors, and vice president. Member of Lawn Lodge No. 815, Chicago, Ill., receiving degrees April-June, 1942; 32° AASR (NJ) at Cleveland, Ohio; Al Koran Shrine Temple, Cleveland and O.E.S. at Lakewood, Ohio.

John Gilbert (1897-1936) Movie actor. b. July 10, 1897 at Logan, Utah. He was educated in grammar schools, and at Hitchcock Military Acad. in San Rafael, Calif. He was identified with the stage from early childhood, and later became a writer, director and cutter of motion pictures. As an actor he was a leading character in many movies including Big Parade and Merry Widow. Mason. d. Jan. 9, 1936.

Levi Gilbert (1852-1917) Editor of Daily Christian Advocate,

1900-1917. b. Aug. 23, 1852 in Brooklyn, N.Y. He was ordained a Methodist minister in 1897, and served pastorates in Minn., Seattle, Wash., Cleveland, Ohio, , and New Haven, Conn. He was a delegate to the general conferences in 1904 and 1908, and a delegate to the Federal Council of Federated Churches of Christ in America in 1908 and 1912. Mason. d. Dec. 24, 1917.

Mahlon N. Gilbert (1848-1900) Episcopal Coadjutor Bishop of Minnesota. b. March 23, 1848 at Laurens, N.Y. He attended Hobart Coll., but was forced to leave before the end of the course because of illness. He later graduated from Seabury Divinity School in 1875. He then supervised the School of the Good Shepherd at Ogden, Utah. He was ordained deacon in June, 1875, and priest in Oct. of the same year. He was rector of St. James, Deer Lodge, Mont., from 1873-78; St. Peters, Helena, Mont., 1878-81, and Christ Church, St. Paul, Minn. from 1881-86. He was consecrated bishop on Oct. 17, 1886. He was initiated in Tienuderrah Lodge No. 605 of New York, and affiliated with Ancient Landmark Lodge No. 5 of St. Paul, Minn. d. in 1900.

Sir William S. Gilbert (1836-1911) English playwright who as a librettist, collaborated with Sir Arthur Sullivan, q.v., another Freemason, to write many famous light operas. b. Nov. 18, 1836 in London, he received a B.A. from London U. in 1857, and was called to the bar in 1863. His first literary work was *Bab Ballads* in 1869. The first Gilbert-Sullivan work was a burlesque entitled Thespis, published in 1871. Among the more famous of their comic operas are: *H.M.S. Pinafore; The Pirates of Penzance; The Mikado*; and *The Gondo-liers*. He also wrote the following independently: *The Palace of Truth; Pygmalion and Galatea; The Wicked World; The Happy Land; Charity* and *Broken Hearts*. Gilbert was raised in Lodge St. Machar, No. 54 of Aberdeen, Scotland, June 23, 1871. d. May 29, 1911.

Albert W. Gilchrist (1858-1926) Governor of Florida, 1909-13. b. Jan. 15, 1858 at Greenwood, S.C. He was graduated from Carolina Military Inst. at Charlotte, and was a cadet in the U.S. Military Academy for three years. He engaged in real estate and orange growing, and was a member of the Florida state legislature four terms, being speaker in 1905. In 1898 he resigned as a brigadier general of the Florida militia, and enlisted as a private with the 3rd U.S. Volunteer Infantry and served in Cuba, being mustered out with rank of captain in 1899. In 1911 he was grand master of the Grand Lodge of Florida. Member of Punta Gorda Lodge No. 115, Punta Gorda, Fla., receiving degrees, April 26, May 7, and May 24, 1890. d. May 16, 1926.

William H. Gilder (1838-1900) Arctic explorer and journalist. b. Aug. 16, 1838 in Philadelphia, Pa. He enlisted as a private in the 5th New York volunteers during the Civil War, and was later on the staff of General Thomas W. Egan. In June, 1878 he accompanied Lt. Schwatka, as second in command, on his expedition to King Willliam's Land in search of the relics of Sir John Franklin. The expedition was marked by the longest sled journey on record at that time - 3,251 miles. The expedition proved the loss of Franklin, and found some of the ill-fated expedition's records. In June, 1881 he accompanied the Rodgers expedition in search of the Jeannette. When their ship, the

Rodgers, burned on Nov. 30, he made a midwinter journey from Bering Strait across Siberia, to telegraph the news of the disaster to the secretary of the Navy. He then joined in the search on the Lena delta for the survivors of the Jeannette. During these expeditions he was correspondent for the New York Herald. Gilder was a member of the "explorers" lodge, Kane No. 454 of New York City.

Malcolm R. Giles (1894-1953) Supreme Secretary, Loyal Order of Moose, 1925-49. b. May 3, 1894 in Somerset Co., Md. He was with the U.S. postal service until 1915, when he became associated with the Loyal Order of Moose, first as chief clerk, then district supervisor. He was an executive director from 1945-49, and director general from 1949. During WWI he served with the A.E.F. for 14 months. Affiliated March 15, 1932 with Jerusalem Temple Lodge No. 90, Aurora, Ill. from Tangia Lodge No. 159 of Deals Island, Md. d. Sept. 29, 1953.

Peter W. Gilkes (1765-1833) English Masonic ritualist. b. May 1, 1765 in London. He was named after Lord Petre, q.v., a Roman Catholic grand master of the Grand Lodge of England. Gilkes himself was a Roman Catholic. He was initiated in British Lodge No. 4 (now 8) in 1786. After achieving financial independence as a merchant, he devoted his life almost entirely to Freemasonry. As an active instructor in ritual, he was prominent in the Emulation Lodge of Improvement for Master Masons. He was a member of many lodges, and served as an officer in ten of them. He was master of St. Michael's Lodge No. 211 at the time of his death. He served 11 years on the board of general purpose and finance, but de-

clined rank in the grand lodge. d. Dec. 11, 1833.

Joseph A. Gill (1854-1933) U.S. District Judge and Chief Justice of Indian Territory Court of Appeals, 1899-1908. b. Feb. 17, 1854 at Wheeling, W.Va. He was admitted to the bar in 1880, and practiced in Illinois, Oregon and Kansas. He was one of the three commissioners on the organization of Indian Territory as part of the state of Oklahoma. Received his degrees in St. Thomas Lodge No. 306 of Colby, Kans., May 4, June 15, and July 20, 1894, affiliating with Vinita Lodge No. 5, Vinita, Okla., June 1, 1901. He was a lodge officer from 1913 until 1916 when he served as master. d. March 23, 1933.

Alexander G. Gillespie Brigadier General, U.S. Army. b. Aug. 19, 1881 at Gaines, Mich. Graduate of U.S. Military Academy in 1906. Served in the U.S., Philippines and France from 1906-19. He was corps area ordnance officer at Chicago from 1924-28, and then professor of ordnance and gunnery at U.S. Military Academy until 1933, when he commanded the Rock Island (Ill.) Arsenal, and later the Watervliet (N.Y.) Arsenal until 1945. He retired in 1947. Member of William B. Warren Lodge No. 209 of Chicago, Ill.

Dean M. Gillespie (1884-1949) Business executive and U.S. Congressman to 78th and 79th Congresses, (1944-47) from Colorado. b. May 3, 1884 at Salina, Kans. He was manager of the western district for White Motor Co. from 1913-25, and president of Dean Gillespie and Co. since 1937. He was also president of the Power Equipment Co. and Motoroyal Oil Co. A Mason, he was both a Knight Templar and Scottish Rite member. A member of the Society for

Research of Meteorites, he owned one of the largest private collections of meteorites in the world. Raised in Temple Lodge No. 84, Denver, Colo., June 15, 1911; exalted in Denver Chapter No. 2, R.A.M., June 24, 1915; greeted in Denver Council No. 1, R. & S.M. Oct. 2, 1916; and knighted in Colorado Commandery No. 1, K.T., Aug. 8, 1924. d. Feb. 2, 1949.

Guy M. Gillette U.S. Senator from Iowa, 1936-54. b. Feb. 3, 1879 at Cherokee, Iowa. Graduate of Drake U. (Ia.). Admitted to bar in 1900, he practiced in Cherokee, Ia. He served in the Spanish-American War as a sergeant, and as a captain in WWI. A member of the state senate from 1912-16, he was U.S. congressman to 73rd and 74th congresses from the 9th Ia. dist. A member of Speculative Lodge No. 307 at Cherokee, Iowa, he received his 50-year recognition in 1955.

King C. Gillette (1855-1932) Organizer and president of the Gillette Safety Razor Co. b. Jan. 5, 1855 in Fond du Lac, Wis. He was educated in the public schools of Chicago. He invented the Gillette razor and was president of the firm from 1901 until 1931. Mason. d. July 9, 1932.

Wilson D. Gillette (1880-1951) U.S. Congressman, 77th to 81st Congresses (1941-51) from 14th Pa. dist. b. in Sheshequin, Pa. He began as a clerk in a general store, and was a dealer of automobiles from 1913. Member of Union Lodge No. 108, Towanda, Pa., receiving degrees, Nov. 17, Dec. 16, 1909, and Jan. 19, 1910. d. Aug. 7, 1951.

George W. Gillie U.S. Congressman, 76th to 80th Congresses (1939-48) from 4th Ind. dist. b. Aug. 15, 1880 in Berwickshire, Scotland, coming to U.S. in 1882, and becoming naturalized in 1890. Graduate of Ohio State U. in 1907 in veterinary medicine. Practiced in Allen Co., Ind. from 1914. Received degrees in Summit City Lodge No. 170, Fort Wayne, Ind. in 1909; 32° AASR (NJ), and past potentate of Mizpah Shrine Temple.

Frank Gillmore (1867-1943) Actor and union executive. b. May 14, 1867 in New York City. Educated in Chiswick Collegiate School, London, England. He first appeared on the stage in 1879, playing the English provinces for three years, and on London stage five years. He then alternated appearances in U.S. and England for several years. He was leading man with Minnie Fiske, Henrietta Crosman, Mary Mannering, Bertha Kalich, and others. From 1918-29 he was executive secretary of the Actors Equity Association, an affiliate of the American Federation of Labor, and president of same from 1929-37, and later international president of the Association of Actors and Artists of America. Mason. d. March 29, 1943.

James C. Gillmore (1854-1927) Commodore, U.S. Navy, Congressional Medal of Honor winner (Spanish-American War). b. July 10, 1854 in Philadelphia, Pa. Graduate of U.S. Naval Academy in 1876. He advanced to rank of commodore, and retired at his own request, July 1, 1911, after 40 years service. He saw service in China, Alaska, Panama, Asia, Cuba, and Europe. His last command was of the battleship Illinois. He was an esoteric Buddhist. Mason. d. June 14, 1927.

Charles Gilman (1793-1861) Grand Master of New Hampshire and Maryland, he also was tendered the grand-mastership of California. b. Dec. 14, 1793 in Meredith, N.H. He studied law and became well known in his field. He was grand treasurer of the Grand Chapter, R.A.M. of New Hampshire from 1830-1833; grand secretary of the Grand Chapter of Maryland, 1836-41; general grand secretary of the General Grand Chapter, R.A.M., and general grand recorder of the General Grand Encampment, K.T., holding both of these offices for 15 years. He served as general grand high priest of the General Grand Chapter from 1856-59, and presided at the meeting in Chicago in 1859, when that organization was stripped of its power and reduced to an advisory body. d. Sept. 9, 1861.

Nicholas Gilman (1755-1814) Signer of the Federal Constitution of 1787 and U.S. Senator from New Hampshire from 1805-14. b. Aug. 3, 1755 in Exeter, N.H. He fought in the Revolutionary War, first as an adjutant in Col. Scammell's regiment, and was for some time a member of Washington's military family. It was his duty to account for the prisoners surrendered by Cornwallis at Yorktown. He was a member of the Continental Congress from 1786-88, and after the adoption of the Constitution, a representative from N.H. from 1789-97. He became a member of St. John's Lodge No. 1, Portsmouth, N.H., March 20, 1777. d. May 2, 1814.

Albert F. Gilmore (?-1943) Editor of Christian Science weekly and monthly magazines, 1922-29, and president of The Mother Church, 1922-23. b. in Turner, Maine. He was a graduate of Bates Coll. He was first a high school principal, and then with a book company. From 1914-17 he was first reader of the First Church of Christ Scientist at Brooklyn, N.Y. Mason. d. June 8, 1943.

Joseph A. Gilmore (1811-1867) Governor of New Hampshire, 1863-65. b. June 10, 1811 in Weston, Vt. Opened a wholesale grocery in Concord, N.H. in 1842. He became a construction agent, later superintendent of the Concord and Claremont Railroad, and eventually superintendent of the Concord Railroad. He held this position until 1866. He served two terms in the state senate. Holding the governorship at a difficult time (Civil War), his health broke and he was forced to retire from office in June 1865. His rise in Masonry was speedy, indeed. He was made a Mason "at sight," April 28, 1863, but there is no record of his affiliating with a lodge. Received the 33° AASR (NJ), May 7, 1863. d. April 17, 1867.

Patrick S. Gilmore (1829-1892) American bandleader and composer of marches and songs. b. Dec. 28, 1829, in Dublin, Ireland. He was associated with bands from the age of 15. He came to Canada with an English band, and then went to Salem, Mass., where he led a brass band. Later, settling in Boston, he organized "Gilmore's Band," which became one of the most famous of that era. He took his band on extensive tours, and in 1861 accompanied the 24th Mass. regiment to the field; in 1863 he was placed in charge of all the bands in the department of Louisiana by General Banks. He wrote When Johnny Comes Marching Home Again under the pseudonym of Louis Lambert. He was a member of Essex Lodge, Salem, Mass. His band participated in the centennial anniversary procession of Union Lodge at Nantucket, Mass.

Ray B. Gilmour (1888-1947) President of American Osteopathic Association, 1926-27. b. Feb. 27, 1888 at Blackfoot, Idaho. Graduate of American School of Osteopathy, Kirksville, Mo. in 1908. Began practice in Kirksville, Mo. in 1908, and settled in Sioux City, Ia. in 1910. He served as president of Osteopathic associations in Iowa, central states, and Northwest Iowa. Mason, 32° AASR (SJ), and Shriner. d. March 5, 1947.

George Gilpin Colonel in the American Revolution. A member of Alexandria Lodge No. 22, Alexandria, Va., he served as one of the pall-bearers at George Washington's funeral.

Curvin H. Gingrich (1880-1951) Astronomer and editor of Popular Astronomy since 1926. b. Nov. 20, 1880 at York, Pa. Graduate of Dickinson Coll. (Pa.) and U. of Chicago. He taught mathematics in colleges in Mo. and Kans. from 1903-12, and has been a professor of mathematics and astronomy since 1912. He taught at Carleton Coll., Mt. Wilson Observatory, Adler Planetarium, McCormick Observatory. He was assistant editor of Popular Astronomy from 1912-26, and editor from that date. His work at Goodsell Observatory of Carleton Coll. was principally micrometric measures of comet positions and double stars, also celestial photography and photographic determinations of positions of asteroids. Member of Social Lodge No. 48, Northfield, Minn., receiving degrees, Jan. 20, Feb. 14, March 31, 1913 and master of lodge in 1933. Member of Corinthian Chapter No. 33, RAM., and high priest in 1938; member of Northfield

Council No. 12, R. & SM., all of Northfield, Minn. d. June 17, 1951.

L. Holmes Ginn, Jr. Brigadier General, U.S. Army Medical Corps. b. Sept. 3, 1902 in Berryville, Va. A graduate of Medical College of Virginia in 1927, he interned in Walter Reed General Hospital. Commissioned in 1928, and advanced through grades to brigadier general in 1952. As a major at Fort Knox, Ky., he developed organization of the medical service for armored troops, and the mobile surgical truck used successfully in WWII. Became 1st surgeon of 1st Armored Division in 1940, serving with it in North Ireland, invasion of North Africa (1942) and Tunisian campaign (1943). Then assigned to 15th Army Group, and was senior U.S. Medical Officer for Sicilian campaign. Surgeon of II Corps in Italy; of 15th Army in Western Europe. Established "Cordon Sanitaire," or quarantine at Rhine River to stop spread of typhus to Western Europe at close of WWII. Named surgeon of the Third Army in Southeastern U.S. in 1950. Transferred to Korea in 1952 as surgeon of Eighth Army. Now surgeon, Fourth Army at Fort Sam Houston, Texas, and commanding general of William Beaumont, q.v., Army Hospital. A member of Army Lodge No. 1105, San Antonio, Texas, he was initiated May 18, passed Aug. 5 and raised Sept. 2, in 1955. 32° AASR (SJ) in San Antonio. Member of Alzafar Shrine temple and special deputy to potentate to Armed Services in 1957. Honorary member of El Maida Temple at El Paso. Member of National Sojourners and Heroes of '76.

Stephen Girard (1750-1831) Philanthropist. b. May 20, 1750 near Bordeaux, France. The son of a sea captain, he sailed to the West Indies as a cabin-boy at an early age, and thence to New York. He became a mate, captain, and then part owner of a ship, and in 1769 settled in Philadelphia where he established himself in trade, and was alternately a shipmaster and a merchant. In 1812 he founded the Bank of Stephen Girard to take over the business of the Bank of the United States. During the War of 1812, he financed 95% of the war's cost by making five million dollars available to the U.S. government. He aided in establishing the Second Bank of the United States in 1816, of which he was a director, and largely influenced its policy. He amassed a fortune of nine million dollars by the time of his death—more than any other American. Personally, he was an enigma. He pinched pennies; gave his help no more than their just wages; was parsimonious and lived a frugal life. On the other hand, he gave his entire fortune to charity and public improvement, including $20,000 for Masonic charity which is still administered by the Grand Lodge of Pennsylvania. The most famous of his bequests was to Girard College at Philadelphia, a home for "poor, white, male orphans." One clause in his will regarding the college specified: "I enjoin and require that no ecclesiastic, missionary or minister of any sect whatsoever, shall ever hold or exercise any duty whatsoever in the said college; nor shall any such person ever be admitted for any purpose, or as a visitor, within the premises appropriated to the purposes of the said college. . . . I desire to keep the tender minds of orphans . . . free from the excitements which clashing doctrines and sectarian controversy are so apt to produce." This would, as he explained, leave them free in future life to choose "such active religious tenets as their matured reason may enable them to prefer." His Masonic affiliations are equally strange. The records of Royal Arch Lodge No. 3 of Philadelphia show the following on Sept. 7, 1778: "Capt. Stephen Girard was duly balloted for, unanimously approved of, initiated and accordingly paid his dues, twenty dollars, into the hands of the treasurer." Again we find that he was made a Mason "at sight" in Union Blue Lodge No. 8, Charleston, S.C. on Jan. 28, 1788 when he was entered, passed, and raised on that date. It has been suggested that Girard was unable to prove himself to be a Mason in 1788, and was initiated a second time—an irregular proceeding, but not impossible in that formative period of the Craft. In 1809 he was appointed to the board of trustees of the Grand Lodge of Pennsylvania, and subscribed the final five thousand dollars necessary to complete the Masonic hall. Two days after his death (Dec. 26, 1831) a public notice appeared in the newspapers requesting the attendance of the Grand Lodge of Pennsylvania and subordinate lodges listed as well as other benevolent associations. Almost 400 Masons assembled for the funeral which was held in the German Roman Catholic Church of the Holy Trinity. When the Masons appeared, the priests refused to perform the burial rites and, after waiting for some time, the brethren then removed the body from the church and placed it in the vault as had been desired by Girard. His body was removed in Jan. 1851 to the Girard College, and at the request of the commissioners of his estate, the Grand Lodge of Pennsylvania participated. The coffin was borne by eight past masters, and a Masonic funeral dirge was composed expressly for the occasion. The heirs had objected to the removal of the remains from the church, but were ruled against by the courts.

Mordecai Gist (1743-1792) Brigadier General of the American Revolution. b. in Baltimore, Md. His ancestors were early English emigrants to Maryland. At the beginning of the Revolution he was elected captain of the "Baltimore Independent Co.," the first raised in Maryland. In 1776 he was appointed major of a battalion of Maryland regulars, and was with them in the battle near Brooklyn. In Jan. 1779, congress appointed him brigadier general in the Continental Army, and he took command of the 2nd Maryland brigade. He fought at the battle of Camden, S.C. in 1780, joined the southern army under Greene, and was given a light corps to command. In 1782 he rallied the broken forces of the Americans under Laurens at the battle of the Combahee and defeated the British. After the war, he lived on his plantation near Charleston, S.C. He had two children whom he named "Independent" and "States." A member of Lodge No. 16, Baltimore, Md., he received his degrees March 14, April 11, and April 25, 1775. He was the first master of Army Lodge No. 27 of the Maryland Line, chartered by the Grand Lodge of Pennsylvania in April, 1780. He was the president of the convention of Army lodges held in Morristown, N.J. which suggested the election of Washington as general grand master. He was deputy grand master of South Carolina in 1787, and grand master of the Grand Lodge of South Carolina from 1789-92. d. Sept. 2, 1792.

Peter Maurice Glaire (1743-1819) b. in Switzerland. He went to Poland in 1764, and eventually became a confidant of King Stanislaus Poniatowski, who sent him on numerous diplomatic missions. While in Poland, he established a rite of seven degrees. He returned to Switzerland in 1788, and in 1810 was elected grand master for three years—at the end of which term he was elected to the position for life in the Grand Orient of Helvetia.

James Glaisher (1809-1903) English astronomer and meteorologist. He was chief of the magnetic and meteorological department at Greenwich from 1838-74 and pioneered balloon ascents to obtain meteorological data. He was admitted to Royal Union Lodge No. 382, Uxbridge, England, Jan. 16, 1864. Before this he had been a member of Britannic Lodge No. 33. **Carter Glass** (1858-1946) Secretary of the Treasury under President Wilson, and U.S. Senator from Virginia. b. Jan. 4, 1858 at Lynchburg, Va. Educated in public and private schools at Lynchburg, he later received honorary doctorates from 13 colleges and universities. He was the owner of the Daily News and Daily Advance of Lynchburg. He was a member of the state legislature several terms before serving as U.S. congressman to the 57th to 65th congresses (1902-19). He resigned from congress in 1918 to become secretary of the Treasury in Wilson's cabinet, serving until 1920, when he resigned to accept senatorship by appointment of Virginia's governor. He served from 1920 until his death in 1946, his last re-election being in 1942. He was president pro-tem of the senate from 1941. He was chairman of the important appropriations committee of the senate and member of the foreign relations committee. He declined the secretaryship of the Treasury under F. D. Roosevelt. He was a member of Hill City Lodge No. 183 of Lynchburg; he received the 32° AASR at Lynchburg, Aug. 16, 1929. He was later coroneted 33°. In 1940 he wrote his lodge as follows: " ... It seems to me I was taken in Hill

Lodge considerably more than 50 years ago. I was lectured for entrance by the late Thomas N. Davis, one of the most brilliant Masons who ever wielded a gavel; and, before I entered public life 40 years ago, I could recite the ritual backward as well as forward, and took the in-tensest interest in Masonic work. I have never ceased to regard the Masonic fraternity in a little less reverential vein than my church. No good Mason could fail to be a good churchman, and no churchman should omit to become a good Mason." d. May 28, 1946.

William E. Glasscock (1862-1925) Governor of West Virginia, 1909-13. b. Dec. 13, 1862 near Arnettsville, W. Va. Admitted to the bar in 1902. Taught school in Ia., Nebr. and W. Va., and was county superintendent of schools of Monongalia Co., 1887-90. Was U.S. collector of internal revenue for W. Va., 1905-08. Member of Acacia Lodge No. 157, Fairmont, W. Va. as well as the York Rite bodies of that city, and a Shriner. d. April 12, 1925.

Benjamin Gleason (1777-1847) One of the first appointed Masonic lecturer in the U.S. He was graduated from Brown U. in 1802. His original lodge is not known, but he was a member of Mount Lebanon Lodge of Mass. on June 2, 1807. He received his appointment as grand lecturer of the Grand Lodge of Mass. in 1805, holding the office until 1842. He received the lectures from Thomas Smith Webb, q.v., and, next to his mentor, he was probably the foremost ritualist in the U.S. At one time Gleason visited the Grand Lodge of England and exemplified the work, where it was declared to be accurate. Gleason taught John Barney, who in turn taught Samuel Willson. Jonathan Heart, q.v., was appointed as lecturer

in Conn. by a convention of lodges in 1783. George Richards of N.H. may also have served as lecturer before Gleason's time.

Edwin F. Glenn (1857-1926) Major General, U.S. Army. b. Jan. 10, 1857 near Greensboro, N.C. Graduate of U.S. Military Academy in 1877. Promoted through grades to brigadier general in 1917, and major general in same year. He instituted military training at the U. of Minnesota in 1888. He was a member of the Minn. bar. He commanded exploring and relief expeditions into Alaska in 189899. He served first with the judge advocate's department, and in WWI, organized Camp Sherman, Ohio, and the 83rd Division in 1917, commanding that division in France in 1918, and retiring at his own request in 1919. Member of St. Paul Lodge No. 3, St. Paul, Minn. d. Aug. 5, 1926.

Robert B. Glenn (1854-1920) Governor of North Carolina, 1905-09. b. Aug. 11, 1854 in Rockingham Co., N.C. Engaged in law practice, first at Danbury, N.C., and later as counsel for Southern Railway and Western Union. Served as state solicitor and member of state legislature. The Grand Lodge of North Carolina attended his inauguration as governor in a body. He was a member of Winston Lodge No. 167 of Winston-Salem, receiving his degrees Dec. 27-29, 1904, and transferring to Raleigh Lodge No. 500, Raleigh, N.C., May 19, 1905. He was a member of Raleigh Chapter No. 10, R.A.M., Raleigh Commandery No. 4, and Oasis Shrine Temple. d. May 16, 1920.

William M. Glenn Newspaper editor and co-founder of the national professional journalism fraternity, Sigma Delta Chi (1909 at DePauw U.). b. April 21, 1888 at Hillsboro,

Ohio. Graduate of DePauw U. in 1910. From 1910-14 he was a reporter on newspapers in Indiana and Illinois, becoming editor of Orlando Morning Sentinel (Fla.) in 1914, until 1925, when he became publisher. In 1931-34 he was editorial writer for the Daily Times of Tampa and returned as publisher of the Orlando paper from 1939-43. Since 1943 he has been an editor with the Florida Sun of Miami Beach. Mason, he is past commander of Olivet Commandery, K.T. of Orlando, Fla. He is the author of several books.

John, Viscount of Glenorchy Grand Master Mason of Scotland, 1824-25. Later became 2nd Marquis of Breadalbane.

Glenn F. Glezen U.S. Lieutenant Commander and Arctic explorer. Member of the Byrd Antarctic Expedition of 1955-58, as administrative officer on staff of Admiral George Dufek, commanding Task Force H-3 in operational control of ships. Has served in the Navy since age of 17, and was commissioned in WWII. He is the former secretary of Cherrydale Lodge No. 42, Cherrydale, Va.

Carl Glick Writer, director, lecturer. b. Sept. 11, 1890 at Marshalltown, Iowa. Graduate of Northwestern U. in 1915. Started as an actor with Donald Robertson Players, Chicago Art Institute, 1909 and later toured in Shakespearian repertoire. From 1915-17 he was a drama instructor in Fairmount Coll. (Kans.) and then director of the community theatre, Waterloo, Ia. He has directed theatre groups in Sarasota, Fla., York, Pa., Columbia, S.C., Schenectady, N.Y. Glick has taught at U. of Montana; U. of Colo.., and since 1955 at California Western U. at San Diego. Served in U.S. Army in WWI. Among his writings are Shake Hands with the Dragon; Three Times I Bow; Swords of Silence; The Secret Societies of China (with Hong Sheng-Hwa); The Secret of Serenity; Death Sits In; and the Masonic volume, A Treasury of Masonic Thought. Member of St. John's Lodge No. 1, New York City; Darius Chapter No. 143, R.A.M., San Diego, Calif. and member of advisory council, Point Loma Chapter, Order of DeMolay.

George W. Glick (1827-1811) Eighth Governor of Kansas, 1883-85. b. July 4, 1827 in Fairfield Co., Ohio. Admitted to bar in 1850, and practiced in Ohio until 1859. He enlisted for Mexican War, but saw no service; he served in the Civil War a short time. He went to Kansas in 1859 where he engaged in farming and stock raising. He was a member of the Kansas legislature from 1863-66, 1876 and 1882. A member of Washington Lodge No. 5 of Atchison, Kans., he was junior warden of same in 1863, and 1864. He was also a member of Washington Commandery No. 2, K.T. of Atchison.

William Henry, Duke of Gloucester and Edinburg b. 1743. He was a son of Frederick, Prince of Wales, q.v., and grandson of King George II. He married Maria, widow of James, Earl of Waldegrave, a natural daughter of Sir Edward Walpole. Their only son was Prince William Frederick of Gloucester, q.v. He was a brother of King George III, q.v. He was initiated in Royal Lodge No. 313, later known as Royal Alpha No. 16 on Feb. 16, 1766. The meeting was held at the Horn Tavern of London and he received all three degrees the same evening, conferred by Lord Blayney, the grand master.

Earl of Gloucester (See Clare de Gilbert).

William Frederick, Prince of Gloucester (1776-1834) b. Jan. 15, 1776 at the Teodoli Palace, Rome, son of William Henry, Duke of Gloucester and Edinburgh, q.v., nephew as well as son-in-law of King George III, and great grandson of George II. Was educated in Trinity Coll., Cambridge, and entered the army as a captain in 1789, later becoming a major general. He married his cousin, Mary, in 1816 and died childless in 1834. He was initiated in Brittanic Lodge No. 29 (now No. 33) on May 12, 1795; became a Royal Arch Mason on Jan. 7, 1797 and a Knight Templar on Jan. 11, 1797.

Aquila Glover (?-1849) A rescuer of the ill-fated Donner Party in 1847. He crossed the plains from Missouri by ox team with his family in 1846 and spent part of fall and winter of 1846-47 at Sutter's Fort where he met James F. Reed. Reed recognized him as a Mason and requested that he go with the relief party and assist in bringing out the Reed family from the snows of Donner Lake. Glover is reported as saying: "Brother Reed, I will go with the first relief party, and I pledge you on my honor and word as a Master Mason, that I will rescue your family even at the risk of my life and do just the same for them as I would for my own." He was true to his word and did his utmost to accomplish the rescue of the entire Reed family. He could not, however, bring them all out of the mountains. He did rescue Mrs. Reed and two of her four children. Reed, himself, brought the other two children out shortly afterward. Glover moved to San Francisco in the spring of 1847 and lived there with his family in a tent. He helped organize the first Methodist church in San Francisco. He went to the mines at Coloma and died there Nov. 18, 1849. Sherman, in his history of the Grand Lodge of California, stated that Glover was probably a member of a lodge near Warsaw, Benton Co., Mo. and that his Masonic regalia was burned in a house on the Gish road, one mile north of San Jose in 1854 or 1855.

John Glover (1732-1797) Brigadier General of the American Revolution. b. Nov. 5, 1732 in Salem, Mass. At the beginning of the Revolution he raised 1,000 men and joined the army at Cambridge. He commanded the 21st and later the 14th regiment, the latter being one of the first as well as one of the best in the Continental Army. It was composed almost entirely of fishermen and it was called the "amphibious regiment." On the retreat from Long Island, it manned the boats and crossed the entire army in safety. These troops also manned the boats and led the advance over the Delaware River on the night before the victory at Trenton. As a colonel, he participated in the battle of Stillwater, and was with Washington at Valley Forge. He was appointed brigadier general, Feb. 21, 1777, and in July, joined Schuyler in the campaign against Burgoyne. In 1778 he joined Greene's division in N.J. and later detached to R.I. under Sullivan. He was a member of the court that sentenced Major Andre to hang. A member of Philanthropic Lodge of Marblehead, Mass., he is recorded as visiting St. John's Lodge in Providence, R.I. when he was stationed there. d. Jan. 30, 1797.

Charles Gloyd (?-1869) Husband of Carrie Nation, of barsmashing fame. Signed petition to organize Holden Lodge No. 262, Holden, Mo. on July 31, 1867 and was first master of same in 1868. Record shows a dimit from Ward Lodge No. 281 of Piqua, Ohio dated April 9, 1867. d. March 20, 1869.

John P. S. Gobin (1837-1910) Brigadier General in Civil War and Spanish-American War. b. Jan. 26, 1837 at Sunbury, Pa. Received law degree from Susquehanna U. Following the Civil War, he practiced law at Lebanon, Pa., and was one of the organizers of the G.A.R., serving as its commander-in-chief in 1897. He was lieutenant governor of Pa. in 1898 and commanded the national guard of that state during the coal strike of 1902. He was made a Mason in Sunbury Lodge No. 22 on Jan. 9, 1860, and affiliated with Williamson Lodge No. 307 of Womelsdorf, Pa. on May 4, 1881, and served as its master. A member of Hermit Commandery No. 24, K.T., he was its commander, and was the 15th grand master of the Grand Encampment, K.T. of the U.S. in 1889. He received the 33° AASR (NJ) on May 9, 1906. d. May 1, 1910.

Chester W. Goble Major General, U.S. Army. b. Nov. 25, 1891 at Columbus, 0. He enlisted in Troop B of the Ohio national guard in 1908, and later was commissioned first lieutenant. He served overseas in WWI with the 136th heavy field artillery. In 1940 he was commissioned a lieutenant colonel, and in July, 1955, was retired with the rank of major general. In his 47 years in the military service he served with the cavalry, field artillery, quartermaster corps, and finance corps. In 1947-48 he was adjutant general of Ohio, and for many years before retirement, director of selective service for Ohio. He was raised in Humboldt Lodge No. 476, Columbus, Ohio on April 18, 1913;

exalted in Ohio Chapter No. 12, R.A.M. Jan. 21, 1926; greeted in Columbus Council No. 8 R. & S.M. March 19, 1926; knighted in Mt. Vernon Commandery No. 1, K.T. March 12, 1926. Received 32° AASR in Aug., 1917 and 33° Sept. 26, 1951. Member of Aladdin Shrine Temple at Columbus.

Arthur Godfrey Radio and television personality. b. Aug. 31, 1903 in New York City. He served in the Navy from 1920-24, and in the Coast Guard 1927-30; he is a commander in the Naval Reserve. He began in radio as an announcer and entertainer over Station WFBR of Baltimore in 1930, and was with NBC from 1930-34. Since 1934 he has been freelance. His daily program on radio, Arthur Godfrey Time has run for years. His television programs over CBS have been Arthur Godfrey's Talent Scouts and Arthur Godfrey and His Friends. Member of Acacia Lodge No. 18, Washington, D.C.; E.A. Feb. 9; FC March 23; MM April 27, 1937. He was raised by Arch McDonald, a radio sports announcer. Member of Albert Pike Consistory, AASR and joined Almas Shrine Temple on May 19, 1937.

Edward S. Godfrey (1843-1932) Brigadier General, U.S. Army and Congressional Medal of Honor winner. b. Oct. 9, 1843 at Kalida, Ohio. Enlisted as a private in Co. D, 21st Ohio Inf. in 1861 and was graduated from U.S. Military Academy in 1867. Promoted through grades to brigadier general in 1907. He was awarded the Congressional Medal for "most distinguished gallantry" at Bear Paw Mountains against Chief Joseph and the Nez Perce Indians on Sept. 30, 1877. He was in all the campaigns and Indian fights of his regiment under General Custer, until the latter's death. He originated "cossack" and "rough riding" for the Army and was a member of the board of officers that devised drill regulations for the infantry, cavalry, and artillery. He served in Cuba and the Philippines. Mason, 32° AASR and Knight Templar. d. April 1, 1932.

Frank J. Goebel Vice President of Baltimore and Ohio Railroad in charge of personnel. b. Sept. 26, 1893 at Princeton, Ind. A lawyer, he was first secretary and assistant counsel of the Cincinnati, Indianapolis, and Western Railroad. In 1927 he went with the B & 0 as assistant general solicitor, became director of personnel, and vice president since 1947. Mason.

Henry Goering Premier of Germany, and anti-Mason, who in 1934 issued an official decree to the three largest grand lodges in Germany, stating that their existence was no longer necessary and that lodges must be dissolved. The three grand lodges mentioned were known as the Christian grand lodges because they admitted only members of the Christian faith.

Hermann Goering (1893-1946) Nazi Field Marshal and anti-Mason. Served in German air force in WWI and commanded the Richthofen squadron. He was involved in the National Socialist uprising at Munich in 1923. In Hitler's government, he became Reich Minister of the air force, minister of interior and general of infantry. He was made economic dictator of Germany in 1937, and field marshal in 1938. He committed suicide in jail, while awaiting trial for war crimes. In an interview with grand master von Heeringen on April 7, 1933, Goering told him "In a National Socialist state . . . there is no place

for Freemasons." Later, German Masonic heads reported "if the intention of Minister Goering should find general approval in the Reich cabinet, there need be no question of the continuance of our grand lodge of Freemasons." Next followed the rules under which Freemasonry might carry on—discontinuation of the use of the words "Freemason" and "Lodge"; breaking off all international relations; requirement that all members be of German descent; removal of the requirement of secrecy; and elimination of those parts of the ritual which were of Old Testament origin. As a result, the National Grand Lodge changed its name to "The National Christian Order of Frederick the Great."

August von Goethe (1789-1830) Son of the German poet, Johann Wolfgang von Goethe, q.v. He was a government official and chamberlain to the grand duke of Saxe Weimar. His wife was Ottilie, Baroness von Pogwisch. After the death of his wife, in 1816, he took care of his father in his last years; however, he died two years before his father. He was initiated in his father's lodge—Lodge Amelia in Weimar on Dec. 5, 1815. This was the last time his father was able to attend lodge.

Johann Wolfgang von Goeth (1749-1832) German poet and intellectual. b. at Frankfurt am Me ln, he was educated at Leipzig and studied law at Strasbourg. He was the dominant influence of his era on the development of the German literature. His *Gotz von Berlichingen*, a tragedy published in 1773, inaugurated the romantic school and established the Shakespearean form of drama on the German stage. *His Die Leiden des Jun.gen Werthers*, a romantic love story published in 1774 as a result of an affair with Charlotte

Buff, established the romantic school. His *Faust*, 1808 and 1832, heralded the modern spirit of German literature. He settled in Weimar in 1775 on the invitation of Charles Augustus, heir to the duchy of Saxe-Weimar. It was then the literary and intellectual center of Germany. He was a close friend of Schiller, q.v., who inspired many of his works. Goethe made an extended trip with the Duke of Weimar during the closing months of 1799 and found evidence of the advantages of Masonic membership. He addressed a petition, of his own composition and handwriting, to the master of Lodge *Amalia in Weimar* and received the first degree on June 23, 1780. He received the second degree exactly one year later (June 23, 1781), although at that time an entered apprentice was required to wait three years before advancing. Goethe, however, had written a letter to the master calling his attention to the efforts he had put forth to render himself worthy. He received the third degree on March 3, 1782. He subsequently received the higher Templar degrees of the Rite of Strict Observance. At this time the development of the many so-called higher degrees brought strong differences of opinion and caused the closing of Goethe's lodge in 1783, and it did not open again until 26 years later. Goethe's interest in Freemasonry never wavered during these years, and when the reorganization meeting took place on June 27, 1808, he received three out of the 12 votes cast for master. He was one of those who signed the petition to the lodge in the neighboring city of Rudolstade asking their cooperation in securing a charter from the Grand Lodge of Hamburg. His advice was sought by the newly elected officers and although he could not be present at the reopening of the lodge on Sept 24, 1808, he sent a special message bearing his best wishes and assuring the brethren of his interest. For the next four years he attended its, meetings regularly. He attended lodge for the last time on Dec. 5, 1815 when his son, August, q.v., was initiated. On June 23, 1830 the lodge celebrated the 50th anniversary of Goethe's admission. Old age and infirmities prevented his attendance, but he wrote a special poem, *Fifty Years Today Are Over*, which was read. Goethe's writings, especially *Wilhelm Meister*, contain numerous Masonic allusions and references. He gives many Masonic references in his collected works. His best known Masonic work is the short poem *Mason Lodge* which may be found in most collections of his works. One biographer writes that on his deathbed his speech became less and less distinct and that the last words audible were More Light.

Nathan Goff, Jr. (1843-1920) Secretary of the Navy and U.S. Senator from West Virginia. b. Feb. 9, 1843 at Clarksburg, W.Va. He served in the Union army during the Civil War from 1861-65, and was admitted to the bar in 1866. He served one term in the lower house of W.Va., was U.S. district attorney, U.S. circuit judge, and U.S. congressman to 48th to 50th Congresses (1883-89). He was elected governor of W.Va. in 1888 by a plurality of 130 votes, but when his opponent contested the vote, he lost the election by vote of the state legislature. In 1881 he was secretary of the Navy in the cabinet of President Hayes. He was U.S. senator from W.Va. from 1913-19. Member of Hermon Lodge No. 6, Clarksburg, W.Va. d. April 24, 1920.

Norris Goff The "Abner" of Lunt and Abner comedy team. Both Goff and Chester Lauck (Lum) are memhers of Dallas Lodge No. 128, Mena, Ark.

Maurice Goldblatt President of Goldblatt Bros., Inc., Chicago department store, from 1914-45, and chairman of the board since 1945. b. Dec. 17, 1893 at Staszow, Poland. Active in hospital and health societies, he is executive director of the American Heart Association. Mason.

Maurice H. Goldblatt Violinist, composer and art expert. b. May 30, 1883, in Tallinn, Estonia, he was brought to America at age of six. A graduate of the Chicago Music Coll., he has an honorary doctorate from Notre Dame. He made his debut as a violin soloist in St. Louis when he was 13 years old. He has been concert meister of the Italian Grand Opera Co. of New York and Chicago Philharmonic Orchestra. He was first violinist of the Chicago Opera from 1915-18 and has taught violin at the Chicago Musical Coll. since 1910. He is director of the art gallery of Notre Dame U. and art expert for the Beaumont Galleries of Chicago and Metropolitan Galleries of New York. He was decorated by the French government for establishing authorship of four paintings in the Louvre in 1927. He is said to be the first to employ black light and spectographic analysis, and is the inventor of the "lightoscope." He has composed numerous pieces for violin and piano. Mason.

Nathan Goldblatt (1895-1944) Department store executive. b. March 24, 1895 in Staszow, Poland, he was brought to the U.S. in 1904. When 19 he and his brother Morris, q.v., established a small dry goods store in Chicago with a capital of $2,000. They opened a second store in 1928, and others in 1929-30, and in 1936 acquired the Loop store

known as The Davis Co. He was also the owner of stores in Hammond, Gary (Ind.) and Joliet (Ill.). He was secretary and treasurer of Goldblatt Bros., Inc. Received degrees in Emblem Lodge No. 984, Chicago on Jan. 22, Feb. 19, and March 2, 1919 affiliating Oct. 23, 1922 with Pilgrim Lodge No. 1079—now known as Pilgrim Jonas Lodge No. 1079. d. Nov. 3, 1944.

Frank Goldman President of B'nai B'rith, 1947-53 and honorary president since that date. b. Dec. 4, 1890 in Lowell, Mass. Graduate of Boston U. summa cum laude in 1910 and admitted to Mass. bar in 1912, practicing in Lowell. A member of B'nai B'rith since 1920, he served as president of the Lowell lodge, district president, national vice president, 1941-47. He has been the editor of The National Jewish Monthly since 1947. Active in civic and Jewish charity organizations. Mason and 32° AASR (NJ).

John R. Goldsborough (1808-1877) Commodore, U.S. Navy. b. July 2, 1808 in Washington, D.C. He became a midshipman in 1824, rising to commodore in 1867. While a midshipman on the sloop Warren, he captured the schooner Helene (of four guns manned by 58 Greek pirates) by engaging them with a launch with 19 men. In the Civil War he commanded the steamer, Union, and was employed in the blockade of the southern coast. He captured and sunk the Confederate schooner, York, and later commanded the Florida and Colorado. He retired in 1870. He was a member of Federal Lodge No. 1, Washington, D.C. and Columbia Chapter No. 15, R.A.M. of Washington, but later withdrew from both. d. June 22, 1877.

Robert H. Goldsborough (1779-1836) U.S. Senator from Maryland, 1813-19 and 1835-36. b. Jan. 4, 1779 near Easton, Md. He was made a Mason in St. Thomas' Lodge No. 37 at Easton, Md. about 1800. In 1807 this lodge became dormant, but was revived again in 1823 at Coats' Lodge No. 76, Goldsborough being one of the charter members and its master in 1824. He was senior grand warden of the Grand Lodge of Maryland in 1824. d. Oct. 5, 1836.

Barry M. Goldwater U.S. Senator from Arizona, from 1953. b. Jan. 1, 1909 in Phoenix, Ariz. Attended Staunton Military Academy and U. of Arizona. Has been with Goldwater's, Inc., since 1929; president, 1937-53, and now chairman of the board. From 1948-50 he was a member of the advisory committee on Indian Affairs of the Department of Interior. In WWII he served as a pilot in the Air Force from 1941-45, and was chief of staff of the Arizona national guard, 1945-52. He received the U.S. Junior Chamber of Commerce award in 1937. Raised in Arizona Lodge No. 2, Phoenix, April, 1930; 32° AASR (SJ) at Tucson and 33° in Oct., 1959. Member of Shrine and Eastern Star. His uncle, Morris Goldwater (1852-1939) was the 8th grand master of the Grand Lodge of Arizona; grand high priest of the Grand Chapter of Arizona and grand master of the Grand Council of Arizona.

Pavel I Golenischev-Kutusov (1767-1829) Russian General and politician. He was curator of the Moscow University, member of the Senate and a general of great personal courage. He was the chief founder and first master of the Lodge Neptune at Moscow in 1803. This lodge was an "inner order" of the outer circle represented by a lodge called Harpocrat. A Rosicrucian, he was a Mason of the old school, being initiated in another lodge called "Neptune" which was founded in Kronstadt in 1779. Members of his lodge belonged to the Moscow nobility and included some professors of the university and a few young army officers.

Freire de Andrade de Gomez (see under Freire).

Samuel Gompers (1850-1924) One of the founders and first president of the American Federation of Labor, serving from 1886-1924. b. Jan. 27, 1850 in London, England. A cigar-maker by trade, he was an advocate of the rights of labor from the time he was 14 years old. He helped develop the Cigar makers International Union, and was one of the founders of the Federation of Trades and Labor Unions in 1881, being president of same for three years. He probably did more for American labor than any other man. He fought socialism relentlessly. In his autobiography, he relates that his Masonic affiliation frequently protected him. He said "In my Masonic life I have visited lodges in many lands, and I have learned that Freemasonry in many countries, particularly in Latin countries, is the principal means whereby freedom of conscience, of thought, and of expression is preserved." A member of Dawson Lodge No. 16, Washington, D.C. he received his degrees on Feb. 8, March 28 and May 9, 1904, and the 32° AASR (SJ) in Albert Pike Consistory of Washington, D.C. on Feb. 10, 1906. Samuel Gompers Lodge No. 45, Washington, D.C. is named for him. d. Dec. 13, 1924.

Marie F. P. Gonthier (see under Maine de Biran).

Antonio Gonzales Philippine lawyer who was first grand high priest of the Grand Chapter, R.A.M. of the Philippines and first grand master of the Grand Council, R. & S.M. of the Philippines. b. Aug. 28, 1895 in Manila. Graduate of San Beda Coll. and Escuela de Derecho. Initiated in Luzon Lodge No. 57 in 1920, he became a charter member of Luz Oceanica Lodge No. 85, served as master and elected grand master of the Grand Lodge of the Philippines in 1932. From 1939-53 he was grand secretary of the grand lodge. A charter member of Manila Chapter, U.D. in 1949, he was appointed deputy for the general grand high priest for the Philipines in 1951. Greeted in Trenton Council No. 37, Trenton, Mo. in 1951. Received Order of High Priesthood in St. Louis, Mo., Sept. 2, 1951 and was instrumental in forming a Philippine convention of same; past commander of Far East Commandery No. 1, K.T. Manila; past sovereign of Asoka Conclave, Red Cross of Constantine and intendant general for Philippines in 1951. He has presided over all the Scottish Rite bodies in the Philippines.

Manuel Gonzalez (1833-1893) President of Mexico, 1880-84, and General. b. near Matamoros, Tamaulipas. As early as 1853 he was fighting in guerilla wars with the reactionary party. Many times wounded, his right arm was amputated. When Mexico was invaded by the French, English and Spanish in 1861, he joined Juarez, q.v., accompanied the president in his flight from the capital as far as San Luis Potosi, and established himself in the mountains of Hidalgo, where he stayed until 1865. Cutting through the French forces, he joined Escobedo, q.v., and marched south with him. In 1869 he was appointed governor by Juarez, holding that office until 1871, when arrested for complicity in the disappearance of Maximilian's, q.v., gold and silver from the palace. He escaped in the revolution of 1871 and joined the forces of Diaz, q.v. He was a determining factor in the winning of the revolution and was named full general and made secretary of War. In the latter position he did much to improve the Mexican army. He resigned his cabinet position in 1880 and was declared elected president and appointed Diaz as secretary of public works. His administration was distinguished by financial mismanagement which grew so had that he was forced by Diaz to resign in 1884. He then served as governor of the state of Guanajuato. He was a member of the Supreme Council AASR of Mexico.

Tom C. Gooch (1880-1952) President of The Times Herald, Dallas, Texas, and editor in chief from 1910. b. Jan. 25, 1880 in Bonham, Tex., he was the great grandson of Mrs. Mabel Gilbert, the first white woman to come to Dallas. Began as a reporter on Ft. Wayne News (Ind.) and became associated with the Dallas Times in 1901. Member of Dallas Lodge No. 760, Dallas, Texas, receiving degrees on July 15, Sept. 21, 1903 and Mar. 4, 1904. In 1912 he affiliated with Trinity Valley Lodge No. 1048, Dallas, as a charter member; 32° AASR (SJ) and KCCH. d. June 13, 1952.

Edward E. Good (1862-1937) Justice, Supreme Court of Nebraska from 1923. b. May 13, 1862 in Bloomfield, Ia. Graduate of State U. of Iowa in 1885. Began law practice at Wahoo, Nebr. in same year. He affiliated Oct. 9, 1886 with Wahoo Lodge No. 59, Wahoo, Nebr. and was master of same in 1894. His original lodge is unknown. d. Aug. 4, 1937.

James W. Good (1866-1929) Secretary of War under President Hoover and U.S. Congressman, 61st to 67th Congresses (1909-23) from 5th Ia. dist. b. Sept. 24, 1866 at Cedar Rapids, Ia. He was a graduate of Coe Coll. (Ia.) and the U. of Michigan. He resigned from congress to practice law in Chicago. He was raised in Mt. Hermon Lodge No. 263 of Cedar Rapids, Ia. on Feb. 3, 1898 and received the 32° AASR (SJ) in that city on Feb. 8, 1909. d. Nov. 18, 1929 in Washington, D.C.

Albert G. Goodall (1826-1887) President of the American Bank Note Co. b. Oct. 31, 1826 at Montgomery, Ala. Orphaned at the age of 15, he entered the Texas navy as a midshipman, serving three years. In 1848 he moved to Philadelphia and learned copper plate engraving. He then went to New York and became associated with a firm which later became the American Bank Note Co. He was president of the company the last 12 years of his life. In 1858 he went to Europe on a business mission and returned with orders from many countries to make their currency. Greece was his first customer and Russia was next. He also secured orders from several South American countries. In 1860 he went to Russia to teach them the American method of engraving and was decorated by Alexander II. He was a proficient linguist and translated many foreign grand lodge proceedings for the American Craft. He was initiated in Montgomery Lodge No. 19, Philadelphia on Sept. 19, 1854 and was exalted in Jerusalem Chapter No. 3, R.A.M. of Philadelphia on Oct. 31, 1826. Made 33° AASR (NJ) Sept. 16, 1864 and active member May, 1867. After removing to New York, he affiliated with Holland Lodge No. 8 and with Morton Commandery No. 4 and Jerusalem Chapter No. 8, R.A.M. He was cornmander of the commandery in 1872-73, was active in the Grand Commandery of New York and was deputy grand commander when he died. He was high priest of the chapter in 1884. d. Feb. 19, 1887.

Reginald H. Gooden Protestant Episcopal Bishop. b. March 22, 1910 at Long Beach, Calif. Graduate of Stanford U. and Berkeley Divinity School (Conn.) and studied at U. of Madrid (Spain). Ordained to ministry in 1934. Served as dean of the Holy Trinity Cathedral in Havana, Cuba from 1939-45, and has been bishop of the missionary district of the church in the Panama Canal Zone since 1945. Mason.

John M. Goodenow (1782-1838) Judge, Supreme Court of Ohio from 1830. b. in Mass., he studied law and was admitted to the bar, practicing in Steubenville, Ohio where he developed a large practice. In 1819 he published American. Jurisprudence in Contrast With the English Common Law. He was elected to U.S. congress in 1929, but resigned the following year to become supreme court judge. He was a member of Old Erie Lodge No. 3 of Ohio.

Frank R. Gooding (1859-1928) U.S. Senator from Idaho, 1921-28, dying in office. b. Sept. 16, 1859 in Teverton, England and came to the U.S. with parents in 1867. He went to Calif. at the age of 15, and to Idaho when 21, where he engaged in stock and farming business for 20 years, being one of the largest sheep raisers in the state and farming several thousand acres. He was governor of Idaho from 1905-07. He was a member of Lincoln Lodge No. 59, Gooding, Idaho, receiving the degrees on April 27, 1916, June 14 and June 28, 1917, and was a member of this lodge at the time of his death on June 24, 1928.

Walter S. Goodland (1862-1947) Governor of Wisconsin, 1943-47, dying in office. b. Dec. 22, 1862 at Sharon, Wis. Admitted to Wis. bar in 1885, and began practice at Wakefield, Mich. He founded the Wakefield Bulletin in 1887, and the Ironwood Times (Mich.) in 1889. He was part owner of the Beloit Daily News (Wis.), and became editor and publisher of the Racine Times (Wis.) in 1900. He was Samuel G. Goodrich state senator of Wis. from 1926-34; lieutenant governor from 1938-42. A member of Belle City Lodge No. 92, Racine, Wis., he received his degrees in Ironwood Lodge No. 389, Ironwood, Mich. on Nov. 7, 1889; April 26 and Sept. 25, 1890. He affiliated with the Ironwood Lodge on Sept. 28, 1926. d. March 12, 1947.

E. Urner Goodman Boy Scout Executive and Founder of Order of the Arrow in 1915. b. May 15, 1891 at Philadelphia, Pa. He became a scout field executive at Philadelphia in 1915, and was scout executive at Philadelphia from 1917-27, and at Chicago from 1927-31. He was national program director from 1931-51 and national field scout commissioner. He wrote Leaders Handbook for the Boy Scouts of America. Raised in Lamberton Lodge No. 487, Philadelphia, Pa. about 1917.

William M. Goodman Major General, U.S. Army. b. Sept. 8, 1892 at Norfolk, Va. Graduate of Virginia Military Inst. in 1912 and various army service schools. Advanced through grades from second lieutenant in 1916 to major general in 1944.

Served overseas in WWI. He was on the General Staff from 1937-42, and in charge of supply division of New York port of embarkation until 1945, and then the San Francisco port of embarkation until 1946. Retired. Mason.

Aaron Goodrich (1807-?) First Chief Justice of the Minnesota Territory, 1849-51. b. July 6, 1807 in Sempronius, N.Y. Studied law and practiced in Tenn. where he was a member of the state legislature in 1847-48. In 1849 he was appointed chief justice of the newly organized territory of Minnesota by President Taylor. He subsequently practiced law in St. Paul, and after Minnesota achieved statehood, was on the commission to revise the laws and prepare a system of pleading and practice. In 1861 Lincoln appointed him secretary of the U.S. legation at Brussels, Belgium, and he served in that capacity for eight years. He was a member of Dover Lodge No. 39, Dover, Tenn. and later of St. Paul's Lodge No. 3, St. Paul, Minn., being past master of the same and deputy grand master of the Grand Lodge of Minnesota at his death. He was buried by the grand lodge.

Herbert F. Goodrich Judge of the U.S. Court of Appeals, Third Circuit since 1940. b. July 29, 1889 at Anoka, Minn. Graduate of Carleton Coll. (Minn.) and Harvard. Taught law at State U. of Iowa, U. of Michigan; U. of Pennsylvania. He has edited and written for many bar journals. Mason.

James P. Goodrich (1864-1940) Governor of Indiana, 1917-21. b. Feb. 18, 1864 at Winchester, Ind. Educated at Notre Dame, De Pauw, and Wabash. Admitted to Indiana bar in 1886, practicing in Winchester and Indianapolis. He was chairman of the

Republican state central committee for ten years, and of the national executive committee eight years. He was a member of the executive committee of the Great Lakes-St. Lawrence Tide Water Assn., chairman of the Indiana-St. Lawrence Waterways Commission, and appointed by president as member of the international St. Lawrence Waterways Commission. Received his degrees in Winchester Lodge No. 56, Winchester, Ind. on Feb. 20, May 14, June 23, 1892 and in 1902 became a charter member of Summers Lodge No. 638 at Winchester. d. Aug. 15, 1940.

Samuel G. Goodrich (1793-1860) American author who wrote under the pen name of "Peter Parley." b. Aug. 19, 1793 in Ridgefield, Conn. After traveling abroad, he settled in Hartford, Conn. where he published books, particularly juveniles. He then moved to Boston where from 1828-42 he edited the original annual, *The Token*. The encouragement he gave to young writers became proverbial. Among these was Nathaniel Hawthorne. He served in the Mass. senate in 1838-39, and from 1841-54 edited Merry's Museum and Parley's Magazine. From 1851-55 he was U.S. consul in Paris, France by appointment of Filmore. He published about 200 volumes, 170 of which were under the name of "Peter Parley." He retired from active authorship in 1859. Member of St. John's Lodge No. 4, Hartford, Conn. d. May 9, 1860.

Angier L. Goodwin U.S. Congressman, 78th to 81st Congresses (1943-50) from 8th Mass. dist. b. Jan. 30, 1881 at Fairfield, Maine. Graduate of Colby Coll. and Harvard U. Admitted to Maine bar in 1905 and practiced in Boston from 1906. Served in both state legislative

bodies. Member of Fidelity Lodge of Melrose, Mass. and past master of same. Member of Waverly Chapter, R.A.M., Melrose Council, R. & S.M. and Hugh de Payens Commandery, K.T. all of Melrose; Past master of the council; 32° AASR (NJ) in Boston; member of Shrine and Eastern Star.

Frederick D. Goodwin Protestant Episcopal Bishop. b. Nov. 5, 1888 in Cismont, Va. Graduate of William and Mary Coll. and Virginia Theol. Sem. Ordained deacon in 1917, and priest in 1918, serving churches and parishes in Virginia. In 1930 he was named bishop coadjutor of Virginia, and has been bishop of Virginia since 1944. Mason.

Godfrey G. Goodwin (1873-1933) U.S. Congressman, 69th to 72nd Congresses (1925-33) from 10th Minn. dist. b. Jan. 11, 1873 at Nicollet Co., Minn. Graduate of U. of Minnesota in 1895. Admitted to bar in 1896 and practiced at Cambridge, Minn. Raised on Jan. 16, 1920 in Helios Lodge No. 273, Cambridge, Minn. 32° AASR (NJ) and Shriner. d. Feb. 16, 1933.

Ichabod Goodwin (1796-1882) Governor of New Hampshire, 1859-61. b. Oct. 10, 1796 at North Berwick, N.H. He entered the service of Samuel Lord, a merchant and ship owner of Portsmouth, and became master of a ship, following the sea until 1832, when he established himself as a merchant in Portsmouth. He served six terms in the state legislature between 1838-56. He also served on two constitutional conventions. He became a member of St. Johns Lodge No. 1, Portsmouth on Nov. 1, 1819. d. July 4, 1882.

Philip A. Goodwin (1882-1937) U.S. Congressman, 73rd and

74th Congresses (1933-36) from 27th N.Y. dist. b. Jan. 20, 1882 at Athens, N.Y. Engaged in lumber and construction business. Received his degrees in Wadsworth Lodge No. 417, Albany, N.Y. on Jan. 23, Feb. 7, Feb. 27, 1907 and on April 16, 1917 affiliated with Ark Lodge No. 48, Coxsackie, N.Y. In 1921-22 he was district deputy grand master of Greene-Ulster district; 32° AASR (NJ). d. June 6, 1937.

Alvin L. Gorby Major General, U.S. Army Medical Corps. Surgeon with the 10th Corps at Inchon landing in Korea. Member of Takoma Lodge No. 29, Takoma Park, D.C.

Bazil Gordon (1768-1847) Sometimes "Basil." Said to have been America's first millionaire. b. May 15, 1768 in Kirkudbright, Scotland. His monument in the Masonic Cemetery at Fredericksburg, Va. is most pretentious and the monument to his daughter is even more exquisite. He was a member of Fredericksburg Lodge No. 4, of Fredericksburg, Va. d. April 20, 1847.

George Gordon (see Earl of Aboyne).

George H. Gordon (1825-1886) Union Major General in Civil War. b. July 19, 1825 at Charlestown, Mass. He was graduated from the U.S. Military Academy in 1846, and took part in the Mexican War, seeing action at the battles of Cerro Gordo, Vera Cruz, Contreras, Chapultepec, and Mexico City. He was twice wounded. He was on frontier duty from 1850-54, resigning in the latter year. He then studied law and entered practice in Boston. At the beginning of the Civil War, he raised the 2nd Mass. regiment and became its colonel. He fought at the second battle of Bull Run, Antietam; Virginia, and Maryland campaigns; military governor of Harper's Ferry; opened communications with Little Rock, Ark. by the White river, and took part in the actions against Charleston and Mobile. He was made brigadier general in 1862 and major general in 1865. He retired to his law practice at Boston and published several books on the Civil War. Member of Bunker Hill Army Lodge No. 5 of Mass. d. Aug. 30, 1886.

John B. Gordon (1832-1904) Governor and U.S. Senator from Georgia; Lieutenant General in Confederate Army. b. Feb. 6, 1832 in Upson Co., Ga. Attended U. of Georgia and admitted to bar. He rose from captain to lieutenant general in the Confederate Army, and was shot eight times, being severely wounded at Antietam. He was U.S. senator from 1873-80 and 1891-97. He was governor of Georgia from 1887-90. At one time he was commander-in-chief of the United Confederate Veterans. A Mason, his lodge is not known, but thought to have been in Atlanta. He was a visitor to Cherokee Lodge No. 66 at Rome, Ga., on two occasions.

Sir Robert Gordon-Gilmour Brigadier General in the British Army and 81st Grand Master Mason of Scotland from 1917-19.

Thomas F. Gordon (1787-1860) Historian and author. b. in Philadelphia, Pa., he was a member of the Philadelphia bar, but devoted much of his time to historical and archaeological research. Among his writings are Digest of the Laws of the United States; History of Pennsylvania From Its Discovery to 1776; History of New Jersey From Its Discovery to 1789; History of America; Cabinet of American History; History of Ancient Mexico and others. Member of Columbia Lodge No. 91, Philadelphia. d. Jan. 17. 1860.

William C. Gordon Banker and Grand Master of the Grand Encampment, Knights Templar, 1952-55. b. Aug. 11, 1878 at Waverly, Mo. Graduate of Missouri Valley Coll. and Harvard U. After a period of teaching school, he succeeded his father as president of the Farmers Savings Bank of Marshall, Mo. He has served as treasurer, vice president and president of the Missouri Bankers Association and organized the agricultural work of that organization. He served a number of years on the agriculture commission and executive council of the American Bankers' Association. He has served as president of the Marshall Chamber of Commerce and a member of the board of trustees of Missouri Valley Coll. as well as president of John Fitzgibbons Hospital. He was raised Feb. 12, 1900 in Trilumina Lodge No. 205 of Marshall and served as master in 1913; exalted in Saline Chapter No. 74, R.A.M. on July 12, 1900, he served as high priest in 1911; greeted in Centralia Council No. 34, Jan. 19, 1914 and knighted in Missouri Commandery No. 36, K.T. of Marshall on Aug. 22, 1900, serving as commander in 1912 and grand commander of Missouri in 1932-33. d. Jan. 10, 1959.

Christopher Gore (1758-1827) Governor and U.S. Senator from Massachusetts. b. Sept. 21, 1758 in Boston. His father was banished as a loyalist in 1778, but was restored to citizenship in 1787. He was graduated from Harvard in 1776, and acquired a lucrative law practice in Boston. In 1789 Washington appointed him the first district attorney for Mass. and he held the office until

1796. He spent eight years in London, first to settle American claims, and later as charge d'affaires. He returned to Boston in 1804, and was appointed governor of Mass. in 1809, serving one year. He served in both branches of the state legislature, and in 1813, was elected U.S. senator, serving until 1816. For a time he was Daniel Webster's tutor in law. He left valuable bequests to several organizations, including Harvard, which named its library building for him. He was a member of Massachusetts Lodge of Boston, being admitted Feb. 13, 1781. d. March 1, 1827.

Howard M. Gore (1887-1947) Secretary of Agriculture in Coolidge cabinet (1924-25) and Governor of West Virginia, 1925-29. b. Oct. 12, 1887 at Clarksburg, W.Va. Graduate of West Virginia U. in 1900. He was in agriculture and livestock raising as well as hotel, banking, and mercantile business. He served as assistant secretary of agriculture in 1923-24, and was commissioner of agriculture for W.Va. in 1931-33. He was active in many national farm organizations and was a founder and patron of boys' and girls' organization work. He was a member of Hermon Lodge No. 6, Clarksburg, W.Va. d. June 20, 1947.

George Gorham American captain of the Revolution who helped stretch the cable across the Hudson river to obstruct the British in their attempt to get ships up the river. Member of King Hiram Lodge No. 12, Derby, Conn.

Howard W. Gorham Established the Perfect Craftsmen Quarry Degree in 1919 as degree for Fellowcraft clubs. b. Oct. 7, 1888 in South Norwalk, Conn. Worked for Bridgeport Brass Co. from 1905-24 rising to production manager. In 1924 he succeeded his father as owner and manager of The Gorham Press, Inc. at South Norwalk. He wrote the 36 page ritual for the Perfect Craftsmen in code. Its use has spread to 40 clubs in Conn. and to numerous states. In 1922 he organized the first chapter of DeMolay in New England at Bridgeport. He organized the Norwalk Lions Club formed organization committee which founded Norwalk Everyman's Bible Class (enrollment of 600); started Norwalk Chamber of Commerce; formed committee to establish Norwalk Community Chest; started Norwalk Town Hall Association; organized committee for better housing for Negroes; organized the Carver Foundation, Inc. in Norwalk; organized United War and Community Fund of Norwalk; and founded the Norwalk Historical Society. Raised in St. John's Lodge No. 3, Bidgeport on May 24, 1911; exalted in Jerusalem Chapter No. 13, R.A.M. in 1913; greeted in Jerusalem Council No. 16 R. & S.M. in 1913. Made honorary life member of his lodge in 1922 for service to Freemasonry. Knighted in Clinton Commandery No. 3, K.T., Norwalk in 1936. Received AASR (NJ) 32° in 1937 and 33° on Sept. 25, 1957. Received the National Cross of Honor from DeMolay in 1930; Shriner and member of Grotto.

William A. Gorman (1814-1876) Union Brigadier General in Civil War, and Territorial Governor of Minnesota. b. Jan. 12, 1814 near Flemingsburg, Ky. A graduate of the U. of Indiana, he was admitted to the bar and practiced in Bloomington, Ind. He served in the Mexican War as a major and colonel with the 4th Indiana regiment which he commanded in several battles. He was severely wounded at Buena Vista. In 1848 he was civil and military governor of Puebla. From 1849-53 he was U.S. Congressman from Indiana. In 1853 he was appointed governor of the territory of Minnesota and ex-officio superintendent of Indians, holding the offices until 1857. He practiced law in St. Paul until 1861 when he was appointed brigadier general of volunteers. He led a bayonet charge at Fair Oaks and commanded a brigade at South Mountain and Antietam. He was mustered out of service in 1864 and returned to St. Paul to practice law. He became a member of Federal Lodge No. 1, Washington, D.C. on July 2, 1850. d. May 20, 1876.

John Gorrie (1803-1855) American inventor. b. in Charleston, S.C. On May 6, 1851 he took out a patent on an artificial refrigeration process containing the basic principle of present day mechanical refrigerators. His statue appears in Statuary Hall of the U.S. Capitol. A bridge, a high school, an elementary school, a chapter of Order of Eastern Star, and a Liberty ship were named in his honor. He was a physician. He was a charter member of Franklin Lodge No. 6, Apalachicola, Fla. and was later its secretary and treasurer.

Henry H. Gorringe (1841-1885) U.S. Naval Commander who brought the famous Egyptian obelisk in New York's Central Park to America in 1880. b. Aug. 11, 1841 in Barbados, W.I., he came to U.S. at an early age and entered the merchant marine service. He served through the Civil War with distinction, rising in rank from a common sailor to lieutenant commander in 1868. He commanded the sloop Portsmouth in the South Atlantic, and in 1876-78 the Gettysburg in the Mediterranean. When the Egyptian government presented the obelisk to the U.S., Gorringe was given charge of transporting it to America. William H. Vanderbilt paid for the expense of its removal ($103,732). Gorringe dug it out of the old location by removing 1,730 cubic yards of earth. Then by an ingenious device of his own invention, lowered it to a horizontal position and cut a hole in the iron steamer Dessoug, purchased from the Egyptian government, through which the obelisk was placed in the hold. The 69 foot shaft which was erected by Thothmes III at Heliopolis about 1600 B.C. was removed to Alexandria in 22 B.C. It has often been claimed that the stone has "Masonic" markings on its base. Subsequently Gorringe criticized naval matters in public, and when called to account, offered his resignation, which was accepted. He then entered the shipbuilding field, but his venture failed. He was a member of Anglo-Saxon Lodge No. 137 of New York City. The lodge at one time tendered him a reception. d. July 7, 1885 as the result of an accident.

Freeman F. Gosden Radio entertainer. The "Amos" of Amos and Andy show. b. May 5, 1899 at Richmond. Va. He began as a tobacco salesman. He became associated with Charles J. Correll in the promotion of amateur theatricals. In 1925 they started their famous comedy team as Sam n' Henry with radio station WGN, Chicago, and two years later they transferred to station WMAQ of Chicago, under the title of Amos and Andy. Broadcast over a national network since 1929, it has probably had the longest life of any show on radio. Gosden is a member of Petersburg Lodge No. 15, Petersburg, Va., affiliating on June 30, 1922.

Charles A. Goss (1863-1938) Chief Justice Supreme Court of Nebraska, 1927-38. b. Dec. 10, 1863 at Edinburg, Ohio. Graduate of Mt. Union Coll. (Ohio). Admitted to bar in 1887, and practiced at Omaha until 1920. He served as U.S. attorney and district judge. Member of Covert Lodge No. 11, Omaha, Nebr., receiving degrees on March 13, April 22, June 15, 1895; 32° AASR. d. Aug. 13, 1938.

Evan B. Goss (1872-1930) Justice Supreme Court of North Dakota, 1911-16. b. Dec. 8, 1872 at Rockford, Mich. Graduate of U. of Michigan. Practiced law first at Bottineau, and later Minot, N.D. Raised Sept. 9, 1898 in Tuscan Lodge No. 44, Bottineau, N.D.; exalted Jan. 23, 1902 in Mystic Chapter No. 13, R.A.M., Towner, N.D.; charter member June 30, 1904 of Phoenicia Chapter No. 17, R.A.M., Bottineau; affiliated Jan. 14, 1913 with Bismarck Chapter No. 10, R.A.M. Bismarck, N.D.; greeted June 28, 1917 in Lebanon Council No. 2, R. & S.M., Rugby, ND.; knighted April 23, 1906 in DeMolay Commandery No. 10, K.T., Minot, N.D. Charter member, Nov. 1909 of Kern Shrine Temple at Grand Forks, N.D. d. March 23, 1930.

Benjamin B. Gossett Cotton textile executive. b. Aug. 18, 1884 at Williamston, S.C. In cotton manufacturing since 1907, he has been president of the following companies at one time or another: Riverside Mfg. Co.; Toxaway Mills; Panola Cotton Mills; Cohannet Mills; Chadwick-Hoskins Co.; Martinsville Cotton Mill Co.; Gossett Mills; Calhoun Mills; Hoskins Corp. He has also been a director or officer in 19 other corporations. Mason, Knight Templar and Shriner.

Charles C. Gossett Former Governor of Idaho. b. Dec. 2, 1888 at

Hillsboro, Ore. He received his degrees in 1921 in Golden Rule Lodge No. 147, Nyssa, Ore.; suspended in 1935, he reinstated in May, 1937, and dimmitted in Dec. 1937, to affiliate with Ashlar Lodge No. 90 of Nampa, Idaho on June 24, 1938.

Frank C. Goudy (1881-1944) Justice, Supreme Court of Colorado, 1942-44. b. Feb. 16, 1881 at Ouray, Colo. Graduate of Stanford and Columbia universities. Admitted to Colorado bar in 1915. Raised April 13, 1891 in Union Lodge No. 7, Denver, Colo.; exalted in Denver Chapter No. 2, Jan. 16, 1892; affiliated with Colorado Chapter No. 29, Denver, on Sept. 21, 1893; knighted in Colorado Commandery No. 1, on May 2, 1892 and affiliated with Coronal Commandery No. 36, Denver on Sept. 21, 1917. Member of consistory in Denver. d. Oct. 14, 1944.

Arthur R. Gould (1857-1946) U.S. Senator from Maine, 1926-31. b. March 16, 1857 at East Corinth, Maine. Engaged in lumber business at Presque Isle and built an electric railroad from that city to Caribou. He was president of the Aroostook Valley Railroad. He served one term in the Maine senate. Raised June 3, 1889 in Trinity Lodge No. 130, Presque Isle, Maine, from which he dimmitted on Dec. 21, 1931; exalted Oct. 25, 1889 in Garfield Chapter No. 48, R.A.M. at Caribou from which he dimmitted on March 13, 1936; greeted on Feb. 20, 1891 in St. Croix Council No. 11, R. & S.M., Calais, dimmitting on March 10, 1892 to become a charter member of Aroostock Council No. 16, Presque Isle; knighted Jan. 3, 1890 in St. Aldermar Commandery No. 17, K.T., Houlton; joined Kora Shrine Temple March 19, 1903 and dimmitted to Anah Temple in 1921. d. July 24, 1946.

Benjamin A. Gould (1824-1896) American astronomer. A graduate of Harvard in 1844, he founded the Astronomical Journal in 1849, which he edited until 1861, and again from 1886-96. He was director of the longitude determinations of the U.S. Coast Survey of 1852-67, and director of the Dudley Observatory of Albany, N.Y. from 1855-59. At the invitation of the Argentina government, he instituted the national observatory at Cordoba in 1870. While there, he made an extended study of the magnitudes of the southern stars, which was published in *Uranometrica Argentina* in 1879. He was a member of St. Andrew's Lodge of Boston and a 33° AASR (NJ).

Robert Freke Gould (1836-1915) English soldier and Masonic historian. He entered the British Army at the age of 18 in 1854, and the same year was commissioned as a lieutenant, serving with distinction in North China in 1860-62. On his return to England, he studied law and qualified as a barrister in 1868. He was initiated in Royal Navy Lodge No. 429 at Ramsgate in 1854. He joined the Friendship Lodge at Gibraltar in 1857, and also served as master of Inhabitants' Lodge No. 153 at Gibraltar. He was first master of Meridian Lodge No. 743, a military lodge attached to his regiment. Traveling to different countries with his regiment, Gould continued his Masonic activities wherever he went. In 1863 he was master of Northern Lodge No. 570 of China, and was grand "Z" of Zion Chapter No. 570, R.A.M. in Shanghai in 1865. Returning to England in 1865, he became a member of Moira Lodge No. 92 and served as its master as well as head of Moira Chapter No. 92, R.A.M., in 1874. He was a founder of the famous Quatour Coronati Lodge No. 2076 of London, in 1884, and became its second master in 1887. He was appointed senior grand deacon of the Grand Lodge of England in 1868, and served many years on the board of general purposes. In his Masonic writings he set a high standard of scholarship. In 1879 he wrote The Four Old Lodges and in 1899 Military Lodges. His greatest work is his *History of Freemasonry*, published in three volumes from 1882 to 1887. It has since been revised twice, first in five volumes by Dudley Wright, and again in four volumes by the Rev. Herbert Poole. The third edition is considered better than the first. He also published *A Concise History of Freemasonry* in 1903. d. March 25, 1915.

John J. J. Gourgas (1777-1865) First Secretary General and third Sovereign Grand Commander of the Northern Jurisdiction, AASR. b. May 23, 1777 of French Huguenot parents in Geneva, Switzerland. The family, fleeing from persecution, later moved to England and then to Mass. in 1803. He was initiated in La Union Francaise Lodge No. 14 (now 17) of New York City on May 19, 1806. On July 29, 1806 he became a member of the Sovereign Chapter of Rose Croix at New York, and on Aug. 4, 1806 received the 32° from Antoine Bideaud, a SGIG from de Grasse's 1802 Supreme Council in the Qest INdies. When Bideaud established a grand consistory two days later, Gourgas was its secretary. On Aug. 5, 1813, Emanuel De La Motta established the Northern Supreme Council, and Gourgas was elevated to the rank of sovereign grand inspector general, 33°, and became the first grand secretary general. In 1832 he became grand commander and served in that position until Aug. 25, 1851. His memory is perpetuated in the northern jurisdiction by the Gour-

gas Medal, the highest honor it confers. d. Feb. 14, 1865.

Thomas E. Grady Judge, Supreme Court of Washington, 1942-45. b. Nov. 19, 1880 at Chippewa Falls, Wis. Graduate of U. of Minnesota in 1904. Admitted to Washington bar in 1905; he was judge of the superior court of Washington from 1911-17. Mason and 32° AASR (SJ).

Theodore Graebner (1876-1950) Anti-Masonic writer. b. Nov. 23, 1876 at Watertown, Wis. Graduate of Luther Coll., New Ulm, Minn. in 1893, Concordia Coll., Ft. Wayne, Ind., 1894, and Concordia Seminary, St. Louis, 1897. Was a professor of theology at Concordia Theological Seminary, St. Louis, from 1914. Member and ordained minister of the Missouri Lutheran Synod. He was editor of the Lutheran Witness from 1914-49, and Bible Student from 1921. Wrote many anti-Masonic tracts and pamphlets which represented the Missouri Synod's attitude towards Freemasonry including Is Masonry a Religion? in 1946. d. Nov. 14, 1950.

Joseph V. Graff (1854-1921) U.S. Congressman to 54th through 61st Congresses, 1895-1911 from Ill. b. July 1, 1854 in Terre Haute, hid. He moved to Delavan, Ill. in 1873 and engaged in mercantile pursuits. He studied law and was admitted to the bar in 1879, practicing at Delavan and later at Pekin. Following his terms in the legislature, he continued law practice at Peoria, where he moved in 1899. Knighted in Peoria Commandery No. 3, K.T. on Nov. 23, 1897. d. Nov. 10, 1921.

Edwin Grafton Active Member, Supreme Council, 33° AASR (SJ) and Sovereign Grand Inspector

General in Montana. Received 32° in 1919; KCCH in 1925; 33° in 1934; appointed deputy in Montana in 1951 and crowned an active member in 1957. He is administrator of the Montana Children's Home and Shodair Crippled Children's Hospital.

David C. Graham Clergyman, scientist. b. March 21, 1884 at Green Forest, Ark. From 1911 to 1948 he was an evangelistic and educational missionary to China. He taught in the West China Union U. and was curator of the museum of that institution. He was a collector for the Smithsonian Institution and sent them many natural history specimens, including many new species and nine new genera. He also collected two live pandas which were presented by the Chinese government to the American people in 1941. He has written several books on the life and religion of Szechwan Province, China. Mason.

Horace F. Graham (1862-1941) Governor of Vermont, 1917-19. b. Feb. 7, 1862 in New York City. Graduate (cum laude) of Columbia Law School in 1888. He practiced law at Craftsbury, Vt. He served as state's attorney, and in the state legislature for two terms. In 1900 he was a presidential elector. From 1902-17 he was auditor of accounts for Vermont. He was a member and past master of Meridian Sun Lodge No. 20 of Crafts-bury, Vt. d. Nov. 23, 1941.

J. Clark Graham President of Yankton College (S.D.) 1945-54. b. Feb. 9, 1894 at Aledo, Ill. Graduate of Grinnell Coll. (Ia.) and Columbia U. He was with Ripon Coll. (Wis.) from 1916-45, successively as instructor in English, associate professor, professor and head of dept. of psychology and education. Since 1954 he has been English professor at Drury Coll.

(Mo.). He became a member of Lafayette Lodge No. 52 at Montezuma, Ia. in 1915 and received the 32° AASR (SJ) at Yankton, S.D. on Nov. 21, 1948.

Louis E. Graham U.S. Congressman to 76th to 80th Congresses (1939-49) from 25th Pa. dist. b. Aug. 4, 1880 in New Castle, Pa. Graduate of Washington and Jefferson Coll. in 1901, he began law practice in Beaver, Pa. He was U.S. attorney of the Western district of Pa. from 1929-33, and special assistant to U.S. attorney general in 1934-35. Received degrees in St. James Lodge No. 457, Beaver, Pa. on March 16, April 13, May 18, 1905; life member, past master in 1909; and secretary from 1911-19. Life member of Eureka Chapter No. 167, R.A.M., Rochester, Pa. and member of Beaver Valley Council No. 54, R. & S.M. and Beaver Valley Commandery No. 84, K.T., both of Beaver Falls, Pa. Life member and 32° AASR (NJ) at New Castle, Pa. Life member of Syria Shrine Temple at Pittsburgh and honorary member of Almas Temple in Washington, D.C.

William J. Graham (1872-1936) Presiding Judge of U.S. Court of Customs and Patent Appeals, Washington from 1924. b. Feb. 7, 1872 at New Castle, Pa. Graduate of U. of Illinois in 1893 and practiced law at Aledo, Ill. from 1895. Member of the 65th to 68th congresses (1917-25) from 14th Ill. dist. Member of Aledo Lodge No. 252 at Aledo, Ill., receiving degrees on May 14, June 25 and Oct. 22, 1895 and serving as master in 1899. d. Nov. 10, 1936.

Elijah S. Grammer (1868-1936) U.S. Senator from Washington, 1932-33. b. April 3, 1868 in Hickory Co., Mo. In logging and construction business in Washington most of his life. President and manager of Grammer Investment Co. Mason. d. Nov. 21, 1936.

George McInvale Grant U.S. Congressman to 75th to 81st Congresses (1939-51) from 2nd Ala. dist. b. July 11, 1897 at Louisville, Ala. Graduate of U. of Alabama in 1922, and admitted to bar in same year, practicing in Troy. Served in U.S. Army in WWI. Was state commander of the American Legion in 1929 and national secretary of Pi Kappa Phi fraternity from 1922-25. Mason and Shriner.

James Grant (1720-1806) British General and First Governor of Florida under English rule. b. in Ballendalloch, Scotland. He was a major of the Montgomerie Highlanders in 1757. In 1758 he led 800 men to reconnoiter Fort Duquesne, but was surprised and defeated with a loss of 295. He was appointed governor of East Florida in 1760, and lieutenant colonel of the 40th Foot. He defeated the Cherokee Indians in a severe battle at Etchoe in 1761. In the Revolutionary War he commanded the 4th and 6th British brigades at the battle of Long Island in Aug. 1776. In December of that year, Lord Howe gave him command of the British troops in N.J. at a critical period, and the American victories of Trenton and Princeton followed. In 1777 he was made a major general and commanded the 2nd brigade. He fought at Brandywine and Germantown, and in 1778 was detached with a strong force to cut off Lafayette on the Schuylkill, but was unsuccessful. He defeated Lee at Monmouth and shortly thereafter sailed for the French West Indies in command of the troops in that sector. He was made governor of Stirling Castle and a lieutenant general in 1782, and full

general in 1796. While in Florida, Grant, with three others, petitioned the Grand Lodge of Scotland for a charter to establish Grant's East Florida Lodge at St. Augustine. It was also requested that Grant be commissioned as the provincial grand master over the lodges in the southern district of North America. The petition was granted March 15, 1768. In 1771, Grant as grand master, issued a charter to St. Andrew's Lodge No. 1, at Pensacola, West Florida, formed by ten brethren who belonged to Lodge No. 108 of Scottish registry to be held in the 31st Regiment of Foot of the British Army. This lodge continued for ten years until the city and port were captured by the Spaniards in 1781. When Florida was ceded back to Spain in 1783, in exchange for the Bahama Islands, the English settlers abandoned their homes, and the Grand Lodge of the Southern District of North America ceased to exist. d. April 13, 1806.

Jesse R. Grant Father of Ulysses S. Grant, q.v. Member of Bethel Lodge No. 61, Bethel, Ohio.

Robert A. Grant U.S. Congressman to 76th to 80th Congresses (1939-49) from 3rd Ind. dist. b. July 31, 1905 in Marshall Co., Ind. Graduate of U. of Notre Dame in 1928 and 1930. Admitted to bar and practiced in South Bend in 1930. Member of South Bend Lodge No. 294 at South Bend, Ind., receiving his degrees on Feb. 8, Feb. 15 and March 8, 1935. Shriner.

Ulysses S. Grant (1822-1885) Eighteenth President of the United States. Not a Freemason, although he had a number of close associations with the craft. His father, Jesse R. Grant, was a member of Bethel Lodge No. 61, Bethel, Ohio and his father-in-law, Lewis Dent, was a member of Amith Lodge No. 5, Zanesville, Ohio. Even Grant's original name had Masonic significance for he was baptized Hiram Ulysses. His mother was Hannah Simpson, who married Jesse R. Grant in June, 1821, in Clermont Co., Ohio. When Thomas L. Hamer, q.v., appointed him to West Point, he did not know that he was known by his middle name and he presumed his middle name was from his mother's family, so his official appointment was in the name of Ulysses S. When Grant called it to the attention of the West Point officials, they did not feel authorized to correct it, and it became the name by which he was known.

A.F.A. de Grasse-Tilly (See under de Grasse).

Charles Gratiot (1788-1855) Brigadier General in War of 1812. b. in Missouri. A graduate of the U.S. Military Academy in 1806, he served with distinction in War of 1812 as chief engineer with Harrison's army. He was engaged in the defense of Fort Meigs in 1813 and the attack on Fort Mackinack in 1814. In 1815 he was superintendent of the fortifications on the Delaware River, and later those in Hampton Roads, Va. He was breveted brigadier general in 1828, and appointed inspector of West Point, holding that office for ten years. He was dismissed for having failed to pay into the treasury certain balances of money placed in his hands for public purposes. After holding a clerkship in the land office at Washington, D.C. from 1840-55, he went to St. Louis, where he died destitute. Fort Gratiot on the St. Clair River in Michigan and the villages of Gratiot in Michigan and Wisconsin were named for him. He was senior warden of Comfort Lodge No. 143 (now defunct) at Old Point Comfort, Va. d. in St. Louis May 18, 1855.

Henry Grattan (1746-1820) Irish orator and statesman. b. in Dublin, he was called to the Irish bar in 1772. He was a member of the Irish parliament from 1775-97, and of the British parliament from 1805-20. He was a champion of Irish independence and Catholic emancipation. He particularly opposed the union with England in 1800. He was elected a member of First Volunteer Lodge of Ireland in 1784.

John J. Gravatt Protestant Episcopal Bishop. b. Oct. 3, 1881 at Hampton, Va. Graduate of U. of Virginia in 1903. He taught school for two years and was ordained a deacon in 1908, and priest in 1909. He was rector in Rapidan, Va. and Frankfort, Ky., and a chaplain in the U.S. Army overseas in WWI. After the war he was rector in Staunton, Va. until 1939 when named bishop of Upper South Carolina. Mason.

William L. Gravatt (1858-1942) Protestant Episcopal Bishop of West Virginia from 1916. b. Dec. 15, 1858 in Port Royal, Va. Graduate of Virginia Theol. Sem. in 1884; Washington and Lee U. in 1904. Ordained deacon in 1884 and priest in 1885. Served churches in Richmond, Va., 1885-87; Norfolk, Va., 1887-93 and Charles Town, W. Va., 1893-99. Was elected coadjutor bishop of W. Va. in 1899 and bishop in 1916. He was grand chaplain of the Grand Lodge of West Virginia from 1917-35; grand chaplain of the Grand Chapter, R.A.M. of W. Va. from 1909-29 and grand prelate of the Grand Commandery, K.T. of W. Va., 1916-40. Was a member of Beni Kedem Shrine Temple and a 33° AASR of the

Southern Jurisdiction. d. Feb. 14, 1942.

Bib Graves (1873-1942) Governor of Alabama, 1927-31 and 1935-39. b. April 1, 1873 at Hope Hull, Ala. Graduate of U. of Alabama and Yale. Admitted to bar in 1897 and practiced at Montgomery. Served as Colonel in WWI. He was adjutant general of Alabama from 1907-11. He was raised in Andrew Jackson Lodge No. 173 of Montgomery in Feb., 1897 and received the 32° AASR (SJ) Oct. 7, 1921 at Montgomery and KCCH Oct. 18, 1927. d. March 14, 1942.

Duncan M. Gray Protestant Episcopal Bishop. b. May 5, 1898 at Meridian, Miss. Graduate of U. of the South at Sewanee, Tenn. in 1925. Ordained deacon in 1925, and priest in 1926, serving as rector of churches in Rosedale, Cleveland, Canton, Lexington, Columbus, Macon, Greenwood, and Winona (all Miss.) until he was elected bishop of Mississippi in 1943. Mason.

Gordon Gray Secretary of the Army, 1949-50. b. May 30, 1909 at Baltimore, Md., he graduated from the U. of North Carolina and Yale. He practiced law in N.C. and published the Winston-Salem Journal and Twin City Sentinel. He also operated radio station WSJS from 1935-47. He was assistant secretary of the Army from 1947-49. For eight months in 1950 he was special assistant to the president of the U.S. In 1950 he was president of the U. of North Carolina. He was assistant secretary of defense for internal security affairs from 1955-57 and since 1957 has been director of the office of defense mobilization. He served in the Army 1942-45, first as a private and later an officer. Member of Winston Lodge No. 167, he re- ceived his degrees on April 12, July 12 and Aug. 2, 1940.

Harold Gray Cartoonist and creator of *Little Orphan Annie*. b. Jan. 20, 1894 at Kankakee, Ill. Graduate of Purdue U. in 1917. He joined the staff of the *Chicago Tribune* as an artist in 1917 and entered the Army in 1918. Discharged as a second lieutenant in 1918, he returned to the *Tribune*. In 1920 he started his own commercial art studio and was assistant to Sidney Smith on The Gumps cartoon. He began drawing his famous *Little Orphan Annie* strip in 1924. It first appeared in the *New York News* and *Chicago Tribune*, but is now published in more than 250 newspapers. Charter member of Lombard Lodge No. 1098, Lombard, Ill., where he still maintains membership.

Cary T. Grayson (1878-1938) Rear Admiral, U.S. Navy. b. Oct. 11, 1878 in Culpepper Co., Va. Graduate of the U. of the South, Medical College of Virginia and U.S. Naval Medical School. Commissioned assistant surgeon in 1903, he was promoted to medical director with rank of rear admiral in 1916. He was surgeon on the presidential yacht, Mayflower, and was attending and consulting physician at the Naval dispensary in Washington during the Roosevelt and Taft administrations. He was physician to President Wilson. In 1935 he was chairman of the American National Red Cross. He retired from the Navy in 1928. He was raised in Temple Noyes Lodge No. 32, Washington, D.C. on July 13, 1911. d. Feb. 15, 1938.

John Greaton (1741-1783) Brigadier General in Revolutionary War. b. March 10, 1741 in Roxbury, Mass. Before the war he was an innkeeper and officer of militia in Rox-bury. On July 12, 1775 he was ap-pointed colonel of the 24th regiment, and the following October, colonel of the 36th. Still later he became colonel of the 3rd Mass. regiment on the con-tinental establishment. During the siege of Boston he led an expedition which destroyed the buildings on Long Island in Boston harbor. On April 15, 1776 he was ordered to Canada and in December joined Washington in N.J., and was after-wards transferred to Heath's division at West Point. Congress made him a brigadier general Jan. 7, 1783. It is thought that he was admitted a mem-ber of Masters' Lodge of Albany, N.Y. in 1777, while stationed at West Point. He was present in American Union lodge as a visitor on June 24, 1779. d. Dec. 16, 1783. G.L. of Mass. met in his tavern in 1761. Was J.W. of Washington Lodge No. 10 (Military) in the Mass. brigade when organized at West Point in 1779.

Horace Greeley (1811-1872) American journalist, political leader and anti-Mason. b. in Amherst, N.H. He moved to New York in 1831, where with Jonas Winchester, he founded the New Yorker, a weekly journal, in 1834. In 1841 he founded the New York Tribune and merged the two papers. The Tribune was an outstanding success and in turn it gave him influence in molding thought in the people of the North. He sup-ported the Free Soil movement; en-couraged antislavery sentiment; sup-ported the administration in the Civil War. After the war, he was an advo-cate of universal amnesty and suf-frage, believing that the long impris-onment of Jefferson Davis without trial was a violation of Davis' constitu-tional rights. He accepted the nomi-nation for the presidency by a body of liberal Republicans and was en-dorsed by the Democrats, but badly beaten in the election of 1872. His biographer, Patton, thus refers to his attitude on Freemasonry: "Our ap-prentice (Greeley) embraced the anti-Masonic side of this controversy, and embraced it warmly. It was natural that he should. And for the next two or three years he expended more breath in denouncing the Order of Freemasons, than upon any other subject—perhaps than on all other subjects put together. To this day secret societies are his special aver-sion."

Adolphus W. Greely (1844-1935) Arctic Explorer and Major Gen-eral, U.S. Army. b. March 27, 1844 at Newburyport, Mass. He served in the Civil War from private to major and was three times wounded. After the war he remained in the army and rose to brigadier general and chief signal officer in 1887, and major gen-eral in 1906. From 1876-79 he con-structed 2,000 miles of telegraph line in Texas, Dakotas, and Montana. In 1881 he was placed in charge of a U.S. expedition to establish a chain of 13 circumpolar stations, and his party of 25 reached the northernmost point yet achieved (83° 23'), and discov-ered new land north of Greenland, crossing Grinnell Land to the Polar Sea. Two relief parties failed to reach them, and by the time the third party found them, all but seven had starved to death. He was later in charge of building telegraph lines in Cuba, China, Philippines, and Alaska. He was in charge of relief operations in the San Francisco earthquake of 1906. He authored many books in-cluding Three Years of Arctic Service; Handbook of Polar Discoveries; and Polar Regions in the Twentieth Cen-tury. A member of St. Marks Lodge of Newburyport, Mass., he was knighted in Newburyport Commandery, K.T. on

June 17, 1867, and on June 24, following, carried the banner of the commandery in the procession in Boston
at the occasion of the dedication of
the Masonic temple. He was made an
honorary member of Kane Lodge No.
454 (the explorer's lodge) of New
York City. The lodge tendered him a
reception, April 28, 1885, and he was
given an illuminated certificate of
membership in the lodge. While at
Fort Conger, Grinnell Land, he made
a Masonic flag which was carried by
Lieutenant Lockwood and Sergeant
Brainard of his command, to the
shores of the Polar Sea on the Northwest coast of Greenland, and there
displayed at Lockwood Island on May
13th and 15th. It was afterwards presented to Kane Lodge No. 454, New
York City.

Allen P. Green (1876-1956)
Founder of the world's largest fire
brick company. b. in Jefferson City,
Mo. on a site now included in the
state capitol grounds. Shortly after he
was graduated from the Missouri
School of Mines at Rolla, he bought a
local company in Mexico, Mo. and
built the world's largest fire brick
plant—the A. P. Green Fire Brick Co.
He expanded the company into an
international industry, with 15 domestic and Canadian plants. Its sales
organization has reached into 54 foreign countries. He pioneered many
developments in the refractories industry, and was the leader in making
Missouri the fire clay center of the
world. In 1928 he gave $100,000 to
the School of the Ozarks at Hollister,
Mo. He was a national director of
both the Y.M.C.A. and the Boy
Scouts; director of the Wabash Railroad; vice president of the Missouri
State Historical Society, and a member of the advisory board which developed the Missouri Conservation
Commission. An enthusiastic Free-

mason, he gave of his time and
money to Masonic purposes. The lot
on which the new Masonic Temple in
Mexico stands is his gift to the local
bodies of that city. He was a member
of Hebron Lodge No. 354, Mexico
Chapter No. 27, R.A.M. and Crusade
Commandery No. 23, K.T. all of Mexico. He was exalted on Jan. 18, 1939,
and knighted, May 1, 1939. Before
his death he set up a foundation
which granted $350,000, of which the
major part went to medical research
in Parkinson's disease. In his will the
foundation was left about two million
dollars. Thousands of dollars in other
bequests were made, including
$1,000 to the Grand Lodge of Mis-
souri. d. June 9, 1956.

Charles M. Green President
of the Sperry Gyroscope Co. since
1955. b. March 31, 1891 at Camp
Dennison, Ohio. He began as an apprentice machinist in 1906, and was
subsequently a clerk, accountant,
general storekeeper, assistant production superintendent for a chemical
company, service manager for Peters
Cartridge Co., and works manager for
same. From 1934-44 he was with
Remington Arms Co. as works manager, production manager, and plant
director. He went with Sperry in 1944
as vice president. He is also vice
president of the Sperry Corporation
and president of Sperry Farragut
Corp., Sperry Gyroscope Co. of Canada. Member of Mason Lodge No.
678, Mason, Ohio, and former junior
warden of same. Member of Mason
Chapter No. 494, O.E.S. and past
patron.

Dwight H. Green (1897-
1958) Governor of Illinois, 1940-49. b.
Jan. 9, 1897 at Ligonier, Ind. Graduate of U. of Chicago. Admitted to bar
in 1922 and practiced at Chicago until
1926. He then went with the bureau

of internal revenue as a special counsel and served as special assistant to U.S. attorney in Northern Ill. in charge of income tax matters. He conducted prosecutions against notorious gangsters and public office holders charged with acceptance of bribes. He was the keynote speaker at the National Republican convention of 1948. In WWI he was a second lieutenant in the Air Service, and a pilot and flying instructor. Member of Ligonier Lodge No. 185, Ligonier, Ind. 32° AASR (NJ) in Oriental Consistory of Chicago on Nov. 8, 1934 and 33° on Sept. 29, 1943 at Buffalo, N.Y. Member of St. John's Conclave No. 1, Red Cross of Constantine, and Shriner of Medinah Temple, Chicago. Member of Lincoln Park Chapter No. 177, R.A.M.; Chicago Council No. 4, R. & S.M.; Chicago Commandery No. 19, K.T. d. Feb. 20, 1958.

Fred W. Green (1872-1936) Governor of Michigan, 1927-31. b. Oct. 20, 1872 at Manistee, Mich. Graduate of U. of Michigan in 1898. Began practice of law at Ypsilanti in 1899, and became identified with the Ypsilanti Reed Furniture Co.; he moved with it to Ionia in 1904. He was vice president of the National Rattan & Willow Co. He served in the Spanish-American War as a first lieutenant and was with the Michigan national guard 14 years, rising to brigadier general. He was a member of Phoenix Lodge No.13, Ypsilanti, and received the 32° AASR (NJ) at Detroit in Oct. 1928.

James S. Green (1817-1870) U.S. Senator from Missouri, 1857-61. Sometimes called "Missouri's greatest orator." b. Feb. 28, 1817 in Fauquier Co., Va. Admitted to bar and practiced at Canton, Mo. He served in the U.S. congress from 1847-51, and was named charge d'affaires in Colombia, S.A. in 1853, and consul in 1854; but he tired of the position and returned to the U.S. in 1856, and was again elected to congress, but did not take his seat, having been chosen to the senate. His senatorial career was brilliant. No one could surpass him as a reasoner or excel him as an orator, and few equaled him. He was one of the few senators who could stand up against Stephen A. Douglas, q.v., and in 1859 defeated him in a debate. He was the champion of the slave interests and states' rights. He was dropped from the senate because of his slavery views, and was under surveillance by both the Union and Confederacy—the former, to quiet his secession activities, and the latter, requiring an oath that he would not take up arms against them. He moved to St. Louis and practiced law, dying there Jan. 9, 1870. He was a member and past master of Canton Lodge No. 100, Canton, Mo.

Jesse Green (?-1834) Delaware political and military leader. A Roman Catholic, he was the second grand master of the Grand Lodge of Delaware, serving three terms from 1809-11. His great, great grandmother was Helen Calvert, daughter of the first Lord of Baltimore, q.v. He was elected eight times to the lower house from Sussex Co., Del. (1797-1807), and was speaker in 1804. He was adjutant general of Delaware from 1808 to 1814. When the War of 1812 broke out, he helped raise a regiment of Delaware and Maryland troops and was present at the British bombard merit of Lewes. He owned some 7,000 acres of land. He was raised in Washington Lodge No. 3 (Md. charter). This lodge was originally chartered in 1770 by Pa. as No. 15, Fells Point, Md., then the easternmost part of the city of Baltimore. It is still in existence. On Sept. 18,

1792, he became charter master of St. John's Lodge No. 10 at Georgetown, Del. The lodge became dormant in 1796, but was revived June 23, 1800, and Green was again named as first master of the lodge, then known as Hope Lodge No. 31, at Laureltown, Del. After he was grand master, he served as the first master of Temple Lodge No. 9, Milford. d. Aug. 21, 1834.

Robert S. Green (?-1895) Governor of New Jersey. He was raised in Washington Lodge No. 33, Elizabeth, N.J. on April 18, 1855 and three days later affiliated with Princeton Lodge No. 38, Princeton, N.J., to become warrant master. He was again reelected master in 1856. On Jan. 2, 1857 he reaffiliated with Washington Lodge No. 2, and from 1859-63 was grand pursuivant of the Grand Lodge of New Jersey. d. May 7, 1895.

Thomas Green (1816-1864) Confederate Major General in Civil War. b. in Virginia. His father was chief justice of Tenn. and president of Lebanon law college. Thomas moved to Texas in early manhood, and was a ranger in the war of Texan independence; he also served in the Mexican War. From 1855-58 he was clerk of the supreme court of Texas. He joined the Confederate army and fought in the battles of Valverde, Bisland 'and Galveston. In the campaign of 1863 he commanded the cavalry under Gen. Richard Taylor and repulsed the Union forces at the battle of Bayou la Fourche. He was made major general after this action and placed in command of the cavalry of the trans-Mississippi dept. In April, 1864, he commanded the Texas infantry in the Red River campaign. He was mortally wounded near Pleasant Hill, April 12, 1864, from a shot by a Union gunboat. Member of Austin Lodge No. 12 (Texas).

Thomas E. Green (1857-?) Churchman, lecturer, and author. b. Dec. 27, 1857 at Harrisville, Pa. He was first a Presbyterian minister in Mt. Carmel, Chicago, and Sparta, Ill. (1880-86), and then became a Protestant Episcopal priest in 1887, serving first a Chicago church and later, Grace Church of Cedar Rapids, Iowa. In 1898 he was elected bishop of Iowa, but declined. He began lecturing in 1903, and journeyed around the world in 1910-11 in the interest of international peace. He was a delegate at large to the 4th American Peace Conference of 1913 and a special lecturer for Carnegie Endowment for Peace, the American Red Cross, U.S. Treasury dept. and other organizations. Received many foreign decorations. He was chaplain of the Republican national convention in 1884, and of the Democratic national conventions of 1889-92-95-98. Mason, Knight Templar and 32° AASR, he was grand prelate of the Grand Commandery, K.T. of Iowa in 1897-99 and 1901. He wrote *The Mason as a Citizen*. Other books included *The Hill Called Calvary; In Praise of Valor; The War Trust; The Burden of Nations; War Facts and Peace; The Salt of the Earth* and many others. Deceased.

Warren E. Green (1870-1945) Governor of South Dakota, 1931-33. b. March 10, 1870 in Jackson Co., Wis. He engaged in farming and stock raising near Hazel, S.D. from 1895. He served three terms in the state senate and was a member of the state board of charities and corrections from 1913-19. He was made a Mason April 17, 1918, in Sioux Valley Lodge No. 125, Castlewood, S.D. Received 32° AASR (SJ) in Oriental Consistory, Yankton, S.D., in Nov. 1931.

William M. Green (1876-1942). Protestant Episcopal Bishop. b. July 12, 1876 at Greenville, Miss. Graduate of the U. of the South. Ordained deacon in 1899, and priest in 1900. From 1900 to 1919 he served various churches in Miss. and Tenn. He was consecrated bishop coadjutor of Miss. in 1919, and bishop of Miss. by succession on Nov. 2, 1938. Member of King Solomon Lodge No. 333, Meridian, Miss., receiving degrees on July 13, 1906, Nov. 19, 1907, and April 8, 1908. d. Nov. 12, 1942.

Christopher Greene (1737-1781) Colonel of the American Revolution known as the "hero of Red Bank." b. May 12, 1737 in Warwick, R.I. He served in the R.I. legislature in 1772-74. He was made a major by the state legislature in 1775 and given a company, which he marched to Cambridge, and subsequently was placed in command of the first battalion under Benedict Arnold, q.v., by Washington. He was with Arnold in Quebec. Captured in the attack on that city, he was prisoner for eight months. After his release, he was made a colonel and placed in charge of Fort Mercer on' the Delaware. When the fort was assaulted by Hessians in Oct. 1777, he repulsed them with heavy loss, including the mortal wounding of their leader, Count Donop. For this, congress voted Greene a sword. In 1778 Greene and his troops were detached for duty in R.I. and put under command of Gen. John Sullivan. On May 13, 1781 his headquarters on the Croton river was surrounded by loyalists and he was killed. A monument to his memory was erected near Red Bank, N.J. in 1829 by N.J. and Pa. volunteers. He

was initiated March 3, 1779 in St. John's Lodge, Providence, R.I.

Frank L. Greene (1870-1930) U.S. Senator from Vermont, 1923-30, dying while in office. b. Feb. 10, 1870 at St. Albans, Vt. He began as an errand boy in a railway office and became stenographer, and later chief clerk of the freight department. In 1891 he entered the newspaper business as a reporter on the St. Albans Daily Messenger, and was editor of the same from 1899 to 1912. He was U.S. congressman to the 62nd to 67th congresses (1912-23) from first Vt. dist. He served in the Spanish-American War from 1888-1900 and was captain of Co. B, 1st Vt. Inf. Vols. Greene was a member of Englesby Lodge No. 84, St. Albans, Vt. receiving his degrees on April 4, April 11, April 18, 1891. d. Dec. 17, 1930.

Henry A. Greene (1856-1921) Major General, U.S. Army. b. Aug. 5, 1856 at Matteawan, N.Y. Graduate of U.S. Military Academy in 1879. Rose through ranks to brigadier general in 1914, and major general in 1917. He served in Texas and in Montana, organizing and commanding for nearly three years a company of Sioux Indians. He commanded a company in the Spanish-American War in Cuba, and also in the Philippine insurrection. In 1903 he was a member of the board to select the first general staff of the Army, and was first secretary of the staff. He later commanded departments in Oklahoma City, St. Louis, Alaska, Indiana, Canal Zone, Chicago, Arizona, and Washington. He was on observation duty with French and English forces in WWI. Retired in 1918. Mason. d. Aug. 19, 1921.

Nathanael Greene (1742-1786) General of the American Revolution. b. June 6, 1742, at Potowomut (Warwick) , R.I. He and Washington, along with Putman, Gates and Heath were the only general officers who served throughout the War. He was made a brigadier general in the Continental Army in June, 1885, and a major general in Aug., 1776. He led the left wing of the American force at Trenton on Dec. 24, 1776 and captured the Hessians. In 1778 he was made quartermaster general of the Army. When criticized by Congress in 1780, he resigned, but at Washington's insistence took over the command of the Army of the South from Gates, q.v. Here he conducted a strategic retreat in 1781, and finally turned and forced the British out of Georgia and the Carolinas, and back to three coastal bases. He was considered a military genius by Washington. A Quaker, he was disciplined by them for his military activities. Masonic scholars are still searching for his connection with the fraternity. It is claimed by some that he was a member of a Rhode Island Lodge, and by others, a member of a military lodge. Throughout the revolution he wore a Masonic medal that was presented to him by Lafayette, q.v., and this medal is now in the possession of the Grand Lodge of Rhode Island. A Masonic apron, said to have been worn by him, was presented to Lakewood Lodge No. 601, Lakewood, Ohio in 1937, by William Greene, a descendant and member of that lodge. On March 21, 1825 the Grand Lodge of Georgia united with Lafayette in laying the cornerstone of a monument to Greene in Savannah (also one to Pulaski, q.v.). With his family, he retired from public life to a plantation in Savannah, Ga. His Savannah monument's cornerstone was laid with Masonic ceremony, making the most of the presence of Lafayette in that city. However it was dedicated to the

"Saviour of the South" and not to a "brother." Obviously he did not wear any Masonic medal presented to him by Lafayette "throughout the Revolution" as Lafayette was not in this country until the middle of 1777. Historian James R. Case asks "And where were Lafayette and Greene associated —and when?" Greene and Washington were not the only general officers to serve "throughout the Revolution"; Putnam, Gates and Heath were others. d. June 19, 1786 at Savannah.

Samuel D. Greene Anti-Mason and Anti-Masonic writer. Originally a member of Batavia Lodge No. 433, Batavia, N.Y., he was expelled on Feb. 8, 1827. This was shortly after the disappearance of William Morgan, q.v., of Batavia who had written an expose of Freemasonry which started the anti-Masonic movement in the U.S.

Lawrence N. Greenleaf (1838-1922) Masonic author. b. Oct. 4, 1838 in Boston, Mass. He was initiated in Columbia Lodge of that city in 1863. In that same year he moved to Denver, Colo., where he affiliated with Denver Lodge No. 5. He was in the mercantile business until 1893, when he purchased and edited the Masonic monthly Square and Compass. He retired in 1917. He served as master of the lodge five times; exalted in Denver Chapter No. 2, R.A.M., he was twice high priest. He received the cryptic degrees in Boston Council in 1868, and was a charter member of Denver Council No. 1, R. & S.M., and master in 1901. Knighted in DeMolay Commandery at Boston in June, 1868, he affiliated with Colorado Commandery No. 1, K.T., July 17, 1883, and was commander in 1890. He was grand master of the Grand Lodge of Colorado in

1880; grand high priest in 1867, and grand master of the grand council in 1907. He was mainly responsible for organizing the AASR (SJ) in Colorado and was deputy for Colorado in 1878 and 33° in 1880. His best known Masonic poems are Lodge-Room Over Simpkins' Store; Hands Across the Sea; and Live On, 0 Masonry! d. Oct. 25, 1922.

Simon Greenleaf (1783-1853) Lawyer and author. b. Dec. 5, 1783 in Newburyport, Mass. Moved with his family to Maine in 1801 and studied law. In 1806 he moved to Standish, and later to Gray, practicing in both places. In 1818 he moved to Portland, and in 1820, after the admission of Maine to the Union, he became reporter of the supreme court, holding that office until 1832, when appointed royal professor of law in Harvard. He remained at Harvard until 1848. He was considered one of the foremost legal authorities. He was made a Mason in Cumberland Lodge in 1804 and was master in 1807. He is considered the leading spirit in establishing the Grand Lodge of Maine, and was its second grand master in 1823. He wrote Origin and Principles of Freemasonry. His greatest legal work is Treatise on the Law of Evidence. d. Oct. 6, 1853.

Clifford C. Gregg Director of Chicago Natural History Museum since 1937. b. July 9, 1895 at Cincinnati, Ohio. Graduate of U. of Cincinnati in 1917. He was assistant to the director of the Field Museum of Natural History (now Chicago Natural History Museum) from 1926-37. Served as an Infantry lieutenant in WWI, and WWII rose to colonel, serving with 6th Corps Area in Chicago, and later at Tank Destroyer Center, Camp Hood, Texas, and Army Ground Forces, Washington, D.C. He has been vice

president, trustee, and general secretary of Beta Theta Pi social fraternity. Member of Vattier Lodge No. 386, Cincinnati, Ohio, receiving degrees on May, 18, 1918, Feb. 17 and March 31, 1919; received 32° AASR (NJ) in Massachusetts Consistory; Aleppo Shrine Temple, Boston and past president of Camp Hood (Texas) Chapter No. 208, National Sojourners.

John Gregg (1828-1864) Confederate General of the Civil War who was the last to command the famous Texas Brigade in Lee's Army. b. Sept. 2, 1828. A member of Fairfield Lodge No. 103, Fairfield, Texas, he received the degrees in May, Aug. and Oct., 1854, and was senior warden in 1855; member of Palestine Commandery No. 3, K.T. He was killed on Oct. 7, 1864.

Clifford V. Gregory (1883-1941) Editor of the Prairie Farmer, Chicago. b. Oct. 20, 1883 at Mason City, Ia. He was a professor at Iowa Agricultural Coll. before becoming associated with the Prairie Farmer Publishing Co. in 1911. He became vice president of the company which published Prairie Farmer and owned station WLS from 1911-37. In the latter year he became associate publisher of Wallace's Farmer and Iowa Homestead. Member of Wheaton Lodge No. 269, Wheaton, Ill., receiving degrees on Aug. 24, Aug. 31 and Oct. 13, 1915. d. Nov. 18, 1941.

David T. Gregory (1889-1956) Bishop, United Brethren Church. b. July 16, 1889 at Martinsburg, W.Va. Graduate of Lebanon Valley Coll. (Pa.) in 1917. Served churches in W.Va., Va., and Pa. from 1914-17. From 1920-21 he was associate editor of Religious Telescope, and president of Shenandoah Coll.

1922-26. He was pastor of the Euclid Ave., U.B. Church of Dayton from 1926-36, and superintendent of the Miami Conference from 1932-37. From 1937-50 he was executive secretary of the church's national council of administration and was named bishop in 1950. Member of Stillwater Lodge No. 616, Dayton, Ohio, receiving degrees on July 9, Sept. 10 and Sept. 27, 1928; 32° AASR (NJ). d. Dec. 27, 1956.

Luther E. Gregory Rear Admiral, U.S. Navy. b. Jan. 9, 1872 at Newark, N.J. Entered the U.S. Navy as a civil engineer in 1898, and rose to rank of rear admiral. He was chief of the bureau of yards and docks of the Navy from 1922-29. Retired. Member of William H. Upton Naval and Military Lodge No. 206, Bremerton, Wash., Washington Chapter No. 3, National Sojourners, 33° AASR, Knight Templar, and member of St. Alban's Conclave No. 18, Red Cross of Constantine, Seattle.

William Gregory (1849-1901) Governor of Rhode Island in 1901, dying in office. b. Aug. 3, 1849 in Astoria, N.Y. A manufacturer, he was president of the Wickford Natl. Bank and director of the Union Trust Co. of Providence. He served in both of the houses of the state legislature and was lieutenant governor from 1898-1900. Member of Franklin Lodge No. 20, Westerly, R.I.

William V. Gregory (1877-1936) U.S. Congressman to 70th to 74th Congresses (1927-37) from 1st Ky. dist. b. Oct. 21, 1877 in Graves Co., Ky. Graduate of West Kentucky Coll. in 1896. Was superintendent of schools in Mayfield, and began law practice there in 1902. Received his degrees in Mayfield Lodge No. 679 on Nov. 4, 1907, March 3 and April

20, 1908. On June 21, 1923 this lodge consolidated with Hinton Lodge No. 369 and became Mayfield Lodge No. 369. d. Oct. 10, 1936

Ludwig Greinemann A Dominican monk and Anti-Mason. While preaching Lenten sermons at Aix-la-Chapelle in 1779, he claimed that the Jews who crucified Jesus were Freemasons, and that Pilate and Herod were wardens of a Masonic lodge. Judas, he stated, had been initiated in the synagogue, and the 30 pieces of silver was the amount of his initiation fee. He stated that he would slay every Freemason he met with his own hands, and so aroused the people that the authorities were forced to issue an edict against Freemasons' meetings. Eventually authorities of neighboring districts calmed him down by stating that if he did not cease his practices he would not be allowed to collect alms in their territory.

Perry E. Gresham President of Bethany College (W.Va.) since 1953. b. Dec. 19, 1907 at Covina, Calif. Graduate of Texas Christian U. in 1930, with graduate work at Columbia and U. of Chicago. He was a teacher of Greek and philosophy at Texas Christian and ordained to the ministry of the Christian church in 1931. He served churches in Fort Worth, Seattle, Detroit, and Glasgow, Scotland. He was later a feature writer for the Detroit Free Press on Middle East affairs and a lecturer at many universities. In 1949 he was a delegate to the founding assembly of the World Council of Churches at Amsterdam, and delegate to conventions in 1950-51-52. Mason, 32° AASR and Knight Templar.

Jean Baptiste Greuze (1725-1805) French portrait and genre painter. b. Aug. 21, 1725. He was a member of the famous Lodge of the Nine Sisters (les Neuf Soeurs) at Paris, his name appearing on the list for 1779. He was held in high regard as an artist. d. March 4, 1805.

Robert E. Gribbin Protestant Episcopal Bishop. b. Feb. 21, 1887 at Windsor, S.C. Graduate of Military Coll. of South Carolina and Coll. of Charleston. Ordained deacon in 1912 and priest in 1913. He served churches in Charleston, Atlanta, Wilmington, and Winston-Salem, from 1912-34. Consecrated bishop of Western North Carolina on Jan. 25, 1934. Now retired. Served as chaplain in both World Wars. Mason.

Aleksandr Sergeevich Griboedov (1795-1829) Russian poet and statesman. He is known chiefly as the author of a satirical comedy in verse depicting the struggle between two generations. It is variously translated into English as The Misfortune of Being Clever, or Woe From Wit. He was a member of the Lodge of United Friends in Russia about 1820. He was murdered at Teheran, with members of the embassy staff, by a mob.

Jeremiah Gridley (1702-1767) Lawyer, teacher and author of pre-Revolutionary period. Often called "Jeremy," he was a brother of Richard Gridley, q.v., a major general in the Revolution. b. March 10, 1702 in Boston, Mass. He was graduated at Harvard in 1725, and for several years was an assistant in a grammar school in Boston. He studied theology and occasionally preached. He then studied law and was admitted to the bar. For a year he edited a weekly newspaper called The Rehearsal. This was the first newspaper published in America having substantial claim to literary merit. He was elected a member of the general court from Brookline, and became an opponent of the British policies. Notwithstanding, he was appointed attorney general for the province of Massachusetts Bay. In 1761, while in this office, he defended the "writs of assistance" which the British custom officers had applied for to enable them to enter the dwellings of suspected individuals at their discretion. He handled it with such dignity that he did not lose his popularity. He was proposed to the first lodge (Mass.) by none other than Henry Price, q.v., past grand master on April 13, 1748; elected April 27 and made May 11. On Dec. 7, 1750 he was raised in Masters Lodge. He was elected junior warden of Masters Lodge, Dec. 1, 1752, and senior warden July 6, 1753, retiring from office in that lodge on Dec. 7, and receiving the unanimous election as master of the First Lodge on Dec. 26, 1753. On Oct. 1, 1755, he was appointed grand master of North America, an office which he held until his death on Sept. 10, 1767.

Richard Gridley (1711-1796) Major General in American Revolution. b. Jan. 3, 1711 at Boston, Mass. Brother of Jeremiah Gridley, q.v., Earned a reputation as an artillerist, and on Sept. 20, 1775 was commissioned major general in command of the Continental artillery, serving until November of the same year. He served as an engineer in the reduction of Louisburg in 1745, and in 1755 became chief engineer and colonel of infantry in the British army. The following year he was with the expedition to Crown Point, and constructed the fortifications at Lake George. He served under Amherst in 1758, and later under Wolf on the plains of Abraham, being at the capture of Quebec. At the conclusion of the

French-Indian War, he received Magdalen Island from the British government for his services, with half-pay for
life. He sided with the colonies in
1775, and planned the works at Bunker Hill the night before the battle of
June 17, 1775. Although 65, he
fought in the entire engagement and
was wounded. He was made a Mason in St. John's Lodge of Boston,
Mass. on April 4, 1746 and was master of the lodge in 1757. On Jan. 27,
1769 he was appointed deputy grand
master of Mass., and subsequently
was grand master of the Grand
Lodge of Massachusetts. d. June 20,
1796.

Ruel C. Gridley (1829-1871)
Humanitarian of the Civil War who
was famous for his "sanitary sack of
flour." b. Jan. 23, 1829 in Hannibal,
Mo. Although six years older, it is
claimed that he was a boyhood friend
of Mark Twain, q.v. He served in the
Mexican War while still in his teens.
His experiences were wide and varied and he earned his living at mining,
merchandising, banking, and newspaper publishing. Married in 1850 to a
girl from Louisiana, Mo., he made his
way overland to California in 1852,
and his family joined him a year or
two later by way of Panama. He
moved about the state and was a
member of six Calif. Masonic lodges,
and two in Nevada. In 1866 he
opened a store at Paradise and the
following year became postmaster.
While living in Austin, Nev. during the
war, Gridley, a Democrat, bet a sack
of flour that David E. Buel would be
elected over his Republican opponent, Charles Holbrook. The bet was
taken by Dr. H. S. Herrick, with the
understanding that the loser would
carry it from Clifton to Upper Austin, a
distance of about a mile and a half.
Gridley lost, and paid the bet. The
newly elected officials marched be-

hind him, followed by most of the
local citizenry with the town band
playing John Brown's Body. At the
end of the journey a dispute arose as
to what should be done with the flour.
Gridley solved it by auctioning off the
flour to raise money for the Sanitary
Commission—a forerunner of the
Red Cross. The idea caught the fancy
of the crowd and the sack was auc-
tioned and re-auctioned, none wish-
ing to keep it. This gave Gridley an
idea, so shouldering the sack, he
went through the country of Nevada,
and into California, auctioning the
flour. It is said that the last auction
brought $15,000, and that he raised a
total of $275,000 for relief of the Civil
War's sick and wounded. In doing
this, however, Gridley ruined his
health. His business was gone, and
his wife was also in poor health. They
moved to Stockton, Calif.—he on a
mattress in the wagon bed. His wife
hobbled to town each day on
crutches to obtain the necessities of
life. When it was learned that he was
a Mason, and of his charitable deeds,
the people of Stockton presented
them with a comfortable home. Gridley died Nov. 24, 1870, and in 1886
the Grand Army of the Republic
erected a life-size statue of him over
his grave in the Stockton Rural cemetery. It is not clear where he was
made a Mason, but it is known that
wherever he established residence in
Calif. and Nevada, he affiliated with
the nearest lodge. Thus we find him
belonging to the following lodges in
order: Diamond No. 29 of Diamond
Springs; St. John's No. 37 of Yreka;
Oroville No. 103 of Oroville; Table
Mountain No. 124 of Oroville (now
Paradise); Lander No. 8 of Austin,
Nevada; Morning Star No. 68 of
Stockton; and Sacramento No. 40, of
Sacramento.

Meade F. Griffin Justice, Supreme Court of Texas. b. March 17, 1894 at Cottonwood, Tex. Graduate of U. of Texas. Admitted to bar in 1917, he practiced at Tulia and then Plainview. Served in WWI as a major, and in WWII as a colonel. He was chief prosecutor at Wiesbaden, Germany in 1945. Raised in Alamo Lodge No. 44, San Antonio, Texas in 1917, and presently a member of Plainview Lodge No. 709, Plainview, Texas. Served as junior and senior deacon in 1924-25. Member of Plainview Chapter No. 228, R.A.M. and Plainview Council No. 164, R. & S.M. both of Plainview, Texas.

Calvin R. Griffith President and owner of the Washington Senators baseball team. Adopted son of Clark C. Griffith, q.v., he succeeded his father as president of the team on the former's death in 1955. He is a member of Harmony Lodge No. 17, Washington, D.C., the same lodge in which his father held membership.

Clark Griffith (1869-1955) Owner of Washington Senators baseball club and one of the organizers of American League in 1901. b. Nov. 20, 1869 in Vernon Co., Mo. Known as the "Old Fox" of baseball, he was one of the game's best known personalities. Under his direction the Senators captured three American League pennants and one world series. Griffith became president in 1919. An outstanding pitcher in his day, he was elected to the Baseball Hall of Fame at Cooperstown, N.Y. in 1946. He won a total of 236 games and lost only 139, playing in both the American and National leagues with Chicago, New York, Cincinnati, and Washington. While still playing and managing, he helped organize the American League in 1901. That year he piloted the Chicago White Sox to a

pennant. He also managed Cincinnati and New York before casting his lot permanently with Washington. An active and interested Freemason, he was a member of Harmony Lodge No. 17 of the District of Columbia and an honorary member of the Grand Lodge of the District of Columbia. His adopted son, Calvin R. Griffith, q.v., who succeeded him as owner of the Washington team, is also a member of that lodge. He allowed the stadium to be used for the Craft-sponsored "Night of Thrills" and gave liberally to Masonic charities. He died Oct. 27, 1955, and graveside services were conducted by his lodge. Masons acting as pallbearers were Phil Howser, Jim Ritchie, Ossie Bluege, Billy Werber, Billy Jurges and George Case—all active in baseball or former big leaguers.

David W. Griffith (1880-1948) Known as the "Father of the Film Art," he produced the famous *Birth of a Nation*, the world's first successful film, which grossed about 50 million dollars. b. in La Grange, Ky. He was the son of Confederate Brigadier General Jacob W. Griffith. For two years he tried acting, but was unsuccessful. He entered the motion picture business in 1908, and was a director for Biograph Film Co. Other pictures he produced were *Intolerance; Hearts of the World; Way-Down East; Broken Blossoms; Orphans of the Storm* and *America*. He was a member of St. Cecile Lodge No. 568 of New York City. d. July 23, 1948.

Griffith J. Griffith (1850-1919) Philanthropist and mine owner. b. Jan. 4, 1850 in Glamorganshire, South Wales. He came to America in 1865, and after being educated in public schools of Pa. and Fowler Inst. of N.Y., he moved to Calif. in 1873, where he was associated with the

Herald Publishing Co. of San Francisco. He later engaged extensively in mining in Mexico. In 1882 he purchased the Los Feliz Rancho of 4,074 acres near Los Angeles and acquired extensive realty holdings in the city. In 1896 he donated 3,016 acres of his ranch to Los Angeles for a public park without restriction. In 1912 he gave $100,000 for the erection of an observatory on Mt. Hollywood for public use and scientific research. Mason. d. July 6, 1919.

Paul H. Griffith Public relations counselor and national commander of the American Legion, 1946-47. b. April 8, 1897 at Uniontown, Pa. From 1919-32 he was a partner of D.A. Griffith & Son, Uniontown, Pa., and from 1946-49, a partner in a business consultant firm, establishing his own company, Paul H. Griffith Associates in Washington, D.C. From 1935-40 he was executive director of the American Legion. He served as an enlistedman with the 28th Division in WWI, participating in all major engagements, and in WWII served as an executive under the secretary of War, advancing to colonel in 1944; he retired from active duty in 1945. Served as military advisor on a mission to India, and later as chief of the veterans personnel division of the Selective Service. He was in every theatre of operation during WWII. Mason and past master of his lodge.

Thomas Griffith (1680-1744) Irish actor, and first grand secretary of the Grand Lodge of Ireland, 1725-32. He first came to Masonic notice by singing the Entered Apprentice's Song at a theatre entertainment following the installation of the Earle of Rosse as grand master of Ireland in 1725. It is thought by some historians that Griffith may have been the author

of the words. He later found himself in trouble with the grand lodge for "chusing so vile and obscene a play" as Wycherley's The Country Wife for a benefit performance. Lord Southwell, grand master, gave him the official appointment of "Tide Waiter" (customs officer) and as such it was his duty to keep an eye on the comings and goings of the "wild geese" and other Jacobite sympathizers, of whom Lord Rosse was rumored to be one.

Allan K. Grim U.S. Judge, Eastern District of Pennsylvania, since 1949. b. Oct. 15, 1904 at Kutztown, Pa. Graduate of Harvard. Admitted to Pa. bar in 1929 and practiced in Reading. Raised in Huguenot Lodge No. 377 at Kutztown, Pa. in 1929 and past master of same. 32° AASR (NJ) at Reading, Pa. and member of the Shrine.

Alexander V. Griswold (1766-1843) Protestant Episcopal Bishop. b. April 22, 1766 in Simsbury, Conn. Of unusual learning ability, he could read at age of three. Studied law, but gave it up to enter ministry, and was ordained deacon and priest in 1795. For the next ten years he served parishes at Plymouth, Harwinton, and Litchfield, Conn. In 1804 he went to a church in Bristol, R.I., and six years later to Litchfield. In May, 1810 he was elected bishop over the "Eastern Diocese" which included Maine, New Hamp., Vt., Mass., and R.I. He was the first and only bishop to serve this diocese. In 1836 he became the presiding bishop of the church. He was raised in Aurora Lodge No. 35 of Harwinton, Conn., and on removal to Bristol, R.I., affiliated with St. Albans Lodge No. 6, which he served as master in 1805. He was grand chaplain of the Grand Lodge of Rhode Island from 1815-26.

He was exalted in Solomon Chapter No. 3, R.A.M., Darby, Conn. on June 17, 1799 and knighted in Providence Encampment, K.T. Jan. 5, 1826. d. Feb. 15, 1843.

Dwight P. Griswold (1893-1954) Governor and U.S. Senator from Nebraska. b. Nov. 27, 1893 at Harrison, Nebr. Graduate U. of Nebraska in 1914. With First Natl. Bank of Gordon, Nebr., 1912-44; editor and publisher of the Gordon Journal, 1922-40, and president of the Gering (Nebr.) Natl. Bank, 1951-54. Was chief of American Mission for Aid to Greece in 1947-48. Served in both houses of state legislature and was Governor three terms, 1940-46. U.S. Senator from 1952. Member of Arcana Lodge No. 195 of Gordon, Nebr., receiving degrees on Jan. 4, Feb. 1, March 1, 1915, and served as master. He was a member of Occidental Chapter No. 48, R.A.M., Zerubbabel Council No. 27, R. & S.M. and Melita Commandery No. 22, K.T., all of Chadron. Received his Scottish Rite degrees in Guthrie, Okla. and affiliated with bodies at Omaha in 1919. Received KCCH in Oct., 1943 and 33° in 1949. d. April 12, 1954.

Glenn Griswold Editor and vice president of Midwest Television, and manager of station KFEQ-TV, St. Joseph, Mo. since 1956. b. June 19,1886 at Benton Harbor, Mich. Was publisher of country newspaper at 17 and was later associated with the *Inter-Ocean, Examiner, Tribune, Journal of Commerce*, all of Chicago. He was editor and publisher of the latter in 1922-31; vice president of Fox Film Corp. in 1931; editor of Business Week, N.Y. 1933-38; and from 1938, head of Glenn Griswold Associates. Mason, Knight Templar, and Shriner.

Alexander J. Groesbeck (1873-1953) Governor of Michigan three terms, 1921-27. b. Nov. 7, 1873 in Macomb Co., Mich. Graduate of U. of Michigan in 1893 and admitted to bar in same year. Served as attorney general of Mich. from 1916-20. Raised in Corinthian Lodge No. 241 and became a life member on Nov. 4, 1938; 33° AASR (NJ) on Sept. 19, 1922. d. March 11, 1953.

Ferde Grofe (Ferdinand Rudolph von Grofe). Composer and conductor. Known for his Grand Canyon Suite. b. March 27, 1892 at New York City. Studied in Germany, New York and Calif. Has been radio orchestra conductor and made personal appearances at many places. Among his compositions are: *Tabloid Suite; Mississippi Suite; March for Americans; Kentucky Derby; Knute Rockne; Three Shades of Blue Suite; Christmas Eve; Ode to the Star-Spangled Banner; Cafe Society Ballet; Symphony in Steel; Hollywood Suite; Blue Flame; Miss Mischief; Free Air; Templed Hills; Daybreak; Broadway at Night;* and many others. Raised in Silver Trowel Lodge No. 414, Los Angeles, and member of St. Cecile Lodge No. 568, New York City.

Francis Grose (1731?-1791) English antiquarian. Published Classical Dictionary of the Vulgar Tongue. Mason.

H. R. Gross U.S. Congressman to 81st Congress (1949-51) from 3rd Ia. dist. b. June 30, 1899 at Arispe, Ia. Attended U. of Missouri. He was newspaper reporter and editor, 1921-35, and radio news commentator (WHO) 1935-48. Served in Mexican border campaign and with A.E.F. in WWI. Member of Twilight Lodge No. 151, Afton, Iowa, and

Petworth Chapter No. 16, R.A.M., Washington, D.C.

Milt Gross Cartoonist and author. b. March 4, 1895 at New York City. Started as an office boy for *New York American* in 1912, and was then a comic artist for the *American Press Association, New York Evening Journal,* and *New York Tribune.* With the *New York World* since 1922. Drew daily news cartoon *Banana Oil,* and is creator of *Gross Exaggerations* and *Nize Baby.* Served as infantry private in WWI. Author of *Nize Baby; Dunt Esk; Famous Fimales From Heestory.* Member of Dirigo Lodge No. 30, New York City.

Moses H. Grossman (1873-1942) Lawyer and founder of Arbitration Society of America in 1922. b. Feb. 18, 1873 at New York City. Graduate of New York U. in 1894. Admitted to bar in 1894 and practiced in New York City. He is the donor of a rare collection of 13th century English legal documents to the New York U. Law School. Member of Centennial Lodge No. 763, New York City, receiving degrees on Feb. 12, Feb. 26 and March 12, 1895; master in 1908; grand representative to Minn., 1923-26; member of Mecca Shrine Temple. d. June 6, 1942.

Thomas Grosvenor (1744-1825) Revolutionary patriot. b. in Pomfret, Conn. Graduate of Yale in 1765. Was a lieutenant under Putnam in 1775 and later a colonel. He was wounded at Bunker Hill and John Trumbull's painting, *Death of General Warren* at Bunker Hill, shows Grosvenor being helped off the field by his servant, Peter Salem. He was a lawyer, judge and state legislator. Made a Mason in American Union Lodge, Redding, Conn. and served as secretary and senior deacon.

Galusha A. Grow (1823-1907) U.S. Congressman from Pennsylvania (1851-63). Speaker of the House from 1861-63. b. Aug. 31, 1823 in Ashford, Conn. Family moved to Pa. when he was ten. Was graduated from Amherst in 1844, studied law in Montrose, and admitted to bar in 1847. Later moved to Houston, Texas, as president of International and Great Northern Railroad, remaining there until 1875, when he returned to Pa. In 1876 he declined the position of U.S. minister to Russia. He was a member of Lodge No. 51 (no name) of Philadelphia, Pa., receiving degrees on Jan. 26, Feb. 23 and March 23, 1871. d. March 31, 1907.

Peter Hermann Gruber (1851-?) Jesuit Abbe and anti-Mason. b. Feb. 5, 1851 at Kufstein in Austria. Educated in the Jesuit schools of Austria, Germany, Holland, and England; he entered the Society of Jesus in 1868, and was ordained in 1879. He is known mainly in America for his article on Freemasonry in the *Catholic Encyclopedia* (now *Catholic Dictionary*). He spent his adult life fighting the Craft. In Europe, he wrote many books, hundreds of articles, gave speeches, and carried on a wide correspondence in which he undertook to show that Freemasonry is the enemy of Christianity. When the Fascists in France and Italy, the Phalangists in Spain, and the Nazis in German began to burn and pillage lodge rooms, mob and shoot Freemasons, he urged moderation, but his efforts were difficult as the encyclical of Pope Leo XIII, q.v., (Humanum Genus) was a virtual invitation for Roman Catholics to use once again the machinery of the Holy Inquisition against Freemasonry. He attacked Freemasonry on the grounds of "liberalism," "naturalism" and "Deism." In June, 1928, several prominent Free-masons from Europe and the U.S. held a day-long meeting with him in Aachen, Germany. At that time he expressed a hope that anti-Masons in Europe and anti-Roman Catholics in America would raise the debate to a more dignified level. Ossian Lang, of New York, who attended the meeting, stated that the abbe regretted that his career had been to make war on Freemasonry, which he had come to admire, but that his superiors had started him off with a collection of inferior and misleading books, and that he was afraid his article in the *Catholic Encyclopedia* had lowered him in the eyes of impartial scholars. Deceased.

Frederick G. Gruen (1872-1945) A founder and president of the Gruen Watch Co. b. April 15, 1872 at Delaware, Ohio. Student at Ohio State U. and graduate of Horological Institute, Dresden, Germany. Founder of modern watchmakers' guild idea, and life member of Horological Insti-tute of America. Member of Hansel-mann Lodge No. 208, Cincinnati, Ohio, receiving degrees on May 29, Oct. 16, Nov. 20, 1916; 32° AASR (NJ). d. Sept. 15, 1945.

Felix Grundy (1777-1840) Attorney General of the U.S., 1838-39, and U.S. Senator from Tennes-see, 1829-37, 1838-40. b. Sept. 11, 1777 in Berkeley Co., Va. The family moved first into Pa. and then Ky., and in both places were exposed to Indian depredations, three of his brothers being killed by the Indians. Elected to Kentucky constitutional convention in 1799, and was a member of the legis-lature from 1799-1806. Appointed judge of supreme court of errors in 1806, and became chief justice the next year. Moved from Bardstown,

Ky., to Nashville, Tenn. in 1808, where he practiced law and achieved a reputation as a criminal lawyer. He defended 105 criminal cases and only one client was executed. He was elected to U.S. congress in 1811, and reelected in 1813, but resigned the next year due to health of wife. Served in Tenn. state legislature in 1819, and in 1829 was elected U.S. senator. Grundy Co., Mo. is named in his honor. He was raised Oct. 29, 1803, in Washington Lodge No. 6 of Bardstown, Ky., although the pro-ceedings of that grand lodge list him as an entered apprentice of Lexington Lodge No. 1 in 1802. He was secre-tary of the lodge as well as senior warden in 1804. He later became a member of Hiram Lodge No. 7, Franklin, Tenn., and Cumberland Lodge No. 8, Nashville, Tenn. at one time. In 1814 was deputy grand mas-ter, pro-tem of the Grand Lodge of Tennessee (1814). d. Dec. 19, 1840.

Pedro Gual Twelfth President (provisional) of Republic of Vene-zuela for a short term during the Civil War in 1861. He was a Mason and 18° AASR.

Hezekiah A. Gudger (1850-1917) Consul General to Panama, 1897-1905 and Chief Justice, Su-preme Court of Canal Zone, Panama, 1905-14. b. May 27, 1850 at Mar-shall, N.C. Engaged in law practice at Asheville, N.C. from 1871. Served in both houses of the state legislature. Resumed law practice in Asheville after term in Canal Zone supreme court. Mason. d. Sept. 22, 1917. Initi-ated, passed and raised in French Broad Lodge No. 292, Marshall, N. Car. in 1870. Dimitted from same on Oct. 22, 1915 and affiliated with Mount Hermon Lodge No. 118, Ashe-ville, N. Car. on Dec. 2, 1915.

Louis Guenther (1874-1953) Publisher of *The Financial World* from 1905. b. Aug. 4, 1874 in London, Eng. Was in advertising business from 188699, and established a monthly trade paper, The Mail Order Journal, in 1892, with his father. Received degrees in Roome Lodge No. 746, New York City, April 23, May 14, and June 11, 1898; affiliated March 28, 1902 with Mystic Tie Lodge No. 272, New York City. d. March 11, 1953.

Vincente Guerrero (1783?-1831) Mexican president and patriot. He became grand master of the York Grand Lodge of Mexico, established through the efforts of Joel Poinsett, q.v., American minister to that republic. He teamed up with Augustin de Iturbide, q.v., to liberate Mexico from the Spaniards, setting up the Plan of Iguala. They forced the Spanish government to capitulate with the Treaty of Cordoba, in 1821, which assured Mexican independence. Iturbide set himself up as Emperor Augustin I, from 1822-23, and his harsh measures of repression led to a revolution by Santa Anna, q.v., Guerrero, and others. Iturbide abdicated, fleeing to Europe, but returned, and was captured and shot, July 19, 1824. Guerrero became vice president of Mexico from 1824-28, and was chosen president by congress in March, 1829, serving until December of that year when a revolution broke out against him, led by Bustamante, q.v. Guerrero was captured and shot, Feb., 1831.

Olindo Guerrini (1845-1916) Italian poet who wrote under the pseudonym "Lorenzo Stecchetti" and also "Beni." His works include poems and lyrics. Many of them contained humorous Venetian dialects. The bulletin of the International Masonic Congress of 1917 states that he was a Freemason.

William A. Guerry (1861-1928) Protestant Episcopal Bishop of South Carolina from 1908. b. July 7, 1861 in Clarendon Co., S.C. Graduate of the U. of the South in 1884. Ordained deacon in 1889, and priest in 1890. He served churches in Florence, Marion, and Darlington, S.C., from 1888-93, when he became professor of homiletics at the U. of the South. In 1908 he was named coadjutor bishop of S.C. Made a Mason "at sight." d. June 9, 1928.

Edgar A. Guest American Poet. b. Aug. 20, 1881 in Birmingham, England. He was brought to the U.S. in 1891 where he received a grammar and high school education in Detroit. He has been connected with the Detroit Free Press since 1895, for which he conducts a column of verse and humorous sketches. His "folksy" poems have earned him the title of "foremost poet of the 20th century" from many admirers. Among his best known poems are: *A Heap o' Livin'; Just Folks; Over Here; Path to Home; When Day Is Done; All That Matters; The Passing Throng; Rhymes of Childhood; The Light of Faith; Harbor Lights of Home; The Friendly Way; Life's Highway; Collected Verse; All in a Lifetime; Today and Tomorrow; Living the Years*; and *Home*. At the height of his productivity he was making nearly $130,000 a year—a fact which caused the long-haired poets with scarcely a penny in their jeans to use him as their favorite punching bag. He has been writing a poem a day since 1916, and they total now well over 15,000. Guest was made a Master Mason in Ashlar Lodge No. 91 of Detroit; exalted in Peninsular Chapter No. 16, R.A.M.; greeted in Monroe Council No. 1;

knighted in Detroit Commandery No. 1, K.T.; and received 32° AASR (NJ) in Valley of Detroit—all of Detroit, Mich. He was crowned a 33°, honorary, Sept. 20, 1921. He is a member of St. Clement Conclave No. 39, Red Cross of Constantine, and Moslem Shrine Temple. In 1954 he received the gold medal of the General Grand Chapter, Royal Arch Masons, the highest honor of this national body. Many of his poems are Masonic in character and as a result of his attachment to the fraternity, he was created a Blue Friar in 1954 (an organization for Masonic authors). Guest has said: "Masonry has greatly enriched my life. It has given me friendships that I cherish dearly. It has, I think, whispered subconsciously to me in the silent hours, words of caution and encouragement. I like going back to my lodge. I have found it refreshing and good to step aside out of the path of my busy life and sit again with the Masons who have carried on in my absence." d. Aug. 5, 1959.

Baron von Gugomos A Masonic imposter, who, in 1775, called together a Masonic congress at Wiesbaden, Germany, which was attended by many influential Freemasons, in spite of the warnings given them by their more conservative brethren. Gugomos claimed that he had been designated by certain unknown superiors of the Holy See at Cyprus to establish a new Order of Knights Templar with himself at the helm. His claims became so absurd that he left Wiesbaden. It is imposition, saying that he had been said that in 1786 he confessed the employed by the Jesuits in an effort to harm Freemasonry.

Samuel A. Guiberson, Jr. Oil producer and engine manufacturer. b. Sept. 20, 1873 in Calif. He began as

an oil worker in 1894, and has been in the oil business on his own since 1906 as president of the Home Ranch Petroleum Co. In 1930 he began the manufacture of radial diesel aircraft and tank engines, and is president of the Guiberson Diesel Engine Co., Dallas, Tex. Mason, Knight Templar and Shriner.

Jean Francois Guichard (1731-1811) French author. b. May 5, 1731 at Chartrettes, France. He wrote a number of books including some comic operas and verse. He was a member of the famous Paris Lodge of the Nine Sisters, being on the roster of 1779 and 1806. d. Feb. 23, 1811.

Curtis Guild (1860-1915) Governor of Massachusetts, 1906-09, journalist, soldier, diplomat. b. Feb. 2, 1860 at Boston, Mass. Graduate of Harvard, summa cum laude, in 1881. He entered the office of the Commercial Bulletin, Boston, which was founded by his father. He rose from bill collector to editor, and was sole owner of the paper from 1902. He was also president of the Anchor Linotype Printing Co. He was a brigadier general of Mass. militia at the outbreak of the Spanish-American War, in which he served as inspector general of the 7th Army Corps and later inspector general of Department of Havana, until the break-up of corps in Cuba. He declined many national jobs offered him. In 1910 he was a special ambassador to Mexico, and from 1911-13 was U.S. ambassador to Russia. He was a member of Columbia Lodge of Boston, being initiated on April 6, 1899. He was also a member of St. Andrew's Chapter, R.A.M. and Boston Commandery, K.T., both of Boston. He was a member of the Scottish Rite bodies in Boston, and was master of Lafayette Lodge of Perfection in 1910, and coroneted 33° AASR (NJ) on Sept. 18, 1906. d. April 6, 1915.

Cato Maximilian Guildberg (1836-1902) Norwegian mathematician and professor of mathematics at Oslo U. At the age of 28 he formulated the famous law of mass termed "The Law of Guildberg and Waage" on which physical chemistry is built. He was master of the Lodge St. Olaus den hvide Leopard in Olso from 1887-92 and was K.C. of the Order of King Charles XIII.

Comte A. C. Guileminot French General and commander of a division under Napoleon. In 1838 he was Lieutenant du Souveran Grand Commandeur of the Supreme Council, Scottish Rite of France.

Joseph Ignace Guillotin (1738-1814) French physician and deputy to the French assembly in 1789. Although the guillotin used for executions was named after him, it is neither true that he invented it nor met his death by it, as often stated. b. May 28, 1738 at Saintes, France. As a deputy to the States-General, he was the first to demand a doubling of the representatives of the Third Estate. It was in that assembly on Dec. 1, 1789 that he urged capital punishment should be inflicted as speedily and painlessly as possible, and argued for a machine designed for this end. The guillotin was invented by Antoine Louis, secretary of the Academy of Surgeons, and a mechanic named Schmidt. Guillotin was one of the founders of the Grand Orient of France, and was first the orator of the Chamber of the Provinces, becoming president on Oct. 27, 1775. He was master of Concorde Fraternelle Lodge of Paris, his name being on the list of that lodge in 1776 with his address as "the Schools of Medicine."

He was also a member of the famous Lodge of the Nine Sisters, and in 1784 was on a committee with Benjamin Franklin and Sylvain Bailly, a French astronomer, to report on the animal magnetism claims of Mesmer. In 1778 he was the founder of the society which became the Academy of Medicine. d. March 26, 1814 in Paris.

Isaac Guion (1755-1823) Revolutionary War soldier and governor of Natchez under American rule. b. in New Rochelle, N.Y. of a Huguenot family. He was commissioned an ensign in Lamb's Artillery at the outbreak of the revolution. He accompanied Gen. Montgomery's expedition into Canada in 1775, and was in the general's party at the ill-fated attempt to take Quebec when the general was killed. Guion was taken prisoner but permitted to attend Montgomery's funeral. He was soon exchanged, and served until the end of the war in Thomas Machin's artillery company, being discharged in 1783 as a captain. He reentered the army in 1792, and in 1797 was ordered by General Wilkinson, q.v., down the Mississippi to occupy Natchez and receive that territory from the departing Spanish garrison. He served as military governor of Natchez until relieved by Winthrop Sargent, q.v., the first civil governor of the territory. It was at this time that Guion was called upon to entertain the Duke of Orleans, later Louis Phillippe, q.v., Emperor of France and his entourage. It is said that Guion was singularly handsome, had excellent manners, and was a brilliant linguist. A contemporary described him as "impetuous but cool; resolute, inflexible, extremely courteous" and another said he was "one of the most fastidious, circumspect and courtly officers in the army." His original lodge is not known, but he was a visitor to American Union Lodge at Morristown in 1780 and again at West Point in 1783. He visited Lodge No. 22, Burlington, N.J. in 1782, and was master of Military Lodge No. 58, Pennsylvania charter. He was also master of Lodge No. 4, New York City in 1789. He assisted at the installation of Nova Caesarea Lodge No. 10 at Cincinnati, and soon after his arrival at Natchez, was one of the petitioners for Harmony Lodge No. 7 (later No. 33, but now No. 1) under Kentucky charter. As the last survivor of the siege of Quebec, he returned 50 years later to identify the burial place of General Montgomery, whose body was removed to New York City by Governor DeWitt Clinton, q.v., then grand master. There was another Isaac Guion, also a Revolutionary soldier. He was a surgeon and belonged to St. John's Lodge No. 3, New Bern, N.C. They are often confused.

Charles P. Gulick (1885-1955) President and chairman of board of National Oil Products Co. b. May 21, 1885 at Newark, N.J. Began as clerk with National Oil & Supply Co. of Newark, N.J. and was later treasurer of the National Red Oil & Soap Co. He became associated with present company in 1912 as treasurer and has been president since 1947. He was also president of the Metasap Chemical Co.; Rare Chemicals, Inc.; Admiracion Labs; The Vitex Labs; and a director of other companies. Member of Northern Lodge No. 25, Newark, N.J.; 32° AASR (NJ) at Jersey City and member of Salaam Shrine Temple, Newark. d. Sept. 4, 1955.

Emil Gumpert Judge, Superior Court of California. b. Jan. 14, 1895 at Stockton, Calif. Studied at Columbia and Washington & Lee U.

and admitted to bar in 1916. He practiced at Stockton until 1947. Named superior court judge in 1956. He is a founder of the American College of Trial Lawyers and was president of same in 1950-51. Mason and Shriner.

Carl Gunderson (1864-1933) Governor of South Dakota, 1924-25. b. June 20, 1864 in Clay Co., Dakota Territory. Graduate of U. of South Dakota in 1890. He was a member of the S.D. senate for five terms, and from 1904-12 was U.S. Indian allotting agent. He served two terms as lieutenant governor (1921-24). Member of Incense Lodge No. 2, Vermillion, S.D. d. Feb. 26, 1933.

George P. Gunn Protestant Episcopal Bishop. b. Oct. 11, 1903 at Winona, Miss. Graduate of Episcopal Theological Seminary at Alexandria, Va. in 1930. Ordained deacon in 1929, and priest in 1930, he was consecrated a bishop in 1948. From 1948-50 he was bishop coadjutor of Southern Virginia, and senior bishop (diocesan) since April, 1950. Member of Campbell Lodge No. 316, Altavista, Va., receiving degrees in 1932.

James Gunn Contemporary English portrait painter. Has painted portraits of King George VI, Queen Elizabeth, the Queen Mother, and the present reigning Queen Elizabeth, the latter hanging at the headquarters of the Royal Regiment of Artillery, of which she is captain-general. He painted the Earl of Scarbrough, present grand master of the Grand Lodge of England. In 1953 the grand lodge lent this painting to the Royal Academy for exhibition.

James Gunn (1739-1801) General in American Revolution and U.S. Senator from Georgia. b. in Virginia. He received a common school education, studied law, was admitted to the bar, and moved to Savannah, Ga. where he practiced. He was elected U.S. senator to the first congress, and was reelected in 1789. He was one of the members of congress who voted for establishing the seat of government at Washington. He fought a duel with General James Jackson. Both belonged to Solomon's Lodge No.1 of Savannah. He also twice challenged General Nathanael Greene, q.v., to a duel, but George Washington refused to let Greene duel. d. July 30, 1801.

Walter T. Gunn (1879-1956) Justice, Supreme Court of Illinois, 1938-51. b. June 4, 1879 in LaSalle Co., Ill. Admitted to bar in 1902. Member of Olive Branch Lodge No. 38, Danville, Ill. receiving degrees on Sept. 22, Oct. 20 and Nov. 5, 1903. d. Oct. 13, 1956.

Royal Arch Gunnison (1873-1918) U.S. Federal Judge, 1st Alaska District, 1904-09. b. June 24, 1873 at Binghamton, N.Y. On the evening of June 24, 1873, his father, Christopher B. Gunnison, attended a meeting of his chapter, Binghamton No. 139, and returning home, found that he was the father of a boy whom he promptly named "Royal Arch." He was graduated from Cornell in 1896, and was admitted to the N.Y. bar in 1897. From 1909 until his death, he was in private practice in Juneau, Alaska. He served as food administrator of Alaska under Herbert Hoover during WWI. A member of Osteningo Lodge No. 435 of Binghamton, N.Y., he received his degrees on June 26, Aug. 30 and Sept. 20, 1894, and received the Royal Arch Degree in his father's chapter on July 12, 1898, withdrawing on Sept. 12, 1916. He belonged to the AASR (NJ) in Binghamton and affiliated with the Scottish Rite bodies

of Seattle, Wash. on Oct. 27, 1911. Received KCCH Oct. 20, 1915 and 33° on April 13, 1916. His son, Royal Arch, Jr. became a radio commentator and writer. d. June 15, 1918.

Julius C. Gunter (1858-1940) Governor of Colorado 1917-19. b. Oct. 31, 1858 at Fayetteville, Ark. Admitted to Colo. bar in 1881, and practiced in Trinidad. He served as a district judge on the court of appeals, and from 1905-07 was a justice of the Colorado supreme court. He was president and trustee of Tillotson Academy of Trinidad; Clayton Coll. Denver, and a regent of the U. of Colorado from 1913-15. Raised Dec. 8, 1906 in Union Lodge No. 7, Denver, Colo. d. Oct. 26, 1940.

Willis H. Gurley President of Borden Food Products Co. since 1951. b. Jan. 4, 1894 at Altmar, N.Y. He began as a clerk in a general store in 1904; and later worked as a telegraph operator, in highway construction, operated a rural milk plant, and was cashier in a dry goods store. In 1919 he was employed by Merrell-Soule Co. and rose from accountant to sales manager. The company was taken over in 1928 by the Borden Co., and he became vice president in 1946. Served in Army in WWI. Mason.

Chandler Gurney U.S. Senator from South Dakota, 1939-51. b. May 21, 1896 at Yankton, S.D. He was secretary and treasurer of House of Gurney, Inc. (seeds and nursery stock) at Yankton from 1918-33, and president of the Chan Gurney Oil Co., Sioux Falls, 1933-35. He has been a member of the Civil Aeronautics Board since 1951, and was chairman of same in 1954. From 1927-32 he operated radio station WNAX. Served in WWI as a sergeant. He is a member of the Scottish Rite bodies (SJ) at Yankton and is a KCCH.

William Gurney (1821-1879) Union Brigadier General of Civil War. b. Aug. 21, 1821 in Flushing, N.Y. At the beginning of the Civil War he was in business in New York City. He entered the army in April, 1861, and, after three months with the 7th regiment, accepted a commission as captain in the 65th New York and served with it through the early campaigns of the war. In 1862 he raised the 127th New York regiment, which he headed as part of the 23rd Corps. In October of that year he commanded the 2nd Brigade of General Abercrombie's division. Wounded at Devoe's Neck in S.C. and assigned to command the Charleston post, being promoted to brigadier general of volunteers for gallantry in action. After the war he returned to Charleston and established himself in business. He was a member of Continental Lodge No. 287, New York and served as its master. d. Feb. 3, 1879.

Gustavus III (1746-1792) King of Sweden from 1771-92. He followed his father, Adolphus Frederick, q.v., on the throne, becoming king when royal power was low and party strife intense. In 1772 he arrested the council in a body, retained power, and waged a useless war against Russia in 1788. In 1789 he received more power from the diet. He was assassinated by J. J. Anckarstrom, an army officer, in a conspiracy of nobles. He was the author of dramatic works and poems of merit. He became interested in Freemasonry in 1780, and through his instigation the IX Province of the Rite of Strict Observance was established in Sweden. He named his brother, the Duke of Sudermania, as grand master in 1780. The duke succeeded him

as regent after his assassination, and later became Charles XIII, q.v., on the deposition of Gustavus IV, q.v., his nephew. Under the grandmaster-ship of Gustavus III, Swedish Freemasonry took a particular form which it has always preserved. He received the title of Vicarius Saiornortis (Vicar of Solomon), or "protector."

Gustavus IV Adolphus (1778-1837) King of Sweden, 1792-1809. Son of Gustavus III, q.v., and grandson of Adolphus Frederick, q.v. He ascended the throne on the assassination of his father, under the regency of his uncle, the Duke of Sudermania. His uncle, in turn, became Charles XIII, q.v., when Gustavus Adolphus was dethroned in 1809. He served under the regency for eight years, and was actually crowned in 1800. Actuated by a hatred of Napoleon, he entered into a coalition against him in 1805, and as a result, lost Swedish Pomerania and German possessions. He received help from England, but lost Finland to Russia in 1808. Dethroned in 1809, he wandered about Europe and died in poverty at Saint Gallen, Switzerland. He was initiated into Freemasonry at the hands of his regent and uncle, Charles, on March 10, 1793, in Stockholm. On March 9, 1803 he issued an edict which required all secret societies in his dominions to register themselves with local authorities, giving the nature of their oaths and the objects of their associations. They were also required to submit to inspection at any time by government officials. At the end of the decree, however, the king stated: "The Freemasons, who are under our immediate protection, are alone excepted from this inspection, and from this ordinance in general."

Gustavus V (1858-1950) King of Sweden, 1907-50. Better known as "Gustaf." Son of Oscar II, q.v., of the Bernadotte dynasty, he was born in Drottningholm and educated at Uppsala. He married Victoria, daughter of Frederick William Louis, Grand Duke of Baden. In 1892 he was a lieutenant general. He often acted as regent during his father's absence from the throne, especially in 1899-1900. He strongly favored the allies in WWI, but kept Sweden neutral. A popular sovereign, he was presented one million dollars by his people on his 80th birthday in 1938. Tall, thin, and athletic, he played tennis well past his 80th year, and his favorite hobby was knitting altar pieces for churches. He was made a Mason, Jan. 13, 1877, and served as grand master of Sweden until his death. An active Freemason, he took part in the ritual work. In 1947 he was made an honorary past grand master of the Grand Lodge of England. In 1949 he received the Gourgas Medal from the AASR (NJ)of the United States. This is the highest honor of the Scottish Rite (NJ) and Gustavus was the third person to be so honored.

Ludovic Gutakovsky President of the State Council, Duchy of Warsaw, the political entity set up by Napoleon I, q.v. When the Grand Orient of Poland was reestablished on March 22, 1810, Gutakovsky headed it.

William E. Guthner (1884-1951) Brigadier General, U.S. Army. b. Dec. 18, 1884. Entered army in 1901 and served from a private to brigadier general in National Guard and same rank in U.S. Army 1941. From 1934-42 he was commanding general of the 89th Infantry Brigade of the 45th Division. From 1942-46 he was director of security and intelligence of the VI Corps Area at Chicago. From 1934-40 he was director of public safety, Denver, Colo., and from 1946-49, secretary of the Illinois Highway Traffic Safety Comm. In 1936 he was national chief of staff of the Veterans of Foreign Wars. Mason. d. Jan. 24, 1951.

George W. Guthrie (1848-1917) Ambassador to Japan, from 1913. b. Sept. 5, 1848 at Pittsburgh, Pa. He was graduated from Western U. (now U. of Pittsburgh) in 1866 and 1868. Admitted to bar in 1869 and practiced at Pittsburgh. Mayor of Pittsburgh 1906-09. Member of Franklin Lodge No. 221, Pittsburgh, receiving degrees on Sept. 18, Nov. 6 and Dec. 18, 1873; master of the lodge in 1880 and grand master of the Grand Lodge of Pennsylvania in 1910-11; Received 33° AASR (NJ) in Sept., 1885. d. March 8, 1917.

James Guthrie (1792-1869) U.S. Secretary of Treasury and U.S. Senator from Kentucky. b. Dec. 5, 1792 in Nelson Co., Ky., he was educated at Bardstown, Ky., and studied law under John Rowan. In 1820 he entered practice at Louisville. He served in both houses of the Kentucky state ASR Felix X. Gygax legislature between 1827-40, and in the latter year was president of the convention that formed the state constitution. He was secretary of the Treasury from 1853-57 under the administration of Franklin Pierce. In 1865 he was elected U.S. senator, but resigned in 1868 due to poor health. From 1860 to 1868 he was president of the Louisville and Nashville Railroad. A member of Clark Lodge No. 51 of Louisville, he is listed as a past master in the proceedings of 1850. He was also a member of Louisville

Chapter No. 5, R.A.M. d. March 13, 1869.

Jacinto Gutierrez Provisional President of the Republic of Venezuela in 1879. Under the control of Blanco, q.v. A 33° AASR.

Tomas Guardia Gutierrez (1832-1882) President of Costa Rica, 1870-76 and virtual dictator, 1876-82. His administration proved of great benefit to the country. His principal work was the construction of rail lines. He abolished the death penalty in Costa Rica. He was a member of Caridad Lodge No. 26 and was "Protector of the Order."

Walter C. Guy Imperial Potentate of the Shrine, 1955-56. b. April 9, 1891. Taught school nine years in Illinois and Missouri, traveled for a building materials concern in Oklahoma, and was with the U.S. Veterans Bureau in St. Louis from 1921-26, when he reentered sales work with Remington Rand, and later became regional manager of that concern, with offices in Memphis, Tenn. In 1931 he returned to Little Rock and became president of the Arkansas Printing and Lithographing Co. as well as three allied firms. Past master of Trinity Lodge No. 694, Little Rock; 33° AASR (SJ); Knight Templar; past potentate of Scimitar Shrine Temple; member of DeMolay Legion of Honor and Court No. 12, Royal Order of Jesters.

Ulysses S. Guyer (?-1943) U.S. Congressman to 68th Congress (1923-25) and 70th to 77th Congresses (1927-43) from 2nd Kans. dist. b. in Pawpaw, Ill. From 1897-1901 he was principal of the St. John, Kans. high school, and was admitted to the bar in 1902, practicing in Kansas City. Member of Wyandotte Lodge No. 3, Kansas City, Kans., receiving degrees on Dec. 11, 1905 and March 3 and May 12, 1906. He became a member of Wyandotte Chapter No. 6, R.A.M. in 1906 and Ivanhoe Commandery No. 21, K.T. in 1908, withdrawing from both in 1924. Active in Scottish Rite, he was a member of Caswell Consistory in Kansas City, Kans. and Abdallah Shrine Temple. d. June 4, 1943.

Felix X. Gygax Rear Admiral, U.S. Navy. b. March 30, 1884 at Twin Creek, Kans. Graduate of U.S. Naval Academy in 1906. Commissioned ensign in 1908, and advanced through grades to rear admiral in 1940. Served on U.S.S. Kearsarge on round the world cruise of battle fleet in 1907-09; naval attache to Switzerland in 1911; duty with submarines from 1913-20. He pioneered as officer in charge of Submarine School, New London, Conn., and established the submarine base at Pearl Harbor, T.H. From 1926-27 he was commander in chief of the U.S. Fleet, and secretary of the War Plans division of the Chief of Naval Operations, 1927-28. He was director of the Naval reserve from 1937-40, and commanded Cruiser Division No. 2 in the Pacific, 1940-41. From 1941-44 he was commandant of the Norfolk Navy Yard, and from 1944 to retirement in 1946, was commandant of the 1st Naval District and Boston Navy Yard. Received the three degrees in fall of 1918 at San Pedro, Calif. as a courtesy to Saqui Lodge No. 160, Osborne, Kans., while en route with submarine division from San Francisco to Panama; on dimit since 1946.

H

Haakon VII (1872-1957) King of Norway, 1905-1957. Second son of Frederick VIII, q.v., King of Denmark. In 1896 he married Maud, the daughter of King Edward VII, q.v., of England. When Norway was separated from Sweden in 1905 he was chosen king and crowned at Trondheim in 1906. When the Nazis invaded Norway, he fled to England in 1940, and returned in 1945. He was initiated into Freemasonry by his father, as were his two brothers, King Christian X, q.v., of Denmark and Prince Harald, q.v., of Denmark. He only received two degrees and, after becoming king, did not continue. d. Sept. 21, 1957.

James Habersham (1712-1775) Acting Governor of Georgia, 1769-72. b. in Yorkshire, England. He arrived in Savannah, Ga. on May 7, 1738 in company with his friend, George White-field, the evangelist, and opened a school for orphans and destitute children at Bethesda, nine miles from that city. In 1744 he became a merchant. In 1750 he was appointed to serve with one other, as a committee of two, to advance the culture of silk in the colony. In 1754 he became secretary of the province and one of the councilors. In 1767 he was one of the presidents of the upper house of assembly, and from 1769-72 served as governor during the absence of Sir James Wright. He raised the first cotton in the state at Bethesda and sent the first few bales grown to England. He was a member of Solomon's Lodge No. 1 of Savannah and grand treasurer of the Grand Lodge of Georgia in 1787. d. Aug. 28, 1775. His sons, John, q.v., and Joseph, q.v., were both members of the same lodge.

John Habersham (1754-1799) Officer of the American Revolution. b. in Savannah, Ga., the son of James Habersham, q.v. He engaged in mercantile pursuits and took an active part in the pre-Revolutionary movements, and was later a major of the 1st Georgia Continental Regiment. He was greatly trusted by the Indians and after the Revolution, Washington appointed him Indian agent. He was a member of the Continental Congress from Georgia in 1785-86, and was collector of customs at Savannah in 1789-99. Member of Solomon's Lodge No. 1, Savannah, as were his father and brother, Joseph, q.v. d. Nov. 19, 1799.

Joseph Habersham (1751-1815) Third Assistant Postmaster General of the U.S., 1795-1801. b. July 28, 1751 in Savannah, Ga., son of James Habersham, q.v. He was one of first members of the commission appointed by the Friends of Liberty in Georgia in 1774, and upon hearing of the skirmish at Lexington, they seized the powder in the royal magazine at Savannah. He was a member of a party that captured a government ship with munitions, including 15,000 pounds of powder, in July, 1775. On Jan. 18, 1776, while a member of the state assembly, he raised a body of volunteers who took Gov. Wright prisoner and confined him to his house under guard (his father had served as governor of Georgia 1769-72 during the absence of Wright). As a major of the 1st Georgia battalion he defended Savannah from a British naval attack in March, 1776. When Savannah fell to the British, he moved with his family to Va., but returned to participate in the disastrous attack on Savannah in 1779. Attained rank of lieutenant colonel at close of war and later served in the state assembly, being its speaker in 1785 and 1790. He was a member of Solomons Lodge No. 1, Savannah as were his father and brother John, q.v. d. Nov. 17, 1815.

George, 11th Earl of Haddington (1827-1917) Seventy-third Grand Master Mason of Scotland, 1892-93.

Lord George Haddo Thirty-Fifth Grand Master Mason of Scotland, 1784-85.

Countess Hadik-Barkoczy (see under Barkoczy).

Henry H. Hadley (1841-1903) Prohibitionist. b. 1841 in Ohio. He served in the Civil War with the Ohio volunteer infantry from 1862-66, rising from private to lieutenant colonel. Graduate of National Law U. at Washington in 1875. When "converted" in 1886, he went into the rescue mission work, organizing 60 rescue missions and several total abstinence societies. He raised $258,000 for their support and addressed over 5,000 audiences on the subject of total abstinence. Raised in Progressive Lodge No. 354, Brooklyn, N.Y. on March 20, 1871, he affiliated with Metropolitan Lodge No. 273, New York City on May 11, 1882, and became unaffiliated Dec. 9, 1886. d. in 1903.

Herbert S. Hadley (1872-1927) Governor of Missouri, 1909-13.

b. Feb. 20, 1872 at Olathe, Kans. Graduate of U. of Kansas and Northwestern U., with honorary doctorates from U. of Missouri, Mo. Valley Coll. and Harvard. Was in general law practice in Kansas City from 1894-98. As attorney general of Mo., from 1905-09, he prosecuted cases against several large trusts and race track gamblers of St. Louis. After term as governor, he resumed practice in Kansas City. From 1917-23 he was professor of law at the U. of Colorado and chancellor of Washington U., St. Louis from 1923-27. He was the author of Rome and the World Today, a scholarly treatise, for which he was honored by the Italian government. He was raised in Temple Lodge No. 299, Kansas City, Mo., and withdrew on Dec. 20, 1916, affiliating with Columbia Lodge No. 14 of Boulder, Colo., March 6, 1921. He was a member of this lodge at the time of his death. In 1913 he was the grand orator of the Grand Lodge of Missouri. In 1924 he presided over a Flag Day service at the Scottish Rite Temple in St. Louis. He was a member of Orient Chapter No. 102, R.A.M. Kansas City, receiving his degrees, Nov. 23, Nov. 29, and Dec. 13, 1895, and withdrawing on Dec. 26, 1916. Also member of Oriental Commandery No. 35, K.T. of Kansas City, receiving the orders on Nov. 22 and Dec. 2, 1899 and withdrawing on Jan. 5, 1917. d. Dec. 1, 1927.

Hiram E. Hadley (1854-1929) Chief Justice, Supreme Court of Washington, 1907-09. b. Jan. 16, 1854, at Sylvania, Ind. Practiced law in Bloomington, Ill. (1877-81) and Rockville, Ind. (1881-89), moving to Whatcom, Wash. in 1889. Served as supreme court justice from 1901-09, declining reelection to resume practice. Mason. d. Jan. 13, 1929.

Lindley H. Hadley (1861-1948) U.S. Congressman to 64th to 72nd Congresses (1915-33) from 2nd Wash. dist. b. June 19, 1861 near Sylvania, Ind. Admitted to Ind. bar in 1889, moving to Whatcom, Wash. in 1890 where he established law practice. He was a brother of Hiram E. Hadley, q.v., Mason, Knight Templar. d. Nov. 1, 1948.

Fitzhugh W. Haensel (1879-1944) Impresario. b. Jan. 11, 1879 at Richmond, Va. He first entered newspaper work in New York City, specializing in musical reviews and criticism. In 1905 he founded and was president of Haensel & Jones. He was director and vice president of Columbia Concerts Corp., and president of Community Concerts Corp. Member of Holland Lodge No. 8, New York City, receiving degrees on Oct. 25, Nov. 8 and Nov. 22, 1921; Knight Templar, 32° AASR (NJ) and Shriner. d. May 3, 1944.

Harold C. Hagen (1901-1957) U.S. Congressman, 78th to 81st Congresses (1943-51) from 9th Minn. dist. b. Nov. 10, 1901 at Crookston, Minn. Started as newspaper reporter in 1920, and was a publisher of weekly newspaper from 1928-32; salesman until 1934, and congressional secretary from 1934-42. Member of Crookston Lodge No. 141, Crookston, Minn. being raised June 30, 1944. d. March 25, 1957.

Lawrence W. Hager Newspaper publisher. b. May 28, 1890 in Louisville, Ky. Graduate of Centre Coll., Danville, Ky. President and editor of the Owensboro Inquirer and Owensboro Messenger (Ky.). Has been with the former since 1910 and the latter since 1929. He is also president of the Owensboro Broadcasting Co. since 1938. He was na-tional chairman of the American Legion publicity committee which launched The National Legionnaire, a weekly newspaper, in 1935. Member of the American Legion publications committee since 1939. Mason and Knight Templar.

Maurice S. Hague (1862-1943) Artist. b. May 13, 1862 in Richmond, Ohio. Studied medicine for three years but abandoned it for art. He was a portrait painter until 1895, when he switched to landscape painting. He was self-educated in art. His works are in private collections throughout the country. He exhibited at Boston, St. Louis, Minneapolis, Buffalo, Cleveland, and Columbus. From 1888-1903 he was a basso in the Scottish Rite Quartet, and was a member of the Orpheus Club, a noted malechorus. Mason 32° AASR (NJ). d. Feb. 3, 1943.

Ernest H. Hahne (1890-?) President of Miami University, Oxford, Ohio. b. Oct. 20, 1890 at Walker, Kans. Graduate of U. of Nebraska, Harvard and U. of Chicago. Admitted to Nebraska bar in 1913. He has taught at Dakota Wesleyan U. and Northwestern U., serving as assistant dean of the College of Liberal Arts of the latter from 1925-30. Mason. Deceased.

Samuel Hahnemann (1755-1843) German physician and founder of homeopathy. His full name was ChristaM Friedrich Samuel. He practiced at Leipzig, Germany from 1816-22, but retired to Cothern after being driven from Leipzig by apothecaries, for dispensing medicines. In 1835 he moved to Paris. While translating *Cullen's Materia Media* into German, he noticed the similarity between the effects of Peruvian bark (cinchona) on a healthy person and the symptoms of disease cured by the bark. After further investigations, he announced the principle that a disease could be cured by a drug that would produce symptoms in a healthy person similar to those in a diseased one. He expounded the homeopathic system of medicine in his *Organon der Rationellen Hefikunde* (1810). He was initiated in a lodge in Hermanstadt, Germany in 1777, and affiliated with the Lodge Minerva in Leipzig in 1817. b. April 10, 1755 at Meissen, Saxony and d. July 2, 1843 in Paris.

Douglas Haig (1861-1928) British Field Marshal, created 1st Earl of Haig in 1919. b. June 19, 1861 in Cameronbridge, Fife, Scotland. He served in the Sudan in 1898, and the Boer War from 1899 to 1902, and in India from 1903-06. He was made a major general in 1904; lieutenant general in 1910; general in 1914; and field marshal in 1917. In WWI he commanded the 1st Army from 1914-15, and was commander-in-chief of the expeditionary forces in France and Flanders from 1915-19. After the war he was commander-in-chief of the Home Forces in Great Britain until 1921. He was initiated in Elgin Lodge No. 91 at Leven, Scotland on Dec. 27, 1881. After 43 years, he was passed on Feb. 2, 1924, and raised on March 4, 1924. Haig was installed master of Elgin Lodge, Dec. 1, 1925. He also received the Mark Master degree in his lodge in 1925. On Dec. 3, 1924 he was installed as junior grand deacon of the Grand Lodge of Scotland. He was elected an honorary member of Lodge Canongate Kilwinning No. 2, Edinburgh in May, 1924. d. Jan. 29, 1928.

Henry H. Haight (1825-1878) Governor of California, 1867-71. b. May 20, 1825 in Rochester, N.Y. His father was U.S. judge for the district of California. Haight was graduated from Yale in 1844, studied law and was admitted to the bar at St. Louis in Oct., 1846. He moved to California in 1850. He was appointed U.S. district judge by President Lincoln. He resumed private law practice after his term as governor. He was a member of Pacific Lodge No. 136 of San Francisco and served as grand orator of the Grand Lodge of California. He was also a member of San Francisco Chapter No. 1, R.A.M. d. Sept. 2, 1878.

Harry L. Haines (1880-1947) U.S. Congressman, 72nd to 75th Congresses (1931-39) from 22nd Pa. dist. b. Feb. 1, 1880 at Red Lion, Pa. He was a cigar manufacturer from 1906. Member of Red Lion Lodge No. 649, Red Lion, Pa., receiving degrees on March 8, May 3 and May 31, 1917. d. March 30, 1947.

William T. Haines (1854-1919) Governor of Maine, 1913-14. b. Aug. 7, 1854 at Levant, Maine. Graduate of U. of Maine in 1876, and Albany Law School (N.Y.) in 1878. He began practice in Waterville, Maine, in 1879. He served as a member of both state legislative bodies and was attorney general from 1897-1901. Raised Aug. 29, 1877 in Kenduskeag Lodge No. 137, Kenduskeag, Maine, and affiliated with Messalonskee Lodge No. 113, Oakland in 1879, and on April 27, 1893, affiliated with Waterville Lodge No. 33, Waterville, Maine. He was exalted on May 20, 1880 in Drummond Chapter No. 27, R.A.M. of Oakland, and became a charter member of Teconnet Chapter No. 52, Waterville in 1893; knighted May 13, 1881 in St. Omer Commandery No. 12, K.T. of Waterville. Joined Maine Consistory, AASR (NJ) May 29, 1908 and Kora Shrine Temple Dec. 8, 1898. He was active in building the mosque at Lewiston. d. June 4, 1919.

Sherrill Halbert Federal Judge. b. Oct. 17, 1901 at Terra Bella, Calif. Graduate of U. of California, and admitted to bar in 1927. Practiced in Porterville, Calif. from 1927-36; San Francisco, 1942-44 and Modesto, 1944-49. He was judge of the superior court of Calif. from 1949-54, and since 1954, has been U.S. district judge of Northern Calif. Mason.

John A. Halderman (1833-?) Union Major General in Civil War and diplomat. b. April 15, 1838 in Mo. and spent his boyhood in Ky. He emigrated to Kans. in 1854, and served as private secretary to that state's first governor. He served in both houses of the Kans. legislature and was twice mayor of Leavenworth. He entered the army as a major and advanced to major general, being named in official orders for conspicuous gallantry in action. He was one of the leaders in Kans. to abolish slavery. He was U.S. consul in Bangkok, Siam in 1880, later consul general, and from 1882-85 minister resident in Siam. He received his degrees in Leavenworth Lodge No. 2, Leavenworth, Kans. on Oct 6, 1855, Feb. 6 and Feb. 23, 1856. He served the lodge as junior warden in 1863, and was first grand orator of the Grand Lodge of Kansas in 1856. He also served in four grand lodge committees. He dimitted July 18, 1870, and there is no Masonic record of him after that date.

Fletcher Hale (1883-1931) U.S. Congressman to 69th to 71st Congresses (1927-31) from 1st N.H. dist. b. Jan. 22, 1883 at Portland, Maine. Graduate of Dartmouth U. in 1905. Admitted to bar in 1908, and practiced at Littleton, N.H. until 1912, and from that time at Laconia. Member of Mount Lebanon Lodge No. 32, Laconia, N.H., receiving degrees on June 6, Oct. 3 and Nov. 20, 1917. d. Oct. 22, 1931.

Garth Hale (See Albert B. Cunningham).

Harry C. Hale (1861-1946) Major General, U.S. Army. b. July 10, 1861 at Knoxville, Ill. Graduate of U.S. Military Academy in 1883, and rose through grades to major general in 1921. In 1891 he was in charge of the Sioux Indian prisoners of war in S.D. During the Manila campaign, he was aide to General Merritt and during the Philippine Insurrection of 1899-1902, he was battery commander of the 44th U.S. Volunteers. After this action, he joined the General Staff, but returned to the Philippines from 1906-09. In WWI he first commanded Camp Zachary Taylor at Louisville, Ky., and then the 84th Division overseas. From 1922 to his retirement in 1925, he commanded the 6th Corps Area in Chicago. He was raised in Dearborn Lodge No. 310 of Chicago on Feb. 12, 1925. d. March 20, 1946.

Nathan Hale (1755-1776) American Revolutionary patriot, whose last words before being hanged by the British as a spy were: "I only regret that I have but on life to lose for my country." b. June 6, 1755 at Coventry, Conn. He was graduated from Yale in 1773 and taught school until 1775, when shortly after the Battle of Lexington, he was commissioned a lieutenant in the Continental army. In 1776 he was promoted to a captain. He volunteered for hazardous spy duty behind the British lines on Long Island in response to a call from General Washington. He was caught and ordered executed by Sir William Howe, who refused his request for a Bible or a chaplain. He was hanged Sept. 22, 1776 in an orchard at the present junction of Market St. and East Broadway in New York City. It is almost certain that Hale was not a Freemason although he is often referred to as such. James R. Case, Conn. Masonic historian believes that the confusion is caused by the initiation of Colonel Nathan Hale of New Hampshire (d. 1780) in St. John's Lodge of Portsmouth. The martyr, Nathan Hale is sometimes referred to as a member of "St. John's Regimental Lodge of New York City."

Oscar Hale Judge, Supreme Court of Iowa from 1939. b. Feb. 27, 1867 at Wapello, Iowa. Admitted to the bar in 1893, and practiced at Wapello until 1913, when he became a judge of the district court. Mason and Knight Templar.

Samuel W. Hale (1823-1891) Forty-second Governor of New Hampshire. b. April 2, 1823 at Fitchburg, Mass. A manufacturer of chairs at Keene, N.H. He was inaugurated governor on June 7, 1883. Member of Social Friends Lodge No. 42, Keene, N.H. receiving his degrees Feb. 4, April 8, and July 15, 1861. d. Oct. 16, 1891 at the home of his brother, John M. Hale, in Brooklyn, N.Y.

Theodore Hale Vice President of International Harvester Co. in charge of sales since 1944. b. Oct. 26, 1896 in Madison, Wis. He started with International Harvester in 1915 as a warehouse helper. Served in France during WWI with 164th Infantry. Mason, 32° AASR (NJ) and Shriner.

William W. Hale Vice President of Southern Pacific Railroad in charge of freight traffic since 1942. b. March 15, 1887 at Solomon, Kans. With Southern Pacific since 1901. Mason.

James A. Haley President and Director of Ringling Bros., Barnum & Bailey Circus, from 1946-48, and U.S. Congressman to 83rd and 84th Congresses from 7th Fla. dist. b. Jan. 4, 1899 at Jacksonville, Ala. From 1920-33 he was an accountant at Sarasota, Fla., and from 1933-43 was general manager of John Ringling estate. From 1943-45 he was 1st vice president of Ringling Circus, and president of same from 1946-48. Member of Sarasota Lodge No. 147, Sarasota, Fla.

Arthur E. Hall Vice President, Treasurer and General Manager of Chicago Daily News since 1953. b. Oct. 22, 1898 at Covington, Ky. He was a public accountant from 1920-29, becoming associated with the Chicago paper on the latter date as a auditor, and rising as controller, assistant treasurer, circulation director. Mason.

Charles B. Hall (?-1883) First President of American Bankers Association in 1875. He served three terms and asked to be relieved of a fourth. Member of Revere Lodge, Boston, Mass. in 1858. d. May 8, 1883.

Charles B. Hall (1844-1914) Major General, U.S. Army. b. April 29, 1844 at Portland, Maine. He was commissioned a second lieutenant in the 25th Maine Volunteer Infantry in 1862, and in 1867 commissioned second lieutenant in the U.S. Army, serving in the 28th Infantry. He was promoted through the grades to major general in 1908, and retired that year. Was twice cited in Civil War for gallantry. He later commanded the Infantry, Cavalry and Signal Schools as well as the Army Staff Coll. Served as master of Hancock Lodge No. 311, Ft. Leavenworth, Kans. d. May 11, 1914.

Charles F. Hall Episcopal Bishop of New Hampshire since 1948. b. April 20, 1908 in Dorchester, N.B., Canada. Graduate of Springfield Coll., Episcopal Theol. School and Tufts Coll. Ordained deacon in 1936, and priest in 1937, he served churches in Worcester and Medford, Mass. and Concord, N.H. from 1936-48. Mason and received 33° AASR (NJ) in 1952.

Cyrus Hall Brigadier General (brevet) in Civil War. Served with the 14th Illinois Infantry. Listed in the 1864 lodge roster for Jackson Lodge No. 53, Shelbyville, Ill.

David Hall (1714-1772) Printer and business partner of Benjamin Franklin, q.v. b. in Edinburgh, Scotland. He learned the printing trade in that city and later worked in London. He came to America about 1747 and entered into a partnership with Franklin until May, 1766, when it was dissolved, and he formed another with William Sellen. As a member of these firms he was one of the printers of the Pennsylvania Gazette. The latter firm printed the paper money issued by Congress during the Revolutionary War. After his death, his sons, William, q.v., and David became the partners of Sellen. Hall was a member of Lodge No. 2 in 1760, and in 1761 was senior warden of the Provincial Grand Lodge of Pennsylvania. d. Dec. 24, 1772.

David Hall (1752-1817) Governor of Delaware, 1802-05. b. Jan. 4, 1752 in Lewes, Del. He was the son of David Hall, q.v., the printer and partner of Benjamin Franklin, q.v. He was admitted to the bar in 1773. During the Revolution he served as a captain in Haslet's Delaware regiment in 1776, and the following year was made colonel of the Delaware regiment. He was wounded at the Battle of Germantown, Oct. 4, 1777, sent home, and never returned to active duty. He was raised in Lodge No. 18 at Dover, Del. on May 18, 1776 (under Pa. charter). He was later master of Hirams Delaware Regimental Lodge No. 30 under Pa. charter, and was charter master of Lodge No. 63, Lewes, Del. whose charter was granted May 28, 1794. d. Sept. 18, 1817.

Elijah Hall Naval Captain of Revolutionary War, who was a lieutenant under John Paul Jones, q.v., on the Ranger. He commanded a marine battery during the siege of Charleston, S.C. Hall was second in command to Jones in the naval battle between the Bonhomme Richard and the Serapis of Flamborough Head in 1779. He was raised in St. John's Lodge No. 1, Portsmouth, N.H., on June 26, 1777.

Henry C. Hall (1820-1901) Foreign service officer. b. Aug. 17, 1820 in Dutchess Co., N.Y. He had nearly 30 consecutive years in the consular and diplomatic service of the U.S. in Cuba and Central America. He was known as the "father of the Nicaragua canal," and was instrumental in breaking up the coolie slave trade in Cuba. He was initiated in Sylvan Grove Lodge No. 274 of N.Y.C., on March 25, 1856. His father-in-law, Antonio Echeverria, a Cuban merchant of Italian descent, claimed that his life was saved by a pirate captain who had once seized his ship. Just before "walking the plank," he recognized the pirate captain as a Mason. The pirate spared his life and all the men in the crew. At Hall's death, the secretary of the lodge wrote Mrs. Hall, "In his death, this lodge has lost one of its oldest members, an upright and true Mason, an honor to the fraternity and this lodge." d. Oct. 29, 1901.

James F. Hall (1822-1884) Union Brigadier General in Civil War. b. Jan. 31, 1822 in New York City. In 1861 he assisted the state of N.Y. to equip 28 regiments for the field and with that completed, equipped one for himself, which he led as colonel. He was prominent at the taking of Port Royal; constructed the works on Tybee Island; was present at the capture of Fort Pulaski, Ga.; mentioned for gallantry at Pocotaligo and Olustee, Fla.; was present at capture of Morris Island; and cooperated with Sherman against Savannah and Charleston. For two years he was provost marshal general of the Dept. of the South. Was brevetted brigadier general of volunteers in Feb., 1865. Member of Kane Lodge No. 454, New York City.

John Hall (1767-1833) Judge, Supreme Court of North Carolina, 181832. b. in Waynesboro, Va., he went to N.C. at an early age and was educated at William and Mary Coll. He settled in Warrenton in 1792 and became eminent as a lawyer. He was judge of the superior court of N.C. from 1801-18. Member of Johnson Caswell Lodge No. 10 of Warrenton, he was grand master of the Grand Lodge of North Carolina from 1805-07. d. Jan. 29, 1833.

Lee D. Hall Justice, Supreme Court of Mississippi since 1948. b. Nov. 20, 1893 at Laurel, Miss. Graduate of Mississippi Coll. in 1912, and U. of Mississippi in 1915. Admitted to bar in 1915 and practiced in Columbia until 1948. He received his degrees in St. Alban's Lodge No. 60, Columbia, Miss. and served as master of the same. A member of Columbia Chapter No. 123, R.A.M. and Columbia Council No. 25, R. & S.M., both of Columbia, he served as high priest of the chapter. Member of Hattiesburg Commandery No. 21, K.T. Hattiesburg; 33° AASR (SJ) at Jackson; Wahabi Shrine Temple of Jackson and St. Leonard Conclave No. 64, Red Cross of Constantine, Jackson.

Leicester C. Hall (1874-1950) Saved from hanging by a Masonic sign. As an attorney representing the city of Los Angeles in a water project, he was kidnapped by a band of Bishop, Calif. citizens and ranchers, Aug. 29, 1924, taken to the outskirts of the town, and strung up to the limb of a tree. As he was dangling in the air, Hall gave a Masonic signal of distress, and was immediately cut down and revived by his kidnappers, whose names he refused to reveal in the face of an Inyo Co. jury inquiry. He died of natural causes at the Sawtelle Veterans Hospital, Glendale, Calif., 26 years after having been "hanged."

Leonard W. Hall U.S. Congressman, 76th to 81st Congresses (1939-51) from 2nd N.Y. dist. b. Oct. 2, 1900 at Oyster Bay, N.Y. Was graduated from Georgetown U. in 1920, admitted to bar the following year and began practice in New York City. Mason.

Luther E. Hall (1869-1921) Governor of Louisiana, 1912-16. b. Aug. 30, 1869 at Morehouse Parish, La. Graduate of Washington and Lee U. and Tulane U. Began law practice at Bastrop, La. in 1892, and served in the state senate from 1898-1900. He served as a district judge from 1900-06, judge of the court of appeals from 1906-10, and justice of the supreme court from 1910. Received his degrees in Mt. Gerizim Lodge No. 54, Bastrop, La. on April 24, May 29, June 26, 1893. He served as master of this lodge. On Feb. 6, 1917 he affiliated with Ideal Lodge No. 367, New Orleans, as a charter member. He was past district deputy grand master of the Grand Lodge of Louisiana. d. Nov. 6, 1921.

Lyman Hall (1724-1790) Signer of Declaration of Independence and Governor of Georgia one term (1783). b. April 12, 1724 at Wallingford, Conn. He was graduated from Yale in 1747, studied medicine, and moved to Georgia in 1752, where he acquired a large practice. He took an active part in the pre-Revolutionary movements and was influential in causing Georgia to join the other colonies. In 1775 he was elected by the parish of St. John to congress and served until 1780. When the British took possession of Georgia, he moved with his family to the north, and all his property was confiscated by the Crown. He returned to Georgia in 1782. It is thought that he was a member of Solomon Lodge No. 1, Savannah, Ga., but the records of that lodge from 1734-84 were destroyed by the British and his membership cannot be proved. d. Oct. 19, 1790.

Manly P. Hall Founder-President of The Philosophical Research Society, Inc., an educational corporation devoted to the study of comparative religion, idealistic philosophy and analytical psychology. b. March 18, 1901 in Peterborough, Ont., Canada. He has been an author, lecturer, editor and teacher at Los Angeles, Calif. since 1919. He has lectured in Carnegie Hall, Town Hall, India, England. He is the discoverer of a unique Azted manuscript named *Coder Hall*. He has made numerous radio and television appearances and is a motion picture writer and technical consultant. Among his many writings are *An Encyclopedic Outline of Masonic, Hermetic, Quabbalistic and Rosicrucian Symbolical Philosophy; The Lost Keys of Freemasonry; Freemasonry of the Ancient Egyptians*, and *Masonic Orders of the Fraternity*. He was raised in Jewel Lodge No. 374, San Francisco on Nov. 22, 1954 and 32° AASR (SJ) in Valley of San Francisco. Made knight patron of the Masonic Research Group of San Francisco in 1953.

Peirson Hall U.S. District Judge for Southern California since 1942. b. July 31, 1894 at Armour, S.D. Admitted to bar in 1916 and practiced in Los Angeles until appointed to bench as judge of the superior court of Los Angeles Co. in 1939. Mason.

Prince Hall (1748-1807) First Negro Freemason in the United States and one for whom the Negro Prince Hall Grand Lodges are named. b. Sept. 12, 1748 in Bridgetown, Barbadoes, British West Indies. He was the son of Thomas Prince Hall, an Englishman, whose wife was a free Negro of French descent. "Prince" is not a title, but a first name. Other sources place his birth date as 1735, and also 1738. In 1765 he arrived in Boston, and through eight years of frugal living, he saved enough money to become a freeholder and voter. In 1774 he was converted under the preaching of two pioneer Methodists, Richard Bondman and Joseph Gilmore. Using his evenings for study, Hall became an ordained Methodist preacher in Cambridge, Mass., and a leader of his race in New England. On March 6, 1775, he was made a Master Mason, together with 14 other free Negroes of Boston, in a British Army lodge of Irish register that was attached to one of General Gage's regiments. The lodge gave them the privilege of meeting, marching in procession, and burying their dead, but not to confer degrees. In the Revolutionary War, he espoused the cause of the Colonies and as the spokesman for the Negroes, he won Washington's approval of the service of free Negroes in the Continental Army. Five thousand responded. In March, 1784, Hall petitioned the Grand Lodge of England for a charter which was issued Sept. 29, 1784, but was not delivered until April 29, 1787. Delivery was made by Captain James Scott, a seafaring man, who was a brother-in-law of John Hancock, q.v. On May 6, 1787, African Lodge No. 459 was established. Four years later-on June 24, 1791-the African Grand Lodge was formed with Prince Hall as grand master. The name was changed on June 24, 1808 to the M.W. Prince Hall Grand Lodge, F. & A.M. of Massachusetts, honoring their first grand master who had died on Dec. 4, 1807 (this has been given as both Dec. 7 and 1808 by some authors). The original charter of African Lodge No. 459 is still preserved. It was issued by the authority of the Duke of Cumberland, q.v., and attested to by William White, q.v., grand secretary of the Grand Lodge of England. Today there are 38 Prince Hall grand lodges in the U.S. and one

each in Canada, Liberia and Africa. All claim descent from the original Mass, grand lodge. In 1864 the Prince Hall Masons of Mass. purchased a plot of ground in Arlington, Mass. for a cemetery, and a year later erected a monument to the memory of Prince Hall on Copp's Hill. Hall led the movement to secure educational facilities for Negro children and was a passionate advocate of equality before the law. He is described as an eloquent, persuasive speaker, an ardent patriot and a devoted Freemason. Unquestionably he is the "father of Negro Freemasonry" in the United States.

Reynold T. Hall (1858-1934) Rear Admiral, U.S. Navy. b. Nov. 5, 1858 at Philadelphia, Pa. He was appointed assistant engineer in the Navy in 1880 and advanced through grades to rear admiral in Dec. 1914, retiring in 1922. He was chief engineer of the U.S.S. Petrel under Dewey in the Battle of Manila Bay, May 1, 1898, and manager of Cavite Navy Yard during the Spanish-American War of 1898. He was made a Mason in Merchantville Lodge No. 119, Merchantville, N.J. on April 20, 1880, dimitted April 14, 1916, and on May 31, same year affiliated with Franklin Lodge No. 34, Philadelphia, Pa. He was master of this lodge in 1921. He was exalted in Jerusalem Chapter No. 8, R.A.M. of New York City, May 15, 1908, received the 32° AASR (NJ) in New York City, Jan. 5, 1909, and 33°, Sept. 21, 1920. He served as first vice president and trustee of the National Sojourners. d. Feb. 10, 1934.

Robert H. Hall (1837-1914) Brigadier General, U.S. Army. b. Nov. 15, 1837 at Detroit, Mich. Graduate of U.S. Military Academy in 1860. He was breveted brigadier general of volunteers in 1898, and in regular army in 1901. Serving throughout the Civil War, he was cited for bravery in the battles of Lookout Mountain and Weldon (Va.). After the war he served on the frontier until 1871, and at the U.S. Military academy 1871-88. He later commanded Ft. Sheridan, Ill., and served in the Philippines during the 1899-1900 insurrection. Mason. d. Dec. 29, 1914.

Robert S. Hall (1879-1941) U.S. Congressman 71st and 72nd Congresses (1929-33) from 6th Miss. dist. b. March 10, 1879 at Williamsburg, Miss. Admitted to bar in 1900 and practiced at Hattiesburg. Was member of state senate one term, and district judge for eleven years. Raised in Hattiesburg Lodge No. 397, Hattiesburg, Miss. on Feb. 26, 1912. Suspended twice for NPD; last one on Aug. 8, 1934. Member of Hattiesburg Chapter No. 114, R.A.M. and Liberty Council R. & S.M., suspended in each in 1920. d. June 10, 1941.

T. Graham Hall Grand Sword Bearer, Supreme Council, 33° AASR (SJ) and Sovereign Grand Inspector General in Tennessee. Received his 32° in 1908; KCCH in 1911; 33° in 1917; appointed deputy in Term. in 1946 and crowned active member in 1949. He was appointed to his present office in 1957. He is engaged in the general insurance business in Nashville.

Willard Hall (1780-1875) U.S. District Judge and founder of the public school system of Delaware. b. Dec. 24, 1780 in Westford, Mass. He was graduated from Harvard in 1799 and was admitted to the bar in 1803. He moved to Dover, Del., in that year and practiced there for 20 years. He served two terms as secretary of state for Delaware, and in the U.S.

congress from 1817-21. He was appointed U.S. district judge for Delaware by President Monroe in 1823, holding this office until retirement in 1872. He revised the state laws by order of the general assembly in 1829, and in 1831 was a member of the state constitutional convention. He advocated the establishment of public schools, and suggested the plan that was adopted in 1829. Member of Union Lodge No. 5, of Middletown, Del., and was grand master of the Grand Lodge of Delaware from 1817-19. d. May 10, 1875.

William Hall (1774-1856) Governor of Tennessee and Major General of militia. b. in Virginia. He served in the Indian wars and commanded a regiment of Tenn. riflemen under General Jackson, q.v., in the War of 1812. He served in the state legislature for a number of years and became governor on the resignation of Samuel Houston, q.v., in 1820. He served in the U.S. congress from 1831-33. Member of King Solomon Lodge No. 6, Gallatin, Tenn. d. in Oct. 1856.

William P. Hall (1864-1937) Founder and President of The Hall Signal Co., he introduced automatic block signals on many American railways. b. Feb. 1, 1864 at Stamford, Conn. A prominent lay evangelist of the Methodist Episcopal Church, he was vice president of the American Bible Society, and president of the Bible League of North America. Past master of Acacia Lodge No. 85, Greenwich, Conn. and Knight Templar. d. Aug. 14, 1937.

Fitz-Greene Halleck (1790-1867) American Poet. b. July 8, 1790 in Guilford, Conn. Original family name was "Hallock." He was interested in poetry from early childhood.

He served as a bank clerk in New York City from 1811-29, and in 1832 entered the employment of the fur baron, John Jacob Astor, q.v., as a confidential clerk. He was able to retire in 1849 with a yearly stipend of forty pounds granted him by Astor. He then lived with a maiden sister in his home town of Guilford, Conn. He was best known for Fanny, a satire on fashion; Green Be the Turf Above Thee, an eulogy on the death of a friend; Marco Bozzaris; Poetical Works; and Alnwick Castle, With Other Poems. His portrait was painted by Jarvis, Morse, Inman, Waldo, Elliott and Hicks. In May 1877, a life-size bronze statue of him was dedicated in Central Park, New York—the first statue to a poet in the new world. Attending the ceremonies were the president of the U.S., his cabinet, and many prominent citizens including the poets Bryant, Boker, Bayard Taylor, and John G. Whittier. He was made a Mason in Holland Lodge No. 8, New York City in 1815. He was a member of Columbian Commandery, No. 1, K.T. of New York City and must have been suspended at one time, for he reinstated in the same, on Dec. 13, 1833. He was grand standard bearer of the Grand Commandery, K.T. of New York in 1817-18. d. Nov. 19, 1867.

Harry L. S. Halley Justice, Supreme Court of Oklahoma since 1949; Chief Justice, 1953-55. b. Sept 5, 1894 at Antlers, Okla. Graduate of U. of Oklahoma in 1917. Practiced in Tulsa from 1918-49. He served in WWI as an Infantry captain, and in WWII as a lieutenant colonel in Africa, Italy, and France. Received his degrees in Delta Chapter No. 425, Tulsa, Okla. in 1923; 32° AASR (SJ) at Guthrie; Shriner and member of High Twelve.

John H. Halliburton Vice President of Eastern Airlines, Inc. in charge of flight operations since 1957. b. May 21, 1906 in Brownsville, Tenn. Graduate of U. of Tennessee in 1929. Began with Ford Motor Co. as an engineer in the flight test department of the airplane division in 1929. From 1930-31 he was a pilot for the Curtiss Flying Service. Has been with Eastern since 1931 as line captain, director of military training and operations manager. Received degrees in College Park Lodge No. 545, College Park, Ga. Presently a member of Coral Gables Lodge No. 260, Coral Gables, Fla. and master of same in 1942.

James G. Halliwell-Phillips (1820-1889) English antiquarian, librarian I On A. S. Hall-Johnson and Shakespearean scholar. Although not a Mason, the fraternity owes him a debt of gratitude, for in his work he found a document erroneously catalogued as "A Poem of Moral Duties," which was actually a Masonic constitution. Experts believe it was written about 1390, making it the oldest known Masonic document. It was called the Regius Manuscript or Regius Poem, but more often The Halliwell Manuscript, in his honor. He published it in 1840, with a brochure entitled On the Introduction of Freemasonry Into England. His original name was "Halliwell," but in 1872 he added his wife's surname of "Phillips." As librarian of Jesus College, Cambridge, he concentrated on the writers Camden, Percy, and Shakespeare, collecting many of their works and rarities. He also published Nursery Rhymes of England; Dictionary of Archaic and Provincial Words; and Outlines of Life of Shakespeare.

A. S. Hall-Johnson Masonic lecturer and writer. b. July 25, 1891 in

Bingham, Nottinghamshire, England. A long time resident of Argentina, he was initiated into Excelsior Lodge No. 617, Buenos Aires, on Dec. 7, 1922. He is grand representative of the grand lodges of Connecticut and Colorado at the Grand Lodge of Argentine. Holds honorary memberships in many lodges; 18° AASR and prominent in Royal Arch, Mark and Knight Templar work. He has written and privately printed more than 50 papers on Masonic subjects which he has distributed free throughout the world. He is a Fellow of the Royal Geographical Society; Royal Society of Arts; Royal Economic Society; honorary life president of the Johnson Society River Plata and member of many learned societies. A veteran of WWI, he is a licensed reader of the Church of England.

Charles G. Halpine (1829-1868) Author and poet. b. Nov. 20, 1829 in Oldcastle, County Meath, Ireland. His father was editor of the Evening Mail, the chief Protestant paper of Dublin. Was graduated at Trinity Coll. Dublin, in 1846. Came to New York in 1852, where he worked on the New York Herald. For a time he was assistant editor of the Boston Post, and finally associate editor of the New York Times. In 1856 he became part owner and editor of the New York Leader. He served in the Civil War as a major, and was with the 69th New York Infantry, and later, on General Hunter's staff. As the result of his war experiences he later wrote under the pseudonym of "Private Miles O'Reilly." He wrote Life and Adventures of Private Miles O'Reilly; Baked Meats of the Funeral and others. After the war he became editor and proprietor of The Citizen, a New York City paper that advocated reforms in the civil administration of that city. He was a member of Hol-

land Lodge No. 8, New York City. d. Aug. 3, 1868.

Frederick Halsey (1870-1952) Canon of Church of England. Graduate of Magdalen Coll., Oxford, he was ordained in 1894. He succeeded his brother, Admiral Lionel Halsey, q.v., as deputy grand master for the province of Hertfordshire in the Grand Lodge of England, on the former's death in 1949, and was installed Jan. 19, 1950. His father, Sir Thomas F., q.v., held that position for 50 years. He was deputy grand master of the Mark Grand Lodge of England from 1936. A Mason for 60 years, he was initiated in Apollo University Lodge No. 357 at Oxford while still a student. He was also past grand chaplain of the Grand Lodge of England. d. Jan. 31, 1952.

Sir Lionel Halsey (1872-1949) Admiral of British Navy. In WWI he took part in the Battles of Helgoland Bight (1914) and Dogger Bank (1915), and from 1917-18 was third sea lord. He commanded the Australian navy from 1918-20. Promoted to vice admiral in 1921 and admiral in 1926. From 1920-36 he was comptroller and treasurer to the Prince of Wales. He was deputy grand master of Hertfordshire for 19 years and was succeeded by his brother, Canon Frederick Halsey, q.v., in this position. Previously, their father, Sir Thomas F. Halsey, q.v., served in that capacity for 50 years.

Sir Thomas F. Halsey (1839-1927) Deputy Grand Master of United Grand Lodge of England from 190327. b. Dec. 9, 1839 at Temple Dinsley, Hertfordshire, England. Educated at Eton and received M.A. degree from Christchurch Coll., Oxford. He represented the county of Hertfordshire in the house of commons from 1874-85, and the Watford division of the country from 1885-1903. In 1901 he was appointed a member of the privy council of Great Britain. Initiated in Apollo University Lodge. No. 357 at Oxford in Jan., 1861, he joined Westminster and Keystone Lodge No. 10, London, and was master in 1867, and master of Watford Lodge No. 404 the following year. He was a founder of the Hertfordshire Imperial Yeomanry Lodge No. 3192 and a joining member of Berkhampstead Lodge No. 504. In 1873 he was appointed provincial grand master for Hertfordshire and held this position for 50 years. Two of his sons were named to this office: Sir Lionel Halsey, q.v., and Canon Frederick Halsey, q.v. He was also first master of Hertfordshire Masters Lodge No. 4090 in 1920. He was exalted in Watford Chapter, R.A.M. on Sept. 28, 1863 and was first principal in 1871, and in 1903 was second grand principal of the Supreme Grand Chapter of England. d. Feb. 12, 1927.

Joseph S. Halstead (1818-1925) A pioneer physician who at one time was the oldest Freemason in the world, living to be 107 years of age and a Mason for 80 years. b. March 4, 1818 at Lexington, Ky., he worked his way through the Transylvania Medical Coll., and traveled through Kentucky, Indiana, and Illinois before coming to Missouri to establish a practice. In Missouri, he looked over the towns of Boonville and Chillicothe, but finally settled in Richmond. His wife was the daughter of Gov. Wickliffe, q.v., of Ky. Henry Clay was among Dr. Halstead's patients, and the latter prided himself on their correspondence. He later practiced in Lexington, Mo., but in 1860 moved to Caldwell Co., where he practiced farming near Breckenridge. He received his 50-year pin from the grand

master of the Grand Lodge of Missouri. d. 1925.

Joseph E. Hamblin (1828-1870) Union Major General (brevet) in Civil War. b. in Yarmouth, Mass. He was a member of the 7th N.Y. regiment many years prior to the Civil War. At the outbreak of hostilities, he became adjutant of the 5th N.Y. regiment, and in Nov., 1861 transferred to the 65th N.Y. regiment. Participated in Grant's campaign of 1864 and then to the Shenandoah Valley to resist pressure on Washington and Maryland. Was severely wounded at Cedar Creek, and for this action was made brigadier general (brevet) and placed in command of a brigade. In the spring of 1865 he was promoted to full rank and participated in all subsequent engagements of the Army of the Potomac to the surrender at Appomattox. For bravery at Sailor's Creek (last engagement between North and South) he was brevetted major general and mustered out in Jan., 1866. Member of Kane Lodge No. 454, New York City. d. July 3, 1870.

Thomas L. Hamer (1800-1846) Brigadier General, U.S. Army. b. in Northumberland Co., Pa. in July, 1800. He moved to Ohio, studied law and was admitted to the bar in 1821. He practiced at Georgetown, Ohio. He served several years in the lower house and was its speaker at one time. He served in the U.S. congress from 1833-39, and as a congressman nominated Ulysses S. Grant to the U.S. Military Academy. (See interesting story under "Grant" on how Hamer made an error in his name that he carried thereafter.) He volunteered as a private in the Mexican War; however, he had to serve only one day as such, for the following day (July 1, 1846), his commission as brigadier general arrived. He distinguished himself at Monterrey, and commanded General Butler's division after the latter was wounded. He died in Monterrey, Mexico, on Dec. 2, 1846. Hamer was a member of New Caesarea Harmony Lodge No. 2 of Cincinnati, Ohio and was a Royal Arch Mason.

Alexander Hamilton (1757?-1804) American statesman and first U.S. Secretary of the Treasury (1789-95). b. on island of Nevis of Leeward Islands, West Indies. He served through the Revolution and was secretary and aide-de-camp to Washington. He showed a remarkable grasp of governmental, financial, and administrative problems. He was a member of the Continental Congress in 1782-83 and 1787-88. As secretary of the Treasury he planned and initiated policies establishing a national fiscal system, strengthened centr al government, stimulated trade, and developed national resources. In 1789 he was appointed inspector general of the Army with the rank of major general. In 1800 he was instrumental in defeating Aaron Burr for the presidency and for the governorship of New York in 1804. In a duel with Burr, q.v., on July 11, 1804, he was wounded, and died the next day. His Masonic membership has never been determined, although the majority of authorities believe he was never a Freemason. The latest work on this is by James R. Case in 1955, in which he comes to the conclusion that Hamilton was never a member of the Craft. Those who state that he was a Freemason base their claims principally on the fact that he was recorded among the visitors of American Union Lodge (military) at Morristown, N.J., on Dec. 27, 1779, at which time Washington is supposed to have raised General Lafayette, q.v.

It is stated that it must have been the Alexander Hamilton because he was the only one of that name then holding a commission in the Army under Washington. It is also claimed in the painting The Petition, which shows the presentation of a petition to Washington to become general grand master of the United States, that Lieut. Col. Alexander Hamilton of New York is standing next to Washington. His youngest son, Philip, q.v., was a Mason and past master of his lodge.

David G. Hamilton (1842-1915) Railroad president and capitalist. b. Jan. 10, 1842 at Chicago, Ill. Graduate of Asbury (now DePauw) U. in 1865,1868. He was president of the Anglo-American Land & Claim Assn. of Texas in 1890; president of Texas & Mexican Central R.R.; president of National Railway of Illinois and subsidiary companies, and president of the Chicago City R.R. Co. Member of Home Lodge No. 508, Chicago, Ill., receiving degrees on May 22, June 5 and June 12, 1874. He served the lodge as senior warden in 1877 and master in 1878. d. Feb. 16, 1915.

Duke of Hamilton (see Marquis Wm. Douglas).

Alexander, 10th Duke of Hamilton and Brandon Fifty-third Grand Master Mason of Scotland, 1820-21.

George E. Hamilton (?-1945) Author of the "Iowa Corn Song." He is said to have derived his inspiration from the tune Traveling, which he had heard Shrine bands play. Strange to say, it was the last line of his chorus (That's where the tall corn grows) that gave him the most trouble in composing. It was this line which really made a "hit" of the song. He taught it to the various Iowa Shrine Temples and they serenaded Los Angeles with their new song, carrying printed ears of corn. The success of the song in Iowa was gradual. In 1921 Prof. J. T. Beeston, director of the Za-Ga-Zig band, wrote three new verses which retained the Shrine theme. Hamilton never got around to copyrighting it because he did not realize he had written a hit tune. Beeston's verses and Hamilton's chorus were printed in sheet music for the first time in 1921. A member of the chapter and council, Hamilton took the part of Nebuchadnezzar in the cryptic work for 35 years at Des Moines. He was secretary of the Des Moines Chamber of Commerce for 24 years, retiring in 1938. d. March 14, 1945.

Henry DeWitt Hamilton (1863-1942) Soldier, lawyer, and General I 17 Philip Hamilton Grand High Priest of the General Grand Chapter, R.A.M. in 1927. b. Feb. 26, 1863 in Whitehall, Ill. Educated at West Point and Columbia U. He was admitted to New York bar in 1884, and Rhode Island bar in 1923. He enlisted as a private in the New York national guard in 1884, and served in the Spanish-American War as a major. In 1913-14 he was adjutant general of New York; in WWI served as an Infantry colonel. In 1924 he was placed on the reserve list of the New York national guard as a brigadier general. In Dec., 1923 he was appointed adjutant general of Rhode Island. He was a close friend of Senator Gerry, q.v., and active in Democratic politics. He was raised in United States Lodge No. 207, March 6, 1889 (N.Y.C.) and became master in 1892. He served as district deputy grand master of the Grand Lodge of New York in 1906-07. He was exalted in Constellation Chapter No. 209,

Brooklyn on April 28, 1890 and served as high priest in 1899 and grand high priest in 1905. He was also a member of Adelphic Council, R. & SM., Clinton Commandery No. 14, K.T., and 33° AASR (NJ). He also belonged to Kismet Shrine Temple and Azim Grotto. d. Aug. 18, 1942.

James Hamilton (1710?-1783) Pre-Revolutionary Governor of Pennsylvania, and son of the famous Andrew Hamilton, the lawyer who made American legal history by his defense of the printer, John Peter Zenger, in 1735. James became a member of St. Johns Lodge, Philadelphia in 1734, and was grand master in 1735. He was elected to the provincial assembly in 1734 and re-elected five times. He was mayor of Philadelphia in 1745, and a member of the provincial council in 1746. He was residing in London in 1748, when he was commissioned by the sons of William Penn as lieutenant governor of the province and territories. He resigned in 1754, when the news of the Indian outrages reached Philadelphia, and entered actively on the work of erecting a chain of forts and blockhouses. He was again deputy governor from 1759-63, and on the departure of John Penn, he administered the government as president of the council until the arrival of Richard Penn in Oct., 1771. He was acting governor for the fourth time in 1773. d. Aug. 14, 1783.

John W. Hamilton (1845-?) Methodist Bishop. b. March 18, 1845 at Weston, Va. He was licensed to preach in the Methodist Episcopal Church in 1865; a deacon in 1868, and elder in 1870. He held pastorates at Newport, Ohio, Maplewood, Mass., Sommerville, Mass. Was made bishop in May, 1900. He was chancellor of the American U. at Washington, D.C. from 1916-22 and emeritus from that date until his death. Mason, deceased.

Paul Hamilton (1762-1816) Governor of South Carolina, 1904-06, and Secretary of Navy, 1809-13. b. in St. Paul's parish, S.C., Oct. 16, 1762. He rendered important services during the Revolution and was comptroller of S.C. from 1799-1804. As secretary of the navy under James Madison, his policy was to keep our frigates in port to prevent their capture in the War of 1812, and the first great American victory of the Constitution was gained because Hull did not obey Hamilton's mandate "to remain in Boston until further orders!" He was a member of Lodge No. 8, Charleston, S.C. and past master of the same. In 1806 he was grand master of the Grand Lodge of South Carolina. d. June 30, 1816.

Philip Hamilton (1802-1884) Youngest son of Alexander Hamilton, q.v. Sometimes confused with the oldest son of the same name, who was killed in a duel, Nov. 24, 1801, on the same spot where his father was killed by Aaron Burr, q.v., three years later. The second "Philip" was born June 1, 1802. He was assistant district attorney in New York City, and for some time was judge advocate of the naval retiring board in Brooklyn. He was a member of Albion Lodge No. 26, being master of the same (New York City) in 1829. d. July 9, 1884.

Wilson H. Hamilton Justice, Supreme Court of Iowa. b. May 1, 1877 at Delta, Ia. Graduate of Drake U. in 1900. Admitted to bar in 1900 and practiced at Sigourney, Ia. Became associate justice of the supreme court in 1935, and was chief

justice in 1937-38. Returned to private practice in Sigourney. Mason.

Joe B. Hamiter Justice, Supreme Court of Louisiana since 1943. b. Nov. 16, 1899 at Shreveport, La. Graduate of Louisiana State U. in 1923, and in private law practice in Shreveport until 1935, when appointed judge of court of appeal, 2nd circuit. Mason, Knight Templar and Shriner.

Harry G. Hamlet Rear Admiral, U.S. Coast Guard. Member and past master of Semper Paratus Lodge No. 49, Washington, D.C., and of National Sojourners. Received 33° AASR (SJ) on Oct. 19, 1943.

Leonidas L. Hamline (1797-1865) Methodist Episcopal Bishop. b. May 10, 1797 at Burlington, Conn. Early in life he moved to Ohio where he was admitted to the bar and practiced at Lancaster. He became a member of the Methodist church in 1828, and was soon afterward licensed to preach. He became assistant editor of the Western Christian Advocate at Cincinnati in 1836, and when the Ladies' Repository was started in 1840, he was its editor. He was ordained a bishop at the general conference in New York in June, 1844. It was at this meeting that the rupture between the northern and southern organizations started, and it is thought that a speech delivered by Hamline, at the time, greatly advanced the split. In 1852 he was released from his office as bishop at his own request, due to ill health. He was a member of Lafayette Lodge No. 79 of Zanesville, Ohio. d. March 23, 1865.

Wilbur E. Hammaker Methodist Bishop. b. Feb. 17, 1876 at Springfield, Ohio. Ordained to Methodist Episcopal ministry in 1901, and served churches in Dayton, Middletown, and Youngstown, Ohio from 1901-36, being elected bishop in the latter year. He was assigned to Nanking, China area from 1936-39, and then to the Denver area in 1939. He was reassigned in 1940, and retired in 1948. He was president of the National Temperance and Prohibition Council of the Methodist Church since 1948. Member of Jefferson Lodge No. 90, Middletown, Ohio, receiving degrees on April 19, May 17 and June 21, 1907; received 50-year medal from Grand Lodge of Ohio; 32° AASR (NJ).

John Hammill (1875-1936) Governor of Iowa three terms, 1925-31. b. Oct. 14, 1875 at Linden, Wis., moving with his family in boyhood to Hancock Co., Ia. Graduate of State U. of Iowa in 1897, he was admitted to the bar that same year and practiced at Britt. From 1908-12 he was a member of the state senate and lieutenant governor, 1920-24. He was a member of Darius Lodge No. 431 of Britt and past master of the same. He was also a member of chapter, commandery and 32° AASR (SJ). d. April 6, 1936.

Benjamin Hammond Commander of the privateer schooner, Greyhound in the Revolutionary War. Member of Essex Lodge of Salem, Mass.

James Hammond, Jr. Business executive. b. Aug. 1, 1892 at Tolu, Ky. Served as bank cashier from 1912-18. Treasurer of Lord & Taylor, N.Y., 1922-26; president of Gimbel Bros., department store at Pittsburgh from 1927-32; president and publisher of Detroit Times, 1932-33, and of the Commercial Appeal (Memphis, Tenn.) 1933-36. Chairman of the board of Cleveland (Ohio) Automatic Machine Co. Mason, Knight Templar, 32° AASR and Shriner.

John Hays Hammond (1855-1936) American mining engineer who was consulting engineer for Cecil Rhodes, q.v. b. March 31, 1855 in San Francisco, Calif. Graduate of Yale. As a mining engineer he examined properties in all parts of the world. While in South Africa as a consulting engineer to Consolidated Gold Fields and Randfontein Estates Gold Mining Co., he was one of the four leaders in a reform movement in the Transvaal (1895-96). For this he was arrested and sentenced to death. The sentence was commuted to 15 years and he was later released on payment of a fine of $125,000. In London, he became interested in many mining companies. When he returned to the U.S. in 1900, he became associated with some of the most important financial groups in the country, purchasing and promoting several of the largest mining properties in the U.S. and Mexico. He was also active in hydro-electric and irrigation projects. In 1911, he was appointed by President Taft as special ambassador to the coronation of King George V of England. He was raised in Oriental Lodge No. 144, San Francisco, Calif. on June 20, 1893. d. June 8, 1936.

Winfield S. Hammond (1863-1915) U.S. Congressman to 60th to 63rd Congresses from 2nd Minn. dist. b. Nov. 17, 1863 at Southboro, Mass. Graduate of Dartmouth Coll. Served as high school principal and superintendent of schools in Minn. until 1890, when he was admitted to the bar and practiced at Madelia, and later St. James. Member of Libanus Lodge No. 96 at St. James, Minn. d. Dec. 30, 1915.

Walter Hampden American Shakespearean actor. b. June 30, 1879 in Brooklyn, N.Y. His real name is Walter Hampden Dougherty. Attended Yale U. and was graduated from Poly. Inst. of Brooklyn in 1900. He first appeared on the stage in England in 1901, and for three years was leading man at the Ade1phi Theatre in London. He returned to the U.S. in 1907 and appeared in The Tempest, Macbeth, Othello, Salome, Romeo and Juliet, Taming of the Shrew, and others. In 1925 he leased the Colonial Theatre (N.Y.) and renamed it "Hampden's." He appeared there in 1925-26, co-starring with Ethel Barry-more in Hamlet and Merchant of Venice. He alternated appearances on the legitimate stage of New York with tours throughout the country, presenting his revived Cyrano de Bergerac. The New York stage saw him in the leading roles of a dozen plays and dramas. He also did motion picture and radio work. Member of Howard Lodge No. 35, New York City.

John Francis Hamtramck (1756-1803) Colonel of American Revolution; military commander of Detroit. b. Aug. 16, 1756 in Quebec, Canada, the son of French refugees. He was baptized Jean Francois. Parents later settled just north of Lake Champlain in N.Y. In Sept. 1775 he joined General Montgomery's army marching on Montreal, and was appointed continental commissary. He was commissioned a lieutenant early in 1776, and on Nov. 21 captain of the 5th N.Y. continentals. Became a major Jan. 1, 1781; lieutenant colonel and commander of the first sub-legion under General Anthony Wayne on Feb. 18, 1793. When Detroit was occupied by the Americans under Article 2 of Jay's Treaty, Colonel Hamtramck was ordered to descend the Maumee River, and on July 13, assumed command of Detroit. On July 24, 1775 Dr. Peter Middleton, provincial deputy grand master of New York, issued a warrant to form St. John's Regimental Lodge No. 1. From the diary of Ensign John Barr of the N.Y. Line on Feb. 3, 1780 we learn: "Our lodge (St. John's) formed at Captain Hamtramck's hut." This was while in camp near Morristown, N.J. St. John's Lodge is now settled at Clark's Town in N.Y. Later we find Hamtramck as a member of Union Lodge No. 1 (now Mt. Vernon No. 3 of Albany), having signed the register of that lodge as "No. 63," with no date shown. Hamtramck, Mich., a suburb of Detroit, was named in his honor, and it is interesting to note that as the largest Polish city in America, even today it does not possess a Masonic lodge because of its heavy Catholic population. d. April 11, 1803 and is buried at Mt. Elliott Cemetery in Detroit.

John Hancock (1737-1793) First signer of the Declaration of Independence; first Governor of Massachusetts; Major General of the American Revolution. b. Jan. 12 (some sources say the 23rd), 1737 at Quincy, Mass. He received a good education and was graduated from Harvard in 1754. He entered the counting house of an uncle by the same name, who adopted him, and at his uncle's death in 1764, he fell heir to his business which was worth £70,-000. He was probably the wealthiest man in Boston. He was chairman of the committee which protested the "Boston Massacre" to the royal governor and demanded the removal of British troops from the city. In 1774-75 he was president of the first and second provincial congresses. He was one of the few men who was excluded from an offer of general amnesty by the British as he was "too flagitious a nature to admit of any other consideration," and the expedition sent by General Gage to Lexington and Concord in April, 1775 was to capture Hancock, as well as destroy the materials of war. He was a member of the Continental Congresses from 1775-80, being its president from May, 1775 to Oct., 1777. When asked why he wrote his name so boldly on the Declaration of Independence, he replied, "So that George III may read it without putting on his glasses." In 1776 he was commissioned a major general of militia in Mass., and in August, 1776, he commanded the Mass. troops in the effective Rhode Island expedition. His military leadership, however, was not as outstanding as his abilities in the political field. He was elected the first governor of the commonwealth of Massachusetts in 1780, and served for nine terms (1780-85 and 1787-93), being governor at the time of his death. Honorary degrees were conferred on him by Yale, Princeton and Brown Universities. He was treasurer of his own university, Harvard, and presented it with a valuable library. He went to London in 1760 on business and, while on a similar mission to Quebec, he was made a Freemason in Marchants Lodge No. 277, in 1762. On his return to the colonies, he affiliated with St. Andrew's Lodge of Boston on Oct. 14 of the same year. d. Oct. 8, 1793.

Winfield S. Hancock (1824-1886) Major General, U.S. Army. b. Feb. 14, 1824 in Montgomery Square, Pa. Graduate of the U.S. Military Academy in 1844, he was commissioned and sent West where under General Scott, he participated in the Mexican War. In 1855 he was ordered to Florida as a captain to participate in the fights against the Seminole Indians. From there he went to Kansas and then to Utah, where serious trouble had developed between the Mormons and the Gentiles. When the Civil War broke out, he was stationed in Calif. and immediately requested to be sent to the zone of operations. He was made brigadier general of volunteers, and aided in the organization of the Army of the Potomac. From this point on he became one of the most respected general officers, fighting in major engagements of the war: Fredericksburg; Chancellorsville (lost 2,000 of his 5,000 men); Gettysburg (lost 4,000 out of 10,000); Spottsylvania Court House (took 4,000 prisoners). He was appointed brigadier general in the regular Army in 1864 and major general in 1866. A popular man, he was almost president of the United States. In the election of 1880, he received 4,444,952 votes as the Democratic candidate and was defeated by James A. Garfield, the Republican, with 4,454,416 votes. He received all three degrees by special dispensation in Charity Lodge No. 190 of Norristown, Pa. on Oct. 31, 1860 while on leave. He was also a member of Norristown Chapter No. 190, R.A.M. and Hutchison Commandery No. 32, K.T., both of Norristown, Pa. d. Feb. 9, 1886.

Edward Hand (1744-1802) Brigadier General and Adjutant General of Continental Army. b. Dec. 31, 1744 in Clyduff, King's Co., Ireland. In 1774 he accompanied the 18th Royal Irish regiment to this country as a surgeon's mate, but resigned and settled in Pennsylvania where he practiced medicine. At the start of the Revolution, he joined Thompson's brigade as a lieutenant colonel, serving at the siege of Boston, and in the battles of Long Island and Trenton.

He was appointed brigadier general in 1777. He succeeded General Stark in command at Albany in 1778, and soon afterward served with General Sullivan in his expedition against the Indians in central New York. Near the close of the war he succeeded Alexander Scammell as adjutant general. He was a member of the U.S. congress in 1784-85 and a signer of the Pennsylvania constitution of 1790. He was a member of the Pennsylvania Military Lodge, now Montgomery Lodge No. 19. Served as master of his lodge. d. Sept. 3, 1802.

Thomas M. Hand U.S. Congressman to 79th to 81st Congresses (1945-51) from 2nd N.J. dist. b. July 7, 1902 at Cape May, N.J. Admitted to bar in 1924 and practiced at Cape May City, N.J. Hand also published a newspaper, and was mayor of the city from 1937-44. Mason.

George Handley (1752-1793) Governor of Georgia in 1788. b. Feb. 9, 1752 in Sheffield, England. He arrived in Savannah in May, 1775, where he joined the Georgia continental battery as a captain in 1776, rising to lieutenant colonel. He was actively engaged in S.C. and Ga. during the Revolution, was captured at Augusta, and sent to Charleston as a prisoner of war. He was afterward sheriff of Richmond Co., and often a member of the state legislature. A member of Solomon Lodge No. 1 of Savannah, he was grand treasurer of the Grand Lodge of Georgia in 1786. d. Sept. 17, 1793.

Levin I. Handy (1861-1922) U.S. Congressman from Delaware, 1896-98. b. Dec. 24, 1861. A teacher, superintendent of schools (Kent Co.) and lawyer. He also edited the Wilmington Every Evening paper. He was raised in Harmony Lodge No. 13,

Smyrna, Del. and later affiliated with Hiram Lodge No. 25, Dec. 27, 1897. In 1906 he was grand master of the Grand Lodge of Delaware. d. Feb. 3, 1922.

William C. Handy (1873-1958) American Negro composer known as "Father of the Blues." b. Nov. 16, 1873 at Florence, Ala. He taught school from 1892-93, becoming a teacher-bandmaster in the latter year. In 1900 he was with the music department of the A. & M. College, Normal, Ala. until he became an orchestra leader for minstrel shows in 1903. In 1912 he started devoting all his time to composing and publishing as president of the Handy Bros. Music Co., Inc., N.Y.C. Among his most famous blues songs are *St. Louis Blues; Memphis Blues; Beale Street Blues*; and the march, *Hail to the Spirit of Freedom*. He was author of *Negro Authors and Composers of the United States; W. C. Handy's Collection of Negro Spirituals; Father of the Blues* (an autobiography); and *Unsung Americans Sung*. Handy was a member of Prince Hall and a 33° AASR. d. March 31, 1958. Buried with Masonic rites.

Charles B. Hanford (1859-1926) American Shakespearean actor. b. May 5, 1859 at Sutter Creek, Calif. He worked for a time in the U.S. pension office in Washington, D.C. and then as a private secretary of a Calif. congressman; he began his first season as an actor at New London, Conn. in 1882. Through the years as a legitimate actor, he starred with such famous actors of the day as William Stafford, Thomas W. Keene, Edwin Booth, Julia Marlowe, Louis James, and Kathryn Kidder. In 1917 he volunteered for naval duty and was assigned to the office of Naval Intelligence. He was detailed to duty with Thomas A. Edison. Member of King Solomon Lodge No. 31 (Daylight Lodge), Washington, D.C. and received 32° AASR (SJ) in Albert Pike Consistory, Washington, D.C. on Feb. 28, 1922. d. Oct. 16, 1926.

Louis B. Hanna (1861-1948) Governor of North Dakota two terms, 1913-17. b. Aug. 9, 1861 at New Brighton, Pa. He moved to N.D. in 1881 and became president of the First National Bank of Page. He served in the lower house from 1895-97, and in the state senate from 1897-1901, and 190509. Hanna was a member of the 61st and 62nd U.S. congresses (1909-13) as a delegate at large. In WWI he served with the American Red Cross in France. He was appointed by President Hoover as a member of the Mount Rushmore National Memorial Commission. He was the first grand tyler of the Grand Lodge of North Dakota and the last surviving member of the charter members of that grand lodge. A member of Hiram Lodge No. 20, Page, N.D., he was raised Oct. 20, 1885; exalted in Casselton Chapter No. 2, R.A.M. on Feb. 21, 1890, he affiliated with Keystone Chapter No. 5, Fargo on Nov. 25, 1918; greeted May 2, 1907 in Fargo Council No. 1, R. & S.M.; knighted in Auvergne Commandery No. 2, K.T. Dec. 29, 1894; 32° AASR (SJ) at Fargo Dec. 7, 1894 and 33° in 1903. Joined El Zagal Shrine Temple Dec. 7, 1894. Served the Grand Lodge of North Dakota as grand tyler (1889), grand pursuivant (1896), grand junior steward (1897) and grand senior steward (1898). d. April 23, 1948.

Robert Hanna (1786-1858) U.S. Senator from Indiana, 1825-1832. b. April 6, 1786 in Laurens, S.C. His parents moved to Indiana in 1802, and settled in Brookville. He

was sheriff of the eastern district from 1809 until the organization of a state government, and a member of the Indiana constitutional convention of 1816. He was registrar of the land office and general of militia. For many years he was a member of the state legislature. In 1835 he moved to Indianapolis. He was a member of Harmony Lodge No. 11 of Brookville. On Nov. 19, 1858 he was killed by a train while walking on the railroad tracks at Indianapolis.

John A. Hannah President of Michigan State College since 1941. b. Oct. 9, 1902 at Grand Rapids, Mich. Graduate of Michigan State in 1923. He was an extension specialist in poultry husbandry at Michigan State from 1923-33, and manager of the Federal Hatchery Coordinating Committee at Kansas City, Mo. from 1933-35. In 1935 he returned to Mich. as secretary of the State Board of Agriculture of the state college, serving until named president in 1941. He has been a U.S. delegate to the World Poultry Congresses in London, Rome, Leipzig, and Copenhagen. In 1948-49 he was president of the Association of Land Grant Colleges and Universities. Mason.

William Hanna (1833-1907) Brigadier General (brevet) in Civil War. b. June 23, 1833 in Lexington, Ind. He moved to Camp Point, Ill. in 1857, where he engaged in the mercantile business until the Civil War. He assisted in raising troops and was made captain of the 15th Regiment, Ill. Vol., becoming major, lieutenant colonel, colonel and brevetted brigadier general for bravery at the Battle of Altoona. After the war he lived at Golden, Ill. and was postmaster there for many years. Raised in Justice Military Lodge U.D. (Ill.) in 1862 or 1863, affiliating with Benjamin Lodge

No. 297 and later with La Prairie No. 267 of Golden. He was exalted in Quincy Chapter No. 5, R.A.M., and knighted May 12, 1875 in Delta Commandery No. 48, K.T., of Clayton, serving as commander. d. Aug. 4, 1907.

Wallace Hannah English Anti-Mason. In 1955-56 the Rev. Hannah, curate of St. Augustine's church at Kensington, England since 1952 shocked the English newspaper readers with a vicious personal attack on the Archbishop of Canterbury in particular, and Freemasonry in general. Shortly thereafter he announced that he had taken steps for his "immediate admission" into the Roman Catholic Church.

Allen B. Hannay U.S. District Judge, Texas since 1942. b. Feb. 14, 1892 at Hempstead, Tex. Graduate of U. of Texas in 1913. Practiced law in Hempstead and Houston 1913-30. He was judge of Waller Co. from 1915-17; judge of 113th dist. of Texas 1930-42. Mason, 32° AASR (SJ) and Shriner.

Edward A. Hannegan (1807-1859) U.S. Senator from Indiana, 1843-49. b. June 25, 1807 in Hamilton Co., Ohio. He was educated in Ky., where he spent his boyhood; he began law practice in Covington, Ind. He was a frequent member of the Indiana legislature and served as U.S. Congressman one term. In 1849-50, he was U.S. minister to Prussia. He has been described as eloquent, brilliant, and erratic. In 1852, while under the influence of liquor, he killed his brother-in-law, Capt. Duncan. Afterwards he moved to St. Louis, Mo. where he spent the remainder of his life. His original lodge is not known, but he was a charter member of LaPorte Lodge No. 41, LaPorte, Ind. in 1838, and, in

1850, affiliated with Fountain Lodge No. 60 at Covington, Ind. and served as master of the same in 1851. d. Feb. 25, 1859.

Arthur T. Hannett Governor of New Mexico, 1925-27. b. Feb. 17, 1884 at Lyons, N.Y. Graduate of Syracuse U. in 1910, he began law practice in Gallup, N.M. in 1911. He served as city attorney and mayor of Gallup, and was chairman of the state highway commission from 1923-25. He is a member of Lebanon Lodge No. 22, Gallup; 32° AASR (SJ) at Santa Fe and Ballut Abyad Shrine Temple at Albuquerque.

Ernest Augustus, King of Hanover (see under Duke of Cumberland).

Henry C. Hansbrough (1848-1933) U.S. Senator from North Dakota three terms, 1891-1909. b. Jan. 30, 1848 at Prairie du Rocher, Ill. Moved to Calif. in 1867, where he learned the printing trade and published a daily paper at San Jose from 1869-70. Following that, he was with the San Francisco Chronicle until 1879, and then published a paper at Baraboo, Wis. for two years. He moved to the Territory of Dakota in 1882, where he engaged in journalism, and was twice mayor of Devil's Lake. He served in the 51st U.S. congress from N.D. He was a member of Minnewaukan Lodge No. 21 at Devil's Lake and Doric Chapter NO: 8, R.A.M. as well as Cyrene Commandery No. 7, K.T. all of Devil's Lake. He received the 32° AASR (SJ) in 1897. d. Nov. 16, 1933.

Charles R. Hanscom (1850-1918) Shipbuilder. b. June 6, 1850 at Portsmouth, N.H. He was an assistant draftsman and draftsman in the navy yards at New York, Philadelphia, Boston, and Washington from 1873-80, and naval expert with U.S. Navy Dept. at Washington from 1880-90. From 1890-1900 he was superintendent and general superintendent of the Bath (Maine) Iron Works, and president of the Eastern Shipbuilding Co. of New London, Conn. from 1900-06, retiring in the latter year. He designed and built many steam yachts for private owners and also the large steamships Minnesota and Dakota. Mason and Knight Templar. d. Oct. 31, 1918.

Agner B. Hansen (1896-1948) President of Northern Paper Mills. b. June 7, 1896 at Racine, Wis. Began as a chemist for paper company working his way to the vice presidency of Northern Paper Mills in 1935, and president in 1941. He was also president of four other allied companies. Served as ensign, U.S. Navy in WWI. Received his degrees in Belle City Lodge No. 92, Racine, Wis. on July 13, July 27 and Aug. 10, 1918 and affiliated with Washington Lodge No. 21, Green Bay, Wis. on Jan. 6, 1939. Member of Scottish Rite bodies (NJ) at both Green Bay and Milwaukee. d. July 4, 1948.

Niels E. Hansen (1866-1950) American horticulturist and developer of new strains of fruits, grasses and plants. b. Jan. 4, 1866 near Ribe, Denmark, coming to U.S. with parents in 1873. Graduate of Iowa Agriculture Coll. in 1887. Was professor of horticulture, first at Iowa Agriculture Coll., and then at the S.D. Agriculture Coll. and Experiment Station, 1895-1937. He made many exploratory expeditions to Russia, China, Siberia, Transcaucasia, Lapland, Finland, Manchuria, Japan, North Africa, Mongolia, and Turkestan, collecting new varieties of hardy seeds and plants. He was the originator of new

fruits, especially the Hansen hybrid plums, named in his honor. He introduced Turkestan, Siberian and many other alfalfas and also introduced and named the Cossack alfalfa, now widely grown on the Northwest prairies. It was developed from a spoonful of seed in 1906, to over 1000 bushels of seed in 1916. Member of Brookings Lodge No. 24, Brookings, S.D., receiving degrees on Oct. 10, 1896, Feb. 6, June 1, 1897; suspended April 1, 1924; reinstated April 5, 1927. d. Oct. 5, 1950.

Ole Andreas Hansen A giant. *The Mystic Star*, in Sept. 1869 quoted a story from the Glasgow Herald (Scotland) of an emergency meeting of Clyde Lodge No. 468 in that city at which Major Ole Andreas Hansen of the U.S. Army and a native of Norway, was initiated, passed and raised. His height was given as eight feet and weight 33 stones.

William C. Hansen President, State Teachers College, Stevens Point, Wis. since 1940. b. July 4, 1891 at Neenah, Wis. Graduate of U. of Wisconsin. Was teacher, principal and superintendent of schools in Wis. cities. Initiated May 8, 1924 in Neillsville Lodge No. 163, Neillsville, Wis., and presently a member of Evergreen Lodge No. 93, Stevens Point, Wis. 32° AASR (NJ) in Madison, Wis.

Roger W. Hanson (1827-1863) Confederate Brigadier General in Civil War. b. Aug. 27, 1827 at Winchester, Ky. At the age of 20 he served in the Mexican War under John S. Williams. After returning home he fought a duel in which he was crippled for life. He studied law and was admitted to the bar and then went to Calif. as a gold-seeker, returning to Ky. in 1850, where he practiced law at Winchester. In 1853 he was elected to the state legislature and gained considerable distinction as a lawmaker. Later he moved to Lexington and continued his law practice there. At the beginning of the Civil War he entered the Confederate Army and was made colonel of the 2nd Kentucky Inf. After the battle of Fort Donelson, he was promoted to brigadier general for bravery. He participated in numerous battles and was mortally wounded at the Battle of Murfreesboro (Tenn.) on Jan. 2, 1863 and died on the 4th of the same month. He was a member of Good Samaritan Lodge No. 174, Lexington, Ky., from the date of his initiation in 1856 until he left for Army service in 1861.

Prince Harald of Denmark (1876-1949) b. Oct. 8, 1876, the third son of King Frederick VIII of Denmark,q.v. The king, an interested Freemason and grand master for many years, initiated all three sons—Harald, Christian X, q.v., and Haakon, q.v. Harald was initiated April 4, 1896 in Lodge Nordstjernen at Copenhagen. He served as pro-grand master for many years and succeeded his brother Christian X as grand master, being installed, Sept. 18, 1947, in the presence of about 800 brethren. He was known as the "Hussar Prince" as he was a lieutenant general in the Danish Army Hussars. He married Princess Helena, April 28, 1909. He frequently took part in the work of all degrees. d. March 30, 1949.

Count Agoston Haraszthy de Mokcsa (1812?-1869) An Hungarian pioneer in America who founded the town of Sauk City, Wis. about 1841. He migrated to Calif. in 1849, and there introduced Tokay, Zinfandel, and Shiras grapes into Calif., thereby creating the grape and wine industry of that state. He became a member of Madison Lodge No. 5, Madison, Wis. in 1845.

James G. Harbord (1866-1947) Lieutenant General, U.S. Army and President of Radio Corporation of America. b. March 21, 1866 at Bloomington, Ill. Graduate of Kansas State Agriculture Coll. Entered army as an enlisted man in 1889, and commissioned second lieutenant in 1891. Fought in Spanish-American and First World Wars. Made brigadier general in 1917, major general in 1919, and retired as lieutenant general in 1942. He was chief of staff, A.E.F. in France, and commanded the Marine Brigade near Chateau Thierry and the 2nd Division in the Soissons offensive. From 1923-30 he was president of R.C.A., and chairman of the board from 1930-47. He was a member of Council Grove Lodge No. 36, Council Grove, Kansas (Dec. 8, 1898), and received the 32° AASR (SJ) on Dec. 5, 1909 at Ft. Leavenworth, Kans. while stationed there. He was a member of the Grand Council, Order of DeMolay. d. Aug. 20, 1947.

Cary A. Hardee Governor of Florida, 1921-25. b. Nov. 13, 1876 in Taylor Co., Fla. He was a teacher in the Florida public schools until 1900, when he was admitted to the bar and practiced at Live Oak, Fla. Was a member and speaker of the lower house from 1915-17. Mason, member of Live Oak Commandery, K.T.

Karl August von Hardenberg (1750-1822) Prussian prince and statesman. He was councilor at Hanover from 1779-82, and later in service of state at Brunswick, and administrator of principalities of Ansbach and Bayreuth. Served in war against France in 1792-95, and concluded the peace at Basel in 1795. In cabinet of Frederick William III, q.v., from 1798-1804, and foreign minister of Prussia from 1804-06. From 1810-17 he was chancellor of Prussia, and was made a prince in recognition of his part in the War of Liberation (1813-14). He was active in the Holy Alliance, and his policy in later years was reactionary. Said by the Bulletin of the International Masonic Congress (1917) to have been a member of the Craft.

Wesley Hardenbergh President of American Meat Institute since 1939. b. July 14, 1894 at Youngsville, N.Y. Graduate of Columbia U. in 1918. In 1919 he edited the Liberty Register (N.Y.), and the following year joined the public relations staff of the American Meat Inst. He was made vice president in 1928. In 1944-45 he was president of the American Trade Association Executives. Mason.

Delmar S. Harder Vice President of Ford Motor Co. b. March 19, 1892 at Delhi, N.Y. He started in the automotive industry with the Durant Motor Co. in 1915, and was later with Budd and Fisher Body Division of General Motor Corp. In 1945 he was president of the E. W. Bliss Co. He has been a Ford vice president since 1947; first, in charge of manufacturing, and since 1955 in charge of basic manufacturing groups. He is also a director of the Ford Motor Company. Mason.

Frederick A. Hardesty Rear Admiral, U.S. Navy. b. Jan. 16, 1893 at Astoria, Oreg. Graduate of U. of Oregon in 1915. He taught school until entering the Naval reserve in 1917, advancing to captain in 1943, and retired as rear admiral in 1947. In WWI he served on the U.S.S. Ohio and was commanding officer of the

U.S. Schuylkill in 1943-44 and U.S.S. Rocky Mount in 1944-45. Mason.

James Hardie (1750?-1826?) Masonic author, who in 1818 published The New Freemasons' Monitor and Masonic Guide. Mackey thought it more valuable than the monitors of Webb and Cross, qq.v. Although credited with membership in New York, the records of that jurisdiction fail to reveal any record of New York membership. He was born either in 1750 or 1760 and 1826 is the probable year of his death.

Charles H. Hardin (1820-1892) Governor of Missouri, 1875-1877. b. July 25, 1820 in Trimble Co., Ky. The family moved to Missouri in 1821, and his father was the first postmaster of Columbia. His mother was the sister of Dr. William Jewell, for whom William Jewell Coll. is named. He attended the Columbia schools, the U. of Indiana, and graduated from Miami U., Oxford, Ohio in 1841. While in college at Miami, he was one of the founders of the Greek letter fraternity, Beta Theta Pi, now a national organization. He was admitted to the bar in 1843, and practiced law in Fulton, 1848-52. In 1852 he was a member of the lower house and served three terms. In 1860 he was state senator. He was against secession, and in the "Rebel Legislature" which met at Cassville, was the only senator who voted against it. From 1865-71 he practiced law at Mexico, Mo. and was again elected state senator in 1872. His administration as governor was marked by reduction of debt, enforcement of criminal laws, and erection of the state penitentiary. He issued his famous "grasshopper proclamation," designating June 3, 1875, as a day of "fasting and prayer" for relief from grasshoppers which had again invaded Mo. after ruining crops the year before. In 1873 he founded Hardin College for women at Mexico, and in 1889 was active in the establishment of Missouri Military Academy at Mexico. He was initiated Jan. 26, 1852, passed Feb. 3, and raised March 2, in Fulton Lodge No. 48. He was elected senior warden in 1854, and became master in 1855. d. July 29, 1892 in Mexico, Mo. and his body was moved in 1893 to the Jewell Graveyard, two miles south of Columbia, Mo.

John J. Hardin (1810-1847) Colonel in Mexican War. b. Jan. 6, 1810 in Frankfort, Ky., the son of Martin D. Hardin, q.v., U.S. senator from Kentucky. He was educated in Transylvania U. (Ky.), studied law and moved to Jacksonville, Ill., where he practiced. He was prosecuting attorney for several years, and a member of the state legislature from 1836-42. In 1842 he was elected to the U.S. congress and served one term. He volunteered when the Mexican War began and was appointed colonel of the 1st Illinois regiment. He was killed on the second day of the battle of Buena Vista while leading his men in a charge. Hardin Military Lodge No. 87, chartered by the Grand Lodge of Mo., was named for him when it was organized in N.M. d. Feb. 27, 1847.

John R. Hardin (1860-1945) President of Mutual Benefit Life Insurance Co. from 1924. b. April 24, 1860 in Sussex Co., N.J. Graduate of Princeton U. in 1880 and 1883. Admitted to bar in 1884, and practiced at Newark, N.J. from that date. Mason. d. Dec. 7, 1945.

Martin D. Hardin (1780-1823) U.S. Senator from Kentucky, 1816. b. June 21, 1780, Monongahela River,

Pa. He was educated in Transylvania Academy (Ky.). He practiced law in Franklin Co. and served several terms in the state legislature. During the War of 1812 he joined the army and served under General Harrison, being promoted to major of the Kentucky volunteers. He was a Mason and member of Washington Chapter No. 11, R.A.M. His son, John J. Hardin, q.v., was a U.S. congressman from and was killed in the War with Mexico. d. Oct. 8, 1823.

Warren G. Harding (1865-1923) Twenty-ninth President of the United States. b. Nov. 2, 1865 at Corsica, Ohio. A newspaperman, he published the Marion Star (Ohio) from 1884. He was a member of the Ohio senate from 1900-04, and lieutenant governor of Ohio, 1904-06. He was U.S. senator from Ohio for the term 1915-21, resigning in 1920. He was nominated for president by the Republicans in 1920, and elected for the term 1921-25, but died Aug. 2, 1923. He was initiated in Marion Lodge No. 70, Marion, Ohio on June 28, 1901, and after 19 years he was passed, Aug. 13, 1920, and raised Aug. 27, 1920. On May 4, 1921 he was made an honorary member of Albert Pike Lodge No. 36 of Washington; made honorary member of Washington Centennial Lodge No. 14, Washington, on Feb. 16, 1922; and honorary member of America Lodge No. 3368, London, England in 1922. A member of Marion Chapter No. 62, R.A.M., he received his degrees, Jan. 11 and 13, 1921. He was knighted in Marion Commandery No. 36, K.T. on March 1, 1921, and made honorary member of Columbia Commandery No. 2, K.T. in Washington, March 4, 1921. He had been elected to receive his degrees in Marion Council No. 22, R. & SM., but died before they could be conferred. In the Scottish Rite, he received the 32° (NJ) at Columbus, Ohio, Jan. 5, 1921, and was elected to receive the 33° on Sept. 22, 1921, but died before receiving it. He joined Aladdin Shrine Temple of Columbus, Ohio, Jan. 7, 1921, and was made an honorary member of Almas Temple of Washington, March 21, 1921. He was associate honorary member of the Imperial Council of the Shrine in June, 1923. Kallipolis Grotto MOVPER conferred the degrees on him at the White House on May 11, 1921, and made him a life member. Washington Chapter No. 3, National Sojourners, made him a member at the White House on May 28, 1923, and he was made a member of Evergreen Forest No. 29, Tall Cedars of Lebanon, at Milford, Del. on June 9, 1923. Harding visited many Masonic groups from Alaska to the Canal Zone. On July 8, 1923 he laid the cornerstone pf Ketchikan Lodge No. 159, Ketchikan, Alaska; laid the cornerstone of the Masonic Temple at Birmingham, Ala. on Oct. 26, 1921; and addressed the National League of Masonic Clubs in Washington at the Willard Hotel on May 12, 1921. He stated: "No man ever took the oaths and subscribed to the obligations with greater watchfulness and care than I have exercised in receiving the various rites of Masonry, and I say it with due deliberation and without fear of breaking faith, I have never encountered a lesson, never witnessed an example, never heard an obligation uttered which could not be proclaimed to the world." At the cornerstone laying in Birmingham, Ala. he said "I have been a better citizen for being a Mason. There is nothing in Masonry that a free, religious, and just American could not be proud to subscribe to, and be a better citizen for so doing." When he received the Royal Arch degree he inscribed the Bible of a friend with the

following: "With grateful and happy remembrance of the occasion when this Holy Book was employed in revealing the exalting impressions of Royal Arch Masonry." He was scheduled to deliver an address on Aug. 2, 1923, in Hollywood, Calif. to Hollywood Commandery No. 56, K.T. on the occasion of the presentation to them by him own cornmandery, Marion No. 36, of the International Traveling Beauseant. He was on death's doorstep, and his secretary, Sir Knight George B. Christian, delivered the address. This was his last message to the American people. He died Aug 2, 1923, and on Aug. 8, the body was conducted from the White House to the Capitol with the six commanderies of Knights Templar of Washington, D.C. being in the funeral cortege. The asphalt container in which his body was placed was the gift of Boumi Shrine Temple of Baltimore, Md.

William L. Harding (1877-1934) Governor of Iowa, 1917-19. b. Oct. 3, 1877 at Sibley, Iowa. Graduate of U. of South Dakota in 1905. Began law practice in 1905. He was a member of the lower house in Iowa from 190713, and lieutenant governor from 1913-17. Member of Morningside Lodge No. 615, Sioux City, Iowa. d. Dec. 17, 1934.

Thomas Douglas Harington (1808-1882) Deputy Receiver General of old Canada in 1858-78. b. June 7, 1808 at Windsor, England. He served in the Royal Navy and with the East India Company's navy. Raised Dec. 13, 1843 in Duke of Leinstat Lodge No. 283 (Irish) at Kingston, Ontario and later affiliated with lodges in Montreal, Kingston, Quebec and Ottawa. Was provincial grand master of Lower Canada in 1853; provincial grand master of

Canada East (Scot.), 1853; past grand master of Ancient Grand Lodge of Canada West in 1856; grand master of Grand Lodge of Canada in 1859. Was grand first principal of Grand Chapter of Canada in 1859-71; grand master of Cryptic Rite, Ontario, 1871; honorary provincial grand master of Cryptic Rite, Ontario, 1871; honorary provincial grand master of Grand Conclave, K.T., Ontario, 1859-71 and first sovereign grand commander of Supreme Council, Scottish Rite in Canada, 1874. d. Jan. 13, 1882.

John H. Hardy (1847-1917) Justice Superior Court of Mass. from 1896. b. Feb. 2, 1847 at Hollis, N.H. Graduate of Dartmouth in 1870 and admitted to bar in 1872. Raised in Hiram Lodge, Arlington, Mass. on Oct 17, 1872, dimitted March 22, 1888. d. Oct 10, 1917.

Oliver Hardy (?-1957) Comedian of stage and screen. Gained worldwide recognition with his partner Stan Laurel in the team of "Laurel and Hardy." He was a member of Solomon Lodge No. 20 in Jacksonville, Fla. and was a frequent visitor at Hollywood and Mount Olive Lodges in California.

Samuel Hardy (1758?-1785) American statesman, who, in 1784, was nominated by President Jefferson as minister plenipotentiary to Europe, to assist John Adams and Benjamin Franklin in negotiating treaties of commerce. b. in the Isle of Wight Co., Va. Educated at William and Mary Coll. in 1776-81, he entered law practice. He was a member of the Continental Congress from Va. in 1783-85, and for a time, lieutenant governor of Va. A county in the northern part of Va. is named for him. He received his Entered Apprentice

degree in Williamsburg Lodge No. 6 at Williamsburg, Va. on Dec. 12, 1778. d. Oct., 1785.

Ray M. Hare Brigadier General, U.S. Army. b. Aug. 19, 1893 at Louisville, Ky. Graduate of Harvard U. in 1936. Commissioned in 1917, he advanced through grades to brigadier general in 1950. During WWI he served in France and Germany. From 1937-42 he was member of staff of secretary of War, and from 1942-45 was chief of ordnance. In 1945 he was in the Western Pacific, and since 1950, assigned to chief ordnance of European command. Member of Alamo Lodge No. 44, San Antonio, Texas; 32° AASR (SJ) at Galveston; Arabia Shrine Temple, Houston; National Sojourners. Was senior warden of Laneck Lodge, U.D. (Texas) at Coblentz, Germany in 1920 during occupation of Germany.

Earl of Harewood (1882-1947) Full name was Henry George Charles, Viscount Lascelles. He later became the 5th earl of Harewood. He was a brother-in-law of King George VI, q.v., and one of the richest men in England. He served with distinction in WWI and was wounded three times. He married Princess Mary in 1922. By the time he was 40 years old, the earl—nicknamed "Lucky Lascelles"—was the husband of a king's sister, possessor of a fortune estimated at 12 million dollars, and owner of about 27,700 acres, three country houses and a town house. One day, in 1915, while on leave from France, he met his great-uncle, the wealthy, eccentric marquis of Clanricarde. Lord Lascelles, as he was then, took his uncle out to lunch and had a chat about antiques. Not long afterward, when again at the front, Lascelles received a telegram telling him that the marquis had left him his estate amounting to some ten million dollars. Thirteen years later he inherited $1,200,000 from his father. It was often rumored that the earl and the duke of Windsor, q.v., were not on the friendliest of terms. The duke was once reported to have said: "Every day I get commoner and commoner, and every day Lascelles gets royaller and royaller." He served as provincial grand master for West Yorkshire and on June 1, 1943, he was installed by his brother-in-law, King George VI, as grand master of the United Grand Lodge of England at an especial meeting of that body in the Grand Temple at Freemasons Hall. Previous to that he had been pro-grand master from 1935-42. d. May 24, 1947.

Sir Henry Harford (1762?-?) Owner of the Province of Maryland, and provincial grand master of Maryland. He was the natural son of Frederick, the sixth and last Lord Baltimore, and Hester Wheland. When Frederick died in 1771, he had no legitimate children, and he willed the province of Maryland to Harford, then a child about nine years of age. Harford's interests in Maryland were represented by Robert Eden, as proprietary governor, until the Revolution. In the Book of Constitutions (1783) of the Maple T. Had Grand Lodge of England, Harford's name appears as provincial grand master for Maryland. It also appeared in the calendars published from time to time by the grand lodge, and strange to say, even appeared after the Grand Lodge of Maryland was formed and working. He is recorded as having given £25 to the FreeMasons' Hall. He returned to America after the war and attempted to recover some of his property, but was unable to do so. He then returned to England, and that country indemnified him to the amount of £90,000 for his losses.

George Harison (1719-1773) Fourth Provincial Grand Master of New York (English constitution). b. in England. He changed the spelling of his family name which had contained two "r's." His father, the Hon. Francis Harrison, Esq. of Berkshire, England, came to N.Y. with Governor Lovelace in 1708, where he served as a member of the provincial council, recorder of the City of New York, and judge of the admiralty court. He later fell into political disfavor and returned to England, leaving his family in America. Son George visited him in England in 1738, and returned home with an appointment to the office of surveyor of customs in N.Y. He married Jane, daughter of Richard Nicholls, a prominent N.Y. citizen, on Sept. 3, 1740. On June 8, 1753 he was made provincial grand master of New York by Baron Carysfoot. He was in charge of the celebration of St. John the Baptist on June 25, 1753, at the King's Arms Tavern, and again that fall, at the celebration of the Feast of St. John the Evangelist. A full account of these ceremonies was published in the New York Mercury on Dec. 31, 1753. The paper was owned by Hugh Gaine, secretary of the grand lodge, and he took the opportunity to refute the charges against Freemasonry by drawing attention to their acts of public and private charity. Freemasonry grew under Harison's leadership, and by 1771 there were seven lodges in New York City, two at Albany, one at Johnstown, one at Fairfield, Norfolk, Stratford, and Stamford, Conn. and even one at Detroit, Mich.—all deriving their authority from New York. He was one of the original vestrymen of Old Trinity Church and was also the owner of the brigantine, Charming Sally, with 12 guns, which his brother, Capt. Merely Harison, commanded. In 1765 he went into the brewing business with his father-in-law and James Leedbeater, a professional brewer. d. April 18, 1773.

Thomas J. Harkins Grand Commander, Supreme Council, 33° AASR, Southern Jurisdiction from 1952-55, succeeding John H. Cowles, q.v. b. Jan. 15, 1879 in Buncombe Co., N.C. He was a student at U. of North Carolina from 1897-1901. Admitted to the Oklahoma bar in 1901, he practiced at Weatherford, Okla., and at Asheville, N.C. since 1907. Member of Republican National Congressional Committee, 1912-14, and delegate to Republican National Convention in 1916. From 1922-26 he was special assistant U.S. attorney, and U.S. attorney for Western N.C. dist. from 1927-31. In 1931 he served as special assistant to the attorney general of the U.S. Member of Mount Hermon Lodge No. 118 of Asheville, N.C.; he served as its master in 1926, and grand master of the Grand Lodge of North Carolina in 1940-41. He received the 32° in 1904; KCCH in 1911; 33° in 1915 and was named deputy for N.C. in 1918. He became an active member of the supreme council in 1921.

Maple T. Harl National Commander of Disabled American Veterans of the World War in 1937. b. Feb. 4, 1893 at Marshall, Mo. Graduate of William Jewell Coll. (Mo.). He is a former president of the Harl Mortgage Co., Denver Safe Deposit Co. and Sun Investment Co. From 1939-45 he was state bank commissioner of Colorado. He enlisted as a private in the Army in 1917, and rose to major, being discharged in 1919. Served with the A.E.F. Mason, Knight Templar, 32° AASR and Shriner.

John M. Harlan (1833-1911) Justice of U.S. Supreme Court, 1877-

1911. b. June 1, 1833 in Boyle Co., Ky. Was graduated from Transylvania U. in 1853. He served in the Civil War as Union colonel in the 10th Kentucky Infantry. From 1863-67 he was attorney general of Ky. He was probably made an Entered Apprentice in Hiram Lodge No. 4, Frankfort, Ky. in 1858. He is carried as such in the proceedings of the Grand Lodge of Kentucky for 1858-67 inclusive, but disappears from the list of Entered Apprentices of Hiram Lodge after 1867. d. Oct. 1, 1911.

William W. Harllee Confederate General in Civil War. Member of Clinton Lodge No. 60, Marion, S.C.

Richard C. Harlow Football coach and professor of zoology. b. Oct. 19, 1889 at Philadelphia, Pa. Graduate of Pennsylvania State Coll. 1912 and 1913. From 1913-17 he was football coach and instructor of zoology at Pennsylvania State Coll., and again from 1919-21. From 1921-25 he was football coach and assoc. professor of ornithology at Colgate U. From 1925-34 he was football coach and athletic director of Western Maryland Coll. From 1934-49 he was football coach at Harvard U. and curator of zoology. He returned to Western Maryland Coll. and became head coach of track and advisory football coach. In 1936 he was voted "coach of the year" by U.S. football coaches and writers. He served with the U.S. Army in WWI and was discharged as an Infantry lieutenant. In WWII he was a lieutenant commander in the Naval Reserve. Mason.

Arthur F. Harman (1875-1948) President of Alabama State College for Women, 1935-47. b. Aug. 10, 1875 at Lexington, S.C. Was teacher, principal, superintendent of schools, and state superintendent of education for Alabama. Mason. d. Oct. 12, 1948.

Josiah Harmar (1753-1813) Brigadier General and General-in-Chief of the Army in 1789. b. in Philadelphia, Pa. He was educated in a Quaker school and entered the Continental army as a captain in 1776, serving in the 1st Pa. regiment. He served until the close of the war, being brevetted brigadier general by congress in 1787. He was with Washington's army in 1778-80, and in Greene's division in the south in 1781-82. After the war he was Indian agent for the northwest territory, and in 1790 commanded a force against the Miami Indians. He resigned his commission in 1792, and was appointed adjutant general of Pa. He was made a Mason in Lodge No. 3 of Philadelphia on July 2, 1778. He is also reported as a member of Pennsylvania Union Lodge No. 29, and was one of the petitioners for Nova Caesarea Lodge No. 10 (now N.C. Harmony Lodge No. 2 of Cincinnati). d. Aug. 20, 1813.

Henry G. Harmon College President. b. June 14, 1901 at St. Paul, Minn. Graduate of Cotner Coll. (Nebr.); Transylvania Coll. (Ky.); and U. of Minn. Taught school in China for two years, returning to America to teach in Culver Stockton Coll. (Mo.). From 1934-41 he was president of William Woods Coll., Fulton, Mo. and has been president of Drake U. since 1941. Member of Craft Lodge No. 287, Canton, Mo. 33° AASR (SJ) at Des Moines, and Shriner.

Judson Harmon (1846-1927) Governor of Ohio two terms, 1909-13, and U.S. Attorney General under Cleveland, 1895-97. b. Feb. 3, 1846 at Newton, Ohio. Graduate of Denison U. in 1866, and Cincinnati Law

School in 1869. He served as mayor of Wyoming, Ohio, judge of court of common pleas, and judge of the superior court. Member of Walnut Hills Lodge No. 483, Cincinnati, and elected honorary member of American Union Lodge No. 1 at Marietta on July 18, 1910. d. Feb. 22, 1927.

Reginald C. Harmon Major General, U.S. Air Force and first Judge Advocate General of U.S. Air Force in 1948. b. Feb. 5, 1900 at Olney, Ill. Admitted to bar in 1928, and practiced at Urbana, Ill. Commissioned second lieutenant in the U.S. Army in 1926, and advanced through grades as major general in regular Air Force in 1948. In WWII he was in charge of legal representation of U.S. government in industrial expansion program of the Air Force. Mason and Knight Templar.

Forest A. Harness U.S. Congressman to 76th to 80th Congresses (1939-49) from 5th Ind. dist. b. June 24, 1895 at Kokomo, Ind. Graduate of Georgetown U. in 1917, he has practiced law at Kokomo, Ind. since 1919. In 1933-34 he represented the U.S. in the extradition of Samuel Insull from Greece. Served in WWI with the 80th Infantry division, as a first lieutenant. Mason.

Cornelius Harnett (1723-1781) American Revolutionary patriot and governor of North Carolina, 1775-76. b. April 20, 1723. A resident of Wilmington, N.C., he first became known in public affairs through his opposition to the stamp act. He represented Wilmington in the provincial assembly of 1770-71. As the Revolution approached, Harnett became its leading spirit in the Cape Fear region. In the provincial congress of 1775 he represented his old constituents of Wilmington, and when Governor Martin was forced to abdicate, he was made president of the council, and thus acting governor of N.C. In 1776 Sir Henry Clinton appeared in Cape Fear River with a British fleet and offered a general pardon to all residents except Harnett and Robert Howe. In 1778 he was elected to fill Caswell's seat in the congress, and his signature is found on the "articles of confederation and perpetual union." When the British subsequently took possession of the Cape Fear region, Harnett was taken prisoner, and died in a British prison at Wilmington on April 20, 1781. He was a member of St. John's Lodge No. 213 under English constitution and St. John's Lodge No. 1, under North Carolina constitution (at Wilmington). This was the first lodge to be established in N.C. At one time he was deputy provincial grand master of America under the provincial grand master, Joseph Montfort, q.v.

Edwards Harper First Grand Secretary of the United Grand Lodge of England. He shared this position with William Henry White. Harper served as deputy grand secretary under Leslie in the grand lodge of the "Ancients" from 1801-13. White became grand secretary of the grand lodge of the "Moderns" in 1810. They served the United Grand Lodge jointly until 1838 when Harper retired on a pension. White then continued alone as grand secretary until 1856. They also acted as secretaries to the Lodge of Reconciliation from 1813-16.

Roy W. Harper U.S. District Judge of Missouri from 1947. b. July 26, 1905 at Gibson, Mo. Graduate of U. of Missouri in 1927 and 1929. Practiced law first at Steele, Mo., and later at Caruthersville. He enlisted in the U.S. Air Corps in 1941, and served with 35th Fighter Group in the Southwest Pacific from 1942-44. In 1945 he became a colonel in the Air Corps Reserve. Mason, 32° AASR and Shriner.

Thomas Harper (1736-1832) Deputy Grand Master of the grand lodge of the "Ancients" (Athol). At the union of the grand lodges, he opened the especial grand lodge as deputy grand master, and by unanimous accord was requested to continue in office until the installation of a grand master. When the Duke of Kent was installed, he appointed Harper as his deputy. The latter also had a footing in the "Moderns," as he was a member of the Lodge of Antiquity from 1792, and served as grand steward in the Moderns' grand lodge in 1796. He was expelled by that body in 1803 for nonattendance at the committee of charity. This action hurt the attempt at union between the two grand lodges. Harper was a jeweler by trade, and many old lodges still possess lodge jewels struck by him.

William R. Harper (1856-1906) President of University of Chicago from 1891. b. July 26, 1856. He was graduated from Muskingum Coll. when he was 14 years old (1870) with a B.A. degree, and delivered the commencement oration in Hebrew. He was graduated from Yale in 1875, with a Ph.D. degree. He first taught and was principal of the Masonic Coll., Macon, Tenn. (1875-76). His field was Semitic languages, and he was a professor of the same at the Baptist Union Theol. Sem. of Chicago; Yale U.; Chautauqua Coll.; and U. of Chicago. He helped organize the U. of Chicago and guided it as president during its early years. He was a member of Ashlar Lodge No. 308, Chicago, El.

Edward Henry Harriman (1848-1909) Capitalist. b. Feb. 25, 1848 at Hempstead, L.I., N.Y. He received a common school education, and became a broker's clerk in Wall Street at the age of 14. He later became a stock broker, and was admitted to the exchange in 1870. He was president of the following companies: Union Pacific Railroad (and chairman of executive committee); Oregon Railroad & Navigation Co.; Portland & Asiatic Steamship Co.; Oregon Short Line Railroad; Southern Pacific Co.; Texas & New Orleans Railroad; Southern Pacific Coast Railroad; Western Railroad. He was an officer and director in numerous other large corporations, including chairmanship of executive committee of Wells-Fargo & Co. Member of Holland Lodge No. 8, New York City.

Walter Harriman (1817-1884) Governor of New Hampshire, 1867-68, Brigadier General (Union) in Civil War. b. April 8, 1817 at Warner, N.H. He began as a teacher but became a Universalist clergyman. He abandoned the ministry in 1851, and entered a life of politics. He was state treasurer in 1853-54; was on a presidential commission to classify Indian lands in Kansas; and served in both the N.H. lower house and senate. In 1860 he was elected to the state senate over his opponent—who was his brother! He canvassed Michigan for Buchanan, in company with General Lewis Cass, q.v., and was an earnest supporter of Stephen A. Douglas, q.v. In 1861 he became publisher of the Union Democrat at Manchester, N.H., and advocated immediate action against the seceding states. He became colonel of the 11th N.H. regiment and was taken prisoner in the Battle of the Wilderness on May 6, 1864, sent to Macon, Ga. and removed to Charleston. He

was exchanged in March, 1865, and brevetted brigadier general in 1865. In 1868 he toured the mid-west and west campaigning for General Grant, q.v. d. July 25, 1884. Member of St. Peters Lodge No. 31, Bradford, N.H.

Frank L. Harrington President of Paul Revere Life Insurance Co. since 1945. b. Jan. 17, 1902 at Worcester, Mass. Graduate of Dartmouth and Harvard. He entered the insurance field with the Mass. Protective Association in 1927, and has been with the Revere Company since 1930, starting as a claim examiner. Member of Acacia fraternity and a Mason.

Jonathan Harrington The last survivor of the Battle of Lexington. He was made a Mason in King Solomon Lodge of Charlestown, Mass., March 7, 1797, and was a charter member of Hiram Lodge at Lexington, Mass. He was buried Masonically.

Charles K. Harris (1865-1930) Composer and music publisher who wrote After the Ball. b. May 1, 1865 at Poughkeepsie, N.Y. Moved to Milwaukee after attending public schools in East Saginaw, Mich. He wrote more than 100 songs including After the Ball (in 1892), and was head of the Charles K. Harris Publishing Co. of Milwaukee, and later of New York, with many American and foreign branches. He also wrote Can Hearts So Soon Forget? He authored several plays including A Limb of the Tree, The Luckiest Man in the World, The Barker, and The Heart of a Man. He was raised in Arcana Lodge No. 246 of New York City on Jan. 15, 1906, and was a member of the Mecca Shrine Temple, N.Y. d. Dec. 22, 1930.

Everette B. Harris President of Chicago Mercantile Exchange since 1953. b. April 19, 1913 in Norris City, Ill. Graduate of U. of Illinois, and U. of Chicago. He was an economist with the department of labor from 1938-46, and director of personnel of Mandel Bros. department store of Chicago from 1946-49. From 1949-53 he was executive secretary of the Chicago Board of Trade. Member of May Lodge No. 718, Norris City, Ill.; 32° AASR (NJ) at Chicago; and member of Medinah Shrine Temple, Chicago.

Frederic R. Harris (1875-1949) Rear Admiral, U.S. Navy. b. April 10, 1875 in New York City. He was commissioned lieutenant, j.g. in 1903, rear admiral in 1916, and retired in 1927. In WWI he was in charge of navy war construction in U.S. and abroad. He was general manager of the Emergency Fleet Corp., of the U.S. Shipping Board and in charge of war emergency merchant marine construction. He specialized in bridges, harbor and river work. After retiring from Navy, he was president of Frederic R. Harris, Inc., and was a consulting engineer to the Navy from 1939-45, and to the British admiralty. He designed water-front facilities and some of the largest floating dry docks in the world. Place of Masonic membership not known, but he was a member of the National Sojourners. d. July 22, 1949.

Frederick Harris Lieutenant General, British Army. b. in 1891, he was educated at Coleraine school in Northern Ireland, and attended Trinity Coll. of Dublin U. He saw service in WWI at Gallipoli, Egypt, France and Italy, winning the Military Cross, and being wounded twice. In WWII he was on the staff of the Northern Command in India, and after serving

as deputy director of the medical service in Burma, was appointed director general of the Army Medical Service in 1952. He was created a companion of the Order of the Bath in 1949. He was an honorary surgeon to King George VI from 1946 until his death. He is a commander of the Order of the British Empire. He is a member of Royal Thames Lodge No. 2966, Gerrard's Cross, Buckinghamshire.

Frederick B. Harris Chaplain of U.S. Senate, 1942-46 and since 1949. b. in Worcester, England, he was graduated from Dickinson Coll. (Pa.) with A.B., A.M. and D.D. degrees, holds honorary doctorates from several universities. He was ordained to the ministry of the Methodist Episcopal church in 1912, and served churches in Trenton and Long Branch, N.J.; Grace Church in New York City; and Foundry church in Washington, D.C. He has been at the latter since 1924. Member of Pentalpha Lodge No. 23 of Washington, D.C.

Lord George St. Vincent Harris Fifth Baron Harris. The barony of Harris, Seringapatam, and Mysore was created in 1815, with a land tenure in Belmont, Kent. It was awarded to his ancestor George, 1st Baron Harris who was wounded at the Battle of Bunker Hill in 1775, captured Seringapatam, and conquered Mysore in 1799. The baron succeeded his father in 1932. He was educated at Eton and Christ Church Coll. of Oxford. Lord Harris was installed deputy grand master of the Grand Lodge of England in 1952. He is also grand master of the Mark Grand Lodge of England. He was grand master of the Knights Templar, and 33° AASR, being grand inspector general of the same. Previously he had been provincial grand master for the provinces of Surrey and Kent.

Henry B. Harris (1866-1912) Theatrical manager. b. Dec. 1, 1866 at St. Louis, Mo. He was educated in the public schools of that city and in Boston. As an associate of Rich & Harris, he undertook the management of May Irwin, and later managed Pete Daily, Lily Langtry, and Amelia Bingham in The Climbers, and launched Robert Edeson as a star. He became manager of the Hudson Theatre in 1903, the Harris Theatre in 1906, and the Follies Bergere in 1911. During the season of 1910-11 he had 18 companies on tour. Included in the productions he managed were The Lion and the Mouse; The Traveling Salesman; The Third Degree. He was a member of Munn Lodge No. 190, the Scottish Rite, and Mecca Shrine Temple, all of New York City. He was lost in the sinking of the Titanic on April 15, 1912.

Isham G. Harris (1818-1897) U.S. Senator and Governor of Tennessee. b. Feb. 10, 1818 at Tullahoma, Tenn. Of poor parents, he became a merchant in Tippah Co., Miss. By studying law at nights, he was able to pass the bar in 1841. He served in the state legislature from 1847-49, and was U.S. congressman from Tenn. for two terms, 1849-53. He was elected governor three times, serving from 1857-62. It was a turbulent period, and he joined the staff of General A. S. Johnston as an aide, and was with the Army of the West during most of the war. He was captured, broke parole, and went to Mexico, and then to England. He returned to the U.S. in 1867 and resumed law practice in Memphis, Tenn. He lost his fortune of $150,000 in the war. In 1876 he ran for the U.S. Senate, won, and took his seat in 1877. He served

in the senate until his death on July 8, 1897, and was president pro tern of that body from 1893-97. A member of Paris Lodge No. 108, Paris, Tenn., he was elected grand orator of the Grand Lodge of Tennessee in 1851, but was unable to serve.

Nathaniel E. Harris (1846-1929) Governor of Georgia, 1915-17. b. Jan. 21, 1846 at Jonesboro, Tenn. Graduate of U. of Georgia in 1870. He enlisted in the Confederate forces in 1862, and served to the close of the Civil War, being on the staff of the Army of Northern Va. part of that time. He began law practice at Sparta, Ga. in 1872, and moved to Macon in 1873. He served in both branches of the state legislature, and was superior court judge of the Macon circuit in 1912. In 1885, he founded the Georgia School of Technology, and for a long time was chairman of the trustees. He was also trustee of the U. of Georgia, and Wesleyan Female Coll. Member of Macon Lodge No. 5, serving as master in 1914. Also a member of Constantine Chapter No. 4, R.A.M. of Macon. d. Sept. 21, 1929.

Oren Harris U.S. Congressman to 77th to 81st Congresses from 7th Ark. dist. b. Dec. 20, 1903 at Belton, Ark. Graduate of Henderson State Coll. (Ark.), and Cumberland U. Admitted to Ark. bar in 1930, and since practiced law at El Dorado. Member of El Dorado Lodge No. 13 and El Dorado Chapter No. 114, RAM., El Dorado, Ark.; 32° AASR (SJ) at Little Rock, Ark.; Shriner and Jester.

Overton Harris (1856-1931) Cattleman and banker. b. July 3, 1856 at Harris, Mo. A farmer from boyhood, he owned 3,000 acres in Sullivan Co., Mo. He started breeding

Hereford cattle about 1890, and won most of the prizes offered for cattle with show herd at St. Louis Exposition in 1904. His herd developed into one of the foremost in the U.S. In 1888 he organized and was president of the Harris Banking Co., Harris, Mo. Member of Arcana Lodge No. 389, Harris, Mo.; exalted Milan Chapter No. 103, R.A.M., April 30, 1885; and charter member of St. Bernard Commandery No. 52 K.T. of Milan, in April 1889. Withdrew from chapter and cornmandery in 1923. Member of Scottish Rite. d. April 14, 1931.

Ray Baker Harris Masonic author and librarian. b. Dec. 31, 1907 in Manila, Philippines. Educated in public schools of New York City, the Massanutten Acad. (Va.), and George Washington U. He was on editorial staff of Doubleday, Doran & Co., publishers, N.Y. from 1928-30, and from 1930-39 was in charge of the publications section of The Library of Congress. Since 1939 he has been librarian of the Scottish Rite Supreme Council Library (SJ) at Washington, D.C. A contributor of historical and biographical articles to *Encyclopaedia Britannica*, historical quarterlies, magazines, and newspapers, he founded the Romanian Collection at Kent State U. (Ohio). In WWII he was with the 109th Inf. regiment and 28th Inf. Div. hdqs. in the Rhineland, Alsace, and German campaigns. A member of Potomac Lodge No. 5, Washington, D.C., he was master in 1947, and grand master of the Grand Lodge of District of Columbia in 1957. He is past secretary of Potomac-Hiram Chapter No. 8, R.A.M., and past recorder of Columbia Council No. 3, R. & S.M. He belongs to Potomac Commandery No. 3, K.T. Harris received the 33° honorary, in the AASR (SJ) in 1947, and is past wise master of Evangelist Chap-

ter of Rose Croix. He also belongs to Almas Shrine temple, American Lodge of Research (active member), National Sojourners, Tall Cedars and O.E.S. He is the author of A Century and a Half of Freemasonry in Georgetown, and editor of *Bibliography of the Writings of Albert Pike*.

Reginald V. Harris Lawyer and Masonic author. b. March 21, 1881 at Londonderry Mines, N.S., Canada. Holds B.A. from Trinity U. (Toronto), and M.A. from Toronto U. and King's College (Windsor), with two honorary doctorates. Admitted to Nova Scotia bar in 1905, and has practiced in Winnipeg (Man.) and Halifax (N.S.) Active in the Church of England for 50 years, he was elected prolocutor in 1946, being first layman in Anglican Communion to hold this office. A founder and past president of the Commercial Club of Halifax; founder of Canadian Cancer Society; governor of King's College; school commissioner for Halifax; alderman, Halifax; founder and past president of Halifax Welfare Bureau; past member of provincial and national Red Cross council. Created officer of Order of St. John in 1917, and commander in 1943; received King's Coronation medal in 1937. In 1909 he won first prize in the Empire-wide competition for essay on Standard of Empire. Among his many writings are The *Trial of Christ from a Legal Standpoint; History of Knight Templarism in Canada; The Beginnings of Freemasonry in Canada (1606-1800)*; and over 200 histories of Masonic bodies in Canada. He has written a number of plays including ten Masonic ones. Raised in St. Andrew's Lodge No. 1, Halifax, Oct. 7, 1913, he served as master and secretary. He was grand master of Nova Scotia from 1932-35, and has been grand secretary of the Grand Lodge of Nova Scotia since

1945. Exalted in St. Andrew's Chapter No. 2 in 1915, he was grand high priest in 1926-27; Knighted in Antiquity Preceptory No. 5, K.T., he was supreme grand master in 1937-39. A member of the Nova Scotia Consistory, Scottish Rite, he was made honorary 33° in 1932, and was active 33° from 1954-56.

Robert LeRoy Harris (1874-1948) Episcopal Bishop. b. Feb. 12, 1874 at Cleveland, O. Graduate of Kenyon Coll. (Ohio) in 1896. Ordained Episcopal deacon in 1899, and priest in 1900. He served churches in Toledo, Ohio; Newport, Ky.; Cincinnati, Ohio; and Cheyenne, Wyo. He was elected bishop of Marquette in 1917, and later served as bishop in charge of Episcopal churches in Europe. Member of Sanford L. Collins Lodge No. 396, Toledo, Ohio; Toledo Chapter No. 161, R.A.M.; Toledo Council No. 33, R. & S.M.; Toledo Commandery No. 7, K.T. Received Scottish Rite degrees in Valley of Cincinnati in 1905, and in 1908 affiliated with the bodies at Cheyenne, Wyo., returning to Valley of Toledo in 1918. He was crowned 33° (NJ) on Sept. 16, 1919. d. Feb. 6, 1948.

Rufus C. Harris President of Tulane University since 1937. b. at Monroe, Ga. in 1897. Graduate of Mercer U. in 1917. He was professor of law at Mercer U. from 1923-27, and from 1927-37 was dean and professor of law at Tulane U. Has been director of U.S. Federal Reserve Bank at Atlanta, Ga. since 1938. Served in WWI as a first lieutenant of Infantry in France. Member of General Warren Lodge No. 20, Monroe, Ga., being raised on May 11, 1920.

Thaddeus M. Harris (1768-1842) Colonial clergyman and Ma-

sonic writer. b. July 7, 1768 at Charlestown, Mass. His father was a Revolutionary patriot, who died during the war, leaving his family destitute. He entered the school of Dr. Morse, who prepared him for college; and in 1787 he was graduated from Harvard U. Through the influence of friends he was invited that year to become private secretary to General Washington, but was prevented from accepting by an attack of smallpox. He taught at Worcester a year, studied theology and in 1781 was appointed librarian at Harvard. He served until 1793, when he became pastor of the First Unitarian church at Dorchester, where he remained until three years before his death. His son, Thaddeus W., q.v., later became librarian at Harvard. He wrote Discourses in Favor of Freemasonry (1803). Other writings were: Biographical Memoirs of James Oglethorpe; A Natural History of the Bible; Journal of a Tour of the Territory Northwest of the Alleghany Mountains; and others. He was the first grand chaplain of the Grand Lodge of Massachusetts from 1797-98, drafted the "Harris Constitutions" for his grand lodge; was junior warden in 1800, and grand secretary from 1800-10. He was made a Mason in King Solomon Lodge, Charlestown in 1790. d. April 3, 1842.

Thaddeus W. Harris (1795-1856) Entomologist and librarian. b. Nov. 12, 1795 at Dorchester, Mass., the son of the Rev. Thaddeus M. Harris, q.v. He was graduated from Harvard in 1815, studied medicine, and practiced at Milton Hill, Mass. until 1831, when he was appointed librarian of Harvard. He served in this capacity until his death in 1856. His father had been librarian of Harvard 1781-93. In 1837 he was appointed to make a zoological and botanical survey of Mass., and after much research, published a catalog of insects that numbered 2,350 species. He was a member of Union Lodge at Dorchester. d. Jan. 16, 1856.

Thomas L. Harris (1816-1858) U.S. congressman to 31st and 34th-35th Congresses, 1849-51, and 1855-58 from Ill. b. Oct. 29, 1816 in Norwich, Conn. Graduate of Trinity Coll., Hartford, Conn. in 1841, studied law and began practice in Petersburg, Ill. Served as major in 4th Reg. Ill. Vol. Inf. in Mexican War and was presented with a sword by Ill. for gallantry at the Battle of Cerro Gordo. Was elected to 36th Congress, but died before taking office. Served as master of Clinton Lodge No. 19, Petersburg, Ill. in 1849. d. Nov. 24, 1858.

William L. Harris (1817-1887) Methodist Episcopal Bishop. b. Nov. 4, 1817 at Mansfield, Ohio. Admitted to the Michigan conference of the church in 1837, and in 1840, when boundaries between Mich. and Ohio were adjusted, became a member of the Northern Ohio conference. He served pastorates in Ohio for eight years and became an instructor in Ohio Wesleyan U., and later principal of Baldwin Inst. at Berea. Ordained bishop in 1872. In 1872-73 he circumnavigated the world on a visit to various missions. He was recognized as an expert on Methodist church law. The place and dates of his degrees are unknown, but in 1842, he was a member of Mount Zion Lodge No. 9, (Ohio) and in 1848 was a member of Toledo Lodge No. 144, Toledo, Ohio. d. Sept. 2, 1887.

Alexander C. Harrison An aide to General Washington during the Revolution. Member of Hiram Lodge No. 28 of Maryland. During the Revolution, Washington had a total of 32 aides at one time or another. Some were military and others were secretaries. Seven of them have been identified as Freemasons.

Benjamin Harrison Federal Judge, Southern District of California since 1940. b. Dec. 18, 1888 at San Bernardino, Calif. Admitted to bar in 1914, and practiced at Needles, and then San Bernardino. Raised in Needles Lodge No. 326, Needles, Calif. in Jan., 1922; exalted in Keystone Chapter No. 56, R.A.M. of San Bernardino; greeted in Valley Council No. 56, R. & SM., San Bernardino; and knighted in St. Bernard Commandery No. 23, San Bernardino. He went through the chairs in the chapter. Member of Al Malaikah Shrine Temple, Los Angeles.

Byron P. "Pat" Harrison (1881-1941) U.S. Senator from Mississippi (four terms) 1919-43, dying in office. b. Aug. 29, 1881 at Crystal Springs, Miss. Attended Louisiana State U.,and began law practice at Leakesville in 1902, and later at Gulfport. He was a member of the 62nd to 65th U.S. congresses (1911-19) from the 6th Miss. dist. He was chairman of the senate finance committee. Member of Gulfport Lodge No. 422, Gulfport, Miss. Received 32° AASR (SJ) on Oct. 12, 1923 in Gulfport Consistory. d. June 22, 1941.

Carter H. Harrison (1860-1953) Lawyer, publisher, and five times mayor of Chicago (1897-1905, 1911-15) b. April 23, 1860. He was the son of Carter Henry Harrison, who also served five terms as mayor of Chicago, and was killed by an assassin, Oct. 28, 1893. Graduate of St. Ignatius Coil. (Loyola U.) in 1881. He first practiced law, then engaged in the real estate business, and from 189194 was editor and publisher of the *Chicago Times*. Member of Auburn Park Lodge No. 789 of Chicago, receiving degrees on Feb. 10, March 12, and March 18, 1898; Knight Templar. d. Dec. 25, 1953.

Francis B. Harrison (1873-?) Former Governor General of the Philippines. b. Dec. 18, 1873. He replaced Governor General Forbes in 1913. A member of Manila Lodge No. 1, he was made "at sight" by Grand Master Taylor on July 11, 1916. He received the 32° AASR in August, 1916, dimitted in 1927, reinstated in 1946, and again dimitted in 1949.

George P. Harrison Confederate General of Civil War. Was deputy grand master of Grand Lodge of Alabama in 1892-93, and grand master in 1894-95.

Henry B. Harrison (1821-1901) Governor of Connecticut, 1885-86. b. in New Haven, Conn. Graduate of Yale at head of class in 1846, receiving LL.D. from same in 1885. A lawyer, he was often in the state legislature, and was one time speaker of the house. He assisted in the organization of the Republican party in Conn. in 1885-86. Member of Hiram Lodge No. 1, Franklin Chapter No. 4, and New Haven Commandery No. 2, K.T., all of New Haven, Conn.

Roland R. Harrison (1878-1940) Managing editor of the Christian Science Monitor. b. June 10, 1878 at Smithville, N.Y. Graduate of Cornell U. in 1903. From 1903-22 he was with the following newspapers: Brooklyn Standard Union; New York Times; New York Herald. He joined the Monitor staff at Boston in 1922, and was executive editor from 1924-29, and administrative editor from 1939. He was manager of the Christian Science Publishing Society from 1929-39. Mason. d. Jan. 16, 1940.

William H. Harrison Judge, Supreme Court of New Brunswick. b. Sept. 25, 1880 in St. John, N.B., Canada. Graduate of U. of New Brunswick and Harvard Law School. Called to the bar in 1903, and became King's counsel in 1923. From 1908-19 he edited the N.B. Law Reports. He served in the provincial legislature from 1925-33, when appointed attorney general of N.B. on the latter date. Supreme court judge since 1935. In WWI he commanded the 3rd New Brunswick Royal Canadian Artillery, and was awarded the D.S.O. Mason.

William Henry Harrison (1773-1841) Ninth President of the United States. Anti-Mason.

Archibald C. Hart (1873-1935) U.S. Congressman to 62nd to 64th Congresses (1911-17) from 6th N.J. dist. b. Feb. 27, 1873 at Lennoxville, P.Q. Canada. Admitted to N.J. bar in 1896. Served in Spanish-American War with 2nd N.J. Volunteer Infantry. Raised in Pioneer Lodge No. 70, Hackensack, N.J. on March 16, 1900. d. July 24, 1935 (grand lodge records say July 23rd).

Joel Hart Dr. Hart was U.S. consul to Scotland in 1817. Member of Jerusalem Chapter No. 8, R.A.M. of N.Y.C. and high priest in 1812.

John E. Hart (1825-1863) Lieutenant Commander, U.S. Navy. A truce was called while his erstwhile enemies gave him Masonic burial services. b. in New York City. Appointed midshipman in the navy, Feb. 23, 1841. At the outbreak of the Mexican War he was serving on the famous Constitution. He entered the U.S. Naval Academy, and was the

92nd man to graduate from that newly formed school, in 1847. In 1856 he served on the sloop James-town off the African coast. He was apparently granted a leave, for he was made a Mason in St. George's Lodge No. 6, Schnectady, N.Y. in 1857. He married the daughter of Abraham A. Van Vorst, who was three times mayor of Schenectady, and master of the lodge in 1855-56. Thereafter Hart made Schenectady his home. He served on the receiving ship New York in 1857, and was promoted to lieutenant commander Aug. 5, 1862, and assigned com-mand of a small side-wheel gunboat Albatross. As a part of Farragut's squadron, he received orders to shell the town of St. Francisville, La. on the Mississippi River. He became deliri-ous with fever and shot himself to death in his cabin. Before dying, he requested that he be given a Masonic funeral instead of having his remains consigned to the river. Fellow officers, respecting his request, ran up the flag of truce, and rowed to Bayou Sara, where they contacted Capt. William W. Leake, the senior warden of Fe-liciana Lodge No. 31. Leake was home on leave from the Confederate Army. Leake, Samuel, and Benjamin White (local residents), and the Ma-sons of the Albatross conducted the Masonic services. In the ensuing years the lone Union grave in a field of Confederate dead was cared for by Leake, who passed the job on to his daughter, Mrs. Camilla Barrow, when he died in 1912. Mrs. Barrow was still living when on Jan. 8, 1956, a dele-gation from St. George Lodge of Schnectady, N.Y. and St. Francisville Masons, gathered to dedicate a new marker on the 93-year-old grave, and to hear repeated the strange story of how once the bonds of Masonry stretched across the enemy lines. Two dates are given for Hart's death.

Navy records state it was June 11, 1863, while Feliciana Lodge records say it was April 11, 1863.

Louis F. Hart (1862-1929) Governor of Washington. b. Jan. 4, 1862 at High Point, Mo. Admitted to the bar in 1884, he first practiced at California, Mo. and then in Snoho-mish, Wash. from 1889. He was lieu-tenant governor of Washington from 1912-19, and governor from 1919-25. He was grand secretary of the Grand Lodge I.O.O.F. of Washington from 1901-14. He was a member of Fern Hill Lodge No. 80 of Tacoma, and Afifi Shrine Temple of that city. d. Dec. 5, 1929.

O. Frank Hart (1879-1950) General Grand Master, General Grand Council, R. & S.M., 1927-30. He was a druggist before accepting the grand secretaryship of the state bodies of S.C. Made a Master Mason in Richland Lodge No. 39, Columbia, S.C. in 1903. Member of Columbia Chapter No. 5, RAM.; Columbia Commandery No. 4, K.T. Served as grand high priest of the grand chapter and grand commander of the grand commandery of S.C., secretary and recorder of grand lodge, chapter, council and commandery; grand commander, grand commandery of S.C. in 1927. d. Nov. 28, 1950.

Oliver J. Hart Protestant Episcopal Bishop of Pennsylvania. b. July 18, 1892 at York, S.C. Graduate of Hobart Coll. (N.Y.) in 1913. Or-dained minister in 1917, and served churches in Charleston, S.C.; Macon, Ga.; Chattanooga, Tenn.; Washing-ton, D.C.; and Boston, Mass. He was elected bishop coadjutor of Tenn. in 1937, but declined. In 1938 he was made bishop of Delaware, and in 1942 bishop of Pennsylvania. He served as a chaplain in both World

Wars. Received degrees in Philanthropic Lodge No. 32, York, S.C. on Oct 3, Nov. 6, 1917, and Feb. 4, 1918. Later affiliations have been Macon Lodge No. 5, Macon, Ga. (1920-37); Temple Noyes Lodge No. 32, Washington, D.C.; St. Andrew's Lodge, Boston, and since 1946, University Lodge No. 610, Philadelphia, Pa. Exalted in Carolina Chapter No. 1, R.A.M. of Charleston, S.C., April 22, 1920, and later affiliations have been in Macon, Ga., Mt. Pleasant Chapter No. 13, R.A.M., D.C., and University Chapter No. 256, R.A.M., Philadelphia. He was knighted in South Carolina Commandery No. 1, Charleston, S.C. on May 29, 1920, affiliating with Chattanooga Commandery No. 32, K.T. Chattanooga Tenn., Dec. 26, 1930, and later, with Mary Commandery No. 36, K.T. at Philadelphia. He has been grand chaplain of Grand Lodge of Pennsylvania since 1949. Received the 32° AASR (NJ) in Philadelphia and 33° in Boston on Sept. 27, 1951.

William L. Hart Judge, Supreme Court of Ohio from 1934. b. Feb. 5, 1867 at Salineville, Ohio. Graduate of Mt. Union Coll. and U. of Michigan, he was admitted to the bar in 1897, and has since practiced at Alliance. Member of Conrad Lodge No. 271, Alliance, receiving degrees on May 23, Oct. 2, and Oct. 16, 1913.

Dow W. Harter U.S. Congressman to 73rd to 77th Congresses (1933-43) from 14th Ohio dist. b. Jan. 2, 1885 at Akron, Ohio. Practiced law first at Akron, and later in Washington, D.C. Mason.

Roland H. Hartley (1864-1952) Governor of Washington, 1925-33. b. June 26, 1864 at Shogomoc, N.B., Canada. Educated in public schools of Minneapolis, Minn. In 1897

he was private secretary to his father-in-law, Governor David M. Clough of Minn. Moved to Everett, Wash. in 1903, where he engaged in the lumber business. He was mayor of Everett in 1910, served in the lower house in 1915-16. He was president of Clough, Hartley Co. Mason, Shriner, and member of St. Alban's Conclave No. 18, Red Cross of Constantine. 33° AASR (SJ) on Oct. 22, 1897. He was raised Nov. 26, 1885 in Cataract Lodge No. 2 of Minneapolis, and served as master in 1897. He was later a member of Cass Lodge No. 243 of Cass Lake, Minn. and served as master in 1901. In 1898 he was district deputy grand master of the Grand Lodge of Minn. He had also served as high priest of his chapter, commander of his commandery, potentate of his Shrine Temple and grand commander of the Grand Commandery, K.T. of Minn. in 1902-03. d. Sept. 21, 1952.

Leroy L. Hartman Dentist, and after 18 years of research, discoverer of formula for desensitizing dentine of teeth (1935), known as "Hartman's Solution." b. Jan. 20, 1893 at Victoria, B.C., Canada. Received dental degree from Northwestern U. in 1913. Naturalized in 1919. Practiced dentistry in Victoria and in Seattle, Wash., and was professor of operative dentistry at Columbia U. Mason, 32° and Shriner.

John F. Hartranft (1830-?) Governor of Pennsylvania, 1872-78, and Major General in Civil War. b. Dec. 16, 1830, in New Hanover, Pa. Graduate of Union Coll. in 1853, he was admitted to the bar in 1859. At beginning of Civil War he raised the 4th Pa. regiment, and commanded it. He later organized the 51st Pa. regiment, which he commanded and led in the charge of the stone bridge at

Antietam. He fought at Fredericksburg, Campbell's Station, the defense of Knoxville, Vicksburg, and with Sherman in his march to Jackson, Miss. He commanded a brigade in the battles of the Wilderness and Spottsylvania, and was made brigadier general of volunteers in 1864. In Aug. 1864, he commanded a division and was brevetted major general for services in recapturing Fort Steadman. He was postmaster of Philadelphia in 1879, and collector of the port in 1880. Member of Charity Lodge No. 190 at Norristown, Pa. Deceased.

Joseph C. Hartzell (1842-1929) Methodist Episcopal Bishop. b. June 1, 1842 at Moline, Ill. Graduate of Illinois Wesleyan U. and Garrett Bible Inst. Ordained to ministry in 1866, and served churches in Pekin, Ill., and New Orleans, La. from 1869-82. He founded the *Southwestern Christian Advocate* in 1875. Served as missionary bishop of Africa from 1896-1916. At one time he was special envoy to U.S. and England in behalf of the Republic of Liberia, and succeeded in averting a crisis between that country and Germany. He was made Knight Commander, Order of Redemption of Africa by the Liberian government. Mason. d. Sept. 6, 1929.

Matthew Harvey (1781-1866) Governor of New Hampshire in 1830, serving but one year. He resigned to accept appointment of President Jackson, q.v., as Federal judge of the district court. b. June 21, 1781 in Sutton, N.H. Graduate of Dartmouth U. in 1806, he practiced law in Hopkinton. He served in the state legislature from 1814-20, and in U.S. Congress from 1821-25. From 1825-28 he was president of the state senate. Member of King Solomon's Lodge No. 14,

Elkins, N.H. (formerly of Scytheville). d. Concord, April 7, 1866.

William W. Harvey Chief Justice, Supreme Court of Kansas. b. Nov. 21, 1869 in Madison Co., Ky. and reared in Shawnee Co., Kans. He taught school in Silver Lake, Rossville, and Ellsworth, Kans. before being admitted to the bar in 1898. He first practiced law at Topeka, but moved to Ashland in 1906. Harvey served on the supreme court bench from 1923-56, and was chief justice from 1945-56. He was initiated in Ellsworth Lodge No. 146, Ellsworth, Kans., May 2, 1898, passed Aug. 1, and was raised Oct. 11. On May 20, 1903 he was admitted to Topeka Lodge No. 17, Topeka, and on Jan. 2, 1907, was admitted to Ashland Lodge No. 277, Ashland. He served the latter lodge as junior warden in 1908 and master in 1909.

Charles Harwood (1880-1950) Governor of Virgin Islands, 1941. Federal Judge of Canal Zone, 1937. b. May 24, 1880 in Brooklyn, N.Y. He was graduated from the New York Law School and was admitted to the bar in 1904. He practiced in New York City until 1935, when he became special assistant to the U.S. attorney general for two years. Raised in Marchants Lodge No. 709, Brooklyn, April 18, 1907; became dual member of Harrison Lodge No. 1093, Feb. 2, 1949. Received 32° AASR (NJ), May 24, 1907, and joined Kismet Shrine Temple, May 31, 1907. d. Oct. 23, 1950.

Kittredge Haskins (1836-1916) U.S. Congressman to 57th to 60th Congresses (1901-09) from 2nd Vt. dist. b. April 8, 1836 at Dover, Vt. Admitted to bar in 1858. During the Civil War, he served with the 16th Vt. regiment from 1862-63. He practiced law in Brattleboro after 1866. He was a U.S. district attorney from 1880-87, served in the state legislature, and was speaker of the house in 1898, and member of state senate, 1892-94. He was raised in Social Lodge No. 38, Wilmington, Vt., June 7, 1857, affiliating with Columbian Lodge No. 36 at Brattleboro in 1865; exalted in Fort Dummer Chapter No. 12, R.A.M. in 1865; knighted in Beauseant Cornmandery No. 7, all of Brattleboro. He was grand master of the Grand Lodge of Vermont from 1895-97; grand high priest of the Grand Chapter of Vermont in 1883; and grand commander of the Grand Commandery of Vermont in 1891. Received 33° AASR (NJ) in 1899. d. Aug. 7, 1916.

Daniel H. Hastings (1849-1903) Governor of Pennsylvania, 1895-99. b. Feb. 26, 1849 at Salona, Pa. Reared on a farm, he practiced law from 1875-88. He was largely interested in coal mines and banking. In 1887-91 he was adjutant general of Pa., and as such had charge of the relief measures in the Johnstown flood of 1889. His home was at Bellefonte, Pa. and he was a member of Bellefonte Lodge No. 268; he served as commander of Bellefonte Commandery, K.T.

Daniel 0. Hastings U.S. Senator from Delaware, 1928-37. b. March 5, 1874 at Somerset Co., Md. Admitted to bar in 1902, he served as deputy attorney general of the state, and as secretary of state. In 1909 he was appointed associate justice of the state supreme court, and served until 1911, when he resigned. He was appointed by the governor as U.S. senator in 1928, and won the next term by election. Now practices law in Wilmington. Member of Armstrong Lodge No. 26, Newport, Del. and 32° AASR (NJ) at Wilmington since 1914.

Francis, 1st Marquis of Hastings (see Earl of Moira).

S. Clinton Hastings (1814-?) Chief Justice of Iowa and California; philanthropist. b. Nov. 14, 1814. He was educated at Gouverneur Academy (N.Y.) and studied law, beginning practice in Iowa. He was a member of the Iowa legislature and was one of the first U.S. congressmen from Iowa, serving from 1846-47. He was appointed chief justice of Iowa supreme court in 1848, but only served one year, moving to Calif. where he was elected chief justice of Calif. by the unanimous vote of the state legislature. He designed the first seal of Calif. which showed an altar with a square and compass on it. In 1878 he founded and endowed Hastings Coll. of Law in the U. of Calif. He paid $100,000 in gold to the state treasury for use in legal education of students. He also gave $6,000 in property to the foundation of St. Catherine Academy in Benicia. He belonged to two California lodges, Tehama No. 3 and Jennings No. 4 of Sacramento. The latter lodge had a short but tempestuous life. It was originally chartered as New Jersey Lodge, U.D. under the Grand Lodge of N.J. (1849), and then as Berryman Lodge No. 4 under Calif. in 1850, and a short time later changing its name to Jennings No. 4. Both the lodge names were in honor of Berryman Jennings, the first grand treasurer of the Grand Lodge of California. Due to expenses of building a lodge hall ($3949) and charity to sojourning brethren ($14,000), it was forced to close its doors after three years. Hastings was one of the names on the note to make good the money advanced the lodge by Jennings.

Samuel M. Hastings (1860-1943) President of Dayton Scale Co. and director of International Business Machines Corp. b. Aug. 14, 1860. Was in manufacture and sale of computing scales at Chicago from 1893, and president of the Dayton Scale Co. until 1927, when it merged with I.B.M. and he became director of the latter organization. Received the degrees in Braidwood Lodge No. 704, Braidwood, Ill., Nov. 15, Dec. 6, and Dec. 31, 1883. Affiliated with Streator Lodge No. 607, Streator, Ill. in 1885, dimitting Feb. 5, 1890, and on Feb. 7, 1918, affiliating with A.O. Fay Lodge No. 676, Highland Park, Ill. d. April 1, 1943.

William W. Hastings Rear Admiral, U.S. Navy. b. Feb. 18, 1889 at Geneva, Nebr. Graduate of Mass. Inst. of Tech. in 1925 in naval architecture and marine engineering, he entered the naval service in WWI and advanced through grades to rear admiral in 1947. He was with the Naval Construction Corps from 1918 until his retirement in 1947. Mason, Knight Templar and Royal Arch Mason.

Charles H. Haswell (1809-1907) First Engineer-in-Chief of the U.S. Navy, 1844-52. b. May 22, 1809 in New York City. He was a member of the board that designed the steam frigates Missouri and Mississippi. Before the naval engineering corps was established in 1844, he had served as chief engineer from 1836. He was a consulting engineer in New York City from 1852, and a trustee of the New York and Brooklyn Bridge in 1877. He wrote Mechanic's and Engineer's Pocket-Book; Mechanic's Tables; and others. He was a past master of Hiram Lodge No. 10, Washington, D.C. Exalted in Jerusalem Chapter No. 8, R.A.M. of New York City in 1888 at the age of 79. He was master of Kane Lodge U.D. (now 454) in 1858. He published a volume of reminiscences of New York life and society from 1816-35. In 1836 he was engineer of the first steam war-vessel in the U.S. Navy.

Carl A. Hatch U.S. Senator from New Mexico, 1933-49; U.S. District Judge for New Mexico from 1949. b. Nov. 27, 1889 at Kirwin, Kans. Graduate of Cumberland U. He first practiced law at Eldorado, Okla., but moved to Clovis, N.M. in 1912. He was assistant attorney general in 1917-18, and judge of the 9th judicial dist. from 1923-29. He again practiced law at Clovis from 1929-33. Received his degrees in Clovis Lodge No. 40, Clovis, N.M., and life member of same; 32° AASR at Santa Fe, and member of Ballut Abyad Shrine Temple at Albuquerque, N.M.

William B. Hatcher (1888-1947) President of Louisiana State University from 1944. b. Dec. 12, 1888 at Ripley, Miss. Graduate of Louisiana State U. in 1916. He served as principal of high school in Baker, La. and superintendent at Baton Rouge before going to Louisiana State U. as a history professor in 1936. Received his degrees in Plains Lodge No. 135, Zachary, La. on Oct. 8, Nov. 12, and Dec. 3, 1915. Dimitted Dec. 3, 1940. d. April 3, 1947.

Henry D. Hatfield Governor of West Virginia, 1913-17, and U.S. Senator, 1929-35. b. Sept. 15, 1875 in Logan Co., W. Va. Received medical degree from U. of Louisville (Ky.) in 1895 and from N.Y. University in 1904. Was Medical Corps major in WWI. He joined all the Masonic bodies early in life, but after his term as governor expired he bought a hospital, and when the Shrine started to build its hospitals for crippled children, Dr. Hatfield thought it would hurt his business, so he dropped all Masonic affiliations.

Mark 0. Hatfield Governor of Oregon from 1959. b. July 12, 1922 in Dallas, Oreg. Graduate of Willamette U. in 1943 and Stanford in 1948. Was resident assistant at Stanford U., 1947-49; instructor at Willamette U., 1949, and dean of students and associate professor of political science at the latter, 1950-56. Mason and Shriner. Member of the Scottish Rite in Salem, Oreg. He placed the name of Richard Nixon in nomination for the presidency at the Republican convention of 1960.

Ichiro Hatoyama Prime Minister of Japan. b. Jan. 1, 1883 in Tokyo. He studied at the Tokyo Imperial U. and practiced law in Tokyo from 1907-15. He served many years in the Japanese house of representatives, starting in 1915, and was chief secretary of the cabinet in 1927-29. In 1931-34 he was minister of education. He was elected prime minister of Japan in 1954. He was made a Master Mason, March 26, 1955, while prime minister. This was widely publicized in the Japanese newspapers, for it was an about face of policy from 15 years previous, when the Japanese government forbade any national to become a member of the fraternity. Local attacks upon Freemasonry went as far back as 1921, when Jiro Imai, faculty member of Tokyo Imperial U., warned against "this dangerous and subversive secret society." The ceremony was jointly conducted by the Grand Lodge of the Philippines and the district grand lodge of Japan. Five officers from the Philippines attended, including Grand Master Warner Schetelig, and Grand Secretary Antonio Gonza-

les. The Nippon Times stated that General John E. Hull, General Paul E. Rusto, General K. P. McNaughton, and Venezuelan Minister Rodriguez-Jiminez participated in the ceremony. Messages of congratulations poured in from people all over the world to Hatoyama, including ex-president Truman and General Douglas MacArthur. MacArthur's wire read: "As basic morality is the foundation of Freemasonry it is a source of deep satisfaction to me to see its progress in Japan. No more reassuring indication of its growing strength could be evidenced than the conferring of its third degree upon the Prime Minister. Please extend my felicitations to him on this significant occasion not only personally, but as the political representative of the great Japanese race."

Jacob Hvinden Haug Major general in Norwegian army; he was in charge of the Oslo (Grand area when the Germans occupied Norway). Master of the Grand Lodge of Norway 1945-1957, at which time he resigned because of ill health. He was distinguished for his work in rebuilding Freemasonry in Norway after WWII. Grateful brethren from all parts of Norway presented him with a gold medal upon his resignation in 1957 as grand master. He was K. and C. of the Order of King Charles XIII. b. in 1880.

David N. Hauseman Brigadier General U.S. Army and president of Houndry Process Corp. b. March 4, 1895 at Pottstown, Pa. Graduate of U. of Pennsylvania, Mass. Inst. Tech. and Harvard U. He enlisted in the Army as a private in 1917, and advanced through grades to brigadier general in 1944, retiring in 1946. Following WWII he was in charge of the general staff supervision of settling war contracts and disposal of surplus property for Army Service Forces and Air Force. He was vice president of Temple U. and president and director of that institution's research institute from 1946-48. Mason.

Samuel T. Hauser (1833-1914) Governor of Montana, 1886-88. b. Jan. 10, 1833 in Falmouth, Ky. Educated as a civil engineer, he was an engineer on Missouri Pacific Railroad in 1854, and a prospector along the upper waters of the Missouri and Columbia Rivers in 1862. He opened a bank at Virginia City, Mont. in 1865, and from 1866 was president of the First National Bank of Helena, Mont. He was a prominent member of the Vigilance Committee in the pioneer days. Mason. d. Nov. 10, 1914.

John W. Haussermann Capitalist, known as the "Gold King of the Philippines." b. Dec. 14, 1867 in Clermont Co., Ohio. Graduate of U. of Cincinnati in 1889. Admitted to Ohio bar in 1889, and later practiced in Leavenworth, Kans., where he was city attorney; in 1898, he enlisted with the 20th Kansas volunteers, and served in the Philippines as a second lieutenant. In 1902 he was appointed by Governor Taft to prepare a charter for the city of Manila. He served as assistant attorney general for the Philippines in 1902-03, and resigned to enter private practice of law. Since 1915 he has engaged principally in gold mining. He has been president of the Benguet Consolidated Mining Co. since that time. On his 90th birthday, he offered his Ohio estate, known as the Pond Run Farm, to the Masons of Ohio. Member of Corregidor-Southern Cross Lodge No. 3, F. & A.M. in Manila, Philippines; Luzon Chapter No. 1, R.A.M. and Oriental Council No. 1, R. & S.M., Manila; Nile Shrine Temple, Seattle, Wash.; and

Asoka Conclave No. 30, Red Cross of Constantine, Manila.

John F. Haussmann (1873-1955) University coach, baseball player, and professor of German. In early life he was a member of the St. Louis Cardinals. He was an uncle of Clemens Haussmann, Boston Red Sox pitcher, and of George Haussmann, 2nd baseman with New York Giants. He studied at Washington U. (Mo.); Elmhurst Coll. (Ill.) and was graduated from U. of Michigan in 1902, with Phi Beta Kappa honors. He played on Michigan's baseball team. After study in Germany, he taught German at the U. of Wisconsin where he earned a master's and doctor's degree. In 1908 he was the university's baseball coach. He retired in 1948. Made a Mason in Hiram Lodge No. 50 of Three Rivers, Mich. on April 14, 1917, he was buried by that lodge following his death on Dec. 30, 1955.

Henry Havemeyer (1838-1886) Sugar magnate. b. July 25, 1838 in New York City. He became a member of the family sugar refining firm, which controlled more than half of the entire sugar interest of the country. He was also engaged in tobacco commerce. He was one time engaged of the Long Island Railway. Member of Holland Lodge No. 8, New York City. d. June 2, 1886.

Joseph E. Haven (1885-1937) U.S. Consul. b. Jan. 19, 1885 at Chicago, Ill. Entering consular service in 1904, he served at St. Christopher, W.I.; Crefeld, Germany; Roubaix, France; and Catania, Turin and Trieste, Italy. d. May 4, 1937.

Benjamin C. Hawkes (1875-1931) President of Standard Playing Card Co. from 1898, and President of U.S. Playing Card Co. from 1929-30.

b. Oct. 8, 1875, at Chicago, Ill. Educated in Chicago public schools, Northwestern U., and Chicago Coll. of Law. Admitted to bar in 1896, and practiced at Chicago until 1906. He was also president of the Caxton Printing Ink and Color Co., and Great Northern Lumber Co. Mason. d. Dec. 16, 1931.

Alan S. Hawkesworth (1867-1942) Mathematician and clergyman. b. Aug. 10, 1867 in New Orleans, he was taken to England when four years old, and educated in Church Missionary Coll. of London. He went to San Antonio, Texas in 1891. Ordained deacon in Protestant Episcopal church in 1892, he went to Buenos Aires, S.A., and was ordained priest in 1894. He was rector at Sao Paulo and Santos, Brazil, Georgetown, St. Vincent, B.W.I. and Pittsburgh, Pa. from 1893-1917. From 1917-1923 he was a mathematician in the Bureau of Naval Ordnance. He discovered and published nearly 100 new theorems in geometrical conics. He traveled in nearly all countries of the world. In 1908 he was a member of the 4th International Mathematical Congress at Rome, and a perpetual fellow of the Circolo Matematico di Palermo. Mason. d. Oct. 31, 1942.

Edward L. Hawkins (1851-1913) English Masonic author. b. Aug. 10, 1851. He was raised in Apollo University Lodge No. 357, Oxford, in 1881. He was an early member of the Quatuor Coronati Lodge No. 2076, joining in 1886. However, he resigned at the first meeting after its consecration, and did not again affiliate for 20 years. He served as its senior warden in 1912. He wrote *A History of Freemasonry in Oxfordshire* (1882); *A Concise Cyclopaedia or Handbook of Masonic Reference* (1908); started the publication

Miscellanea Latomorunt in 1911; and prepared a revised edition of *Mackey's Encyclopaedia of Freemasonry* in 1911. d. March 17, 1913.

Albert H. Hawley (1866-1931) Labor leader. b. May 13, 1866 at Davenport, Iowa. He was a hotel employee from the age of 13 to 19, and a railroad fireman and engineer from 1885-1901. From 1901-09 he was an inspector for the Interstate Commerce Commission, and from 1909 was general secretary and treasurer of the Brotherhood of Locomotive Firemen and Engineers. Mason. d. May 28, 1931.

Joseph R. Hawley (1826-1905) Governor, Congressman, Senator from Conn. Was brigadier general (1864), and brevetted major general (1865), in Civil War. He served as governor of Conn. in 1866, U.S. congressman several times, and U.S. senator from 1881-1905. He is referred to as a Mason, but no record is found of his membership.

Paul R. Hawley Major General, U.S. Army Medical Corps, and now chief executive officer of Blue Cross and Blue Shield programs. b. Jan. 31, 1891 at West College Corner, Ind. Graduate of Indiana U., 1912, U. of Cincinnati, 1914, Johns Hopkins, 1923. He was commissioned a first lieutenant in the Medical Corps in 1916, and advanced through grades to major general in 1944. From 1943-47 he was chief medical director of the U.S. Veterans Administration. He is director of the American College of Surgeons. He has received many decorations and awards, both foreign and domestic. Served in WWI in France, and in WWII was chief surgeon of Army Air Force in British Isles and European theatre. Mason.

Willis C. Hawley (1864-1941) U.S. Congressman to 60th to 72nd Congresses (1907-33) from 1st Oregon dist. b. May 5, 1864 near Monroe, Oreg. Held a B.S., LL.B., A.B., A.M. and LL.D. from Willamette U. of Salem, Oreg. He was president of the Oregon State Normal School from 1888-91, and 1893-1902. From 1902-05 he was vice president and dean of Willamette U. He was admitted to the bar in 1894. Member of Pacific Lodge No. 50, Salem, Oreg., receiving degrees on Nov. 25, 1903, March 30 and April 27, 1904. d. July 24, 1941.

Frank W. Hawthorne Justice, Supreme Court of Louisiana from 1945. b. June 2, 1900 at Springhill, La. Graduate of Louisiana State U. in 1924, he was admitted to the bar in that year and practiced at Winnsboro for a short time, and then at Bastrop from 1924-33. Received the degrees in Simcoe Walmsley Lodge No. 359, Cypress, La. on Sept. 10, Dec. 4, Dec. 15, 1921; affiliated with Mt. Gerizim Lodge No. 54, Bastrop, La., May 21, 1928; 32° AASR (SJ).

Arthur D. Hay (1884-1952) Justice of Supreme Court of Oregon, 1942-52. b. Oct. 24, 1884 in Scotland, he came to the U.S. in 1906, and was naturalized in 1918. He studied at the Heriot Watt Coll. of Edinburgh, and graduated from U. of Oregon in 1911, being admitted to the bar in that year. He first practiced in Portland, then Klamath Falls (1912-15), and Lakewood (1915-33). He served as district attorney and circuit judge. He received his degrees in Lakeview Lodge No. 71, Lakeview, Oreg., Feb. 19, April 13 and June 8, 1921, serving as master of same, 1924-32, and grand master of the Grand Lodge of Oregon in 1941. He

held dual membership in Research Lodge No. 198. d. Dec. 19, 1952.

Marion E. Hay (1865-1933) Seventh Governor of Washington, 1909-13. b. Dec. 9, 1865 in Adams Co., Wis. After clerking in a store in Minn. for seven years, he moved to Washington Territory in 1888, and entered the mercantile business in Davenport, moving to Wilbur in 1889, and Spokane in 1908. Elected lieutenant governor in 1908, and became governor on the death of Governor Cosgrove. He was a member and past master of Tuscan Lodge No. 81 of Wilbur. d. Nov. 21, 1933.

Count Tadasu Hayashi (1850-1913) Japanese diplomat and statesman. He was minister to China from 1896-98; minister to Russia from 1898-99; minister to Great Britain, 1899-1906. He was created a count in 1907, for being largely responsible for the treaties of the Anglo-Japanese alliances of 1902 and 1905. He was a delegate to the International Peace Conference at The Hague in 1899. He was made a Freemason in Empire Lodge No. 2108 of London, England.

Carl Hayden U.S. Senator from Arizona since 1926. Now in his sixth term. b. Oct. 2, 1877 at Hayden's Ferry — now Tempe, Ariz. Served as member of town council of Tempe, treasurer and sheriff of Maricopa Co. In WWI he was an infantry major in the national guard. He was a member of the 62nd to 69th U.S. congresses (1912-27) from Arizona at large. He has specialized in legislation relating to irrigation of arid lands and Federal aid for highways. Member of Tempe Lodge No. 15, Tempe, Ariz.

Franz Joseph Haydn (1732-1809) Austrian composer, regarded as the first great master of the symphony and the quartet. He sang in the cathedral choir of St. Stephen's at Vienna from 1740-49. From 1760-90 he was kapel/meister in the service of the Esterhazy family, and it was during this period that he wrote some of his greatest music, operas, Masses, piano sonatas, symphonies and overtures. He had a long friendship with Mozart, q.v., beginning in 1781. Mozart's influence aided him in developing a fuller mastery of orchestral effects in his later symphonies. While in England from 1791-92, he wrote and conducted six symphonies, and again in 1794-95, wrote another six symphonies while in that country. He was a resident of the Vienna suburbs from 1795, where he wrote his last eight Masses, his finest chamber music, the Austrian national anthem, and the two great oratorios, The Creation, and The Seasons. It is probable that his association with Mozart led him to petition Freemasonry, as it happened three years after their close association started. Haydn received his Entered Apprentice degree on Feb. 4, 1785 in the lodge Zur Wahrn Eintracht at Vienna and Mozart was present on that occasion.

N. W. J. Haydon (1871-1950) Librarian, Grand Lodge of Canada, 1923-50. b. Devonshire, England, Oct. 1, 1871. Raised in North Lodge, Lowell, Mass. in 1886, and was the first affiliate of Riverdale Lodge No. 494 of Toronto, Canada in 1910. He formed the Toronto Society for Masonic Research in 1920, and was greatly interested in the literary side of Freemasonry. d. Dec. 12, 1950.

Charles M. Hayes Founder of the "Schoolboy Patrol" and long-time President of the Chicago Motor Club. b. June 9, 1877 in Cincinnati, Ohio. First employed by Standard Oil Co.,

he later owned Chicago agency for the Halliday car. He was elected president of the Chicago Motor Club in 1914. In 1922 Hayes interested Ill. and Ind. public and parochial schools in a project whereby volunteers were assigned to direct pupils at street crossings while going and returning from school. The resultant reduction in deaths and injuries was followed by an adoption of the plan throughout the nation, and in foreign countries. In 1954 the government issued a 3c stamp on the 50th anniversary of the American Automobile Assn., featuring the Schoolboy Patrol. He was raised in Alpha Lodge No. 155, Galesburg, Ill. in April, 1904. He was exalted in Galesburg Chapter No. 46, R.A.M. the same month, and knighted in Galesburg Commandery No. 8, K.T. in May, 1904. He received the 32° AASR (NJ) at Galesburg in Nov. 1904. Moving to Chicago he transferred his memberships to Dearborn Lodge No. 310; Chicago Chapter No. 127, R.A.M.; Englewood Commandery No. 59, K.T. He is also a member of Medinah Shrine Temple, Chicago. In Sept., 1953 he received the 33° AASR (NJ) and later he and his wife contributed $5,000 to the benevolent foundation of the Supreme Council, AASR. d. Oct. 16. 1957.

Charles R. Hayes Judge, Supreme Court of South Dakota from 1947-51. b. Dec. 24, 1899 at Deadwood, S.D. Graduate of U. of South Dakota in 1924, and admitted to bar in that year, practicing at Deadwood, and at Miami, Fla. from 1925-30. He was a member of the state legislature (SD.) from 1937-38, and circuit judge 1939-47. In private practice at Deadwood since 1951. Mason and master of Deadwood Lodge No. 7, Deadwood, in 1937. A 32° AASR (SJ), he headed the Black Hills Consistory from 1947-50. Member of NAJA Shrine Temple.

Isaac I. Hayes (1832-1881) Arctic explorer. b. March 5, 1832, in Chester Co., Pa. A medical graduate of the U. of Pennsylvania in 1853, he was with the E. K. Kane, q.v., expedition, 1853-55, as surgeon and naturalist. In May, 1854 he crossed Kane Sea, and was the first white man to place foot on Grinnell Land. On this trip his boat, the Advance, was frozen in, and but for the charity of the Etah Esquimaux, he and his companions would have frozen and starved to death. In 1860-61 he headed his own Arctic expedition, financed by Henry Grinnell, which led to important knowledge of polar geography. It was undertaken in the ship United States. In May, 1861 he crossed the Kane Sea and again set foot on Grinnell Land, attaining, on May 18th, a point which he called Cape Lieber (latitude 80° 15' N; longitude 70° W). On this date he planted a Masonic flag, together with the American flag. It was on this trip that he was the first white man to set foot on Ellesmere Land. His third expedition to the Arctic was with William Bradford in the Panther, in 1869. For his Arctic work he received the founder's medal of the Royal Geographic Society and the gold medal of the Paris Society. In 1862 he was commissioned a surgeon of volunteers, and served in the Civil War until 1865, as a lieutenant colonel. He moved to New York City, and was there an assemblyman for five years. He published *An Arctic Boat-Journey; The Open Polar Sea; The Land of Desolation*, and others. Although his original membership is not known, he was made an honorary member of Kane Lodge No. 454 (the explorer's lodge) of New York City in 1875. d. Dec. 17, 1881. Initiated in Lodge No. 51, Philadelphia on Feb.

24, 1859 while lodge was under dispensation. This interesting information has been found on page 263 of Memoirs of Lodge No. 51, F. & A.M. of Philadelphia, Pa. "At our meeting on Nov. 28, 1861, Bro. Isaac I. Hayes, a physician, who was initiated on Feb. 24, 1859 (by dispensation, in Lodge No. 51, A.Y.M.) was present, having then recently returned from an Arctic expedition. The W.M. called upon Bro. Hayes, who thanked the brethren for their assistance rendered the undertaking at a critical moment. . . . He stated the fact of his having displayed his Masonic flag on land at a higher Northern latitude than had yet been greeted by the Compass and the Square, namely 81° 35', etc."

Moses M. Hayes (1739-1805) Early Boston merchant. His original membership is not known. He first appears on Masonic records, Dec. 6, 1768, when Francken appointed him deputy inspector general of the Rite of Perfection for the West Indies and North America. On Feb. 17, 1769, George Harrison, provincial grand master of the New York "Moderns," issued a warrant for King David's Lodge in New York City, in which Hayes, "A Hebrew of Masonic distinction," was named master. Apparently, Hayes later took the warrant to Newport, R.I., and opened a lodge there. He eventually became grand master of the Grand Lodge of Massachusetts. As grand master he ruled with a firm hand, and urged caution in the admission of candidates, and insisted upon secretaries keeping proper records.

Paul H. Hayne (1830-1886) American poet. b. Jan. 1, 1830 at Charleston, S.C. His father, a naval officer, died at sea when Paul was an infant, and he was educated by his uncle Robert Y. Hayne, U.S. Senator and Governor of S.C. Graduate of Coll. of South Carolina at an early age, and at 23, was editor of *Russell's Magazine*, and afterward the *Charleston Literary Gazette*. He served for a time in the Civil War as an aide to Gov. Pickens; his home and all family effects were burned in the bombardment of Charleston. He then moved to Augusta, Ga., where he supported himself by his literary efforts. His last years were spent in virtual poverty and poor health. He became known as the "Laureate of the South." His published volumes are: *Poems; Sonnets and Other Poems; Avolio, a Legend of the Island of Cos; Legends and Lyrics; The Mountain of the Lovers, and Other Poems.* He was raised in Landmark Lodge No. 76 of Charleston, S.C. about 1851. d. July 6, 1886.

Caleb V. Haynes Brigadier General, U.S. Air Force. b. March 15, 1895 at Mt. Airy, N.C. Graduate of Wake Forest Coll. in 1917. Served in WWI as a private in the aviation section of Signal Corps, U.S. Army, and commissioned second lieutenant in 1918, advancing through grades to brigadier general in 1942. Has been flying since WWI, and never crashed a plane. He set world record for flight for altitude with greatest pay load, in 1939, and record for load distance (2,000 kilograms for 5,000 kilometers), non-stop in 1939. In WWII he helped set up the ferrying commands between the U.S. and England and Africa-Middle East. He personally directed the evacuation of Burma, and was named chief of U.S. Army Bomber Command in China to assist Chiang Kai-Shek, and General Chennault's American Volunteer group in China. He was commanding general of Indian Air Task Force operating against Japanese in Burma. Mason, 32° AASR and Shriner.

Eli S. Haynes (1880-1956) Astronomer. b. July 12, 1880 at Trenton, Mo. Received A.B. and A.M. from U. of Mo. and Ph.D. from U. of Calif. Instructor in astronomy at U. of Mo., 1908-11, and in U. of Calif. 1912-13. From 1913-14 he was a Martin Kellogg fellow at the Lick observatory, and professor of astronomy at Beloit Coll. from 1915-23, as well as director of Smith observatory. He returned to Mo. in 1923 as professor of astronomy and director of Laws observatory at the university, retiring in 1950. Member of board of trustees of Christian Coll., Columbia, Mo. from 1937. He made valuable contributions to science on variable star photometry, orbits of comets, and asteroids, and orbits of spectroscopic binaries. Raised in Acacia Lodge No. 602, Columbia, Mo., Sept. 6, 1910; master in 1932; DDGM from 1933-35; charter member of Mo. Lodge of Research; exalted in Columbia Chapter No. 17, R.A.M. Nov. 5, 1925; high priest in 1939, and grand treasurer of the Grand Chapter of Missouri from 1944-56; greeted in Centralia Council No. 35, R. & S.M. in 1926, and master in 1937; knighted in St. Graal Commandery No. 12, Dec. 13, 1935 and was commander in 1940. d. Sept. 13, 1956.

Roy A. Haynes (1881-1940) Federal Prohibition Commissioner, 1921-27. b. Aug. 31, 1881 at Hillsboro, Ohio. He was editor of the Dispatch at Hillsboro, O., from 1908, and an active worker in prohibition campaigns for many years. From 1927-28 he was president of the Economy Fire Insurance Co. Author of Prohibition Inside Out. Member of Highland Lodge No. 38, Hillsboro, Ohio, receiving degrees June 29, 1905, July 2, and Aug. 14, 1914; dimitted June 1, 1931. d. Oct. 20, 1940.

William B. Haynes Sports writer. b. May 29, 1881 at Akron, Ohio. He is widely acquainted with fish and game grounds of America, and contributor of illustrated articles to sportsmen's magazines. Author of *Ducks and Duck Shooting*; co-author of *Duck Shooting and Hunting Sketches*, and *Supreme Duck Hunting Stories*. Mason.

Brooks Hays U.S. Congressman, 78th to 84th Congresses from 5th Ark. dist. b. Aug. 9, 1898 at Russellville, Ark. Graduate of George Washington U. in 1922, and U. of Arkansas in 1919. Admitted to bar in 1922, practicing first at Russellville, and then at Little Rock. Attorney general of Ark. in 1925-27. President of the Southern Baptist Convention in 1957. Received his degrees in Russellville Lodge No. 274, Russellville, Ark. in 1922. Received 33° AASR (SJ) in 1957.

Frank L. Hays Justice, Supreme Court of Colorado from 1946. b. Feb. 12, 1889 at Council Bluffs, Iowa. Graduate of Creighton U. at Omaha, Nebr. in 1918. Admitted to bar in 1920 and practiced in Denver. Mason.

George W. Hays (1863-?) Governor of Arkansas, two terms, 1913-17. b. Sept. 23, 1863 near Camden, Ark. Began law practice in Camden, Ark. in 1894, and was circuit judge from 1906-13. Mason. Deceased.

Harry T. Hays (?-1876) Confederate Brigadier General in Civil War. Received all his degrees in Louisiana Lodge No. 102, 1860 (New Orleans). d. Aug. 21, 1876.

Norman R. Hays Judge, Supreme Court of Iowa since 1946. b. Nov. 9, 1891 at Knoxville, Iowa. Graduate of Grinnell Coll. (Ia.) and Harvard U. Admitted to bar in 1919. He served as county attorney and district judge. In WWI he was a captain in the Army. Mason.

Will H. Hays (1879-1954) Postmaster General of the U.S. under President Harding (1921-22) and "czar" of the motion picture industry 1922-45. b. Nov. 5, 1879 at Sullivan, Ind. Graduate of Wabash Coll. (Ind.) in 1900 and 1904. Admitted to bar in 1900. Active in Republican politics, he was chairman of the National Committee in 1918-21. As president of the Motion Picture Producers and Distributors of America, Inc. he accepted the job at a time when the film industry was beset with public criticism which threatened its independence. He ruled the "Hays Office" with firmness and fairness, and was credited with having saved the industry from government regulation. He retired in 1945, but acted as advisor until 1950. He was raised in Sullivan Lodge No. 263; he was a member of both York and Scottish Rites. He received the 33° AASR (NJ) in Sept. 1945. He received his 50-year service emblem from the grand lodge in 1950. d. March 7, 1954.

Charles D. Hayt (1850-1927) Justice, Supreme Court of Colorado, 1889-98. b. May 20, 1850 at Poughkeepsie, N.Y. He practiced at Walsenburg, Garland City, Alamosa, and Denver, in that order. Served as district judge and district attorney. Was chief justice of the supreme court from 1892-98. His original lodge is not known, but on May 6, 1899 he affiliated with Denver Lodge No. 5.

Alvin Hayward Early California miner. He purchased an interest in a mine in 1853, and after working it four years, his four partners abandoned the claim as worthless. Hayward persevered under the most discouraging conditions, and when poverty stricken and without credit, struck an immensely rich vein of gold, and became the richest man in the state at that time. He was principal sojourner of Volcano Chapter No. 11, R.A.M., which changed its name to Sutter Chapter No. 11 (Sutter Creek) in 1860. He worked his way through the chairs and became high priest. He presented the chapter with a golden altar and a set of solid gold jewels which are still in use.

Harry LeRoy Haywood (1886-1956) Masonic author. b. Nov. 1, 1886 in Mulberry, Ohio. He was graduated from the Cedarville, Ohio high school at the age of 13, and attended the Theological Seminary, Dayton, and Lawrence College, Appleton, Wis. Ordained a minister at 18, he gave up preaching in 1919. Although without a college degree, he taught and lectured on religion and anthropology for 13 years in many major colleges of the U.S. In 1917 he became editor-in-chief of *The Builder*, official journal of the National Masonic Research Society. From 1925-30 he was editor of the *New York Masonic Outlook*. At the time of his death he was engaged in research and writing for the Grand Lodge of Iowa at Cedar Rapids. He was considered the dean of Masonic historians and writers of his generation. He has written at least 30 books and 1500 articles on Masonry. Among his books are: *Symbolical Masonry* (his first in 1916); *Vol. 3 of Mackey's Encyclopedia; A History of Freemasonry* (with James Craig); *The Newly-Made Mason; More About Masonry; Free-* *masonry* and *Roman Catholicism; Well-Springs of Freemasonry*. He was raised in Acacia Lodge No. 176 at Webster City, Ia., June 7, 1915. He later affiliated with Waterloo Lodge No. 105, and with Publicity Lodge No. 1000 of New York City. Returning to Iowa, he became a member of Mizpah Lodge No. 639 at Cedar Rapids. He was a member of Tabernacle Chapter No. 42, R.A.M. at Waterloo, and 32° AASR (SJ) at Zarephath Consistory in Davenport. d. Feb. 25, 1956.

John Haywood (1753-1826) Judge of Supreme Courts of both North Carolina and Tennessee. b. in Halifax Co., N.C., his father was an officer in the Revolution. He entered law practice at an early age and was attorney general of N.C. in 1791, and supreme court judge in 1794, holding the latter office until 1809, when he resigned to defend James Glasgow, the secretary of state, on charge of fraud. His defense of Glasgow caused much criticism, and he left the state to settle in Tenn. in 1810. By 1812 he was judge of the Tenn. supreme court and held that office until his death. He authored A Manual of Laws of North Carolina; Haywood's Justice and North Carolina Law Reports; Tennessee Reports; Natural and Aboriginal History of Tennessee, and The Civil and Political History of Tennessee From Its Earliest Settlement to 1796. In 1813 he was reported as a member of St. Andrews Lodge No. 57, Louisburg, N.C. d. in Dec., 1826.

William H. Haywood (1801-1852) U.S. Senator from North Carolina, 1843-46. b. in Wake Co., N.C., he graduated from the U. of North Carolina in 1819, studied law and established a practice in Raleigh. He was a member of the state legislature from 1831-36. He resigned from the U.S. senate and returned to practice, but poor health forced him to retire. Member of Hiram Lodge No. 40 of Raleigh. He represented his lodge at grand lodge as early as 1823, and was grand lecturer in 1825-27. d. Oct. 6, 1852.

Joseph C. Hazen Baptist clergyman. b. April 5, 1874 at Beaver Co., Pa. Graduate of Bucknell U. (Pa.) and U. of Chicago. Ordained to ministry in 1903, and served churches in Ill., Wis. and N.J. Corresponding secretary of Northern Baptist Convention 1940-51; president of New Jersey Baptist State Convention, 1927-41; member of executive committee and radio commentator of Federal Council of Churches of Christ in America, 1930-45; chairman of the general commission on Army and Navy chaplains, Washington, 1947-50. Mason, 32° AASR and Shriner.

Natt Head (1828-1883) Governor of New Hampshire, 1879-80. b. May 20, 1828 in Hookset, N.H. He was a railroad and general building contractor. Was a member of the state legislature in 1861-62, and was adjutant general from 1864-70. In the latter capacity he published a four-volume set containing the records of every officer and enlisted man in the Civil War from N.H. He was president of the New Hampshire Agricultural Society. In 1876-77 he served in the state senate, being president of same in last year. Under the new law providing for biennial elections, he was chosen governor in 1879. He received his degrees in Washington Lodge No. 61, Manchester, N.H. in 1857, and was a member of Mt. Horeb Chapter, RAM., Adoniram Council, R. & S.M., Trinity Commandery, K.T., all of Manchester, and 33° AASR (NJ). d. Nov. 12, 1883.

T. Grady Head Justice, Supreme Court of Georgia since 1945. b. July 4, 1897 at Tunnel Hill, Ga. Graduate of Chattanooga Coll. of Law (Tenn.) and admitted to Georgia bar in 1925, practicing at Ringgold. He was attorney general of the state in 1942. Received degrees at Tunnel Hill Lodge No. 202, Tunnel Hill, Ga. in July-Aug., 1918, and presently a member of Buckhead Lodge No. 712, Atlanta; past master of Tunnel Hill Lodge.

Walter W. Head (1877-1954) Founder and President of the American Life Insurance Co. of St. Louis, 1933-54. b. Dec. 18, 1877 near Adrian, El. He first taught public schools in DeKalb Co., Mo. and entering the banking business, was officer of banks in St. Joseph, Mo., Omaha, Nebr., and Chicago, Ill. From 1931-33 he was president of the Morris Plan Corp. of America. From 1926-46 he was president of the National Council, Boy Scouts of America, and thereafter honorary life vice president. From 1942-46 he was state chairman of the Missouri War Finance Comm. Active in hospital, youth, educational, and community projects. He was a member of St. Johns Lodge No. 25 of Omaha, Nebr. and later affiliated with Wellington Lodge No. 22, DeKalb, Mo. He was exalted in Ringo Chapter No. 6, R.A.M. of DeKalb (now defunct) and on Dec. 9, 1839 affiliated with Kilwinning Chapter No. 50 of St. Louis. He was knighted in Hugh de Payens Commandery No. 4, K.T. of St. Joseph, Mo., Dec. 16, 1912; also 32° AASR and Shriner. d. May 3, 1954.

John W. Headley (1901-1957) College President. b. May 5, 1901 at Filley, Nebr. Taught in public schools of S.D. from 1921-29, and with Gen. Beadle State Teachers Coll. from 1929-45. From 1931-38 he was superintendent of schools at Colman and Winner, S.D. From 1945-47 he was president of the State Teachers Coll. at Mayville, N.D. and from 1947-51, president of State Teachers Coll. at St. Cloud, Minn. He was president of South Dakota State College from 1952-57. He was initiated in Garden City Lodge No. 146, Garden City, S.D. and affiliated with Evergreen Lodge No. 17 of Madison, S.D.; member of Cyrus Chapter No. 26, R.A.M. and Madison Commandery No. 20, K.T., both of Madison, S.D. He was a past master of Evergreen Lodge. A 32° AASR (SJ) and member of El Riad Shrine Temple, both in Sioux Falls, S.D. d. Nov. 29, 1957.

Charles J. Heale (1900-1949) President and General Manager of Iron Age and Hardware Age. b. May 20, 1900 at Brooklyn, N.Y. Began as office boy with Iron Age in 1916, becoming vice president and editor in 1934, and president and general manager in 1946. Member of Sandalphon Lodge No. 836, Brooklyn, N.Y., receiving degrees, March 29, Nov. 15 and Dec. 6, 1923. d. Dec. 1, 1949.

George W. Healy, Jr. Editor of *The Times-Picayune*, New Orleans, La. since 1952. b. Sept. 22, 1905 at Natchez, Miss. Graduate of U. of Mississippi in 1926. He began as a correspondent for Associated Press while in college, and later was reporter on the *Knoxville Sentinel* (Tenn.). With *The Times-Picayune* since 1926, first as a reporter, city editor and managing editor. He is also managing editor of *The Times-Picayune New Orleans States* and treasurer of Times-Picayune Publishing company since 1939, and vice

president since 1942. Elected national president of the American Society of Newspaper Editors in 1958. Member of Louisiana Lodge No. 102, New Orleans, receiving degrees Feb. 19, April 10, and April 15, 1948.

Jack W. Heard Major General, U.S. Army. b. March 6, 1887 in New York City. He was graduated from U.S. Military Academy in 1910, and advanced through grades to major general in 1941. He served in the cavalry, 1910-15; aviation section of Signal Corps 1915-19; Motor Transport Corps, 1919-20; cavalry, 1920-32; U.S. Bureau of Budget, 1932-33; Cavalry 1933-40; armored Force, 1940-43 and manpower board of War Department, 1943-46. Received his degrees in June, 1920 in Mt. Vernon Lodge No. 151, Baltimore, Md. and became a member of Jerusalem Chapter No. 9, R.A.M., Baltimore. Has not maintained membership since 1925.

Oscar E. Heard (1856-1940) Justice, Supreme Court of Illinois, 1924-33. b. June 26, 1856 at Freeport, Ill. Attended Northwestern U. and admitted to Ill. bar in 1879, practicing at Freeport. Was circuit judge and appellate judge. From 1927-28 and 1932-33 he was chief justice of the supreme court of Ill. Member of Evergreen Lodge No. 170, Freeport, Ill., receiving degrees, March 22, April 2, April 9, 1888, and was master in 1892. d. July 15, 1940.

Jonathan Heart (1744-1791) Officer of American Revolution. b. in Kensington, Conn., he was graduated from Yale in 1768, taught school in N.J. for a year or two, and returned to Kensington district and entered merchandising business with a local minister. The business was about to fail when the Revolution came on. He was a Lexington volunteer, but was shortly given a commission and served throughout the war from Bunker Hill to Yorktown, being discharged as a captain in 1783. He remained out of the army only a year or so and returned to be commissioned in the newly organized 1st American Regiment of the regular army, staying with it until his untimely death in 1791. His importance, however, stems from the fact that he was an original member of the famous American Union Lodge (Military), first secretary, and third and last master, bringing that lodge to the Northwest Territory. When the lodge was organized in the Connecticut line in 1776, he was its first secretary; elected senior warden in Feb., 1779, and master the following June, continuing as such until his death in 1791. He carried on an extensive Masonic correspondence; was well informed on the ritual and Masonic history. In 1783 he was selected by a general convention to visit and instruct the several lodges in the state of Conn. His long tenure of office saw him presiding in the East at many famous meetings, when such personalities as Washington were present. It was Heart who called a convention of army lodges at Morristown in 1780, when the idea of a national grand lodge was proposed. When the Grand Lodge of Mass. chartered Washington Lodge No. 10 (military) he was designated as deputy grand master for the elaborate institution ceremonies at West Point. The original minutes of American Union Lodge are largely in Heart's handwriting, and still preserved. They contain the records of nearly 500 visiting Masons. According to his own record, he was made a Mason in the lodge at Wallingford, Conn. (now Compass No. 9) shortly after his graduation from Yale in 1769. Heart carried the records of American Union Lodge in his field

chest during the War. He was one of the early members of the Mark lodge attached to St. John's Lodge No. 2 of Middletown, Conn. and registered his mark in the form of a "heart." When he affiliated with a chapter in the same town he is recorded as "a very well-known, vouched-for Royal Arch Mason." He was also interested in Frederick Lodge, formed by his comrades in arms at Farmington, and it was with them that he left the records of American Union Lodge. His Army service took him to the Northwest Territory (Ohio), and while stationed at Fort Harmer, near Marietta, he invoked his commission, called the brethren in the community, and again resumed labor as American Union Lodge, thus introducing Freemasonry into that territory. He was succeeded as master by General Rufus Putnam, q.v., who later became first grand master of Ohio. His battalion was ordered on a punitive expedition against the Indians under General St. Clair. Lack of security measures and generalship resulted in the massacre of 900 men, including Heart, on Nov. 4, 1791. Due to the deep snow, the bodies were not recovered until the following January. Fort Recovery monument is now on this spot on the Wabash River.

Edwin R. Heath (1839-?) Explorer, physician, and diplomat. Won recognition as a South American explorer while secretary to the American legation in Chile. A river which forms part of the boundary line between Bolivia and Peru is named in his honor. By charting 90 miles of a mysterious river he opened a passage for Bolivia to the Atlantic, and a Bolivian holiday was declared in his honor. After his legation service, he became chief surgeon for the Pacasymo Railroad, employing 45,000 men. A Royal Arch Mason from 1880, he was a member of Wyandotte Chapter No. 6, Kansas City, Kans., serving as high priest of that chapter five times. He was a member of Palmyra Lodge No. 248, Palmyra, N.Y. His death date is not known, but he lived at least into his 92nd year.

Fred H. Heath Chemist, who discovered selenium mustard gas in 1918. b. Feb. 25, 1883 at Warner, N.H. Graduate of U. of New Hampshire, 1905, and Yale, 1909, studying later in Germany. He taught chemistry in M.I.T., Case School of Applied Science, Wesleyan U., U. of North Dakota, U. of Washington, U. of Florida. Mason.

Leonard D. Heaton Lieutenant General, U.S. Army Medical Corps. b. Nov. 18, 1902 at Parkerburg, W.Va. Received medical degree from U. of Louisville in 1926, and entered the medical corps that year as a first lieutenant, advancing through grades to lieutenant general in 1948. He has been commanding general of Walter Reed Army Hospital since 1959. He has served in Army hospitals in El Paso, Texas, San Antonio, Texas, Fort Warren, Wyo., Hawaii, Staunton, Va., Blandford, England, and commanding general of Letterman Hospital, 1946-52. With Walter Reed Hospital, 1952-59. Member of Hancock Lodge No. 311, Fort Leavenworth, Kansas; received 32° AASR (SJ) at Fort Leavenworth in 1938, and 33° in 1957.

Paul 0. Hebert (1818-1880) Governor of Louisiana, 1853-56, and Brigadier General, C.S.A. in Civil War. b. Nov. 12, 1818 in Bayou Goula, La. He graduated from U.S. Military Academy in 1840. For the next two years he taught at the academy, and from 1843-45 was sent with the Army engineers for work on the

Mississippi River. He resigned from the army in 1841, and was appointed chief engineer of the state of Louisiana, holding this office until the Mexican War, when he was appointed lieutenant colonel of the 14th volunteer infantry, and participated in battles of Contreras and Chapultepec, as well as Molino del Rey. In 1851 he was U.S. commissioner to the Paris World's Fair. He was a member of the convention for the state constitution of 1852. In 1861 he was appointed a brigadier general in the provisional Confederate army, and the rank was afterwards confirmed by the Confederate congress. He was first in command of Louisiana, and then the trans-Mississippi and Texas departments. Member of Iberville Lodge No. 81, Plaquemine, La. d. Aug. 29, 1880.

Gabriel A. J. Hecart (1755-1838) French Masonic writer and developer of the "Hecart System" of Masonic degrees. His system included five degrees—Knight of the Prussian Eagle, Knight of the Comet, The Scottish Purifier, Victorious Knight and Scottish Trinitarian, or Grand Master Commander of the Temple. It was never accepted or practiced by any Masonic group.

Cornelius Hedges (1831-1907) "Father" of Yellowstone National Park. b. Oct. 28, 1831 at Westfield, Mass. Graduate of Yale in 1853, and in law from Harvard in 1855. Admitted to Mass. bar in 1855, moving in that year to Independence, Iowa, where he practiced until 1864. In 1864 he walked to Virginia City, Mont. and the following year moved to Helena, bringing his family in 1867. When the territorial government was established, he served a term as U.S. district attorney. Hedges once said "It could not be said that every vigilante was a Mason, but it could be said that every Mason was a vigilante without deviating far from the truth." He served as superintendent of public instruction for six years, and was one of the original founders of the Helena public library in 1868. He was a senator from Lewis and Clark Co. in the first Montana legislature. He was a member of the Washburn-Doane-Langford expedition of 1870 that first explored the area which later became Yellowstone National Park. Both Washburn and Langford, qq.v., were Freemasons; the latter was grand master of the Grand Lodge of Montana. On the last night in the area, on the Firehole River, Hedges remarked that "this area must be set aside for the use and benefit of the people." His words are incised in the granite arch at the northern entrance to the park, where the party first entered. The park was established in 1872, as the first national park, largely through the efforts of Langford and Hedges. Hedges was raised in Independence Lodge No. 87, Independence, la., Oct. 27, 1858, withdrawing on June 7, 1865 to affiliate and become master of Helena City Lodge, U.D. under the Grand Lodge of Colorado, on Aug. 17, 1865. He was again master in 1874. He was exalted in Aholiab Chapter No. 21, R.A.M., Independence; withdrew on April 18, 1867 to become charter member of Helena Chapter No. 2, R.A.M., and its first scribe. He received the council degrees in Springfield, Mass. and affiliated with Helena Council No. 9, R. & S.M. under California jurisdiction, serving as master in 1869. Hedges was knighted in Helena Commandery, U.D., K.T., March 25, 1869, and was commander in 1873 and 1879. A moving factor in the organization of the Grand Lodge of Montana in Jan., 1866, he was its first senior grand warden, and its fifth grand master from 1870-71. In 1871

he became grand historian, and on June 24, 1872 was appointed grand secretary, serving in that capacity until his death. He wrote Montana's correspondence reports for 36 years. He represented Montana at the Masonic congress of Chicago in 1893. He was grand recorder of the Grand Cornmandery of Montana from its organization in 1888, until his death, with the exception of the years 1896-1904. In 1896 he was grand commander of the Grand Commandery of Montana. He was grand secretary of the Grand Chapter of Montana from its organization in 1891 until his death. He was crowned 33° AASR by Albert Pike on Sept. 10, 1885. d. April 29, 1907.

William S. Hedges Vice President of National Broadcasting Co. b. June 21, 1895 at Elmwood, Ill. He began as a reporter for the Chicago Daily News in 1914, and in 1922 became director of that paper's radio service. In 1929 he became president of station WMAQ of Chicago, and from 1932-33 managed WMAW and WENR of Chicago for NBC. The following two years he managed station KDKA of Pittsburgh, and in 1934 became general manager of the NBC stations in New York. In 1937 he became vice president of Crosley Radio Corp. and general manager of their station WLW in Cincinnati. He has been vice president of NBC since Nov. 1937. Received his degrees in Standard Lodge No. 873, Chicago, in 1918; 32° ASSR (NJ) at Freeport, Ill.; life member of Medinah Shrine Temple of Chicago and member of national headquarters chapter of the National Sojourners.

Joseph J. Hedrick President of Natural Gas Pipeline Co. of America; Texas-Illinois Natural Gas Pipeline Co. since 1949; and of Natural

Gas Storage Co. of Ill. and Texoma Production Co. since 1951. b. Nov. 8, 1898 at Olathe, Kans. Graduate of LaSalle U. and John Marshall Law School. Admitted to Okla. bar in 1921, and became general counsel of Natural Gas Pipeline Co. in 1930. He is also president of Kimswick Development Co. and Peoples Production Co. A life member of Bartlesville Lodge No. 284, Bartlesville, Okla., he received his degrees on Sept. 5, Oct. 26, and Dec. 5, 1922; exalted in Bartlesville Chapter No. 55, R.A.M. March 22, 1923. He served as senior deacon of the lodge at one time. Member of Bartlesville Chapter No. 142, O.E.S.

Adolphus L. Heermann (1822?-1865) Naturalist and ornithologist. b. about 1822 in S. Car. Moved to Philadelphia, Pa. in the 1840's. Elected a member of the Philadelphia Academy of Natural Sciences in 1845. In 1846 he received a medical degree from the U. of Maryland. In 1843 he had crossed the Rockies, possibly with Fremont. In 1848 he made a trip to Florida, collecting bird specimens, and in 1849 made the trip to Calif. by way of the Isthmus. Here he collected and studied birds for three years, returning to Philadelphia with 1,200 specimens, nests and eggs. Each winter from 1854-56 was spent in Calif., and this was followed by an expedition with the Pacific Railroad survey parties seeking passes through the mountains, Heermann being surgeon and naturalist for the trips. About 1862 he moved permanently to San Antonio, Texas. Several birds of the West coast are named for him—Larus heermanni and Melospiza cinerea heermanni; also the snake Pityophis heermanni. He became a member of Lodge No. 51, Philadelphia, Pa., on April 22, 1847. d. in Sept., 1865.

Roy C. Heflebower Brigadier General, U.S. Army Medical Corps. b. Oct. 25, 1884, in Washington, D.C. Received medical degree from George Washington U. in 1906, and is an honorary graduate of U.S. Army Medical School in 1910. Began medical practice in 1906, and was commissioned in Medical Corps Reserve in 1909, advancing through grades to brigadier general in 1941; he retired in 1946. Now with Anderson Hospital for Cancer Research. Mason, 32° AASR, Shriner and National Sojourner.

J. Thomas Heflin (1869-?) U.S. Senator from Alabama, 1920-31; U.S. Congressman to 59th to 66th Congresses from 5th Ala. dist. b. April 9, 1869 at Louina, Ala. Admitted to bar in 1893. Served in Alabama legislature 1896-1900. First elected to senate to fill term of John H. Bankhead, q.v. After senate terms, he resumed law practice in Lafayette, with Heflin & Heflin. A member of Solomon Lodge No. 74 of Lafayette, he received his degrees, Jan. 1, Dec. 28, 1898, and Jan. 4, 1899. Received 32° AASR (SJ) in Albert Pike Consistory, Washington, D.C. on April 20, 1923.

Robert A. Hefner Justice Supreme Court of Oklahoma, 1926-33. b. in Hunt Co. Texas. Graduate of U. of Texas, 1902. Practiced law in Beaumont, Texas. Moved to Ardmore, Okla., where he was city attorney, mayor and president of board of education. From 1939-47 he was mayor of Oklahoma City, Okla. Mason, Knight Templar, Shriner and member of grand council of DeMolay.

Albert F. Hegenberger American aviator, who with Lester J. Maitland, q.v., was the first to make a successful flight from Hawaii to the United States. Member of Stillwater

Lodge No. 616, Dayton, Ohio, receiving degrees, June 16, Sept. 29, 1919, and Feb. 16, 1920; suspended NPD July 27, 1936.

Rolf Magnus von Heiden-stam (1884-1958) Swedish industrialist and lord in waiting to the King of Sweden. B.C.V.O. (British). He was managing director of the Aga Co. from 1937-50; president of board of same, 1950-58. He was president of the board of the Svenska Handelsbanken, Swedish Ford Motor Co., Swedish Shell Co., Dunlop Rubber Co. He had served as vice president of the Stockholm Chamber of Commerce, chairman of the Swedish National Committee of the International Chamber of Commerce (1948-51) and president of the International Chamber of Commerce (1951-53). He was president of the General Export Association of Sweden, member of the Board of the Federated Swedish Industries and chairman of the Swedish Trade Mission to the U.S. and Canada in 1943-44. He was Swedish delegate to the conference on international trade in Havana, Cuba in 1947-48. Past master of lodge St. Erik in Stockholm (1938-43), grand secretary of the Grand Lodge of Sweden, 1938-43 and grand chancellor of same, 1943-58. d. Aug. 6, 1958.

Julius P. Heil (1876-1949) Governor of Wisconsin, 1938-43. b. in Dusemond, Germany. He began in a Wis. general store at age of 12, and was later a drill press operator, blacksmith, and welder with International Harvester. Became an expert welder and traveled throughout the country, completing welding contracts, building street railways in Buenos Aires, Argentina. He founded the Heil Co. in 1901, and served as president until 1946. Was head of the NRA of Wis. A

member of Independence Lodge No. 80, Milwaukee, 32° AASR (NJ) Wisconsin Consistory, and Tripoli Shrine Temple. He was Shrine potentate in 1927, and chairman of finance, and member of building committees. d. Nov. 30, 1949.

Frank A. Heileman Major General, U.S. Army. b. Mar. 13, 1891 at St. Louis, Mo. Graduate of U. of Missouri in 1914. He was commissioned second lieutenant of Infantry in 1917, transferred to engineer corps in 1923, and promoted through grades to major general in 1945. He was with the general staff in 1940; headquarters Army Service Forces in 1942; director of supply in Western Pacific in 1945, and chief of transportation Department of Army, 1948-53; now retired. Acacia fraternity; Acacia Lodge No. 602, Columbia, Mo. (about 1914); former member of Columbia Chapter No. 17 R.A.M. (1915), Columbia, Mo.

Van Campen Heilner Explorer, naturalist, and author. b. July 1, 1899 at Philadelphia, Pa. Graduate of Trinity Coll. (Conn.) in 1927. He is an associate editor of Field and Stream, sportsman's magazine. He was field representative in ichthyology of American Museum of Natural History, on an expedition to Peru and Ecuador in 1924-25, and leader of the Heilner Far Western Alaskan expedition for American Museum of Natural History in 1927. He made another expedition for same museum to Cienaga de Zapata on the south coast of Cuba in 1934, and in 1948 an expedition for the Peabody Museum of Yale to Tiena del Fuego and Straits of Magellan. He is the first naturalist to make successful motion pictures of the roseate spoonbill in its natural haunts, and discovered several new species of West Indian fishes. He is the author of *The Call of the Surf; Adventures in Angling; Beneath the Southern Cross; A Book on Duck Shooting; Our American Game Birds*. Member of Spring Lake Lodge No. 239, Spring Lake, N.J.; 32° AASR and member of Lu Lu Shrine Temple, Philadelphia, Pa.

Adolphus Heiman (?-1863) Confederate Brigadier General of Civil War. b. in Potsdam, Prussia, he became a member of Cumberland Lodge No. 8, Nashville, Tenn. on Jan. 31, 1843. He was a member of Cumberland Chapter No. 1, R.A.M., and Nashville Commandery No. 1 (1847) of Nashville. d. at Jackson, Miss.

Edward 0. Heinrich Criminal expert. b. April 20, 1881 at Clintonville, Wis. Graduate of U. of Calif. in 1908. Became a chemical-legal expert, and expert in criminal investigation. Entered chemical engineering practice at Tacoma, Wash. in 1908. Later moved to Calif., and was chief of police of Alameda. In 1918-19, was mayor of Boulder, Colo.; he has practiced in San Francisco since 1919. Lecturer at U. of Calif. on criminal investigation and political science. He was an expert on questioned documents and other evidence in Hindu Ghadr revolution trials; U.S. vs. Jack Dempsey; U.S. vs. Levin;- people vs. Roscoe Arbuckle; the d'Autremont train bandits; Black Tom cases; U.S. vs. Harry Bridges; and other celebrated cases. Mason and Knight Templar.

Charles E. Heitman (1874-1948) Manager of Christian Science Publishing Society, and director of The Mother Church, 1st Church of Christ, Scientist, Boston. b. Nov. 12, 1874 in McLean Co., Ky. He was first reader of 2nd Church of Christ, Scientist, at New York City from 1918-

21, and president of the Mother Church in 1923-24. From 1926-27 he was associate editor of the Christian Science Monitor. Served as corporal in Roosevelt's Rough Riders in Spanish-American War. Member of Marble Lodge No. 702 at Tuckahoe, N.Y., and 32° AASR in Boston, Mass. d. Oct. 1, 1948.

Friedrich Heldmann (1770-1838) German Masonic philosopher and professor of political science in the academy of Bern, Switzerland. He was initiated at Freiburg in 1809, and in studying Fessler, q.v., and other Masonic writers, decided to establish a system founded on a collation of all the rituals which would be more in accordance with the design of the Craft. For this purpose, he organized the Lodge Zur Brudertreue at Aarau, Switzerland in 1816, and prepared a manual for it. When the Swiss authorities demanded an inspection of it, he refused, and withdrew from the lodge. He later published The Three Oldest Memorials of the Ge7- mart Masonic Brotherhood at Aarau in 1819. It is in this work that the constitutions of the stone masons of Strausburg were published for the first time.

John R. Heller, Jr. Director of National Cancer Institute since 1948. b. Feb. 27, 1905. Received B.S. at Clemson Coll. (S.C.) in 1925, and M.D. from Emory U. (Ga.) in 1929. He became associated with the U.S. Public Health Service in 1931, and in 1943 became medical director and chief of the division of venereal disease. He has been a professor and lecturer at George Washington U. since 1944. Member of Atlantic Lodge No. 82, Brunswick, Ga., receiving degrees in 1931.

John L. Helm (1802-1867) Governor of Kentucky, 1850-52. b. July 4, 1802 in Hardin Co., Ky. Studied law and admitted to bar. He served in both state legislative branches, and was lieutenant governor in 1848. He was made president of the Louisville and Nashville Railroad in 1854. After the Civil War, he was again chosen governor of Kentucky, and was inaugurated at his residence in Elizabethtown Sept. 3, 1867, five days before his death. Member of Morrison Lodge No. 76, Elizabethtown, and Eastern Star Chapter No. 34, R.A.M. of same city.

Claude Adrien Helvetius (1715-1771) French philosopher. He was appointed farmer general in 1738. In 1741 he married Anne Catherine de Ligniville d'Autricourt, and shortly afterward retired to his country estate to devote himself to study. His great work is de VEsprit, published in 1758, in which he expounds his doctrine of sensationalism or sensualism. The book was condemned by the Sorbonne and publicly burned in 1759. Member of the Lodge of the Nine Sisters in Paris.

John Michael Hely-Hutchinson (see Earl of Donoughmore).

Samuel Hemming (1767-1832) One of the leaders in the uniting of the "Ancients" and "Moderns" into the United Grand Lodge of England in 1813, and its first senior grand warden. He was master of the Lodge of Reconciliation (1813-16), which was formed to bring about a union of the two groups. At this time the Prestonian lectures were practiced by the Moderns, while the Ancients, or Atholl Freemasons, recognized higher degrees and varied their ritual. After the union, the Prestonian system was abandoned and Hemming formed a new set of lectures, known as "Hemming Lectures," which was adopted. In it he abolished the dedication to the two Saints John, and substituted a dedication to Solomon. He is also credited with defining Freemasonry as "a beautiful system of morality,veiled in allegory and illustrated by symbols." d. in 1832.

Fay Hempstead (1847-1934) Lawyer, Masonic writer, and grand secretary. b. Nov. 24, 1847 in Little Rock, Ark. He attended St. John's College, a Masonic institution at Little Rock, and following the Civil War, graduated in law at the U. of Virginia in 1868. He practiced his profession in Little Rock until 1881, when he retired to devote his entire time to Freemasonry. He was grand high priest of the Grand Chapter, R.A.M. of Arkansas in 1891, and served as grand secretary for 35 years. He was grand master of the Grand Council, R. & S.M. in 1889 and general grand master of the General Grand Council from 1921-24, and grand secretary for 35 years. He was grand commander of the Grand Commandery, K.T. of Arkansas in 1919, and grand recorder of same 34 years. His grand secretaryship of the Grand Lodge of Arkansas lasted 53 years. He was sometimes called the "poet laureate of Freemasonry." d. April 24, 1934.

Stephen Hempstead Second Governor of Iowa, succeeding Ansel Biggs, q.v. He received all three degrees in Dubuque Lodge No. 3 in June, 1843, being raised June 30. He served as master in 1845, and was instrumental in forming the Grand Lodge of Iowa, serving as grand junior warden in 1848. He was a member of Dubuque Chapter No. 3, R.A.M., and served as secretary of the same. He was a charter member of Siloam Commandery No. 3, K.T.

Alexander   Henderson Commodore, U.S. Navy during Spanish-American War. Member of Nepparhan Lodge No. 736, Yonkers, N.Y.

Byrd E. Henderson President of Household Finance Corporation, 1933-51; Chairman of Board since 1951. b. Jan. 9, 1889 at Louisville, Ky. and educated in Louisville high school. Began as an investigator for Mackey Finance System at Louisville in 1907, and rose to executive vice president in 1925. Owner of the Everett Resort and Everett Golf Club at Eagle River, James Pinckney Henderson Wis. Mason, Knight Templar, and Shriner.

Charles Henderson (1860-1937) Governor of Alabama, 1915-19. b. April 26, 1860 in Pike Co., Ala. In business at Troy, Ala. as Charles Henderson & Co. He was president of the Troy Bank & Trust Co. and Standard Telephone and Telegraph Co. He was also director of other organizations, and president of the Alabama Railroad Commission from 1906-15. Mason. d. Jan. 7, 1937.

Charles B. Henderson U.S. Senator from Nevada, 1918-21; Director of Reconstruction Finance Corporation, 1934-47. b. June 8, 1873 at San Jose, Calif. He was graduated from U. of Michigan in 1895, and began practice of law at Elko, Nev. in 1896. He was a member of the state legislature in 1905-07, and regent of U. of Nevada from 1907-17. Raised in Elko Lodge No. 15 on April 4, 1899. Shriner.

David B. Henderson (1840-1906) Speaker of the U.S. House of Representatives, 1899-1903. b.

March 14, 1840 at Old Deer, Scotland. He was brought to Ill. in 1846. and to Iowa in 1849. He entered the Civil War as a private in the 12th Iowa volunteers, was wounded in the Battle of Donelson, lost a leg at the Battle of Corinth, and was then discharged. He reentered the army as a colonel in 1864. Admitted to the bar in 1865, he served as collector of revenue, 3rd Iowa dist., and U.S. attorney of northern district of Iowa. He served in the U.S. congress from 1883-1903, but withdrew from ticket in 1902, when re-nominated. He was made a Mason in Mosaic Lodge No. 125 of Dubuque, June 23, 1883; exalted in Dubuque Chapter No. 3, April 29, 1889, and knighted in Siloam Commandery No. 3, May 8, 1899. He joined El Kahir Shrine Temple of Dubuque, May 22, 1901.

Howard A. M. Henderson (1836-1912) Clergyman and soldier. b. Aug. 15, 1836 in Paris, Ky. Graduate of Ohio Wesleyan U. in 1858. Ordained to Methodist Episcopal ministry in 1856, he served pastorates in Newberne and Demopolis, Ala., until 1861, when he entered the Confederate army as a captain of Co. E, 28th Ala. Infantry. In 1864 he was assistant adjutant general, C.S.A., and in 1864-65 was assistant commissioner of exchange of prisoners of war. Following the war, he was pastor at Frankfort and Lexington, Ky., and then state superintendent for public instruction of Kentucky from 1871-79. He then served churches in San Francisco, Calif., Hannibal, Mo. (1881-83), Jersey City, N.J., New York City, Cincinnati, Ohio, and Hartwell, Ohio. In 1872 he founded the system of Negro schools in Kentucky. He was grand master of I.O.O.F. in Kentucky, and grand chaplain of the Grand Lodge of Kentucky from 1867-79. He first appeared as a Mason in the records of Hiram Lodge No. 4 in 1868, and was suspended, Aug. 24, 1893. H. A. M. Henderson Lodge No. 515, chartered Oct. 24, 1872 at Bethlehem, Ky. was named for him.

James Pinckney Henderson (1808-1858) First Governor of Texas after statehood, and U.S. Senator. b. March 31, 1808 in Lincoln Co., N.C. He studied law and was admitted to the bar in 1829. Moving to Miss. in 1835, he remained there until the Texas difficulties began, when he volunteered in the Texan army, and was appointed brigadier general in 1836. He was appointed attorney general by President Sam Houston, q.v., and was subsequently secretary of state in 1837-39. In 1839 he visited England and France to procure the recognition of Texan independence. He resumed his law practice in 1840, in partnership with Gen. Thomas J. Rusk, q.v. He was "special minister" to the United States in 1844, to negotiate the annexation of the Republic of Texas, and was a member of the state constitutional convention in 1845. He again took up arms in the Mexican War, and for action at Monterrey, received a sword and the thanks of congress. In 1857 he was appointed U.S. senator to fill the unexpired term of his partner, Rusk, who had died. He took his seat in March, 1858 but died before the end of the session. He was a member of Redland Lodge No. 3, San Augustine, Texas. d. June 4, 1858.

John Henderson (1795-1857) U.S. Senator from Mississippi. He practiced law in Woodville, Miss., and in 1835 served in the state legislature. In 1849 he was elected to the U.S. senate as a Whig. At the expiration of his term, he allied himself with the politicians of the extreme southern school that favored annexation of Texas, the conquest of Mexico and Cuba, and was connected with General John A. Quitman, q.v., in these enterprises. In 1851 he was arrested with Quitman, and tried before a federal court in New Orleans for violating the neutrality laws of 1818 by his complicity with the Lopez expedition against Cuba. He was acquitted, but retired from public life. Henderson was a member of Washington Lodge No. 3, Port Gibson, Miss. d. at Pass Christian, Miss. in 1857.

Leon Henderson Economist and Administrator of Office of Price Administration. b. May 26, 1895 at Mill-vine, N.J. Graduate of Swarthmore Coll. (Pa.) in 1920. First employed as economies instructor in Wharton School (Pa.), and Carnegie Inst. of Tech., then director of consumer credit research for Russell Sage Foundation, N.Y.C. 1925-43. Entering the government field in 1934, he was with the N.R.A.; advisor to U.S. senate; advisor to Democratic National Committee; W.P.A.; Council of National Defense; OPA, 1941-42; director of Civilian Supply Division of O.P.M., and War Production Board. He then became chief economist for Research Institute of America; president of International Hudson Corp., and since 1955, has been president of American Leduc Uranium Corp. Served in WWI from private to captain in ordnance. Raised in Shekinah Lodge No. 58, Millville, N.J. on Jan. 21, 1920.

Leonard Henderson (1772-1833) Chief Justice, Supreme Court of North Carolina from 1829. b. Oct. 6, 1772 in Granville Co., N.C. He was clerk of the district court at Hillsborough for several years after his admission to the bar, and became judge of the appellate court in 1808. He was elevated to the supreme court bench in 1818. He conducted a law-school throughout his judicial career that was the most popular in the state. Member of Malta Lodge No. 24, Williamsburgh, Granville Co., N.C., and was its senior warden in 1797. d. Aug. 13, 1833.

L. Manuel Hendler Director of The Borden Co. b. Feb. 10, 1885 near Baltimore, Md. From 1905-12 he was the owner of T. A. Hendlers (ice cream) at Baltimore. In 1912 he established Hendler Creamery Co. of which he is still president. In 1929 he became chairman of the Southeastern division of The Borden Co.; director of same in 1930, and member of the executive committee in 1940. Mason and 32° AASR (SJ).

Eldo L. Hendricks (1866-1938) President of Central Missouri State Teachers' Coll., 1915-30. b. Oct. 2, 1866 at Rossville, Ind. Graduate of Franklin Coll. (Ind.) He served as school superintendent in Indiana before coming to Mo. He was a member of the fact finding commission to Indians in 1930-31. Mason. d. Nov. 22, 1938.

William W. Hening (1767-1828) Lawyer and author. b. in Virginia, he was admitted to the bar on April 30, 1789, in the district court at Fredericksburg, at the same time as John Marshall and James Monroe. He moved to Albemarle Co., and in 180405, represented it in the legislature. He later became a member of the state executive council, and deputy adjutant general. During his later years he was clerk of the chancery court for Richmond district. An accomplished writer, he compiled Hening's Justice; edited Francis' Maxims of Equity, and several volumes of reports from the Va. court of appeals. His greatest work was the 13-volume

set of Statutes at Large of Virginia, which contained the laws beginning with the colonial period. Raised March 19, 1796, in Richmond Lodge No. 10, he later became master of the Door of Virtue Lodge No. 44 at Charlottesville. He was grand master of the Grand Lodge of Va. in 1805-06. Exalted in Richmond Chapter No. 2, RA.M., Dec. 22, 1805, he served as high priest; he was the second grand high priest of Virginia in 1810, and assisted in the formation of the Grand Chapter of Virginia. d. April 1, 1828.

Edward J. Henning (1868-1935) Federal judge. b. Dec. 28, 1868 at Iron Ridge, Wis. Graduate of U. of Wisconsin (1894) and Columbian U. (1896). He practiced law in Milwaukee until 1912, when he moved to San Diego, Calif. He was judge of the Eastern District of Wis. from 1901-10 and of Southern District of Calif. from 1925-29. From 1921-25 he was assistant secretary of Labor. A member of Damascus Lodge No. 290, Milwaukee, Wis., he received his degrees on July 1, Aug. 31 and Sept. 30, 1905; member of Wisconsin Chapter No. 7, Milwaukee and Ivanhoe Commandery No. 24, K.T., Milwaukee; 32° AASR (NJ) Valley of Milwaukee. d. Sept. 6, 1935.

Andrew Henry (1775-1833) Western explorer, fur trader, and discoverer of the South Pass through the Rockies. b. in York Co., Pa., he lived for a time at Nashville, Tenn. He moved to St. Genevieve, Mo. And while here became one of the first three petitioners of Western Star Lodge No. 107 at Kaskaskia, Indian Territory (across the river). On Dec. 27, 1806 he was one of the petitioners for Louisiana Lodge No. 109 (from Pa.) at St. Genevieve—the first lodge west of the Mississippi River. He is listed among the 13 charter members and as senior warden in 1808. Old records of the lodge bear witness to his wanderings and one financial report states "absent two years and six months; dues have been remitted, $4.62." Francois Valle, also formerly of Lodge No. 107 and charter member of 109, evidently accompanied Henry on this expedition, for the same entry was made at the same time concerning him. Henry was interested in lead mining while at St. Genevieve. On March 7, 1809 he joined with several others including Pierre Chouteau, Jr. and William Clark, qq.v. in establishing the Missouri Fur Co. He was with the first expedition of 150 men that set out three months later for the west. They reached the Rockies at a place called Three Forks (confluence of Madison, Jefferson and Mo. Rivers) and set up a post. Indians, however, forced them to leave after losing 30 men. Henry then led his group across the Rockies into what is now the state of Idaho, and wintered at a post they set up on the North fork of the Snake River, known as Henry Fork. They returned home in 1811. On another expedition in 1822, with General William Ashley, he reached the mouth of the Yellowstone and discovered the South Pass through the Rockies. He returned to Missouri in 1824, and settled between Caledonia and Potosi, Mo., where he returned to lead mining.

Henry VI (1421-1471) King of England, 1422-61 and 1470-71. His reign was marked by the Statute of Laborers, which prohibited the congregations of Freemasons.

Henry Frederick (see Duke of Cumberland).

Horace C. Henry (1844-1928) Pioneer railroad builder. b. Oct. 6, 1844 at Bennington, Vt. Served in Civil War from 1862-63, and fought at Cemetery Ridge. Entered the railway contracting business at Minneapolis in 1866, and with associates built about 2,500 miles of railway in the Northwest. He moved to Seattle, Wash. in 1890, and built lines for the Northern Pacific, Great Northern, and Chicago Milwaukee & St. Paul, involving over 20 million dollars, and employing 10,000 men. He erected an art gallery and gave his collection of 160 paintings to the U. of Washington. He was honored by the French government with the Cross of Legion of Honor for his aid in supporting 1,800 French orphans. Mason. d. June, 1928.

Isaac N. Henry An early Missouri journalist, who, in 1819, established the Enquirer at St. Louis, which was edited at one time by Col. Thomas H. Benton, q.v. Henry was a member of Missouri Lodge No. 12 (under Tenn.) and on Oct. 4, 1819 attended an annual communication of the Grand Lodge of Tennessee, representing his lodge. In 1820 he printed 1,200 copies of the state constitution for $100.

Henry Louis Frederick, Prince of Prussia (see under Frederick).

Patrick Henry (1736-1799) American Revolutionary leader famous for his words "Give me liberty, or give me death." There are many references to his being a Freemason, particularly by grand lodge orators in the 1800's, but no satisfactory evidence of his membership. It is possible that he was a member of old Tappahannock Lodge of Virginia whose records are lost. There was at one time a Patrick Henry Lodge No. 140 in Patrick Co., Va. There is a Masonic apron in existence that is reported to have belonged to him. It was exhibited at one time in Lexington Lodge No. 1, Lexington, Ky.

Thomas P. Henry (1877-1945) President of American Automobile Association, 1923-45. b. Dec. 28, 1877, at Brookhaven, Miss. As a newspaperman he worked on papers in Miss., New Orleans, and on the Chicago Tribune, New York Times, and Detroit Free Press. In 1906 he founded the Thomas P. Henry Co. at Detroit. Raised Oct. 15, 1913 in Zion Lodge No. 1, Detroit, Mich. d. Sept. 7, 1945.

William Henry (1761-1824) Soldier of the Revolution and War of 1812. b. in Charlotte Co., Va., he entered the army when very young and fought at Guilford, the Cowpens, and Yorktown in the Revolutionary War. He then moved to Kentucky, and took part in many conflicts with the Indians. He was appointed a major general of Kentucky volunteers in Aug., 1813, and commanded a division in the Battle of the Thames in Oct. of that year. He also served in Scott's and Wilkinson's campaigns. He served in both houses of the Kentucky legislature, and was a member of the constitutional convention of that state. He was raised in Union Lodge No. 43 of Pa. and admitted to Lexington Lodge No. 1 of Lexington, Ky. in 1803. d. Nov. 23, 1824.

David Henshaw (1791-1852) U.S. Secretary of the Navy, 1843 under Tyler. b. April 2, 1791 in Leicester, Mass. Was apprenticed to a druggist in Boston at 16, and was in the drug business for himself from 1814-29. Gained prominence as a political writer, served in both houses of state legislature, and was a collector of Boston customs from 1830. He was active in promoting the early railroad enterprises in Mass. Appointed secretary of the Navy by Tyler, July 24, 1843, he served for seven months, and was then rejected by the senate. Member of Columbian Lodge, Boston, Mass. d. Nov. 11, 1852.

Samuel J. Hensley (?-1866) California pioneer. b. in Lexington, Ky., he emigrated to Platte Co., Mo. as a small boy, and in 1843 went overland to Calif. as a member of the Chiles-Walker party. He worked for John Sutter and became a Mexican citizen so he could obtain a land grant; however, he was one of the promoters of the Bear Flag revolt. In the war with Mexico, he joined Fremont's battalion and rose to rank of major. At the close of the war he went to Washington, D.C. as a witness at Fremont's court martial, returning to Calif in 1848, after the discovery of gold. He engaged in general store and banking business, and then turned to real estate and water transportation, organizing the California Steam Navigation Co. in 1854. This company virtually controlled all traffic on San Francisco Bay. On July 19, 1851, Henry Eddy, veteran of the Donner Party, presented Hensley's petition to San Jose Lodge No. 10. He received his degrees, Aug. 23, Nov. 8, 1851, and Feb. 21, 1852. Late in 1855 he was exalted in California Chapter No. 5, R.A.M. of San Francisco, but when Howard Chapter No. 14, R.A.M. was organized in San Jose in 1856, he was one of its charter members—and the only one who had received all chapter degrees in Calif. d. Jan. 7, 1866.

William N. Hensley, Jr. (1881-1929) Pioneer aviator. Free balloon pilot, kite balloon pilot, observer, airship and airplane pilot. b. Oct. 18, 1881 at Columbus, Nebr.

Graduate of U.S. Military Academy in 1905. Commissioned second lieutenant in cavalry in 1905, and rose to major in 1920. He organized a division of Philippine national guard in 1917, and was commander of the army balloon school at Pasadena, Calif. in 1918-19. He was the first American to make a non-stop flight from U.S. to Europe (on return trip of R-34 from England in July 1919). In 1919 he made a study of the Zeppelin Airship Line in Germany, and furnished the U.S. War Dept. with the first detailed authentic information on the L-72, the giant dirigible built at Friedrichshafen for the bombing of New York City, in WWI. The dirigible was almost completed when armistice was signed. Mason. d. March 21, 1929.

Josiah Henson (1789-1883) The Negro slave whose life formed the basis of Harriet B. Stowe's famous novel, Uncle Tom's Cabin. References on his birth and death dates differ. His tombstone in Dresden, Ont. states: "In memory of the Rev. Josiah Henson, died May 5, 1883, born July 15, 1789. Aged 93 years, 10 months and 5 days." Another reference states he was born June 15, 1787 at Port Tobacco, Md., and died in 1881. Born as a slave, he took all his first master's slaves to a relative in Kentucky to prevent their passing into the hands of creditors. He escaped with his wife and two children to Cincinnati, and then across the wilderness to Sandusky where they were conveyed to Canada by schooner. He settled at Colchester, Ont., and during the Canadian rebellion, was the captain of a company of colored men. He later farmed near Dresden, and was the pastor of a church. At the age of 55 he began to learn to read and write. He made three trips to England, and at one time was entertained at Windsor Castle by Queen Victoria. It is not known whether Henson was a Mason—either regular or Prince Hall affiliation. It is possible that he could have been either—possibly in Canada or even England. However his gravestone carried the square and compasses in the fellowcraft position with one point of the compasses above the square.

Matthew A. Henson (1866-1955) Negro explorer who was with Admiral Peary, q.v., when he reached the North Pole in 1909. b. Aug. 8, 1866 in Charles Co., Md. He was associated with Peary for 20 years. In his final dash to the pole, Peary said this of Henson: "When each man has led me and my men to a certain point, within striking distance of the pole, their work is done. They shall no longer be needed. But Henson is not to return. I can't get along without him." Commander Donald MacMillan said of him: "A carpenter, he built sledges; a mechanic, he made the alcohol stoves; an expert dog driver, he taught us to handle our dogs. Highly respected by the Eskimos, he was easily the most popular man on board the ship. .. . Henson, strong physically, and above all fully experienced, was of more real value to our commander than Bartlett, Marvin, Borup, Goodsell and myself put together. Matthew Henson went to the pole with Peary because he was a better man than any one of us." Henson, the last survivor of the expedition, died in 1955. He was a member of Celestial Lodge No. 3, of Prince Hall jurisdiction in New York City. He is the author of A Negro Explorer to the North Pole.

William P. Hepburn (1833-1916) U.S. Congressman from Iowa to 47th to 49th Congresses (1881-87), and 53rd to 60th Congresses

(1893-1909), introducing the bill to carry out President Theodore Roosevelt's Pure Food and Drug Act in Dec., 1905. b. Nov. 4, 1833 at Wellsville, Ohio. He was taken to Iowa Territory in 1841, and educated there. Admitted to bar in 1854, he was county prosecuting attorney, clerk of the Iowa house of representatives, and district attorney. He served in the Civil War as a lieutenant colonel of the 2nd Iowa Cavalry from 1861-65, and lived at Memphis, Tenn. from 1865-67. He returned to Iowa in 1867, and remained at Clarinda until his death on Feb. 7, 1916. His absence from the 50th to 52nd congresses was due to his position as solicitor for the Treasury during these years (1888-93). Member of Nodaway Lodge No. 140 at Clarinda, Iowa.

James M. Herbert (1863-1923) President of Colorado, Wyoming & Eastern Railway, 1914-16 and St. Louis Southwestern Railway, 1916-23. b. Jan. 15, 1863 in Westmoreland Co., Pa. Began as a telegraph operator in 1881, and worked up as dispatcher, chief dispatcher, and trainmaster. In 1897 he became superintendent of the Grand Trunk Railway of Canada, and of the Missouri Pacific in 1901. He was later manager of the Southern Pacific and Denver and Rio Grand Western. Mason. d. Aug. 5, 1923.

Percy Mark Herbert (see under Bishop of Norwich).

Thomas J. Herbert Governor of Ohio, 1947-48, and Justice, Supreme Court of Ohio since 1956. b. Oct. 28, 1894 at Cleveland, Ohio. Admitted to Ohio bar in 1919, he served as assistant county prosecutor and assistant attorney general. Specialized in public utilities. Was attor-

ney general of Ohio from 1938-44, and president of the National Association of Attorneys General in 1943-44. Served as a lieutenant in the Air Force in WWI; wounded in 1918, and discharged in 1920. He organized the 17th Aviation Division of the Ohio National Guard in 1927. A member of Master's Lodge No. 675 of Cleveland, he received his degrees, July 13, July 27, and Sept. 27, 1921; is 32° AASR (NJ).

Johann Gottfried von Herder (1744-1803) German philosopher and man of letters. Upon Goethe's q.v., recommendation, he was called to Weimar as general superintendent of the church district, serving there from 1776 to 1803. Among his works are *Kritische Waller* (1769); *Abhandlung uber den Ursprung der Sprache* (1772) ; and various editions of German folksongs. He was made a Mason at Riga in the lodge Zurn Schwert in 1766.

Frank E. Hering (1874-1943) Credited as first nationwide sponsor of Mother's Day; President of Fraternal Order of Eagles, 1909-12. b. April 30, 1874 in Northumberland Co., Pa. Graduate of U. of Notre Dame in 1898 and 1902. He was a trustee of the U. of Notre Dame, and national president of the Alumni Assn. U. of Notre Dame in 1930-31. He was a teacher of English and history at U. of Notre Dame from 1898-1904. He was managing editor and advertising manager of The Eagle magazine from 1912. He was active in promoting mothers' pension laws and old age pension laws. A bronze tablet was erected in his honor at the English Opera House of Indianapolis, Ind. commemorating the first Mother's Day address on Feb. 7, 1904. Member of South Bend Lodge No. 294, South Bend, Ind. d. July 11, 1943.

Nicholas Herkimer (1715-1777) Brigadier General of American Revolution, who was fatally wound-ed in the Battle of Oriskany. His name is anglicized from the German Herchheimer. His father, John Jost Herkimer, was one of the Palatine Germans that settled Herkimer Co., N.Y. At the age of 30 he was a lieu-tenant of militia, and was in command at Fort Herkimer (his home), when the French and Indians attacked German Flats in 1758. He later lived in the Canajoharie district, and was made colonel in 1775, and brigadier general in 1776. He was made a Mason April 7, 1768, in St. Patricks Lodge No. 8 (now 4) of Johnstown, N.Y. The master of this lodge was Sir John Johnson, q.v., who was also Indian agent for the British and pro-vincial grand master of New York. The Indian, Joseph Brant, q.v., was a protégé of Johnson's. At the Battle of Oriskany Herkimer opposed Johnson, Brant, and Col. Butler, q.v., another member of St. Patricks Lodge. In 1777 when General St. Leger in-vested Fort Stanwix (afterwards Fort Schuyler), Herkimer took his militia to the relief of Gen. Gansevoort. At a point some six miles from Ft. Stanwix, Herkimer fell into an ambush. His horse was killed and he was badly wounded, a leg being broken. Drag-ging himself to a stump, he encour-aged his men to the last, but sus-tained a loss of 200 men. He was removed from the field to his home at Little Falls, and died, Aug. 16, 1777, ten days after the battle, from an un-skilled amputation of his leg. The town, township, and county in New York are named for him.

Raphael Herman (1865-1946) Manufacturer and active in promotion of peace and international relations. b. Dec. 15, 1865 near Konigsburg, Germany. Educated in Germany, he came to America in 1890, and engaged in business in New York state. In 1901 he was offi-cial of the Buffalo Pan-American Ex-position. From 1895-1903 he pub-lished the Acetylene Journal. He was president of the Diamond Power Specialty Co., Detroit; Power Effi-ciency Corp.; Calorizing Corp. of America. He was an organizer and trustee of the Detroit Tuberculosis Sanitarium; founder of the Detroit Museum of Art; founder and trustee of the Los Angeles U. of International Relations; and member of the board of the World Federation of Educa-tional Associations and American Museum of Natural History (N.Y.) He was national vice president of the League of Nations Association. He was the donor of a $25,000 competi-tive peace prize. Mason and 32° AASR. Deceased.

Leo D. Hermle Lieutenant General, U.S. Marine Corps. b. June 30, 1890 in Hastings, Nebr. Graduate of U. of California in 1914 and 1917. Commissioned lieutenant in Marine Corps in 1917, and rose to major general in 1944. In WWI he com-manded a Marine company in France, and commanded the 6th Ma-rines in Iceland in 1941. He was chief of staff of the 2nd Marines on Gua-dalcanal in 1943; assistant division commander at Tarawa in 1943, and assistant division commander of 5th Marines in 1945. He landed at Iwo Jima on D-Day and was island com-mander of Guam in 1946. Raised in Oakland Lodge No. 188, Oakland, Calif., Nov., 1914; member of AASR (SJ) in Oakland and the Shrine.

Don Manuel Diaz Hernandez (1774-1863) Catholic priest, Freema-son, patriot, and liberal. He was made a Mason in 1810, and later became master of his lodge and a member of the Scottish Rite. He always wore the insignia of his Scottish Rite chapter on his cassock—a pelican, a cross and a rose. Because of his liberal activity, he was banished to Teneriffe in 1820 by King Ferdinand VII, q.v. In 1825 he was allowed to return and his parish was restored. In 1894 the people of Santa Cruz de Palmas, in the Canary Islands, erected a monument in his honor. The base states "Diaz—his grateful fatherland," and the statue shows him in his cassock with the Masonic emblems.

Chesley C. Herndon Executive Vice President of Skelly Oil Co. b. Aug. 26, 1886 at Clarksville, Tenn. Graduate of Cumberland U. (Tenn.) in 1909, and admitted to bar in that year, practicing in Nashville until 1910, when he moved to Oklahoma and took up practice at Chickasha, and later Tulsa. He became an attorney for Gulf Oil Corp.; and vice president of Skelly Oil Co. in 1919, and executive vice president and director from 1948. Affiliated with Chickasha Lodge No. 94, Chickasha, Okla. on April 6, 1911, dimitting from same on Oct. 22, 1915 and affiliating with Delta Lodge No. 425, Tulsa on April 18, 1916.

Charles N. Herreid (1857-1928) Governor of South Dakota two terms, 1900-04. b. Oct. 20, 1857 in Dane Co., Wis. Graduate of U. of Wisconsin in 1882. Settled in McPherson Co., S.D. in 1883, where he served as county judge and state's attorney. He was lieutenant governor from 1892-96. After his governorship, he practiced law at Aberdeen. He was past grand chancellor of the Knights of Pythias. Received degrees in Acacia Lodge No. 108, Eureka, S.D. on June 21, July 25 and Aug. 17, 1894. Affiliated with Aberdeen

Lodge No. 38, Aberdeen, S.D. on Feb. 1, 1916. d. July 6, 1928.

Thomas W. Herren Lieutenant General, U.S. Army. b. Aug. 9, 1895 in Dadeville, Ala. Graduate of U. of Alabama in 1917, and commissioned second lieutenant in that year, advancing through grades to lieutenant general in 1954. He served overseas in WWI with the field artillery, and in WWII was commander of the 106th Cavalry regiment and commandant of the Cavalry School. He later became assistant division commander of the 70th Infantry division; G-3 of the 4th Army; chief of staff of U.S. Army forces in Korea; commanding general of military district of Washington; commanding general of Northern area in Europe; commanding general of first army; and since 1954, senior member of Military Staff Committee of United Nations. Now retired. Member of Rockford Lodge No. 102, Rockford, Ill., but his work was completed at Burlington, Vt. Member of National Sojourners at Springfield, Mass.

Dionisio Herrera (1790?-1850) Elected President of three countries —president of Honduras from 1824-27; president of Nicaragua from 1829-34. He retired in 1833 to live in El Salvador, and in 1835 was elected president of that country, but refused. Mason.

Lott R. Herrick (1871-1937) Justice, Supreme Court of Ill., 1933-37. b. Dec. 8, 1871 at Farmer City, Ill. Graduate of U. of Ill. (1892), and U. of Michigan (1894). In law practice at Farmer City, Ill. from 1894-1933. Member Farmer City Lodge No. 710, Farmer City, Ill. d. Sept. 18, 1937.

Samuel Herrick Brigadier General in War of 1812. He affiliated with Amity Lodge No. 5 of Zanesville, Ohio about 1813, dimitting on June 19, 1824 to affiliate with LaFayette Lodge No. 79, Zanesville on May 25, 1825, withdrawing on Dec. 30, 1830.

Frederick W. Herring (1821-?) American artist. b. Nov. 24, 1821, the son of James Herring, q.v., who was also an artist. He studied art with his father and Henry Inman, and devoted himself to portrait painting. Member of St. John's Lodge No. 1, New York City, N.Y.

James Herring (1794-1867) Artist. b. Jan. 12, 1794, in London, Eng. He came to America with his family in 1804. He began his career by coloring prints and maps. He lived in Philadelphia for a time, but returned to New York where he settled in Chatham Square as a portrait painter. He illustrated (with Longacre) American biography in the National Portrait Gallery. His son, Frederick W. Herring, q.v., was also a painter. James was initiated in Solomon's Lodge, Somerville, N.J. in 1816, and was master of Clinton Lodge, N.Y.C., in 1827-28-32-34, during the period when the anti-Masonic spirit was at its height. He, with the remaining members of Clinton Lodge, united with St. John's No. 1 of N.Y.C. on Dec. 18, 1834. He was grand secretary of the Grand Lodge of New York from 1829-46. When the grand lodge split, June 5, 1849, he became grand secretary of the Phillips (or Herring) group and held that office until 1858. He was exalted in Jerusalem Chapter No. 8, R.A.M., New York City, Jan. 5, 1817; knighted in Columbian Commandery No. 1, K.T.; and was 33°, sovereign grand inspector general, AASR (NJ). He was high priest of his chapter, and served for a time as general grand secretary of the General Grand Chapter of the U.S. He

was also grand master of the Grand Encampment, K.T. of the U.S. d. Oct. 8, 1867 in Paris, France.

Arthur W. S. Herrington President of Marmon-Herrington Co., 1931-42 and chairman of board since 1940. b. March 30, 1891 in Coddenham, England, he was brought to the U.S. in 1896. Served in WWI. He designed several types of military trucks with four and six wheel drives, as well as track laying vehicles for U.S. Army and Marine Corps. In 1942 he was technical advisor for the U.S. Mission to India. Member of Madison Lodge No. 93, Madison, N.J. and 32° AASR (NJ) at Indianapolis, Ind. Member of Murat Shrine Temple of Indianapolis.

Alexander Herrman (1844-1896) Magician. b. Feb. 11, 1844 in Paris, France. He died suddenly while en route from Rochester, N.Y. to Bradford, Pa., and was buried with Masonic ceremonies in Woodlawn Cemetery, near New York, by Munn Lodge No. 190, N.Y.C. d. Dec. 11, 1896.

Francis J. Herron (1837-1902) Major General in Civil War. b. Feb. 17, 1837 in Pittsburgh, Pa. He was graduated from Western U. (Pa.) in 1853, and moved to Dubuque, Ia. in 1856, where he was in the mercantile business. He organized a military unit in 1861, and in Sept. of that year, was made lieutenant colonel of the 9th Iowa regiment. He saw action in the campaigns in Mo., Ark., and Indian Tern Was wounded in Battle of Pea Ridge. As a brigadier general he commanded the Army of the Frontier at Battle of Prairie Grove, Ark., and was made major general of volunteers in Nov., 1862. He subsequently captured Van Buren, Ark., invested Vicksburg, and captured Yazoo City.

He negotiated and received the surrender of the Confederate forces west of the Miss. In 1865 he was appointed commissioner to negotiate treaties with the Indians. After the war he practiced law in New Orleans, and was U.S. marshal of dist. of La. in 1872-73. He later practiced law in New York City. Charter member of Mosaic Lodge No. 125, Dubuque, Iowa, dimitting April 9, 1872. 32° AASR. d. Jan. 8, 1902.

Ira G. Hersey (1858-1943) U.S. Congressman to 65th to 70th Congresses (1917-29) from 4th Maine dist. b. March 31, 1858 in Hodgdon, Maine, he began law practice in that city in 1880. He served in both bodies of the state legislature, and was president of the senate in 1915-16. After his term as congressman, he practiced law in Washington, D.C. Member of Monument Lodge No. 96, Houlton, Maine, receiving degrees on Oct. 17, 24 and Nov. 14, 1894. In lodge line from 1896, serving as master in 190506. d. March 6, 1943.

Mark L. Hersey (1863-1934) Major General, U.S. Army. b. Dec. 1, 1863 at Stetson, Maine. Graduate of U.S. Military Academy in 1887, and received A.M. from Bates Coll. in 1902. Commissioned in 1887 he advanced through the grades to major general in 1924, retiring in November of that year. He was with the Philippines constabulary from 1905-14, and chief of the Mindanao constabulary from 1909-14. In WWI he commanded the 155th Infantry brigade in the St. Mihiel offensive, and the Bois des Loges defensive in the Meuse-Argonne. Given command of the 4th Division in Oct., 1919, he served with it on the march to the Rhine, and throughout the occupation service. He was a member of Pacific Lodge

No. 64, Exeter, Maine, and New England Chapter of National Sojourners. d. Jan. 22, 1934.

Lewis B. Hershey Lieutenant General, U.S. Army, and Director of Selective Service. b. Sept. 12, 1893 in Steuben Co., Ind. Graduate of Tri-State Coll. (Ind.) in 1914. He began as a country school teacher in 1910, and was high school principal of Flint, Ind. from 1914-16. He entered the Indiana National Guard in 1911as a private, and advanced through grades to lieutenant general in 1956. In the regular Army, he was promoted to major general in 1942, and retired on physical disability in 1946. He was a member of the War Department General Staff from 1936-40. He was appointed deputy director of the Selective Service System in 1947, and made director in 1948. Member of Northeastern Lodge No. 210, Freemont, Ind.

Paul L. Hershfield President of Mississippi Glass Co. since 1949. b. July 11, 1908 at Montrose, Ill. He was associated with Anchor-Hocking Glass Corp., from 1934-40. Has been chairman of board of Walsh Refractories Corp. since 1951. Mason, Knight Templar, 32° AASR, and Shriner.

Jean Hersholt (1886-1956) Actor. b. July 12, 1886 in Copenhagen, Denmark. Educated in Knud Coll. at Copenhagen, he received honorary degrees from several American colleges. He began acting in the Dagmar Theatre of Copenhagen in 1904, and continued on the European stage until 1913, when he came to the U.S. and was naturalized in 1920. Under contract to the Metro-Goldwyn-Mayer Film Corp., he played in more than 400 pictures including Four Horsemen; Greed; Stella Dallas; Old Heidelberg; Emma; Old Soak;

Alias the Deacon; Men in White; Grand Hotel; The Country Doctor; Sins of Man; Reunion and Heidi. He received the Academy of Motion Picture Arts' award (Oscar) in 1939-49-50, and was president of the academy from 1945-49. From 1937 he starred in the Dr. Christian radio series. He was knighted by King Christian X, q.v., of Denmark in 1946 for his work as president of the American-Denmark Relief, Inc. during WWII. He was a partner of the Sol Lesser Productions, Inc. of Hollywood. He authored a complete translation of Hans Christian Anderson's *Fairy Tales*. Member of Hesse-Darmstad of Palms Lodge No. 512, Hollywood, Calif. d. June 2, 1956.

Christian A. Herter Governor and Congressman of Massachusetts; and Under Secretary of State, Department of State since 1957. b. March 28, 1895 in Paris, France. Graduate, cum laude, of Harvard in 1915. During 1916-17 he was an attaché of the American embassy in Berlin, and a special assistant to U.S. Dept. of State in 1917-18. He was secretary of the American commission to negotiate peace at Paris in 1918-19. In 1919-24 he was assistant to Herbert Hoover, secretary of Commerce. Became U.S. Secretary of State in April, 1959, succeeding John Foster Dulles. He edited *The Independent* from 1924-28, and was assistant editor of The Sportsman, Boston, from 1927-36. Herter served in the Mass. legislature from 1931-43, and was a member of the 78th to 82nd Congresses from 1943-53, from 10th Mass. dist. He served as governor of Mass. from 1953-57. Member of Mount Tabor Lodge; St. Paul's Royal Arch Chapter; Council of R. & S.M.; St. Bernard Commandery, K.T. all of Boston. In Scottish Rite he is member of Boston Lafayette Lodge of

Perfection; Giles F. Yates Council, Princes of Jerusalem; Mount Olivet Chapter of Rose Croix and Mass. Consistory. He became a 33°, honorary member of the Northern Supreme Council on Sept. 23, 1953 at Chicago, Ill. He became a charter member of Nantascot Lodge, Hull, Mass. Received the Gourgas Medal of the Scottish Rite on Oct. 23, 1959.

Earl of Hertford (see Clare de Gilbert).

Harcourt Hervey Major General, California National Guard. b. Sept. 2, 1892 at Los Angeles, Calif. He was graduated from U. of California in 1916. Commissioned in that year, he advanced through grades to lieutenant colonel, and was with the A.E.F. from 1916-18, resigning to enter the banking profession. He became vice president of Security National Bank of Los Angeles. He entered the national guard in 1922, and advanced through grades to major general. He saw overseas duty in WWII from 1942-45, in Europe, Asia, Pacific, and Korea. A member of Pentalpha Lodge No. 202 of Los Angeles, he received his degrees, Jan. 6, June 9, and June 23, 1914, and 32° AASR (SJ), March 18, 1917, in Kansas, affiliating with Los Angeles AASR bodies on Nov. 4, 1917.

William R. Hervey (1870-1953) Judge of Superior Court of California in 1909. b. March 26, 1870 in Somerville, Tenn. Graduate of U. of Arkansas in 1890, and U. of Michigan in 1894. Practiced law in Los Angeles from 1894-1907. He was president of American Savings Bank from 1908-11, and superior court judge from 1901-11. He was also vice president of two other banks and a building and loan concern. He was grand master of the Grand Lodge of California in

1917-18. He was a 33° AASR (SJ), and grand inspector general for Calif.; Knight Templar, and past potentate of Al Malaikah Shrine Temple. He was raised in Pentalpha Lodge No. 202 on June 10, 1895. d. Feb. 1, 1953.

Rudolph Hess Nazi third deputy to Hitler, second only to Goering in line of succession to supreme power in German dictatorship. An anti-Mason. b. in 1894 in Alexandria, Egypt. Followed Hitler from 1921, becoming secretary and bodyguard to Hitler in 1925. He took down *Mein Kampf* from Hitler's dictation. He was designated by Hitler as head of the political section of the National Socialist party in 1932 and admitted into the newly formed cabinet council in 1934. He created a world sensation by a solo flight in 1941 to Scotland where he was held as a prisoner of war. In 1946 at the Nurnberg trials, he was convicted as a war criminal and sentenced to life imprisonment. Among the documents used by the prosecution in this trial was an article in the Voelkischer Beobachter, Aug. 28, 1939, reporting a speech by Hess at Graz on Aug. 26, which included the statement "Jews and Freemasons want a war against this hated Germany, against the Germany in which they have lost their power."

William E. Hess U.S. Congressman to 71st to 74th, and 76th to 80th Congresses, from 2nd Ohio dist. b. Feb. 13, 1898 at Cincinnati, Ohio. Attended U. of Cincinnati and Cincinnati Law School, being admitted to the bar in 1919, and practiced since at Cincinnati. Member of Hanselmann Lodge No. 208, Cincinnati, Ohio, receiving degrees on March 1, April 5 and May 15, 1920. 32° AASR (NJ) and Shriner.

Prince of Hesse-Cassel (see under Frederick).

Prince of Hesse-Cassel (see under "Karl").

Dukes of Hesse-Darmstad (see under "Ludwig").

Prince of Hesse-Darmstadt (see under George Karl).

Landgrave of Hesse-Homburg (see under Frederick Ludwig).

Edouard Gregory Hesselberg (D' Essenelli) (1870-?) Pianist. b. May 3, 1870 at Riga, Russia. Graduate of the Conservatory of Music and Dramatic Art, Moscow, with honors in 1892, and later studied under the famous Rubinstein. He came to America in 1892, and was naturalized in 1900. He taught in the Ithaca (N.Y.) Conservatory of Music, 1895-96, and at U. of Denver, and Dick's Normal Coll. (Denver), from 1896-1900. He was director of music at Wesleyan Coll. Conservatory, Macon, Ga., 1900-05, and at Belmont Coll., Nashville, Tenn., 1905-12. Later he taught at London, Ontario, and Chicago, Ill. He composed a new national hymn, America, My Country, in 1916. He composed many songs and compositions for piano, violin, and orchestra. Mason. Deceased.

Prince of Hesse-Philippsthal-Barchfeld (see under Frederick William).

Hugh B. Hester Brigadier General, U.S. Army. b. Aug. 4, 1895 at Hester, N.C. Graduate of U. of North Carolina in 1916. Commissioned in 1917, he advanced through grades to general rank in 1944. Served in Quartermaster department, and was in Southwest Pacific and Australia in WWII. Later he was with military government in Germany, and military attaché in Australia. He has commanded the Philadelphia Quartermaster depot since 1948. Member of Army Lodge No. 1105, Fort Sam Houston, San Antonio, Texas; 32° AASR (SJ).

Henry Heth (1825-1899) Confederate Major General in Civil War. b. in Virginia, he was graduated from U.S. Military Academy in 1847, and joined the 6th Infantry. He was promoted to captain in 1855. At the out-break of the Civil War, he resigned and entered the Confederate Army as a brigadier general, and was commissioned major general in May, 1863. He commanded a division under General A. P. Hill in Virginia, and was in the battle of Gettysburg, and the campaigns of 1864-65. After the war he engaged in business in South Carolina. He was first a member of Rocky Mountain Lodge No. 205, Camp Floyd, Utah, and served as its senior warden at one time. He affiliated with Benjamin B. French Lodge No. 15, Washington, D.C. about 1891. He was buried Masonically by Richmond Lodge No. 10, Richmond, Va., at the request of Benjamin B. French Lodge. d. Sept. 27, 1899.

Jacob A. W. Hetrick President of New York Medical College since 1942. b. April 22, 1895 at Asbury Park, N.J. He was graduated from New York Medical Coll. in 1918. He became associated with the college in 1927 as a professor, and later served as registrar, assistant dean, and dean. Received his degrees in Kane Lodge No. 454, New York City in spring of 1931.

Frederick L. Hetter Rear Admiral, U.S. Navy. b. Jan. 25, 1907

at Rock Island, Ill. Graduate of U.S. Naval Academy in 1927. Advanced through grades to rear admiral in 1952. His specialty is Naval aircraft supply. He served in the Central Pacific in WWII, and since the war has been executive officer of supply depots at Philadelphia, with the Atlantic fleet, and at Bayonne, N.J. since 1956. Raised in Rock Island Lodge No. 658, Rock Island, Ill. in Oct., 1928. He was a DeMolay in Rock Island, Ill. as a youth. Member of Mt. Vernon Chapter No. 8, R.A.M.; Warren Council No. 5, R. & S.M. and Hugh de Payens Commandery No. 1, K.T., all of Jersey City, N.J.

Ralph D. Hetzel (1882-1947) College president. b. Dec. 31, 1882 at Merrill, Wis. Graduate of U. of Wis-.1.1 A Howard R. Hick consin in 1906 and 1908. A professor of English and political science, he became president of the New Hampshire Coll. of Agr. and Mechanic Arts, 1917-23, and president of U. of New Hampshire, 1923-26. He was president of Pennsylvania State Coll. from 1927. Made a Mason "at sight" by R. R. Lewis, grand master of Pa. in Masonic Temple at Philadelphia on Dec. 27, 1938. Became member of State College Lodge No. 700. d. Oct. 3, 1947.

Joseph Hewes (1730-1779) Signer of the Declaration of Independence. b. Jan. 23, 1730 in Kingston, N.J. His family were farmers and Quakers, but at the beginning of the Revolution, he gave up his ties with the Society of Friends and devoted himself to the war. In 1776 he was a member of the secret committee of the committee on claims, and was virtually the first secretary of the Navy. At an early age he moved to Philadelphia where he engaged in business, but moved to Edenton,

N.C. in 1763. He was in the state senate that year, and in 1774 was a delegate to the Continental Congress and assisted in the preparation of the report on "The Statement of Rights." With General Washington, he conceived the plan of operations for the ensuing campaign. He was again chosen a delegate to congress in 1776, but illness prevented him from serving. He was again returned to congress in 1779, but died in the second month of his term. His funeral was attended by Washington, and he was buried in Christ Church, Philadelphia. His lodge is not known, but he is recorded as a visitor at a meeting of Unanimity Lodge No. 7 of Edenton, N.C. on Dec. 27, 1776, just after his return from the Continental Congress. d. Nov. 10, 1779. Was buried with Masonic honors.

Weldon B. Heyburn (1852-1912) U.S. Senator from Idaho, 1903-09, 1909-15. b. May 23, 1852 in Delaware Co., Pa. Admitted to the bar in 1876, and practiced in Shoshone Co., Idaho from 1883. He was a delegate to three national Republican conventions. Member of Shoshone Lodge No. 25, Wallace, Idaho. d. Oct. 17, 1912.

Melville L. Hibbard President of Minnesota Power and Light Co. 193354 and now chairman of board. b. Feb. 21, 1883 at Farnham, Quebec, Canada, coming to the U.S. in 1908; was naturalized in 1921. He was employed by utility companies in San Antonio, Texas, Fargo, N.D., and Minneapolis, Minn. He was president of the Idaho Power Co., 1931-33. Member of Shiloh Lodge No. 1, Fargo, N.D. receiving degrees on Feb. 28, March 28 and April 29, 1919. Member of Keystone Chapter No. 20, R.A.M. and Duluth Commandery No. 18, K.T., both of Duluth, Minn.; 32°

AASR at Fargo, ND.; El Zegal Shrine Temple, Fargo; past director of Duluth Court No. 55, Royal Order of Jesters; Aad Shrine Temple, Duluth; St. George Conclave No. 6, Red Cross of Constantine and DeMolay Legion of Honor.

Philip Hichborn (1839-1910) Rear Admiral, U.S. Navy and inventor of Franklin Life Buoy. b. in Charleston, Mass. He served five years as an apprentice in the Boston Navy Yard, and took a special course in ship construction in the Navy. He went to Calif. in 1860, where he entered the Mare Island Navy Yard and became a master shipwright in 1862. He entered the Navy in 1869, and became chief naval constructor, 1893-1901, retiring in the latter year. He was master of Naval Lodge No. 87 at Vallejo, Calif. in 1866, but withdrew in 1872. d. 1910.

Howard R. Hick Grand Master of the Grand Lodge of the Philippines (1958-59). Born in England March 8, 1910. In 1915 while England and France were at war his parents moved to the United States, coming on the last voyage of the Lusitania before it was sunk.

Bourke B. Hickenlooper Easton, Pa., where after graduation from high school he attended New York U., graduating with a B.S. in aeronautical engineering. Was captain and member of 1932 track team at Olympic tryouts in Los Angeles. He was an instructor in Pacific Military and Elsinore Naval Academies. He was naturalized in 1933; he engaged in research work in Greece, India and the Philippines; he spent three years in Santo Tomas internment camp. He is president and general manager of the Peter Paul Philippine corporation. Made a Freemason in 1946, he advanced rapidly, becoming grand master in 1958. He had a large part in securing an agreement in the Japanese-Philippine grand lodge controversy.

Bourke B. Hickenlooper Governor and U.S. Senator from Iowa since 1945. b. July 21, 1896 at Blockton, Iowa. Graduate of Iowa State Coll. in 1920, and received law degree from U. of Iowa in 1922. Admitted to bar in latter year, and has since practiced in Cedar Rapids. He was lieutenant governor of Iowa from 1939-43, and governor 1943-44. He served in the lower house 1935-39. During WWI he was a second lieutenant with the 339th Field Artillery and served in France. Member of Mizpah Lodge No. 639, Cedar Rapids; received 32° AASR (SJ) in Army Consistory No. 1, Kansas, April 2, 1918, and affiliated with the Cedar Rapids consistory, Jan. 21, 1925. Shriner.

Doyle 0. Hickey Major General, U.S. Army. b. July 27, 1892 at Rector, Ark. Graduate of Hendrix Coll. Conway, Ark. in 1913. He was commissioned in 1917, in officers reserve corps, and in the regular army in 1920. He advanced through grades to major general in 1948. Mason, 32° AASR, and Shriner.

John E. Hickman Chief Justice, Supreme Court of Texas since 1948. b. Mar. 28, 1883 at Liberty Hill, Texas. He taught school, and was admitted to bar in 1910. He practiced in Erath and Stephens Co. until 1926, when he became a justice of the court of civil appeals. He served as chief justice of this court from 1928-34. He became associate justice of the supreme court in 1945. Mason.

Henry D. Hicks Prime Minister of Nova Scotia, 1954-56. b. Mar. 5, 1915 at Bridgetown, N.S. Graduate of Mount Allison and Dalhousie universities, he was a Rhodes scholar at Oxford in 1943. Admitted to the bar in 1941, he practiced at Bridgetown. He has been a member of the Nova Scotia legislature since 1945; was minister of education, 1949-54; provincial secretary in 1954, and leader of the Liberal Party since 1956. In WWII he served as an artillery captain, from 1941-45, in the Canadian Army. He was initiated in Rothsay Lodge No. 41, Bridgetown, in 1947, and is a member of the Scottish Rite.

Joseph W. Hicks Public relations and industrial relations counsel. b. July 18, 1899 in Oliver Springs, Tenn. He was graduated from U. of Oklahoma in 1923, and is the author of Cheer Oklahoma, the U. of Oklahoma's song. Starting as a newspaper man and editor, he was on papers in. Topeka, Kans., Seattle, Wash., San Francisco, Calif., and Oklahoma City, Okla. He was also a correspondent of the United Press from 1921-23 and International News Service, 1923-24. He entered the public relations field at Chicago in 1925, and taught in the Medill School of Journalism of Northwestern U. from 1927-33. In private practice since 1941, he is president of the Joseph W. Hicks Organization. Served in WWI in artillery. Member of Siloam Lodge No. 276, Oklahoma City, Okla.; chapter, council and commandery in Evanston, Ill. and 32° AASR (NJ) in Chicago. Member of Medinah Shrine Temple, Chicago. 226 Archibald T. Higgins Raymond M. Hicks Steamship executive. b. at Kingston, N.Y. in 1898. He is executive vice president and director of Number One Broadway Corp.; U.S. Lines Co.; and Roosevelt Steamship

Co. Member of Columbia Lodge No. 3, Washington, D.C.

Thomas H. Hicks (1798-1865) Governor and U.S. Senator from Maryland. b. Sept. 2, 1798 in Dorchester Co., Md. Reared on a farm, he entered the mercantile business in 1831. As governor of Maryland from 1858-62, he strongly opposed secession. He was first appointed to the senate, and later elected, serving from 1863-65. He was a member of Cambridge Lodge No. 66, Cambridge, Md. and served several terms as master. He was deputy grand master of the Grand Lodge of Maryland in 1849. He was also a member of Livingston Chapter No. 14, Cambridge. His commandery membership is not known, but he was buried with Knights Templar ceremonies from the senate chamber of the U.S. Capitol. d. Feb. 13, 1865.

Miguel Hidalgo (see also Miguel Hidalgo y Costilla). Catholic priest and liberator of Mexico. Although it is claimed that he was a member of Arquitechtura Moral Lodge, receiving his Entered Apprentice degree in 1808, there is no documentary evidence to support the belief. This lodge met at 5 Calle de las Ratas (today 7th and Bolivar) in Mexico City. It was a Scottish Rite lodge established in 1806. It is claimed that immediately after Hidalgo received the degree, all the papers and books of the lodge were destroyed.

Anton Hieronymus It is said that in the examination of a German steinmetz, or stonemason, this was given as the name of the first Freemason. Mackey says that it is unquestionably a corruption of Acton Hiram.

Joseph Hiester (1752-1832) Governor of Pennsylvania, 1821-23. b. Nov. 18, 1752 in Bern township, Pa. Had a common school education, and worked as a farm laborer, and then as a clerk in Reading, Pa. At the beginning of the Revolution he raised and equipped that town with a company which took part in the battles of Long Island and Germantown. He was a colonel, and at one time was captured and held prisoner. Hiester was a member of the constitutional convention of 1776. He served five-terms in the state house, and four in the state senate of Pa. In 1807 he was appointed one of the two major generals to command the quota of Pa. military militia called for by the president. He served in the U.S. congress from 1797-1805, and again from 1815-20. A member of Lodge No. 62 of Reading, Pa., he served as junior and senior warden, and was treasurer in 1811. d. June 10, 1832.

Ranulf Higden (?-1364) A monk of Chester, England, who is buried in the Chester cathedral. He was the compiler of Polychronicon, a world history, drawn upon for some details in the very imaginary history of Masonry found in the Old Charges. Polychroniccm was written in Latin, but an English version was printed by Caxton in 1482.

Andrew J. Higgins (1886-1952) Shipbuilder, who during WWII was identified with the construction of amphibious landing boats. b. Aug. 28, 1886 in Columbus, Nebr. He was a lumber mill owner and operator in Ala. and Miss. from 1908-15; then a lumber broker and exporter at -New Orleans from 1915-20. From 1920-30 he was president of the Higgins Lumber and Export Co., and from 1930 was president of the Higgins Industries, Inc., builders of motor boats, planes, engines, ship radios, etc. at New Orleans. He was the inventor of some 30 improvements for amphibious landing craft and vehicles. Mason. d. Aug. 1, 1952.

Archibald T. Higgins (1893-1945) Justice, Supreme Court of Louisiana from 1934. b. Oct. 31, 1893 in Algiers, La. He graduated from Tulane U. Law School and Loyola U. Admitted to the bar in 1916, he practiced at Gretna. He served in the lower house from 1920-24 and was judge of the court of appeals, Orleans Parish, 1929-34. He received his degrees in St. John Lodge No. 153, New Orleans on Dec. 19, 1919, April 20, and Oct. 7, 1920. Became charter member of William De White Lodge No. 408 in 1922 and was master in 1923. Exalted in Orleans-Delta Chapter No. 1, R.A.M.; knighted in Jacques de Molay Commandery No. 2, K.T.; 32° AASR (SJ) on July 27, 1929. Was grand master of the Grand Lodge of Louisiana in 1937. d. Oct. 3, 1945.

Frank W. Higgins (1856-1907) Governor of New York, 1905-07. b. Aug. 18, 1856 at Rushford, N.Y. He was in the mercantile business at Stanton, Mich. from 1875-79 and in Olean, N.Y. in 1879. He served as state senator from 1894-1902, and was lieutenant governor from 1903-05. A member of Olean Lodge No. 252, Olean, New York, he was past commander of St. John's Commandery No. 24, K.T. of Olean. d. 1907.

William L. Higgins (1867-1951) U.S. Congressman to 73rd and 74th Congresses (1933-37) from 2nd Conn. dist.; physician. b. March 8, 1867 at Chesterfield, Mass. Received M.D. degree from U. of City of New York in 1890, and began practice at

Willimantic, Conn., moving after a short time to South Coventry, Conn. Served seven terms in the lower house, and one term as state senator. He was Corm. secretary of state two terms, 1929-33. Member of Uriel Lodge No. 24, Merrow, Conn., receiving 3rd degree on Feb. 24, 1923. Member of Trinity Chapter No. 9, R.A.M. and St. Johns Commandery No. 11, both of Willimantic. 32° AASR (NJ) at Norwich and member of Sphinx Shrine Temple, Hartford. d. 1951.

Ben Frank Hilbun President of Mississippi State College from 1953. b. Nov. 14, 1890 in Laurel, Miss. Graduate of Miss. State Coll. in 1923. He became associated with the college in 1925, as director of publicity, and later served as registrar and assistant to president. Member of Abert Lodge No. 89, Starkville, Miss. since 1922 and J. J. Brooks Chapter No. 151, Starkville. Past master of his lodge. Son, Ben Frank, Jr. member of same bodies.

Oscar F. Mild (1901-1950) Member of the International Executive Board of American Federation of Musicians since 1940. b. Feb. 15, 1901 at Cincinnati, Ohio. Student at U. of Cincinnati, 1926-30. From 1916-30, he was an instrumental musician with various bands and orchestras, including the Chicago Opera, and Cincinnati Symphony Orchestra. In 1931 he was business agent of the Cincinnati Union of Musicians, and president since 1932. He was manager-director of the Cincinnati Summer Opera which presents the only summer grand opera season in America. Mason and Knight Templar. d. April 24, 1950.

Horace A. Hildreth Governor of Maine, 1945-49, and Ambassador to Pakistan, 1953-57. b. Dec. 2, 1902 at Gardiner, Maine. Graduate of Bowdoin Coll. (1925), and Harvard Law School (1928). Admitted to the bar in 1928, he first practiced in Boston, Mass., and after 1936, in Portland, Maine. He served one term each in the state house and senate, being president of the senate in 1943. From 1949-53, he was president of Bucknell U. Member of Casco Lodge No. 36 of Yarmouth, Maine.

Melvin A. Hildreth (1859-1944) Brigadier General of National Guard, and Congressional Medal of Honor winner. b. Oct. 27, 1859 at Whites-town, N.Y. Began practice of law in Watertown, N.Y. in 1883, and moved to Fargo, N.D. in 1888. He was U.S. attorney for N.D. from 1914-24. He enlisted in the N.D. National Guard in Oct., 1890, serving in the Spanish-American War, and in the Philippine Insurrection of 1898-99, as a colonel. He was a member of the commission, under treaty to settle military affairs with the Spanish government in the Philippines in 1899. Elevated to brigadier general in 1908. Member of Shiloh Lodge No. 1 of Fargo, ND., and made life member on Nov. 16, 1942. Member of Keystone Chapter No. 5, R.A.M., Auvergne Commandery No. 2, K.T. and El Zagal Shrine Temple of Fargo, N.D. d. Jan. 13, 1944.

Arthur M. Hill Chairman of executive committee of The Greyhound Corp. b. March 23, 1892 at Charleston, W.Va. He is chairman of board of Atlantic Greyhound Corp.; president and chairman of the Charleston Transit Co.; and chairman of the board and director of Capitol Greyhound Lines. He is an officer in a number of other corporations. From 1935-48 he was a director of the U.S. Chamber of Commerce, and is presi-

dent of the National Assn. of Motor Bus Operators. He was an officer in WWI with the 77th Infantry Division, and in WWII was special assistant to the secretary of the Navy. Mason, 32° AASR (SJ), and Shriner.

Claude E. Hill (1874-1957) Disciples of Christ minister. b. Jan. 11, 1874 in Pike Co., Mo. Graduate of U. of Chicago in 1901. Ordained minister in 1896, and served churches in Ala., Tenn., and Okla. From 1906-18 he was national superintendent of Christian Endeavor, Disciples of Christ, and a member of the executive commission of the International Convention, Disciples of Christ in 1923-26. In 1926 he was chairman of the Peace Commission of that church. He was a delegate to the Churches of Christ in Great Britain in 1932. Author of *Keeping the Faith: Plea of the Disciples of Christ for Christian Unity*. Member of Chattanooga Lodge No. 199, Chattanooga, Tenn. and John Bailey Nicklin Chapter No. 49, Chattanooga. Member of Trinity Commandery No. 20, K.T., Tulsa, Okla. and grand prelate of Grand Commandery of Oklahoma in 1932. Shriner. d. Feb. 10, 1957.

David G. Hill President of Pittsburgh Plate Glass Co. since 1955, and member of executive committee. b. June 6, 1902 at Pittsburgh, Pa. Graduate of Cornell in 1924. He began with Pittsburgh Plate Glass Co. as an engineer in 1924, and advanced as assistant to vice president, 1929-40; general superintendent, 1940-52; vice president, 1952-55. He is also a director of many large corporations. Member of Shekinah Lodge No. 257, Festus, Mo.

Isaac Hill (1788-1851) U.S. Senator and Governor of New Hampshire. b. April 6, 1788 in Somerville,

Mass. He was employed in the printing office of the Amhurst, N.H. Cabinet, at the age of 14, and in 1809 went to Concord, N.H., where he purchased the American Patriot, changing its name to New Hampshire Patriot. After serving in both branches of the state legislature, he was second comptroller of the treasury, from 1829-30, when he was elected U.S. senator, holding this office until 1836, he resigned to become governor of New Hampshire. He served as governor until 1839. He was a member of Blazing Star Lodge No. 11, Concord, and King-Trinity Chapter No. 2, R.A.M. of Hopkinton, N.H. In 1826 he was grand senior warden of the Grand Lodge of New Hampshire. d. March 22, 1851.

James J. Hill (1838-1916) Railroad president who was known as the "Empire Builder of the Northwest." b. Sept. 16, 1838 near Guelph, Ont., Canada. He left his father's farm for a business life in Minn. He became associated with a steamboat office in St. Paul in 1856, and later established a fuel and transportation company of his own. His Red River Transportation Co., established in 1870, was the first to open communication between St. Paul and Winnipeg. He organized a syndicate which secured control of the St. Paul & Pacific R.R. from Dutch owners, and reorganized it as the St. Paul, Minneapolis & Manitoba Railway Co., serving as general manager from 1879-81; vice president, 1881-82; and president 1882-90. It became part of the Great Northern system in 1890. Hill was the moving force in the construction of the Great Northern Railway from Lake Superior to Puget Sound on the Pacific, with Northern and Southern branches, and direct steamship connections to China and Japan. He was president of the entire

Great Northern system from 1889-1907, and chairman of the board from 1907-12. He was the owner of one of the finest collections of modern French paintings in the world. He contributed half a million dollars to the erection and endowment of the St. Paul Theological Seminary. Member of Ancient Landmark Lodge No. 5, St. Paul, Minn. d. May 29, 1916.

Jim Dan Hill President, State Teachers College, Superior, Wis. from 1931, and major general, 32nd Division (Wis. N.G.). b. Feb. 4, 1897 in Leon Co., Texas. Graduate of Baylor U., U. of Colorado, and U. of Minn. Was principal of high school, in Texas, and commandant of Gulf Coast Military Acad. in Miss. He then taught English in the N.M. School of Mines, and English and economics in the Michigan Coll. of Mines. In WWI he was a seaman in the Navy. During WWII he was granted a leave of absence from the college for military service. Raised in Eldorado Lodge No. 890, Eldorado, Texas in Feb., 1918 and presently a member of H.H. Grace Lodge No. 324, Superior, Wis.

John F. Hill (1855-1912) Governor of Maine two terms, 1901-05. b. Oct. 29, 1855 at Eliot, Maine. He received an M.D. degree from Bowdoin in 1877. He served in both branches of the state legislature, and was a member of the executive council from 1898-99. Member of Augusta Lodge No. 141, Augusta, Maine. d. March 16, 1912.

Lister Hill U.S. Senator from Alabama since 1938. b. Dec. 29, 1894 at Montgomery, Ala. Graduate of Stark Univ. School (Ala.); U. of Alabama; and Columbia U.; he began law practice in Montgomery in 1916. Served in U.S. Army in WWI from 1917-19. U.S. congressman, 68th to

75th congresses (1923-39) from 2nd Ala. dist. During 77th-79th congresses, he was the majority whip in the senate. Received 32° AASR (SJ) at Montgomery, Ala. on Nov. 24, 1924.

Matthew W. Hill Chief Justice, Supreme Court of Washington. b. June 26, 1894 at Bozeman, Mont. Graduate of U. of Washington in 1917; admitted to bar in 1918, and practiced in Seattle, 1919-45. He was elected justice of supreme court in 1947, and reelected to term ending 1959. He is now chief justice (1957-58). In 1955-56 he was first vice president of the American Baptist Convention, and a member of the general council, 1957-58. Mason, he was grand master of the Grand Lodge of Washington in 1940-41; 33° AASR (SJ). Coroneted 33° Dec. 8, 1945. Active in York Rite, Red Cross of Constantine.

Robert P. Hill (1874-1937) U.S. Congressman, 63rd Congress (1913-15) from 25th Ill. dist. b. April 18, 1874 at Ewing, Ill. Admitted to bar in 1904, and practiced at Marion, Ill. Member Fellowship Lodge No. 89, Marion, Ill. Suspended NPD in 1918. d. Oct. 29, 1937.

Samuel B. Hill Judge of Tax Court of the U.S. b. April 2, 1875 at Franklin, Ark. was graduated from U. of Arkansas, and practiced law in that state five years before moving to Waterville, Wash. in 1904. He was judge of the superior court of Washington, 1917-23, and member of the 68th to 74th U.S. congresses from 5th Wash. dist. (1923-37). In 1936 he was appointed to the U.S. Board of Tax Appeals (now the Tax Court of the U.S.), and reappointed for a term ending in 1960. Mason.

Thomas R. Hill President, director and general manager of Rexair, Inc., Detroit, since 1935. b. Dec. 15, 1894 at Williamstown, Ky. Graduate of Georgetown Coll. in 1915. From 1915-18 he was a coach, high school principal and superintendent of schools. From 1915-18 he was a lecturer on the Redpath Chautauqua circuit and from 1927-31 with the RKO Lyceum Bureau. He is also president, director and general manager of Martin-Parry Corp., Detroit, since 1941. Raised in Jellico Lodge No. 527, Jellico, Tenn. in 1916. He is a member of Kentucky-Tennessee Chapter No. 148, R.A.M. of Williamsburg, Ky. and Pineville Commandery No. 39, K.T., Pineville, Ky., as well as Eastern Star, Shrine and White Shrine.

Wilson S. Hill (1863-1921) U.S. Congressman to 58th to 60th Congresses (1903-09) from 4th Miss. dist. b. Jan. 19, 1863 in Choctaw Co., Miss. Graduate of Cumberland U. (Tenn.). Admitted to bar in 1884 and practiced first at Winona and later at Greenwood. Received degrees in Winona Lodge No. 48, Winona, Miss. in 1898; suspended in 1909; reinstated in 1915; dimitted in 1915. d. Feb. 15, 1921.

Michael Hillegas (1729-1804) First Treasurer of the U.S. b. in Philadelphia on April 22, 1729, son of an early German emigrant. He engaged in sugar refining and became a man of some wealth. In June, 1774, he became treasurer of the committee of safety, of which Benjamin Franklin was president. In 1775, he was appointed by the Continental Congress as treasurer of the U.S. and held this office until 1789. Member of St. John's Lodge (Moderns), Benjamin Franklin's lodge. His name appeared on the original subscription list for the erection of Freemason's Hall, March 13, 1754. The only documentary evidence of any meetings of the "Moderns" during or after the Revolution is a communication to the grand lodge dated Oct. 30, 1782, wherein it gives Hillegas as junior warden of the lodge. d. Sept. 28, 1804.

Jeffrey P. Hillelson U.S. Congressman, 83rd Congress from 4th Mo. dist. b. March 9, 1919 in Ohio, he graduated from U. of Kansas City in 1947. Served in WWII as a captain (1942-46). From 1947-52 he operated a grocery store in Independence, Mo. For a time he was executive assistant to the postmaster general, resigning in 1956. In 1957 he was named postmaster of Kansas City, Mo. Member of Independence Lodge No. 76, Independence, Mo.; exalted in Independence Chapter No. 12, R.A.M. on April 17, 1954 and knighted in Palestine Commandery No. 17, K.T. on June 4, 1954, both of Independence, Mo.

Benjamin C. Hilliard (1868-1957) Chief Justice, Supreme Court of Colorado, 1939-41. b. Jan. 9, 1868 near Osceola, Ia. Graduate of State U. of Iowa in 1891. He practiced law in Kansas City, Mo. in 1890-93 and moved to Denver, Colo. in 1893. He was a justice of the supreme court of Colorado from 1931. Member of Highlands Lodge No. 86, Denver, Colo., receiving degrees on Oct. 19, Nov. 16, and Dec. 14, 1894, and master of same in 1901. Grand orator of the Grand Lodge of Colorado in 1934-36 and grand master, 1941-42. Received 32° AASR (SJ) in Colorado Consistory No. 1, in Feb., 1936. d. Aug. 1, 1957.

Otto Hillig (1876-1954) Transatlantic flyer and philanthropist.

b. in Germany in 1876. He came to this country at the age of 13, worked at odd jobs and took up photography commercially. Living frugally he amassed a fortune of approximately $100,000. In 1931, he flew from his home in Liberty, N.Y. to Copenhagen, Denmark, with Maj. Holger Hoiriis as his pilot. On the trip he carried a letter from the grand master of New York to the King of Denmark. He constructed a German type "castle" on a mountain top near Liberty to remind him of his homeland. In his will he left this to the Grand Lodge of New York. Once a year, his home lodge, Mongaup No. 816 of Liberty, N.Y., met in the building. He also left bequests to six other lodges in that county. Other bequests in his will were to a dozen churches and many friends and associates. d. Oct. 2, 1954.

Charles C. Hillman Physician and Brigadier General, U.S. Army. b. Aug. 27, 1887 at Almyra, Ark. Graduate of U. of Arkansas (B.S. 1907) and Rush Medical Coll. (M.D. 1911). He became a contract surgeon with the Army in 1912. He was commissioned the following year and advanced through grades to brigadier general in 1942. During WWII he was commanding general of Letterman General hospital, San Francisco; retired in 1947. Member of Mt. Zion Lodge No. 135, Metuchen, N.J.; 32° AASR at Bloomsburg, Pa. (NJ) and Irem Shrine Temple, Wilkes-Barre, Pa.

James N. Hillman President of Emory and Henry College, 1922-41. b. Nov. 6, 1883 in Coeburn, Va. Received A.B., M.A. and LL.D. from William and Mary Coll. He served as high school principal in Williamsburg, Va.; Latin instructor in William and Mary; superintendent of schools in Wise Co., Va.; and secretary of the state board of education, 1917-22. As president of Emory and Henry College, he was privileged to sign and confer degrees on all four of his children as well as his son-in-law, brother, and niece. He was grand master of the Grand Lodge of Virginia in 1938; grand high priest of the Grand Chapter of Virginia in 1947. He was raised March 19, 1906 in Williamsburg Lodge No. 6; past high priest of Coeburn and Highland Park Chapter No. 37; past commander of Cyrene Commandery No. 21, Norton, Va. Received KCCH in 1948 and 33° AASR, (SJ) in 1951, being a member of Dalcho Consistory. Member of Acca Shrine Temple, Richmond, St. Poly-carp Conclave, Red Cross of Constantine, Royal Order of Scotland, and master of Virginia Lodge of Research No. 1777 since 1950.

Thomas Hilson (1784-1834) Actor. b. in England in 1784, his family name was Hill. He first appeared in this country at the Park Theatre in New York City in 1809 as Walter in The Children of the Wood. He continued as a member of the company until August, 1833, performing a wide range of character in comedy, tragedy and opera-bouffe. Paul Pry, Touchstone and Tony Lumpkin were among his most successful renderings. It is said that "his forte was low comedy, but he sometimes lowered it to vulgarity." Member of Holland Lodge No. 8, New York City. d. July 23, 1834.

William 0. Hiltabidle, Jr. Commodore, U.S. Navy. b. Nov. 2, 1896 at Glyndon, Md. Graduate of Lafayette Coll. in 1919. He was a civil engineer from 1919-21; was commissioned in the Navy in that year, advancing through grades to commodore in 1945. He has been stationed at Naval yards and installations in New York City, Washington, D.C., Guam, Hawthorne, Nev., Pearl Harbor, San Diego, Quantico, Va., Newport, R.I. and Marianas Islands. In 1947-48 he was assistant chief of Bureau of Yards and Docks. Mason and National Sojourner.

Charles C. Hilton (1843-1905) Early day Chicago hotel owner. b. Oct. 24, 1843 in Madison, Maine. He came to Chicago in 1865 to become the manager of the old Briggs House. From this hostelry, he went to the Sherman House when it was built and subsequently with the Tremont, Palmer House, and Grand Pacific hotels. At the time of his death he was the proprietor of the Hotel Hilton. He served as a private in Co. K. of the 5th Mass. Inf. in the Civil War, and later was adjutant general of Ill. He was initiated in 1866 in William B. Warren Lodge No. 309 and was a member of Apollo Commandery No. 1, K.T., both of Chicago. d. June 28, 1905.

Clifford L. Hilton (1866-1946) Justice, Supreme Court of Minn. from 1928. b. Dec. 8, 1866 in Kenyon, Minn. Graduate of U. of Wisconsin in 1888, entering law practice at Fergus Falls, Minn., that year. He served two terms as attorney general of the state. Member of Corner Stone Lodge No. 99, Fergus Falls, Minn. Was Knight Templar, 33° AASR (NJ) and Shriner. d. April 5, 1946.

David C. Hilton (1877-1945) Surgeon and Brigadier General, National Guard. b. April 22, 1877 at Saline Co., Nebr. Received A.B. and A.M. from U. of Nebraska and M.D. from Rush Medical Coll. He practiced medicine in Lincoln, Nebr. from 1903. Served as a captain in medical corps in WWI and was division surgeon of 35th Division, Nebr. National Guard,

1927-40. Made brigadier general, unassigned, in 1940. He was U.S. delegate to International Congress of Military Medicine and Pharmacy at Warsaw, Poland in 1927 and in 1929 to same in London, England. Member of Acacia fraternity. Initiated in Siloam Lodge No. 780, Chicago, Ill. in 1903, he affiliated with Lincoln Lodge No. 19, Lincoln, Nebr. and served as master in 1917-18. Exalted in Lincoln Chapter No. 6, R.A.M. in Sept., 1914, he was high priest in 1925 and grand high priest of Grand Chapter, R.A.M. of Nebraska in 1945-46. Knighted in Mt. Moriah Commandery No. 4, K.T., Lincoln in Nov. 1914, he served as commander in 1938; greeted in Lincoln Council No. 4 R. & S.M. in Dec. 1914. Was sovereign of Coeur de Lion Conclave No. 10, Red Cross of Constantine in 1941. Received 32° AASR (SJ) in 1906, KCCH in 1915 and 33° on Oct. 24, 1919. d. Dec. 12, 1945.

James W. Hilton Brigadier General, U.S. Army (retired); Manager of industrial relations at Wisconsin Steel Works, International Harvester Co. A combat infantryman in WWI and WWII, he served as an enlisted man in the same regiment during the first war that he commanded in the second. Retired as brigadier general in March, 1951. He is past master of South Park Lodge No. 662, Chicago; past president and member of board of governors of Chicago Chapter, National Sojourners; member of Logan Chapter No. 196, R.A.M.; Englewood Commandery No. 59, K.T.; Chicago Court No. 48, Royal Order of Jesters; 32° AASR (NJ) Valley of Chicago, being chancellor of Oriental Consistory and chairman of fraternal relations committee; potentate of Medinah Shrine Temple, Chicago in 1958.

Joseph H. Himes Business executive and U.S. Congressman to 67th Congress (1921-23) from 16th Ohio dist. b. Aug. 15, 1885 in New Oxford, Pa. He rose from a cinder pitman in the Pittsburgh steel mills to an executive position. He is founder and president of Group Hospitalization, Inc., Washington, D.C.; president of Joseph H. Himes Co., Inc.; director of Acacia Mutual Life Ins. Co.; special partner in brokerage firm of Merrill, Lynch, Pierce, Fenner & Beane, N.Y. and director of a number of corporations. Mason. 32° AASR and Shriner.

John H. Hinds Major General, U.S. Army. b. Feb. 9, 1898 at Ft. Monroe, Va. Graduate of U.S. Military Academy in 1918 and advanced through grades to brigadier general in 1943. He has served in France, Philippines, Hawaii, North Africa, United Kingdom, Belgium, Germany and Czechoslovakia. In WWII he was with the War Dept. general staff, corps artillery commander, and artillery officer of 12th army group. From 1946 he was liaison officer to the Atomic Energy Commission. Retired. Member of Leonard Wood Lodge No. 105, Philippines.

Edward N. Hines (1870-1938) Highway pioneer who designed and built the first mile of concrete road in the U.S. b. Jan. 13, 1870 in St. Louis, Mo. He entered the printing business in 1889 and incorporated in as Speaker-Hines-Printing Co., of which he was president and general manager from 1925. He was road commissioner of Wayne Co., Mich. from 1906. In 1911 he originated the white line device to separate traffic lanes, and in 1893 he compiled and published the first road tour book. He sponsored the adoption of county road law in Mich. in 1893, and was organizer of American Road Builders Assn. in 1903. Member of Ashlar Lodge No. 91, Detroit, Mich., receiving degrees on Nov. 2nd, 9th, and Dec. 28, 1893. d. June 4, 1938.

Frank T. Hines Brigadier General, U.S. Army; Administrator of Veterans' Affairs; U.S. Ambassador to Panama. b. April 11, 1879 in Salt Lake City, Utah. He entered the service as an enlisted man in the Utah Light Artillery (N.G.) in 1898 and advanced through grades to brigadier general (N.G.) in 1918. In the Philippine insurrection, he served in 24 engagements and was recommended for the Congressional Medal of Honor. He assisted in the return of 3,100 American citizens from Europe in 1914 at the start of WWI. In 1918 he was chief of the embarkation service and the following year appointed chief of the Transportation Service, U.S. Army. In this position he was largely responsible for the transporting of over two million men to Europe in 18 months and returning them home in eight months. He was made permanent brigadier general in 1919 and resigned in 1920. From 1923-30 he was director of the U.S. Veterans' Bureau, and from 1930-44 was administrator of Veterans' Affairs. He was appointed ambassador to Panama in 1945. Raised in Temple Noyes Lodge No. 32, Washington, D.C. on Jan. 10, 1929; 32° AASR (SJ) and KCCH. d. April 3, 1960. d. April 3, 1960.

James F. Hinkle (1864-1951) Governor of New Mexico, 1923-25. b. Oct. 20, 1864 in Franklin Co., Mo. Educated in U. of Missouri. From 1885-1911 he was a cattle raiser in New Mex. He entered the banking business in 1911 and became president of First National in Roswell. He served three terms in the lower state house and was elected to the territorial senate in 1901. Member of Roswell Lodge No. 18, Roswell, N.M., receiving degrees on Sept. 27, Dec. 27, 1890, and March 25, 1891. Knight Templar, received 33° AASR (SJ) on Nov. 23, 1933. Shriner. d. March 26, 1951.

Thomas Hinkle Wagon boss for pioneer firm of Russell, Majors and Waddell, the great freighting firm of the prairies which started the Pony Express. Its owners and employees were predominantly Freemasons. Hinkle was a first sergeant in the Lexington, Mo. company of Doniphan's regiment in the Mexican War. In the Civil War, he was a colonel under General Sterling Price, q.v., and directed placing of the bales of hemp to form a moveable breastworks behind which Price's troops stormed the Masonic College in the Battle of Lexington in 1861. He was an early member of Lexington Lodge No. 32, petitioning, Oct. 25, 1841, and receiving the first degree, Nov. 23, 1841, and the next two, Dec. 3, 1841. This lodge later consolidated with Lexington No. 149.

Alonzo G. Hinkley Justice, Supreme Court of N.Y., 1920-47. b. Sept. 27, 1876 in Buffalo, N.Y. Admitted to bar in 1898. He served as official referee for the supreme court of New York following his retirement from the bench in 1947. Member of Washington Lodge No. 240, Buffalo, N.Y. receiving degrees on Feb. 23, April 7, and 27, 1899. District deputy grand master, 1922-23. Received 33° AASR (NJ) on Sept. 19, 1922. Shriner. Received 60-year lodge palm in 1959. Past potentate of Ismailia Shrine Temple; past monarch Zuleika Grotto. Received 60-year palm from his lodge in 1959. Is past potentate of

Ismailia Shrine Temple and past monarch of Zuleika Grotto.

Eugene E. Hinman (1875-1937) Masonic Author, physician. b. May 23, 1875 in Albany, N.Y. Received M.D. degree from Albany Medical College in 1899. Raised in Temple Lodge No. 14, Albany, N.Y. in 1901; served as master in 1919. He was grand master of the Grand Council, R. & S.M. of New York in 1917. He was co-author of *History of Cryptic Masonry*. d. Jan. 20, 1937.

George E. Hinman Justice, Supreme Court of Connecticut 1926-40. b. May 7, 1870 in Alford, Mass. He edited the Willimantic Journal for three years and was admitted to the bar in 1899, practicing in Willimantic, Conn. He served terms as attorney general of the state and justice of the superior court. After retirement from bench in 1940 he was state referee. Member of Cincinnatus Lodge, Great Barrington, Mass.; Trinity Chapter No. 9, R.A.M. and St. John's Commandery No. 11, K.T. (past commander) in Willimantic, Conn.

Carl Hinshaw (1894-1956) U.S. Congressman to 76th to 81st Congresses from Calif. (1939-51). b. July 28, 1894 in Chicago, Ill. Graduate of Princeton U. and U. of Michigan. From 1920-28 he was a salesman in Chicago, first with motor vehicle companies and later investment companies. In 1928-29 he was in real estate and investments in Tucson, Ariz., moving to Pasadena, Calif. in 1932 in the same business. Mason and 32° AASR (SJ). d. Aug. 5, 1956.

William W. Hinshaw (1867-1947) Singer, conductor and operatic producer. b. Nov. 3, 1867 near Union, Iowa. Graduate of Friends Academy (Ia.) and Valparaiso U., he also stud-

ied singing in U.S. and Germany. At the age of 15 he was the leader of a boys' band. From 1890-99 he taught music in Chicago and Valparaiso U. He made his debut with Castle Square Opera Co. as Mephisto in *Faust* at St. Louis in 1899. From 1903-07 he was president of the Chicago Conservatory of Music, and for the following two years, of the Hinshaw Conservatory in Chicago. He was the leading American baritone with the Metropolitan Opera Co. of New York from 1910-13. He sang in Austria, Germany, and Canada, and in 1920 organized his own company, giving Mozart operas in English (800 performances). In 1926 he retired from musical activities and devoted himself to publishing an encyclopedia of American Quaker genealogy. Mason, Knight Templar, 32° AASR and Shriner. d. Nov. 27, 1947.

Frank Hiscock (1834-1914) U.S. Senator from New York, 1887-93. b. Sept. 6, 1834 at Pompey, N.Y. He was admitted to the bar in 1855. A member of the state constitutional convention of 1867, he served in the 45th to 49th U.S. congresses (1877-87). Following his term as senator, he resumed private practice at Syracuse, N.Y. d. June 18, 1914.

Arthur M. Hitch (1875-1956) President of Kemper Military School, Boonville, Mo. b. Feb. 26, 1875 at Cuba, Mo. He attended the Rolla School of Mines (Mo.) and was graduated from the U. of Missouri in 1897. He began his teaching career in 1897 and was with Kemper from 1899. He was vice president and principal from 1907-27; superintendent from 1927-49; and president from 1934. A member of Cooper Lodge No. 36, Boonville, Mo.; he was exalted in Boonville Chapter No. 60, R.A.M. on Feb. 20, 1904; served as high priest in 1907-08-09 and received his 50-year chapter pin; member of Olivet Cornmandery No. 53, K.T., Boonville, he was knighted on April 2, 1904; member of Ararat Shrine Temple of Kansas City, he was past president of the Boonville Shrine Club. d. Feb. 20, 1956.

Herbert E. Hitchcock (1867-1958) U.S. Senator from South Dakota, 1936-38. b. Aug. 22, 1867 in Maquoketa, Iowa. Attended Iowa State College and College of Law, Chicago, moving to Mitchell, S.D. in 1884 and was admitted to bar in 1896, practicing in Mitchell. Member of the state senate three terms. Member of Resurgam Lodge No. 31, Mitchell, S.D., receiving degrees on May 16, 1898, Jan. 21 and Feb. 22, 1899. Received 32° AASR (SJ) in Oriental Consistory Oct. 5, 1919. d. Feb. 17, 1958.

Phineas W. Hitchcock (1831-1881) U.S. Senator from Nebraska, 1870-77. b. Nov. 30, 1831 in New Lebanon, N.Y. He was admitted to the bar and settled in Omaha, Nebr. in 1857. In 1861 he was appointed U.S. marshal of the Territory of Nebraska, holding this office until his election as a delegate to congress in 1864. He was a member of the national committee appointed to accompany the remains of Lincoln to Illinois. On the organization of Nebraska as a state in March, 1867, he was appointed surveyor-general, and held that office two years. Member of Capitol Lodge No. 3, Omaha, Nebr. d. July 10, 1881.

Raymond Hitchcock (1865-1929) Star of the comedy stage. b. in Auburn, N.Y. Member of St. Cecile Lodge No. 568, New York City.

Adolf Hitler (1889-1945) Anti-Mason. German chancellor and Fuhrer. Dorothy Thompson, writing about him for the Ladies Home Journal in Oct. 1955 thought that he was suffering from paranoia and a persecution complex: "Those whom he imagines to be conspiring against him may be individuals. But his enemies may also be `they'—a whole society, or some section of it. Priests, Freemasons, Jews, or 'the crowned heads of Europe.' " Hitler not only forbade meetings, but even membership, and established a museum which was to depict the foolishness of Freemasonry. The following is part of Hitler's official decree against Freemasonry in 1942 that was presented during the Nuremburg trial: "Freemasons and the ideological enemies of National Socialism who are allied with them are the originators of the present war against the Reich. Spiritual struggle according to plan against these powers is a measure necessitated by war. I have, therefore, ordered Reichsleiter Alfred Rosenberg to accomplish this task in cooperation with the Chief of the High Command of the armed forces. To accomplish this task, he has the right to explore libraries, archives, lodges, and other ideological and cultural establishments of all kinds for suitable material and to confiscate such material for the ideological tasks of the N.S.D.A.P. for scientific research work. The regulations for the execution of this task will be issued by the Chief of the High Command of the armed forces in agreement with Reichsleiter Rosenberg."

George Hoadly (1826-1902) Governor of Ohio, 1883-85. b. July 31, 1826 at New Haven, Conn. In 1830 he moved to Cleveland, Ohio with his parents. Was graduated from Western Reserve Coll. in 1844 and studied at Harvard Law School. Admitted to the bar in 1847, he practiced in Cincinnati. After 1887 he practiced law in New York. Mason and 32° AASR. d. 1902.

William D. Hoard (1836-1918) Governor of Wisconsin, 1889-91. b. Oct. 10, 1836 at Stockbridge, N.Y. Moved to Wis. in 1857, where he engaged in farming and in nursery business at Columbus from 1865-70. Was publisher of Jefferson County Union, Lake Mills, 1870-73, moving it to Ft. Atkinson in latter year. He also published Hoard's Dairyman. He served as president of Farmers National Congress and National Dairy Union; president of board of regents, U. of Wis. 1907-11. Member of Billings Lodge No. 139, Fort Atkinson, Wis. at time of his death, Nov. 22, 1918.

James Hoban (1762?-1831) Architect who designed and supervised the construction of the White House, Washington, D.C. (1792-1800). When it was destroyed by the British in 1814, he designed the one replacing it (1815-29). b. at Tullamore, near Callan, in County Kilkenny, Ireland, his exact birth date is unknown. He studied architecture under Thomas Ivory, and in 1785 arrived in Philadelphia. He then went to Charleston, S.C., where he built several public buildings, and the state house at Columbia. For this he was recommended to President Washington, and he went to Philadelphia to confer with Washington about developing the Federal City. His plan for the White House was accepted, and he received the contract to supervise the construction at 200 guineas a year. Hoban collaborated with William Thornton, q.v., in constructing the U.S. Capitol, and, in 1797, was named superintendent of the execu-

tive buildings to be erected, including the Treasury, State, War, and Navy buildings. He married Susanna Sewell in 1799, and they had ten children. Although a devout Catholic, he was ardently interested in Masonry. Bishop Carroll stated, in a letter in 1794, with reference to prohibitory edicts, that they would not be enforced in his diocese. James Hoban laid the cornerstone of the White House with Masonic ceremonies, Oct. 12, 1792. It is not known where he received his degrees, but under his leadership a group of Irish Catholics and Scotch Presbyterians organized Federal Lodge No. 1, Washington, D.C. and he became its first master, and afterwards, treasurer. The lodge also participated in the laying of the cornerstone of the Capitol by Washington, Sept. 18, 1793. He was a member of an early Royal Arch "encampment" in the Dist. of Columbia. d. Dec. 8, 1831, and his body was interred in the graveyard of St. Patrick's Church, but reinterred in Mt. Olivet by his grandson in 1863.

Garrett A. Hobart (1844-1899) Twenty-fourth Vice President of the United States, 1897-1901. b. June 3, 1844 in Monmouth Co., N.J. He was graduated from Rutgers Coll. in 1863, taught school, studied law, and was admitted to the bar in 1869. He practiced at Paterson, N.J. He was a member of the state legislature from 1873-78, and state senator, 1879-85. A member of Falls City Lodge No. 82, Paterson, N.J., he received his degrees, July 9, Oct. 31, 1867, and raised Dec. 8, 1868. He was exalted in Cataract Chapter No. 10, R.A.M., Paterson, Nov. 6, 1871, and knighted in St. Omer Commandery No. 13, K.T. of Paterson in the same year. He became a charter member of Adelphic Chapter No. 33, R.A.M. of Paterson, Oct. 13, 1874, and a charter member of Melita Commandery No. 13, Paterson, May 10, 1876; at one time he served as generalissimo of this commandery. On Dec. 23, 1896 he became a life member of Washington Commandery No. 1, K.T. at Washington, D.C.; received 32° AASR (NJ) in New Jersey Consistory, Jan. 31, 1876. d. Nov. 21, 1899.

Thomas Walter Hobart (see under Inskip).

Sam Francis Hobbs (1887-1952) U.S. Congressman to 74th to 81st Congresses (1935-51) from 4th Ala. dist. b. Oct. 5, 1887 at Selma, Ala. Graduate of U. of Alabama in 1908, and practiced law in Selma from 1908-21, when he became a circuit judge. He resumed law practice in 1926. Mason. d. May 31, 1952.

William P. Hobby Newspaper publisher and Governor of Texas, 1917-21. b. March 26, 1878 at Moscow, Texas. He served an apprenticeship on the Houston Post, and in 1924 became president of the board, resigning in 1955 to become chairman. From 1907-21, he published the Beaumont Enterprise. He was lieutenant governor of Texas in 1914-17, then governor. His wife, Oveta Culp Hobby, was the commanding officer of the WAC organization (Woman's Army Corps) in WWII, and has succeeded him as publisher of the Post. Member of Beaumont Lodge No. 286, Beaumont, Texas, receiving degrees on March 5, May 26, and June 23, 1913, dimitting May 28, 1931.

Homer Hoch (1879-1949) Judge, Supreme Court of Kansas from 1939, and U.S. Congressman to 66th to 72nd Congresses (1919-33) from 4th Kans. dist. b. July 4, 1879 at Marion, Kans. Graduate of Baker U.

and Washburn Coll. Member of Center Lodge No. 147, Marion, Kans. d. Jan. 30, 1949.

August F. Hockenbeamer (1871-1935) President of Pacific Gas & Electric Co. 1927-35. b. March 6, 1871 at Logansport, Ind. Worked for Pennsylvania, B. & O. and C.R.I. & P. railroads from 1887-1903; N. W. Halsey & Co., investment bankers, 190307; went with the Pacific Gas and Electric Co. in 1907. Was vice president of Bond & Share, and a trustee of Edison Electric Inst. Mason. d. Nov. 11, 1935.

Thetus H. Hocker Vice President of George A. Hormel & Co. (meat packers) from 1944, and director since 1938. b. Oct. 5, 1902 at Monroe, Ind. Graduate of U. of Indiana in 1924. Member of Fidelity Lodge No. 39, Austin, Minn., 32° AASR (SJ), Winona, Minn. and Osman Shrine Temple, St. Paul, Minn.

John R. Hodge General, U.S. Army. b. June 12, 1893 in Golconda, Ill. He was commissioned a second lieutenant in 1917, and advanced through the grades to general in 1952. In WWI, he served in France in 1918-19. In WWII he was in the Pacific Theater from 1942-48, commanding the 24th Corps from activation in 1944, to Aug., 1948. He commanded the U.S. Army forces in Korea from 1945, until the Korean government was formed in 1948. He was in the landings at Leyte and Okinawa. Hodge accepted the surrender of the Japanese army in Korea. In 1950-52 he commanded the Third Army in the U.S., and was chief of army field forces, 1952-53. Now retired. A member of E. A. Minor Lodge No. 603, Atlanta, Ga., he was raised Nov. 18, 1950. In 1954 he was created an honorary member of the Grand Lodge of Mississippi. In 1951 he addressed the Grand Lodge of Alabama and in part said: "I think the proudest day of my life is the day I was raised and could call myself a Mason. The obligations exemplified the things that I always believed in, so I was not embarrassed at any stage." Also a member of Phoenix Chapter No. 2, R.A.M.; Fayetteville Council No. 27, R. & S.M.; and Palestine Commandery No. 20, K.T., all of Fayetteville, N.C. 32° AASR (SJ) in Atlanta, Ga. and Yaarab Shrine Temple, Atlanta.

Walter H. Hodge U.S. Federal Judge. b. Aug. 29, 1896 at Auburn, Ind. Graduate of U. of Washington, 1919, admitted to Washington bar in 1919, and Alaska bar in 1935. In private practice at Seattle from 1929-34, and Cordova, Alaska, 1935-54. Named judge of U.S. district court, second div. at Nome in 1954, and has served since that time. Received degrees in Mount Baker Lodge, Mount Vernon, Wash. about 1925. Past master of Mount McKinley Lodge No. 183, Cordova, Alaska and present chaplain of Anvil Lodge No. 140, Nome, Alaska. 32° AASR at Juneau; member of Nile Shrine Temple, Seattle, Wash.; and Cordova Chapter No. 4, O.E.S. at Cordova.

George H. Hodges (1866-1947) Governor of Kansas, 1913-15. b. Feb. 6, 1866 at Orion, Wis., moving with parents to Kans. in 1869. He began as a lumber yard salesman and bookkeeper at Olathe in 1886. He became senior member of Hodges Bros., owning 12 lumber yards, 12 hardware stores, and the Johnson County (Kans.) Democrat. As a member of the Kansas senate he authored the Hodges hard surface road law. As governor, he inaugurated a movement to collect food and supplies for the Belgians; the state and its citizens donated 50,000 barrels of flour, meal, and food that were delivered in 90 days. He advocated a constitutional amendment abolishing the two-house legislature by substituting a single body of 12 men to pass and repeal the laws of the state (failed). At his death he had been a Mason 55 years, and had received his 50-year button. He was a charter member of Caswell Consistory of Kansas City, Kans., Aug. 19, 1898; he had received the 33°. Member of Olathe Lodge No. 19, Olathe, Kansas. d. Oct. 7, 1947.

Henry C. Hodges (1831-1917) Brigadier General, U.S. Army. b. Jan. 14, 1831 in Vt., he was graduated from the U.S. Military Academy in 1851 and was promoted through grades to brigadier general in 1904, when he retired. He saw early service on the frontier, and in 1853-54 was on the Pacific Railroad explorations. In the Civil War he was chief quartermaster of the Army of the Cumberland, and on the staff of Gen. Rosecrans in the Tenn. campaign. Later he was quartermaster general after the war until he retired. A member of Willamette Lodge No. 2, Portland, Oreg., he received the first two degrees on Dec. 9, 1853 and the third the following night. d. Nov. 3, 1917.

Luther H. Hodges Governor of North Carolina since 1954. b. March 9, 1898 in Pittsylvania Co., Va. Graduate of U. of North Carolina in 1919. An executive in the mill industry (fabrics). He delivered an address at the laying of the cornerstone of the new Masonic temple at Winston-Salem, March 19, 1955. He delivered the principal address at the General Grand Chapter banquet in 1954.

Silas H. Hodges (1804-1875) Commissioner of Patents 1852-53, and examiner-in-chief of U.S. patent office, 1861-75. b. Jan. 12, 1804 in Clarendon, Vt. He studied law and was admitted to the bar in 1825. In 1832 he abandoned his profession, studied theology, and became a Congregational clergyman, preaching until 1841, when he resumed his law practice in Rutland, Vt. Member of Center Lodge No. 6, Rutland. d. April 21, 1875.

Richard M. Hoe (1812-1886) Inventor of the rotary press (1847), web press (1847), and improvements that made possible the modern newspaper press. b. Sept. 12, 1812 in New York City. He entered his father's printing press manufacturing business at the age of 15, and became senior member of the firm in 1833. Of an inventive mind, he made many improvements on the prevailing flatbed press of that day. His new rotary press was known as Hoe's "lightning press." He was a member of Columbia Lodge No. 91, Philadelphia, being initiated, Oct. 23, 1854, and remaining a member until his death, June 7, 1866.

Heinrich Hoepker (1874-1956) Active in the rejuvenation of the Masonic groups in Germany in 1949, forming the United Grand Lodge of Germany, after the Nazi regime. b. June 28, 1874, he was initiated in Urania zur Unsterblichkeit Lodge in May, 1911, serving as master of the lodge in 1922-26. He was deputy grand master of the Grosseloge von Preussen (Royal York) from 1925-31. He served as representative of the Grand Lodge of New York from 1926 until his death. In 1929 he was chairman of the Verein Deutscher Freimauer. d. Feb. 10, 1956.

Charles B. Hoeven U.S. Congressman to 78th to 85th Congresses (1943-59) from 8th Ia. dist. b. March 30, 1895 at Hospers, Ia. Graduate of Iowa State U. in 1920. Admitted to bar in 1922, and practiced at Alton. He was a member of the Iowa state senate from 1937-41, and president of same last three years. Served in WWI with 88th Div. in France. Raised in Floyd Lodge No. 537, Orange City, Iowa in 1921 and past master of same; 32° AASR (SJ) at Sioux City, Iowa; and member of Abu Berk Shrine Temple, Sioux City.

Clyde R. Hoey (1877-?) Governor of North Carolina, 1937-41, and U.S. Senator, 1945-1951. b. Dec. 11, 1877 at Shelby, N.C. Attended U. of North Carolina, and was admitted to bar in 1899. He began in a printing office at age of 12, and later edited a county newspaper. He served in both houses of the state legislature, and was U.S. congressman to 66th congress (1919-21) from the 9th N.C. dist. He declined congressional renomination, and resumed law practice in 1921. A member of Cleveland Lodge No. 202, Shelby, N.C. he received his degrees, Sept. 20, Oct. 18, and Nov. 22, 1907. He was trustee of his lodge from 1931-36; grand orator of the Grand Lodge of North Carolina, 1932-33, addressing that body on April 18, 1933.

Harold G. Hoffman Governor of New Jersey, 1935-37. b. Feb. 7, 1896 at South Amboy, N.J. He enlisted as a private in WWI, and was promoted to captain in the 114th Infantry. In WWII, he was colonel in the Transportation Corps. Was mayor of South Amboy, 1925-26, and U.S. congressman to 70th and 71st congresses (1927-31) from 3rd N.J. dist. From 1930-35 he was commissioner of motor vehicles in N.J. Member of

St. Stephen's Lodge No. 63, South Amboy, being initiated March 7, 1927.

John T. Hoffman (1828-?) Governor of New York, 1868-72. b. Jan. 10, 1828 at Sing Sing, N.Y. Graduate of Union Coll. in 1846, he studied law, and was admitted to the bar in 1849. He acquired an extensive practice in New York City; joined the Tammany organization in 1854. He was mayor of New York City from 1865-69. Mason. d. March 24, 1888.

Paul G. Hoffman Corporation executive and Economic Cooperation Administration. Administrator, 1948-50. b. April 26, 1891 at Chicago, Ill. Honorary degrees from many universities. He began as an automobile salesman for Studebaker Corp. in 1911, and became president of same, serving from 1935-48; chairman of board in 1953; chairman of board Studebaker-Packard Corp. 1954-56. Chairman of board of Hoffman Specialty Mfg. Co.; president and trustee of Ford Foundation, 1951-53. Director of many large corporations including New York Life Ins. Co., Encyclopedia Britannica, Time, Inc., and United Air Lines. Member of Wilshire Lodge No. 445, Los Angeles, Calif., receiving his degrees in 1926.

Roy Hoffman (1869-1953) Lawyer, judge, and Major General, National Guard. b. June 13, 1869 in Neosho Co., Kans. Founded the *Guthrie (Okla.) Daily Leader* in 1889; was admitted to the bar in 1892; was district judge, 1908-12; and U.S. attorney for Okla. in 1903-07. He enlisted in army during Spanish-American War, and rose to captain. In Mexican Border conflict he was a colonel; became brigadier general, U.S. Army, in 1917. In WWII he commanded Ft. Sill, Okla.; 61st Depot Brigade, Camp Bowie, Tex.; and

organized, commanded, and went overseas with the 93rd Division. Following the war he commanded Camp Shelby, Miss., and was discharged March, 1919. Retired as major general, commanding 45th Division, National Guard. Member of Oklahoma's Hall of Fame. Mason; received 32° AASR (SJ) on Aug. 5, 1898.

John William Hofmann (1824-?) Union Civil War General. b. Feb. 18, 1824 in Philadelphia, Pa. He recruited the 23rd Regiment of Pa. Vols. and was later lieutenant colonel of the 56th regiment. As a colonel, he gave the orders to open fire at the Battle of Gettysburg (July 1, 1863). A member of. Lodge No. 51, Philadelphia, he received the degrees Feb. 24, March 24 and May 26, 1853. At that time he was 29 and his occupation was given as a storekeeper.

James Hogan (see under Hogun).

William Hogarth (1697-1764) English painter and engraver famous for his caricature and satirical paintings. b. Nov. 10, 1697, in St. Bartholomew parish of London. He was apprenticed to Ellis Gamble, a silversmith of Cranbourne St., Leicester Fields, London. His talents soon found another outlet; his first sketch was of a drunken fray which he happened to witness in a tavern on the road to Highgate. His extremely ludicrous sketch set the pattern for his future efforts—to exhibit vice in all its deformities, strip villainy of its cloak, and ridicule all excesses offensive to the moral code. Hogarth was an active Freemason, and not only served as grand steward of the Grand Lodge of England in 1735, but designed the jewel of the Grand Stewards Lodge that is still used today. He is shown on the records of the grand stewards as having been a member of the lodge at the "Bear and Harrow," Butchers' Row in 1730, and at the "Hand and Apple-tree," Little Great Queen St. in 1725. In 1729 he secretly married Jane, daughter of Sir Thomas Thornhill, q.v., a painter under whom he studied. Thornhill became senior grand warden of the Grand Lodge of England in 1828. Hogarth painted his father-in-law's portrait in Masonic attire as a grand officer. His best known Masonic engraving is entitled Night, being the last of a series known as The Four Times of the Day. It represents Restoration Day (May 29) in Hartshorn St., Charing Cross (now part of Northumberland Ave.), with an inebriated master, or past master being assisted down the street by a tyler. It is thought that the master is Sir Thomas DeVeil, q.v., past master of Hogarth's first lodge, and the tyler was Bro. Montgomerie, the grand tyler, or as he was then called, "garder of ye Grand Lodge." The painting Sleeping Congregation(1736) represents Dr. Desaguliers, grand master in 1720, preaching to a congregation. Among the sleepers are a number of grand lodge officers and Masonic notables whom Hogarth knew well through his attendance at the quarterly sessions of grand lodge, and in the dozen London lodges. The Mystery of Masonry Brought to Light by the Gormogons (1742), shows Dr. James Anderson, q.v., and the Duke of Wharton, q.v., grand master in 1722-23. The Roast Beef of Old England, or The Gate of Calais, was the result of Hogarth's visit to France, shortly after the peace of Aix-la-Chapelle. While sketching the gate, Hogarth was arrested as a spy and returned to England. The friar depicted in it is none other than John Pine, official engraver to the grand lodge in 1746. He also made an engraving of Martin Folkes, q.v., deputy grand master of the grand lodge in 1724. He executed a savage portrait of Bro. John Wilkes, q.v., who had been initiated in prison, and one of Lord Lovat (1746), who was connected with the Rite of Strict Observance and executed April 9, 1747 for treason. Hogarth died Oct. 25, 1764.

Moses D. Hoge (1819-1899) Virginia clergyman, said to have been the most eloquent speaker in the southern Presbyterian church. He was made a Freemason on his deathbed. b. Sept. 17, 1819 near Hampden Sidney Coll., Va.; he was graduated from that institution in 1839. He was licensed to preach in 1844. He served the 2nd Presbyterian church of Richmond most of his life. During the Civil War he ran the blockade to England in order to provide Bibles for the Confederate Army, and the Earl of Shaftesbury granted him £4,000 for this purpose. He declined the presidency of Hampden Sidney Coll. at one time. From 1862-67 he edited the Central Presbyterian with Rev. Thomas Moore. Details of his deathbed initiation from the minutes of Dove Lodge No. 51, Richmond, Va. A called communication of the lodge was held in the office of the grand secretary of the grand lodge at the Masonic Temple in Richmond on Nov. 22, 1898. The master announced that the lodge had been called for the purpose of conferring the degrees upon the Rev. Hoge. The grand master then stated that in consequence of the physical disability of the candidate that permission was given the lodge under dispensation which he personally granted to meet at the residence and without charter. The son, Moses D. Hoge, Jr. met the lodge members at his father's residence (N.E. corner of Main & 5th) and Grand Master R. T. W. Duke, Jr.

then conferred the three degrees "dispensing with such portions of the ceremony as in his opinion the physical condition of the candidate required." At the completion of the ceremonies, Rev. Hoge stated he desired to become a member of Dove Lodge No. 51, and without any ballots being taken the Master appointed him chaplain of the lodge. He died Jan. 6, 1899. He died at Richmond, Va., Jan. 6, 1899.

Palmer T. Hogenson (1899-1955) President of Webber College, Babson Park, Fla. since 1949; economist. b. Dec. 25, 1899 at Stewartville, Minn. Graduate of St. Olaf Coll., Harvard, and American U. He traveled and studied in China, Philippines, Sumatra, Ceylon, Italy, France, and England. He was professor of economics at Missouri Valley Coll., (Marshall, Mo.) 1927-30; same at Bradley U., 1930-44, and economist with the War Dept. in Washington, 1944-47. Mason, 32° AASR. d. Oct. 8, 1955.

James Hogg (1770-1835) Scottish poet known as the "Ettrick Shepherd." b. in Ettrick, Selkirk, Scotland, he was a friend of Scott, Byron, John Wilson, Wordsworth, and Southey. He settled in Edinburgh in 1810, and at Eltrive Lake in Yarrow in 1816. Among his works are *Donald M'Donald; Scottish Pastorals; The Mountain Bard; Forest Minstrel; The Queen's Wake; Pilgrims of the Sun; The Poetic Mirror;* and *Queen Hynde.* He was made a Mason in Lodge Canon-gate Kilwinning, Edinburgh, May 7, 1831.

Jean Baptiste N.M. de la Hogue (see under Delahogue).

James Hogun (?-1781) Brigadier General in American Revolution. b. in Ireland, he served in the

Georgia and North Car. militia and was appointed brigadier general on Jan. 9, 1779. He was taken prisoner at Charleston, S.C. on May 12, 1780 and died while a prisoner, Jan. 4, 1781. Member of Lodge No. 3, Philadelphia, Pa., he received his degrees on April 13, 15 and 17th, 1779. He signed the by-laws on April 16th, 1779 as James Hogun; however, the minutes refer to him as Hogan. Two other officers received the degrees at the same time. They were General J. P. G. Muhlenberg, q.v., and General William Thompson, q.v., the latter while a prisoner on parole, en route to N.Y.

John A. Holabird (1886-1945) Architect. b. May 4, 1886 at Evanston, Ill. was graduated from U.S. Military Academy in 1907. Was member of firm of Holabird & Root which designed the Palmolive, Daily News, and Board of Trade buildings in Chicago; courthouse in St. Paul, Minn.; Lafayette building, and Staffer Hotel in Washington, D.C. After service in the regular army as a lieutenant, he served as a captain in the Ill. National guard, until 1917, when he reentered the army as an artillery colonel, serving in WWI until 1919, and receiving the Distinguished Service Medal. Member Evans Lodge No. 524, Evanston, Ill. 32° AASR (NJ). d. May 4, 1945.

Ross E. Holaday (1869-1929) U.S. Consul. b. July 14, 1869 at Westboro, Ohio. Clerked in post office at Wilmington, Ohio, and taught public schools before being admitted to Ohio bar in 1898. He practiced law at Wilmington from 1898-1902, and was a member of the Ohio legislature. From 1902-15 he was U.S. consul at Santiago de Cuba, and at Manchester, England, from 1915. Member of Wilmington Lodge No. 52, Wilmington, Ohio, receiving degrees on Aug. 1, 16 and Sept. 5, 1905. d. Nov. 26, 1929.

Moses Holbrook (1783-1844) Fourth Grand Commander of the Southern Supreme Council of the Scottish Rite (1826-1844). By profession he was a physician. A man of learning, he was at one time (1811) preceptor of a Portland, Maine, Academy. He was initiated in Middlesex Lodge at Framingham, Mass., Nov. 13, 1804, and in 1808, was created a Knight Templar in Washington Encampment, K.T. at Roxbury, Mass. He moved to Charleston, S.C. in 1822, and was "admitted to the Supreme Council," Nov. 15, 1822. He is listed as a past master of Washington Lodge No. 7 in 1823, and from 1824-36 was treasurer of the Grand Lodge of South Carolina. He was present at the formation of a "grand encampment," Knights Templar for S.C., and became the first grand commander of that jurisdiction. d. Dec. 1, 1844 in Florida.

Marcus H. Holcomb (1844-1932) Governor of Connecticut three terms, 1915-21. b. Nov. 28, 1844 in New Hartford, Conn. Admitted to the bar in 1871, and practiced at Southington, 1872-93, and at Hartford, 1893-1910. He was a probate judge more than 30 years. He served in both state legislative bodies, and was attorney general, and judge of the superior court. Initiated in North Star Lodge No. 58, Hartford, Conn. in 1867 and was master in 1872. Affiliated with Friendship Lodge No. 33, Southington, Conn. in 1875. 32° AASR at Hartford, Conn. d. March 5, 1932.

Albert J. Holden (1841-1916) Organist and composer. b. Aug. 17, 1841 at Boston, Mass. He studied entirely in New York, and was organist over 47 years at the Church of the Divine Paternity (Universalist), and the Church of the Puritans. He was one of the founders of the American Guild of Organists. He composed more than 300 anthems, hymns, and other church music. He edited and compiled numerous collections of music, both sacred and secular. Mason. d. July 16, 1916.

John B. Holden (1873-1928) Justice, Supreme Court of Mississippi, 1919-28. b. Jan. 5, 1873 in Franklin Co., Miss. He was admitted to the bar in 1894, and practiced for 20 years at Summit and McComb City, Miss. He was mayor of Summit, prosecuting attorney of Pike Co., and circuit judge of 14th dist. Received degrees in Summit Lodge No. 231, Summit, Miss.; dimitted in 1912 to affiliate with McComb City Lodge No. 382 on Nov. 6, 1913; dimitted from same Oct. 4, 1917. d. Jan. 7, 1928.

Oliver Holden (1765-1831) Psalmist and author of *Confidence and Coronation* hymns. b. Sept. 18, 1765 in Shirley, Mass. While engaged in the carpenter's trade, he published his first book of sacred music, arranged in three and four parts, entitled *The American Harmony* (1793). Most of this volume was original. Soon afterward he *published Union Harmony, or a Universal Collection of Sacred Music.* He was a member and past master of King Solomon's Lodge, then at Charlestown, but now at Somerville, Mass. d. 1831.

William W. Holden (1818-1892) Governor of North Carolina, 1865-70. b. Nov. 24, 1818 in Orange Co., N.C. Admitted to the bar in 1841; in 1843, he bought The Raleigh Standard, and was its editor 25 years. He was appointed, by President Johnson, provisional governor of N.C. in 1865, and was elected to that office in 1868. In 1869-70 reports of the Ku Klux outrages caused him to proclaim Alamance and Caswell counties to be in a state of insurrection, and the militia placed several persons under arrest. He refused to deliver the prisoners to the civil authorities under a writ of habeas corpus. This culminated in the state senate and house of representatives ordering him removed, Dec. 20, 1870, for "high crimes and misdemeanors," and ordering that he "be removed from the office of governor, and disqualified to hold any office of trust, honor or profit under the state of N.C." He moved to Washington, where he edited the National Republican, but later returned to Raleigh, and was postmaster. He was made a Mason "at sight" in 1865, by Grand Master John McCormick, in Wake Co., and affiliated with New Light Lodge No. 215. A year previous he had applied to Hiram Lodge No. 40 of Raleigh, but was rejected. The exact date of his application to this lodge is not known, for the records of Hiram lodge were burned. He dimitted in 1877. d. March 1, 1892.

Edward E. Holland (1861-1941) U.S. Congressman, 62nd to 66th Congresses (1911-21) from 2nd Va. dist. b. Feb. 26, 1861 in Nansemond Co., Va. Graduate of Richmond Coll. and Elon Coll. Admitted to bar in 1882, and practiced at Suffolk, Va. Served in state senate, and was active nationally in the Democratic party. Mason. d. Oct. 22, 1941.

George Holland (1791-1871) Comedian and actor. b. Dec. 6, 1791 in London, England. He began as a small parts actor in 1817 in Drury Lane Theatre, and in 1820 played at the London Olympic. His first appearance in this country was in the Bow-

ery Theatre in New York, Sept. 12, 1827. After several seasons in New York he made prolonged tours of the southern and western theatres, and settled in New Orleans, where he became treasurer of the St. Charles Theatre. Returning north, he formed a connection with Mitchell's Olympic Theatre from 1843-49. From 1849-52 he lost his professional identity by attaching himself under an assumed name to Wood's and Christy's Negro minstrels. In 1852 he reappeared as an actor in Placide's Varieties, New Orleans, but soon returned to New York to become a member of Wallack's Theatre. He made his final appearance, May 15, 1870, at the Fifth Avenue Theatre; he died destitute. *The Loomis Musical and Masonic Journal* (March, 1871, p. 147) states that he was made a Mason May 20, 1824. It must have been, therefore, in England. d. Dec. 20, 1871. At Holland's death, a Madison Avenue (NY) minister refused to officiate at the funeral and suggested there was "a little church around the corner" where the funeral might be held. Since that date actors have been going to *The Little Church Around the Corner* which has become known as the "Actor's Church." Properly it is the Protestant Episcopal Church of the Transfiguration. Holland's son, Joseph Jefferson Holland, q.v., was also an actor and Mason.

James B. Holland (1857-1914) U.S. Federal Judge, Eastern District of Pennsylvania from 1904-14. b. Nov. 14, 1857 in Montgomery Co., Pa. Admitted to the bar in 1887. Member of Fritz Lodge No. 420, Conshohocken, Pa. receiving degrees on Oct. 16, Nov. 13 and Dec. 11, 1883 and was master in 1895. d. April 24, 1914.

John H. Holland (1785-1864) Louisiana lawyer, who as grand master of Louisiana received General Lafayette, q.v., in that grand lodge. b. May 23, 1785 in Hartford, Conn., he settled in New Orleans early in life, and practiced law in that city. He was often called the "Father of Louisiana Masonry," and was active in every branch and rite. He became grand master of Louisiana in 1825, and, by virtue of that office, was also grand high priest, serving in both capacities for 12 years. He presided at the convention which organized the Grand Council R. & S.M. of Louisiana in 1856, and was the first grand master, holding that office the remainder of his life. For many years he was commander of Indivisible Friends Commandery No. 1, K.T., and under proxy from Benjamin B. French, q.v., organized the Grand Commandery of Louisiana, and became its first grand prelate. He was commander-in-chief of the grand consistory in New Orleans, and 33° in the Supreme Council of Louisiana. Participated in the Concordat of 1855 merging the Supreme Councils of Charleston and New Orleans. d. March 29, 1864.

Joseph J. Holland (1860-1926) Actor. b. Dec. 20, 1860 in New York City, the son of George Holland, q.v., an early day comedian and actor. He first appeared on the stage at the age of six as the footman with fairy coach in Cinderella, at the Olympic Theatre in New York, and later as the boy in Grandfather Whitehead. After serving as a clerk in commercial houses, he returned to the stage permanently in 1878, with George Ringold in Shakepeare's Henry V. He played various roles in New York, Philadelphia, and San Francisco. He starred with his brother, E. M. Holland, in The Social Highwayman, under management of Richard Mansfield, and starred alone in The Mysterious Mr. Bugle. He retired in 1904. Mason. d. Sept. 25, 1926.

Louis E. Holland Business executive and association president. b. June 20, 1878 in Parma, N.Y. Organized Holland Engraving Co., Kansas City, Mo. in 1916; chairman of board since 1945. Served as president of the American Automobile Assn., 1949-51; National Better Business Bureau, 1926; Kansas City Chamber of Commerce, 1925-27; Associated Advertising Clubs of World, 1922-25. Member of Mt. Washington Lodge No. 614, Mt. Washington, Mo., and master in 1916. 32° AASR (SJ) in Kansas City and life member of Ararat Shrine Temple, Kansas City. DeMolay Legion of Honor.

Ray P. Holland Editor of Field and Stream, 1924-41; writer under name of "Bob White," and conservationist. b. Aug. 20, 1884 in Atchison, Kans. He was educated in the public schools of that city. Began writing for sportsmen's magazines in 1903, and since has contributed hundreds of articles, writing under the name, "Bob White." He joined the staff of the U.S. Bureau of Biology in 1914, and was district enforcement inspector of federal migratory bird legislation. The test case of State of Mo. vs Ray P. Holland was carried to the supreme court of the U.S.; it settled the question of jurisdiction of the federal government over wild game. He is the author of *My Gun Dogs; Nip and Tuck; Shotgunning in the Uplands; Shot-gunning in the Lowlands; My Dog Lemon; Goodshot; The Master; But Listen, Warden; Bird Dogs; Scatter-gunning.* Member of Washington Lodge No. 5, Atchison, Kans. since about 1905.

Spessard L. Holland U.S. Senator and Governor of Florida. b. July 10, 1892 at Bartow, Fla. Graduate of Emory Coll. (now Emory U.) in 1912. He taught from 1912-16 in Warrentown, Ga., and U. of Florida; he was admitted to the bar in 1916, practicing in Bartow. He served as governor of Florida from 1941-45, was appointed to the U.S. senate in 1946, and elected in 1946, and each term since that time. He served with the 24th Squadron, Air Corps, in France in WWI, and was awarded the DSC in 1918. A member of Tuscan Lodge No. 6, Bartow, Fla., he is a 32° AASR, receiving the KCCH in 1957; Shriner.

John H. Holliday (1846-1921) Founder and president of Indianapolis News. b. May 31, 1846 in Indianapolis. Graduate of Hanover Coll. He served in the 137th Ind. Volunteers in the Civil War. In 1869 he founded the newspaper and was editor until 1892. In 1899 he founded the Indianapolis Press with Wm. J. Richards, which was consolidated with the News in 1901. He also founded and headed the Union Trust Co. in 1893. Member of Mystic Tie Lodge No. 398, Indianapolis, Ind. d. Oct. 20, 1921.

Ernest F. Hollings Governor of South Carolina since 1958. b. Jan. 1, 1922 in Charleston, S. Car. Graduate of The Citadel in 1942 and U. of South Carolina in 1947. Admitted to the bar in 1947. Member of state house of representatives, 1948-54 and speaker pro tern, 1950-54. Lieutenant governor of S. Car., 1954-58; governor from 1958. A member of La Candeur Lodge No. 36 of Charleston, he was made a life member of the lodge on Dec. 16, 1959.

Victor S. Holm (1876-1935) Sculptor. b. Dec. 6, 1876 in Copenhagen, Denmark; came to America in 1890. He was a pupil of Lorado Taft, and studied at the Art Institute of Chicago, and in New York. He was an instructor of sculpture and lecturer on the history of art at the St. Louis School of Fine Arts (Washington U.) from 1909. His principal works include the Missouri State monument at Vicksburg, Miss.; in St. Louis are to be found the Halsey C. Ives Memorial, Barnes Memorial, The Crucifixion and the Papal Trophy in St. Pius Church, Washington U. War Memorial, Musicians' Memorial Fountain in Forest Park, Emile Zola Memorial, Dr. Beaumont Memorial, and a statue of Washington for the St. Louis Masonic Temple. Member of Clayton Lodge No. 601, Clayton, Mo., receiving degrees on Nov. 17, Dec. 21, 1922 and Feb. 17, 1923. d. Nov. 11, 1935.

Rufus C. Holman U.S. Senator from Oregon, 1939-45. b. in Portland, Oreg. Began as a farmer, and engaged successively in teaching, steamboating, bookkeeping and accounting. Active in the paper industry and many civic activities. Received his degrees in Willamette Lodge No. 2, Portland, Oreg. on Dec. 11, 1911, Jan. 15 and May 13, 1912; 32° AASR in Portland and potentate of Al Kadar Shrine Temple in 1934.

William H. Holman President of Jitney Jungle Stores, Inc. (a chain of 224 grocery stores in ten states). b. Sept. 19, 1889 in Hemingway, Miss. Started with brother in grocery business in Jackson, Miss. in 1911, and with brother and cousin, began chain of cash and delivery stores in 1917, and later the first self-service stores, called Jitney Jungle, in 1919. Mason and Shriner.

Randle Holme (1627-1699) The third of a line of five heraldic painters of Cheshire, England, who bore this name. He was the author of The Academie of Armory (1688). In that work are several references to the pre-grand lodge Freemasonry, which are of historical interest. One, for instance, states: "I cannot but Honor the Fellowship of the Masons because of its Antiquity; and the more as being a Member of that Society, called Free-Masons." He belonged to the old Chester Lodge, which seems to have been in the process of transition from operative to speculative at that time. A list of its members is found in a fragment of the Harleian MS.

Gabriel Holmes (1769-1829) Governor of North Carolina three terms, 1821-1824. b. in 1769 in the colony of North Car., in what is now Sampson Co. He was educated under a clergyman in Iredell Co., N.C., and studied at Harvard; being admitted to the bar, he practiced in Clinton, N.C. He was a member of the state legislature from 1793-1813, and in 1821 that body elected him governor. At the close of his term he was chosen a member of congress and served from 1825-29. A member of Saint Tammany Lodge No. 30, Wilmington, his initiation dates are unknown. The only recorded proof of his membership is that he was a visitor in St. John's Lodge No. 1, Jan. 20, 1817. d. Sept. 26, 1829.

Guy E. Holmes (1873-1945) Composer and musician. b. Feb. 14, 1873 at Baraboo, Wis. Studied music under private teachers. He was a former flute soloist with Weldon's Band, and director of the Ben Hur Band; teacher of harmony and instrumentation, Prior's Conservatory, Danville, Ill., and arranger with Vogel's Minstrels. He wrote over 200 military marches and overtures for band and orchestra, and many songs and characteristic pieces. His March Courageous was dedicated to the United Nations of WWII. Mason. Member of Olive Branch Lodge No. 38, Danville, Ill. d. Feb. 10, 1945.

John Holmes (1773-1843) U.S. Senator from Maine, 1820-33. b. March 14, 1773 in Kingston, Mass. He was graduated from Brown in 1796, studied law, and was admitted to the bar in 1799, settling in Alfred, Maine. While Maine was still a part of Mass. he served in the house of representatives (1802-03) and senate, 1813-17. In 1817 he was a U.S. congressman, until Maine was admitted as a state. He was a member of the convention to form the first state constitution. A Mason, he delivered an address at Dover, N.H., Oct. 23, 1817, at the installation of Stafford Lodge, and another address at Somersworth, Great Falls, June 24, 1829, before the N.H. lodges. He was buried Masonically. d. July 7, 1843.

Leslie A. Holmes President of Northern Illinois State Teachers College (DeKalb) since 1948. b. Dec. 19, 1902 at Freeport, Ill. Graduate of U. of Illinois. Worked as a geologist for Kelly Oil Co., taught high school in Argo, Ill., and was dean of men at Dodd-Harris Jr. Coll., Chicago. Later he taught geology at Illinois State Normal, and was assistant to the president from 1943-48. Member of Excelsior Lodge No. 97 at Freeport, Ill.

Pehr G. Holmes (1881-1952) U.S. Congressman, 72nd to 80th Congresses (1931-47) from 4th Mass. dist. b. April 9, 1881 in Sweden, coming to U.S. in 1886. Organizer, in 1909, and owner of the Holmes Electrotype Foundry. Director of several banks; mayor of Worcester, Mass.; ex-president of Mass. Highway Association. Member of Athelstan Lodge, Worcester, Mass., receiving degrees on Sept. 3, Nov. 12, 1913, and Jan. 14, 1914. Member of Chapter, council and commandery at Worcester and 32° AASR (NJ) at Boston. Also member of Aleppo Shrine Temple and Aletheia Grotto.

Prince of Holstein-Gottorp (see under George Ludwig).

Elmer W. Holt Former Governor of Montana. Member of Yellowstone Lodge No. 26, Miles City, Mont., and Al Bedoo Temple, Mystic Shrine, Billings, Mont.

Homer A. Holt Governor of West Virginia, 1937-41. b. March 1, 1898 at Lewisburg, W.Va. Graduate of Washington and Lee U. in 1918 and 1923. He joined the university staff in 1920, as math instructor; in 1925 entered law practice in Fayetteville. From 1933-37, he was attorney general of the state. Following his term as governor, he resumed law practice at Charleston. He is vice president of Union Carbide and Carbon Corp., New York, and general counsel since 1947; also a director of Acacia Mutual Life Insurance Co. since 1941. Received his degrees in Greenbrier Lodge No. 42, Lewisburg, W.Va. in 1920-21 and 32° AASR in Charleston, W.Va. on April 28, 1938. Member of Beni Kedem Shrine Temple, Charleston.

Ivan Lee Holt Methodist Bishop, 1938-44, and Bishop in charge of Methodist conferences in Missouri from 1944. b. Jan. 9, 1886 in DeWitt, Arkansas. Graduate of Vanderbilt and U. of Chicago. Traveled and studied in Europe, and has received honorary degrees from many

institutions. Ordained minister in Methodist Episcopal Church, South, in 1909; held pastorates in St. Louis and Cape Girardeau, Mo. He taught four years in Southern Methodist U. at Dallas, Tex., and returned to St. Louis as pastor of St. John's Church from 1918-38, being ordained a bishop on the latter date. Active in national Jrid international church affairs, he was at one time president of the Federal Council of Churches of Christ in America. Member of Tuscan Lodge No. 360, St. Louis, and 33° AASR (SJ) in St. Louis. He is a past grand chaplain of the Grand Lodge of Missouri and gave the dedicatory address at the St. Louis Masonic Temple. He received his degrees in Cape Girardeau, Mo. being raised in 1916. Member of Hella Shrine Temple, Dallas, Tex.

Thomas M. Holt (1831-1896) Governor of North Carolina 1891-93. b. July 15, 1831 in Orange Co., N.C. He received his degrees in Alamance Lodge No. 133, Graham, N.C. in 1863, and served as junior warden in 1865. In 1878 this lodge became inactive, and in 1898 it was reconstituted as Thomas M. Holt Lodge No. 492, in honor of the former governor. He was a member of Graham Chapter No. 28, R.A.M. of Graham, and served as master of the third veil for three years. d. April 11, 1896; did not have a Masonic funeral.

Francis W. Honeycutt (1883-1940) National fencing champion and Brigadier General, U.S. Army. b. May 26, 1883 in San Francisco, Calif. Was a graduate of U.S. Military Academy in 1904, and advanced through grades to brigadier general in 1938. Was with the field artillery of the A.E.F. in WWI. He was intercollegiate fencing champion in 1903-04, and captain of the American

Olympic Fencing Team at Antwerp in 1920; national foil champion in 1921, and captain of the American team vs. the British in 1921 and 1923. Mason. d. Sept 20, 1940.

Saint John Honeywood (1763-1798) American poet and lawyer. b. Feb. 7, 1763 in Leicester, Mass. His father, an English physician, who had settled in Leicester, Mass., was killed at Ticonderoga in 1776, while a surgeon in the Army. His son was left destitute, but was educated by friends, and was a Yale graduate of 1782. He taught in an academy in Schenectady, N.Y. in 1783-84, after which he studied law in Albany, and practiced in Salem, N.Y. He was one of the presidential electors that chose John Adams as the successor to Washington. His poems, which centered around political topics such as the refusal of Washington to serve a third term and Shays' rebellion, were published after his death. Member of St. George's Lodge No. 6, Schenectady, N.Y., receiving his degrees, Sept. 13, Oct. 4, and Oct. 15, 1783. He later be-came No. 238 on the roll of Union Lodge at Albany (Now Mt. Vernon No. 3). d. Sept. 1, 1798.

John H. Honour (1802-1885) Sixth grand commander of Supreme Council AASR, Southern Jurisdiction, 1846-58. b. Dec. 20, 1802 in Charleston, S.C. He founded the Methodist Episcopal Church in Charleston about 1834, and was ordained to the ministry in 1836. He became president of the Charleston Insurance and Trust Co., in 1846. He later became a member of the Lutheran Church, and was president of the Lutheran Synod for a year. He edited the Lutheran Visitor. He was initiated Nov. 2, 1824 in Orange Lodge No. 14, Charleston, served as master in 1826 and 1850-

52, and was an honorary member of Strict Observance Lodge No. 73 in 1851. He was recording grand secretary of the Grand Lodge of South Carolina from 1837-41; grand treasurer, 1842-62. He served as high priest of both Carolina and Zerubbabel Chapters, and was grand high priest of the Grand Chapter of South Carolina, R.A.M. in 1843-53; Knighted in 1841 in South Carolina Encampment No. 1, he was commander in 1844-45. When he resigned as grand commander of the Southern Jurisdiction, he was appointed treasurer general. d. Nov. 26, 1885.

Clifford F. Hood President of U.S. Steel Corp., 1953-56 and present chairman of executive committee. b. Feb. 8, 1894 at Monmouth, Ill. Graduate of U. of Illinois in 1915. He associated himself with the American Steel & Wire. Co. in 1917, and with the exception of military service in WWI, was with the company until he became president in 1938. In 1949 he became president of the Carnegie-Illinois Steel Corp., and executive vice president of U.S. Steel in 1951. Mason.

Charles R. Hook President of Armco Steel Corp., 1930-48, and chairman of board since that date. b. July 12, 1880 in Cincinnati, Ohio. Started as office boy in Cincinnati Rolling Mill & Tin Plate Co. in 1889, and has been with Armco Steel Corp. since 1902, working his way up from night superintendent. Received degrees in Jonesboro Lodge No. 109, Jonesboro, Ind., on July 29, Aug. 29, and Sept. 23, 1901, affiliating with Jefferson Lodge No. 90, Middletown, Ohio on Feb. 3, 1908.

Theodore E. Hook (1788-1841) English humorist and novelist.

He edited John Bull in 1820 and New Monthly Magazine from 1836-41. He wrote under several pseudonyms such as Richard Jones, Mrs. Ramsbottom, and Vicesimus Blenkinsop. His books included Maxwell; Gilbert Gurney; Jack Grag; Exchange No Robbery; and others. Several references to Masonry are found in his works. His own lodge is not known, but he was a visitor at Royal Somerset House and Inverness Lodge No. 4, London, March 8, 1813. His apron is in the Grand Lodge of England Museum.

Ben W. Hooper Governor of Tenn. Member of Newport Lodge No. 234, Newport, Tenn.

Frank A. Hooper Federal judge, Northern District of Georgia since 1949. b. April 21, 1895 at Americus, Ga. Admitted to Georgia bar in 1916. In private practice at Atlanta from 1919-43. He has served on the court of appeals and superior court. He was an ensign in the U.S. Naval reserve in WWI. Member of Malta Lodge No. 641, Atlanta, Ga. receiving degrees on June 11, June 25 and Aug. 13, 1919. 32° AASR (SJ) and Shriner.

Robert L. Hooper, Jr. (1709-1785) Deputy Quartermaster General in American Revolution (1778). b. in 1709, his father was chief justice of N.J. from 1724-28. Robert, Jr. was a member of the first committee of nine on July 19, 1782, and delivered an ad-dress to "prevent trade and intercourse with the enemy." He was county clerk of Somerset Co. from 1765-74. He was initiated in Lodge No. 2 at Philadelphia, but after the formation of the Grand Lodge of N.J., he affiliated with Trenton Lodge No. 5; was its first senior warden, and the first deputy grand master of the

Grand Lodge of N.J. d. April 25, 1785.

William Hooper (1742-1790) Signer of the Declaration of Independence. b. June 17, 1742 in Boston, Mass. A graduate of Harvard in 1760, he studied law under James Otis, and in 1767 settled in Wilmington, N.C. He represented Wilmington in the general assembly of 1773, and in 1774 was elected to the Continental Congress and placed on two important committees. He lived at Masonboro, N.C. (about eight miles from Wilmington), until the British occupied the area. He returned in Nov., 1781, but shortly afterward moved to Hillsboro. He was a member of Hanover Lodge at Masonboro, which ceased to exist in 1787. d. Oct., 1790.

Frank G. Hoover (1883-1954) President of the Hoover Co. (vacuum cleaners) from 1948. b. April 4, 1883 in New Berlin, Ohio. Educated in Oberlin Coll. and Ohio State U. He was with the Hoover company from 1904. He was vice president of the National Boy Scout Council. Member of William McKinley Lodge No. 431, Canton, Ohio and 33° AASR (NJ). d. Dec. 3, 1954.

Gilbert C. Hoover Rear Admiral, U.S. Navy, retired. b. July 25, 1894 at Columbus, Ohio. Graduate of U.S. Naval Academy in 1916, and advanced through grades to rear admiral in 1947. In WWI he served with the British Grand Fleet and on the U.S.S. Wyoming. In 1929-30 he was naval aide at the White House under Pres. Hoover. In WWII he commanded a destroyer division in the battles of Coral Sea and Midway, and the U.S.S. Helena in the battles of Cape Esperance and Guadalcanal. He retired in 1947. Received degrees in Overseas Lodge No. 40, Providence, RI. and now affiliated with St. Albans Lodge No. 6, Bristol, R.I. Received 32° AASR in Denver, Colo. and presently member of Scottish Rite in Providence, R.I. Member of Narragansett Bay Chapter No. 14, National Sojourners.

Hubert D. Hoover Brigadier General, U.S. Army. b. Oct. 15, 1887 at Bedford, Ia. Graduate of U. of California in 1909 and 1911. He entered the Army as a reserve officer in 1917, and was commissioned captain in the regular Army in 1920, advancing through grades to brigadier general in 1947. He was with the Judge Advocate General's Dept. Mason.

J. Edgar Hoover Director of Federal Bureau of Investigation since 1924. b. Jan. 4, 1895 in Washington, D.C. He was graduated from George Washington U. in 1916, and 1917, and holds honorary degrees from many other institutions. He entered the Department of Justice in 1917, and from 1919-21 was special assistant to the attorney general of the U.S. From 1921-24 he was assistant director of the FBI. He became a member of Federal Lodge No. 1, Washington, D.C., Nov. 9, 1920, and is a charter member of Justice Lodge No. 46 (Dec. 15, 1926). He was exalted in Lafayette Chapter No. 5, R.A.M., and knighted in Washington Commandery No. 1, K.T., both of the District of Columbia. He received the Scottish Rite degrees (SJ), and is a 33°, honorary. He belongs to Almas Shrine Temple of the district, and is an active member of the grand council, Order of DeMolay. On May 2, 1950, he received the Grand Lodge of New York's Achievement Award, and in 1954 was awarded the gold medal of the General Grand Chapter, Royal Arch Masons. d. May 2, 1972.

Clifford R. Hope U.S. Congressman to 70th through 84th Congresses (1927-56) from 5th and 7th Kans. districts. b. June 9, 1893 at Birmingham, Ia. Was graduated from Washburn Law School (Kans.) in 1917, and began law practice at Garden City, Kans. He was a member of the state house of representatives from 1921-27, and was speaker of the house, 1925-27. He served in WWI as a lieutenant in the 35th and 85th divisions overseas. He was a member of the U.S. delegation to the Inter-parliamentary Union meeting in Stockholm in 1949, and Istanbul in 1951. Member of Tyrian Lodge No. 246, Garden City, Kansas, since about 1925; 32° AASR (SJ) at Wichita; Midian Shrine Temple at Wichita and Cyrus Grotto at Hutchinson, Kans.

Albert J. Hopkins (1846-1922) U.S. Senator from Illinois, 1903-09. b. Aug. 15, 1846 in DeKalb Co., Ill. Graduate of Hillsdale Coll. (Mich.) in 1870. Admitted to the bar in 1871, he practiced at Aurora, Ill. He was a U.S. congressman to 49th through 57th congresses (1885-1903). He later practiced law in Chicago. He was a member of Aurora Lodge No. 254, Aurora, Ill. d. Aug. 23, 1922.

Fred M. Hopkins (1875-1954) Newspaper editor, owner. b. July 12, 1875 at Epworth, Iowa. Graduate in law of U. of Iowa in 1895. Practiced law at Dubuque, Ia., 1895-1903, and was later a federal court reporter at Toledo, Ohio. He became editor of the Toledo Blade, and then the Toledo Times. From 1913-43 he was editor and publisher of the Fostoria Daily Review (Ohio); in 1943 he purchased the Fostoria Daily Times and combined it with the Review. Served as mayor, and postmaster of

Fostoria. Member of Fostoria Lodge No. 288, Fostoria, Ohio, receiving degrees on April 17, May 21 and June 11, 1918. 32° AASR (NJ) d. Dec. 15, 1954.

James H. Hopkins (1832-1904) U.S. Congressman from Pa. 1875-77 and 1883-85. b. Nov. 3, 1832 in Washington, Pa. He was the 10th Grand Master of the Grand Encampment, K.T. of the U.S. in 1874-77. Member of Franklin Lodge No. 221, Pittsburgh, Pa., receiving degrees on Oct. 21, Nov. 6 and Dec. 4, 1856; exalted in Zerubbabel Chapter No. 162, R.A.M. of Pittsburgh, Oct. 2, 1860; 33° AASR (NJ), Sept. 19, 1872. d. June 18, 1904.

Jay Paul Hopkins Brigadier General, U.S. Army, who was chief of the anti-aircraft service in 1918. b. Nov. 2, 1875 at Mattawan, Mich. Was graduated from U.S. Military Academy in 1900, and advanced through grades to brigadier general, retiring in 1940 to become president of First National Bank of Cassopolis, Mich. Member of Backus Lodge No. 55, Cassopolis, Mich., receiving degrees on July 6, July 20, Aug. 3, 1903. Became life member on Nov. 10, 1947.

John Henry Hopkins (1792-1868) Protestant Episcopal Bishop. b. Jan. 30, 1792 in Dublin, Ireland. Came to U.S. with parents in 1801. Entered the iron business in western Pa., first at Bassenheim, near Economy, and later in Ligonier Valley. After the War in 1812, he studied law and was admitted to the bar in Pittsburgh in 1818. Taking up the ministry, he became a deacon and priest in 1823-24. He served seven years in churches of Western Pa., and in 1826 would have been elected assistant bishop, but for his refusal to vote for himself. He went to Boston as a min-

ister in 1831, and in 1832 was elected first bishop of Vermont. He was rector of St. Paul's Church, Vermont for 27 years, and established the Vermont Episcopal Inst. He was a talented painter in oil and water color, and a voluminous author. Member of Ohio Lodge No. 113, Pittsburgh, receiving degrees on Feb. 11 and April 8, 1818. d. Jan. 9, 1868.

John J. Hopkins (1893-1957) President and chairman of board of General Dynamics Corp. b. Oct. 15, 1893 at Santa Ana, Calif. Graduate of U. of California, and Harvard. Practicedlaw in New York City. Was special assistant to Ogden L. Mills, secy. of Treasury in 1932-33. Was managing director of Canadair Ltd., and director of other corporations. Enlisted as a seaman in WWI, and later commissioned as an ensign in U.S. Naval reserve. He was founder and president of the International Golf Assn. Member of Kane Lodge No. 454, New York City, receiving degrees on Feb. 5, 19 and March 4, 1924. 32° AASR (NJ) and Knight Templar. d. May 3, 1957.

Richard J. Hopkins (1873-1943) Federal Judge, Kansas, 1929-43. b. April 4, 1873 in Jefferson City, Mo. Graduate of U. of Kansas and Northwestern U. He began practice of law in Chicago in 1901, and later, with his father, in Garden City, Kans. (1906). He was a member of the lower house in 1909, attorney general of the state from 1919-23; and associate justice of supreme court of Kansas from 1923-29. Member of Tyrian Lodge No. 246, Garden City, Kans., Knight Templar, 32° AASR (SJ) and Shriner. d. Aug. 28, 1943.

Samuel Hopkins (1750-1819) Pioneer, soldier and U.S. Congressman. b. about 1750 in Albemarle Co., Va. He was an officer in the Continental Army of the American Revolution, and fought with distinction at Princeton, Trenton, Monmouth, and Brandywine. His battalion of light infantry was nearly annihilated at the battle of Germantown. He was an officer of the 10th Virginia regt. at the siege of Charleston, and on the death of Col. Richard Parker, became its colonel. He was made a prisoner at the surrender of Charleston, May 20, 1780. In 1798 he settled on Green River in Kentucky, and served several times in the state legislature. During the War of 1812 he led several large groups of volunteers against the Indians on the Illinois and Wabash rivers. He was called "general," but the title was probably honorary. He served in congress from Ky. in 1813-15, but after one term, retired to his farm in Hopkins Co., Ky., which was named in his honor. He was a member of Jerusalem Lodge No. 9 of Henderson, Ky. d. in Oct., 1819.

Francis Hopkinson (1737-1791) Signer of the Declaration of Independence. b. Sept. 21, 1737, the son of Thomas Hopkinson, q.v., who was grand master of the Grand Lodge of Pennsylvania in 1736. Although no proof of Francis' membership can be found, he is often referred to as a Freemason. d. May 9, 1791.

Thomas Hopkinson (1709-1751) Lawyer and scientist who was the father of Francis Hopkinson, Declaration of Independence signer. b. April 6, 1709 in London, England. He was the son of a London merchant. He studied law; emigrated to Pennsylvania in 1731, where he was deputy clerk of the orphans' court, and later, clerk. He became prothonotary of Philadelphia Co., and judge of the admiralty. He participated in all the public enterprises of the time, and was one of the incorporators of the library company and original trustee of the College of Philadelphia. He was first president of the Philosophical Society, and his attainments in natural philosophy were recognized by Benjamin Franklin, who said: "The power of points to throw off the electrical fire was first communicated to me by my ingenious friend, Mr. Thomas Hopkinson." He was a member of St. John's Lodge, Philadelphia, and served as grand master of the Grand Lodge of Pennsylvania in 1736. d. Nov. 5, 1751.

Russell J. Hopley (1895-1949) President of Northwestern Bell Telephone Co., 1942-49. b. April 28, 1895 at Blue Island, Ill. He was associated with the telephone company as a collector in 1915, at Fort Madison, Ia., and became manager at offices in McGregor, Waterloo, and Des Moines, Iowa. He became district manager at Des Moines in 1925; supervisor at Omaha, Nebr. in 1929; and general manager of Nebr. and S.D. in 1937. Served in WWI with the A.E.F., and in WWII as civilian advisor for army air service. Member of Claypoole Lodge No. 13, Fort Madison, Iowa, receiving degrees on June 2, 23, 30, 1916. Was 32° AASR (SJ), Shriner and Jester. d. Nov. 23, 1949.

DeWolf Hopper (1858-1935) Comedian. b. March 30, 1858 in New York City. He was noted for his recitation of Casey at the Bat on the nation's stages, making both himself and the poem famous. His debut was in *Our Boys* in 1879. He was later with Frohman's Madison Square Company, and McCaull Opera Co. He starred in comedy rolls at the head of his own company, and was later with Weber & Fields, q.v. Back with his own company, he starred in

Wang; Happyland, The Matinee Idol; Pinafore; Patience; The Pirates of Penzance; The Mikado; Iolanthe; The Better 'Ole; Ermine, etc. He lectured and was on concert tour in 1930-31, and was author of *Once a Clown, Always a Clown.* He was raised in Pacific Lodge No. 233, New York City, in 1890; was 32° AASR (NJ), and member of Mecca Shrine Temple, New York City. d. Sept. 23, 1935.

Herbert G. Hopwood Admiral, U.S. Navy and present commander-in-chief of U.S. Pacific fleet. b. Nov. 23, 1898 at Mt. Carmel, Pa. Graduate of U.S. Naval Academy in 1919, advancing through grades to vice admiral in 1955. He was director of budget and reports of Navy, 1946-50; deputy comptroller of Navy, 1950-52; commander of cruiser destroyer in Pacific force, 1952; commanded First Fleet in 1955; deputy chief of naval operations (logistics) in 1956. A member of Shamokin Lodge No. 255, Shamokin, Pa. since 1920, he has two sons who are members of the same lodge.

Walter F. Horan U.S. Congressman, 78th to 80th and 83rd to 85th Congresses from 5th Wash. dist. b. Oct. 15, 1898 at Wenatchee, Wash. Graduate of Washington State Coll., 1925. He is an orchardist. He served in the U.S. Navy in WWI. Mason.

Alexander J. Horlick (1873-1950) President of Horlick's Malted Milk Corp. b. Oct. 3, 1873 in Racine, Wis. He was associated with Horlick's Co. from 1893, later serving as president, and chairman of the board. Member of Belle City Lodge No. 92, Racine, Wisc. and 32° AASR (NJ). d. June 6, 1950.

T. Newell Horn (1868-1923) Brigadier General, U.S. Army. b. Jan. 18, 1868 in Brooklyn, N.Y. Graduate of U.S. Military Academy in 1891, advancing through grades to brigadier general in 1918. He commanded the 7th Field Artillery of the 7th Division during WWI. Mason. d. May 5, 1923.

Donald W. Hornbeck Business executive; secretary and director of the Cleveland (Indians) Baseball Co. since 1949. b. Jan. 16, 1903 in London, Ohio. Graduate of Ohio State U. in 1926, and admitted to the bar in 1926, practicing in Cleveland. He is chairman of the board of Allen Electric Co.; chairman of executive committee, and director of Chicago & Eastern Ill. R.R. Co.; secretary of Midland Steamship Line; and director of a number of corporations. Member of Chandler Lodge No. 138, London, Ohio, receiving degrees on June 19, July 28 and Oct. 7, 1925. 32° AASR (NJ), Jester and Shriner.

Stanley K. Hornbeck Educator, diplomatic advisor, and U.S. Ambassador to the Netherlands, 1944-47. b. May 4, 1883 in Franklin, Mass. Graduate of U. of Denver in 1903; Rhodes scholar at Oxford in 1904-07; B.A. in 1907; Ph.D., U. of Wisconsin in 1911. A political science expert, he has taught at Harvard, U. of Wisconsin, U. of Michigan, Williamstown Inst., Institute of Pacific Relations, and Lowell Inst. He was a member of the American mission to Armenia in 1919, and has acted as special advisor to department of State on many occasions. Member of Albert Pike Lodge No. 36, Washington, D.C., since 1922.

Henry Horner (1878-1940) Governor of Illinois, 1933-41, dying in office. b. Nov. 30, 1878 in Chicago.

Graduate of Chicago-Kent Coll. of Law in 1898, and received honorary degrees from many institutions. He began law practice in Chicago in 1899. From 1914-33 he was probate judge of Cook Co., Ill. He was raised in Chicago Lodge No. 437, Oct. 3, 1900, and was master in 1907. He was grand orator of the Grand Lodge of Illinois in 1924, and served on various committees. Received 33° AASR (NJ), Sept. 26, 1934. d. Oct. 6, 1940.

Joseph P. Horner (1837-1893) Lawyer; General Grand High Priest of General Grand Chapter, R.A.M. 1891-93. b. March 18, 1837 in New City. He was reared in New Orleans, La. When his mother died, he lived with an aunt in Philadelphia where he attended school. First apprenticed in a machine shop, he turned to law and had a lucrative practice in New Orleans. Served in Confederate Army in Civil War as a private in Fenner's Battery. Raised in Marion Lodge No. 68, New Orleans, June 14, 1860, he served as its master for many years, and was reelected for the last time while on his death bed. He was grand master of the grand lodge of Louisiana in 1886. Exalted in Orleans Chapter No. 1, R.A.M., he was grand high priest in 1873; member of Louisiana Council No. 1, R. & S.M., he was grand master in 1871; knighted in Orleans Commandery No. 3, he was grand commander in 1869, '70, '74, and grand standard bearer of Grand Encampment of U.S. in 1874-77. d. Jan. 24, 1893.

Odus C. Homey (1866-1957) Brigadier General, U.S. Army, who designed and developed the famous Springfield rifle. b. Sept. 18, 1866 in Lexington, Ill. Graduate of U.S. Military Academy in 1891. From 1894-1930 he was with the ordnance department retiring in the latter year. In addition to the famous caliber 30 rifle, he pioneered the 16 inch rifle in the U.S., and built and put into operation the pioneer Army Smokeless Powder Plant. Received degrees in Alamo Lodge No. 44, San Antonio, Texas, Aug. 12, Sept. 20, Oct. 20, 1921, affiliating with Mechanicsburg Lodge No. 113, Mechanicsburg, Ohio on Feb. 7, 1922. Received 32° AASR (NJ) at Philadelphia on Nov. 18, 1922, and member of Lu Lu Shrine Temple of Philadelphia. d. Feb. 16, 1957.

Rogers Hornsby One of the original members of the Baseball Hall of Fame at Cooperstown, N.Y. b. April 27, 1896 in Fort Worth, Texas. Nicknamed "Rajah," he was baseman for the St. Louis National League club from 1915 to 1933, with the exception of 1927-32, when he played for the New York, Boston, and Chicago National League teams. From 1933-37 he was manager-player with the American League team in St. Louis. He was the National League batting champion for seven years (1920-25 and 1928). His lifetime batting average of .358 was the highest in the National League history, placing him second to Ty Cobb's q.v., lifetime average of .367. In 1926 he managed the Cardinals of St. Louis to the world championship, and was named the most valuable player in 1925 and 1929. He was raised in Beacon Lodge No. 3, St. Louis, Mo., Aug. 16, 1918; exalted in Bellefontaine Chapter No. 25, R.A.M., Feb. 27, 1922; knighted in Ivanhoe Commandery No. 8, May 15, 1922.

Samuel Horowitz Installed master of a lodge on his deathbed. By special dispensation of the grand master of the Grand Lodge of California, Horowitz was able to realize one of the ambitions of his life on his deathbed. He was elected master of Ionic Lodge No. 520, Los Angeles, but was taken sick before the installation occurred. He was installed master in a hospital at 11:00 a.m., and died at 6:00 p.m. the same day.

Harry M. Hosier Vice president of Corning Glass Works, 1943-54. b. May 21, 1886 at Corning, N.Y. He began with Corning Glass in 1905, as a machinist and die maker, advancing as development engineer, production superintendent, factory manager, production manager, and assistant to president. Now honorary vice president and advisor on industrial relations. Member of Painted Post Lodge No. 117, Corning, N.Y., receiving degrees on Feb. 20, March 5 and 19, 1912. 32° AASR (NJ) and Shriner.

John. D. C. Hoskins (1846-1937) Brigadier General, U.S. Army. b. Jan. 19, 1846 in Potosi, Mo. Graduate of U.S. Military Academy in 1868, advancing through grades to brigadier general in 1908 and retiring at own request after 44 years of service. Mason. d. March 1, 1937.

Hezekiah L. Hosmer (1814-1893) First Chief Justice of Montana, appointed by President Lincoln in 1864. b. Dec. 10, 1814 in Hudson, N.Y. He studied law in Cleveland, Ohio, and at one time was editor of the Toledo Blade. He was the author of the novel Octoroon, from which Boucicault took his play of the same name. In 1887 he published Bacon and Shakespeare in. the Sonnets. In 1861 he served as secretary of the house committee on territories in Washington, D.C. As the presidential appointee as first chief justice of the Territory of Montana, he opened the first court of record in the dining room

of a hotel in Virginia City on the first Monday of Dec., 1864. He was initiated in Wood County Lodge No. 112, Ohio, going ten miles into the woods for the degrees (the Morgan incident still causing bitterness). He was exalted in Circleville Chapter No. 20 in 1845, and knighted in Toledo Commandery No. 7, K.T. He became grand king of the Grand Chapter of Ohio, R.A.M.; grand orator of the Grand Lodge of Ohio, and then deputy grand master. In 1865 he was the first master of Montana Lodge No. 2, and for six years commander of Virginia City Commandery No. 1. He was chairman of the foreign correspondence committee of the grand lodge for several years, and grand secretary of the grand lodge in 1870-71. He later moved to Calif., and at his death had been prelate of Golden Gate Commandery No. 16, San Francisco, for thirteen years, and grand prelate of the Grand Commandery of California for ten years. d. Oct. 31, 1893.

Stephen T. Hosmer (1763-1834) Chief Justice, Supreme Court of Connecticut and first Grand High Priest of the Grand Chapter, R.A.M. of Connecticut. b. at Middletown, Conn. in 1763. He was graduated from Yale in 1782, and practiced law at Middletown from 1785. For two years he was a member of the council of state, and after the adoption of the state constitution, was chief justice of Conn. from 1815-1833. A member of St. John's Lodge No. 2, Middletown, Conn., he served as master in 1794-95; 1809-10, and 1815-16. He was high priest of Washington Chapter No. 6, R.A.M. of Middletown from 1796-1809, and again in 1811. d. Aug. 5, 1834. G.M. of Conn. for 18 years (1798-1816).

Timothy Hosmer (1745-1815) Pioneer surgeon and uncle of Stephen T. Hosmer, q.v. b. in Middletown, Conn. in 1740. Was brother of Stephen T.'s father, Titus. He was an officer in the Continental Army of the Revolution, and for two and a half years was surgeon on General Washington's staff. Was a surgeon in the 6th Conn. Regt. in the Revolution and attended and certified the death of Major John Andre, the British spy in 1780. He moved to Ontario Co., N.Y., where he established one of the first two settlements in that wilderness. In 1798 he was appointed first judge of the county. He became a member of the lodge at Waterbury, Conn. (now King Solomon No. 7 of Woodbury) sometime between 1765-1775. In 1787 he became the first senior warden of Frederick Lodge, Farmington, Conn. (now No. 14 of Plainville, Conn.) when it was organized in 1787. On Aug. 20, 1779 he became a member of the famous military lodge, American Union No. 1, signing the by-laws on that date. In 1792 he became charter master of Ontario Lodge No. 23, Canandaigua, N.Y., the oldest lodge in Ontario Co. d. in Canandaigua, N.Y. in 1820.

H. Stuart Hotchkiss (1878-1947) President of U.S. Rubber Plantations; vice president of U.S. Rubber Co.; chairman of board of General Rubber Co.; president of Cambridge Rubber Co. b. Oct. 1, 1878 in New Haven, Conn. In 1932-33 he was representative in Europe of trustee in bankruptcy of International Match Corp., and industrial advisor to Swedish liquidators of Kreuger and Toll, 1934-35. Served in A.E.F. in WWI. Mason. 32° AASR. d. Sept. 16, 1947.

Johann Jakob Hottinger (1783-1860) Swiss historian who was initiated in 1813 and became the first grand master of the Grand Lodge Alpina.

Harry Houdini (1874-1926) Magician and escape artist. b. April 6, 1874 in Appleton, Wis., the son of Rabbi Mayer S. Weiss. He took his stage name from the great French prestidigitator, Robert Houdin, and later had it legalized. He began as a trapeze performer in 1882, and made several tours of the world, performing before many rulers and notables. He was the inventor of a diving suit. In 1910 he was awarded a prize by the Australian Aeronautic League for being the first successful flier in Australia. He is the author of *The Right Way to Do Wrong; Unmasking of Robert Houdin; Miracle Mongers; Paper Prestidigitation; Rope Ties* and *Escapes; A Magician Among the Spirits*. He was a member of St. Cecile Lodge No. 568, New York City, receiving his degrees July 17, 31, and Aug. 21, 1923; became a life member Oct. 30, 1923. Member of Mecca Shrine Temple, N.Y.C. d. Oct. 31, 1926.

Jean Antoine Houdon (1740-1828) French sculptor. b. March 20, 1740 in Versailles. He studied art under Michel Ange Slodtz, and later under Pigale. While in the Ecole des Beaux Arts, at the age of 19, he took the first prize for sculpture, which involved a residence in Italy. He spent ten years in Rome at a period when the excavations of Herculaneum and Pompeii gave a new impulse to art. Here he finished the colossal statue of St. Bruno, of which Pope Clement XIV said, "He would speak, if the rule of his order did not prescribe silence." Returning to Paris, he executed many masterpieces in the next 15 years which placed him in the front rank of French sculptors, and earned his admission into the academy. In 1785 he accompanied Benjamin Franklin to the U.S. to prepare a model for the statue of George Washington, which had been ordered by the state of Virginia. He spent two weeks at Mount Vernon. The statue bears Houdon's legend "Fait par Houdon, citoyen Francais, 1788." It is now in the capitol at Richmond, Va., and there is a replica in the American Hall of Fame. Many personal friends of Washington stated that it was the best representation of him ever made. Among Houdon's later works were busts of Napoleon and Josephine, and the noted statue of Cicero in the palace of Luxembourg. After the execution of the latter work he lost his memory and was compelled to give up his profession. His bust, Voltaire Assis, is in the foyer of the Theatre Francais, Paris, and is considered one of the finest works of its kind in modern art. Among his other portrait busts are Catherine II, Turgot, Moliere, Rousseau, Buffon, d'Alembert, Franklin, Lafayette, Louis XVI, and Mirabeau. A member of the famous Lodge of the Nine Sisters at Paris, his name appears in its list of members in 1779, 1783, 1784, and 1806. He was listed on the latter date as the "imperial sculptor, member of the institute and professor." d. July 16, 1828.

Jean Pierre L. L. Houel (1735-1813) French engraver and painter. b. in Rouen about 1735. He studied in Italy. He wrote four volumes entitled Voyage Pittoresque de Sidle, de Make, et de Lipari between 1782-87. He was a member of the Lodge of the Nine Sisters at Paris, and is listed on the rolls in 1783, 1784, and 1806. d. Nov. 14, 1813.

Frederick W. Houser (1871-1942) Justice, Supreme Court of California. b. April 15, 1871 in Jones Co.,

Ia. Graduate of U. of Southern Calif. in 1899. Practiced law in Los Angeles. Served as judge of superior court, justice, and presiding justice of court of appeal, and associate justice supreme court of Calif. from 1937. Raised Dec. 2, 1899 in East Gate Lodge No. 290, Los Angeles, Calif. Knight Templar, 32° AASR (SJ) and Shriner. d. Oct. 12, 1942.

John Houston (1744-1796) Member of Continental Congress and Governor of Georgia, 1778-87. b. Aug. 31, 1744 in Waynesboro, Ga. In 1774 he was one of the four citizens who called the first meeting of the Sons of Liberty in Savannah. In 1775 and 1776 he was a member of the Continental Congress, and would have signed the Declaration of Independence, but was called to Georgia to counteract the influence of another delegate who had left his seat to oppose the movement. In 1777 he cooperated with General Robert Howe in an invasion of Eastern Florida, which failed. He was appointed judge of the state supreme court in 1792. Member of Solomon's Lodge No. 1, Savannah, Ga. d. July 20, 1796.

John M. Houston U.S. Congressman to 74th through 77th Congresses Sam Houston (1935-43) from 5th Kans. dist. b. Sept. 15, 1890 at Formosa, Kans. He spent six years as an actor, and later engaged in the retail lumber business at Newton, Kans. (1919). Member of Reno Lodge No. 140 Hutchinson, Kans., receiving degrees on April 5, May 13 and June 14, 1912. Shriner.

Robert G. Houston (1867-1946) U.S. Congressman to 69th through 72nd Congresses (1925-33) from Del. b. Oct. 13, 1867 in Milton, Del. Admitted to bar in 1888 and practiced at Georgetown, where he was also the owner and editor of the Sussex Republican from 1893. Member of Franklin Lodge No. 12, Georgetown, Del. being raised July 22, 1890. d. Jan. 29, 1946.

Sam Houston (1793-1863) American patriot and political leader who was governor of Tennessee (1827-29) ; president of the Republic of Texas (1836), and governor of Texas (1861). b. in Rockbridge Co., Va., March 2, 1793. At the death of his father, his family moved to Tenn. near the Cherokee territory and he spent his early years with the Indians, being adopted by one of them. After serving in the 39th Infantry from July, 1813 to May, 1818, he resigned and studied law at Nashville, being admitted to the bar in a few months, and practiced at Lebanon. He was elected to congress in 1823 and 1825, and in his last year fought a duel with Gen. White, whom he wounded. He was elected governor of Tenn. in 1827. He fell into disfavor in 1829, partially due to a mysterious marriage that lasted only a few weeks. Leaving the state, he made his way up the Arkansas to the mouth of the Illinois, where he lived for three years with his former Cherokee father-by-adoption. In 1832 he went to Texas where he was a member of the first convention, April 1, 1833, and was elected general of the militia. On March 2, 1836 he was a member of the convention that declared absolute independence and named him commander-in-chief of the armed forces. Following the slaughters at the Alamo and Goliad, Houston defeated the Mexicans at San Jacinto and took Santa Anna prisoner. He was elected first president of the Republic of Texas, Oct. 22, 1836, and even though his candidacy was announced only twelve days previously, he received 4,374 of the total 5,104 votes. His term expired Dec. 12, 1838. He served again as president from Dec. 12, 1841 to Dec. 9, 1844. He labored for the admission of Texas to the Union, which was accomplished Dec. 29, 1845; and in March, 1846 he was elected to the U.S. senate, serving until 1859. He was governor of Texas from 1859 to 1861, but took no part in public affairs after that date. There has been much misinformation on the religious status of this great Texas Freemason. To set the record straight, we quote from a letter written by his grandson, Temple H. Morrow, past high priest of Z. E. Coombes Chapter No. 421, R.A.M. of Dallas and 33° AASR (SJ). . . . "I am calling your attention to the last sentence in the biographical sketch concerning Sam Houston . . . this sentence reads: 'Houston died a Roman Catholic.' I have never been guilty of parading my relationship to the illustrious dead, but in order to identify myself I will state that my mother was the second child and oldest daughter of General and Mrs. Houston and I was named for the youngest member of the family. The facts concerning his church relationship are as follows. When Antonio Lopez de Santa Anna became president of Mexico, he immediately discarded the constitution of his country and assumed the role of a dictator. His unreasonable decrees and edicts worked untold hardship on the people of Texas, one of which was that no one would be allowed to become a citizen and land-owner unless he was a member of the Roman Catholic Church. General Houston was then living with his old friends, the Cherokees, in what is now Oklahoma. He decided to come to Texas and assist the patriots throw off the yoke of despotism, tyranny and oppression which Santa Anna had placed upon them. Arriving at Nacogdoches, he met an old friend, Adolphus Sterne, who told him of the edict which required every emigrant to be a member of the Catholic Church. Not to be thwarted in his intention to become a citizen of Texas, he told Mr. Sterne to get a priest and he would go through a short form ceremony necessary to become a member. This was done at the home of Mr. Sterne and only took a few minutes. If General Houston ever entered a Catholic Church, I have never heard of it. Mrs. Houston was a devout member of the Baptist Church, and I have many letters she wrote him when he was serving in the U.S. senate, urging him to become a Christian. In the year 1854, while at his home in Independence, Texas, he attended a service in the Baptist Church, and at the invitation of the minister he came forward, knelt at the altar and arose to make his profession of faith. He was baptized by Rev. Rufus C. Burleson in Rocky Creek. He became an active member of that church, thereafter lived an exemplary Christian life and died in that faith." He received his degrees in Cumberland Lodge No. 8, Nashville, Tenn., April 19, June 20, and July 22, 1817. He dimitted from Cumberland Lodge, Nov. 20, 1817, and re-affiliated June 21, 1821. It is thought that during this period he was a charter member of Nashville Lodge No. 37. He served as junior warden, and in 1824 attended grand lodge as a past master. In one place he is recorded as having dimitted from Cumberland Lodge, Jan. 20, 1831; however, he is listed in the proceedings of 1828 (p. 236) as suspended for unmasonic conduct! He affiliated with Holland Lodge No. 36 of La. in 1837, and this became Holland Lodge No. 1 of Texas. On Dec. 20, 1837 he presided over the meeting which established the Grand Lodge of Texas. He dimitted from Holland Lodge July 14, 1842, and was next reported as a member of

Forest Lodge No. 19, Huntsville, Texas, in 1851. He was undoubtedly a Royal Arch Mason, for he was knighted in Washington Commandery No. 1, Washington D.C., Feb. 23, 1853. He is recorded as a visitor to the Grand Lodge of Kentucky in 1825 and the Grand Lodge of Alabama, Dec. 6, 1849. He was present at the dedication of Washington-Centennial Lodge No. 14, Washington, D.C. on Jan. 13, 1853. d. July 1, 1863.

William Houstoun Delegate to Continental Congress in 1784 and 1787, and member of the convention that framed the Federal Constitution. He refused, however, to sign that document. Member of Solomon's Lodge No. 1 Savannah, Ga.

Walter Hoving Corporation executive. b. Dec. 2, 1897 in Stockholm, Sweden. Brought to the U.S. by parents in 1903, he was graduated from Brown U. in 1920. He was with R. H. Macy & Co., New York City from 1924-32, being vice president, 1928-32; from 1932-36 he was vice president of Montgomery Ward & Co., and a member of the board from 1934-36. He was president of Lord & Taylor, New York City, 1936-45; and since 1946 has been president of Roving Corp. He was chairman of the organizing committee to form the U.S.O., and was president of same in 1940, and chairman of board in 1941. Raised in Holland Lodge No. 8, N.Y.C. in 1931 and member of AASR (NJ) in Brooklyn, N.Y.

Benjamin Chew Howard (1791-1872) Officer in War of 1812; congressman. b. Nov. 5, 1791 in Baltimore Co., Md. He was graduated from Princeton in 1809, studied law, and practiced in Baltimore. In 1814 he assisted in organizing troops for the defense of Baltimore, and commanded the "mechanical volunteers" at the battle of North Point, Sept. 12, 1814. He served in the U.S. congress from 1829-33, and 1835-39. He was chairman of the committee on foreign relations in his last term, and as such drew up its report on the boundary question. From 1843-62 he was reporter of the U.S. supreme court. In 1861 he was a delegate to the peace congress. He became a member of Cassia Lodge No. 45, Baltimore, in April, 1813, and became master shortly after that. In 1815-18 he was grand secretary of the Grand Lodge of Maryland, and served as grand master from 1824-41. Son of John E., q.v., and Margaret Chew. d. March 6, 1872.

Charles Howard (see under Baron of Effingham).

Harvey J. Howard A founder of Acacia Fraternity. b. Jan. 30, 1880 in Churchville, N.Y. He was a graduate of the U. of Michigan (1904) ; U. of Pennsylvania (1908); Harvard (1917); and U. of Colorado (1918). He was internationally known as an ophthalmologist (diseases of the eye). During WWI, as a captain in the Medical Corps, he devised the important depth perception test for flying personnel, which has been continuously used since 1919. He was head of the ophthalmology dept. of the U. Medical School, Canton, China, for six years, and Fellow of the China Medical Board of Rockefeller Foundation at Harvard, 1916-18; and at U. of Vienna in 1923-24, where he engaged in important scientific research. In 1919 he returned to China as professor in Peking Union Medical Coll., and was eye physician to the Boy Emperor, Pu Yi, from 1921-25. From 1927-33 he was head of the ophthalmology dept. at Washington U. School of Medicine in St. Louis,

and in private practice in St. Louis from 1933. In 1925 he was captured by Chinese bandits and held for $100,000 ransom for ten weeks. He wrote of his experiences in Ten Weeks With Chinese Bandits. He was raised in Fraternity Lodge No. 262, Ann Arbor, Mich. He became interested in the Masonic Club and continued with it until the transfer was made to Acacia, when he served on the first chapter house committee and was first treasurer of Acacia.

John E. Howard (1752-1827) Colonel in the Revolution; Governor of Maryland, 1789-92, and U.S. Senator, 1796-1803. b. June 4, 1752 in Baltimore Co., Md. He joined the Continental Army early in the Revolution, and served under Gen. Hugh Mercer, q.v., at the Battle of White Plains (Oct. 28, 1776), as a captain. He was then a major in the 4th Maryland regiment, and was at Germantown and Monmouth. In 1780 as a lieutenant-colonel of the 5th Maryland Regiment, he fought at Camden under Gen. Horatio Gates, q.v., and later in the year, joined the army under Gen. Nathanael Greene, q.v. He saw hand-to-hand fighting in the Battle of Cowpens, Guilford Courthouse, and Eutaw Springs, being severely wounded in the latter, leading the final charge after his command was reduced to 30 men. In 1796 he declined a seat in Washington's cabinet. In anticipation of a war with France in 1798, Washington made him one of his major generals. He was a candidate for vice president in 1816. He married Margaret Chew, daughter of Chief Justice Chew. His six sons were Masons. Although no records remain, it is thought that John E. Howard was a member of. Army Lodge No. 27 of the Maryland Line, which asked for a charter, April 27, 1780, naming Gen. Mordecai Gist, q.v., as charter master. Schultz, in his History of Freemasonry in Maryland (1884) states that he had talked with older Masons who remembered Howard as a Freemason, and that his portrait at one time hung in a lodge room of the Baltimore Temple. d. Oct. 12, 1827.

Martin Howard First Chief Justice of North Carolina. Member of St. John's Lodge No. 2, New Bern, N.C.

Nathaniel L. Howard (1884-1949) President of Chicago, Great Western Railroad, 1925-29. b. March 9, 1884 in Fairfield, Ia. Was graduated from U.S. Military Academy in 1907. Began as a civil engineer for C.B. & Q.R.R. in 1907, rising to division superintendent, and general superintendent of Mo. district. He was general manager of the Chicago Union Station Co. from 1924-25, and chairman of the board, and president of the North American Car Corp. from 1930-36. A colonel in WWI, he was with the U.S. Railway Engineers. Mason, Knight Templar, and Shriner. d. May 6, 1949.

Robert S. Howard Newspaper publisher. b. Oct. 23, 1924 at Wheaton, Minn. From 1945-49 he successively published the *Wheaton* (Minn.) *Gazette*; *Madison* (S.D.) *Daily Leader*; *Highland Park* (Cal.) *News-Herald*, *The Dalles* (Oreg.) *Chronicle*; and *Pocatello* (Ida.) *State Journal*. From 1949-55 he was the general manager of the Scripps League at Seattle, and since 1949 has been president of the Logan (Utah) *Herald Journal*; *Nampa* (Ida.) *Free Press; The Dalles* (Oreg.) *Chronicle; Kalispell* (Mont.) *InterLake; Bozeman* (Mont.) *Chronicle* and *Pocatello* (Ida.) State Journal. Since 1955 he has been president and publisher of *the*

Chester Times, Inc. Served as private in AUS, 1942-43, and as second lieutenant in Air Force, 1944-45. Mason.

Roy W. Howard President of *Scripps-Howard Newspapers*, 1936-52, and chairman of executive committee since 1953. b. Jan. 1, 1883 at Gano, Ohio. He began as a reporter on *Indianapolis News* in 1902, and successively was with the *Indianapolis Star; St. Louis Post-Dispatch* and *Cincinnati Post*. He was New York correspondent for the Scripps-McRae League in 1906, and New York manager of *United Press* in 1907. He became general manager of United Press in 1912, and chairman of board of same in 1921. On same date he became chairman of board of Newspaper Enterprise Assn. and all Scripps-McRae (now Scripps-Howard) newspapers, assuming editorial direction of these properties with Robert P. Scripps in 1925. He negotiated the purchase of the *New York Telegram* in 1927; *New York World* in 1931, and *New York Sun* in 1950, which are now combined as the *New York World-Telegram* and *Sun*, of which he is editor and president. He is a Mason of 50-years standing and 33° AASR (NJ) at Indianapolis. Received 33° in 1946. Raised Jan. 18, 1904 in Mystic Tie Lodge No. 398, Indianapolis, Ind. Member of Murat Shrine Temple, Indianapolis.

Percy R. Howe (1864-1950) Originator of silver reduction treatment for infected dentine and septic roots, used extensively in Army. b. Sept. 30, 1864 in Providence, R.I. Graduate of Bates Coll. in 1887, and D.D.S. Philadelphia Dental Coll., 1890. Began practice at Auburn, Me. in 1890, moving to Lewiston in 1891, and Boston in 1898. Was instructor in pathology at Harvard Medical School, 1925-40. Fellow dental surgeon of

Royal Coll. Surgeons (England). President of American Dental Assn., 1928-29. Mason. d. Feb. 28, 1950.

Robert Howe (1732-1785) Major General of American Revolution. b. in Brunswick Co., N.C. in 1732. He lived in England two years, returning to U.S. in 1766, and was appointed a captain at Fort Johnson, N.C. under the commission of Governor Tryon. He was a member of the assembly in 1772-73, and a member of the Continental Congress that met at New Berne in Aug., 1774. In Aug., 1775 he was appointed colonel of the 2nd N.C. regiment by the colonial congress. With his troops, he drove the loyal governor, Lord Dunmore, from Virginia and was promoted to brigadier general. He joined Henry Lee in Virginia with his regiment in March, 1776. He defended the city of Charleston with his troops, and soon succeeded Gen. James Moore as chief in command of the southern department. In Oct., 1777 he was commissioned major general, and led an expedition against Fla., which ended in disaster, and he was forced to return to Savannah, Ga., but lost that city to the British. For this loss, he was court-martialed, but acquitted. When General Christopher Gadsden publicly criticized him, he challenged the latter to a duel. Gadsden fired into the air and Howe's ball grazed Gadsden's ear (Aug. 13, 1778) at Cannonsburg. They were then reconciled. Major John Andre, the famous British spy, who was hanged by the colonial forces, commemorated the affair with a humorous poem of 18 stanzas. Howe was relieved of the southern department and ordered to join Washington on the Hudson. He was in command at West Point in 1780, and in 1781 led troops to quell the mutiny in the Penn. and N.J. regiments. In May, 1785 he was appointed by congress to treat with the western Indians. Member of Hanover Lodge of Masonborough, N.C., which is now extinct.

Evan Howell U.S. Congressman to 77th through 80th Congresses (1941-49) from 21st Ill. dist. b. Sept. 21, 1905 at Marion, Ill. Graduate of U. of Illinois in 1927 and 1930. Admitted to bar in 1930, and practiced at Springfield, Ill. Judge of U.S. court of claims, 1947-53. Raised in Springfield Lodge No. 4, Springfield, Ill. in 1933. Member of Springfield Chapter No. 1, R.A.M.; Springfield Council No. 2, R. & SM.; Elwood Commandery No. 6, K.T. Ansar Shrine Temple; High Twelve Club; Court No. 20, Royal Order of Jesters (past impresario); and 33° AASR (NJ), all of Springfield, Ill.

Harry D. Howell, Sr. Author. b. May 26, 1880 at Columbia, Tenn. Began as a salesman in Washington, D.C. and later became manager and owner of Howell Motor Co. in Baltimore, Md. (1912-22). A writer from 1912, he moved to Hollywood, Calif. in 1922. He was awarded the bronze medal by Eugene Field Society in 1937. He wrote Strange Negro Stories Charles R. Howland of the Deep South, and sponsored the motion picture, The Land of Whispering Hope. Has contributed fiction to magazines, written and produced plays. Mason, Knight Templar, 32° AASR (SJ), and Shriner; past president of Hollywood Shrine Club.

J. Morton Howell (1863-1937) U.S. Minister to Egypt, 1922-27. b. March 17, 1863 at Uniopolis, Ohio. A physician, he was educated in Starling Medical Coll., Columbus and Ohio Northern U., Ada. He began practice in Washington Court House, Ohio, and settled at Dayton in 1896, where he specialized in surgery. Member of Mystic Lodge No. 405, Dayton, Ohio, receiving degrees on April 23, 1901, Nov. 10 and 24, 1903. d. Dec. 27, 1937.

R. Beecher Howell (1864-1933) U.S. Senator from Nebraska, 1923-35, dying in office. b. Jan. 21, 1864 at Adrian, Mich. He was state engineer of Nebraska in 1895-96, and same for city of Omaha in 1896-97. From 1903-05 he was a member of the state senate. He served as a Naval lieutenant in the Spanish-American War. He became a member of Temple Lodge, Adrian, Mich. about 1886 and afterwards affiliated with Nebraska Lodge No. 1 of Omaha. d. March 11, 1933.

Richard Howell (1753-1802) Governor of New Jersey, 1794-1801. b. in Newark, Del. in 1753. A lawyer, he commanded a company of grenadiers before the war, and was one of the young men who was prosecuted for the burning of a tea cargo at Greenwick, N.J., Nov. 22, 1774. He was commissioned captain in the 2nd N.J. Regiment and present at Quebec. He was promoted to major in 1776, and commanded his regiment until 1779. He was appointed judge-advocate of the Army in 1782, but declined. Resuming his law practice, he was clerk of the state supreme court from 1778 until 1793. When Washington passed through Trenton, N.J., Howell composed an ode of welcome to the general. He was a member of Trenton Lodge No. 5, Trenton, N.J. and past master of same. d. April 28, 1802.

William W. Howes Former First Assistant Postmaster General of U.S. b. Feb. 16, 1887 at Tomah, Wis. Graduate of U. of South Dakota in 1912, being admitted to the bar in

that year and practicing at Wolsey. He moved to Huron in 1927. He was a member of the state senate in 1917-18 and a candidate for governor in 1920. He has been a member of the Democratic Natl. Comm. since 1924. He became 2nd assistant postmaster general in 1933, and first assistant in 1934. Member of Anchor Lodge No. 152, Wolsey, S.D. Knight Templar and Shriner.

Robert G. Howie Inventor of the Howie machine gun carrier. b. Dec. 3, 1890 in Chicago, Ill. Commissioned in 1917, he saw Mexican border service and was a company commander of the 33rd Division in France in WWI. From 1927-30 he was in the Philippines and China, and from 1940-43, was assistant commandant of the Armored Force School. From 1943-46 he was commander of bases in the South Pacific, and from 1946 to retirement in 1950, commanded the Florida military district. Mason and Shriner.

Benjamin Howland (1756-1821) U.S. Senator from Rhode Island, 1804-07. b. in Tiverton, R.I. in 1756. He was educated in the public schools and served as a member of the state general assembly as well as holding several local offices. Howland was admitted a member of Mt. Vernon Lodge No. 4, Providence, RI., April 27, 1802. d. May 9, 1821.

Charles R. Howland (1871-1946) Brigadier General U.S. Army, and Medal of Honor winner. b. Feb. 16, 1871 at Jefferson, Ohio. Graduate of U.S. Military Academy in 1895, and National U. Law School (Washington, D.C.) in 1909. Commissioned in 1895, he advanced through grades to brigadier general in 1927, retiring in 1935 while commanding the 2nd Division. In 1903 he was aide-de-camp to General Arthur MacArthur, q.v.; commanded Alcatraz Island Military Prison, 1914-17. Served in Philippine insurrection and WWI, commanding many units including 28th, 343rd, 165th Infantry regiments, 3rd and 4th brigades, and 2nd Division. Mason. d. Sept. 21, 1946.

William Howley Archbishop of Canterbury, 1828-1848. Member and past master of Jehosaphat Lodge at Bristol, England (now extinct).

Rene Edward D. Hoyle Major General, U.S. Army. b. Sept. 16, 1883 at West Point, N.Y. Raised in Benjamin B. French Lodge No. 15, Washington, D.C. on March 17, 1930.

Henry M. Hoyt (1830-1890) Governor of Pennsylvania, 1879-83. b. in Kingston, Pa. on June 8, 1830.-- ,A graduate of Williams Coll. in 1849. He taught school for three years, and was admitted to the bar in 1853. In the Civil War he helped raise the 52nd Pa. regiment, entering as a lieutenant colonel, and mustering out as a brevet brigadier general. He attacked Fort Jackson by boat, landed, and was captured when support did not come to his aid. Confined at Macon, Ga., he was transferred to Charleston, where he made his escape only to be recaptured. On exchange he rejoined his regiment and remained with it until the close of the war. He resumed law practice in 1867. He was initiated in Lodge No. 61 of Wilkes-Barre, Pa., Dec. 27, 1854; secretary of the lodge in 1859, and 1865; junior warden in 1860; senior warden in 1861, and master in 1862. d. Sept. 30, 1890.

Henry Hubbard (1784-1857) U.S. Senator and Governor of New Hampshire. b. May 3, 1784 in Charleston, N.H. He was graduated from Dartmouth in 1803, studied law, and practiced in Charleston. He served in the state legislature from 1812-27, and was speaker during the last three years. He was U.S. congressman from 1829-35, and in 1834, was speaker pro tem of the house. He was U.S. senator from 1835-41, and governor of New Hampshire in 1841. He was admitted to St. John's Lodge No. 1, Portsmouth, N.H., June 5, 1805. He later became a member of Faithful Lodge No. 12, Charleston, and served as its master in 1816. He was a delegate to the grand lodge of Vermont in 1818, and in 1826-27, was grand master of the Grand Lodge of New Hampshire. He was also a member of Webb Chapter No. 6, R.A.M. of Claremont, N.H. d. June 5, 1857.

Lucius F. Hubbard (1836-1913) Governor of Minnesota, 1882-87. He also had the distinction of serving as brigadier general in two wars—Civil and Spanish-American. b. Jan. 26, 1836 in Troy, N.Y. He learned the tinner's trade and went to Minn. in 1857. He was a newspaper publisher at Red Wing from 1859-61. At the outset of the Civil War in 1861, he enlisted in the 5th Minn. Infantry as a private and was breveted brigadier general in 1864, for "gallant and distinguished services in actions before Nashville." Returning to Red Wing, he entered the grain and milling business; became president of the Cannon Valley Railroad (1878-81); built the Midland Railroad; and built and operated the Duluth, Red Wing & Southern R.R. (1888-1902). In the Spanish-American War he commanded the 3rd Division of the 7th Army Corps. Member of Red Wing Lodge No. 8, La Grange Chapter No. 4, R.A.M. and Red Wing Commandery No. 10, K.T., all of Red Wing, Minn. d. Feb. 5, 1913.

Richard B. Hubbard (1836-?) Governor of Texas, 1876-79, and U.S. Minister to Japan, 1885-89. b. Nov. 1, 1836 in Walton Co., Ga. Graduate of Mercer, Harvard, and U. of Virginia; he went to Texas in 1852, and practiced law at Tyler. He served a time as U.S. attorney for Western Texas, and was in the state legislature from 1859-62. He resigned from the latter to raise the 22nd Texas Inf., and was its colonel in the C.S.A. to the end of the Civil War. As a result, he was disfranchised for some years after the war. When civil disabilities were removed, he entered politics and was president of the Democratic state convention; lieutenant governor, 1873-76. Member of St. Johns Lodge No. 53, Tyler, Texas. Deceased.

William B. Hubbard (1795-1866) Fifth Grand Master of Grand Encampment, K.T., USA. b. Aug. 25, 1795 at Lowville, N.Y. He was raised in Rising Sun Lodge No. 125, Adams, N.Y., Sept. 12, 1821, and served as grand master of the Grand Lodge of Ohio in 1850-53; exalted in Zanesville Chapter No. 9, R.A.M., he became grand high priest of the Grand Chapter of Ohio; knighted in Lancaster' Encampment (Ohio), Oct. 21, 1842, he became grand master of the Grand Encampment from 1847-59. d. at Columbus, Ohio, Jan. 5, 1866.

Carl 0. Hubbell Famous "screwball" pitcher for the New York Giants, elected to the National Baseball Hall of Fame in Cooperstown, N.Y. in 1947. Nicknamed "King." b. June 22, 1903 in Carthage, Mo. He pitched for the Giants his entire career, from 1928-43. In 1934 he was hailed for his impressive performance in an all-star game, when he struck out Ruth, Gehrig, Foxx, Simmons, and Cronin in succession. He won 253 games in the majors, scoring 16 straight in 1936, and compiled a streak of 46% scoreless innings in 1933. He was raised in Meeker Lodge No. 479, Meeker, Okla., in 1929.

George W. Hubbell (?-1831) First U.S. Consul to the Philippines. A native of Mass., he was the first American Mason mentioned in the early history of the Philippines. He died May 3, 1831, and a monument to him was erected in the Plaza Cervantes, downtown Manila. In 1954 the monument was transferred to the grounds of the American embassy on Dewey Blvd., Manila.

Walter B. Huber U.S. Congressman, 79th through 81st Congresses (1945-51) from 14th Ohio dist. b. June 29, 1903 in Akron, Ohio. Member of Akron Lodge No. 83, Akron, Ohio, receiving degrees on Feb. 11, March 23 and April 30, 1927.

J. Klahr Huddle First U.S. Ambassador to Burma (from 1947). b. March 25, 1891 in Senaco Co., Ohio. Before entering the consular service in 1915 he was a high school principal, and did newspaper and commercial work. He was attached to the American commission to negotiate peace in Paris, 1918-19, and with the American consulate in Paris until 1920. He was then sent on assignments to Germany and Poland, and was consul at Hamburg, Germany, 1921-23. From 1925-27 he was chief of the passport division, State Dept, followed by terms as consul general at Cologne, Germany, and Warsaw, Poland. He was inspector of American foreign service in 1935; consul at Bern, Switzerland in 1941. Received his degrees in Fort Recovery Lodge No. 539, Fort Recovery, Ohio in 1915.

James H. Hudson (1878-1947) Judge of Supreme Court of Maine from 1933. b. March 21, 1878 at Guilford, Me. Graduate of Colby Coll. and Harvard. Admitted to the bar in 1903 and practiced in Guilford. Served as county attorney, probate judge, and justice of superior court. Member of Mt. Kineo Lodge No. 109, receiving degrees on April 21, May 5, May 19, 1906. d. Aug. 21, 1947.

Jay W. Hudson (1874-1958) Author and educator. b. March 12, 1874 in Cleveland, Ohio. Studied at Hiram and Oberlin Colleges and received degrees from U. of Calif. (1905), and Harvard (1907). He taught philosophy at U. of Calif., Harvard, and U. of Missouri. He was with the latter institution from 1908 until 1944, when he became professor emeritus. He wrote non-fiction as well as novels. His novel, *Abbe Pierre's People* (1928) was awarded the prize as the best novel of the year by the Catholic Press Ass'n. Another well known novel was *The Eternal Circle* (1925). Other writings were *The College and the New America; The Truths We Live By; Abbe Pierre; Nowhere Else in the World; Morning in Gascony; Why Democracy; The Old Faiths Perish*. He was a member of Acacia Lodge No. 602, Columbia, Mo. and Columbia Chapter No. 17, R.A.M., Columbia, dimitting from the latter in 1940. He was grand orator of the Grand Lodge of Missouri in 1929, 1944, and 1945. d. May 12, 1958.

Manley Ottmer Hudson American jurist and professor of international law, Harvard, from 1923 and director of research in international law at Harvard Law School (1927-1938). b. May 19, 1886. Member of American commission at Paris Peace Conference (1919); member of legal section, Secretariat of the League of Nations (1919-1923). Judge of the Permanent Court of International Justice (1943-46) and author of many volumes dealing with international law. Member of Masonic fraternity. One time instructor in the University of Missouri.

Richard F. Hudson President and publisher of the Montgomery (Ala.) Advertiser and Alabama Journal. b. Oct. 24, 1884 in Jefferson Co., Ga. He began with the Atlanta Journal in 1901, and went with the Montgomery Advertiser in 1903, working his way up until he purchased the paper in 1935. In 1940 he purchased the Journal. Mason.

William A. Hudson American chest surgeon. b. Feb. 23, 1891 at Jasper, Ark. Graduate of Washington U., St. Louis (M.D., B.S.) in 1918 and 1920. He interned at Royal Victoria Hospital, Montreal, and Henry Ford Hospital, Detroit. After study in England, he returned to the Grace Hospital of Detroit and established the first department of thoracic surgery of any general hospital. Since he entered the field, the mortality rate for chest operations has dropped from 60 to 70% to less than 1%. He was the first permanent chairman of the scientific section of the First International Congress on Chest Diseases, held in Rome, Italy in 1950, and named to same position at second congress in Rio de Janeiro. He is past president of American Coll. of Chest Physicians. He served as master of Kismet Lodge No. 489, Detroit in 1943; high priest of Sojourners Chapter No. 164, R.A.M., Detroit, in 1945, and at present (1958) is grand king of the Grand Chapter, R.A.M. of Michigan; member of Monroe Council No. 1 R. & S.M.; 32° AASR (NJ); Detroit Commandery No. 1 K.T.; Moslem

Shrine Temple; Thistle and Rose Council, A.M.D. Elected Grand High Priest of the Grand Chapter, R.A.M. of Michigan in Oct., 1959.

Robert H. Hudspeth Prison warden. b. March 20, 1877 at Lenoir, N.C. Was successively record clerk, superintendent of identification, parole officer, acting warden, deputy warden of Kansas State Prison, Lansing, Kans. 1913-30. He was then assistant deputy warden, deputy warden, and warden of the U.S. Penitentiary, Ft. Leavenworth, Kans., 1930-37, and warden of the Main Federal Prison, Leavenworth, 1937-43, retiring in that year, but returning to prison service as warden of the Kansas State Prison at Lansing in 1944. He retired in July, 1953. Member of Nine Mile Lodge No. 49, Lansing, Kans. since about 1916; 32° AASR (SJ) in Kansas City, Kans.; Abdallah Shrine Temple, Kansas City, Kans.

Remi Paul Hueper Brigadier General, U.S. Army. b. Nov. 19, 1886 at Louisville, Ky. He served as an enlisted man in U.S. Navy in 1902-03, and in 1917 was commissioned a captain in the Quartermaster Dept., U.S. Army. In 1920 he transferred to the Finance Dept., and was assistant chief of finance, U.S. Army from 1941-46. Retired in 1946. Mason.

Clyde R. Huey (1877-1954) U.S. Senator, 1945-54 and Governor of North Carolina, 1937-41. b. Dec. 11, 1877 in Shelby, N.C. He began in printing office at age of 12, and was later editor of county newspaper. He was admitted to the bar in 1899, and served terms in both houses of the state legislature. From 1913-18 he was assistant U.S. district attorney of the Western Dist. of N.C. He served in the 66th U.S. congress, 1919-21,

and resumed law practice in 1921. Mason. d. May 12, 1954.

Christoph Wilhelm Hufeland (1762-1836) German physician who was professor of pathology and therapeutics at Berlin U. He wrote on Wieland, Herder, Goethe, and Schiller as well as on scientific subjects. The 1917 bulletin of the International Masonic Congress lists him as a Freemason.

James W. Huffman U.S. Senator from Ohio, 1945-47. b. Sept. 13, 1894 at Chandlersville, Ohio. Student at Ohio Wesleyan and Ohio State U.; graduate of U. of Chicago in 1922. Began as a high school teacher and superintendent of chautauqua. He was admitted to the bar in 1922, practiced in Chicago, 1922-24, and then moved to Ohio where he was executive secretary to Gov. Donahey from 1924-27; member of public utilities commission of Ohio, 1927-29, and practiced law at Columbus since 1929, specializing in corporation l a w . Served as an officer of the A.E.F. with 83rd and 32nd Divisions. Member of Gauge and Gavel Lodge No. 448, Chandlersville, Ohio, he received his degrees, April 13, June 15, and Sept. 7, 1916. Received 32° AASR (NJ) at Columbus, Ohio in Aug.,1917. Became member of Crescent Shrine Temple, Trenton, N.J. in 1918, and later affiliated with Aladdin Temple of Columbus, Ohio.

William J. Hughan (1841-1911) A foremost English Masonic scholar. b. Feb. 13, 1841 in Devonshire, England. While a boy, he was apprenticed to a draper in Devenport, and later entered a wholesale firm at Plymouth, going later to Manchester and Truro, remaining at the latter place until 1883, when he retired and settled at Torquay to devote himself to Masonic research. A student, particularly of the Old Manuscripts, he did much to take away the many fanciful notions in which its literature abounds. His work made possible the great flowering of English Masonic scholarship which began about 1884. He was a founder of the Quatuor Coronati Lodge, and a collaborator on Gould's History of Freemasonry. He was initiated in St. Aubyn Lodge No. 954 of Devenport in 1863. In 1864 he became a member of Emulation Lodge of Improvement in London, and on moving to Truro in 1864, joined the Phenix Lodge of Honor and Prudence No. 331, which he served for a time as secretary. In 1866 he affiliated with Fortitude Lodge No. 131, and was master in 1868, 1878. He was exalted in Glasgow Chapter No. 50, R.A.M. (Scotland) in 1865 and became a member of Kilwinning Chapter No. 80. He received many honorary titles from the grand lodge and grand chapter of England for his contributions to the Craft, and was an honorary senior grand warden of the Grand Lodge of Iowa, and honorary life member and past high priest of Lafayette Chapter No. 5, Washington, D.C. d. May 20, 1911.

Aaron K. Hughes (1822-1906) Rear Admiral, U.S. Navy. b. March 31, 1822 in Elmira, N.Y. He was appointed acting midshipman in 1838, promoted to passed midshipman in 1844; master, 1853; lieutenant, 1853; captain, 1869; commodore, 1875, and rear admiral, 1882. During the Civil War he served in the South Atlantic and Gulf squadrons. He was a member of Union Lodge No. 95, Elmira, N.Y. d. 1906.

James H. Hughes (1867-1953) U.S. Senator from Delaware, 1937-42. b. Jan. 14, 1867 in Kent Co., Del. He taught school in his home county from 1885-89, studied law and was admitted to the bar in 1890, practicing at Dover. He also engaged in agricultural pursuits and banking. He was secretary of state of Delaware in 1897-1901 and unsuccessful candidate for governor in 1916. Member of Union Lodge No. 7, Dover, Del. d. Aug. 29, 1953.

Matt S. Hughes (1863-1920) Methodist Episcopal Bishop. b. Feb. 2, 1863 in Dodridge Co., Va. (now W.Va.). He attended the U. of West Virginia. He was ordained to the ministry in 1887, and served churches in Portland, Maine, Minneapolis, Minn., Kansas City, Mo., and Pasadena, Calif. from 1890-1916. From 1908-11 he was professor of practical theology of Maclay Coll. of Theology, U. of Southern California. Hughes was elected bishop in 1916. In the Spanish-American War he was chaplain of the 1st. Minn. regiment. Member Corona Lodge No. 324, Calif., affiliating with it on Jan. 7, 1915 from Ancient Landmark Lodge No. 17 of Portland, Maine. d. April 4, 1920.

Morris N. Hughes U.S. foreign service officer. b. Jan. 13, 1901 in Champaign, Ill. Graduate of U. of Illinois in 1922. He entered the U.S. foreign service as a clerk in the American consulate at Montevideo in 1923. He became a vice consul in 1925, and was successively assigned to Rome, Naples, Athens, and Baghdad. He became 3rd secretary at Tokyo in 1933; consul at Addis Ababa, Ethiopia, 1936; 2nd secretary in Albania, 1937; consul, Mexico City, 1939; 2nd secretary in 1941; and commercial attaché in 1942 in Mexico. He was deputy protocol officer at the famous U.N. formation conference in San Francisco in 1945. In 1947 he was consul general of Cuba; counselor of legation, Bern, Switzerland, in 1949; Reykjavick, Iceland, 1951-53; consul general Tunis, Tunisia, 1953-56; and consul general, Paris, since 1956. Member of Western Star Lodge No. 240, Champaign, Ill. receiving degrees in 1922.

Roy 0. Hughes President of Order of Railway Conductors and Brakemen since 1950. b. Sept. 24, 1887 at Portland, N.D. He farmed before becoming a machinist helper on the Great Northern Railroad at Superior, Wis. in 1908. He was later brakeman and conductor on Northern Pacific; Chicago, Milwaukee & St. Paul Railroads. Received his degrees in Ionic Lodge No. 186, Duluth, Minn. in 1912 and presently a member of Trinity Lodge No. 282, Duluth. 32° AASR (NJ) in Milwaukee, Wis.

Comte Joseph Leopold Sigisbert Hugo (1773-1828) French General, and father of Victor Hugo, q.v. He wrote on military subjects, and served in the Revolutionary and Napoleonic armies. Best known for his defense of Thionville in 1813-14. The bulletin of the International Masonic Congress of 1917 states that he was a Freemason.

Victor Marie Hugo (1802-1885) French romantic novelist, best known for his *Les Miserables*, and the *Hunchback of Notre Dame*. Son of Comte J. L. S. Hugo, q.v. Although often referred to as a Mason, there is no proof.

Homer B. Hulbert (1863-1949) Author. b. Jan. 26, 1863 at New Haven, Vt. Graduate of Dartmouth in 1884. He was in the educational service of the Korean government from 1886-1905, and in the diplomatic service of that government from 1905-10. From 1900-06 he was the editor of Korean Review. His

books include: *The History of Korea; The Passing of Korea; Comparative Grammar of Korean and Dravidian; Omjee the Wizard; The Face in the Mist.* Mason. d. Aug. 5, 1949.

Cyrus E. Hull (1830-1936) Masonic veteran who reached the age of 106. b. Oct 28, 1830 in Lebanon, N.Y. He was raised in Hampden Lodge, Springfield, Mass., March 23, 1853. He later became a charter member of East St. Louis Lodge No. 504. He was a Mason for 83 years and 19 days. d. April 11, 1936 in Los Angeles, Calif.

Harry E. Hull (1864-1938) U.S. Commissioner General of Immigration, 1925-33. b. March 12, 1864 in Belvidere, N.Y. Educated in the public schools of Cedar Rapids, Ia. He engaged in the grain business, and was president of the Williamburg (Ia.) Telephone Co., serving as mayor and postmaster of that city. He was a member of the 64th through 68th U.S. congresses (1915-25) from the 2nd Iowa dist. Member of Stellapolis Lodge No. 391, Williamsburg, Iowa, receiving degrees on March 3, 28 and April 24, 1888. d. Jan. 15, 1938.

John A. Hull (1874-1944) Major General, U.S. Army. b. Aug. 7, 1874 at Bloomfield, Ia. Was graduated from U. of Iowa in 1895, and 1896, being admitted to the bar in latter year, and began practice in Des Moines. While serving in the Iowa National Guard, he was made lieutenant colonel of volunteers in judge advocate dept., and advanced to rank of major general in 1924, retiring in 1928. He was legal adviser to the governor general of the Philippines in 1930-32, and associate justice of the supreme court of the Philippines from 1932-36. Mason. d. April 17, 1944.

John E. Hull Major General, U.S. Army. B. May 26, 1895 in Greenfield, Ohio. Graduate of Miami U. (Ohio) in 1917. Commissioned in 1917, he advanced through grades to major general in 1948. Had a long and distinguished service as an officer in both World Wars. In 1946 he was commanding general of the armed forces in the Middle Pacific and Hawaiian Department; in 1947-48 he commanded Joint Task Force 7 which conducted the first atomic weapons test at Eniwetok. In 1948-49 he was commanding general of the U.S. Army in the Pacific. From 1949 to 1953 he was with the office of secretary of Defense and general staff in Washington, being vice chief of staff from 1951-53. In 1953-54 he was commander-in-chief of the United Nations Forces in the Far East, and also commander-in-chief of Far East Command, and governor of Kyukyu Islands. He retired in 1955, and since that date has been president of Manufacturing Chemists Association. On Oct. 5, 1954 he attended the first communication of the district grand lodge for Japan in the Tokyo Masonic building, and addressing the brethren on that occasion said: "What impresses me as most distinctive about Freemasonry, is the ease with which it surmounts the national barriers which plague so many endeavors. The lodges in Tokyo and vicinity, with brethren from varying racial backgrounds are a splendid example of the way in which our Order can develop and exemplify its magnificent principles in an atmosphere of freedom and mutual understanding." Member of Oxford Lodge No. 67, Oxford, Ohio, receiving degrees on Nov. 9, 1916, April 16, 1928 and June 4, 1928.

William Hull (1753-1825) Brigadier General of War of 1812, and officer of American Revolution. b. June 24, 1753 in Derby, Conn. Was graduated from Yale, studied law, and practiced at Litchfield after admission to the bar in 1775. After the news of John E. Hull Major General, U.S. Army. b. May 26, 1895 in Greenfield, the Battle of Lexington reached his town, a company was formed under his charge and he joined Washington at Cambridge as part of Webb's Conn. regiment. He was lieutenant colonel in 1779, and army inspector under Baron Von Steuben, q.v. He fought in the battles of White Plains, Trenton, Princeton, Stillwater, Saratoga, Fort Stanwix, Monmouth, and Stony Point, receiving the thanks of both Washington and congress. Following the war, he became a major general of the 3rd Mass. militia, and a state senator. In 1805 he was appointed by Jefferson as governor of the Michigan Territory, holding that office until 1812, when he was named to command the northwestern army. In attempting to defend Detroit, he failed to receive support or supplies, and when he was forced to surrender that place, the country needed a scape-goat—which turned out to be Hull. Strangely enough, the two officers who effected his downfall were brother Masons, Col. Lewis Cass, q.v., and Gen. Henry Dearborn, q.v. Cass wrote a letter, made public, that criticized the actions of Hull (although his own actions indicated that he supported Hull's decisions). Hull was brought to trial, with Gen. Dearborn as president of the court-martial. Dearborn, instead of cooperating with Hull in the invasion of Canada, had signed the armistice without Hull's knowledge, which allowed the British troops to be sent against Detroit. Hull was found guilty of cowardice, sentenced to be shot, and then told to go home to Newton, Mass. and wait for the execution of the sentence—which never came! Dearborn, incidentally, was relieved of his Northwest command "for political reasons" shortly thereafter. Hull was a member of Washington Lodge No. 10; its charter was granted Oct. 6, 1779, and it was a traveling lodge located at West Point. He must have held previous membership, for he is mentioned as being present at St. John's Day celebration of American Union Lodge at West Point, June 24, 1779, almost four months before Washington Lodge was chartered. He was junior warden of Washington Lodge in 1779. He became first master of Meridian Lodge, Natick, Mass., in 1797. d. Nov. 29, 1825.

William E. Hull (1866-1942) U.S. Congressman, 68th through 72nd Congresses (1922-33) from Ill. b. Jan. 13, 1866 at Lewiston, Ill. Honorary vice president and general manager of Hiram Walker & Son, Inc., distillers, Peoria, Ill. Built Jefferson Hotel and Palace Theater in Peoria, and was postmaster from 1898-1906. In congress he secured the passage of the "deep water way bill from lakes to gulf." Member of Temple Lodge No. 46 at Peoria, Ill. d. May 30, 1942. Initiated in American Union Lodge at Roxbury, Mass. on March 13, 1776.

Edwin W. Hullinger Journalist, author, and motion picture producer. b. Aug. 13, 1893 in Chicago, Ill. Graduate U. of Kansas in 1917. Served on staff of papers in Calif. and Kans., joining United Press in N.Y. in 1917, and made manager of Michigan headquarters in Detroit. Was staff correspondent in England, Paris, and Soviet Russia. He was deported from Russia for insistence on right of freedom of press for foreign correspondents. He was correspondent in Italy for the New York Times from 1925-26. In WWII he was information specialist with OWI, Dept. of Agriculture and FCC. He is the author of *The Reforging of Russia; The New Fascist State; Flesh Alley—A Story of Broadway*; and *Plowing Through*. He produced the motion picture *The Private Life of Mussolini* (1938) and a series entitled *Makers of Destiny* (1946-47). Mason.

Sir Samuel Hulse English Field Marshal. Joined Prince of Wales Lodge No. 259, London, England, July 12, 1787, and was deputy master of the same from 1787-1820.

Russell J. Humbert President of DePauw University since 1951. b. May 26, 1905. Graduate of Coll. of Wooster, and Boston U. Ordained to Methodist ministry in 1930, and served pastorates in Beech City, Ohio, Akron, Toledo, and Youngstown until 1951. Author of A Man and His God, and conducts weekly broadcast entitled "Faith for Today" over Station WIRE, Indianapolis, during the academic year. Member of national committee, Boy Scouts of America. Received his degrees in Coventry Lodge No. 665, Akron, Ohio in 1937. Member of Fort Industry Chapter No. 208, R.A.M.; Grafton M. Acklin Council No. 127, R. & SM.; Toledo Commandery No. 7, KT.; 32° AASR (NJ) and Zenobia Shrine Temple, all of Toledo, Ohio. Worked in the 14° AASR while in Toledo.

Johan Nepomuk Hummell (1778-1837) German composer and piano virtuoso. b. Nov. 14, 1778 in Pressburg, Hungary. He was a member of the Lodge Amalie at Weimar, and a pupil of Mozart, q.v. He wrote sonatas, concertos, chamber music, Masses and nine operas. His lodge published a music book in 1820 which contained two of his songs. d. at Weimar, Germany in 1837.

Arthur L. Humphrey (1860-1939) President of Westinghouse Air Brake Co., 1919. b. June 12, 1860 in Buffalo, N.Y. Began as a farmer, and later machinist's apprentice. He served with five railroads and was appointed western manager of Westinghouse Air Brake in 1903, advancing as general manager, vice president, president, executive director, chairman of board of directors, and chairman of the executive committee. From 1893-95 he was a member of the lower house in Colo., and speaker of same in 1895. He affiliated with George W. Guthrie Lodge No. 691, Pittsburgh, Pa. on Feb. 21, 1918, coming from Colorado Springs Lodge No. 76, Colorado Springs, Colo. where he had been raised on Nov. 9, 1899 and served as treasurer in 1890. d. Nov. 1, 1939.

George D. Humphrey President of University of Wyoming since 1945. b. Aug. 30, 1897 in Tippah Co., Miss. Graduate of Miss. State Teachers Coll., Blue Mountain Coll. (Miss.), U. of Chicago, and Ohio State U. From 1923-33 he was a teacher, principal, and superintendent in various public schools in Miss. From 1934-45 he was president of Mississippi State Coll. Member of Ripley Lodge No. 47, Ripley, Miss., serving as master of same. He was grand marshal of the Grand Lodge of Mississippi for two years. Member of New Albany Chapter No. 45, R.A.M.; New Albany Council No. 3, R. & S.M.; New Albany Commandery No. 29, K.T., all of New Albany, Miss. Shriner and member of Eastern Star.

Lyman U. Humphrey (1844-1915) Governor of Kansas, 1889-93. b. July 25, 1844 in New Baltimore,

Ohio. Served in Civil War with the 76th Ohio Inf. and was wounded. Studied law at U. of Michigan, and began practice in Independence, Kans., in 1871. He served in both branches of the state legislature, and was lieutenant governor 1877-84. Member of Fortitude Lodge No. 107, Independence, Kans. d. Sept. 12, 1915.

Albert E. Humphreys (1860-1927) Capitalist; pioneer in opening up the iron deposits of the Mesaba range (Minn.) and founder of Virginia, Minn. b. Jan. 11, 1860 in Sissonville, W.Va. At the age of 17 he began in the lumber business with his father, but went to Duluth, Minn. in 1891. He prospected widely for minerals and oil in the Rocky Mountains and Southwest. He organized the Merritt Oil & Gas Co. of Oklahoma in 1914, and was associated with F. Julius Fobs, geologist, in many enterprises. He opened the Big Muddy Pool in Wyo., and Mexica field in Texas. He was interested in the coal deposits of W.Va. He built the Boyd Memorial Church in Charleston, W.Va. Member of Palestine Lodge No. 79, Duluth, Baron Karl Gotthelf von Hund Minn., withdrawing on Jan. 18, 1926 with no further record in d. May 8, 1927.

Baron Karl Gotthelf von Hund (1722-1776) A German nobleman, and hereditary landed proprietor in the Lausitz, who devoted his life to the establishment of the Rite of Strict Observance. b. Sept. 11, 1722 in Oberlausitz, Germany. The strict observance system pledged unquestioned obedience to an unknown superior, and was based on the fiction that the Templar secrets had survived the suppression of the order in 1312, when after the execution of Jacques de Molay, eight high-ranking knights escaped to Scotland and reestablished the order. In the latter half of the 18th century the order swept Europe. Himself a man of integrity, Von Hund's faith in the existence of an unknown grand master (he was convinced that it was Charles Edward, the Young Pretender), made him the prey of such imposters as Johnson. In an effort to reconcile the differences between Von Hund's rite and another strict observance rite under Von Starck (who contended only Roman Catholics could be members), a congress was held in 1774, and Von Hund appears to have been divested of much of his authority, as the grand-mastership was conferred on Frederick, duke of Brunswick, q.v. When the clerical branch withdrew and formed an independent order, the strict observance lodges thence forward called themselves the United German Lodges. Authorities disagree on the initiation dates and places of Von Hund. Mackey says he received the first and second degrees, March 20, 1742, in the Lodge of the Three Thistles at Frankfort on the Main. Other sources say it was in 1741, at Ghent, Belgium. Hund was made a Knight Templar in 1743, probably in Paris. In 1749, he erected at his own expense, a lodge on his estates at Kittlitz, near Lobau, to which he gave the name of The Three Pillars. At the same time he built a Protestant church, the cornerstone of which was laid by the brethren with Masonic ceremonies. d. Nov. 8, 1776.

Charles C. Hunt (1866-1948) Masonic writer. b. Nov. 9, 1866 in Cleveland, Ohio. Graduate of Grinnell Coll. (Ia.). Between 1895 and 1917, he held many public offices. He was raised in Lafayette Lodge No. 52, Montezuma, Ia., July 24, 1900. He was grand secretary and grand librarian of the Grand Lodge of Iowa from

1924-45, and was an honorary past grand master of that jurisdiction. He wrote numerous Masonic articles including *Masonic Symbolism.; Landmarks of Freemasonry*, and co-author of the 2-volume *History of the Cryptic Rite*. d. July 24, 1948.

George W. P. Hunt (1859-1934) First Governor of Arizona, 1911-19, and again 1923-28, and 1931-33. b. Nov. 1, 1859 at Huntsville, Mo. He received only eight years of formal schooling. He was a rancher on the Salt River of Arizona from 1890-1900. He became connected with the Old Dominion Commercial Co. in 1890, served as its secretary, and was president from 1900. Hunt served two terms in the lower house, and five in the upper of the state legislature, and was president of the constitutional convention of 1910. He was an exponent of prison reform and president of the Anti-Capital Punishhient League. In 1920-21 he was U.S. envoy and minister to Siam. He was made a Mason, Nov. 18, 1897, in White Mountain Lodge No. 3, Globe, Ariz.; was a Knight Templar, and member of El Zaribah Shrine Temple of Phoenix. d. Dec. 24, 1934.

Lester C. Hunt (1892-1954) U.S. Senator and Governor of Wyoming. b. July 8, 1892 in Isabel, Ill. Received dental degree from St. Louis U. in 1917, and was a dentist in Lander, Wyo. from that date until 1934. He was secretary of state of Wyo. from 1935-43, and governor from 1943-49. He served his state as U.S. senator from 1949 until his death. In 1948-49 he was chairman of the governors' conference. In WWI he was an officer in the Dental Corps of the Army. From 1924-28 he was president of the Wyo. State Board of Dental Examiners. Hunt designed

Wyoming's distinctive "bucking horse" license plate for automobiles in 1936. Member of Wyoming Lodge No. 2, Lander, receiving degrees on Sept. 8, Nov. 6 and Dec. 5, 1919. Member of Scottish Rite in Cheyenne and Shriner. d. June 19, 1954.

George Hunter Indian scout and frontiersman of early West. He wrote Reminiscences of an Old Timer. He was raised in Temple Lodge No. 7, Astoria, Oreg. about 1860; affiliated with Blue Mountain Lodge No. 13, Walla Walla, Wash. about 1868, and affiliated with Columbia Lodge No. 26, Dayton, Wash. about 1877. Withdrew about 1890.

William Hunter (1774-1849) U.S. Senator from Rhode Island, 1811-21. b. Nov. 26, 1774 at Newport, R.I. He first studied medicine in England, but abandoned it for law. On his return to the U.S. in 1795, he was admitted to the bar of R.I. His speeches on the acquisition of Florida and the Missouri compromise gave him a wide reputation in the senate. He resumed his law practice at Newport in 1821 until 1834, when he was named charge d'affaires in Brazil, becoming U.S. minister to that country in 1841, and serving until 1843. Member of St. John's Lodge No. 1, Newport, R.I. d. Dec. 3, 1849.

George C. Hunting (1871-1924) Protestant Episcopal Bishop ,of Nevada. b. Oct. 22, 1871 at Milwaukee, Wis. Graduate of the Virginia Theol. Seminary in 1894. Ordained deacon in 1894, and priest in 1897. He served churches in Virginia City, Nev., Evanston, Wyo., and was hospital chaplain in Salt Lake City. He was general missionary for Nevada and Utah 1898-99. From 1907-12 he was missionary at Ely, Nev. He was consecrated bishop, Dec. 16, 1914.

From 1909-11 he was editor of The Nevada Churchman. Initiated Aug. 7, 1895 in Virginia Lodge No. 3, Virginia City, Nev. Affiliated with Reno Lodge No. 13, Reno. Member of Reno Chapter No. 7, R.A.M., DeWitt Clinton Cornmandery No. 1, K.T., and 32° AASR (SJ), all of Reno. Also member of Kerak Shrine Temple, Reno. Appointed grand chaplain of Grand Lodge of Nevada in June, 1923, but died before the year was over. d. Feb. 6, 1924.

Arthur F. Huntington (1877-1954) Rear Admiral, U.S. Navy. b. Feb. 24, 1877 in Brooklyn, N.Y. Student at U.S. Naval Academy, 1894-97. Commissioned ensign in 1898, he advanced through grades to rear admiral in 1938, and retired in 1941, although he remained on active duty until Aug., 1942. Mason. d. April 19, 1954.

Ebenezer Huntington (1754-1834) Revolutionary soldier and Brigadier General of state militia. b. Dec. 26, 1754 in Norwich, Conn. He entered Yale in 1771, but left to join the army, and was afterward given his degree. He served in Col. Wyllis's regiment, and became brigade major under Gen. Parsons, and deputy adjutant general to Gen. Heath on the Hudson River. In 1777 he was a major in Webb's regiment, which he commanded in R.I. in 1778. He became a lieutenant colonel and commanded a battalion at Yorktown. In 1792 he was made general of the Conn. state militia, and in 1799 Washington named him brigadier general when the war with France threatened. He served in the U.S. congress in 1810-11, and again in 1817-19. He was considered one of the best disciplinarians in the Army. Member of Somerset Lodge No. 34 of Norwich, Conn. d. June 17, 1834.

Was one of the first initiates of American Union Lodge at Roxbury, Mass. (Feb. 20, 1776). A Royal Arch Mason. Became charter member of Somerset Lodge No. 34, Norwich, Conn. in 1795. Was senior grand warden of the Grand Lodge of Connecticut, 1798-1801.

Jabez W. Huntington Charter member of Somerset Lodge No. 34 in 1795.

Jabez W. Huntington (1788-1847) U.S. Senator from Connecticut, 1840-47. b. Nov. 8, 1788 at Norwich, Conn. He was graduated from Yale in 1806, studied in the Litchfield law school, and practiced in that town for thirty years. He was a member of the assembly in 1829, and U.S. congressman from 1829-34, when he moved to Norwich to became judge of the superior court. He was a member of the Masonic convention that met in Washington in 1843. d. Nov. 1, 1847.

Samuel Huntington (1765-1817) Governor of Ohio, 1808-10 and 2nd Grand Master of the Grand Lodge of Ohio in 1809. b. Oct. 4, 1765 at Coventry, Conn. he was the son of Joseph Huntington, but was adopted and educated by his uncle, Samuel Huntington, signer of the Declaration of Independence. He is often confused with his uncle in Masonic history. He was graduated from Yale in 1785, and admitted to the bar in Norwich in 1793. In 1801 he moved to Cleveland, Ohio, and then to Painesville. He was judge of the common court of pleas in 1802-03, and of the superior court in 1803, and later chief justice. A member of the first constitutional convention of Ohio in 1802, he was a senator in its first legislature, serving as speaker. He was one of the original proprietors of Fairport, founded in 1812. He seems to have received his degrees in Somerset Lodge No. 34, Norwich, Conn., for he was a proxy for the junior warden of that lodge at the grand lodge sessions in 1796. There was also a Samuel Huntington present as a guest, Dec. 27, 1790, in St. John's Lodge No. 2 at Middletown, Conn., and it is presumed this was the younger Huntington. In Ohio he became a past master of Scioto Lodge No. 6, Chillicothe. In 1809 he is listed as representing Erie Lodge No. 47 at the grand lodge sessions. In 1813 he is listed as suspended NPD, but evidently reinstated the next year. d. June 8, 1817. Received all three degrees in June 3-4, 1795 in Wooster Lodge, Colchester, Conn. Was G.M. of G.L. of Ohio in 1809.

Marquis of Huntly (see Earl of Aboyne).

Benjamin Hurd, Jr. (1750-1821) Presided over the convention which met to form a General Grand Chapter, Royal Arch Masons in the U.S., and was the second general grand high priest of the same. b. Feb. 1, 1750 in Charlestown, Mass. He was a leather dresser. Initiated, Aug. 14, 1777, in St. Andrew's Lodge in Boston, passed Sept. 11, and raised Dec. 12; served as master in 1794. Received chapter degrees in St. Andrew's Chapter, Boston, March 20, 1789, and immediately was made secretary; became high priest in 1791, and held the position for seven years. In 1798 he was elected first grand high priest of the new Grand Chapter, R.A.M. of Mass. He was a charter member of Boston Encampment, K.T. in March, 1806. He was general grand high priest from 1806-16. He was not present to preside at the septennial of 1816, nor did he appear at the 1819 meeting. d. May 5, 1821.

Nathaniel Hurd (1730-1777) Early American engraver. b. Feb. 13, 1730. His grandfather came from England and settled in Charlestown, Mass. Nathaniel engaged in the business of seal-cutting and die-engraving in Boston and was considered superior to any one in the colonies in this occupation. He was probably the first in this country to engrave on copper, and he engraved the seal of Harvard University. His works often displayed character and humor. A Mason, sources differ, one stating he was a member of the "first lodge of Boston," and another "the second lodge of Boston." d. Dec. 17, 1777.

Stephen A. Hurlbut (1815-1882) Major General of Civil War, and first national commander of the Grand Army of the Republic. b. Nov. 29, 1815 in Charleston, S.C. He was admitted to the bar in 1837, and practiced in Charleston until the Florida War, in which he served as adjutant in a S.C. regiment. In 1845 he went to Illinois, practicing his profession in Belvidere, and taking an active part in politics. He was named brigadier general at the beginning of the Civil War and commanded Fort Donelson after its capture in Feb., 1862. He commanded the 4th Division under Gen. Grant, q.v., and was the first to reach Pittsburg Landing on the Tenn. river, which he held for a week alone. He was promoted to major general for meritorious conduct at the Battle of Shiloh, and then stationed at Memphis. He led a corps under Sherman in 1863, and in 1864 succeeded Gen. N. P. Banks in command of the Department of the Gulf, serving there until 1865, when mustered out. He was U.S. minister to Colombia from 1869-72. After two terms in U.S. congress (1873-77), he was appointed

U.S. minister to Peru in 1881, holding that office until his death (he died in Peru). On Nov. 20, 1866 he was elected first national commander of the GAR. A member of Belvidere Lodge No. 60, Belvidere, Ill., he was grand orator of the Grand Lodge of Illinois in 1865. d. March 27, 1882.

Vincent L. Hurlbut (1829-1896) Eleventh Grand Master, Grand Encampment, K.T. of U.S.A. b. June 28, 1829 at West Mendon, N.Y. A physician, he received the 33° AASR (NJ) at Chicago, May 11, 1865, and made active member of Northern Supreme Council on June 26, 1868. d. July 24, 1896.

Patrick Jay Hurley Major General, U.S. Army; Secretary of War; diplomat. b. Jan. 8, 1883 in Choctaw Indian Territory (now Okla.). He is a graduate of Indian U. (now Bacone Coll.), National U. Law School (Washington, D.C.), and George Washington U. Admitted to the bar in 1908, he practiced in Tulsa, and from 1912-17 was national attorney for the Choctaw Nation. After a year as undersecretary of War, he became secretary of War in 1929, serving until 1933. His military career started as a private in the Indian Terr. Voluntary Cavalry in 1902. He then became captain in Okla. national guard (1914-17), and in WWI rose to colonel, U.S. Army. He participated in the Aisne-Marne, Meuse-Argonne, and St. Mihiel offensives, and negotiated agreement between the Grand Duchy of Luxembourg and the A.E.F. in 1919. At outbreak of WWII he was promoted to brigadier general and was a personal representative of Gen. Marshall, q.v., in Far East. The first three months of 1942 were spent running the blockade between the Philippines and Australia, and, on Feb. 19 he was wounded at Darwin.

In April, 1942, he was U.S. minister to New Zealand, and in Nov.-Dec. was personal representative of the president to Soviet Union, and to Egypt, Syria, Lebanon, Iraq, Iran, Palestine, Trans-Jordon, Saudi Arabia, Afghanistan, India, and China in 1943. He drafted the Iran Declaration of the Teheran conference in Dec. 1943. In 1944 he was made major general and personal representative of the president in China. In Dec. 1944 he became U.S. ambassador to China. He assisted in the organization of the U.S. Chamber of Commerce in 1912. Member of Olive Branch Lodge No. 114, Leesburg, Va., receiving degrees, May 20, 1940, April 7, and July 11, 1941.

Thurman S. Hurst Chief Justice, Supreme Court of Oklahoma, 1947-48. b. April 28, 1889 at Cassville, Mo. Graduate of Oklahoma State U. in 1912, and practiced law at Pawnee, and later Weleetka, Okla. He was associate justice of the supreme court from 1937-46. Now in law practice in Tulsa. Member of Pawnee Lodge No. 82, Pawnee, Okla. since 1920; 32° AASR (SJ) at Guthrie, Okla.

Joseph Huston Missouri pioneer, who with his brother, Benjamin, built S. Arthur Huston the famous Arrow Rock Tavern in Arrow Rock, Mo. He was a native of Augusta Co., Va., coming to Mo. in 1819, and settling on a farm near Arrow Rock. After the death of his first wife (a Brownlee), he married the widow of Bradford Lawless. He was a judge of the county court for several terms, first when the county seat was at Old Jefferson, near Cambridge, and later at Marshall, and Jonesboro. In the early 1830's he built the tavern, which he operated successfully, in connection with a general mercantile

business. The old Santa Fe Trail passed in front of the tavern, and many prominent travelers were overnight guests, including Washington Irving. He was a charter member of Arrow Rock Lodge No. 55, and its treasurer for many years.

S. Arthur Huston Protestant Episcopal Bishop. b. Dec. 10, 1876 at Cincinnati, Ohio. Graduate of Kenyon Coll. and Bexley Theol. Seminary. He was ordained deacon in 1903, and priest in 1904; he served pastorates in Columbus, Ohio; Detroit, Mich.; Cheyenne, Wyo.; Baltimore, Md.; and San Antonio, Tex. from 1903-25. He was elected bishop of Olympia (Wash.), in 1925 and retired from active service in 1947. Mason and 32° AASR.

John B. Hutcheson (1860-1939) Justice, Supreme Court of Georgia, 1934-38. b. Nov. 20, 1860 in Jonesboro, Ga. Began practice of law there in 1886. From 1885-88 he was editor of the Jonesboro News. He was superior court judge from 1919-34. Member of Jonesboro Lodge No. 87, Jonesboro, Ga., receiving degrees in 1886. He served as master from 1891-93, 1897 and 1902. d. May 21, 1939.

Sterling Hutcheson U.S. Judge, Eastern District of Viriginia since 1944. b. July 23, 1894 in Mecklenburg Co., Va. Admitted to the bar in 1919, and practiced at Boydton. Was U.S. district attorney in 1933-44. Mason.

William E. Hutchison (1860-1952) Justice, Supreme Court of Kansas, 1927-39. b. July 14, 1860 in Oxford, Pa. Graduate of Lafayette Coll. (Pa.) in 1883 and 1886. Admitted to Pa. bar in 1886 and Kans. bar in 1887. He first practiced in Ulysses,

Kans. and later in Garden City. He was county attorney, district judge, secretary of state board of bar examiners (1912-27) and pardon attorney of Kans. in 1925. He was raised in Santa Fe Lodge No. 312, Sublette, Kans. on May 14, 1892, was master in 1896 and grand master of the Grand Lodge of Kansas in 1912. He was exalted in Dodge City Chapter No. 75, R.A.M. on Jan. 20, 1895 and affiliated with Garden City Chapter No. 83 as a charter member in 1901, being charter high priest and serving until 1903; grand high priest, Grand Chapter, R.A.M. of Kansas in 1924. Member of Dodge City Council No. 16, R. & SM., having been greeted in Wichita Council No. 12 on Dec. 14, 1920. He was knighted in Dodge City Commandery No. 35, K.T. on July 2, 1895 and became a charter member of Garden City Commandery No. 50, serving as commander from 1905-07 and grand commander, Grand Commandery, K.T. of Kansas in 1928. Member of Red Cross of Constantine and 33° ASSR (SJ). d. April 5, 1952.

William L. Hutcheson (1874-1953) President of United Brotherhood of Carpenters and Joiners, 1915-53. b. Feb. 7, 1874 in Saginaw Co., Mich. He began as a carpenter in 1890, and then became business representative for the union, becoming 2nd vice president, 1st vice president, and then general vice president of the same. He was also vice president of the American Federation of Labor from 1940. He was a member of the War Labor Board, 1917-19, and in charge of the labor division of the Republican party in 1932 and 1936. A Mason, he was a member of both Scottish and York Rites, The Royal Order of Scotland and Red Cross of Constantine. He was a 33° AASR (SJ). Lodge membership was

in Capital City Lodge No. 312, Indianapolis, Ind. d. 1953.

Lester Hutchings (1896-1951) President of Western Auto Supply Co. b. April 7, 1896 in Excelsior Springs, Mo. He became a certified public accountant in 1920, and in 1928 associated with the Western Auto Supply, becoming first vice president in 1937. Served in U.S. Navy in WWI. Mason. d. Feb. 12, 1951.

Elijah C. Hutchinson (1855-1932) U.S. Congressman to 64th through 67th Congresses (1915-23) from 4th N.J. dist. b. Aug. 7, 1855 at Windsor, N.J. He was secretary and treasurer of the Trenton Bone Fertilizer Co. From 1905-08 he was state road commissioner of N.J., and served in both houses of the state legislature. Received the degrees in Column Lodge No. 120, Trenton, N.J. in 1886, dimitting on Dec. 12, 1904 and affiliating with Loyal Lodge No. 181, Trenton as a warrant member on March 23, 1905. d. June 25, 1932.

William Hutchinson (1732-1814) Early English Masonic writer known as "the father of Masonic symbolism." A lawyer by profession, he devoted much of his time to writing,- including several works of fiction and plays. He is best known for his Spirit of Masonry, which did much to elevate the Frank K. Hyatt spirit and character of the Craft. He prepared a series of Masonic lectures about the same time that William Preston, q.v., was similarly employed. He was master of the Lodge of Concord in his home town of Barnard Castle. d. April 7, 1814.

James Hutchison (1752-1793) Surgeon General of Pennsylvania in the Revolution. b. Jan. 29,

1752 in Wakefield, Pa. He received his medical education in London, and at the prospect of war, he espoused the cause of the colonies. Returning home by way of France, he bore important dispatches from Benjamin Franklin to congress. He joined the American Army and served throughout the war as a physician and surgeon. He was a trustee of the U. of Pa. from 1779 until his death, and was secretary of a philosophical society for several years, and professor of medicine at U. of Pa. Member of Lodge No. 2, Philadelphia. d. Sept. 6, 1793.

Joseph C. Hutchison Brigadier General and business executive. b. Sept. 17, 1894 in Cross Hill, S.C. Started as a school teacher and clerk, and since 1935 in own business as J. C. Hutchison & Co. (Fla. and N.Y.). Served in WWI as a private to second lieutenant, and in Fla. national guard was advanced to brigadier general in 1940, and commanded the 62nd Infantry. In WWII he was assistant division commander of the 31st Infantry Division. Member of Sanford Lodge No. 62, Monroe Chapter No. 15, R.A.M. and Taylor Commandery No. 28, K.T., all of Sanford, Fla. Member of Bahia Shrine Temple of Orlando, Fla.

Ralph C. Hutchison College president. b. Feb. 27, 1898 at Florissant, Colo. Graduate of Lafayette Coll., Harvard, Princeton Theol. Seminary, U. of Pennsylvania. Ordained to ministry of Presbyterian church in 1922; secretary of young people's work, Presbyterian board of Christian education, 1924-25; professor of philosophy and religion at Alborz Coll., Teheran, Persia. From 1931-45 he was president of Washington and Jefferson College, and since 1945 has been president of

Lafayette College, Easton, Pa. Served in WWI as a naval aviator. Received 1st degree in Tyrian Lodge No. 246, Garden City, Kans. on Dec. 19, 1919; 2nd and 3rd in Princeton, N.J. on Feb. 13 and May 19, 1922. Now member of Easton Lodge No. 152, Easton, Pa.; 32° AASR (NJ) in Lehigh Consistory, Allentown, Pa.; and member of Tall Cedars of Lebanon, Forest No. 35, Easton, Pa.

Levi W. Hutton (1860-1928) Philanthropist and miner. b. Oct. 22, 1860 at Fairfield, Iowa. He was left an orphan at the age of six and was reared by an uncle. In 1879 he went to Portland, Oreg., where he became a locomotive fireman, and later an engineer on the Northern Pacific railway. He was one of the original owners of the Hercules Mine of the Coeur d'Alene district in Idaho, one of the largest lead-silver producing mines of the country. He built and owned many buildings in Spokane. In 1917 he established near Spokane the Hutton Settlement, a home for orphans, fully endowed, on 300 acres with modern buildings. Mason. d. Nov. 3, 1928.

Walter A. Huxman Governor of Kansas, 1937-39 and member of U.S. Circuit Court of Appeals since 1939. b. Feb. 16, 1887 at Pretty Prairie, Kans. Graduate of Kansas U. in 1914. Admitted to the bar in 1915, and practiced at Hutchinson. Former member of Reno Lodge No. 140, Hutchinson, dimitting on May 31, 1945.

Frank K. Hyatt President of Pennsylvania Military College, Chester, Pa. 1930-52; now emeritus. b. Nov. 19, 1885 at Chester, Pa. He became associated with the college in 1907, as assistant professor, later professor; treasurer from 1916, and vice president, 1917-30. He succeeded his father who was president of the college for many years. Member of Chester Lodge No. 236, Chester, Pa.; Chester Chapter No. 258, R.A.M. and Chester Commandery No. 66, K.T., as well as Tall Cedars of Lebanon.

Arthur M. Hyde (1877-1947) Governor of Missouri, 1921-25, and Secretary of Agriculture in cabinet of President Hoover, 1929-33. b. July 12, 1877 in Princeton, Mo. Graduate of U. of Michigan in 1899, and State U. of Iowa in 1900. He practiced law at Princeton, Mo., 1900-15, and was mayor of that city from 1908-10. In 1915 he moved to Trenton, Mo. He was a member of Mercer Lodge No. 35, Princeton, Mo. and the Royal Arch Chapter in that city, serving as its secretary at one time. When the chapter gave up its charter, he affiliated with Trenton Chapter No. 66, R.A.M., Trenton, Mo. He received the 33° AASR (SJ) at Kansas City, Mo., Nov. 25, 1909. d. Oct. 17, 1947, and buried in Trenton with Masonic honors. After his death, his widow, Hortense Cullers Hyde, gave a memorialentrance to the Trenton Masonic Cemetery.

Laurance M. Hyde Chief Justice, Supreme Court of Missouri, 1949-51. b. Feb. 2, 1892 in Princeton, Mo. He is a brother of Arthur M. Hyde, q.v. Graduate of U. of Missouri in 1914 and 1916. He practiced in Princeton, Mo. from 1916. Supreme court commissioner of Missouri supreme court, 1931-39. Judge of Missouri supreme court, since 1942. Member of Mercer Lodge No. 35, Princeton, Mo. Received chapter degrees in Princeton Chapter No. 31 in 1919, and affiliated with Trenton Chapter No. 66 by consolidation in 1927, dimitting in 1932; 32° AASR (SJ) at Kansas City, Mo.

George B. Hynson (1862-1926) Author of Delaware's state song, Our Delaware. Teacher, lawyer, editorial writer and poet. A collection of his poems has been published under the title of Down Yon. and Therabouts. b. April 2, 1862. Member of Temple Lodge No. 9, Milford, Del. and past master of same. He was grand master of the Grand Lodge of Delaware in 1917. d. Dec. 5, 1926.

I

Ascension Esquivel Ibarra (see under Esquivel).

August W. Iffland (1759-1814) German character actor, director, and dramatist. He was received into Freemasonry in Hamburg, but received only the Apprentice degree. In 1787 he published a Masonic play called Der Magnetismus.

George E. Ijams Drafted plan of soldier insurance used in the field in WWI. b. Sept. 29, 1888 in Baltimore, Md. Served in the Mexican Border conflict and enlisted as a private in WWI, later promoted to lieutenant colonel. He was assigned to the A.E.F. detachment of War Risk Insurance Bureau in WWI, and as risk insurance officer of the 1st Infantry Div., he wrote two hundred million in insurance at the front, some of it under fire. Returning to the U.S. he was assistant director of Bureau of War Risk Ins., and director of the U.S. Veterans Bureau during its last year.

He was assistant administrator of Veterans Administration from its beginning until 1946. He then became director of national rehabilitation service of Veterans of Foreign Wars until 1954. Mason, National Sojourner, Heroes of '76, Knight Templar and Shriner.

Orlando B. Iles (1869-1941) President of International Machine Tool Co., 1923-39. b. May 31, 1869 in Brown Co., Ohio. Graduate of DePauw U. in 1894, he was admitted to the bar in 1897, and practiced in Indianapolis, Ind. In 1899 he entered the wholesale produce business and became manager of the Capitol Gas Engine Co., which later became the International Machine Tool Co. Member of Mystic Tie Lodge No. 398, Indianapolis, Ind. d. April 7, 1941.

Charles F. Inbusch General Grand Master, General Grand Council, R. & S.M., 1946-48. b. Sept. 12, 1885 in Milwaukee, Wis. Graduate of U. of Wisconsin in 1907, followed by law course. For seven years he was in orchard development in Montana, and with the Inbusch Storage and Trucking Co. at Milwaukee for ten years. Since 1936 he has been with the inspection department of New York Life Insurance Co. Life member of Kenwood Lodge No. 303; exalted in Kenwood Chapter No. 90, R.A.M. in 1920; greeted in Kenwood Council No. 34, R. & S.M. in 1920; knighted in Galilee Commandery K.T., 1920 and 32° AASR, 1920. Member of Tripoli Shrine Temple. Was grand master of the Grand Council, R. & S.M. of Wis. in 1936.

Sydney R. Inch President of Electric Bond & Share, 1933-40. b. June 16, 1878 in England. Began with Montana Power Transmission Co. at Butte, Mont. in 1900, and then

with several public service companies, becoming vice president and general manager of Utah Power & Light Co. in 1918-23. He was vice president of Electric Bond & Share from 1924-33. Mason.

William, 4th Earl of Inchiquin Grand Master of the Grand Lodge of England (Moderns) in 1726.

John J. Ingalls (1833-1900) U.S. Senator from Kansas, 1873-91. His statue is in Statuary Hall, U.S. Capitol, Washington, D.C. b. Dec. 29, 1833 in Middletown, Mass. He was graduated from Williams Coll. in 1855, studied law, and was admitted to the bar. In 1858 he moved to Atchison, Kans., where he was a member of the Wyandotte convention of 1859, and secretary of the Territorial Council in 1860. He was a state senator in 1862. From 1887-91 he was president pro tem of the U.S. senate. He received his degrees in Washington Lodge No. 5, Atchison, Kansas in 1862, and is recorded as senior warden the next year. He was evidently suspended NPD at one time, for he was reinstated on April 5, 1869. d. Aug. 16, 1900.

Rufus Ingalls (1820-?) Major General of Civil War, and later Quartermaster General of the Army. b. Aug. 23, 1820 at Denmark, Maine. Graduate of U.S. Military Academy in 1843. He was in the battles of Embudo and Taos, N.M. in 1847, and then served in Calif. and Oreg. He was in Steptoe's expedition across the continent, and from 1856-60 was stationed at Fort Vancouver. At the outset of the Civil War, he was appointed aide-de-camp to Gen. McClellan, and from 1862-65 was chief quartermaster of the Army of the Potomac. He became brigadier general in 1863, and major general in

1865. He was present at the battles of Stone Mountain, Antietam, Fredericksburg, Chancellorsville, and Gettysburg. He became quartermaster general of the Army in 1882, and retired in 1883. He was initiated July 22, 1852 in Willamette Lodge No. 2, Portland, Oreg., but his name disappears from the list after 1856 (when he went to Fort Vancouver). Deceased.

Ebon C. Ingersoll Brother and law partner of Robert G. Ingersoll, q.v., famous agnostic. Member of Peoria Lodge No. 15, Peoria, Ill.

Ralph I. Ingersoll (1788-1872) U.S. Congressman from Connecticut, 1825-33; U.S. Minister to Russia, 1846-48.b. Feb. 8, 1788 in New Haven, Conn. Was graduated from Yale in 1808, and was admitted to the bar in 1811. He practiced in New Haven. Served in lower house of the state for seven years, and in 1825 he was elected to both the lower house and U.S. Congress. He was raised Sept. 19, 1811 in Hiram Lodge No. 1, New Haven, Conn.; served as master in 1814. d. Aug. 26, 1872. Was G.M. of Conn. 1823-24.

Robert G. Ingersoll (1833-1899) American lawyer and agnostic. b. Aug. 11, 1833 in Dresden, N.Y., the son of a Congregational clergyman. His boyhood was spent in Wis. and El. He opened a law office with his brother, Ebon, q.v., at Shawneetown, Ill., moving it to Peoria in 1857. He was a colonel of the 11th Ill. Cavalry in the Civil War and attorney general of Ill. in 1867-69. In 1877 he refused the post of U.S. minister to Germany. He became a noted agnostic lecturer, attacking popular Christian beliefs. Was author of *The Gods and Other Lecturers; Some Mistakes of Moses; Why I Am an Agnostic*; and

Superstition. Although no record can be found of his Masonic membership in Ill., in a speech in San Francisco in 1877 he said that he had received the degrees and that a "Rev. Guard" had attacked him for ridiculing parts of the Bible upon which he took his oath. E. R. Sadowski, Masonic research student of Illinois, believes he was a member and that his membership was hidden as he was highly regarded by the citizens of Peoria who knew him as one of the most sincere persons in the world. d. 1899.

Stuart II. Ingersoll Vice Admiral, U.S. Navy. b. June 3, 1898 in Springfield, Mass. Graduate of U.S. Naval Academy in 1920, and advanced through grades to rear admiral in 1944, and vice admiral in 1955. Commander of U.S. Seventh Fleet. Presently president of Naval War College, Newport, R.I. Member of Portland Lodge No. 1, Portland, Maine, receiving degrees in 1921.

Samuel D. Ingham (1779-1860) Secretary of the Treasury under President Jackson. b. Sept. 16, 1779 in Pa. Managed a paper mill in N.J. for several years. He then served three years in the Pa. legislature, and was U.S. congressman from 1813-18, and 1822-29. Mason. d. June 5, 1860.

Sir Edward Inglefield British Rear Admiral. He served as secretary of Lloyd's of London from 1906-21. A member of Lutine Lodge No. 3049 (composed of employees of Lloyd's). He was provincial grand master of Buckinghamshire in 1917. Deceased.

Sir Edward A. Inglefield (1820-1894) British Admiral and Arctic explorer. He visited the Arctic in search of Sir John Franklin in 1852-

53-54. On the rolls of the Craft in Nova Scotia.

Charles Inglis (1734-1816) First British Angelican Bishop in overseas empire. b. in 1734 in County Donegal, Ireland. Coming to America, he taught school in Lancaster, Pa. from 1754-58. He was ordained in England in 1758

Sir John Eardely Wilmot Inglis (1814-1862) British Major General famous for his gallant defense of Lucknow, India in 1857. b. in Nova Scotia, he served in Canada in 1837, and in the Punjab in 1848-49. He was initiated and passed in a Canadian lodge, but joined Phoenix Lodge No. 257, Portsmouth, England in 1841, and was raised Jan. 26, 1842.

Thomas Walker Hobart Inskip (1876-1947) 1st Viscount of Caldecote (about 1939). English jurist and government official. b. in Bristol. He was educated at Cambridge, and called to the bar in 1899. He served in Admiralty naval intelligence division in WWI, and headed the naval law branch in 1918. He was a member of parliament from 1918-29, and 1931-39; solicitor general, 1922-24, 1924-28, 1931-32; attorney general, 1928-29, 1932-36; minister for coordination of defense, 1936-39; secretary of state for dominion affairs, 1939-40; lord chancellor, 1939-40; and leader of the House of Lords in 1940. He served as junior grand warden of the United Grand Lodge of England in 1941. Deceased in 1947.

Frederick W. Insull (1875-1939) Public utilities executive. b. July 5, 1875 in London, England. He came to the U.S. in 1901, and was naturalized in 1912. He began as a trolley wagon driver with the Winni-

peg Electric Railway in 1891. From 1901-09 he was secretary-treasurer of the North Shore Electric Co. of Chicago. From 1913-39 he was president of the Public Service Co. of Okla., and president of the Southwestern Light & Power Co. from 1928. Received degrees in Oklahoma City Lodge No. 36, Oklahoma City, Okla. on April 13, May 23 and July 9, 1914. Dimitted on May 18, 1925. d. Jan. 14, 1939.

James Iredell, Jr. (1788-1853) Governor and U.S. Senator from North Carolina. b. Nov. 2, 1788 in Edenton, N.C. He was graduated from Princeton in 1806, and then studied law. He served in the War of 1812. He served in the state legislature for many years and was speaker of the house. From 1827-28 he was governor of N.C. and from 1828-31, U.S. senator. He subsequently practiced law in Raleigh and was one of the three commissioners appointed to revise the laws of the state. He was raised in Unanimity Lodge No. 54 at Edenton in 1808, being the 59th signer of the by-laws. He represented his lodge at grand lodge, Nov. 27, 1811, and almost every yearly session from that time until 1844. He held many offices in the grand lodge, and was deputy grand master in 1823. In 1878 the Grand Lodge of N.C. chartered Iredell Lodge No. 362, named in his honor. It went out of existence in 1889. d. April 13, 1853.

Clifford Ireland (1878-1930) U.S. Congressman, 65th through 67th Congresses (1917-23) from 16th dist. b. Feb. 14, 1878 at Washburn, Ill. Admitted to the bar in 1909, he began practice at Peoria. He was president of the Western Live Stock Ins. Co. Served in Spanish-American War in 1898. Member of Washburn

Lodge No. 421, Washburn, El. d. May 24, 1930.

John Ireland The Rev. Ireland was the first chaplain to be commissioned in the U.S. Navy, receiving his appointment on Aug. 16, 1816. He was a member of Fortitude Lodge No. 19, Brooklyn, N.Y.

John Ireland (1827-1896) Governor of Texas, 1882-86. b. Jan. 1, 1827 in Hart Co., Ky. He studied law, and moved to Texas in 1852, practicing at Sequin. He was a member of the convention that passed the ordinance of secession in 1861; and served through the war in the Confederate Army, rising to lieutenant colonel of Infantry in 1862. He was a delegate to the state constitutional convention of 1866, and served a term in both state legislative bodies. He was appointed an associate judge of the supreme court of Texas in 1875. Member of Guadalupe Lodge No. 109, Guadalupe, Texas.

Merritt W. Ireland (1867-1952) Surgeon General, U.S. Army, 191831. b. May 31, 1867 in Columbia City, Ind. Received his M.D. from Detroit Coll. of Medicine in 1890, and another from Jefferson Medical Coll. in 1891. He was appointed assistant surgeon, U.S.A. in 1891, and advanced through grades to major general in 1918. He was in the Santiago Campaign in the Philippines during the insurrection, and was chief surgeon of the A.E.F. in France until Oct. 12, 1918. Mason, he was made a 33° AASR (SJ), Oct. 21, 1921; member of Almas Shrine Temple. Member of Columbia City Lodge No. 189, Columbia City, Ind., being initiated Aug. 6, 1888. d. July 5, 1952.

Leslie L. Irvin Parachute manufacturer. b. Sept. 10, 1895 at Los Angeles, Calif. He founded the Irving Air Chute Co., Inc. at Lexington, Ky. in 1919, and has been president of same since 1946. He is also president of Irving Air Chute, Ltd. of Ontario, and director of Irving Air Chute of Great Britain; Irvin Fallskarmsaktiebolag, Stockholm, Sweden, and Irvin-Bell Helicopter Sales, Ltd., England. Member of Master Builder Lodge No. 911, Kenmore, N.Y. since 1922; 32° AASR in Buffalo, N.Y.; and Ismailia Shrine Temple of Buffalo.

Sir Henry Irving (1838-1905) First English actor to be knighted. His original name was John Henry Brodribb. b. near Glastonbury, England. He was on the stage in Edinburgh from 1857-59, and in Manchester, 1860-65. He scored his first notable success as Digby Grant in Two Roses, on the London stage in 1870, followed by Hamlet, Macbeth, and Othello. He was the manager of the Lyceum Theatre, London in 1878. He was professionally associated with Ellen Terry from 1878-1902, and acted with her in Hamlet; Merchant of Venice; Romeo and Juliet; Much Ado About Nothing; Twelfth Night; King Lear, etc. He made eight American tours, 1883-84, and 1903-04. He was knighted in 1895, and is buried in Westminster Abbey. He was initiated in 1877, at the age of 39, in Jerusalem Lodge No. 197, London, and five years elapsed before he received the 2nd and 3rd degrees in the same lodge. They were conferred by Sir Edward Letchworth, then master. He was a founding member, and first treasurer, of Savage Club Lodge No. 2190, and for 11 years was a member of St. Martin's Lodge No. 2455.

Leonard Irving U.S. Congressman, 81st Congress (1949-51) . b. March 24, 1898 at St. Paul, Minn.

Began in railroad work, became theatre manager in Mont., and later hotel manager in Calif. He entered construction work in Mo. and became business agent for A.F. of L. Construction and General Laborers Union Local No. 264, Kansas City. Mason and Shriner.

William Irving (1766-1821) U.S. Congressman, fur trader, merchant, author, and brother of famed Washington Irving. b. Aug. 15, 1766 in New York City. From 1787-91 he was a fur trader with the Indians in the Mohawk Valley, residing at Johnstown and Caughnawaga. He settled in New York City in 1793, and married a sister of the author, James K. Paulding. He assisted and contributed much to the latter's Salmagundi as well as Mustapha. He was elected to congress three times, serving from 1814-18. He was a member of Holland Lodge No. 8, N.Y.C., and served it as master, 1899-1900. He was also a member of a commandery in New York about 1802. d. Nov. 9, 1821.

Richard W. Irwin (1857-1932) Justice, Superior Court of Massachusetts, 1911-32. b. Feb. 18, 1857 in Northampton, Mass. Graduate of Boston U. in 1885, and practiced law at Northampton. He served in both branches of the state legislature; on governor's council, and was district attorney. Initiated in Pacific Lodge, Amherst, Mass. and later affiliated with Jerusalem Lodge, Northampton, Mass. Also member of Northampton Connmandery, K.T. No. 30 of Northampton. d. March 9, 1932.

Augustin de Iturbide (1783-1824) Soldier and Emperor of Mexico. Said to have been raised in a Mexico City lodge. He commanded the Spanish Army against Vincente Guerrero in 1820, and later joined Guerrero, q.v., in setting up the Plan of Iguala in 1821. Together, they forced the Spanish government to capitulate in the Treaty of Cordoba, which assured Mexican independence. The victory went to Iturbide's head, and he set himself up as Emperor Augustin I from 1822-23. However, his harsh measures of repression led to revolution by Santa Anna, q.v., and Guerrero, q.v., and he abdicated, March 19, 1823, and exiled himself in Europe. He returned and was captured and shot, July 19, 1824.

Alfred Iverson (1798-1873) U.S. Senator from Georgia, 1855-1861. b. Dec. 3, 1798 in Burke Co., Ga. He was graduated from Princeton in 1820, studied law, and practiced in Columbus, Ga. He served in both houses of the state legislature, and was a superior court judge for seven years. In the senate he was one of the leaders of the secession movement. At the beginning of hostilities he entered the Confederate Army, and rose to brigadier general, Nov., 1862. Member of Columbian Lodge No. 8, Columbus, Ga. d. March 4, 1873.

Benjamin F. P. Ivins Protestant Episcopal Bishop. b. Oct. 6, 1884 in South Bend, Ind. Graduate of Nashotah Theol. Seminary, Valparaiso U., and U. of Wisconsin. Ordained deacon in 1909 and priest in 1910. He served pastorates in Plymouth, Ind., Gary, Ind., Kalamazoo, Mich. He was named bishop coadjutor of Milwaukee in 1925, and bishop in 1933. In 1927 he was a joint leader (with English Bishop of Lewes) of Anglo Catholic pilgrimage to the Near East. He received his degrees in Plymouth-Kilwinning Lodge No. 149 of Plymouth, Ind., on Dec. 2, 8, and 13th, 1910. He later dimitted to Lafayette

Lodge No. 265 of Milwaukee, Wis. and is an honorary member of Kenwood Lodge No. 303, Milwaukee. He holds dual membership in Delray Lodge No. 171, Delray Beach, Fla. Exalted on April 26, 1911 in Plymouth Chapter No. 26, R.A.M. of Plymouth, Ind., he is presently member of Kenwood Chapter No. 90, Milwaukee; greeted in Plymouth Council, R. & S.M. on Feb. 29, 1912. Member of Ivanhoe Commandery No. 24, K.T., Milwaukee, but knighted in Plymouth, Ind. In the AASR (NJ) he received 32° in 1932; 33° in 1941; active 33° in 1945; and emeritus since retirement to Florida in 1955. He has served as grand chaplain of the Grand Lodge of Wisconsin; Mark W. Izard grand prelate of Grand Commandery of Wisconsin; master of Rose Croix, AASR and sovereign of Red Cross of Constantine.

Mark W. Izard Territorial Governor of Nebraska. When Francis Burt took the oath of office as the first territorial governor, Oct. 16, 1854, he died two days later, and Izard, then U.S. marshal, succeeded him and served the next two years during the important development period. He was one of the petitioners for a dispensation for Capitol Lodge No. 3 of Omaha, originally No. 101.

J

Daniel C. Jackling (1869-1956) Founder of the Utah Copper Co., the largest single producer of copper in the world. b. Aug. 14, 1869 at Appleton City, Mo. He was orphaned at the age of two, when his

parents were killed in an accident. He was graduated from the Missouri School of Mines at Rolla, Mo. in 1892, and with a borrowed $200, went to Cripple Creek, Colo. and secured a job as a metallurgist. He founded the Utah Copper Co. in 1903, with four others. It later became part of Kennecott Copper Co. Jackling at one time refused the presidency of this firm. Considered a mining genius, he developed a process for extracting copper from low grade ore, and this process now accounts for more than 60% of the world's production. A heroic statue of Tackling was unveiled Aug. 14, 1954, in the Utah State Capitol. He was master of Rocky Mountain Lodge No. 11, Tooele, Utah, in 1899; was a life member of Utah Chapter No. 1, R.A.M. of Salt Lake City, and was knighted in Utah Commandery No. 1, K.T., July 1, 1954, and made a life member. He gave the Grand Chapter of Utah a set of 14 jewels which cost $1400. d. March 13, 1956.

Allan Jackson Vice President of Standard Oil Co. of Indiana. b. July, 1876 in Marseilles, Ill. He began with Standard Oil as a secretary in the Chicago office in 1896, and was with the company 45 years before retirement in 1941. He was a member of the board and vice president in charge of sales in 14 states. Member of Marseilles Lodge No. 417, Marseilles, Ill., Knight Templar; 32° AASR (NJ) in Chicago in April 1900; and 33°, 1955; Shriner.

Andrew Jackson (1767-1845) Seventh President of the United States. b. March 15, 1767 in Washaw settlement between North and South Car. He was admitted to the bar in Salisbury, N.C. in 1787, and, the following year, migrated westward to Nashville, Tenn. Here he became a U.S. congressman (1796-97); U.S. senator (1797-98); judge of the Tenn. supreme court (1798-1804); and major general of Tenn. militia (1802). He defeated the Creek Indians at the Battle of Horseshoe Bend in 1814, and was made major general of U.S. Army and assigned to defend New Orleans in the War of 1812. His defense of that city made him a national hero. He added to his fame by operations against the Seminole Indians in 1818, and involved the federal government by pursuing Indians into Spanish territory, and hanging two English troublemakers. He was governor of Florida Territory in 1821, and again U.S. senator in 1823-25. His first presidential race in 1824 was unsuccessful, but he was elected in 1828, and reelected in 1832. Under his administration the spoils system was introduced, the national debt paid off, the United States Bank overthrown, and the Peggy O'Neale scandal broke up his cabinet. There is doubt as to when and where he received his degrees. An article in The Builder in 1925 states: "The claim of Greeneville Lodge No. 3 of Tenn. (formerly No. 43 of N.C.) seems to be the most weighty. An original transcript of the lodge record for Sept. 5, 1801 shows that he (Jackson) was a member at that time." W. L. Boydon wrote in the *New Age* in Aug. 1920: "The generally accepted belief is that he was made a Mason in Philanthropic Lodge No. 12 at Clover Bottom, Davidson Co., Tenn." Bell, in his Famous Masons states: "Jackson was a member of Harmony Lodge No. 1 (formerly St. Tammany Lodge No. 29 of N.C.) Nashville, as early as 1800, but the date of receiving the degrees has not been learned. He was present at the first meeting of Tennessee Lodge No. 2, Knoxville, March 24, 1800. Charles Comstock, PGM of Tenn. and histo-

rian, believes that he was a member of Harmony Lodge, and records a visit by him to the initial meeting of Polk Lodge, U.D., Knoxville (dispensation granted Jan. 15, 1800) by "Andrew Jackson of Harmony Lodge of Nashville." In 1808 Harmony Lodge No. 1 lost its charter, and here all record of Jackson's Masonic affiliation ceases until 1822. He evidently kept in good standing by paying his dues to the grand lodge, as was then permitted. The proceedings of 1822 credit him with being a past master, but no record has been found of his mastership. He was elected grand master of the Grand Lodge of Tennessee, Oct. 7, 1822, and again in 1823, serving until Oct., 1824. He was elected an honorary member of Federal Lodge No. 1, Washington, D.C., Jan. 4, 1830, and of Jackson Lodge No. 1, Tallahassee, Fla. as well as the Grand Lodge of Florida (Jan. 15, 1833). He was a Royal Arch Mason, as he served the Grand Chapter of Tennessee as deputy grand high priest at its institution, April 3, 1826, but no record exists of his affiliation with any chapter. As was the custom at the time, the Royal Arch degree was probably conferred by a blue lodge. He contributed $35.00 in 1818 to the erection of a Masonic temple in Nashville; requested two lodges to perform funeral services; introduced Lafayette to the Grand Lodge of Tennessee in 1825; while president, assisted Washington's mother lodge to lay a cornerstone of a monument to Washington's mother in Fredericksburg, Va. (May 6, 1833); assisted in the Masonic laying of the cornerstone of Jackson City (across the river from Washington, D.C.) on Jan. 11, 1836; attended the Grand Lodge of Tennessee in 1839; and the same year visited Cumberland Chapter No. 1 of Nashville to assist in the installation of officers. d. June 8, 1845.

Clarence A. Jackson President of American United Life Insurance Co. (Ind.) since 1952. b. June 29, 1891 in Columbus, Ohio. Was a partner of Smith-Jackson Co., wholesalers, from 1918-33. He organized and directed the Indiana State Gross Income Tax Div., 1933-39, and the Indiana State Employment Security Div., 1936-39; director of Indiana State Civilian Defense, 1941-46; and vice chairman of the Indiana Comm. for Economic Development since 1943. Raised in New Castle Lodge No. 91, New Castle, Ind. in 1912, shortly after his 21st birthday.

Conrad F. Jackson (1813-1862) Brigadier General in Civil War. b. Sept. 11, 1813 in Pa. Before the war he was connected with the Pennsylvania and Reading Railroad. He joined the army early in 1861, and was appointed colonel of the 9th regiment of Pa. reserves, which he commanded at the battle of Dranesville, Va., and under Gen. G. A. McCall in the Pa. campaign. He was made brigadier general in July 1862, fought at South Mountain, and was killed at Fredericksburg while commanding the 3rd brigade of McCall's division. d. Dec. 13, 1862. Member of Lodge No. 45, Pittsburgh, Pa.

Ed Jackson (1875-1954) Governor of Indiana from 1925-29. b. Dec. 27, 1875 in Howard Co., Ind. Practiced law at New Castle and Indianapolis. Member of Newcastle Lodge No. 91 of Newcastle, Ind. and also the chapter, council and commandery there. Member of Murat Shrine Temple of Indianapolis. Suspended NPD Dec. 5, 1934. d. Nov. 18, 1954.

Elihu E. Jackson (1837-1907) Governor of Maryland, 1888-92. b. Nov. 3, 1837 in Wicomico Co., Md. He operated a country store at Delmar, Md. from 1859-62, moving to Salisbury in the latter year, where he engaged in the lumber business. He was a member of the state legislature in 1882-83, and state senator, 1884-88. Member of Wicomico Lodge No. 91, Salisbury, Md. d. 1907.

Frank D. Jackson (1854-1938) Governor of Iowa, 1894-96. b. Jan. 26, 1854 at Arcade, N.Y., moving to Iowa in his boyhood. Graduate of State U. of Iowa in 1874. He was secretary of the Iowa senate, 1882-84, and secretary of state, 1884-89. He was president of the Royal Union Life Ins. Co. Jackson received his degrees in Alpha Lodge No. 326, Greene, Iowa, Dec. 6, 1881, March 23, 1883, and April 24, 1883; withdrew in 1901, and affiliated with Capitol Lodge No. 110 of Des Moines in 1904; 32° AASR (SJ) in Des Moines Consistory No. 3 in 1909, and KCCH in 1919. d. Nov. 16, 1938.

George W. Jackson (1861-1922) Engineer. b. July 21, 1861 in Chicago, Ill. In contracting business from 1893. He built the Strickler tunnel through Pike's Peak; the 14-foot subway at Reading, Pa.; pneumatic tube system for Associated Press; 90% of the underground system for Chicago Telephone Co., and many others. Mason, Knight Templar; 32° AASR, and Shriner. d. Feb. 5, 1922.

Gilder D. Jackson, Jr. Brigadier General, U.S. Marine Corps. b. July 5, 1893 at Dover, Del. Commissioned second lieutenant in Marine Corps in 1917, and advanced through grades to brigadier general in 1946. He served in WWI with 2nd Division, and later in China, Haiti, Pearl Harbor, and commanded the 6th regiment at Guadalcanal in 1943. Retired in 1946, he has been purchasing agent for Essex Wire Corp. since 1948. Mason.

Henry M. Jackson U.S. Senator from Washington since 1953. b. May 31, 1912 at Everett, Wash. Graduate of U. of Washington Law School in 1935. Served in the U.S. congress from 77th through 81st congresses from 2nd Wash. dist. Named by President Truman as U.S. delegate to International Maritime Conf. at Seattle in 1946. Member of Everett Lodge No. 137, Everett, Wash. and 32° AASR (SJ) in Everett. A former DeMolay, he is a member of the De-Molay Legion of Honor and Nile Shrine Temple of Seattle, Wash.

James Jackson (1757-1806) Brigadier General; Governor of Georgia, U.S. Congressman and U.S. Senator from Georgia. b. Sept. 21, 1757 in Moreton-Hampstead, Devonshire, England. He came to this country in 1772, studied law in Savannah, Ga., and was active in repelling the British from that city in March, 1776. Joining the Continental Army, he took part in the defense of Savannah, and saw service at Blackstocks, Augusta, Cow-pens, and Long Cane. He was made brigadier general in 1788. He was elected governor of Georgia in 1788, but declined to serve, pleading that he was too young. He was governor of the state from 1798-1801; congressman from 1789-91, and U.S. senator, 1793-95, and 1801-06. He killed lieutenant governor Wells in a duel in March, 1780, and also fought a duel with General James Gunn, q.v., both being members of Solomons Lodge No. 1, Savannah. Jackson served as master of the lodge in 1786 (initiated about 1782), and was grand master of the Grand Lodge of Georgia in 1789. On June 24, 1789 he was a visitor to the Grand Lodge of New York, and on Feb. 5, 1790, was a visitor to Holland Lodge, N.Y.C. d. March 19, 1806.

James S. Jackson (1823-1862) Union Brigadier General in Civil War. b. Sept. 27, 1823 in Fayette Co., Ky. He was a graduate of Jefferson Coll. (Pa.) and Transylvania U. He served in the Mexican War, and while in Mexico had a duel with Col. Thomas F. Marshall. To avoid a court-martial, he resigned, and resumed law practice, first at Greenupsburg, and afterward at Hopkinsville, Ky. In 1860 he was elected to congress as a Unionist, but resigned in the fall of 1861 to organize the 3rd Kentucky cavalry. He took an active part in the battles of Shiloh, Corinth, Iuka, and Athens. Made brigadier general in 1862. He was killed in the Battle of Perryville while commanding a division of McCook's corps. Member of Hopkinsville Lodge No. 37, Hopkins-vine, Ky. d. Oct. 8, 1862.

Jesse B. Jackson (1871-1947) U.S. Consul. b. Nov. 19, 1871 at Paulding, Ohio. He was engaged in real estate business until 1905, when he entered the foreign service of the U.S. He served as consul at Alexandretta, Syria; Aleppo, Syria; Leghorn, Italy; Fort William-Port Arthur, Canada, retiring in 1935 after 30 years' service. In the Spanish-American War, he served in the Ohio Inf. Mason. d. Dec. 4, 1947.

Lee R. Jackson President of Firestone Tire and Rubber Co., 1948-57 and vice chairman of board since 1957. b. in Akron, Ohio in 1891, he was educated in the U. of Akron. He began with Firestone as a salesman in 1913, in Detroit, became district manager at Grand Rapids, Mich; Indianapolis, Ind.; division manager of Pacific Coast and division manager of Northwest. He was successively in charge of manufacturers sales, general sales manager, and vice president. Mason and Shriner.

Robert H. Jackson (1892-1954) U.S. Attorney General; U.S. Supreme Court Justice and American prosecutor at Nuremburg war crimes trials in Germany. b. Feb. 13, 1892 at Spring Creek, Pa. Educated in Albany (N.Y.) Law School, he received honorary degrees from many universities. Admitted to N.Y. bar in 1913, he began practice at Jamestown. He was assistant attorney general of the U.S. 1936-38; solicitor general of U.S., 1938-39; U.S. attorney general, 1940-41; and associate justice U.S. supreme court from 1941. In 1945 he was appointed by President Truman to represent the U.S. in negotiating with Russia, England, and France on agreement for international trials of European Axis war criminals, and was also named chief of counsel for U.S., to conduct prosecution of Goering, Ribbentrop and others. A member of Mt. Moriah Lodge No. 145, Jamestown, N.Y., he received his degrees, Sept. 17, Oct. 1, and Oct. 22, 1929; 32° AASR (NJ) in Nov., 1930 at Jamestown; and member of Ismailia Shrine Temple, Buffalo, N.Y. d. Oct. 9, 1954.

Samuel D. Jackson (1895-1951) U.S. Senator from Indiana in 1944. b. May 28, 1895 in Allen Co., Ind. He was admitted to the bar in 1919, and practiced in Fort Wayne, Ind. From 1940-41 he served as attorney general of Ind., and Jan. 28, 1944, was appointed U.S. senator, serving until Nov. 15, 1944. Raised in Summit City Lodge No. 170, Fort Wayne, Ind. on Jan. 3, 1920. Was

33° AASR (NJ) and deputy for Indiana. d. March 8, 1951.

Thomas J. "Stonewall" Jackson (1824-1863) Confederate Major General of Civil War who gained the sobriquet "Stonewall" by his stand at Bull Run. b. Jan. 21, 1824 at Clarksburg, W.Va. Was graduated from U.S. Military Academy in 1846. He served in the Mexican War but resigned from the army in 1852. He joined the Confederate service at the outbreak of the Civil War, and was made brigadier general in 1861, and major general later in the same year. He led the Confederates in the brilliant Shenandoah Valley campaign in 1862, and was mortally wounded by accidental fire from his own troops after routing the Federal right wing at Chancellorsvile, on May 2. d. May 10, 1863. There is no proof as to his Masonic membership, but many details of his life strongly suggest his membership. His father and other near relatives were active members and officers of the Clarksburg, W.Va. lodge, and his father is thought to have been a past master. At the elder Jackson's death (Jonathan), his family was left in poor circumstances and the lodge contributed to their relief, and provided them with a 3-room house at Clarksburg. Stonewall thus had Masonic antecedents, and became a beneficiary of the Craft at the age of two. When he was a faculty member at the Virginia Military Institute at Lexington, Va. he wrote his sister, Laura Jackson Arnold in 1853, and 1854, concerning a Masonic dependent for whom he hoped to secure aid from the lodge at Staunton. When the local lodge could not help, he wrote his sister that he would be in Richmond "this winter and bring her case before the grand lodge of the state." In Simon Wolf's *Presidents I Have Known* the author tells of seeing Jackson secure food for General Pope's prisoners. Upon their meeting, he gave Jackson the sign of distress, which the general answered, and saw that he was safely across the Union lines. If a Mason, he was probably a member of a traveling military lodge while in the Mexican War.

William H. Jackson (1843-1942) Pioneer photographer, artist and explorer. b. April 4, 1843 at Keeseville, N.Y. He was educated in the public schools of N.Y. and Pa. He began as a photographer in Troy, N.Y. (1858), and later Rutland and Burlington, Vt. (1860-66). He served with a Vt. regiment in the Civil War. After the war he traveled overland to Calif. in 1866-67, returning to Omaha, Nebr. in 1868, where he entered the photography business. As the official photographer with the Hayden Expedition of the U.S. Geological Survey in 1870-78, he was the first to take photographs in the Yellowstone region. He was a photographer in Denver, Colo., 1879-97, and at Detroit, Mich. 1898-1924. Between 1894-96 he went on a photography tour around the world for *Harper's Weekly*. In 1924 he retired from business and moved to Washington, D.C., where he began painting and writing about the covered wagon days of the West. Mason. d. June 30, 1942.

William J. Jackson (1859-1932) President of Chicago and Eastern Illinois Railroad. b. in Toronto, Ont. Began in Grand Trunk Railway shops at Toronto as machinist's helper in 1877, rising as freight clerk, chief claim clerk at Chicago, general freight foreman and assistant agent. Entered the Chicago & Eastern service in 1891, rising as local freight agent to general manager, vice president, receiver, and presi-

dent. During receivership of 1918-20, he was federal manager of the line, and president after reorganization. After 1925 he was chairman of the executive committee. Member of Normal Park Lodge No. 797, Chicago, Ill. d. April 4, 1932.

William P. Jackson (1868-1939) U.S. Senator from Maryland, 1912-14. b. Jan. 11, 1868 at Salisbury, Md. Entered lumber manufacturing business in 1887. He was a member of the Republican National Committee from Md. from 1908-32. In 1918-20 he was treasurer of state of Maryland. Member of Wicomico Lodge No. 91, of Salisbury, Md., being raised in 1900. d. March 7, 1939.

Abraham Jacobs (?-1834) Early Scottish Rite member. A native of New York, he received the second degree on July 22, 1782 in St. Andrew's Lodge of Boston, and was a member of York Lodge No. 197, New York City until his death. He brought a diploma signed by Moses Cohen from Jamaica, showing that he received the "Select Mason of 27." He came to Georgia in 1790 and served Forsythe Lodge of Augusta as master in 1799-1800, and later was master of King Solomon Lodge at Charleston. He conferred the AASR degrees on various persons. In 1801 he was joined by Emanuel de la Motta, q.v., a member of the supreme council and he conferred the "Select of 27" on de la Motta in Nov., 1802. He came to New York in 1804 and continued conferring degrees. In 1810 he ran into trouble with the supreme council when he was expelled for having added, without authority, the words "with power to initiate others" to his patent. d. 1834.

Randall Jacobs Vice Admiral, U.S. Navy. b. Dec. 12, 1885 at

Danville, Pa. Graduate of U.S. Naval Academy in 1907, and advanced through grades to vice admiral in 1946. He commanded battleships, target and repair ships, Yangtze river gunboat, cruiser, and in 1941 was training commander of the Atlantic fleet, and chief of Naval personnel in 1941-45. In 1945-46 he was commander of the 13th Naval district, being retired in Nov., 1946, but returned to active duty as governor of the Naval Home at Philadelphia. Received three degrees at the same time by special dispensation in Mahoning Lodge No. 516, Danville, Pa. in May, 1909. 32° AASR in Bloomsburg, Pa.

Bernhard M. Jacobsen (1862-1936) U.S. Congressman 72nd to 74th Congresses (1931-37) from Iowa. b. March 26, 1862 at Klixbuel, Schleswig, Germany. He came to the U.S. at age of 14. He worked in lumberyard, brickyard, and dry goods store before entering the mercantile business on his own in Clinton, Iowa in 1886. Member of Emulation Lodge No. 255, Clinton, Iowa, receiving degrees on June 8, July 14 and 29, 1891. d. June 20, 1936.

Leonard M. Jacobsen and appointed missionary at Dover, Del. serving there from 1759-65. He became assistant minister and later rector of Trinity Church, N.Y.C., 1776-83. A devoted Royalist, he replied to Paine's Common Sense by pamphlet. Although Washington requested him to omit the prayer for the king and royal family, he refused to do so and after the Declaration of Independence, he closed his church and retired in Aug., 1776 to Flushing, L.I., which was then in the possession of the British. He followed the British Army to N.Y. and was chosen rector of Trinity Church in 1777. In 1781-82

he was chaplain of the 1st battalion of N.J. volunteers and at the evacuation in 1783 went to Halifax, N.S. He was consecrated the first bishop of Nova Scotia in England in 1787, with jurisdiction over the other North American provinces, and as such was the first colonial bishop of the Church of England. In 1767 King's College (now Columbia) conferred upon him the degree of M.A. and in 1770 he became one of the governors of the college. He addressed the Grand Lodge of New York on June 24, 1783 and on other occasions as well, appearing before the Grand Lodge in Nova Scotia. d. Feb. 24, 1816.

Leonard M. Jacobsen Radio sports announcer. b. Oct. 15, 1900 in Brooklyn, N.Y. He was an amateur and professional wrestler until 1947, engaging in 302 matches. Some matches were in the Hollywood Legion Stadium against such greats as Lord Lans Downe, Pat Magill, Duke Pettibrove, Billy Gribbs, etc. He is probably the best known sports announcer on the West coast. Mason, Knight Templar and Shriner.

Albin F. Jacobson Drug executive. b. Sept. 25, 1904 at Ortonville, Minn. Graduate of U. of Minn. in 1926. Started with Walgreen Drug Co. as store manager (Minneapolis), district manager (Rochester), and divisional manager (Chicago). In 1944 he became president of the Sontag Drug Stores, Los Angeles, and when it merged with Rexall Drug Co. he became vice president (1944). He is also president of the Albin Enterprises. Member of North Hollywood Lodge No. 542, Calif., being raised July 26, 1947.

Charles L. Jacobson Vice President of Chrysler Corp. b. May 29, 1896 at Paw Paw, Ill. He began with Ford Motor Co. (1914) in their advertising department, followed by six years with Wills-St. Clair Co. In 1925 he associated himself with the Chrysler Corp. at Minneapolis as regional manager, advancing to general sales manager in 1937, and vice president in 1954. Since 1956 he has been in charge of dealer relations and a director of the corporation. Member of Marysville Lodge No. 498, Marysville, Mich. and Port Huron Chapter No. 27, R.A.M., Port Huron, Mich.

Arthur H. James Governor of Pennsylvania, 1939-43. b. July 14, 1883 in Plymouth, Pa. Graduate of Dickinson School of Law in 1904, and practiced in Plymouth and Wilkes-Barre, Pa. He was lieutenant governor of Pa. in 1927-31, and superior court judge, 1932-39. Member of Plymouth Lodge No. 332, Plymouth, Pa. and Valley Chapter No. 214, R.A.M. of that city; 33° AASR (NJ) .

Benjamin F. James U.S. Congressman, 81st through 85th Congresses from 7th Pa. dist. b. in Philadelphia. He is president of the Franklin Printing Co., which was established by Benjamin Franklin. He served in the Army in WWI. Received degrees in University Lodge No. 610, Philadelphia, Pa. in 1909 and affiliated with Wayne Lodge No. 581, Wayne, Pa. on March 21, 1911 and master of same in 1915. Member of Montgomery Chapter No. 262, R.A.M., Ardmore, Pa. and Delhi Grotto of Upper Darby, Pa.

Thomas L. James (1831-1916) Postmaster General of the U.S. under President Garfield, 1881-82. b. March 29, 1831 in Utica, N.Y. Graduate of Hamilton Coll. in 1863. He learned the printing trade and published a paper at Hamilton, N.Y. from 1851-61. He became the collector of

canal tolls there in 1854, customs inspector of New York in 1861, and later deputy collector of customs. From 1873-81 he was postmaster of New York City. He was chairman of board, Lincoln National Bank of N.Y., and director of Metropolitan Life Insurance Co. Member of Hamilton Lodge No. 120, Hamilton, N.Y. d. Sept. 11, 1916.

Warren W. James (1884-1945) Justice, Supreme Court of New Hampshire, 1933-45. b. March 23, 1884 in Jefferson, N.H. Graduate of Bates Coll. in 1906. Admitted to the bar in 1911, he practiced in Berlin, N.H. Raised Sept. 20, 1920 in Sabatis Lodge No. 95, Berlin, N.H. Knight Templar. d. March 11, 1945.

W. Frank James (1873-1945) U.S. Congressman to 64th through 73rd Congresses (1915-25) from 12th Mich. dist. b. May 23, 1873 at Morristown, N.J. He was a member of the Michigan state senate, 1910-14. Served in Spanish-American War. Mason and 32° AASR (NJ). d. Nov. 17, 1945.

William P. James (1870-1940) Federal Judge, Southern District of California, 1923-40. b. Jan. 10, 1870 in Buffalo, N.Y. Began law practice in Los Angeles, was judge of the superior court of Los Angeles from 190510, and served on California court of appeals, 1910-23. Member of East Gate Lodge No. 290 of Los Angeles, affiliating with Sunset Lodge No. 352 of Los Angeles on Jan. 4, 1904. Suspended in 1922 and restored same year. d. July 28, 1940.

George Jameson (also Jamison) A Seneca Indian chief who received the three degrees in Manhattan Lodge No. 62, N.Y.C., June 5, 1840, and was exalted in Ancient

Chapter No. 1, R.A.M. of N.Y.C., June 8, 1840.

Robert F. Janes General Grand High Priest, General Grand Chapter, R.A.M., 1951-54. b. Jan. 12, 1880 in Boston, Mass. Graduate of Harvard in 1902, and 1904. Admitted to Mass. bar in 1904, and shortly thereafter moved to New York City. He was attorney for the New York Bell Telephone Co. for 39 years, resigning in 1945. He was raised in Charity Lodge of Cambridge, Mass., March 6, 1905, and affiliated with Independent Royal Arch Lodge No. 2, N.Y.C., Dec. 16, 1915. He was exalted in Jerusalem Chapter No. 8, N.Y.C. in June 1915, served as high priest in 1923, and grand high priest of the Grand Chapter of N.Y. in 1933. Greeted in Adelphic Council No. 7, R. & S.M. May 3, 1930, he was master in 1940; knighted in Coeur de Leon Commandery No. 23, N.Y.C., March 24, 1916, he was commander in 1920. He is a charter member of St. Paul's Conclave No. 12, Red Cross of Constantine, and sovereign in 1928; member of Aurora Grata Consistory, Brooklyn, AASR (NJ) , and Mecca Shrine Temple of N.Y.C.

Charles C. Jarchow President of American Steel Foundries, Chicago since 1949 and director since 1943. b. Dec. 22, 1894 at Chicago. He has been associated with the company since 1912. From 1923-24 he was comptroller, vice president from 1943-47. Mason and Shriner.

William M. Jardine (1879-1955) Secretary of Agriculture under President Coolidge, 1925-29 and U.S. Minister to Egypt, 1930-33. b. Jan. 16, 1879 in Oneida Co., Idaho. Graduate of Agricultural Coll. of Utah in 1904, and 1925. He worked on ranches in Idaho and Mont. until 20 years of age. He taught in the agronomy dept. of his alma mater from 1904-07, and later in the agricultural colleges of Kansas and Michigan. From 1918-25 he was president of the Kansas State Agricultural Coll. and president of the Municipal U., Wichita, Kans. from 1934. In 1933-34 he was state treasurer of Kans. Active nationally and internationally in agronomy field. He became a Mason in Lafayette Lodge No. 16, Manhattan, Kans., on July 23, 1915. d. Jan. 17, 1955.

Pete Jarman (1892-?) U.S. Congressman to 75th through 80th Congresses (1937-49) from 6th Ala. dist. b. Oct. 31, 1892 at Greensboro, Ala. Graduate of U. of Alabama in 1913. He was secretary of state of Alabama in 1931-35, and state comptroller from 1935-37. In 1949 he was confirmed as U.S. Ambassador to Australia. Served in WWI as a lieutenant in 327th Inf. A.E.F., and later was a lieutenant colonel of Ala. national guard. Mason. Deceased.

Sanderford Jarman Major General, U.S. Army. b. Nov. 24, 1884 at Boatner, La. Graduate of U.S. Military Academy in 1908, advanced through grades to major general in Oct., 1940, and retired in 1945. Served in field artillery and coast artillery in WWI. From 1934-38 he was on the general staff, and from 1939-41 was commander of the 64th Coast Artillery in Hawaii, and in charge of coast and anti-aircraft commands in the Canal Zone. In WWII he was commanding general of Camp Stewart, Ga.; Anti-aircraft of Eastern defense command; and Saipan. Mason.

Abraham Jarvis (1739-1813) Protestant Episcopal Bishop of Connecticut, 1797-1813. b. May 5, 1739 in Norwalk, Conn. He was graduated from Yale in 1761, and became a lay-reader in Middletown, Conn., while studying theology. He was ordained priest in England, Feb. 19, 1764, by the Bishop of Carlisle. This was made possible by the aid of his parishioners, in 1763, who levied a tax on themselves to send him to England to take the "orders." He became rector in 1762 and second bishop of Conn. in 1797. At the beginning of the Revolution he was torn between his allegiance to the English church and the Colonial cause, as he held that the Declaration of Independence did not dissolve the ecclesiastical obligations of his church to the parent church in England. He presided over a church convention, July 23, 1776, in Conn., which resolved to suspend all public worship because it would be unsafe to continue the reading of the entire liturgy. He was raised in St. John's Lodge No. 2 of Middletown, Conn., Dec. 17, 1783, and received his mark master degree in the mark lodge of St. John's Lodge (first in the U.S.), July 3, 1789. His "mark" was a pulpit. He served as grand chaplain of the Grand Lodge of Connecticut. d. May 3, 1813.

Paul G. Jasper Judge, Supreme Court of Indiana, 1949-53. b. Dec. 15, 1908 in Fort Wayne, Ind. Graduate of Indiana U. in 1932, he practiced at Fort Wayne. Since 1953 he has been general counsel for the Public Service Co. of Ind. Served in the 98th Inf. division in WWII in Central Pacific. Raised in Maumee Lodge No. 725, Fort Wayne, Ind. on Nov. 22, 1933. 33° AASR (NT).

John Jay (1745-1829) First Chief Justice of U.S. Supreme Court, 1789-95. b. Dec. 12, 1745 in New York City. Considered one of the prime builders of the Revolutionary period, he was a member of the Continental Congress in 1774-79, and was its president in the latter two years. In 1779 he was American minister to Spain, and in 1782 was called to Paris by Franklin to negotiate peace with England. He was U.S. secretary of foreign affairs, 1784-89, and joined with Hamilton and Madison in writing the Federalist, explaining the new constitution. In 1794-95 he negotiated "Jay's Treaty" with England, settling outstanding disputes. In 1795-1801 he was governor of New York. There is no proof that he was a Freemason, although many Masonic journals and orators of past years have referred to him as such. On April 21, 1779 he wrote the following letter to Washington that has Masonic significance: "The dissolution of our governments threw us into a political chaos. Time, Wisdom and Perseverance will reduce it into Form, and give it Strength, Order and Harmony. In this work you are (in the style of your professions) a Master Builder, and God grant that you may long continue a Free and Accepted one."

Sir Jamsetjee Jeejeebhoy (1783-1859) Indian Parsi merchant and philanthropist. Founded hospital at Bombay; endowed schools; built public works. He was knighted in 1842 and created a baronet in 1857, being the first native Indian to be thus honored by Great Britain. Mason.

Richard M. Jefferies Governor of South Carolina, 1942-43. b. Feb. 27, 1888 at Gaffney, S.C. Teacher, lawyer and legislator. Member of Unity Lodge No. 55, Waterboro, S.C. and 32° in Dalcho Consistory AASR (SJ) on Nov. 14, 1919.

Clyde G. Jeffers Justice, Supreme Court of Washington since 1939. b. July 2, 1881 in Hampton, Ia.

Graduate of Iowa U. in 1905. Began practice in 1905. Mason.

Bradley C. Jefferson Editor of *Dallas Times Herald* (Tex.) since 1952. b. March 5, 1894 at Fairfield, Texas. Began as a reporter on this paper in 1919; chief editorial writer since 1926, and on board of directors since 1944. Member of Tannehill Lodge No. 52, Dallas, Texas and 32° AASR (SJ) of that city. Member of Hella Shrine Temple and Hi-Noon Club of Dallas.

Joseph Jefferson (1829-1905) American actor, considered to be best comedian of his time. b. Feb. 20, 1829, the fourth generation of actors, and the third to bear the name "Joseph." (His son, an actor of the same name, q.v., was also a Mason.) His first stage appearance was as a child in Pizarro at the age of three. After his father's death, he joined a party of strolling players who played through Texas, and followed the U.S. Army into Mexico. Always known as a good stock actor, his laurels were first earned as Asa Trenchard in *Our American Cousin* in 1858, at Laura Keene's Theatre, N.Y. Other notable parts in which he appeared were: Newman Noggs in *Nicholas Nickleby*; Caleb Plummer *in Cricket on the Hearth*; Dr. Pangloss in *The Heir at Law*; Bob Acres in *The Rivals*; and Dr. Ollapod in *Poor Gentleman*. His greatest success was in *Rip Van Winkle*, playing the leading role in every important city in the U.S., England, and Australia. As a painter he met with fair success, and as an author he wrote his autobiography, and *A Reply to Ignatius Donnelly* on the Shakespeare-Bacon Argument. He received his degrees in Concordia Lodge No. 13, Baltimore, Md. in April 1857 (references disagree as to dates), and became an honorary life member of

the same. He is also famous for making "The Little Church Around the Corner" in N.Y. the actor's church. d. March 23, 1905.

Joseph Jefferson (1869-1919) American actor. b. July 6, 1869 in New York City, the fifth generation of actors and the fourth generation to bear the name "Joseph." His father, q.v., of the same name, was also a Thomas Jefferson Mason. His mother was Sarah A. Warren, second wife of his father. He was educated in the Columbia Grammar School; Challie Institute, N.Y.; English Grammar School, London; and Upson Seminary, Conn. His first appearance on the stage was at Denver in 1885, with his father in *Rip Van Winkle* as a supernumerary. He played Lucius O'Trigger in *The Rivals*; Jim Farren in *Shadows of a Great City*; Chambers in *Pudd'n Head Wilson*; Beverly Clay in *Playing the Game*. In vaudeville he appeared in *Two Vehicles* by William C. de Mille, In 1999, and *Poor Old Jim*. Mason. d. May 1, 1919.

Thomas Jefferson (1743-1826) Third President of the United States. b. April 13, 1743 in Goochland, now Albemarle Co., Va. Graduate of William and Mary in 1762, and admitted to the bar in 1767. As a member of the Continental Congress, he was chairman of the committee that wrote and presented the Declaration of Independence to that body. He was governor of Virginia from 1779-81, and again member of Continental Congress from 1783-85. From 1785-89 he was U.S. minister to France, and secretary of state, 1790-93. He was vice president of the U.S. from 1798-1801, and president, 1801-09, being elected by the house of representatives after a tie vote with Aaron Burr, q.v. Masonic speakers and periodicals, both Masonic and Anti-

Masonic, of the middle 1800's claimed Jefferson was a Freemason. It is, to date, unproven if he was ever a member of the Craft. All claims to membership are based on association, or insinuation, such as "records of this period destroyed"; "closest associates were Freemasons"; "his writings and actions contain Masonic philosophy." It is claimed that the French Dr. Guillotin, q.v., recorded in his diary that he "attended Lodge in company with Mr. Jefferson and Mr. Paine from the American States." There has been an attempt to link his membership with Door to Virtue Lodge No. 44, Albemarle Co., Va., for his son-in-law, Gov. Thomas M. Randolph, q.v., and favorite grandson, Thomas Jefferson Randolph, q.v., were members of that lodge, as well as Peter and Samuel Carr, nephews. He was identified as marching in procession with Widow's Son Lodge No. 60, and Charlottesville Lodge No. 90, Oct. 6, 1817, at the laying of the cornerstone of Central College (now U. of Va.). On August 21, 1801 a dispensation was ordered for a lodge at Surry Court House, Va. to be named Jefferson Lodge No. 65. Some have claimed that he was a member of the Lodge of Nine Muses, Paris. In July, 1826, both the grand lodges of Louisiana and Georgia held funeral orations for Jefferson and, on Aug. 2, 1826, the Grand Lodge of S.C. held a funeral procession for him. A letter from Moses Holbrook, q.v., grand commander of the supreme council, (SJ) to Dr. J. M. Allen, Skaneateles, N.Y. dated Aug. 2, at Charleston, S.C. said: "I have nothing new to write, except tomorrow we have a funeral procession for Thos. Jefferson, and all the societies are invited. I never knew that he was a Freemason."

Olin M. Jeffords Chief Justice, Supreme Court of Vermont since 1955. b. June 8, 1890 at Enosburg Falls, Vt. Graduate of Boston U. in 1918, and admitted to the bar in that year. He was in practice at Rutland until 1934, and a superior court judge until 1938, when he was named to the supreme court bench. Member of Lincoln Lodge No. 78, Enosburg Falls, Vt.

Walter L. Jeffrey Vice President and General Manager of American Motors Corp. since 1955. b. Nov. 7, 1908 at Evansville, Ind. Graduate of Evansville Coll. in 1929. Began in advertising department of Kelvinator, a division of American Motors, in Detroit, 1929, becoming advertising manager, sales manager, and vice president of sales. Member of Ferndale Lodge No. 506, Ferndale, Mich.

John Jeffries (1745-1819) Physician and pioneer balloonist. b. Feb. 5, 1745 in Boston, Mass. He was graduated from Harvard in 1763, and later studied medicine in London and Aberdeen, receiving his medical degree from the latter place in 1769. He then returned to Boston to practice. From 1771-74 he was surgeon of a British ship of the line at Boston, and at the evacuation of that city by the British, he accompanied the troops to Nova Scotia as a Loyalist. In March, 1779, he went to England and was made surgeon major to the forces in America. He served with the British at Charleston, S.C. from March to December of 1780, resigning to return to London where he entered practice. He gained recognition as a scientist and meteorologist. With Francois Blanchard, the French aeronaut, he made the first crossing of the English Channel from Dover to the forest of Guines, France in a balloon on Jan. 7, 1785. He paid the entire expense of the channel voyage ($3,500). In the summer of 1789 he returned to Boston where he delivered the first public lecture on anatomy that was given in New England. At this time public feeling was against dissections and he was forced by mob violence to discontinue his lectures. He received his degrees in St. Andrew's Lodge, Boston, Mass., and in 1770 was charter member, and first junior warden (Dec. 3, 1770) of Massachusetts Lodge, Boston. He became senior warden Dec. 2, 1771; reelected Dec. 7, 1772; elected master Dec. 6, 1773 and reelected master Dec. 5, 1774. d. Sept. 16, 1819.

John, 1st Earl of Jellicoe (1859-1935) Name was John Rushworth. A rear admiral in 1907, he became admiral of the British fleet in 1919. During WWI, he was commander of the grand fleet from 1914-16, and chief of the naval staff in 1917. He commanded the grand fleet in the Battle of Jutland, May 31, 1916. From 1920-24 he was governor general of New Zealand. b. at Southampton, England, Dec. 5, 1859. He did not become a Mason until the age of 63, when he was received into the Lodge Renown of New Zealand while he was governor general of that country. He became grand master of the Grand Lodge of New Zealand in 1922-24. In 1927 he was made past grand warden of the Grand Lodge of England, by the grand master, Lord Connaught, q.v. d. 1935.

Edward H. Jenison U.S. Congressman to 80th and 81st Congresses (1949-51) from 18th Ill. dist. b. July 27, 1907 at Fond du Lac, Wis. Editor of the Paris (Ill.) Daily Beacon News since 1931. Mason.

Reuben E. Jenkins Lieutenant General, U.S. Army. b. Feb. 14, 1896 at Cartersville, Ga. Commissioned in 1918 and advanced through grades to lieutenant general in 1952. In WWI he was company commander in 31st, 77th and 1st Divisions. In WWII he was with GI, War Department; chief of staff G3, Mediterranean Theater, during which time he was responsible for plans and operations in Italy and for plans in landing on the South of France by 6th Army Group; chief of operations, southern France. In 1945-46 he was deputy assistant chief of staff of Army Ground Forces and chief of Joint War Planning Committee, 1946. Assigned to Greece in 1948 as deputy to Gen. James A. Van Fleet for the Greek guerilla war. At close of hostilities he succeeded Van Fleet as director, and remained until 1951. In 1951-52 was assistant chief of Staff, G-3 and in 1952 made commanding general of IX Corps in Korea. In 1953 he commanded the X Corps Group and the I, II and III Republic of Korea Corps of the First ROK Army. He was evacuated in Oct., 1953 for injuries received in the closing campaign and retired in Feb., 1954. Member of Cartersville Lodge No. 63, Cartersville, Ga., he received his degrees on April 17, Dec. 1, and Dec. 4, 1917—the latter by special dispensation of the grand lodge; 32° AASR at Columbus, Ga., where he is an active member of the consistory. National Sojourner. Masonic membership in the Cartersville Lodge is a family tradition.

Frank W. Jenks Executive Vice President of International Harvester Co. b. Aug. 7, 1897 at Richmond, Va. He joined the International Harvester organization at Chicago in 1914 and progressed as assistant branch manager, branch manager, assistant district sales manager, credit manager. He was named vice president in 1944, and executive vice president since 1956. He is past president of the Illinois Chamber of Commerce. Mason and Shriner.

George C. Jenks (1850-1929) Newspaper man and writer who created "Nick Carter," "Diamond Dick," and "Deadwood," as the characters of early dime novels. Wrote much under assumed names. b. April 13, 1850 in London, Eng., he came to America in 1872. He began as a newspaper writer, and was editorial writer for the Pittsburgh. Press for eight years. He went to New York in 1895 where he was a drama critic and New York correspondent of the Pittsburgh Dispatch and Gazette-Times. He authored Official History of the Johnstown Flood; The Climax; The Deserters; Stop Thief. He also wrote plays and motion pictures. Member of Bethel Lodge No. 733, New York City. d. Sept. 13, 1929.

Edward Jenner (1749-1823) English physician who was the discoverer of vaccination. b. at Berkeley, Gloucestershire, England. He was apprenticed to a surgeon near Bristol, and from 1770-72, was a pupil of the famous surgeon, John Hunter. He began his practice in Berkeley in 1773, where he observed that dairymaids who had cowpox did not get smallpox. On May 14, 1796 he vaccinated James Phipps, a boy of eight, with matter from cowpox vesicles on hands of a milkmaid. Several weeks later the boy was inoculated with smallpox but did not contract the disease. He announced his discovery in 1798, in a thesis written on his experiments. Parliament voted him £10,000 in 1803, and £20,000 in 1806. He was master of Royal Faith and Friendship Lodge No. 270, Berkeley, England in 1811-13. He was present at the ceremonial reception of the provincial grand lodge of

Gloucestershire by the Berkeley Masons in the summer of 1822. He was in ill health at the time and died a few months later.

William E. Jenner U.S. Senator from Indiana since 1944. b. July 21, 1908 in Marengo, Ind. Graduate of Indiana U. in 1930, and 1932. Practiced law at Paoli, Shoals, and since 1944, in Bedford. He was state senator from 1934-42. He was an officer in the U.S. Air Force from 1942-44. Raised in White River Lodge No. 332, Shoals, Ind. on July 4, 1939. 33° AASR (NJ), in 1955.

Berryman Jennings (1807-1888) First school teacher in Iowa. b. in Kentucky. He moved to Ill. and in 1830 to Iowa, where he became the first school teacher in the first schoolhouse north of the Missouri and between the Mississippi River and the Pacific Ocean. The dam at Keokuk, Ia. now covers the site of the original school. He became the first grand treasurer of the Grand Lodge of Calif. (1850) and first grand master of the Grand Lodge of Oregon. Was raised in Des Moines Lodge No. 1, Burlington, Ia. in 1845 and affiliated with Multnomah Lodge No. 84 (now 1), Oregon City, Oreg. He lived a short time in Calif. and became senior warden of New Jersey Lodge U.D. at Sacramento, in Dec., 1849. In April, 1850 he was a member of the convention that organized the Grand Lodge of California. He helped establish Willamette Lodge No. 2 of Oreg. and was a member of the convention called to form the Grand Lodge of Oregon. California's New Jersey Lodge was named Berryman and later Jennings No. 4 (now extinct).

John Jennings, Jr. (1880-1956) U.S. Congressman, 76th

through 81st Congresses (1939-51) from 2nd Tenn. dist. b. June 6, 1880 at Jacksboro, Tenn. Graduate of U.S. Grant U. in 1902. Taught school and was county superintendent of public instruction, 1897-1904. In law practice since 1903. Raised May 4, 1903 in Jacksboro Lodge No. 322, Jacksboro, Tenn. Transferred to Jellico Lodge No. 527, Jellico, Tenn. in 1907 and to Masters Lodge No. 244, Knoxville in 1944 where he was in good standing at time of death on Feb. 27, 1956.

Jonathan Jennings (1776-1834) First Governor of Indiana, 1816-22. b. about 1776 in Hunterdon Co., N.J. He emigrated to the Northwest territory, and was the first delegate from Indiana territory to U.S. congress from 1809-16; on the admission of that territory as a state, he was elected the first governor. He was Indian commissioner in 1818, and from 1822-31 was again a member of congress. A member of Pisgah Lodge No. 5, Corydon, Ind., he was grand master of the Grand Lodge of Indiana in 1823-24. d. July 26, 1834.

Newell Jennings Judge, Supreme Court of Connecticut from 1937. b. May 12, 1883 at Bristol, Conn. Graduate of Yale in 1904, and 1907. Admitted to the bar in 1907, and practiced at Bristol until 1922, when named judge of superior court, serving in that capacity until he became a member of the supreme court in 1937. Raised in Franklin Lodge No. 56, Bristol, Conn. in 1904.

W. Pat Jennings U.S. Congressman, 84th and 85th Congresses from 9th Va. dist. b. Aug. 20, 1919 at Camp, Va. Graduate of Virginia Poly. Institute in 1941. He has been president of the Jennings Motor Co. and proprietor of Jennings Farm Supply,

Marion, Va. since 1946, and owner of Mountain Bus Lines and Jennings Transport Co. Served in WWII as a Major, AUS, 1941-46. Member of Marion Lodge No. 31; Marion Chapter No. 54, R.A.M.; Lynn Commandery No. 9, K.T., all of Marion, Va. Member of Kazim Shrine Temple at Roanoke, Va.

Ben F. Jensen U.S. Congressman to 76th through 85th Congresses from 7th Iowa dist. b. Dec. 16, 1892 in Marion, Ia. He has been with the Green Bay Lumber Co. of Exira, Ia. since 1914. In WWI he was commissioned second lieutenant, U.S. Army, at Camp Pike, Ark. in 1918. Raised in Exodus Lodge No. 342, Exira, Ia. in 1922 and past master of same. Member of Amity Chapter No. 93, R.A.M., Audubon, Ia.; Kedron Commandery No. 42, K.T., Atlantic and Za-Ga-Zig Shrine Temple, Des Moines.

Cyril D. Jensen Engineer who is co-originator and developer of underwater welding, and developed arc-oxygen underwater cutting process. b. Aug. 17, 1898 in Brownton, Minn. Graduate of U. of Minnesota in 1921 and 1931, and Lehigh U. in 1929. Licensed professional engineer in Pa. in 1937. Made hydroelectric surveys in Minn. and Wis., and taught civil engineering at Lehigh U., 1925-42. During WWII he was a welding engineer with U.S. Naval Engineering Experiment Station at Annapolis (1942-46), and since that time has been project director for U.S. Army on bomb damage analysis research at Lehigh U. Mason.

Henry Jermyn (see Earl of St. Albans).

Douglas Wm. Jerrold (1803-1857) English playwright and humorist. He published a magazine and newspaper bearing his name, and from 1852 was editor of *Lloyd's Weekly Newspaper*. His most successful plays were Black-eyed Susan (1829); Bride of Ludgate (1831); and Time Works Wonders (1845). Among his contributions to *Punch* magazine, *Mrs. Caude's Curtain Lectures* were best known. He was initiated Nov. 10, 1831 in Bank of England Lodge No. 329. d. June 8, 1857.

Richard H. Jesse (1853-1921) President of University of Missouri, 1891-1908. b. March 1, 1853 in Epping Forest, Va. He studied at U. of Virginia, U. of Munich, U. of Berlin, U. of Tulane, U. of Wisconsin, Mo. Valley Coll., Washington U., and U. of Missouri. He later taught, and was dean at Hanover Academy, Washington Academy, Md., U. of Louisiana, and Tulane U. After his retirement as president of the U. of Missouri, he continued teaching ancient and medieval history at the university under the Carnegie Foundation. Jesse Hall at the university is named in his honor. Member of Twilight Lodge No. 114, Columbia, Mo. d. Jan. 22, 1921.

Beauford H. Jester (1893-1949) Governor of Texas, 1947-49. b. Jan. 12, 1893 at Corsicana, Texas. Graduate of U. of Texas in 1916, and 1920, being admitted to the bar in latter year, and began general practice at Corsicana. He gave up private practice in 1942 to become railroad commissioner of Texas, at Austin, a position which he held until governor in 1947. In WWI he was with the 90th Infantry from organization to demobilization, and participated in engagements at St. Mihiel and Meuse-Argonne. A member of Corsicana Lodge No. 174, Corsicana, Tex., he received his degrees Jan. 10, Feb.

18, and March 28, 1921; a Shriner. d. July 11, 1949.

Thomas S. Jesup (1788-1860) Major General U.S. Army. b. in Virginia in 1788. He was commissioned a lieutenant of Infantry in 1808, and at the beginning of the War of 1812 was adjutant-general to Gen. Wm. Hull. He received successive promotions for bravery, at the Battle of Chippewa in 1814, and at Battle of Niagara in same month. On May 8, 1818 he became quartermaster-general with rank of brigadier general, and ten years later to the day, was made major-general in recognition of ten years' faithful service. He assumed command of the Army in the Creek Nation in May, 1836, and in Dec. of that year, commanded the army in Florida. In 1838 he was wounded in an action with the Seminoles at Jupiter Inlet. Became a member of N.C. Harmony Lodge No. 2, Cincinnati, Ohio, March 13, 1812. d. June 10, 1860.

Ewell K. Jett Federal Communications Commissioner since 1944. b. March 20, 1893 at Baltimore, Md. Served as enlisted man and officer in U.S. Navy from 1911 until retirement in 1929. From 1929-37 he was chief engineer of the Federal Radio Commission, and from 1938-44 chief engineer of Federal Communications Commission. He is vice president and director of radio for the Baltimore Sun papers. In WWII he was a member of the censorship operating board, and chairman of the coordinating comm. of board of war communications. He has been the U.S. representative to several international radio conferences. Mason.

Jesse D. Jewell Rear Admiral, U.S. Navy (Medical). b. July 24, 1891 at Leon, W.Va. He received his

M.D. degree from the U. of Oregon in 1918, and entered the Navy the same year, as lieutenant, j.g. He advanced through the grades to rear admiral in 1944, and retired in 1945. He has served in hospitals, bases, and aboard ships throughout the world. He was awarded the coveted Navy Cross for his service at Pearl Harbor, on Dec. 7, 1941 (day of the Jap sneak attack), when he was stationed on the U.S.S. California. Raised in St. Paul's Lodge No. 14, Newport, R.I. in 1935. Past president of Sinclair Inlet Chapter No. 80, National Sojourners.

Marshall Jewell (1825-1883) Governor of Connecticut and Postmaster General. b. Oct. 20, 1825 in Winchester, N.H. First learned the tanners' trade under his father, and then went to Rochester, N.Y. where he learned telegraphy, then in its infancy. He served three terms as governor of Connecticut (being elected in 1869, 1871, and 1872). He was twice defeated for the office. In 1873-74 he was U.S. minister to Russia. He was recalled in the latter year to serve as postmaster general of the U.S. He later served as chairman of the National Republican Committee. Member of St. Johns Lodge No. 4, and Washington Commandery No. 1, K.T., both of Hartford, Conn.

David Jewett (1772-1842) American who was Admiral of the Fleet in Brazil. b. in 1772 in Montville, Conn. Studied law, but shipped out on a vessel bound for Spain and thereafter followed the sea. He spent two decades in the American naval or merchant service and at one time commanded the American 20-gun Trumbull. In 1952 he entered the employ of the United Provinces along the Rio Plata (now Argentine Republic) and was given command of a naval flotilla. His expedition to the

Falkland Islands and beyond is still cited in support of Argentina's claims to Antarctica territory. In 1832 he transferred to the naval service of Brazil, which had recently become an independent country. He became general of the naval armada, or admiral of the fleet, and here built up the finest navy in South American waters. He remained there until his death at Rio de Janeiro in 1942. Brazil looked upon him as the Americans looked upon Lafayette. Jewett was instrumental in introducing the Ancient and Accepted Rite into Brazil about 1832. There were indications of Freemasonry of a sort before 1800, and as early as 1804 a short-lived Grand Orient of French origin was formed. It was revived in 1822 under Dom Pedro, but fell apart again. Jewett had been created a deputy grand inspector general in 1826 in N.Y. by the DeWitt Clinton-Cerneau Supreme Council. In Brazil he was lieutenant grand commander, yielding the highest office to a native born Brazilian accredited from the Supreme Council of Belgium. Jewett made many trips to the U.S. and while visiting relatives in Conn., he was knighted in Washington Commandery, K.T. of New London on Oct. 18, 1826 at 6 a.m. On Nov. 3, 1826 he received the 33° in N.Y. He appears to have received his craft degrees in Wooster Lodge of Colchester, Conn. and Uriel Lodge No. 24 of Tolland, Conn., being raised Aug. 8, 1793 in the latter.

Hugh J. Jewett (1812-?) Railroad president and lawyer. b. in Deer Creek, Md. Admitted to the bar in 1840, and first practiced at St. Clairsville, Ohio, and later (1848) in Zanesville. Twice state senator, and U.S. district attorney, he served in the U.S. congress one term (1872). He was president of the Little Miami, Columbus, and Xenia Railroad in

1869, and shortly after, the Cincinnati and Muskingum Valley Railroad. On moving to Columbus, he became vice president of the Pittsburgh, Cincinnati, and St. Louis Railroad. He resigned from congress in 1873, to accept the receivership of the New York and Erie Railroad. He ran this railroad for ten years before retiring to Zanesville, Ohio. He was mentioned as a Democratic presidential nominee in 1880. He was a member of Zanesville Chapter No. 9 and Cyprus Commandery No. 10, Zanesville, Ohio. Member of Belmont Lodge No. 16, Clairsville, Ohio, receiving degrees in 1841 and dimitting in 1846.

Leonard B. Job President of Ithaca College (N.Y.) since 1932. b. Dec. 23, 1891 in Putnam Co., Ind. Graduate of Indiana U. in 1919, and PhD from Columbia in 1926. Taught in elementary and high schools of Indiana from 1910-19. With federal and state educational agencies until 1924, and then with Columbia U. (1924-26) and Ohio U. (1926-31). In 1931 he became dean of Ithaca Coll. and president in 1932. Mason.

Joseph Jacques Cesaire Joffre (1852-1931) French Field Marshal who commanded the Allied Armies in France in WWI. He was general of a brigade in 1902, and of a division in 1905. At the outbreak of WWI in 1914, he became commander-in-chief of the French armies. Joffre was the hero of the Battle of the Marne (Sept.1914), in which the German advance on Paris was stopped. In 1917 he was adviser to the general staff, and marshal of France. He received his degrees in Alsace Lorrain Lodge, Paris, while a captain. The dates of the degrees were Nov. 25, 1875, Dec. 28, 1876, and Dec. 26, 1877. At one time he

was orator of the lodge, and was made an honorary member in 1893.

Charles A. Johns (1857-1932) Justice, Supreme Court of Oregon, 1918-21 and Justice Supreme Court of Philippines, 1921-32. b. June 25, 1857 in Jackson Co., Mo. Graduate of Willamette U. in 1878, and admitted to Oreg. bar in 1881, practicing at Dallas. Member of Baker Lodge No. 47, Baker, Oreg., receiving degrees on Dec. 15, 1890, March 12, and April 9, 1891. d. Jan. 11, 1932.

Charley E. Johns Acting Governor of Florida, 1953-55. b. Feb. 27, 1905 in Starke, Fla. Was railroad trainman and conductor, 1923-55; owner of Starke Ice Co. from 1947; president of Presidential Insurance Co., Jacksonville. Member of state legislature in 1935, and state senate, 1937-53. Member of Bradford Lodge No. 35, Starke, Fla., receiving degrees Feb. 1, 1940, March 23 and Aug. 7, 1953. 32° AASR (SJ) and Shriner.

Joshua L. Johns (1881-1947) U.S. Congressman to 76th and 77th Congresses (1939-43) from 8th Wis. dist. b. Feb. 27, 1881 in Eagle, Wis. Graduate of U. of Chattanooga (1906), and Yale (1907). Began as a banker, but later practiced law at Appleton, Wis. He was president of Plumber's Woodwork Co., Algoma, from 1929, and president of Narcor Manufacturing Co., Green Bay, from 1946; also president of Northland Lumber Co, from 1944. Author of resolution creating "I Am an American Day" presented to congress. Member of Waverly Lodge No. 51, Appleton, Wis. at time of his death in March, 1947.

Kensey Johns, Sr. (1759-1848) Chief Justice, Supreme Court of Delaware, 1798-1830. b. June 14, 1759 in Anne Arundel Co., Md. He studied law with Samuel Chase and George Read (the signer), and was admitted to the Del. bar in 1783. In 1792 he was appointed U.S. senator, but the senate refused to seat him on a technicality. Johns became a member of Lodge No. 33 at New Castle, Del. in 1788. In 1795 he was elected master of the lodge, but not installed. d. Dec. 21, 1848.

William H. Johns (1868-1944) President of Batten, Barton, Durstine & Osborn, Inc., advertising agency, 1928-36; chairman of executive committee from 1936, and chairman of board from 1939. b. Feb. 10, 1868 in Redruth, England, and was brought to the U.S. at age of five. Graduate of College of City of New York in 1887. He began in the employment of Funk & Wagnalls, N.Y. in 1887. He was in the advertising business with George Batten from 1892, and started the George Batten Co., Inc., and was president of same from 1918. Received degrees in Cornucopia Lodge No. 563, Flushing, N.Y. in spring of 1904, dimitting Sept. 28, 1922 to become a charter member of Bayside Lodge No. 999, Bayside, N.Y. on that date. d. April 17, 1944.

Johnson (?-1773) A Masonic charlatan of this name appeared on the European scene at Jenna in 1763. His real name was Leucht. He claimed that he was deputized by the heads of Templar Freemasonry in Scotland to introduce reforms into the German lodges. He established a chapter of Strict Observance, and named himself grand prior. Von Hund, q.v., was at first deceived by him, but later found that he had been a servant of a Freemason, whose papers he had stolen, and then assumed his employer's name. He had

been secretary to the Prince of Bernberg, whose confidence he had betrayed. Von Hund denounced him as an imposter and Johnson fled, but was arrested at Magdeburg, and imprisoned at Wartzberg, where he died in 1773.

Alex C. Johnson (1861-1938) Vice President of Chicago and North Western Railroad, 1920-29. b. May 20, 1861 in Crawford Co., Pa. He began with the above railroad in 1892, as a special agent, becoming passenger traffic manager, and general traffic manager. Member of Clark Lodge No. 42, Clark, S.D. d. March 18, 1938.

Andrew Johnson (1808-1875) Seventeenth President of the United States. b. Dec. 29, 1808, near Carter's Station, Tenn. Self-educated, he was apprenticed to a tailor at the age of ten. In 1826 he moved with his family into Tenn., and settled at Greeneville, where he opened a tailor shop. He was a member of the U.S. congress in 1843-53. From 1853-57 he was governor of Tennessee, and U.S. senator from that state 1857-62. He was loyal to the Union during the Civil War, and as military governor of Tenn., held the rank of brigadier general. He was vice president under Lincoln from March 4 to April 15, 1865, and succeeded to the presidency on the death of Lincoln, serving until 1869. He again was elected U.S. senator in 1875, but served only a few months until his death. He was a member of Greeneville Lodge No.119, Greeneville, Tenn., receiving his degrees in 1851 (initiated May 5th), and remained a member of that lodge until his death. At the request of his lodge, G. C. Connor, deputy grand master of the Grand Lodge of Tenn. conducted the Masonic burial service and Coeur de Lion Commandery No. 9, K.T. of Knoxville gave the Templar burial service. His chapter and commandery membership is not known, but he was definitely a Knight Templar as there is a picture of him in Commandery regalia owned by Nashville Commandery No. 1, K.T. Some have Charles H. Johnson claimed his membership was in this commandery, but the record is often confused with another Andrew Johnson who was knighted on July 26, 1859. On June 20, 1867, he received the 4th through 32nd degrees of the Scottish Rite at the executive mansion at the hands of Benjamin B. French, q.v., and A.T.C. Pierson. He thus became the first president to receive the Scottish Rite degrees. He participated in many Masonic functions and cornerstone layings, including a monument to Stephen A. Douglas, q.v., at Chicago, Sept. 6, 1866; Masonic Temple, Baltimore, Nov. 20, 1866; Masonic Temple, Boston, June 24, 1867; Antietam National Cemetery (Md.) Oct. 17, 1867; Masonic Temple, 9th and F Sts., N.W., Washington, May 20, 1868. His close association with Freemasonry was one of the factors that led to his impeachment trial. Thaddeus Stevens, q.v., the anti-Mason, was a ringleader in the impeachment proceedings against Johnson in 1868. d. July 31, 1875.

Axel P. Johnson (1878-1952) Publisher. b. Sept. 24, 1878 in Gefle, Sweden. He came to U.S. with parents in 1888. He began as a reporter on the *Minneapolis Tribune* in 1900. He was successively, advertising manager of the *Minneapolis Times*; the *Milwaukee Sentinel*; general manager of *Chicago Record-Herald*; and publisher and owner of the *Grand Rapids News* (1912-22). From 1921 he was president of the A. P. Johnson Co., publishers and printers. He was raised in King Oscar Lodge No. 855, Chicago, May 1, 1908, and affiliated with York Lodge No. 410, Grand Rapids, Nov. 8, 1935, becoming a life member June 7, 1948; received degrees in Oriental Consistory, Chicago, AASR (NJ) in 1908, and was editor of the *Chicago Scottish Rite Magazine* for several years; received 33° Sept. 21, 1915. He wrote the booklet "Why the Scottish Rite," and a Masonic play, *Darius*, as well as a modern drama for the AASR, entitled *One Wise Man*. In 1944 he founded the *Scottish Rite News* for the Valley of Grand Rapids. He was a member of the York Rite, and past sovereign of the Red Cross of Constantine. He spent much effort in raising money for the George Washington National Masonic Memorial in Va. d. July 9, 1952.

Bernard L. Johnson (1883-1947) Editor. b. Dec. 2, 1883 at Clyde, Mich. Graduate of Kalamazoo Coll. and U. of Chicago. He was the editor of the American Builder (now American Builder and Building Age) from 1908-43, and western editor from 1943. He was editor of Farm Mechanics from 1919-28. He wrote many books on building and home improvement, including *Framing; Radford's Cyclopedia of Construction* (12 vols.); *Farm and Building Guide; Book of Farm Improvements; Small Homes of Charm; Most Popular Homes in America*, etc. Member of Republic Lodge No. 914, Chicago, Ill. Suspended NPD June 26, 1934. d. Dec. 22, 1947.

Charles F. Johnson (1859-1930) U.S. Senator from Maine, 1911-17. b. Feb. 14, 1859 at Winslow, Maine. Graduate of Bowdoin, 1879. He served as principal of high school at Machias, Maine for five years, and was admitted to the bar in

1886, practicing at Waterville. He was elected two terms to the state legislature, defeated for governor twice, and U.S. circuit judge of 1st circuit from 1917. Received his degrees in Herwood Lodge No. 91, Machias, Maine on Jan. 1, Feb. 5 and Feb. 12, 1883. Dimitted on Nov. 8, 1886 and affiliated with Waterville Lodge No. 33, Waterville, Maine on Feb. 7, 1887. Was master of the latter lodge in 1894-95 and grand master of the Grand Lodge of Maine in 1906-07. d. Feb. 15, 1930.

Charles H. Johnson (1870-1948) Past General Grand Master, General Grand Council R. & S.M. b. Oct. 13, 1870 in Brooklyn, N.Y. Graduate of Harvard and Boston U. His life was devoted to social welfare work. He was superintendent of several orphans' and children's homes in New York, deputy warden of Sing Sing; president of American Prison Association; Secretary of N.Y. state board of charities; commissioner of social welfare of N.Y.; and with American relief administration in Russia in 1922. He was a 33° AASR (NJ); past grand master of the Grand Lodge of N.Y.; grand secretary of the grand lodge; president of Masonic Relief Association of U.S. and Canada. He wrote many pamphlets on philanthropic and Masonic topics. d. Oct. 28, 1948.

Clarence W. Johnson President of The Fleischmann Malting Co., Chicago, since 1949. b. Nov. 20, 1898 at Kenosha, Wis. He has been with the Fleischmann company since 1918. Raised in Loyal Lodge No. 1007, Chicago, Ill., Nov., 1920; 32° AASR in Minneapolis, Minn. and member of Zuhrah Shrine Temple, Minneapolis.

David Johnson (1782-1855) Governor of South Carolina in 1847. b. Oct. 3, 1782 in Louisa Co., Va. His family moved to S.C. in 1789. He studied law, and settled in Union Court House. In 1812 he was a member of the state legislature; circuit judge in 1815-24; elevated to court of appeals in 1824, and made chancellor in 1835. A member of Union Lodge No. 43, Union Court House, S.C., he was master of same, and grand master of the Grand Lodge of South Carolina in 1826. d. Jan. 7, 1855.

Eben S. Johnson (1866-1939) Methodist Episcopal Bishop. b. Feb. 8, 1866 in Warwickshire, England. He came to the U.S. in 1889. Graduate of Morningside Coll. (Ia.), he was ordained to the ministry in 1889, and was a pastor in Iowa for many years. In 1916 he was elected missionary bishop of Africa, and bishop in 1920. He served as a chaplain in the Spanish-American War, and on Mexican border in 1916. His extensive missionary travels in Africa included journey across the wilds of Angola and Belgian Congo, 800 miles of which was on foot. Original lodge not known, but was admitted to Kane Lodge No. 377, Ida Grove, Iowa on Dec. 13, 1907; dimitted Oct. 14, 1910 and admitted to Landmark Lodge No. 103, Sioux City, Iowa on Dec. 12, 1910. Was past grand prelate of the Grand Commandery, K.T. of Iowa. d. Dec. 9, 1939.

Edward P. Johnson General Manager of Metropolitan Opera Assn., Inc., 1935-50. b. in Guelph, Ont., Canada. Graduate of U. of Toronto and U. of Western Ontario. Sang in light opera on Broadway for short time, and then studied in Italy under Vincenzo Lombardi, and in Florence. Made his debut at Teatro

Verdi, Padua, in Andrea Chenier, and sang five seasons at La Scala, Milan. In 1914 he was the creator of Parsifal, in Italian, and new roles by Puccini, Alfano, Pizzetti, Zandonai, Montemezzi and Deems Taylor. He has sung in London, Madrid, Lisbon, Buenos Aires, Montevideo, and Rio de Janeiro. He returned to the U.S. with the Chicago Opera Co. in 1920, and was with the Metropolitan from 1922. Member of Adelphic Lodge No. 348, New York City, receiving degrees on Feb. 18, March 4, and April 1, 1902.

Edwin C. Johnson U.S. Senator and Governor of Colorado. b. Jan. 1, 1884 at Scandia, Kans. He began as a railroad laborer in 1901, and was successively, a telegrapher, train dispatcher, homesteader, and manager of farmers cooperative. He was a member of the Colorado legislature four terms (1923-31); lieutenant governor of Colo., 1931-33, and governor two terms, 1933-37. He was U.S. senator from Colorado three terms, 1936-54. Member of Yampa Lodge No. 88, Craig, Colo., he received the 32° AASR (SJ) in Rocky Mountain Consistory, Nov. 15, 1935.

Edwin S. Johnson (1857-1933) U.S. Senator from South Dakota, 1915-21. b. Feb. 26, 1857 in Owen Co., Ind. Began in clothing business with father in S.D. in 1884 and later engaged in banking at Grandview and Armour. He was admitted to the bar in 1891, served as states attorney, and in the state senate. Mason; received 32° AASR (SJ) in Oriental Consistory, Nov. 23, 1911. d. July 19, 1933.

Evan M. Johnson (1861-1923) Brigadier General, U.S. Army. b. Sept. 26, 1861 in Brooklyn, N.Y. Graduate of Mt. Union Coll., 1904. He

enlisted as a private in 1882, and rose through grades to brigadier general in 1917. He served in the campaign against the Apache Indians and Geronimo in Ariz. and N.M. in 1885-86; expedition to Vera Cruz, Mexico in 1914; Spanish-American War in 1898; Philippine Insurrection, 1899-1901, and in WWI commanded the 154th brigade, 158th brigade, 77th and 79th Infantry divisions. He was secretary of the Infantry Assoc. and editor of the Infantry Journal from 1912-14. Member of the New York Scottish Rite bodies. d. Oct. 13, 1923.

Frank T. Johnson (1874-1939) Artist who specialized in Western life paintings. b. June 26, 1874 on a ranch near Big Grove, Iowa. Studied at New York School of Art. He was director of the Biltmore Salon of Los Angeles, and received several national prizes for his paintings. He is represented in the National Art Gallery, Washington, D.C.; Dallas, Texas Art Association; Royal Palace, Copenhagen, Denmark; Dunedin Museum of New Zealand; Municipal Art Gallery, N.Y.C., and other places. Mason. d. Jan. 1, 1939.

George W. Johnson (1811-1862) Governor of Kentucky. b. May 27, 1811 near Georgetown, Ky. Graduate of Transylvania Coll. at Georgetown. Represented Scott Co. in legislature from 1838-40. He first practiced law at Georgetown, but gave this up for farming, later entering politics. He was wounded at the Battle of Shiloh on April 7, 1862. Member of Mt. Vernon Lodge No. 14. d. April 9, 1862.

Guy Johnson (1740-1788) Colonel in British Army during Revolution, and nephew of Sir William Johnson, q.v. b. in County Meath, Ireland in 1740. On the refusal of Sir

John Johnson, q.v. (son of Sir William), to accept his father's office of superintendent of Indian affairs, Guy assumed the office from the time of his uncle's death in 1744, until the end of the Revolution. Previous to this he had served as his uncle's deputy. He married his cousin, Mary, daughter of Sir William. Guy served against the French in 1757, and again in 1759, when he commanded a company of rangers under Sir Jeffrey Amherst. At the start of the Revolution, he fled to Montreal by way of Oswego, with his family and a few faithful Indians. From there he went to England, but returned the following year, remaining several months in N.Y.C., and in 1778, accompanied his old friend Chief Joseph Brant, q.v., on raids in the Mohawk Valley. In Oct. 1779 his estates were confiscated by the New York assembly, and he resettled in Canada. When St. Patricks Lodge No. 8 (now 4) of Johnstown, N.Y. was chartered, May 23, 1766, Guy Johnson was the first senior warden. His uncle, Sir William, was first master, and William's son-in-law, Daniel Claus, was junior warden. Guy had been initiated early in 1766, in Union Lodge No. 1, of Albany, N.Y. On Feb. 7, 1771 he succeeded his uncle as the second master of St. Patrick's Lodge. When he became Indian agent, he made Joseph Brant his secretary, and when he fled to England, he took Brant with him, and was undoubtedly the one who paved the way for Brant to become a member of the Hiram's Cliftonian Lodge No. 417 in London on that trip. It was while he was with Henry Johnson Brant's forces in the Mohawk Valley that Lieutenant Boyd lost his life after appealing to Col. John Butler (first secretary of St. Patrick's Lodge) for mercy. d. March 5, 1788.

Henry Johnson (1783-1864) U.S. Senator and Governor of Louisiana. b. Sept. 14, 1783 in Tenn. He studied law in La., and started practice at Bringiers. In 1809 he was clerk of the territorial court. He was elected to the U.S. senate in place of William C. C. Claiborne, q.v., serving from 1818-24, when he resigned to become governor of La.; he held that office four years. He was elected to the U.S. congress in 1834-39, and again served in the U.S. senate from 1844-49. His original lodge is not known, but he was made an honorary member of Etolie Polaire Lodge No. 1, New Orleans. d. Sept. 4, 1864.

Herschel V. Johnson U.S. Ambassador and foreign service officer. b. May 3, 1894 in Atlanta, Ga. Graduate of U. of North Carolina in 1916, and later attended Harvard Law School. Appointed to the diplomatic service in 1920, first serving in Switzerland. He was then secretary of the legation at Sofia, Bulgaria, and Tegucigalpa, Honduras. He was first secretary of embassy in Mexico City in 1929-30, and then chief of division of Mexican affairs in State Dept., 1930-34. From 1934-37 he was first secretary of embassy in London, and counselor of same from 1937-41 with rank of minister. From 1941-46 he was minister to Sweden. He was U.S. representative on U.N. Security Council from 1946-48, with rank of ambassador. From 1948-53 he was ambassador to Brazil. Now retired. Served as Infantry captain overseas in WWI. A member of Crawfish Spring Lodge No. 300 of Chickamauga, Ga., he received his degrees on April 20, 25 and 27, 1918.

Hiram W. Johnson (1866-1945) U.S. Senator and Governor of California. b. Sept. 2, 1866 in Sacramento, Calif. Began as a shorthand reporter, and studied law in his father's office, being admitted to the bar in 1888. He practiced first in Sacramento, and moved to San Francisco in 1902. He was on the staff of prosecuting attorneys in the boodling cases that involved leading city officials and almost all public utilities in San Francisco. When Francis J. Heney was shot down in court, while prosecuting Abe Ruef for bribery in 1908, Johnson took his place and secured conviction of Ruef. He was governor of Calif. from 1911-15, and reelected for term of 1915-19, but resigned in 1917. He was then U.S. senator from Calif. until his death. A founder of the Progressive Party in 1912, he was vice presidential candidate on that ticket in 1912, and presidential candidate in 1924. Member of Washington Lodge No. 20, Sacramento; he was also a member of Sacramento Chapter No. 3, R.A.M., and Commandery No. 2, K.T. of that city. Member of Islam Shrine Temple, San Francisco. d. Aug. 6, 1945.

Howard A. Johnson Chief Justice, Supreme Court of Montana, 1938-46. b. Dec. 18, 1893 at Beloit, Wis. A.B. and LL.B. from U. of Montana in 1916-17. He served in state legislature, as county attorney, and assistant U.S. attorney. Practiced law at Butte, and resigned from supreme court bench to resume practice. In WWI he was a pursuit pilot with the 638th Aero Squad., A.E.F. Raised in Summit Valley Lodge No. 123, Butte, Mont. in 1920.

James Johnson (1811-1891) Provisional Governor of Georgia in 1865. b. in Robinson Co., N.C. Feb. 12, 1811, he was graduated from the state university in 1832, studied law and was admitted to the bar, practicing in Columbus, Ga. He was U.S. congressman from 1851-53. From 1866-69 he was collector of customs at Savannah, and in 1870, appointed judge of circuit court. Member of Columbian Lodge No. 8, Columbus, Ga. d. Nov. 20, 1891.

Jesse G. Johnson Admiral, U.S. Navy who captured German submarine U-505 intact on June 4, 1944. b. Jan. 9, 1895 at Bridgeton, N.J. Commissioned ensign in 1918, and advanced through grades to admiral in 1947. From 1918-23 he served on destroyers, transports, and the aircraft carrier U.S.S. Langley. A naval aviator, he mapped Wake Island in 1935, and built air base on Russell Islands in 1943. He was executive officer, and assistant task force commander, on U.S.S. Guadalcanal in Atlantic, 1943-44. In 1945 he commanded the U.S.S. Webster in the Pacific; retired in 1947. Author of *Sourdough Flights, a history of Alaskan flights*. Member of Brearley Lodge No. 2, Bridgeton, N.J. since 1917; 32° AASR (SJ) in Norfolk, Va., and Khedive Shrine Temple of that city.

J. Lovell Johnson (1876-1935) President of Iver Johnson's Arms & Cycle Works of Fitchburg, Mass.; Iver Johnson's Arms & Cycle Works of Canada; Iver Johnson Sporting Goods Co. of Boston. b. June 26, 1876 in Worcester, Mass. Began with the Johnson firm in 1896. Member of Charles W. Moore Lodge, Fitchburg, Mass.; 32° AASR (NJ); Thomas Chapter, R.A.M., Fitchburg, and Hiram Council, R. & S.M., Worcester, Mass. d. Nov. 9, 1935.

John Neely Johnson (1825-1872) Governor of California in 1855. b. August 2, 1825 in Indiana. A lawyer, he practiced in Sacramento and San Francisco. Member of Tehama Lodge No. 3, Sacramento. d. Aug. 31,

1872. Also member of Sacramento Chapter No. 3, R.A.M.

Sir John Johnson (1742-1830) British Colonel in Revolutionary War, and last Provincial Grand Master of New York. b. Nov. 5, 1742 at "Mount Johnson" on Mohawk River, N.Y., the son of Sir William Johnson, q.v., the British Indian agent. Educated by clergymen of the Dutch church, and Church of England, chiefly at Albany and N.Y. City, he spent some time in England, during which time he was knighted by George III as a compliment to his father. Hence both bore titles at the same time. It was also while in England that he was initiated in the Royal Lodge of St. James of London. As a youth, he saw considerable militia service under his father, and at the latter's death, he succeeded him as major general of militia (1774), as well as provincial grand master. Between Dec. 5, 1767 and May 3, 1773, he was a frequent visitor to St. Patrick's Lodge No. 4 at Johnstown. This lodge was founded by his father, who was first master. His cousin, Guy Johnson, q.v., was first senior warden, and his brother-in-law, Daniel Claus, junior warden. He fled to Montreal with about 300 of his Scotch-Tory tenants in the spring of 1776 when he learned that Gen. Schuyler was about to capture him. Here he was made colonel, and raised two battalions known as the "Queen's Royal Greens." With them he fought at Fort Stanwix, Oriskany (where Gen. Herkimer, q.v., was killed), and finally were forced to flee back to Canada when the Indians deserted them in fear of Benedict Arnold, q.v. In May, 1780, he desolated Cherry Valley, and in the same year, with Chief Joseph Brant, q.v., and Cornplanter, he raided the Mohawk Valley. At the close of the war his properties were confiscated, and he went to Canada, where the crown appointed him superintendent general of Indian affairs in North America. He spent the year 1784 in England, but returned, and was a member of the provincial council of Canada. In 1789 he became grand master of the Provincial Grand Lodge of Quebec. d. Jan. 4, 1830.

John A. "Jack" Johnson (1878-1946) Negro heavyweight boxing champion of the world. He won the championship by defeating Tommy Burns in 1908. He was defeated by James J. Jeffries in 1910, and lost the title to Jess Willard at Havana, Cuba, in 1915. He was raised in Lodge Forfar & Kincadine No. 225, Dundee, Scotland at 10:00 a.m. October 13, 1911. This meeting was not publicized and Johnson was proposed for membership by a new member of the lodge. Little was known of either the new member or Johnson. Since the members of the lodge had not been notified, and the charter called for no meetings in the morning hours, the charter was suspended from Dec. 21, 1911 to Nov. 1, 1913. When his initiation in a regular lodge became known to American Freemasons, it caused quite a furor.

John L. Johnson (1869-1932) President of Mississippi Woman's College from 1912. b. Aug. 10, 1869 in Spottssylvania Co., Va. Graduate of U. of Miss. and Miss. Coll. Taught school, served as principal and superintendent in public schools, and was president of Hillman Coll. (Clinton, Miss.), 1905-06; professor of modern language in Miss. Coll. 1906-12. Original lodge not known, but affiliated with Hattiesburg Lodge No. 397, Hattiesburg, Miss. on March 7, 1921. d. Feb. 1, 1932.

John M. Johnson Interstate Commerce Commissioner, 1949-56. b. May 5, 1878 in Marion, S.C. In practice as a civil engineer from 1898, specializing in drainage projects. Served in Spanish-American War, and as a colonel in WWI with the Rainbow Division. He was chairman of the S.C. highway commission in 1912-14, and assistant secretary of Commerce, 1935-40. In 1956 he became assistant to the president of the Atlantic Coast Line Railroad. Member of Clinton Lodge No. 60, Marion, S.C. since 1899, which he believes makes him not only the oldest in age but in length of membership of that lodge.

Joseph B. Johnson Governor of Vermont, 1955-58. b. Aug. 29, 1893 in Helsingborg, Sweden. He was brought to the U.S. in 1894, and naturalized in 1900. Graduate of U. of Vermont in 1915. Starting as a draftsman with the Bryant Chucking Grider Co. in 1910, he became chief engineer, general manager, and vice president. He served in the state lower house in 1945-46, and in senate, 1947-50. From 1951-54 he was lieutenant governor of Vermont. Member and past master of St. Johns Lodge No. 41, Springfield, Vt. Member and past high priest of Skitchewaug Chapter No. 21, R.A.M. and member of Springfield Council No. 18, R. & S.M., both of Springfield.

Keen Johnson Governor of Kentucky, 1939-43; Vice president and director of Reynolds Metal Co. b. Jan. 12, 1896 in Lyon Co., Ky. Student at Central Coll. (Mo.) 1914-17, and graduate of U. of Kentucky in 1922. Between 1919 and 1925, he edited the Lawrenceburgh News (Ky.) and Elizabethtown Mirror (Ky.). He has been editor and president of the Richmond Daily Register since 1925. Named vice president of Reynolds

Metal in 1945, he has been director of public relations since 1947. He was lieutenant governor of Ky. from 1935-39, and became governor on resignation of Gov. A. B. Chandler, q.v. In 1946-47 he was undersecretary of labor. He served as a lieutenant in the 89th Division in WWI. Member of Richmond Lodge No. 25, Richmond, Ky.

Leroy Johnson U.S. Congressman to 78th through 84th Congresses from Calif. (3rd and list dists.). b. in Wausau, Wis. Graduate of U. of Wisconsin, and U. of California. Admitted to the bar in 1915, he practiced at Stockton, Calif. In WWI he was a pilot of the 104th Aero Sqn. Mason.

Louis A. Johnson Secretary of Defense, 1949-50; Assistant Secretary of War, 1937-40; National Commander of American Legion, 1932-33. b. Jan. 10, 1891 in Roanoke, Va. Graduate of U. of Virginia in 1912. He began law practice at Clarksburg, W.Va. in 1912. In 1942 he was the personal representative of the President in India. During WWI he served overseas as an Infantry Captain. A member of Clarksburg Lodge No. 155, Clarksburg, W.Va., he received his degrees May 6, June 17, Aug. 1, 1921. Exalted in Adoniram Chapter No. 11, R.A.M. on Oct. 21, 1921 and knighted in Clarksburg Commandery No. 13, K.T. on Jan. 31, 1922—all of Clarksburg, W.Va. Received 32° AASR (SJ) at Wheeling, W.Va. May 24, 1928. Made a member of Osiris Shrine Temple, Wheeling, April 5, 1924. Member of National Sojourners.

Lyndon B. Johnson U.S. Senator from Texas since 1949. b. Aug. 27, 1908 near Stonewall, Texas. He taught in the Houston public schools, 1930-32, and was then secretary to Congressman Richard M. Kleberg until 1935. Was elected to 75th congress to fill unexpired term and reelected to next two congresses, serving from 1937-49. Received Entered Apprentice degree only on October 30, 1937 in Johnson City Lodge No. 561, Johnson City, Texas.

Melvin M. Johnson (1871-1957) Dean of Boston University Law School, 1935-43 and Sovereign Grand Commander, AASR, Northern Jurisdiction, 1933-54. b. May 11, 1871 at Waltham, Mass. Graduate of Tufts and Boston U. Law School. He practiced law from 1895-1939, and gained an international reputation in the defense of the LeBlane-Glover murder case. In 1918 he became associated with the Boston U. Law School as a professor, and was dean emeritus from 1943. He was much in demand as a public speaker. He was raised in Monitor Lodge, Waltham, Mass. in 1892, served as master in 1902, and grand master of the Grand Lodge of Massachusetts from 1914-16. He was a member of all York Rite bodies and many other Masonic organizations. He received distinguished service medals from the grand lodges of Rhode Island, Maine, Connecticut, Massachusetts, New Jersey, North Carolina, Nova Scotia, Czechoslovakia, and Norway, as well as the Gourgas medal from the Northern Jurisdiction, AASR. An author of many Masonic articles, his best known book is *The Beginnings of Freemasonry in America*. Under his leadership the membership of the northern jurisdiction rose from a low of 208,000 to 425,000 in 1954, at the time of his retirement from office. It is through his efforts that the northern jurisdiction set up a foundation for research in schizophrenia, the chief

mental crippler. Since 1934 this foundation has sponsored more than 50 separate projects at research centers across the U.S. and Canada. Johnson was a member of the executive committee of the George Washington National Memorial Association. d. Dec. 18, 1957.

Melvin M. Johnson, Jr. Inventor of the Johnson automatic rifles and machine guns. b. Aug. 27, 1909 in Boston, Mass., the son of Melvin M. Johnson, q.v., former sovereign grand commander of the AASR (NJ). Graduate of Harvard in 1931 and 1934, he was admitted to the bar in 1935. He invented the Johnson semi-automatic rifle in 1936; Johnson light machine gun, 1937; Johnson light machine rifle, 1940; Johnson autocarbine, 1941; and Johnson Indoor Target Gun, 1946. He resigned as president and director of the Johnson Automatics and subsidiaries to join the Winchester Repeating Arms Co., a division of Olin Industries, Inc., in 1939, merging Johnson Arms with Winchester. He has since served as a research consultant to many large organizations, including the U.S. Army. A Marine Corps officer, he engaged in weapons development in WWII. Mason, 32° AASR, National Sojourner, member of Heroes of '76 and DeMolay Legion of Honor.

Napoleon B. Johnson Chief Justice, Supreme Court of Oklahoma. b. Jan. 17, 1891 in Maysville, Okla. He was admitted to the bar in 1921, and practiced in Claremore, Okla. He has been a member of the supreme court of Okla. since 1948, and chief justice, 1955-57. He is president of the Inter-Tribal Council of the Five Civilized Tribes, and a member of the National Hall of Fame for Famous American Indians; member of the surgeon general's advisory committee on Indian health; and president of the National Congress of American Indians of U.S. and Alaska. Member of Claremore Lodge No. 53, Claremore, Okla. since Sept., 1920 and 32° AASR at Guthrie, Okla.

Nels G. Johnson Judge, Supreme Court of North Dakota since 1954. b. April 30, 1896 in Arkanes, Iceland. He migrated to the U.S. in 1900, and was naturalized in 1908. Graduate of U. of North Dakota in 1924, and 1926. He established his law practice in Towner, N.D. in 1926. He was attorney general of N.D. from 1945. Served in WWI as a private in the 82nd Infantry Division. Member of Bismarck Lodge No. 5, and Mouse River Lodge No. 43, and a past grand orator of the Grand Lodge of North Dakota. d. 1958. York Rite Mason; St. Felix Conclave, R.C.C. at Fargo, N.D.

Paul B. Johnson (1880-1943) U.S. Congressman to 66th and 67th Congresses (1919-23) from 6th Miss. dist. b. March 23, 1880 in Hillsboro, Miss. Admitted to the bar, and practiced at Hattiesburg. Served as judge of city court, and for eight years as circuit judge. Democratic nominee for governor in 1939. Member of Hattiesburg Lodge No. 297, Hattiesburg, Miss., and of Scottish Rite (suspended in latter, NPD). d. Dec. 26, 1943.

Richard M. Johnson (1780-1850) Ninth Vice President of the United States, 1837-41. b. Oct. 17, 1780 in Bryant's Station, Ky. Admitted to the bar in 1802, he was a member of the U.S. Congress in 1807-19, and 1829-37. From 1819-29 he was U.S. senator from Ky. In the electoral vote for vice president in 1837, no candidate gained a majority in the electoral college, and the election was thereby thrown into the senate. He was the

only vice president to be thus elected. He was a member of Hiram Lodge No. 4, Frankfort, Ky., but the dates of his degrees are not known. He is listed as a past master in the returns of this lodge of Oct. 1, 1806, and dimitted June 20, 1808. His name appears as a member, and past master, in Mount Vernon Lodge No. 14 in August, 1807. He was evidently a charter member of this lodge. He is also listed as a member of Mount Vernon Chapter (later Georgetown Chapter No. 13, R.A.M.) of Georgetown, Ky., in the proceedings of 1823 to 1827 inclusive. In the resolutions adopted by the anti-Masonic members of the Massachusetts legislature at Boston in 1836 he is referred to as "an adhering Mason." d. Nov. 19, 1850.

Robert L. Johnson President of Temple University since 1941. b. March 25, 1894 in New York City. Graduate of Yale in 1918. From 1922-37 he was vice president of Time, Inc. He is a director of Armstrong Cork Co., Girard Trust Corn Exchange Bank, Penn-Mutual Life Insurance Co., Bell Telephone Co., Avco Manufacturing Co., and others. He served in WWI as a lieutenant in 7th Field Artillery of 1st Division. He was made a Mason "at sight," March 2, 1949, by George H. Deike, grand master of the Grand Lodge of Pennsylvania at a special communication of that grand lodge.

Robert W. Johnson (1814-1879) U.S. Senator from Arkansas, 1853-61. b. in Kentucky in 1814. He moved to Pine Bluff, Ark. where he practiced law. He was a member of the U.S. congress from 1847-53. He withdrew from the U.S. senate in 1861 when Arkansas passed an ordinance of secession, and was elected to the provisional Confederate congress; in 1862 elected to the Confederate senate, in which he was an active member until the close of the Civil War. After the war, he practiced law in Washington, D.C. He was grand orator of the Grand Lodge of Arkansas in 1862, and in 1860 in the proceedings is listed as a member of Union Chapter No. 2, R.A.M. of Little Rock. d. about 1879.

Royal C. Johnson (1882-1939) U.S. Congressman to 64th through 72nd Congresses (1915-33) from 2nd S.D. dist. b. Oct. 3, 1882 in Cherokee, Iowa. Graduate of U. of South Dakota in 1906. He practiced law in High-more, S.D. from 1906 to 1912, when he moved to Aberdeen. In 1911-15 he was attorney general of the state, and in 1929 was appointed a member of the Mt. Rushmore National Memorial committee. He served in WWI as an enlisted man and officer, and was wounded in France and discharged in 1918. Member of Ree Valley Lodge No. 70, Highmore, S.D. d. Aug. 2, 1939.

Samuel Johnson (1709-1784) The great English lexicographer, critic, and conversationalist whose life was immortalized by his biographer James Boswell, q.v., in Life of Samuel Johnson. Johnson's greatest accomplishment was the compilation of the world's first dictionary of the language (1755). This brought him doctorates from Oxford and Dublin universities. b. in Lichfield, he was the son of a book dealer. He opened a school in Lichfield in which David Garrick, q.v., was a student. He contributed heavily to literary magazines of the day and wrote many volumes including *Lives of the Poets* (in 10 volumes); *Journey to the Western Isles of Scotland*; and *Rasselas, Prince of Abyssinia*. He first met Boswell in May, 1763. There is no definite proof that Johnson was a Mason, but as Mackey says, "the probabilities in favor of his having been one are much weightier than the probability against." There was a "Samuel Johnson" who was a member of Old Dundee Lodge No. 18 (formerly No. 9)of Wapping, London. He was proposed May 14, 1767, accepted May 28, 1767, and made a Master Mason July 9, 1767. His name appears thereafter in the records 21 times.

Sir William Johnson (1715-1774) English Baronet who was a most colorful and powerful figure in pre-revolutionary America. b. in Smithtown, County Meath, Ireland. He came to America in 1783 to manage the property of his uncle, Admiral Sir Peter Warren, which was located about 24 miles west of Schenectady. Johnson soon began trade with the Indians, whom he always treated with honesty and justice. His manner was dignified and affable, and he cultivated their friendship by learning their language, assuming many of their manners, and even their dress. His influence, which was greater than any other white man had possessed, earned him the Indian title Wariaghejaghe, or "he who has charge of affairs," and was made a sachem of the Mohawk Tribe. He was a major general of British militia, and distinguished himself in the border warfare with the French, and in Feb., 1748 was placed in command of all New York colonial forces. On April 14, 1755, he was appointed "sole superintendent of the affairs of the Six United Nations, their allies and dependents," holding this position until his death on July 11, 1774. His nephew, Guy Johnson, q.v., replaced him in this office. He became interested in Joseph Brant, q.v., the Mohawk chief, when the latter was about 17 years old. Brant served under

Johnson at the Battle of Fort Niagara on July 25, 1759. He later sent him to school, and took Brant's sister Molly as a common-law wife. He was knighted for his service in the French War, and given 100,000 acres of land in the Mohawk Valley. He was raised in Union Lodge No. 1 (now Mt. Vernon No. 3) of Albany, N.Y., April 10, 1766. On May 23, 1766 a charter was issued to St. Patrick's Lodge No. 8 (now No. 4) to constitute a regular lodge to be held at Johnson Hall in the county of Albany and the province of New York in America. Its first meeting took place Aug. 23, 1776, and Johnson was charter master with his nephew, Guy Johnson, as senior warden, and his son-in-law, Daniel Claus, as junior warden. John Butler, q.v., of Revolutionary fame, was secretary. He established a lodge room on the second floor of his home, Johnson Hall, and it is today a museum with some of the original lodge furniture intact. He later became provincial grand master of New York. On his death, this title was inherited by his son, Sir John Johnson, q.v. On May 4, 1769, the secretary of the lodge recorded that "The Master (Sir William) observed that he had received a commission as Master of a Lodge of superior degrees, which would require his attendance occasionally at Albany." This reference would tend to prove the assertion that he was one of the early founders of the Scottish Rite in America, as he is said to have been master of the "Ineffable Lodge" (of Perfection) at Albany from 1769 to 1773. He was succeeded by his nephew as master of St. Patrick's Lodge on Feb. 7, 1771. d. July 11, 1774.

William E. Johnson (1862-1945) Prohibition lecturer known as "Pussyfoot" Johnson, because of his catlike policies in pursuing lawbreakers in the Indian Territory. b. March 25, 1862 in Coventry, N.Y. He was educated in the U. of Nebraska. He made three trips around the world in the interest of temperance, delivering more than 4,000 lectures. He lost an eye at a prohibition meeting at Essex Hall, London in 1919, by a missile thrown by a member of a mob. As a special officer of the Dept. of Interior to enforce laws in the Indian Territory (1906-11), he secured more than 4,400 convictions. A newspaperman and editor, he was on the staff of the *Lincoln News* (Nebr.) and later manager of the *Nebraska News Bureau*. From 1895-99 he edited the *New York Voice*, and from 1899-1905 the *Chicago Voice*. He was editor of the *New Republic*, 1913-16, and at the same time was managing editor of 35 publications of the Anti-Saloon League. His books on prohibition are numerous. Mason, Knight Templar, and 32° AASR. d. Feb. 2, 1945.

Albert S. Johnston (1803-1862) Confederate General in Civil War. b. Feb. 3, 1803 in Washington, Ky. Graduate of U.S. Military Academy in 1826; served in 2nd Infantry until resignation in 1834. He served in the Black Hawk War. After resignation, he farmed a short time near St. Louis, Mo., but in Aug., 1836, joined the Texas patriots and thereafter considered Texas as his home. He entered the Texas army as a private, and rose in its command as brigadier general. In the Mexican War he joined the regular army under Gen. Zachary Taylor. In 1857 he was ordered to Utah with his Texas regiment to restore order among the Mormons who were revolting against the Federal government. He was breveted brigadier general in the regulars and remained in command of Utah until 1860, when he was sent to Calif. to command the Department of the Pacific. At the start of the Civil War, he resigned his commission and returned to Richmond, Va. where he was given command of the Confederate forces west of the Atlantic states and North of the Gulf states. In the Battle of Shiloh Church, he surprised and defeated the Federal troops under Grant, but was killed in action on April 6, 1862. Masonic Review (Cincinnati) p. 157, Sept. 1868 says he was a Mason, but grand secretary of Grand Lodge of Texas says "definitely not."

Alvanley Johnston (1875-1951) Grand Chief Engineer of Brotherhood of Locomotive Engineers, 1925-51. b. May 12, 1875, in Seeleys Bay, Ontario, Canada, of American parents, coming to the U.S. in 1888. Began as a railroad employee in 1892, and from 1897-1909 was an engineer on the Great American Railroad. He became associated with the labor group in 1909 as general chairman of the engineers of the Great Northern Railroad. Member of both York and Scottish Rites. d. Sept. 17, 1951.

Chester A. Johnston Vice President and General Manager of Wabash Railroad since 1955. b. Sept. 1, 1895 in Logansport, Ind. Educated at Purdue U., and U. of Arizona. From 1917-24 he was with the Pennsylvania Railroad, and has been with the Wabash since 1924. He is vice president and general manager of the Ann Arbor Railroad; Manistique & Lake Superior Railroad; Lake Erie and Ft. Wayne Railroad; vice president of Detroit and Western Railroad; Ann Arbor Boat Co.; Wabash Motor Transport Co. Mason, 32° AASR, and Shriner.

Harris C. Johnston President of Kemper Military Academy

from 1949. b. Feb. 12, 1883 in Boonville, Mo., son of Col. Thomas A. Johnston, the second president of Kemper. He was educated in Kemper and Western Reserve U. He served as athletic director and coach at Kemper for 30 years and was quartermaster of the school from 1904-49. Initiated in Cooper Lodge No. 36, Boonville, in 1920, he served as master in 1927 and grand master of the Grand Lodge of Missouri in 1941-42. Exalted in Boonville Chapter No. 60, R.A.M., May 7, 1920, he was high priest in 1929. Greeted in Centralia Council, R. & S.M. May 12, 1920 and knighted in Olivet Commandery No. 53, K.T., Boonville June 2, 1920, serving as commander in 1923, 1943 and 1944. He is a member of St. Chrysostom Conclave No. 36, Red Cross of Constantine and sovereign in 1939. He is past intendant general of the Red Cross for Missouri. Member of Ararat Shrine, Kansas City and charter member of Kilwinning Council, A.M.D. In 1946 he received a special award for service from the Grand Commandery, K.T. of Mo.

Henry S. Johnston Former Governor of Oklahoma. b. Dec. 30, 1867. Member of Perry Lodge No. 78, Perry, Okla., receiving degrees on June 23, Oct 4 and Dec. 6, 1901. Grand orator of the Grand Lodge of Oklahoma from 1918-21; on appeals and grievances committee, 1916-17; grand master of Oklahoma in 1924. Master of his lodge in 1916. Royal Arch Mason; 32° AASR (SJ) on April 30, 1913; KCCH in Oct. 1919. Elected to receive 33° in 1923, but was never coroneted. The time was not extended in 1925. Living at Perry, Okla.

Olin D. Johnston U.S. Senator from South Carolina since 1944, and Governor of South Carolina,

1937-44. b. Nov. 18, 1896 in Anderson Co., S.C. Graduate of Wofford Coll. (Spartanburg), and U. of S.C. Admitted to the bar in 1924, practicing at Spartanburg. Served as a sergeant with the 43rd Division in France in WWI. Member of Center Lodge No. 37 at Honea Path, S.C., and member of Scottish Rite (SJ) at Charleston, S.C.

Samuel Johnston (1733-1816) Governor of North Carolina, 1787-89, and U.S. Senator, 1789-93. b. Dec. 15, 1733 in Dundee, Scotland. His parents settled in Chowan Co., N.C. in 1736. He was educated in the East and studied law in Edenton where he opened practice. He was elected to the state general assembly in 1759, and served through a dozen sessions prior to 1775. Between 1774 and 1776 he served in four provincial congresses in N.C. and was president of the last two, which launched the Revolutionary government in the state. From 1800-03 he was judge of the superior court. His last years were spent on his plantation. A member of Royal Edwin Lodge No. 5, at Windsor (now Charity No. 5), he affiliated with Unanimity Lodge No. 7 at Edenton when he moved there. He was the first grand master of the Grand Lodge of North Carolina, serving from Dec. 12, 1787-92. On Dec. 10, 1792 he received the Mark and Past Master degrees in Fayetteville. On July 23, 1788 the Johnston-Caswell Lodge No. 10 of Warrenton, N.C., was chartered, honoring the two first grand masters —Johnston and Richard Caswell. This was the first lodge chartered after the Revolution in N.C. d. Aug. 18, 1816.

Wayne A. Johnston President of Illinois Central Railroad since 1945. b. Nov. 19, 1897 at Urbana, Ill.

Graduate of U. of Illinois in 1917. He entered the service of the Illinois Central as an accountant in Champaign, Ill. in 1919, and rose through many positions to assistant general manager in 1942, vice president and general manager in 1944, and president in 1945. He is chairman of board, and director of Madison Coal Corp., Peoria & Pekin Union Railroad, and president and director of Chicago & El. Western Railroad, Paducah & Ill. Railroad. A member of Western Star Lodge No. 240 of Champaign, Ill.; Jackson Park Chapter No. 222, R.A.M., Chicago; St. Johns Conclave Premier No. 1, Red Cross of Constantine; 33° AASR, Valley of Chicago; Medinah Shrine Temple, Chicago. He is also a member of the Illinois Central Square Club, the Illinois Central Shrine Club, and the South Suburban Shrine Club.

William H. Johnston (1874-1937) President of International Association of Machinists, 1912-37. b. Dec. 30, 1874 in Nova Scotia, Canada. Was brought to U.S. in 1885. He was an apprentice machinist with the Rhode Island Locomotive Works, and worked in all branches of the trade. He was a member of the National War Labor Board appointed by President Wilson, 1917-19, and was sent by the President to Great Britain and France in 1918. Mason. d. March 26, 1937.

Al Jolson (1888-1950) Actor and singer. b. May 26, 1888 in St. Petersburg, Russia, as Asa Yoelson. He first appeared on the stage as a member of the mob, in The Children of the Ghetto, at Herald Square Theatre in N.Y.C. on Oct. 16, 1899. Later, he traveled with circuses, vaudeville, and Dockstader's Minstrels. He was particularly noted for his blackface minstrel songs. On the stage he played in LaBelle Paree; The Honeymoon Express; Robinson Crusoe, Jr.; Sin-bad, etc. He starred in the first talking pictures The Jazz Singer; The Singing Fool and Say It With Songs. In 1940-41 he starred in his own production Hold On to Your Hat. A member of St. Cecile Lodge No. 568, New York City, he was raised, July 1, 1913. He died Oct. 23, 1950, in San Francisco after returning from entertaining American troops in Japan and Korea.

Edgar A. Jonas U.S. Congressman to 81st through 83rd Congress (1949-55) from 12th Ill. dist. b. 1885 in Manitowoc Co., Wis. Graduate of Chicago Law School, and admitted to the bar in 1909, practicing in Chicago. He served as assistant state's attorney, judge of municipal court of Chicago, and judge superior court of Cook Co. Raised in Equity Lodge No. 878, Chicago, April 11, 1910, becoming charter member of Sincerity Lodge No. 982 Chicago on Nov. 12, 1915 and serving as master in 1944. Member of Lincoln Park Chapter No. 177, R.A.M., Lincoln Park Commandery No. 64, K.T.; 33° AASR in Oriental Consistory; Medinah Shrine Temple; St. John's Conclave No. 1, Red Cross of Constantine. Was grand orator of Grand Lodge of Illinois in 1940 and has been president of Illinois Masonic Hospital Assn. since 1927.

Ralph Jonas (1878-1952) Philanthropist. b. Nov. 7, 1878 in Brooklyn, N.Y. Active in philanthropic, educational, and civic movements in Greater New York. An organizer of the Brooklyn Chamber of Commerce, as well as the Long Island Chamber of Commerce. He was a leading factor in establishing the Board of Higher Education in N.Y.C., and a leader in establishing a city-maintained college

in Brooklyn. He founded Long Island U. with a gift of $500,000. In 1939 he was one of the incorporators of the New York World's Fair. A director and trustee of many hospitals, schools and civic organizations. Member of Euclid Lodge No. 656, Brooklyn, N.Y., receiving degrees on Jan. 28, Feb. 11, and March 11, 1903. d. April 29, 1952.

Albert M. Jones Major General, U.S. Army. b. July 20, 1890 in Quincy, Mass. Commissioned in 1911, he advanced through grades to major general in 1942. From 1912-15 he was in the Canal Zone; Mexican Border in 1916; Alaska, 1917-18; commander of Ft. George Wright in Spokane, 1919; commanded 19th Infantry, 1921-22; on general staff of 2nd Division, 1924-28. In 1940-41 he was commander of the 31st Infantry at Manila, and in 1941-42, was commanding general of the 51st Division of Philippine Army and 1st Philippine Corps in Luzon and Bataan. He participated in the death march, and spent 40 months in Japanese prison camps. In 1946 he commanded Camp Beale, Calif., and was later military advisor to Republic of Philippines. Mason, 32° AASR, and Shriner.

Andrieus A. Jones (1862-1927) U.S. Senator from New Mexico, 1917-23, and 1923-29, dying in office. b. May 16, 1862 near Union City, Term. Graduate of Valparaiso U. (Ind.) in 1884-85. Taught school in Tenn. two years, and was principal of public schools in Las Vegas, N.M. 1885-87. Admitted to the bar in 1888. From 1913-16 he was first assistant secretary of the Interior. Member of Chapman Lodge No. 2, Las Vegas, N.M., receiving degrees on Sept. 21, 1892 and Jan. 19, Feb. 16, 1893. Was junior warden of his lodge in 1894 and junior grand steward of the

Grand Lodge of New Mexico in 1894. 32° AASR (SJ) and was buried Masonically. d. Dec. 20, 1927.

Anson Jones (1798-1858) Last President of the Republic of Texas, and first Grand Master of Grand Lodge of Texas. b. Jan. 20, 1798 in Great Barrington, Mass. Dr. Jones received his M.D. degree in Philadelphia in 1827, moving to New Orleans in 1832, where he practiced a year before moving to Texas; here, he settled in Brazoria Co. As chairman of a mass-meeting held there in Dec. 1835, he drew up resolutions in favor of a declaration of independence, and for a convention of the people of Texas to form a constitution. He afterward raised a military company with which he fought in the Battle of San Jacinto, and was judge advocate general. In 1837 he was a member of the Texas congress, and minister to the U.S. from Texas in 1837-39. In 1840 he was president of the state senate, and ex-officio vice president of the Republic, and secretary of state from 1841-44. He was president of the republic from 1845 until annexation to the U.S. His personal opposition to the annexation affected his popularity, destroyed his influence, and eventually his reason became unsettled, and he committed suicide. Jones was initiated in Harmony Lodge No. 52, Philadelphia, March 7, passed April 7, and raised in May, 1827. He served the lodge as junior warden in 1830, senior warden in 1831, and master in 1832. He withdrew Nov. 7, 1832, on his removal from the state. While in Philadelphia he became grand master of the Odd Fellows. In March, 1835, Dr. Jones, together with John H. Wharton, Asa Brigham, James A. E. Phelps, Alexander Russell, and J. P. Caldwell met in a grove back of the town of Brazoria at 10 a.m. for the

purpose of applying for a charter from the Grand Lodge of Louisiana. At this time every move in Texas was watched with jealousy and distrust by the Mexican government, and Freemasonry was particularly odious to the Catholic priesthood, whose influence in Texas at that time was all powerful. As a result, a dispensation was granted for Holland Lodge No. 36 (UD)—now Holland No. 1 of Houston. The charter for the lodge was delivered to Bro. John M. Allen, q.v., who was in New Orleans to recruit soldiers for the Texas forces. An orderly had been sent by Gen. Houston, q.v., to meet Allen and advise him of the coming clash with the Mexicans. Allen then set out to join Houston's forces with the charter and other communications from the grand secretary of La. in his possession. He met Dr. Jones on the prairie between Croce's and San Jacinto, and delivered the charter to him. Jones then carried it in his saddlebags through the Battle of San Jacinto. Jones became first master of Holland Lodge, and in 1838 was instrumental in the organization of the Grand Lodge of the Republic of Texas; he served as its first grand master. d. Houston, Texas, Jan. 12, 1858, and was buried with Masonic honors.

Charles A. Jones Chief Justice, Supreme Court of Pennsylvania. b. Aug. 27, 1887 in Newport, Pa. Graduate of Dickinson School of Law, Carlisle, Pa. and admitted to the bar in 1910, practicing at Pittsburgh. From 1939-45 he was judge of the U.S. circuit court of appeals, 3rd circuit. Has been a justice of the supreme court of Pennsylvania since 1945 and chief justice since 1956. Served in the American ambulance service with the French Army in 1917 and in 1918-19 was an ensign in U.S. naval aviation. Was Democratic nominee for governor of Pa. in 1938. He was made a Mason "at sight" on Sept. 1, 1959 by Sanord M. Chilcote, grand master of Pennsylvania, at a stated meeting of Verona Lodge No. 548 at Syria Mosque, Pittsburgh.

Charles "Buck" Jones (1889-1942) Actor and early Western movie star. Member of Henry S. Orme Lodge No. 458, Los Angeles, Calif. d. in December, 1942 in Boston night club fire.

Charles W. Jones (1834-1897) U.S. Senator from Florida, 1875-1887. b. In Ireland in 1834, he was brought to the U.S. when ten years old. After working at his trade as a mechanic, he settled in Pensacola, Fla. in 1854, studied law, and in 1856, was admitted to the bar. He was a member of the Florida legislature in 1874. Member of Santa Rosa Lodge No. 16, and Santa Rosa Chapter No. 6, R.A.M., both of Milton, Fla. d. Oct 11, 1897.

Daniel W. Jones (1839-1918) Governor of Arkansas, 1897-1901. b. Dec. 15, 1839 in Bowie Co., Republic of Texas. He entered the Confederate Army in 1861, and became colonel of the 20th Arkansas Infantry in 1862, and at close of war commanded a brigade. He was admitted to the bar in 1865; served two terms as attorney general, and twice in the state legislature. He resumed law practice on expiration of his gubernatorial term. Member of Mount Horeb Lodge No. 4, Washington, Ark., and senior warden of same in 1866. d. Dec. 25, 1918.

Earle M. Jones Major General, U.S. Army. b. Jan. 6, 1903 in Fresno, Calif. Commissioned in 1924, he advanced through grades to major general in 1951, and since that date

has been adjutant general of Calif. In WWII he was executive officer in operations of S.H.A.E.F., and planner at European Theatre Headquarters. Raised March 4, 1938 in Fresno Lodge No. 247, Fresno, Calif., and past master of same. 32° AASR (SJ) and Shriner.

Edward F. Jones (1828-1913) Union Brigadier General in Civil War, and scale manufacturer. b. June 3, 1828 in Utica, N.Y. He was a colonel in the 6th Mass. regiment—the first in the Civil War. In 1865 he was breveted major general "for meritorious service." His regiment attacked Baltimore and reached Washington on April 19, 1861, where it was met by President Lincoln. Jones operated the Jones Scale Works at Binghamton, N.Y. from 1865, under the corporate name of "Jones of Binghamton." He was the originator of the phrases: "He pays the freight" and "Do it now." Mason. Affiliated with Otseningo Lodge No. 435, Binghamton, N.Y. on Jan. 13, 1887 from St. Paul's Lodge, Mass. d. Aug. 14, 1913.

Francis Jones U.S. Congressman from Tennessee, 1817-23. Received limited education, studied law and practiced at Winchester, Tenn. Member of Winchester Lodge No. 26. Birth and death dates unknown.

Frank C. Jones (1873-1952) Imperial Potentate of the Shrine in 1928. b. April 2, 1873 in Kirksville, Mo. He received the 32° AASR (SJ) in Galveston, Texas, March 4, 1904; KCCH in 1907, and 33°, Oct. 22, 1909. He was past grand master of the Grand Lodge of Texas, and past grand commander of the Grand Commandery, K.T. of Texas. d. Nov. 15, 1952.

George Jones (1766-1838) U.S. Senator from Georgia, 1807. b. Feb. 25, 1766 in Savannah, Ga. Studied medicine with his father and practiced a number of years. Fought in the Revolutionary War and was imprisoned in 1780-81 on an English ship. Member of state house of representatives as well as senate. Served in War of 1812 as a captain of Savannah reserves. Mayor of Savannah, 1812-14. Circuit judge in 1804-07. Member of Solomon's Lodge No. 1, Savannah. d. Nov. 13, 1838. Son of Noble Jones, q.v.

George W. Jones (1804-1896) U.S. Senator from Iowa, 1848-59, and Major General of militia. b. April 12, 1804 in Vincennes, Ind. He was graduated from Transylvania U. (Ky.) in 1825. Admitted to the bar, but never practiced. Moving to Missouri, he was clerk of the U.S. district court in 1826, and served as aide-de-camp to General Henry Dodge, q.v., in the Black Hawk War. He moved to Wis., where he was judge of the county court, colonel, and subsequently general of militia. He was elected to Congress in 1834-37. In July, 1836 he secured a division of Michigan Territory, and the establishment of the Territory of Wisconsin. In 1839 he was appointed by Van Buren as surveyor-general of the Northwest Territory; removed by Harrison, and reappointed by Polk. In 1859 he was named as U.S. minister to New Granada, and on his return in 1861, was charged with disloyalty, and imprisoned for a time. Member of Dubuque Lodge No. 3, Dubuque, Iowa. d. July 22, 1896.

George W. Jones (1806-1884) U.S. Congressman to 28th through 35th Congresses, 1843-59. b. March 15, 1806 in King and Queen Co., Va. Moved with parents to Fa-

yetteville, Tenn., where they settled. He was apprenticed to the saddler's trade. He served in both branches of the state legislature. He was elected to the first house of representatives in the Confederate Congress and served from Feb. 18, 1862 until Feb. 18, 1864. Member of Andrew Jackson Lodge No. 68, Fayetteville and Union Chapter No. 18, R.A.M. In 1847 he was grand scribe of the Grand Chapter of Tennessee. d. Nov. 14, 1884.

Girault M. Jones Episcopal Bishop of Louisiana since 1949. b. June 30, 1904 in Centerville, Miss. Graduate of U. of Mississippi, and U. of the South. Ordained in the Protestant Episcopal Church in 1928, he served first as a rural missionary in Miss. (1928-31), and then pastorates in Pass Christian, Miss., and New Orleans, La. In 1954 he was grand chaplain of the Grand Lodge of Louisiana. Received his degrees in Lumberton Lodge No. 417, Lumberton, Miss. and presently member of Louisiana Lodge No. 102, New Orleans.

Hamilton C. Jones U.S. Congressman to 80th and 81st Congresses (1947-51) from N.C. b. in Charlotte, N.C. Graduate of U. of North Carolina in 1906, and Columbia U. in 1907. Admitted to the bar in 1906, and practiced at Charlotte. Mason.

Howard W. Jones President of Youngstown College, Youngstown, Ohio. b. Sept. 27, 1895 in Palmyra, Ohio. Graduate of Hiram Coll. and Western Reserve U. Mason.

Inigo Jones (1573-1652) English architect. b. July 15, 1573 in London, England. He designed stage sets for court masques written by Ben Johnson, Heywood, Davenant and others. He served as architect to the king under James I, Charles I, and Charles II. He designed the queen's house at Greenwich, Lincoln's Inn Chapel, the banqueting hall at White-hall, reconstruction of St. Paul's Cathedral, Covent Garden piazza and Ashburn-ham House in Westminster. His connection with Freemasonry is based on the statements made by Anderson in his Constitutions of 1723 where he speaks of him as "our great Master Mason Inigo Jones." In his Constitutions of 1738 he goes even further and asserts that Jones was present as grand master at the leveling of the footstone of King James I's banqueting Hall in 1607, and that the Masons then drank to "the King and the Craft." One of the Old Charges is called the Inigo Jones MS, as its frontispiece depicts masons at work and bears the inscription "Inigo Jones Delin, MDCVII," but experts are convinced that this could not possibly have been drawn by him as the manuscript itself can be proved to date not earlier than 1722. Due to Anderson, therefore, he has been claimed as grand master from 1607-18 and 1636-51. Jones did design the building that later became the famous Freemasons' Tavern in London. d. July 5, 1652.

Jacob Jones (1768-1850) Commodore, U.S. Navy. b. in March, 1768, near Smyrna, Del. He studied medicine and started a practice, but became clerk of the Del. supreme court, and in 1799 entered the Navy as a midshipman. He was an officer on the frigate Philadelphia when it was captured in 1803 in the harbor of Tripoli. He remained a prisoner 18 months. Made commander in 1810, he was assigned to the Wasp in 1811. On Oct. 18, 1812 he encountered the British brig Frolic and after an engagement of 43 minutes cap-

tured her. However, the prize was no sooner secured than the British ship Poietiers of 74 guns hove into sight and the 18-gun Wasp was no match. They were captured and carried to Bermuda. This was the first naval engagement of the War of 1812, and the fact that an American ship could best an English ship of approximately the same power was hailed as the destruction Of British invincibility on the seas. For this Congress struck a medal in his honor and awarded the commander and crew of the Wasp a compensation of $25,000. He was buried Masonically by the Grand Lodge of Delaware, the grand master officiating. There is no record of his membership in a Delaware lodge, but it is thought that he was a member of Holland Lodge No. 8, New York City in 1808. The returns of the lodge in that year record his payment of the initiation fee, but no further record is given. d. Aug. 3, 1850.

James K. Jones (1839-1908) U.S. Senator from Arkansas, 1885-1903. b. Sept. 29, 1839 in Marshall Co., Miss. He served as a private in the Confederate forces through the Civil War, and then lived on his plantation until 1873, when he entered law practice. He was a member of the state senate in 1873-79, and president of same the last three years. From 1881-87 he was U.S. congressman, and in 1896 was chairman of the Democratic National Committee. Member of Arkadelphia Lodge No. 19, Arkadelphia, Ark. d. June 1, 1908.

Jesse H. Jones (1874-1956) Secretary of Commerce, 1940-45; Director of Reconstruction Finance Corp., 1932-39. b. April 5, 1874 in Robertson Co., Tenn. In lumber business in Texas, from 1895, and banking business from 1909. Owner and publisher of Houston Chronicle, and large scale real estate investor. From 1936-43 he was chairman of executive committee of Export-Import Bank, and administrator of Federal Loan Agency, 1939-45. Member of National Emergency Council 1933-39, and Economic Defense Board, 1941-45. In recognition of his services to the state and nation, the Texas legislature authorized the painting of his portrait, which was unveiled in the state capitol building at Austin in 1935. He was made a Mason at sight, in an occasional lodge, called by Grand Master Ara M. Daniels of the Grand Lodge of the District of Columbia, Dec. 16, 1941, and was raised by Charles E. Baldwin, past grand master. d. June 1, 1956.

John E. Jones (1840-1896) Former Governor of Nevada. b. Dec. 5, 1840 in Wales. Member of Eureka Lodge No. 16, Eureka, Nev. and master of same in 1885. He was grand master of Nevada in 1893. d. April 10, 1896 in San Francisco, Calif.

John P. Jones (1829-1912) U.S. Senator from Nevada, five terms, 1873-1903. b. Jan. 27, 1829 in Herefordshire, England, coming to U.S. with parents in infancy. He went to Calif. during the gold rush, serving in the Calif. state senate from 1863-67, going to Nevada in the latter year, where he engaged in the development of mines. Mason. d. Nov. 27, 1912.

John Paul Jones (1747-1792) Father of the American Navy. Original name was John Paul. b. July 6, 1747 in Kirkbean, Scotland. He went to sea at the age of 12, and at 19 was first mate of a slaver, and captain of a merchantman three years later. Ill fortune struck, however, when a man, flogged on his

ship, died and another was killed in a mutiny. Hostile witnesses at the inquiry made it rough for him and he next appeared at his brother's home in Fredericksburg, Va., having added the alias of "Jones" to his name. He had been made a member of St. Bernards Lodge No. 122 (now St. Cuthbert No. 41) of Kirkcudbright, Scotland, Nov. 27, 1770. At the outbreak of the American Revolution he obtained a commission in the Continental Navy as a lieutenant. It is said that fraternal connections obtained it for him. He soon became a captain, and acted as commodore of a fleet of privateers through which he established a reputation. Taking the war into European waters, he went to France, and, through Franklin's influence, obtained a vessel named the Bonhomme Richard which first flew the new American ensign in foreign waters. Two days after the fight with the British Serapis (where he is supposed to have uttered the words "I've just begun to fight!"), his ship sank and he made his way back to Paris. While here, he became associated with the famous Lodge of the Nine Sisters, and there are several references to his membership in the lodge records. He was also a visitor to St. Thomas Lodge in Paris. The Lodge of Nine Sisters had a bust of Jones made by Houdon, q.v., the measurements of which were used to identify Jones's body when the remains were removed more than 100 years later. Returning to Philadelphia in 1781, he was named to command the America, a man-of-war then building. Through "defects of taste and character," however, he was not allowed to take the vessel to sea. He again returned to Paris, and finally, in 1787, Congress voted him a medal—the only one awarded a naval hero in the Revolution. After declining service with Denmark, he accepted an appointment as rear admiral in the navy of Empress Catherine of Russia, then at war against the Turks. He was victor in the engagements on the Black Sea, but lost those in the palace corridors. He returned to Paris in 1790, and died of dropsy, July 18, 1792. He was buried in the Protestant cemetery of Paris and his gravesite was forgotten until 1905, when it was rediscovered and the remains were borne in solemn procession through the streets of Paris prior to shipment to America. They were later interred at Annapolis, Md.

John Rice Jones (1759-1824) First lawyer of Illinois and of Louisiana Territory. b. Feb. 10, 1759 in Merionthshire, Wales. He was educated in England and Wales, and was an excellent linguist, mathematician, and lawyer. He emigrated to the U.S. in 1780, settling in Philadelphia where he became acquainted with Benj. Franklin and other prominent men of that city. In 1787 he moved to Vincennes when the Northwest Territory was organized. Here he was instrumental in writing the territorial law. In 1790 he moved to Kaskaskia and practiced law, thus becoming the first practicing lawyer in Illinois. Being a French scholar, he was able to do business with the French of the territory. In 1802 he returned to Vincennes and was appointed U.S. judge of the Indiana Territory, revising the laws of the same in 1807. In 1810 he moved to St. Louis, Mo., residing there only shortly before settling at Potosi in Washington Co., Mo. Here he formed a partnership with Moses Austin, q.v., in the lead business, and erected the first cupola furnace made in the U.S. He was elected from Washington Co. to form the first constitution of Mo. (1819). His son, Rice Jones, fought a bloodless duel with Shadrach Bond, q.v., then the first

governor-elect of Illinois, on an island between Kaskaskia and St. Genevieve. A quarrel with Bond's assistant, Dunlap, led to Rice's murder by Dunlap on the streets of Kaskaskia in 1809. It is not known where John Rice received his degrees, but he is recorded as a member of St. Louis Lodge No. 111, and later of Missouri Lodge No. 12, both of St. Louis. Two of his sons were Freemasons, and one (Augustus) served as grand junior warden of the Grand Lodge of Missouri in 1832. Jones was named supreme court judge of Missouri and held that office at the time of his death in 1824.

Junius W. Jones Major General, U.S. Air Force. b. April 3, 1890 in Jackson, La. Graduate of U.S. Military Academy in 1913, and advanced through grades to brigadier general, U.S. Army, 1941. He commanded several fields including Chanute (Ill.) and Lowry (Colo.), and was air inspector in inspector general's dept. in 1934-38. In 1941 he became commanding general of 5th Air Support Command at Bowman Field, Ky., and air inspector, headquarters, A.A.F., in Washington in 1943. In 1944 he became major general in the Air Force. From 1948-52 he was commanding general of the Sacramento air material area, McClellan Air Force Base, Calif., and in 1952-53 was chief of aircraft section, International Staff, NATO. Now retired. Mason.

Louis R. Jones Brigadier General, U.S. Marine Corps. b. Philadelphia, Pa. Enlisted in Marine Corps in 1914, and commissioned in 1917, advancing through grades to brigadier general in 1942. Mason and National Sojourner.

Marvin Jones U.S. Congressman; U.S. Judge; U.S. Food

Administrator. b. near Valley View, Texas. Graduate of Southwestern U. (Georgetown, Texas) 1905, and U. of Texas, 1907. Admitted to the Texas bar in 1907. Member of 65th to 76th U.S. congresses (1917-41) from 18th Texas dist. Appointed judge U.S. Court of Claims in 1940, and chief justice of same in 1947. Was president of U.N. conference on food and agriculture in 1943, and U.S. Food Administrator 1943-45. Mason.

Mattison B. Jones (1869-1941) Lawyer, teacher and General Grand High Priest, General Grand Chapter, R.A.M. (1936-39). b. June 15, 1869 in Tuttle, Ky. Graduate of U. of Kentucky in 1894. Taught in Kentucky schools from 1887-95, being admitted to the bar in latter year. He then was a professor of mathematics, astronomy, and military science at Cumberland Coll. (Ky.), and U. of Kentucky until 1899, when he moved to Los Angeles, Calif., where he established his law practice. He was a professor in the law school of U. of Southern Calif. from 1904-11; president of First National Bank, Glendale, 1931-32; president of board of trustees of U. of Redlands from founding in 1909 until 1941. An active Baptist, he was president of Southern Calif. Baptist Convention, 1911-13, and Pacific Coast Baptist Conference, 1910-13. In 1931 he was president of the Northern Baptist Convention of the U.S. A Democrat, he was a nominee for governor of Calif. in 1922. Raised in Robinson Creek Lodge, Camp Ground, Ky., June 17, 1891, and dimitted to Southern California Lodge No. 278, Los Angeles in 1900, and to Unity Lodge at Glendale in 1912. In 1928 he was master of Meridian Lodge U.D. He was exalted in London Chapter No. 103, London, Ky., Dec. 31, 1896; affiliated with Signet Chapter No. 57, Los Angeles;

and became charter member of Unity Chapter No. 116, Glendale in 1913, and high priest in 1915. He was grand high priest of the Grand Chapter of California in 1921. Greeted in London Council R. & S.M., London, Ky., Dec. 31, 1896, he affiliated with Los Angeles Council No. 11, in 1910; was master in 1918, and grand master of the Grand Council of California in 1928. Knighted in DeMolay Commandery No. 12, Louisville, Ky., April 10, 1897, he affiliated with Los Angeles Commandery No. 9 in 1904, and became charter member of Glendale Commandery No. 53 in 1914, and commander in 1916. Received 32° AASR (SJ) in Los Angeles, March 8, 1912. d. Oct. 12, 1941.

Melvin Jones Secretary General of Lions International. b. Jan. 13, 1880 in Fort Thomas, Ariz. In the insurance business from 1902-26. He was a founder, in 1917, of the Lions and has been secretary general and treasurer since that time. He is also editor of The Lion, the organization's official paper. Member of Garden City Lodge No. 141, Chicago, Ill.

Noble Jones (1724-1805) Revolutionary patriot, and physician. b. in London, England in 1724. He was the son of Dr. Noble Jones, an early settler of Georgia, who was treasurer of the province and a councilor of state. He was associated with his father in medical practice at Savannah from 1748-56. He held a military commission from early age, and was a member of the assembly in 1761, and subsequently speaker. An active patriot, he was corresponding with Franklin while the latter was in England. He was speaker of the first Georgia legislature and a delegate to the Continental Congress from 1775-76, and again from 1781-83. He lost a son at the capture of Savannah in

1778, and he himself was taken prisoner at the fall of Charleston in 1780, and taken to St. Augustine. Exchanged in July, 1781, he practiced medicine in Philadelphia until Dec., 1782 when he returned to Georgia, and again served in the assembly. He practiced at Charleston from 1783-88 after which he lived in Savannah. He was president of the convention that revised the state constitution in 1795. He is said to have been the first Mason initiated in Georgia, being a member of the old Solomon's Lodge No. 1 of Savannah. Was father of George Jones, q.v. d. Jan. 9, 1805.

Ollie E. Jones Executive Vice President of Swift & Co. since 1952, and director since 1941. b. March 27, 1892 in Wellington, Ill. Has been with Swift since 1912, beginning in accounting department and subsequently a salesman in Lincoln, Nebr., and Chicago; refinery department, and vice president in charge of lard and vegetable oil since 1936; vice president of sales in 1938. Member of Dearborn Lodge No. 310 at Chicago, Ill.

Paul C. Jones U.S. Congressman, 80th through 85th Congresses, 10th Mo. dist. b. March 12, 1901 at Kennett, Mo. Graduate of U. of Missouri in 1923. He has been co-publisher of the Dunklin Democrat, Kennett, Mo. since 1923, and general manager of station KBOA since 1947. Member of Missouri state senate from 1937-45, and chairman of Missouri State Highway Commission from 1945-48. Directed the organization of 6th Mo. Infantry of state guard, and was its commanding officer from 1940-46. Initiated in Kennett Lodge No. 68, Kennett, Mo. in Dec., 1922. Member of Helm Chapter No. 117, R.A.M. of Kennett and Malden Com-

mandery No. 61, K.T. of Malden, Mo. 32° AASR (SJ) in St. Louis, Mo.

Robert E. Jones (1872-) Methodist Bishop. b. Feb. 18, 1872 at Greensboro, N.C. Held degrees from Bennett Coll. (N.C.), Gammon Theol. Seminary (Ga.), and honorary degrees from many others. Ordained to ministry in 1893, serving churches at Lexington, Thomasville, and Reidsville, N.C. From 1897-1901 he was assistant manager of Southwestern Christian Advocate, and editor of same from 1904-20. Was bishop of Methodist church from 1920 until retirement in 1944. Mason and 33° AASR (SJ).

Robert F. Jones Federal Communications Commissioner from 1947. b. June 25, 1907 at Cairo, Ohio. Graduate of Ohio Northern U. in 1929 and admitted to the bar the same year, practicing at Lima, Ohio. Member of the 76th through 80th U.S. congresses (1939-49) from 4th Ohio dist. Received degrees in Rufus Putnam Lodge No. 364, Columbus Grove, Ohio on Sept. 19, 1928, Feb. 2 and March 3, 1929. Affiliated with Fort Amanda Lodge No. 706, Lima, Ohio on June 20, 1935. 32° AASR (NJ) at Dayton and member of Antioch Shrine Temple of Dayton.

Sam Houston Jones Governor of Louisiana, 1940-44. b. July 15, 1897. Began as a deputy clerk in DeRidder, La., 1922. Was assistant district attorney from 1925-34, after being admitted to the bar in 1922. From 1934-40 he was in private practice. Served as Army sergeant from 1917-19 in WWI. Initiated in DeRidder Lodge No. 271, DeRidder, La., Oct. 4, 1918; passed Oct. 5, and raised Oct. 8, same year. His occupation at that time was "soldier," and he was 21 years old. Under consent of the

Grand Lodge of Louisiana, he is also a member of Rudolph Krause Lodge No. 322 of Lake Charles. 32° AASR (SJ) at Lake Charles.

Samuel P. Jones (1847-1906) Famous revivalist known as "Sam Jones." b. Oct. 16, 1847 in Chambers Co., Ala. Received fine education under private tutors and at boarding schools; was admitted to the Georgia bar in 1869. His professional prospects were bright, but he broke down in health due to excessive drinking. This ended his professional career as a lawyer. He professed religion in 1872, and became a Methodist Episcopal clergyman. He held pastoral charges in North Georgia for eight years, and was an agent for the North Georgia Orphanage for 12 years, devoting most of his time to evangelistic work over the nation. His lodge is not known, but he was a member of Rome Commandery No. 8, Rome, Ga., and made a Shriner in Savannah. d. in 1906.

Stephen Jones (1764-1828) Editor, lexicographer and Masonic writer. His well known Muse of Masonry was published in 1797. In 1817, he wrote the article on Freemasonry in the *Encyclopaedia Londinensis*, and four years later edited a new edition of the Illustrations by William Preston, q.v. He was Preston's executor, and belonged to the Lodge of Antiquity No. 2.

Stephen S. Jones Active Member of Supreme Council, 33° AASR (SJ) and Sovereign Grand Inspector General in Kentucky. Received 32° in 1937; KCCH in 1941; coroneted 33° in 1945 and appointed deputy in Kentucky in 1954 and active member in 1955. Is senior member of the law firm of Jones, Keith and Jones and is a judge of the Jefferson circuit court in Louisville.

Thomas A. Jones (1859-1937) Justice, Supreme Court of Ohio, 1915-37. b. March 4, 1859 at Oak Hill, Ohio. Graduate of Ohio U. in 1881. Served as mayor of Jackson, and judge of 4th judicial circuit. Was judge of court of appeals, 4th Ohio dist. 1913-15. Member of Trowel Lodge No. 132, Jackson, Ohio, receiving degrees on Sept. 26, Oct 31, 1884 and Feb. 27, 1885. d. Aug. 31, 1937.

Virgil C. Jones Author and public relations executive. b. June 7, 1906 in Charlottesville, Va. Graduate of Washington and Lee U. in 1930. Editor of *Huntsville Times* (Ala.), 1931-37; reporter *Richmond Times-Dispatch* (1937-41); *Washington Evening Star*, 1941-43. Manager of Washington office of Curtis Publishing Co. from 1945. Author of *Ranger Mosby* (1944); *The Hatfields and the McCoys* (1948). Raised in Waddell Lodge No. 228, Gordonsville, Va. in 1927. Active on degree teams while in college and as a resident of Huntsville, Ala. in the 1930's.

Walk C. Jones Architect. b. Oct. 21, 187,4 at Memphis, Tenn. In continuous practice in Memphis since 1900. Senior member of Walk C. Jones since 1935. Many examples of his work are found in Tenn. and Ky., mostly of government agencies. Raised in Angerona Lodge No. 168, Memphis, Tenn. on March 26, 1907. Received 50-year certificate on Feb. 1, 1957. Exalted in Memphis Chapter No. 95, R.A.M. in 1907 and knighted in Memphis Commandery No. 4, K.T. same year.

William Jones Lieutenant of American Revolution in a Delaware regiment. Killed by Indians at Wyoming, Pa. and later buried Masonically by Military Lodge No. 19, Pennsylvania Artillery.

Charles Stephen Jordan (1700-1745) Secret counselor of the King of Prussia and vice president of the Academy of Sciences in Berlin. In 1740 he founded, jointly with the Baron von Biefeld, q.v., the Lodge of the Three Globes in Berlin. He served as secretary of this lodge until the time of his death in 1745.

Chester B. Jordan (1839-1914) Governor of New Hampshire, 1901-03. b. Oct. 15, 1839 in Colebrook, N.H. Graduate of Kimball Union Academy (Plainfield, N.H.), and Dartmouth. He was clerk of the state supreme court from 1868-74, and was admitted to the bar in 1875. In 1897 he was president of the state senate, and speaker of the lower house in 1881. Member of Evening Star Lodge No. 37, Colebrook, N.H., and at one time was secretary of the lodge. d. Aug. 24, 1914.

George R. Jordan Executive Vice President of International Travelers Assurance Co. b. Sept. 5, 1893 in Kemp, Texas. First a furniture salesman (1914-16); and later insurance salesman, then a general agent (1918-33). Director and member of executive committee of Scottish Rite Hospital for Crippled Children, Dallas. Mason and Shriner.

J. Luther Jordan Banker and General Grand High Priest, General Grand Chapter, Royal Arch Masons, 1957-60. b. Jan. 23, 1895 in Cooper, La. Educated in rural schools; Leesville, La. high school; Louisiana Polytechnic Inst.; Louisiana State U.; and Iowa State U. In WWI he served in the Coast Artillery. He taught two

sessions at Louisiana State U., and served as a member of the Louisiana state board of education. He served as principal of high schools at Simpson, Stonewall, and Mansfield, La. (1916-24); became sales executive of the Trailer Mfg. Co. of Mansfield; and later was general manager of a steel foundry. From 1935-42 he was with the Dept. of Agriculture, and then with the Office of OPA. Next he entered the real estate business in Shreveport, and later returned to his home in Mansfield as vice president of the First National Bank. Raised in Leesville Lodge No. 240 in 1916, he was master in 1921, and grand master of the Grand Lodge of Louisiana in 1942. He was exalted in DeSoto Chapter No. 64, Mansfield, July 1, 1923; was high priest within six months; and grand high priest of the Grand Chapter of Louisiana in 1938. Greeted in Shreveport Council No. 23, R. & S.M. Oct. 29, 1934, he was master in 1942, and grand master of the Grand Council of Louisiana in 1952. Knighted in Bethany Commandery No. 26, K.T., he was commander in 1927, and grand commander of the Grand Commandery of Louisiana in 1948. Received the 32° AASR (SJ) in 1918 at Shreveport. Member of KYCH, Knights Beneficent of the Holy City; El Karubah Shrine Temple; St. Matthew Conclave, Red Cross of Constantine (sovereign in 1947); and grand junior general of United Imperial Red Cross of Constantine in 1958.

L. J. Jordan Master of Daintree Lodge No. 2938 at Wei-hai-Ewi, Shantung, China in 1941, when he was seized and imprisoned by the Japanese. He died in a prison camp. The charter of this lodge was smuggled out of China on a British submarine.

Paul H. Jordan Brigadier General, National Guard and later U.S. Army. b. Aug. 14, 1904 at Chattanooga, Tenn. Owner of Red Bank Hardware, Lumber, and Building Material in Chattanooga. Enlisted in national guard in 1923 and advanced to brigadier general, commanding 30th Infantry division artillery in 1946. With U.S. Army, 1941-45. Mason and past Shrine potentate.

Thomas Jefferson Jordan Major General of Civil War (by brevet). Member of Perseverance Lodge No. 21, Harrisburg, Pa., and master of same in 1856.

Albert N. Jorgensen President of University of Connecticut since 1935. b. March 20, 1899 in Lanark, Ill. Graduate of Coe Coll. (Iowa), U. of Iowa. He served as high school principal in Sabula, Ia., and superintendent of schools at Arlington, Ia. until 1925, when he went with the State U. of Iowa as director of educational administration. From 1927-31 he was professor at Michigan State Normal, and from 1931-35 with U. of Buffalo. Author of several books on education. Mason.

Clifford D. Jory President of the George Washington Masonic National Memorial Association since 1952. b. April 17, 1892 in Sioux Rapids, Iowa. Attended Morningside Coll. at Sioux City three years and was graduated from Iowa U. Law School in 1915. He began law practice in Sheldon, Iowa in that year. Raised in Mistletoe Lodge No. 376, Shelton, Iowa in 1916 and served as master in 1921; grand master of the Grand Lodge of Iowa in 1943. Exalted in Samara Chapter No. 105, R.A.M.; greeted in Chariton Council No. 42, R. & S.M. and knighted in Petros Commandery No. 54, K.T. Member of

the Scottish Rite in Sioux City, Iowa and a 33° (SJ). Member of Red Cross of Constantine. He is an honorary member of Alexandria-Washington Lodge, Alexandria, Va. Past sovereign, Red Cross of Constantine. Has been member of board of directors of the George Washington Masonic National Memorial Assn. since 1946. Received the Henry Price Medal from the Grand Lodge of Massachusetts.

Joseph II (1741-1790) Holy Roman Emperor (1765-90) and King of Germany (1764-90). Son of Francis I and Maria Theresa, q.v. He was co-regent with his mother in Austria from 1765-80, and acquired territory at first partition of Poland in 1772. On his mother's death in 1780, he came into full control of Austria. He prohibited the publication of any new papal bulls, suppressed convents, and reduced the number of clergy. In 1781 he published the Edict of Toleration. As emperor he had many schemes for territorial expansion, but most of them failed. He is one of the best examples of Europe's "benevolent despots." At one time he encouraged Freemasonry, notwithstanding the efforts of the priests to prevent it. It is said that in 1785 he wrote the following decree in his own hand which permitted meetings of lodges. "In return for their compliance with this ordinance, this government accords to the Freemasons, welcome, protection and liberty; leaving entirely to their own direction the control of their members and their constitutions. The government will not attempt to penetrate into their mysteries. Following these directions, the Order of Freemasons, in which body are comprised a great number of worthy men who are well known to me, may become useful to the State." But Joseph did not keep this edict in effect long. At length he yielded to the priesthood, and, in 1789 the above ordinance was rescinded and the lodges were forbidden to meet, under very severe penalties.

John J. Joseph Vice President of Bell Telephone Co. b. July 27, 1899 in Marathon, Ohio. Graduate of Ohio Wesleyan U. and Western Reserve U. Was with Redpath Chautauqua from 1917-28, and political science instructor at Western Reserve U., 1925-28. Admitted to the bar in 1928, he practiced in Cleveland. With Bell Telephone (Ohio) since 1929, and vice president in charge of public relations since 1948. Member of Eastern Star Lodge No. 55, Franklin, Ohio.

Josephine (1763-1814) Empress of France. b. June 23, 1763 in Martinique. Married vicomte de Beauharnais who was executed in the revolution. Married Napoleon Bonaparte, q.v., March 9, 1796. She was active in French adoptive Freemasonry, a woman's organization given quasi-Masonic recognition by the Grand Orient of France. Napoleon promoted adoptive Masonry as a means to consolidate his power, and it rose to favor on his reestablishment of the Empire. In 1805, Empress Josephine was installed as grand mistress of the Loge Imperiale d'Adoption des Francs Chevaliers at Strasbourg, at which time she initiated one of her ladies of honor, Madame F. de Canisy, at a brilliant gathering. In 1805 the androgynous Lodge of Free Knights and Ladies of Paris held a festival at Strasburg in which Josephine assisted Lady Dietrick, the grand mistress. The lodges Saint Josephine of Paris and Josephine of Milan, were named after her. d. May 24, 1814.

John H. Jouett Aviation executive. b. May 14, 1892 at San Francisco, Calif. Graduate of U.S. Military Academy in 1914, advanced to lieutenant colonel, and resigned in 1930. From 1930-32 he was aviation adviser to Republic of China; president of Fairchild Aircraft 1936-38, and executive vice president of Higgins Aircraft, Inc. since Nov. 1, 1942. He is also president of Blue Star Airlines and Caribbean Corp. since 1945. Raised in Republic Lodge No. 690, New York City in 1914; 32° AASR (SJ) at Galveston, Texas in 1929. Member of El Mina Shrine Temple, Galveston.

Arnold E. Joyal President of Fresno State College (Calif.) since 1948.b. Oct. 13, 1902 in Cowansville, Quebec, Canada. Brought to U.S. in 1903 and naturalized in 1927. Received A.B., A.M., and Ph.D. from U. of California. He taught, and was principal, at Wheatland, Calif., and then went with the Federal government in the U.S. Office of Education. He was a professor at U. of Denver and U. of Maryland, 1933-45, and dean of the college of education at U. of Oklahoma, 1945-48. Mason.

Benito Pablo Juarez (1806-1872) Mexican patriot and president. b. March 21, 1806 in San Pablo Guelatao, Oaxaca, Mexico. His parents were pure Indian and died when he was four years old. He was reared by an uncle and received a good education. Admitted to the bar in 1834, he practiced law in Oaxaca until 1846, and was elected governor of that state in 1847. He was expelled by Santa Anna, q.v., in 1853, but returned in 1855 to join Alvarez in a revolution against Santa Anna. As minister of justice under Alvarez, he wrote the "Ley Juarez" in 1855, which abolished special courts and reduced the power of the army and the church, as both had been practically immune under the special courts. When Comonfort became president, he feared the power of Juarez so he named him as governor of Oaxaca. Juarez again made many reforms in finance and education of that state and was regularly elected governor in 1857. He also was elected president of the supreme court at that time, which under the new constitution made him virtually vice president. Comonfort was forced by the liberal press to make him secretary of the interior. He was provisional president of Mexico after Miramon from 1857-61. Three years of civil war followed, but he was elected president for term 1861-65, and by self-proclamation president from 1865-67, as elections were impossible because of the French invasion. He fought against Emperor Maximilian, and the French, and finally captured him and had him shot, June 19, 1867. He was elected president for two more terms - 1867-72, and his later administrations were marked by many reforms and revolutions. For his honesty he is often called the "Washington of Mexico" and for his reforms, the "Lincoln of Mexico." He was prominent in Masonry, serving as master and rising to sovereign inspector general in the Mexican AASR, 33°. His authority seemed to keep the rites together because after his death dissension arose and they broke up. Maximilian is said to have been made a Mason in Austria. He was patron of Masonry in Mexico, but it is not known whether he attended any Masonic meetings there. It is claimed that Maximilian appealed to Juarez as a Mason to save his life but Juarez proved the Emperor was not a Freemason. d. July 18, 1872.

Henry M. Judah (1821-1866) Union Brigadier General in Civil War. b. June 12, 1821 in Snow Hill,

Md. He was graduated from U.S. Military Academy in 1843, and served in the Mexican War with the 8th Infantry. He was commended for bravery in storming of Monterrey, Molino del Rey, and Mexico City. He served with the 4th Infantry against the Indians of California, and Washington and Oregon territories, until the Civil War. He was made brigadier general of volunteers in March, 1862, and acting inspector general of the Army of Tennessee. He resigned his staff appointment to command the 1st Division. He was active in the pursuit of Morgan, q.v., while the latter was making his famous raid into Kentucky, Indiana, and Ohio. He later was inspector general of the Army of Ohio and was mustered out of service in 1865, but reverted to regular status and was commandant of the post at Plattsburg, N.Y. at the time of his death, Jan. 14, 1866. Member of North Star Lodge No. 91, Fort Jones, Calif.

Lawrence M. Judd Governor of Hawaii, 1929-35. b. March 20, 1887 in Honolulu, Hawaii. He was first a salesman for Whiting Paper Co. in New York; buyer for Alexander & Baldwin of Honolulu; director of Theo. H. Davies Co.; and manager of Hawaii Meat Co. In WWI he served as an Infantry major and later as colonel in Hawaii national guard. He was a member of the senate of Hawaii from 1920-27, and president of same in 1923. He is executive vice president of Bowman Deute Cummings, Inc. since 1938. Initiated Dec. 4, 1915 in Hawaiian Lodge No. 21, Honolulu. Shriner.

Walter H. Judd Physician and U.S. Congressman to 75th through 85th Congresses from 5th Minn. dist. b. Sept. 25, 1898 in Rising City, Nebr. Received B.A. degree from U. of Nebraska in 1920, and M.D. in 1923. Had fellowship in surgery, Mayo Foundation, U. of Minn. 1932-34. From 1920-24 he was instructor of zoology at U. of Omaha. From 1925-38 he was medical missionary for Congregational Church in China, and in 1938-40 lectured throughout the U.S. on American foreign policy in the Pacific, advocating boycotting of Japanese goods, and embargo on shipment of war materials to Japan. He practiced medicine at Minneapolis in 1941-42. Served in field artillery in WWI from private to 2nd lieutenant. Member of Composite Lodge No. 81, Rising City, Nebr. 32° and KCCH, AASR (SJ) at Minneapolis, Minn. Shriner.

Frank A. Juhan Protestant Episcopal Bishop. b. April 27, 1887 in Macon, Ga. Graduate of U. of the South and Sewanee Theol. Seminary. Became deacon in 1911, and priest in 1912. He was first a missionary in West Texas, chaplain of Sewanee Military Academy, and rector of Christ Church of Greenville, S.C. He was consecrated bishop of Florida, Nov. 25, 1924. Elected chancellor of U. of the South in 1944. Mason.

Juliana Queen of the Netherlands since 1948. Full name is Juliana Louise Emma Marie Wilhelmina. A daughter of Queen Wilhelmina, she married Prince Bernhard of Lippe Biesterfield in 1937. b. in 1909. When the Grand Lodge of the Netherlands erected an institute for the blind at Bussum in 1932, Queen Wilhelmina, Princess Juliana and the prince-consort attended the ceremonies. The grand lodge's building in The Hague was given them by Prince Frederick of Orange when he was grand master; he also presented the grand lodge with a library of 7,000 volumes. Juliana assumed the title of "Protectress of the Craft." In 1957 she received the grand masters attending an international conference at The Hague.

Niels Juul (1859-1929) U.S. Congressman to 65th and 66th Congresses (1917-21) from Ill. b. April 27, 1859 in Randers, Denmark. He came to Chicago in 1880, graduating from Chicago Coll. of Law in 1898 and admitted to the bar the following year. Elected to state senate in 1898 and served 16 years. Member of Ben Hur Lodge No. 818, Chicago, Ill. d. Dec. 4, 1859.

www.ingramcontent.com/pod-product-compliance
Lightning Source LLC
Chambersburg PA
CBHW020602270326
41927CB00005B/145